THE CONNOISSEUR'S HANDBOOK OF

ANTIQUE
COLLECTING

THE CONNOISSEUR'S HANDBOOK OF

ANTIQUE
COLLECTING

A DICTIONARY OF FURNITURE,
GLASS, CERAMICS, METALWORK, TEXTILES,
TIMEPIECES, ARMS AND ARMOUR

Edited by
HELENA HAYWARD

Revised by
HARRIET BRIDGEMAN AND
ELIZABETH DRURY

With an introduction by
WILLIAM ALLAN
Editor of *The Connoisseur*

BOOK CLUB ASSOCIATES
LONDON

© *The Connoisseur* 1960, 1978

Designed and produced for *The Connoisseur*
by George Rainbird Limited

First published March 1960
Reprinted 1964, 1967, 1969, 1970 and 1972

First published by Book Club Associates 1972
by arrangement with National Magazine Co.

Revised edition published 1978

Printed in Great Britain

Introduction

The 1960s, when this book was first published, were a golden age for collectors; arts magazines such as *The Connoisseur* bulged with advertisements reflecting the vigour and success of the antiques trade and the willingness of wealthy collectors to buy fine objects and works of art. In the salerooms prices soared and scarcely a month passed without records being broken; there was an aura of excitement and prosperity, a sense of opportunity for dealer and collector alike that made antiques into big business and confirmed London as the arts centre of the world.

Nowadays the collecting world is rather different. Few individuals can continue to collect on the grand scale and it is generally only the great museums and institutions who are able to afford Impressionist paintings, Paul Storr silver or the rarest pieces of porcelain. But although these things may be beyond most of our pockets, more people are collecting now than ever before. Though most people cannot afford the thousands of pounds needed for a Sheraton Pembroke table or a Paul de Lamerie ewer, they might be able to afford the few hundreds needed for a Victorian version of the same thing. It is likely to be well made, highly attractive and it is both fun and instructive to compare the piece in a nineteenth-century style with the original, separated as they are by time and a vast gulf in taste. Many dealers are coming to recognize this new balance, and concentrate more on stocking up with interesting, unusual or frankly picturesque items, although inevitably this means that more of the major and 'important' items go abroad, especially to the Continent. Today both collector and dealer are looking to the market below four or five thousand pounds for their staple diet, which makes a collector's handbook of this kind especially valuable.

There are many works of reference and major scholarly studies of the notable cabinet makers, silversmiths, sculptors and craftsmen who traditionally act as still points in the turning world of the antiques trade – Chippendale and Sheraton, de Lamerie and

Storr, Morris and Dresser and a score of others. But there are still remarkably few 'ready reckoners', concise, easily portable guides to the many intricacies, technical terms and points of detail that govern the antique world. This book – now revised and brought up to date in view of the great increase in our knowledge of the decorative arts, and shifts of emphasis and sympathy in their discussion during the last decade – cannot of course be completely comprehensive, but it succeeds very well in providing a nucleus of information, historical and practical, for the better protection of the cautious and circumspect collector.

One might suppose that collecting antiques is a pastime less affected than most by prevailing fashions. In fact, it is peculiarly susceptible; looking back through the advertisement pages of *The Connoisseur* during the past seventy-five years, I am constantly struck by the volatility of taste. In the Edwardian era, walnut furniture, or satinwood, were all the rage; during the 'Twenties, old English oak filled our pages, and in the post-war period mahogany came top of the league. Today, of course, nothing is unfashionable.

In 1975 the committee of the Grosvenor House Fair, one of the decisive events in the trade's calendar, took the bold step of advancing the age of permitted exhibits from 1830 to 1930. The response from the trade was not as warm as they had hoped; superficially disappointing, this absence was in fact a healthy sign, because it became clear that those dealers who specialized in Victorian and later objects were so assured of their clientele, so thoroughly established in their own line of business, that there was no need for them to hire expensive space at the Grosvenor House Fair. For the Victorian period – long derided as the repository of all that is ugly and unsaleable – is no longer out of fashion. As we learn more about this complex and fascinating era, so near to our own times but still so distant in terms of attitudes and preoccupations, we are coming to appreciate the skill and inventiveness of nineteenth-century designers and craftsmen, to banish our dread of the machine-made object and to look more objectively at the cross-current of aesthetic values that produced such a vast wealth of objects. The Victorians, it should be remembered, admired practicality and ingenuity just as much if not more than the Georgians, and they had a great variety of materials with which to work.

Every collector should study the subject of his or her enthusiasm, and handle as many objects and examples as they possibly can, to learn the 'feel' of the different woods, metals and ceramics, and to understand the technology involved, thereby arming themselves against the deceits of generations of dealers and other collectors. In some fields, of course, the unpopularity of the style or type has kept innocence abroad; no one has yet started to fake Gothic Revival furniture (though many pieces have been altered or cut down), because it would be too expensive an undertaking to justify the rewards.

The same goes for many nineteenth-century objects. But for the most part it has been true for many hundreds of years that all is fair in love, war and the antiques trade. That said, it is equally important to remember that most members of the antiques trade are very keen to learn themselves, are themselves often caught out by clever fakes and forgeries, and are still surprisingly dependent on the open-minded curiosity, depth of interest and scholarship of their clients or customers. Indeed, given the number of antique dealers in Britain alone, and the number of objects that pass through their hands each year, it is on the whole surprising that there are not more forgeries and that there is not greater exploitation of that fatal combination of a lack of knowledge and a quite proper desire to hedge against inflation. The remarkable success of Tom Keating and his faked Samuel Palmers showed how gullibility can be born of greed, and how treacherous can be the cry of 'antiques for investment'.

This is a good point at which to stress the availability, through our great national museums, of opportunities for study and verification, which collectors and dealers alike often forget. Not only do the museums organize lectures, study courses and special visits, but their several departments offer 'surgeries' where members of the public can bring objects to be scrutinized by experts. This system is occasionally abused, and museum staff, quite properly, decline to give opinions as to financial worth; but it is their job to try to set a date and origin to pieces brought to their notice in this way, and they are generally delighted to be of help. Of course such a visit can be an occasion for either tears or laughter, but there is no more satisfying feeling than that of knowing you really have picked up a genuine piece of early Bow porcelain masquerading as an ashtray in company with a showy piece inscribed 'Greeting from Clacton'. Bargains are still very much to be had, although so, in another sense, are collectors!

Over the years Europeans have come to regard Americans as the most antiques conscious race on earth. The general view is that Americans combine reverence for the age of an object with an intense interest in its manufacture and historical associations, where any can be proven or safely ascribed. The native art of America has generally been treated as merely imitative or second rate in Europe, partly because American artefacts seldom come on to the market and partly because those American dealers and collectors who travel to Europe are often so effusive in their admiration for every form of art but their own. This picture is, of course, wholly unjust. Not only are there many avid collectors – and fine collections – of American antiques, but the sheer size of the United States, in terms of people as well as area, has meant that American art in the past hundred years has been astonishingly diverse and interesting.

American furniture and art objects do appear from time to time in British salerooms and antique shops, and the purpose of expanding this element in the Handbook is to introduce British readers to distinctively American objects as well as to bring to the attention of prospective American readers some of the more 'collectable' items that are available in Britain. There must inevitably be many omissions, and the editors here have restricted themselves to describing just a few of the most interesting and 'typical' objects that embody the history and traditions of one of the great nations of the world.

There has never been any doubt about the value, both artistic and commercial, of objects and furniture from the Colonial period and the years following the War of Independence. Of special interest, however, are the many artefacts produced during the underrated nineteenth century, from the elegance of the Federal era, through to the pseudo-everything fantasies of the millionaires' mansions in the 1900s. Most people in Britain certainly find it hard to name a characteristically American style or maker between Paul Revere and Tiffany; this may seem a surprising fact in view of the colossal literature on American artists and craftsmen, and the large number of antiques for sale throughout America, but for the average interested Briton who does not have a first-hand acquaintance with American museums there is every opportunity for ignorance. By singling out certain craftsmen and styles I hope it will be possible to give some insight into the course of America's artistic history and confidence to those readers who visit America and have time and money enough to patrol the antique shops or to sit in at the various auction houses.

The overriding influence on American art and artefacts has been the rival traditions of the various immigrant groups, especially the English, Dutch and Germans – the native Indian culture having ceased at a very early date to have any but a purely whimsical influence on taste or design. And, until after Independence at least, the small population, simple habits of life, and a lack of professional craftsmen in the vast tracts of countryside were also predominant factors. The catalogue to the Great Exhibition in London of 1851, noted that 'there were two causes which gave to the productions of American industry displayed in the Great Exhibition a character totally distinct from that which is found in those of many other countries. In the first place whole districts are solely devoted to the pursuit of agriculture, dis-regarding mining, trades and manufacturers; and secondly in the United States, it is rare to find wealth so accumulated as to favour the expenditure of large sums 'upon articles of luxury.' This is almost shocking in view of the conventional view of the United States as the land of wealth and luxury. Nonetheless, even a cursory look at American antiques must bring home the point that until the Civil War and Reconstruction era sophisticated decor and a European standard of design and execution was the privilege of the East Coast minority.

It is worth bearing in mind the consequences of America's dramatic increase in population during the nineteenth century, from five million in 1800 to nearly twenty-three million by 1850, and more than twice that figure by 1900. This rapid expansion, particularly in the last twenty-five years of the century, created a huge market for inexpensive, mass-produced goods, from furni-ture to household utensils, from clocks to fire irons. The inventive-ness was there to follow up the need, and the factories were there to supply the objects designed; everything came together to provide the opportunity for that colossal explosion of wealth which still reverberates around the world.

I very much hope that this book, revised and updated as it has been, will now be of even greater use to those with an interest in antiques. It is particularly pleasing that so many younger people, many of them involved in professions far removed from the arts, should be such keen collectors, and, from the evidence of my postbag, such seekers after knowledge. More people now have an intelligent awareness of the arts than at any point in modern times; concern about our environment has made many people active in the cause of preservation and conservation, of cities and countryside, individual houses and beauty spots, and single items of furniture and other art objects. As we face up to the prospect of an increasingly directed and problem-laden future, it is surely a healthy sign that so many people should care so much about the tangible results of our civilization.

WILLIAM ALLAN
Editor, *The Connoisseur*.

Absolon, William: (1751–1815), pottery decorator and china and glass dealer at Yarmouth. About 1790 he set up a pottery decorating business at a place on the Denes known as 'The Ovens' where he enamelled earthenware and porcelain bought 'in the white' from Staffordshire and Leeds. Absolon's mark, 'Absolon Yarme No 25' painted in red, occurs on wares bought from Turner (q.v.), Wedgwood (q.v.), Shorthose and Leeds (q.v.) and impressed with their marks. In 1808 Absolon purchased a shop at the corner of Market Row (Row No 63) Yarmouth, and he died in Yarmouth in 1815. A painted arrow is also said to be Absolon's mark. There are examples of Absolon's decorated pottery and glass in Norwich Castle Museum.

Acanthus: a stylized leaf ornament adapted for use on furniture and silver from Greek and Roman architecture.

Acid gilding: a process of decorating china with patterns etched into the ware and covered with gold. The design, usually in the form of a narrow border, is transfer-printed (q.v.) to the ware in an acid resist (q.v.). The rest of the plate is then protected, both back and front, and dipped in acid which corrodes away the exposed parts of the design to a certain depth. When the etching is completed, the ware is removed from the acid, the resist and 'stopping' dissolved and washed off and the etched border banded over in gold. After firing the ware is burnished, yielding a polished relief pattern against a duller matt gold background. First introduced by Mintons, 1863. A process which appears similar was invented by the Austrians and acquired, improved and worked by Powell & Bishop of Hanley.

Acid polishing: method of restoring the brilliance to parts of glass that have been cut by briefly dipping the article in a mixture of acids.

Acorn clock: shelf or mantel clock, generally about 60 cm (2 ft) high, with the upper portion shaped somewhat like an acorn. An American type, made by the Forestville Manufacturing Company of Connecticut in the mid-19th cent.

Acorn knop: a knop or protuberance on the stem of a drinking glass, tooled in the form of an acorn and sometimes inverted.

Acosta'd: term derives from Jacob D. Acosta, an 18th-cent. ceramic and glass mender of New York, who also invented the cement he used.

Acqua Fresca, Acqua Matteo: see Chiselled and cut steel.

Act of Parliament clock: a misnomer applied to a timepiece, usually weight-driven, with seconds pendulum (q.v.), having a large unglazed dial and a small trunk. According to legend, these clocks were first put into inns and post taverns for use of the general public, many of whom had sold their clocks and watches when Pitt introduced his Act in 1797 levying 5 shillings a year on all clocks and watches. Such distress was caused in the trade that the Act was repealed in 1798.

Adam, Robert: (1728–92), architect and designer and creator of the English Neoclassical style. He worked at Harewood and Nostell Priory, in Yorkshire; Osterley Park and Syon House, near London; and Luton Hoo, in Bedfordshire, undertaking the design of furniture, carpets and metalwork as well as the architecture and interior decoration.

Adams, William & Sons (Potters) Ltd: a Staffordshire firm operating from the late 18th cent. in Stoke-on-Trent and at Greenfield Works, Tunstall. Concentrated mainly on earthenware and ironstone table services, toilet sets, etc., for the export market.

Admiral Lord Howe jug: a variety of toby jug (q.v.) known as 'Admiral Lord Howe' or 'Admiral Vernon', representing a seated naval figure. Admiral Howe had destroyed Cherbourg in 1758 and in 1794 won a famous victory over the French off Brest.

Adze-surfaced wood: carved wood, especially on Medieval and early Tudor chests, showing the irregular markings of an adze, a tool with an arched blade at right angles to the handle.

Aesthetic Movement: a reaction in England in the 1860s to 1880s to the ornateness of mid-Victorian design, which had been exemplified by objects shown in London at the Great Exhibition of 1851. The intention was to give the decorative arts a simpler, more 'artistic' appearance. It was inspired by the example of the Pre-Raphaelite painters and J. M. Whistler (1834–1903). A variety of styles developed, including Japonisme (q.v.). The principal exponents were E. W. Godwin (q.v.), Philip Webb (q.v.) and W. De Morgan (q.v.).

Affleck, Thomas: (d. 1795), an American cabinet-maker. Born in Aberdeen, Scotland, he learned his trade in London where, as a young man in 1763, he was chosen by John Penn, commissioned governor of Pennsylvania, to go with him to Philadelphia as resident cabinet-maker. He worked in a style adapted from that of Thomas Chippendale (q.v.) and is generally reckoned the most skilful cabinet-maker in 18th-cent. Pennsylvania.

Afghan rugs: rugs woven on Turkestan-Afghanistan border of coarser texture and design, but following the tradition of the other Turkoman types (q.v.), looking rather like a coarse Bokhara rug (q.v.).

After-cast: a bronze figure or article produced not by the *cire-perdue* (q.v.) process but by making moulds from an existing model. After-casts can date from any time between the original production of the article and the present day.

Agata glass: an American type of glass in limited production from 1887–8. The blown glass was stained to produce a mottled effect on the gloss surface and colours ranged from white to rose.

Agate ware: salt-glazed stoneware or lead-glazed earthenware made in Staffordshire in imitation of variegated natural stones, such as agate, by wedging together different coloured clays (early 18th cent.); more refined wares imitating semi-precious stones were made by Josiah Wedgwood (q.v.). A surface agate, known as marbled ware, was produced by combing various coloured slips (q.v.) in the manner of marbled papers.

Aigrette: jewel supporting a feather or imitating it in form, worn in hair or cap since the end of the 16th cent.

Aiguillette: a knot, worn on the shoulder in the 19th cent., often jewelled.

Air-twist stem: a type of stem familiar on 18th-cent. drinking glasses which is found in several forms between *c.* 1740 and *c.* 1770: (a) single-twist spirals in a drawn stem formed by the extension of air bubbles: multiple spirals were common throughout the period, and from 1745 two or four corkscrews; not until about 1750 do we encounter threads of uniform thickness spaced regularly; (b) single-twist in a three-piece glass: between 1740 and 1765 the shank was cut from long lengths made by an extension of air bubbles; from 1750 spirals were made by a mould process, the filaments being finely drawn and coiled with precision in some thirty variations; (c) compound-twist on three-piece glass: between 1760 and 1765 this type is found in a dozen variations.

Single twist   Compound twist

Albarello: a word of obscure derivation used to describe the nearly cylindrical form of the *maiolica* (q.v.) drugpot which was introduced into Italy from Spain, and later copied by English makers of tin-glazed earthenware. Possibly derived from *el Barani*, a vase for drugs. Albarelli were used for ointments and dry medicines and copied in Dutch Delft (q.v.) and English delftware.

Albert: a gold chain intended to hold a watch at one end and fitted with a bar at the other, named after Prince Albert.

Alcora maiolica: tin-glazed earthenware made at Alcora in the province of Valencia at a factory founded in *c.* 1727 by the Count of Aranda, with the help of French potters from Moustiers (q.v.). The early wares are closely akin to those of Moustiers. They achieved a fine quality white enamel.

Ale glass: long, narrow flute for serving strong ale, a highly alcoholic drink; from *c.* 1740 ale glasses were sometimes engraved with the hop and barley motif.

Alençon lace: needlepoint lace (q.v.) was made at Alençon, where the craft was established in 1665 under Venetian tutelage. The early Venetian influence, however, soon became less important than the lighter, fine-threaded Flemish pillow lace (q.v.) notions, but like Argentan lace (q.v.), Alençon was regarded as a heavier winter lace. By 1700 or 1720 the famous grounded *point d'Alençon* was evolved with rich fillings (q.v.) and a stiff *cordonnet* and *picots* (q.v.). This was mainly a narrow lace for borders and caps and was re-introduced in the 19th cent., more

flimsy and often on a spotted ground. A softly looped hexagonal mesh was made first and the pattern put in, worked in close buttonhole stitch. (See *Point de France* and Grounded laces.)

Alentours: (*Fr.*) a term used to describe the borders surrounding tapestries. Except in German examples, these are rarely seen on tapestries until the beginning of the 16th cent. They then began to play a very important part in the general effect, and the best artists of the day were called in to design them. Very beautiful and varied effects were produced, especially in the 16th and 17th cent. In the 18th cent. frame-borders became general, but the *alentours* which surround a subject inset in the main field, and enliven it with Rococo displays of drapery and flowers, create an effect which is really that of an enlarged border. The style of a tapestry border is very important in determining questions of date and workshop and is sometimes a certain indication of this. Normally, borders were woven in one piece with the main field, and it is important to see whether a border has been re-applied. (See also Galloons.)

Allgood family: operated the Pontypool (q.v.) japan works from 1730 until 1818, and Usk (q.v.) from 1763 until early in the 19th cent. They had agents throughout the country and an average turnover of £5000 a year in the 1760s. Few records of prices exist, but 'a basket for cakes' sold for 5 guineas and an oval tray painted with a landscape for 15 guineas.

Alison, Michael: New York cabinet-maker who flourished about 1800–45.

Alloy: a composition of two or more metals intimately mixed by fusion, or a base metal mixed with precious metal to harden it or make it easier to work.

Alma: a chain, worn in the 19th cent., consisting of wide, ribbed links.

Almsdish: a circular dish for ecclesiastical use, usually of silver, brass or pewter (q.v.), with a broad, often ornamented rim. No English examples survive from before the 17th cent., although they were made throughout Europe from the Middle Ages. Almsdishes made after 1840 are often in the Gothic Revival (q.v.) style.

Aluminia Faience Manufactory: the pottery was established in 1863 in Copenhagen. In 1882, the Manufactory bought the Royal Copenhagen Porcelain factory and two years later moved into its own premises. Initially its output was mainly restricted to moderately priced earthenware but after 1900 artistic value was increasingly sought in design with a corresponding increase in the price of its products.

Amberina, or Rose Amber glass: amber lead glass containing gold, which when partially reheated shades from amber to ruby by the action of gold oxide. It was widely manufactured in the United States from 1883 as pressed (q.v.) or patternmoulded table and ornamental ware.

Ambry (aumbry or almery): a recess in a wall, or a compartment or a piece of furniture, with a door. Originally it was a cupboard for food reserved as alms, the door often pierced for ventilation. By the 15th cent. the term was also used to refer to a safe. (See also Armoire.)

Amen glasses: drinking glasses, mostly of the drawn-stem or baluster type, dating from about 1720 to 1745, with one or two verses of a Jacobite hymn engraved upon the bowls, ending with the word 'Amen', and the cipher of James, the Old Pretender.

American Art China Works: established in 1891 at Trenton, New Jersey, and formerly known as the Washington Pottery. Producers of Belleek (q.v.) art wares for professional and amateur china painters.

American Crockery Co.: manufacturers of biscuit (q.v.) or white granite ware from 1876 to 1890 at Trenton, New Jersey. The company also produced porcelain on an experimental basis.

Amorini: cupids of Classical origin, revived as a decorative motif in the Renaissance (q.v.) and again in the 17th and mid-18th cent. on furniture and silver.

Amulet: an ornament worn as a charm or talisman.

Anatolian rugs: see Turkish rugs.

Anchor escapement: a type of clock escapement (q.v.) invented about 1670 by William Clement. It revolutionized timekeeping. With it the pallets (q.v.) are in the same plane as the escape wheel, instead of being at right angles to it, as in the verge escapement (q.v.). It largely eliminated circular error and also made practical the use of long pendulums swinging more slowly, hence with a lesser cumulative error. It is still used to-day for most domestic clocks and particularly in long-case clocks (q.v.) with pendulums beating one second. It is also known as the recoil escapement, in which recoil is seen in the slight shudder at each beat in the seconds hand of long-case clocks so equipped. The vastly improved timekeeping of this escapement made really practical the use of clocks for astronomical purposes. Flamsteed, the first Astronomer Royal at Greenwich in 1675, used clocks made by Thomas Tompion (q.v.), equipped with the anchor escapement. This largely accounted for the far greater accuracy of his observations as compared with those of his contemporaries. From this invention followed, either directly or indirectly, practically all the subsequent improvements in timekeeping.

Anderson carpets: Hiram Anderson (fl. 1840), American dealer in carpets, marked his stock with his name. He sold Brussels (q.v.), ingrain and other carpets at 99 Bowery, New York.

Andirons: the iron fire dog or andiron dates back to Roman times, but the earliest known examples date from the 15th cent. As long as the fireplace occupied the central position in the hall, the fire dog was of purely utilitarian design, but when the fireplace was transferred to a side wall, becoming an important decorative feature, the fire dog also received ornamental treatment. The earliest surviving fire dogs conform to a standard type, whether of English, French, German, or Flemish origin, namely an arched base enriched with Gothic cusping, supporting a pilaster, the front of which is decorated with running scrolls (Fig. A). Sixteenth- and 17th-cent. fire dogs were made to the same design but with Renaissance instead of Gothic ornament (Fig. B).

Fig. A

Fig. B

Fire dogs of this type were made of cast iron, the English ones being produced by the Sussex iron-masters. There seems from an early date to

have been a distinction between andirons and fire dogs. The former term was used for the large dogs, standing three feet or more high, which were intended to decorate the fireplace. Though these andirons could also be used, they were usually accompanied by a smaller pair of fire dogs proper, which stood closer into the hearth and supported the burning logs.

The earlier andirons were of wrought iron, but as early as the 16th cent. they were garnished with silver. In the 17th cent. andirons entirely of silver were produced and there was a fashion for them in England after the Restoration. The Restoration andiron had a particularly handsome baroque form, consisting of a pedestal on volute or claw feet supporting either a flaming vase or a figure. The finest examples are of great magnificence and weight of silver. Similar designs were also produced for the less wealthy in gilt brass. The introduction of the grate in the 18th cent. rendered the fire dog superfluous.

Angell, Joseph, III: (*c.* 1816–*c.* 1891), head of a firm of English silversmiths who produced domestic wares in a variety of original and revival styles and is credited with introducing enamelling on tea sets and cake baskets (q.v.).

Anglo-American pottery: creamware (q.v.) decorated with transferprinted (q.v.) designs relating to American events. Made originally in Liverpool and by Staffordshire potters from *c.* 1815 for the American trade.

Anglo-Venetian glass: glass vessels of fine soda-glass made in London from about 1570 until the last quarter of the 17th cent. These glasses were made in the Venetian manner by immigrant Italian workmen. The number of examples to which an English origin can definitely be attributed is limited, but many vessels probably made in London are mistakenly thought to be Venetian in origin or to have been made in the Netherlands by Venetian workmen. (See also Verzelini, Giacomo.)

Angular knop: a knop or protuberance on the stem of a drinking vessel, of rounded-edge flattened form.

An hua ('secret') decoration: faint engraving or painting in white slip (q.v.), visible only against the light; found on Chinese porcelain especially on early Ming (q.v.) and 18th-cent. white porcelain.

Animaliers: a group of 19th-cent. French sculptors specializing in naturalistic figures of animals. In general they employed the *cire-perdue* (q.v.) method for casting their bronzes. Notable sculptors were A.-L. Barye (q.v.) and P.-J. Mêne (q.v.).

Annealing: (1) a process of toughening flint-glass by raising it to a high temperature and then cooling it gradually. (a) Annealing oven: an oven known as the tower, built above the melting chamber and operated on waste heat from below; (b) annealing tunnel, or leer: a tunnel 4 to 5 m (5 to 6 yds) in length through which newly-made glass passes slowly to cool, toughen, and acquire increased brilliance. (2) Similarly a process of tempering metals. Silver, for example, becomes brittle under hammering during the process of raising from a flat sheet and requires heating to soften it.

Annulated knop: a knop or protuberance on the stem of a drinking glass, of flattened form, sandwiched between two, four or six thinner flattened knops, each pair progressively less in size.

Ansbach porcelain: porcelain was made at a factory set up at Ansbach, Germany, under the protection of the Margrave Alexander of Brandenburg from 1758. The factory was transferred to the castle of the Margrave at Bruckberg in 1762, and although it ceased to have State protection soon after the death of the Margrave in 1791, it actually continued to exist until 1860. Ansbach porcelain is hard-paste made with Passau clay and of fine quality. Many of the figures modelled were taken from Meissen (q.v.) examples, while the table wares were largely influenced by Berlin and Nymphenburg (qq.v.). The mark used from about 1758 to 1762 was a shield surmounted by an A in blue, while an A alone was used from about 1762 to 1785 and later. The figures are often unmarked or bear an impressed shield.

Ansonia Clock Company: American company founded in Ansonia, Connecticut, in 1851; moved to New York in 1879. Noted for wall and shelf clocks in the characteristic Connecticut style. The factory closed *c.* 1930.

Anthemion (honeysuckle motif): a stylized radiating flower or leaf design deriving from the honeysuckle flower. It originated in Greek and Roman architecture and was popular in Neoclassical design of the late 18th cent.

Antwerp lace: pillow lace (q.v.), strong and heavy looking, the patterns outlined in a *cordonnet* (q.v.) of thick untwisted thread and made at the same time as the *fond chant* (q.v.) ground. The style of pattern has given this the name of pot lace or *potten kant*, from the substantial two-handled vase usually prominent in it. This motif was very popular in 18th-cent. embroideries. It appeared also in Normandy laces.

Aogai: Oriental lacquer-work technique in which mother-of-pearl, made from Haliotis shell, is inlaid into the surface of the lacquered wood.

Apostle jug: a straight-sided jug modelled in relief with figures of the Apostles under an elaborate Gothic arcading, made by Charles Meigh in porcellaneous stoneware, *c.* 1845.

Apostle spoon: one of a set of thirteen spoons with a full-length figure of Christ or one of the twelve apostles as the finial (q.v.). Complete, hall-marked (q.v.) sets of the 15th to 17th cents. are rare. This type of spoon was revived in the 19th cent.

Apple-green ground: a trade name for a ground colour used extensively in the decoration of porcelain at Worcester (q.v.) during the Wall period from about 1770 when Sèvres (q.v.) influence was felt. The colour was introduced at Sèvres in *c.* 1757. W. B. Honey describes it as 'pea-green' (*Old English Porcelain*, 1928, new ed. 1948).

Applied ornament: a term used to describe ornament which is worked separately and applied to an object. Carved decoration might be applied to furniture, for example.

Applied work: the sewing of patches on to the surface of a material so that they form a pattern. The edges of the pattern are usually outlined by embroidery. In the Middle Ages applied work was used as a cheaper substitute for tapestry, and during the Renaissance, figured brocades and velvets were imitated by this method. In the 16th and 17th cent. applied work was widely used for altar frontals and vestments, for hangings, chair covers, and horse trappings. In England during the 16th and 17th cent. motifs of animals, floral sprigs and insects were worked in tent stitch on canvas and then cut out and applied to cushion covers and hangings. Needlepoint lace motifs, in silk and metal thread, were similarly applied to work-boxes and embroidered pictures.

Apron piece: an ornamental member, either carved or simply shaped, some-times used below the seat rail of a chair or settle or below the frieze of cabinet stands and dressers.

Aquamanile: metal, usually bronze, ewers used in the Middle Ages for pouring water over the hands of guests after each course of a meal. As forks were not normally employed for conveying food to the mouth, frequent washing of the hands was indispensable. Though originally referring to all kinds of ewer, the term is now confined to a particular type of Medieval ewer of naturalistic form, the most popular being a lion on whose back crouches a dragon, serving as a handle. Other forms include a monster, a knight on horseback wearing a great helm, etc. Medieval aquamaniles of this type were cast by the *cire-perdue* process (q.v.) and no two were exactly alike; many reproductions have, however, been cast from moulds in recent times. The earliest examples date from the 13th cent., but they continued in use until the 16th cent., when they were replaced by the more convenient ewer of helmet shape. They are now objects of extreme rarity.

Aquatint: an indirect method of printing, unlike etching (q.v.) where the engraving tool scratches the lines directly on to the plate, in that an upper surface formed of resin or other substance is placed over the plate, and this is worked on, leaving room for acid to come down on to the plate and eat its way in, thus producing a tonal effect. Aquatint is therefore not a line process but one that produces a more general effect on the plate, and is softer than a line engraving. The aquatint was pioneered in England by Paul Sandby (1725/6–1809). Goya (1746–1828) and some of the Impressionist painters used the etching and aquatint techniques in combination. Aquatints may be hand coloured or colour printed by using a separate plate for each colour.

Arabesque: an ornament of Roman origin, commonly used in the borders and decorative panels of textiles and ceramics, especially Hispano-Moresque and Italian *maiolica* (q.v.). The motif is composed of interlacing naturalistic and abstract elements.

Arbor: the rotating shaft of a clock which carries wheels and pinions.

Arbour group: lovers seated within an alcove or a leafy arbour originally modelled in Germany at Meissen (q.v.), Höchst (q.v.), and elsewhere from 1750 onwards. Made in Staffordshire in white salt-glazed stoneware (q.v.) or Whieldon (q.v.) ware in mid-18th cent. England.

Arcaded decoration: a form of ornament in which a series of arches are represented, supported on columns or pilasters, and frequently found on furniture between 1600 and 1670.

Arcanist: a person knowing the secret of pottery-making in general, and of porcelain-making in particular.

Arcanum: chemical composition and technique of porcelain-making.

Architect's table: a table incorporating a drawing board and drawers for materials.

Architectural clock: a clock in which the hood, in long-case, and the top in mantel clocks, is in the style of a classical pediment, with or without supporting columns. Usually a sign of work in the third quarter of the 17th cent., although these pediment tops were revived for a short period early in the 19th cent.

Arch-top clock case, plain: a case, usually in bracket clocks, where the arch rises directly from the sides of the case.

Arfe family: 16th-cent. Castilian silversmiths famous for their church plate (q.v.) in an architectural style.

Argand lamp: oil lamp devised in the 1780s by the Swiss, Ami Argand (1755–1803). The wick is fitted between two cylindrical tubes, the inner one carrying air direct to the flame. The increased supply of oxygen magnifies the size of the flame and therefore the volume of light.

Argentan lace: needlepoint lace (q.v.) made at a workshop established in 1665. Resembled Alençon lace (q.v.) made ten miles away until they developed meshed grounds. The so-called Argentan lace was made also at Alençon, the work tending to be larger and more perfect than so-called Alençon, with bold patterns and a hexagonal ground, sometimes *picotée*, worked over in tiny buttonhole stitches. (See *Point de France*).

Argentella lace: a needlepoint lace (q.v.), being a variant of *point d'Alençon*, with a large dotted mesh.

Argil: clay, especially potters' clay, hence the trade name Mason's Cambrian Argil used for earthenware allegedly made from Welsh clay by the firm of G. M. and C. J. Mason, *c*. 1820. 'Cambria Clay' occurs in sale notices and means Welsh clay.

Argyle: a silver or plate (q.v.) gravy container, often cylindrical or vase-shaped, resembling a small coffee pot, with either outer lining or central container (sometimes detachable) for hot water. Introduced about 1770; in favour until about 1820.

Arita porcelain: Japanese porcelain made at Arita, where the first Japanese porcelain kilns were established. Two styles of decoration were developed at Arita, both much copied in the West: the Kakiemon style, so called from the Kakiemon family of potters, and the 'Imari', this being the neighbouring port from which the wares were shipped to Europe. (See also Kakiemon and Imari.)

Ark: an early chest with a gabled lid, usually of oak. In the 19th cent., a container for flour or meal.

Armada chest: heavy iron or iron-bound coffer of German manufacture, used in England and elsewhere until the invention of the modern safe in the 19th cent. The name derives from the romantic assumption that they were survivals from the wrecked ships of the Armada. Most of them date from the 17th or 18th cent. and were imported for practical use.

Armet: a type of helmet which probably originated in Italy and appeared in England about 1450. It was lighter than the bascinet (q.v.) and gave better protection. Unlike earlier helmets, which were put on over the head, the lower part was hinged and could be fastened round the head.

Armillary sphere: a construction of rings showing the path of the heavenly bodies, similar in appearance to a skeleton globe. Devised in the 2nd cent. A.D. by Ptolemy, and made until the end of the 16th cent. showing the earth at the centre of the universe. Later models were based on the Copernican system.

Armoire: French term for wardrobe. In France this item of furniture developed out of the cupboard and the cabinet in the late 17th cent. and was treated monumentally by Boulle (q.v.) and his workshop, many examples being made for the Crown and very sumptuously decorated.

From the constructional point of view it consists of a straight, upright cupboard closed by two doors and with one or more shelves in the undecorated interior. It survived into the early Regency, sometimes of plain carved wood, but as rooms became smaller it seems to have disappeared. A number were made in the Boulle technique in the Louis XVI period from earlier designs. Some also were made of plain wood under the Empire.

Armorial china: services of porcelain with coats of arms and crests were popular in the 18th cent., but until 1755 all were made in China at Ching-tê-Chên and ordered through merchants at Canton or through the East India Co. The decoration was done from bookplates, engravings or sketches specially sent to China.

After 1755 some English Armorial services were made, notably at the Worcester factory (q.v.) during the Dr Wall period and also later. Champion produced armorial porcelain at Bristol (q.v.), and most of the factories made pieces as replacements of broken Chinese examples. Some armorial wares were made by Josiah Wedgwood (q.v.) and the Leeds factory (q.v.).

Armorial fan: an ivory or tortoise-shell *brisé* fan (q.v.) enriched with a coat of arms or crest in a floral cartouche (q.v.). Fashionable during the third quarter of the 18th cent.

Arnoux, Léon: (1816–1902), French ceramic chemist and potter. Art director at Mintons (q.v.) from 1848 until his retirement in 1895, his presence at Stoke attracted many leading Continental artists. His achievements included the improvement of the bone porcelain body and glaze (q.v.), the reproduction of ground colours used at Sèvres (q.v.) and the development of *maiolica* (q.v.) colours and techniques.

Arquebus: a term occurring as early as the 15th cent. referring to some type of hand gun. In the late 15th and early 16th cent. it was applied to the earliest type of portable gun fitted with a shoulder butt and a match lock (q.v.). In the late 16th and early 17th cent. it was applied loosely to almost any type of light wheel- or match-lock gun.

Arrasene embroidery: a variation of chenille embroidery used mainly for curtain borders, mantel borders and screens where the pile of the arrasene (a fine wool or silk chenille thread) was not injured by friction. It was worked on canvas, silk, velvet or serge, in tent-stitch, stem or crewel stitch and couching.

Arras lace: pillow lace (q.v.), sometimes spelt 'orris' in old records. Usually associated with a coarser version of Lille (q.v.), but with scalloped edges. George I had 354 yards of it for his coronation. (See *Point de France*.)

Arras tapestry: under the Dukes of Burgundy in the 14th to 15th cent. Arras became a synonym for tapestry (as did Gobelins (q.v.) later) and 'thread of Arras' denoted the highest quality. Only one hanging has survived which can with absolute certainty be attributed to Arras: this is the story of SS Piat and Eleuthère in Tournai Cathedral, dated 1404. Throughout the 14th and 15th cent. Arras, with its great rival Tournai, produced enormous quantities of tapestry besides famous pieces of special quality. The city was razed in 1477, never recovered its position, and was a Habsburg possession from 1493–1640. The Flemish tapestry centre shifted first to Tournai, then to Brussels.

Art glass: mainly coloured glassware with colours shading into one another and with novel surface effects. Major movement in British and American art production between 1870 and 1890, continuing in some cases until the early 20th cent.

Art Nouveau: European and American decorative style of the late 19th and early 20th cent. It was characterized by elongated and flowing forms, combining naturalistic and fantastic elements, and iridescent colouring. The style was variously known as *Jugendstil* (q.v.), *nieuwe kunst* (in Holland and Belgium), *stile Floreale* and *stile Liberty* (in Italy). In Scotland the Glasgow School (q.v.) designers were affiliated to the Movement. (See also Mackintosh, C. R.; Voysey, C. F. A.; Tiffany, L. C.; Guimard, H.; Gallé, E., and Majorelle, L.)

Art pottery: initially inspired in England by the Arts and Crafts Movement (q.v.), the catalyst in both Europe and the United States for original wares was the influence of Japanese art in the last three decades of the 19th cent. Reacting against the industrialization of commercial pottery, workshops arose where a team of experts co-operated on group creations or the artist-potter worked alone on mastering every stage of the process. Wares range from unique pieces to everyday objects.

Arts and Crafts Movement: in the latter years of Queen Victoria's reign a number of guilds and societies were formed with the purpose of fostering a revival of interest in the craftsmanship of the Middle Ages and of developing a greater co-operation between the various crafts. The Arts and Crafts Exhibition Society, formed in 1886, arranged a series of exhibitions which illustrated the many contrasting tendencies of the age. The activities of these groups have come to be known as the Arts and Crafts Movement. The central figure was William Morris (q.v.).

Art Unions: societies formed, under the auspices of the Prince Consort, to promote the sale of works of art. The Art Union of London was established in 1836 and organized the annual lottery of works of art for which members were eligible on payment of an annual subscription.

Art Workers' Guild: an informal group of English artists, designers and craftsmen, formed in 1884, which held discussions on collaboration between the different branches of the decorative arts and on working conditions. An American equivalent was founded at Providence, Rhode Island.

Ashbee, Charles Robert: (1863–1942), an English architect and designer and prominent figure in the Arts and Crafts Movement (q.v.). He was the founder of the Guild and School of Handicraft, for which he designed furniture, silver and jewellery, and a member of the Art Workers' Guild (q.v.). His work is characterized by the combination of various different techniques and materials in a single piece.

Ashburton goblet: goblet pattern pressed in scalloped and other designs by Boston and Sandwich (q.v.) and other American glasshouses of the 19th cent.

Asparagus tongs: silver or plate (q.v.) servers for asparagus with ribbed blades; either in the form of scissors or, like sugar tongs (q.v.), of spring form, often with a guide bracket.

Asprey & Co.: manufacturing and retail firm of jewellers and makers of luxury items such as dressing-boxes (q.v.). Founded in London in 1781.

Assapink Pottery Co.: organized by Henry Speeler at Trenton, New Jersey, the factory produced Belleek ware (q.v.) during the 1860s and 1870s.

Assay: test of purity of a metal. Gold, silver and pewter (q.v.) must be assayed and marked in some countries to show that the article conforms to the legal standard of fineness. (See also Hallmark and Sterling Standard.) Also, a sample piece of work made by a craftsman for acceptance by a guild.

Assisi work: a type of embroidery (so called from the modern embroidery made in Assisi) in which the ground is covered in long-armed cross stitch, leaving the pattern reserved in plain linen. It is usually found in borders or strips, and the earliest examples date from the 16th cent. The patterns include formal designs in typical Renaissance style, figure subjects, including hunting scenes, and stylized birds and animals. Red silk is most commonly used, but green and brown are also found. A similar type of embroidery comes from Azemmour in Morocco, but the designs are more geometric, often of birds, and somewhat bolder in style.

Astbury, John: (1688–1743), John Astbury is almost a legendary figure in Staffordshire pottery history, though little can be stated with certainty about him. Simeon Shaw's stories that he introduced the use of Devonshire white-firing clays and calcined flints into the earthenware body may be true but contemporary evidence in support is lacking. On the strength of tradition John Astbury is credited with the manufacture of red earthenware teapots and other articles with applied white relief decorations, and image toys of musicians, soldiers, etc., made in red and white clays under a lead glaze, sometimes crudely stained with colouring oxides. Both types were made by other Staffordshire potters. He employed as apprentices R. Wood (q.v.) and T. Whieldon (q.v.).

Astbury's name does not occur in Wedgwood's (q.v.) list of early Staffordshire potters; nor are there any authentic examples marked with his name, although the impressed mark ASTBURY is recorded on productions by later members of the Astbury family potting at the Foley, Fenton.

Astbury & Maddock: founded after 1853 at Trenton, New Jersey, from an earlier company. They experimented with porcelain production using kaolin (q.v.) from Missouri and Pennsylvania.

Astbury-type ware: a classification of Staffordshire pottery, produced c. 1730–70, in which red and white clays are combined under a transparent lead glaze. Similar wares, in which the glaze is splashed or dabbed with metallic oxides, are generally called 'Astbury-Whieldon'.

Astbury-Whieldon ware: see Astbury-type ware.

Astragal: a plain semi-circular moulding. The term is used also to describe the glazing bars of cabinet furniture, such as book cases and secretaires, made from about 1750.

Astrolabe: instrument current from c. A.D. 500 to mid-17th cent., formerly used to ascertain the position of the heavenly bodies. Early examples are Arabian and those made in Europe in the Middle Ages emulate the earlier types. Usually made of brass or gilt bronze, finely engraved and pierced. Superseded by more accurate instruments and finally by the sextant.

Astrological dials: these are embodied in many early clocks and watches and reflect the important part that astrology played in the everyday life of the people. They show the relation or aspect of the planets to one another at any time. They are usually shown as related to the moon, whose phases are to be seen through an aperture in the dial for this purpose. The distances in degrees are shown by the Trines △ (120°), Quartiles □ (90°), Sextiles * (60°), Conjunction ♂ (0°), and Opposition ♂ (180°).

Atlanta: a sculptured male figure or half-figure, used as a support, in place of a column, and found on Classical architecture. A motif adopted as a decorative form on oak furniture such as chests, cupboard fronts and beds in the early 17th cent., it regained popularity in the late 18th and early 19th cent. being used by architects, metalworkers, furniture makers, etc. (See also Caryatid.)

Aubusson and Felletin tapestry: it is rare to see tapestries from these workshops in La Marche on the road between Bordeaux and Lyon, which date from earlier than the 18th cent. They also flourished in the 16th and 17th cent. but they lost many workmen abroad in 1685 after the Revocation of the Edict of Nantes. Aubusson tapestry is generally less fine than that of Beauvais (q.v.) and was made for the less pretentious houses of the aristocracy and bourgeoisie. Felletin tapestries tend to be coarser, and at Belegarde, nearby, where the weavers only worked in the winter months, the most rustic of French hangings were

produced. Aubusson copied the *Verdure*, animal, and *Fable* designs of Oudry, Boucher's *Chinoiseries*, and Huet's pastorals, interpreting them very effectively in their somewhat coarser texture. In the late 18th and 19th cent. much tapestry for upholstery was woven.

Aubusson carpets: knotted pile carpets were made at Aubusson from 1742 and at nearby Felletin from 1786. An upright loom was used as at the Savonnerie (q.v.), but the carpets were considerably cheaper. Eighteenth-cent. Aubusson carpets were designed by the Court painters and were of excellent quality. Tapestry or smooth-faced carpets were also made, especially in the 19th cent. With the Revolution the production of moquette carpets (q.v.) was introduced.

Auguste, Robert-Joseph: (*c.* 1736–1805), French jeweller, silversmith and goldsmith who worked in the Rococo (q.v.) and Neoclassical (q.v.) manner. He was Court goldsmith and Crown jeweller to Louis XVI.

Austin, Jesse: (1806–79), English pottery decorator particularly remembered for his decoration of pot lids, notably 'the bear series'.

Automata: mechanically operated figures; the first maker of actual automata as distinct from jacks, and of whom there is a full record, was Jacques de Vaucanson, who exhibited his three mechanical figures before the *Académie des Sciences* in Paris, in 1738, The success that greeted their appearance when they were later shown in London, St Petersburg and in Germany encouraged the making of more automata. The displaying of them became a common feature of the scene in any big city, and the fame of Spring Gardens in London, where Cox (q.v.) showed his pieces, was duplicated in other capitals. (See also Miniature automata and Automata watches.)

Automata watches: not content with following the hours and sounding them, adding a repeater and, perhaps, music, the Swiss craftsmen found space for automata; from a dog that barked quietly, but with realism, at each hour to jousting knights complete with trumpeter, and see-sawing children enjoying themselves before a playing (glass) fountain. Mostly they were cased in gold, and the tiny figures and landscapes made of the same precious metal in different colours.

Automatic winding watch: a pocket watch which is wound up by means of a weight actuated by the motion of the body. A patent was taken out in London in 1780 by Louis Recordon, but prior claim is made for Abraham Louis Perrelet, of Le Locle.

Ave Maria lace: pillow lace (q.v.) made at Dieppe until the mid-19th cent. in long strips with a plaited lozenge ground.

Aventail: see Bascinet.

Aventurine glass: glass rendered opaque, usually of a brown hue, the substance spangled by the addition of metallic particles. Copper oxide and forge-scales are included in the mixture to create this effect. It is said to have been first introduced in Venice in the early 17th cent. by the glass-making family Miotti (q.v.).

Axminster carpets: Thomas Whitty began the weaving of knotted pile carpets, at first inspired by Turkish models and then learning from Parisot at Fulham (q.v.) (1750–5). In 1757–9 he won three awards from the Royal Society of Arts, submitting six carpets for the 1759 competition. His prices were more moderate than Moore or Passavant (see Exeter and Moorfields carpets) and his industry thrived and was continued by his son. The Axminster workshops closed down in 1835, when the looms were taken over by Wilton (q.v.).

Baccarat glassworks: one of the most eminent in France during the 19th cent. All types of paperweights (q.v.) were made there, including encrusted (sulphide), millefiori, mushroom, flowers, fruit and butterfly. No dated weight from the Baccarat factory is known marked earlier than 1846 and, as elsewhere, none later than 1849. The numerals are in red, blue or green in white canes set in a line, and there is often a letter 'B', similarly coloured, above and between the figures '8' and '4'. The glassworks, which takes its name from the town, Baccarat, in which it is situated, is still working.

Bachelor's chest: low chest of drawers with a top consisting of a hinged flap that opens out to form an additional surface.

Back-painting: the art of mounting prints on to the back of glass, making them transparent, and colouring them in from behind. This art, which probably originated in England, dates back to the second half of the 17th cent. It is not known how it originated. There were several variants of the principal method used for making these prints, described in full in the chapter entitled 'Process or Art of Making a Glass Picture' in the book *Polygraphice* (1700) by William Salmon.

The print itself was first soaked in water for four or five hours to remove the size from the paper. A sheet of fine Bristol glass (q.v.) was then covered with an adhesive (usually Venice turpentine) and the print, when dry, laid face down upon it. When it had set, the back of the print was again damped, and the paper rubbed away with a sponge or the finger tips, leaving only a thin tissue with the impression of the print adhering to the glass. After it had again dried out it was coloured in.

The earlier and more beautiful back-paintings owe their clarity to the fact that only the smallest quantity of paper was allowed to remain on the print. Later examples made by amateurs or less skilled professionals have a much more opaque and stodgy appearance, owing to a greater thickness of paper being allowed to remain, the required transparency being partially produced by a white varnish. Back-painting was an anonymous art, although in its earliest days it is almost certain that the engraver of the print himself produced them.

Back-stool: by the end of Queen Elizabeth I's reign it had become fashionable to take meals on joined stools which could be placed round the dining table more conveniently than the Medieval wall benches. To increase comfort a back was added and the stool became known as a back-stool. In the 17th and 18th cent. this term was used to describe a single chair.

Backsword: a sword comparable to a broadsword (q.v.) but having a single cutting edge.

Bacon, John: (1740–99), sculptor and porcelain modeller. Apprenticed to Crispe of Bow Churchyard, 'an eminent maker of porcelain', in 1754. Tradition ascribes to him porcelain figures of Quin as Falstaff, Garrick as Richard III, figures of cooks, and John Wilkes. He is known to have worked for Wedgwood, for Duesbury (qq.v.), who paid his account in 1769, possibly for Champion's Bristol factory and for Enoch Wood of Burslem (qq.v.). He certainly worked, after leaving Crispe, at Coade's Artificial Stone Manufactory (q.v.), of which he eventually became manager.

Baguettes: gemstones of small dimensions cut in narrow rectangles.

Bail handle: half-loop metal handle used on furniture and silver, on a cake basket (q.v.), for example.

Ball-and-claw foot (or **claw and ball**): terminal to a cabriole leg (q.v.), representing a dragon's claw or a bird's claw holding a ball. It is said to be an adaptation from the Chinese dragon's claw grasping a pearl. In use on English furniture from the early until the late years of the 18th cent. and very popular as the foot of American cabriole-leg furniture in the Queen Anne and Chippendale styles.

Ball clay: a plastic clay from Devonshire and Dorset used in the manufacture of earthenware so called from the manner of its excavation.

Ball foot: a round foot in the shape of a ball, used as a terminal to cabinets or table legs in the late 17th cent. and on silver. (See also Bun foot.)

Ball knop: a knop or protuberance on the stem of a drinking glass or other vessel of large spherical form, often found immediately above a shouldered stem. (See Moulded pedestal stem.)

Ballock-knife: see Kidney-dagger.

Balloon-back: a type of chair back common in Britain and the United States in the 19th cent. with a loop back that narrows towards the seat.

Balloon clock: a type of waisted clock popular in the late 18th and early 19th cent.

Balloon seat: see Bell seat.

Ballot box: see Salt kit.

Baluster measure: a pewter tavern measure, bulging below, concave above.

Baluster stem: a type of stem, resembling a baluster, familiar on glass drinking vessels between *c.* 1685 and *c.* 1760 and made in a variety of forms: a stem consisting of a pure baluster form which might be inverted; also a baluster associated with various knopped motifs sometimes with a tear; (a) 1685–1725; heavy inverted baluster with solid bowl-base, the depth of the bowl being almost invariably less than stem length; (b) 1700–25: simple knop such as an angular, annulated, cushioned or

True   Inverted
baluster   baluster

drop knop (qq.v.), with or without a baluster; from 1710 acorn, cylinder, or mushroom knops were usual; from 1715 true baluster alone or with various knops and a pair of balusters placed head to head between a pair of knops; (c) 1725–65: light balusters, true or inverted, supporting bowls with thin bases; illustrated on trade cards of the 1760s. Between 1725 and 1740 the stem and collar baluster is found in which a merese (q.v.) separated bowl from stem. Baluster stems were familiar on silver, wooden, and pewter cups at a much earlier date, while candlesticks of baluster form in a variety of materials were made throughout the 17th and 18th cent.

Baluster turning: a variety of wood turning carried out on the pole lathe in which a number of shapes are achieved by the turner holding the chisel himself and varying the pressure accordingly. A familiar form was the vase-shaped turned support, found particularly on stools and tables of the first half of the 17th cent.

Bamboo turning: furniture made in the Chinese taste in the latter half of the 18th cent. and during the Regency was often constructed of soft wood and painted or japanned, the legs being turned to resemble bamboo.

Bamboo ware: a dark shade of cane-coloured stoneware, made by Josiah Wedgwood (q.v.) in 1770, in imitation of bamboo.

Bandbox: originally a box made of thin band-sawed wood, later of cardboard. Types vary between oval and round, painted, plain and paper-covered.

Banding: a decorative inlaid border, used on late 17th- and 18th-cent. furniture, made of a wood contrasting in colour or grain with that of the surface of the piece. (See also Cross-banded veneer and Herring-bone banding.)

Banford, James: a porcelain painter who first worked at Bristol (q.v.)

although the work that he did then cannot now be identified. He worked for the Derby (q.v.) factory from 1790 until 1795, having also done some work at Wedgwood's (q.v.) decoration workshop at Chelsea. He excelled as a figure painter but also painted flowers, landscapes and birds, turning his hand, in fact, to everything. Most of his painting was done to a small scale with miniature-like delicacy, often upon coffee cans.

Banister-back chair: a chair with a tall back consisting of several splats of split-banister form made in America and widely used there in the early 18th cent. It is usually of maple and often ebonized.

Banjo barometer: barometer with a case resembling a banjo.

Banjo clock: modern name for an American wall clock with a longish pendulum, the whole housed in a case shaped somewhat like a banjo. Invented in the 1790s by Simon Willard, and patented by him about 1800. Made *c.* 1802–60 with a pendulum, round face, painted glass panels and a rectangular base.

Bannock rack: resembles a large toast rack, the silver tray secured to a wooden base. Most surviving date from the second half of the 18th cent. Bannock is a flat home-baked cake made from oatmeal, barley or pease-meal, generally the first, broken into pieces when removed from the girdle and served hot.

Bantam work: a name given to incised lacquer, from the trading station of the Dutch East India Company in Java whence it was exported. Also Dutch and English imitations of the technique dating from the late 17th cent.

Bar-and-heart thumbpiece: a plain, wide thumbpiece (q.v.), pierced by a heart and surmounted by a thick bar found on pewter flagons and tankards.

Barbedienne, Ferdinand: mid-19th cent. French bronze founder, whose mark is sometimes found on small sculptures and *objets de vertu*.

Barberini vase: see Portland vase.

Barber's dish: a wide-rimmed circular dish with a segment notch in the rim to fit the neck, part of the barber-surgeon's equipment.

Barbute: a 15th-cent. open helmet of Italian origin, one of the forms of the sallet (q.v.). It was tall, at first with a pointed apex, later becoming rounded, and extended over the cheeks, leaving only the eyes, nose and mouth exposed. Some examples closely resemble the Classical Greek Corinthian helmet, on which they may perhaps have been directly based.

Bargeman jug: a late and very rare variety of toby jug (q.v.).

Bargueño (or **vargueño**): Spanish cabinet with fall front enclosing drawers and often mounted on a stand. Made of various woods.

Barker of Bath: an artist in sporting scenes, Benjamin Barker was engaged by William Allgood (q.v.) as foreman decorator at the Pontypool Japan works in the late 1770s. He was the father of the celebrated artists, Thomas and Benjamin Barker of Bath, both of whom were born at Pontypool and decorated trays for Allgood. Thomas specialized in rustic groups and figures of shepherds and woodsmen; Benjamin was celebrated for his landscapes. (See Pontypool ware.)

Barley-sugar turning: see Twist turning.

Barm pot: pot for storing barm or yeast (see also Salt kit).

Barnard, Edward, & Sons: London silversmiths established in 1689. They produced church and domestic silver and, after 1842, electro-plated wares under licence from Elkington & Co. (q.v.).

Barnard, Bishop & Barnard: English firm of metalworkers at Norwich, Norfolk. Much of their ornamental work was designed by Thomas Jeckyll (q.v.).

Barnsley, Sydney: (1865–1926), English architect, designer and maker of simple furniture exploiting the natural effects of grain and colouring in the Arts and Crafts tradition. In 1894 he began to work with Ernest Gimson (q.v.). His brother Ernest (1863–1926) was also a designer and craftsman.

Barograph: a self-recording barometer actuated by clockwork.

Baroque: the word appears to derive from the Spanish *Barucca*, meaning a deformed pearl, and describes a style which lasted, in general terms, throughout the 17th cent. Ostensibly based on Classical ideals, Baroque, originating in Italy, is ebullient in spirit and is characterized by rich, decorative effects and the use of prolific foliage, rounded contours and heavy symmetrical volutes. Dynamic movement replaces the restraint of Classic order, plastic form is fully exploited and light and shade are used for dramatic effect. A wide range of individual schools falls under the term, whether of architecture, painting or sculpture while the minor arts too reflect the Baroque spirit. In England the sumptuously carved late-Stuart woodwork and richly embossed silver of the period are manifestations of the Baroque style.

Barum ware: art pottery produced by C. H. Brannam in Barnstaple, Devon, from 1879. Decoration was in *sgraffiato* (q.v.) or painted slip (q.v.), and pieces were normally dated and signed with the initials of the decorator.

Barye, Antoine-Louis: (1796–1875), French sculptor and founder of the group of *Animaliers* (q.v.). His works were principally cast by the *cire-perdue* process (q.v.), and there are many later and inferior copies in existence

Basaltes: unglazed fine-grained black stoneware perfected by Wedgwood. 'A black porcelain biscuit of nearly the same properties with the natural stone, striking fire from steel, receiving a high polish, serving as a touchstone for metals, resisting all acids and bearing without injury a strong fire – stronger indeed than the basaltes itself.' (Wedgwood *Catalogue*, 1787.)

Basaltes was a refinement of the 'dry' black stoneware originally made by Elers (q.v.). Its black colour was due to the presence of iron and manganese in the body (q.v.). In addition to Wedgwood it was made by Adams, Neale & Co., Turner, Hollins, Walton (qq.v.), Palmer, Birch, Mayer and others.

Bascinet: the characteristic light helmet of the 14th and early 15th cent. It was conical in shape and usually had a mail curtain (aventail) laced to its lower edge, protecting the throat and neck. In the second half of the 14th cent. it was often worn with an acutely pointed 'pig-faced' visor.

In the 15th cent. the helmet became more rounded, and the aventail was replaced by a plate gorget; in this form it remained in use for fighting on foot in the lists until the beginning of the 16th cent.

Basin stand: see Washing stand.

Basket-hilted sword: a sword with a hilt in the form of a basket, usually with a broad blade. Introduced at the end of the 16th cent. Much used by the cavalry in the 17th cent. (See Broadsword and Schiavona.)

Basket-top clock case: a pierced metallic and roughly dome-shaped case top, current at the end of the 17th and early in the 18th cent.

Bas relief: a term used in sculpture to describe a modelled decoration in low relief, in which the design is only slightly raised from the surface.

Basse-taille enamel: see Enamel.

Basting spoon: long-handled, with nearly oval bowl, early examples rat-tailed (q.v.), presumed to have been used for basting. Similar in form to early punch ladles and probably of general domestic use.

Batavian ware: Chinese export porcelains with lustrous brown-glazed ground and panels of *famille rose* (q.v.) decoration; named after the Dutch trading station in Java through which they reached Europe in the early 18th cent.

Bateman, Hester: (1709–94), most prominent of a family of English goldsmiths and silversmiths who entered her mark at the Goldsmiths' Hall in 1761. Her mark is often overstruck by that of other makers who undertook work for her.

Baton-cut stones: stones cut in a long narrow rectangle.

Bat printing: process of transfer-printing from engraved copper plates in which a bat of gelatine takes the place of transfer tissue. Used on enamels from about 1780, twenty years after its introduction to England by William Wynn Ryland. Because of its sensitivity to fine engraving the process was extensively used in the first decade of the 19th cent. at Mintons (q.v.), Copeland (q.v.), etc., for transfer printing vignettes of shells and flowers.

Batsto ironware: Furnace in production in New Jersey after 1776 which made fishpots, cookpots, skillets and Dutch ovens which were regarded as superior in quality to those imported from Great Britain.

Battersea enamel: a painted enamel produced at York House (q.v.), Battersea, London, while this factory was controlled by Stephen Theodore

Janssen (q.v.) (1753–6), the firm at first being styled Janssen, Delamain and Brooks. It appears obvious that this association was based on a common belief in the possibilities of decorating the enamels with transfer-prints taken on transfer-papers from engraved copper plates. But Janssen's position in the art world enabled him to call on the services of such exceptionally skilled craftsmen as Ravenet (q.v.). The enterprise was discontinued in 1756, the year in which Janssen was declared bankrupt; the notices of sales, of Janssen's household goods and of the York House stock-in-trade, are the main source of information regarding the types of enamel the firm produced, though engraved copper plates bought at the sales were subsequently used elsewhere. The list included snuff-boxes, pictures, wine-labels, watch-cases, toothpick-cases, coat and sleeve buttons, crosses and 'other Curiosities'.

Battery clock: clock powered by an electric battery, invented by Alexander Bain (1810–77) in 1840.

Baudouine, Charles: New York furniture manufacturer, best known for his pieces in an elaborate Rococo style (q.v.). He also executed, with the assistance of a large staff, a number of pieces in the Renaissance Revival style (q.v.).

Baxter, Thomas: (1782–1821), a china painter. His father was the proprietor of an outside decorating business in London, and he worked for the Worcester porcelain factory. Baxter removed to Worcester in 1814, working as an instructor of apprentices and as an outside artist until 1816 when he went to Swansea. He returned, however, to Worcester, in 1818. He was a painter of landscapes, flowers and figures, subjects which he executed with careful regard to finish and detail. He was particularly successful with shells and feathers.

Baxter licensees: George Baxter (see Baxter prints) granted licences to work his process of colour printing to a number of firms between 1849 and 1854, when the patent expired. The firms were all known as Baxter licensees, and this name seems to have clung to them even after the expiry of the patent. The licensees were Le Blond & Co., J. M. Kronheim, Bradshaw and Blacklock, William Dickens, Joseph Mansell, Myers & Co. The work of all these firms, both in the form of individual prints and in books, has been collected by many. The best-known series, at one time eagerly sought after, were the Le Blond ovals, country scenes, whose shape, of course, gives them the name.

Baxter prints: a process of printing in colours patented by George Baxter (1804–67) in 1835 and used by him with considerable success for a number of years. The impression was made with one engraved copper plate and several, up to twenty, engraved wood blocks, one block for each colour, using oil inks. The process was known as Oil Colour Picture Printing, but the oil is a reference to the inks and does not imply that Baxter prints are like paintings in oils. Many hundreds of Baxter prints appeared up to 1860, in particular in the early 1850s. The first use of Baxter's work was in Mudie's *Feathered Tribes of the British Isles 1834;* the first complete book of Baxter's was *The Pictorial Album or Cabinet of Paintings 1837.* Baxter prints cover almost every possible subject, including some interesting illustrations of the Great Exhibition. They are of all sizes, from folio down to that of a postage stamp.

Bay-leaf garland: a crown of bay-leaves or laurels traditionally worn by classical poets or heroes. Border ornaments composed of stylized leaves, bound with ribbon, were used particularly by goldsmiths in the late 17th cent.

Bayonet: a dagger, or short sword, fitted to a gun to convert it into a pike. Known early in the 17th cent., it was not generally adopted for military purposes until the second half of that cent. At first simply a dagger with round grip, tapered to fit into the musket muzzle, a form which remained in use until well into the 18th cent., but this was gradually superseded by the socket-bayonet, introduced in the late 17th cent. This had a tubular hilt fitting over the muzzle, the blade being set to one side so that the musket could be fired with the bayonet fixed. It was superseded in the 19th cent. by the sword bayonet, attached to a lug on the barrel by a spring-catch and with a hilt like that of a sword.

Bead moulding: a moulding made to simulate a string of beads. Bead mouldings are familiar on 18th-cent. furniture and metalwork.

Beadwork: the earliest surviving English beadwork dates from the 17th cent. Particularly interesting are the shallow baskets, almost tray-shaped, with a flat bottom and sloping sides, decorated entirely with small coloured glass beads sewn on linen canvas. Pictorial subjects, similar to those of the contemporary embroidered pictures, are most common. Looking-glass frames were decorated in this manner, and also caskets, some of which have miniature gardens inside the lid with free-standing flowers made of glass beads mounted on wire. Bead work purses are also found during the 17th, 18th and early 19th cent. Bead work was commonly used to decorate garters.

Beaker: handleless drinking vessel of all periods, usually of tapering cylindrical form. Early examples in silver have engraved or *repoussé* decoration, but later are usually plain.

Bear jug: a jug in the form of a bear hugging a dog, illustrating the sport of bear-baiting. The detachable head was used as a cup. Made in white salt-glazed stoneware in Staffordshire and brown stoneware at Nottingham and in Derbyshire in the 18th cent. Enamelled bear jugs were made in Staffordshire and Yorkshire in the late 18th and early 19th cent.

Beauvais carpets: knotted pile carpets in the Savonnerie (q.v.) manner were made between 1780–*c.* 92 and again for a few years under Napoleon I. Production stopped when high warp looms moved to Gobelins in 1819.

Beauvais tapestry: the factory was founded in 1664 as a private enterprise supported by the State (Colbert). It was to Beauvais that foreign princes and lords had recourse to obtain tapestry' in the French taste and by the best designers of the Courts of Louis XIV, XV and XVI (see Gobelins). Béhagle (who came from Tournai) created the first successful Beauvais period (1684–1704). Particularly popular were the *Grotesques* after Bérain's designs, which are still frequently met with; also the first *Tenture Chinoise*, after Bernansal. An even more prosperous period followed under Oudry, painter at Beauvais from 1726 and inspector from 1734. His own designs included, besides landscape and animal scenes, the famous *Fables de la Fontaine* series, which were particularly popular as an ensemble of hangings and upholstery. Tapestry covers for suites of chairs and *canapés* (q.v.) remained a special feature of Beauvais throughout the 18th and 19th cent. In the 1730s and '40s Boucher's designs attained a pre-eminence which they have never lost, i.e. the *Italian Comedy*, the *Amours des Dieux*, the *Chinese set* (Second *Tenture Chinoise*) representing the most important. The weaving at Beauvais achieved a very fine texture at this time; much silk and finely tinted dyes were used. But it should be remembered that not all Beauvais tapestry is of this excessively fine quality; good but less expensive furnishing tapestry was always produced there. Also, many

18th-cent. designs were reproduced throughout the 19th cent., but as the dyes had been over-refined and an excessive number of tones were used, they easily fade to a rather dull and lifeless uniformity. The last triumph at Beauvais was the *Pastorals* designed by Huet and woven in the decade before the Revolution.

Bed steps: short set of steps made in Britain and the United States, principally in the 18th cent., to facilitate access to high beds.

Bedwarmers: Covered metal containers, normally of brass, with big wooden handles, into which hot embers could be placed. They were occasionally made in silver, but few have survived. In use in Europe from 15th cent.; in England from 16th cent.

Beefeater flagon: a pewter flagon having a lid somewhat resembling the head-dress of the Yeomen of the Tower of London.

Beefsteak dish: similar to an entrée dish (q.v.), and described in a 1797 catalogue of Sheffield plate (q.v.) by John Cadman of Sheffield as fitted with 'the handle to screw off to make a pair of dishes occasionally'.

Beehive clock: a form of small Connecticut shelf clock, also called 'flatiron' clock; so named because of the resemblance of the shape to an old-time beehive or flatiron. Manufactured in Connecticut from *c.* 1847.

Beer-wagon: see Coaster.

Beetham, Isabella: (b. 1750), English silhouettist who had a studio in Cornhill, London.

Beilby, William: (1740–1819) a celebrated enameller of flint-glass vessels who worked with his sister Mary in Newcastle-upon-Tyne from about 1760 to 1776, signing his best work by name and with a lifelike butterfly.

Belcher chain: a chain, worn in the 19th cent., consisting of broad, equally sized links.

Belcher ring: a ring worn in the 19th cent., for securing a neckerchief.

Bell, John: (1811–95), English sculptor and designer of metalwork who executed a number of public monuments. He also made designs for parian (q.v.) figures.

Bellarmine: a stoneware alehouse bottle, big-bellied, narrow-necked, with a bearded mask opposite the handle. It was named after Cardinal Robert Bellarmine (1542–1621). First imported to this country from the Rhineland and Holland, it was later, in the 17th cent., made in England by John Dwight (*c.* 1633–1703) of Fulham and others.

The bellarmine is frequently mentioned or referred to in English 17th-cent. literature, notably by Ben Jonson, Thomas Shadwell and Thomas D'Urfey; and Hogarth figures a bellarmine in the sixth plate of *The Harlot's Progress* (published 1733–4).

It was also known as a Grey Beard or Long Beard.

For its use in witchcraft and magic see Witch bottles.

Belleek: a light, fragile feldspathic (q.v.) porcelain cast in moulds, with lustrous pearly glaze. Invented *c.* 1860 by William Goss of Stoke, improved by William Bromley at the Irish factory of David McBirney & Co. (founded 1857 at Belleek, Co. Fermanagh) which by 1865 won a medal at the Dublin Exhibition. Produced at many American factories 1882–1900 and called Lotus Ware by Knowles of East Liverpool.

Bell-flower ornament: an American term for a conventionalized hanging ('belle') flower bud of three, occasionally five, petals carved or, more often, inlaid one below the other in diminishing size down the legs of a table or chair or, sometimes, a chair splat (q.v.). Seen in American, notably Maryland, furniture of the late 18th cent. It is practically the same as the English 'husk' motif. (See also Husk ornament.)

Bell-form bowl: the bowl of a drinking glass of a deep, waisted form with incurved profile and wide mouth popular during the 18th cent.

Bell metal: bronze used in the casting of bells and some domestic wares.

Bellows: contrivances for making a draught artificially, dating from very early times. Mention is made of bellows in wills from 1500 onwards, but as they suffered hard usage, survivors are seldom from earlier than the 17th cent.; and any of that date are a great rarity. They received their due share of attention and were decorated in many styles. Carved and inlaid wood, wood overlaid with leather or silver, and even finely stitched needlework were used to ornament them. Lacquered examples were made in the first quarter of the 18th cent. Apart from the small hand-bellows, which were often decorative rather than useful, more businesslike machines were made; doubtless for the use of those servants on whom the warmth of the house depended. These standing-bellows were in heavy wooden frames, and rested on the ground firmly, to be worked by means of a lever. Another type, lighter in weight, was operated by turning a wheel which was linked to the mechanism by a cord. This last type dates from the early 19th cent.

The construction of the bellows has not changed in the course of the centuries. It comprises two shaped boards with a spring to keep them apart, held together by a loose leather hinge. One of the boards is pierced in the centre and fitted with a flap of leather on the inside, which acts as a valve, letting air enter but not allowing it to escape except by way of the nozzle. (See also Blowing tube.)

Bell (or **balloon**) **seat:** an American term describing the rounded, somewhat bell-shaped, seat often found in late Philadelphia mid-18th-cent. side chairs.

Bell-top clock case: the top of a clock case where the lower portion is shaped like the bell of a turret clock with concave sides.

Belouchistan rugs: early Turkoman rugs often in prayer designs, the use of blue and lustrous yarn, combining with the coppery red, giving an iridescent effect to otherwise heavy colours.

Belper pottery: a manufacture of coarse brown ware existed here from about 1750. The incised mark 'Belper' is recorded on a mug dated 1775. William Bourne took over the factory about 1800. It was closed down in 1834.

Belter, John Henry: (1804–63), New York furniture maker of German birth who patented a process of laminating and steam-bending wood, subsequently used by Charles Baudouine (q.v.). He worked in the style of the Rococo Revival.

Bended-back chair: name given to chairs with hooped backs and solid splats (q.v.), on account of the curved shape of the splat which allowed the sitter to lean back comfortably.

Beneman, Jean Guillaume: French cabinet-maker, German by birth. Came to Paris c. 1784 but trained prior to this date, when he is first mentioned as being employed by the *Garde Meuble de la Couronne* (q.v.). In 1785 he became a *maître-ébéniste* (see *Menuisiers-Ebénistes, Corporation des*) but without the normal formalities. His employment by the Crown coincides with the disfavour into which Riesener (q.v.) fell owing to his high charges. Beneman made a large amount of furniture for Queen Marie Antoinette and the Court, and was employed also to repair earlier furniture in the possession of the Crown. He collaborated with all the leading craftsmen of the time, including Boizot and Thomire (q.v.), but his furniture retains usually a rather heavy Teutonic appearance. He seems to have specialized in making commodes and *meubles d'entre deux* (q.v.). He was officially employed under the Directoire and Consulate, but his name disappears about 1804. He used the stamp:

G·BENEMAN

Beni: a pink or red pigment used in Japanese prints and obtained from saffron flowers.

Beni-e: Japanese print in which the principal hand-colouring was executed in *beni* (q.v.).

Benizuri-e: Japanese print in which *beni* (q.v.) is one of the colours used in the printing, i.e. a colour print.

Bennett, Edwin: (1818–1908), from 1855 to 1908, Bennett produced parian ware (q.v.) busts, pitchers and figurines. Born in Derbyshire, England, Bennett emigrated to the United States in 1839 to join his brother James's pottery in East Liverpool, Ohio. In 1844 he established his own pottery in Baltimore, Maryland, and traded with his brother William as E. & W. Bennett from 1848–56. Awarded a gold medal at the 1876 Centennial Exposition, Bennett became a major producer of parian ware. By 1886 the factory was also producing Belleek ware (q.v.). In 1890 the company was incorporated as the Edwin Bennett pottery.

Bennington ware: redware (q.v.), stoneware (q.v.), Rockingham (q.v.), and yellow ware (q.v.), but particularly refers to white granite and flint-enamelled ware made at Bennington Vermont.

Benoiton chain: chain suspended from the bonnet or the coiffure to form a loop on the bosom, introduced in England *c.* 1866.

Benson, William Arthur Smith: (1854–1924), English architect and designer of furniture and metalwork, and a founder of the Art Workers' Guild (q.v.). He designed articles for mass production by Morris & Co. (q.v.) and had his own factory at Hammersmith mainly for the production of utilitarian objects.

Bentwood furniture: in the mid-19th cent. Michael Thonet (q.v.) invented a technique for steam-bending solid or laminated wood, especially for the mass production of chairs.

Bérain, Jean: (*c.* 1639–1711), French designer, whose published designs in the Baroque (q.v.) manner were widely followed in silver, furniture, tapestries and the decoration of interiors.

Bergama rugs: Turkish rugs usually with a Mihrab (q.v.) on each end, giving a balanced design. These rugs, woven entirely of very lustrous wool, though not fine in texture, have pleasing colours, the borders bearing a marked affinity to the Caucasian weaves. Made almost exclusively by nomads and sent to town of Bergama for sale.

Bergère: a type of armchair with upholstered sides, frequently with a loose cushion, much favoured in France in the mid- and late-18th cent.

Berlin porcelain: a porcelain factory was started in Berlin in 1752 by Wilhelm Kasper Wegely, a wool merchant, with the encouragement of Frederick the Great, who had long wished to own a porcelain factory. Frederick, however, soon became dissatisfied with Wegely's porcelain and withdrew his patronage in 1757, when the venture was abandoned. Wegely's porcelain was hard-paste (q.v.) and in form and decoration much influenced by Meissen (q.v.). The mark used was a 'W' in blue, sometimes with numerals. A second factory was started in Berlin in 1761 by Johann Ernst Gotzkowsky, which was subsequently purchased by Frederick the Great in 1763 and became the Royal Porcelain Manufactory. After the first World War the title was changed to the State Porcelain Manufactory which exists to the present day. The most important Berlin wares are those made between 1763 and the death of Frederick the Great in 1786. Dinner services with flower painting and mosaic borders are notable, while after 1770 pierced borders were popular and flower painting in a *camaieu* (see *En camaieu*) of two tones. Figure modelling in the best period was in the hands of the brothers Friedrich Elias Meyer (who had previously worked at Meissen) and Wilhelm Christian Meyer. The mark of a 'G' was used from 1761–3, after which a sceptre in blue was introduced.

Berlin woolwork: a type of embroidery in coloured worsteds on canvas in which designs printed on squared paper were copied by counting the squares of the canvas. The designs were published in Berlin and were first imported into England about 1810 but did not reach the country in large numbers until after 1830, the fashion reaching its height about the middle of the cent. The first designs were often worked in silk or glass beads, but the garishly coloured worsteds imported from Berlin (which gave the work its name) became the general medium, and tent or cross stitch the usual method of execution. The designs were usually of flowers, depicted with great naturalism, but pictorial subjects, frequently biblical, were also popular. Samplers on long strips of canvas showing various patterns worked in Berlin wools are also found.

Beshire or **Bushire carpets:** Turkoman carpets (q.v.) actually made in Bokhara City, and providing a variation in the design strongly reminiscent

of the Herat (q.v.) 'fish' design, but the colouring is the usual red, often on dark blue; a strong yellow outlines the design.

Betty lamp: covered, grease-burning lamp, the wick suspended by a metal support. They were made of iron or tin and were in use in Britain in the 17th cent.

Bevelled glass: the angular shaping of the surface at the edges of a mirror-plate, performed by grinding and then polishing the glass. A patent for a method of doing this with the aid of water-power was granted in 1678. Much glass for mirrors had the edges bevelled, but the finish was not always employed for large plates after the middle years of the 18th cent.

Bevor: see Sallet.

Bezel: (1) the metallic framing of a clock or watch glass; (2) the inside rim of the cover or lid of an object; (3) originally the part of a ring which holds the stone, and now generally used to describe the setting of the ring, including the stone.

Bezoar: the gall stone of an animal, usually an ox or a cow, mounted in precious metal and thought to have magical powers.

Bianco sopra bianco: a type of earthenware decoration meaning literally, white on white, but used as a form of white decoration upon a pale grey or blue ground at the Lambeth, Bristol, and Liverpool delftware (qq.v.) factories from about 1750. First used on 16th-cent. Italian *maiolica* (q.v.).

Bibelot: small, often decorative, object; *objet-de-vertu*.

Bible box: oak box with a hinged, often sloping, lid for the family Bible and other books. Generally of small dimensions, and decorated with carving; some examples had a matching stand.

Bibliothèque basse: (*Fr.*) a low cupboard fitted with shelves for books, and doors often of glass but sometimes fitted with grilles.

Bidjar or **Bidshar rugs:** see Kurdish rugs.

Biedermeier style: decorative style of the first half of the 19th cent. particularly associated with Germany and Austria. Used in the design of furniture and glass especially, the style is characterized by a ponderous and sentimental quality that appealed to the taste of the rising middle class.

Bigelow, Erastus Brigham: (1814–79), American industrialist and developer of the power carpet loom which he invented for ingrain carpeting in 1840 at Lowell, Massachusetts. This device was perfected in 1841 and in 1845 he produced his greatest invention, the power loom, for Brussels and Wilton carpeting, establishing a carpet mill at Clinton, Massachusetts in 1849.

Biggin: a form of cylindrical silver coffee pot with short spout, often with stand and spirit lamp.

Bijin-ye: a Japanese term meaning pictures of beautiful girls.

Bilbao (or **Bilboa**): a wall mirror framed in coloured marbles or marble and wood with a scrollwork headpiece and gilded mouldings. American cabinet-makers working in the Adam or Hepplewhite style may have designed them, yet they are believed to have originated in the Spanish seaport of Bilbao.

Bill: see Pole arms.

Billet: see Thumbpiece.

Billies and Charlies: a notorious class of fake lead medallions, figures and amulets (q.v.), made in London about the end of the 19th cent. and commonly known after their inventors William Smith and Charles Eaton of Tower Hill, London, as 'Billies and Charlies'.

Billingsley, William: (*c.* 1760–1828), a china painter and wandering arcanist (q.v.) who discovered the secret of a white and exceedingly translucent porcelain paste which could be produced only at great expense. His career was therefore dogged by disappointment and failure.

Born at Derby and apprenticed as a china painter at the Derby works in 1774; influenced by Boreman (q.v.); became celebrated as a painter of flowers in a new naturalistic style marked by the illusion of depth, and the use of longish sprays of flowers spreading from a central bloom. He left Derby in 1795, entered into association with Coke at Pinxton as an arcanist, then went to Mansfield in 1799 and later to Torksey, Lincolnshire, where he decorated white china bought in Staffordshire. He found employment at Worcester in his trade in 1808 but left once more to become a china-maker at Nantgarw in 1813. His association with Dillwyn at Swansea in 1814 broke down in 1816, and he returned to Nantgarw. In 1819 Rose of Coalport bought his moulds and made use of his ideas.

He died in 1828 in greatly reduced circumstances.

Bilston: early South Staffordshire centre of the enamelling trade, where snuff boxes and similar goods of japanned metal had been produced from the beginning of the cent. The rare japanned snuff boxes with enamel decoration on their lids are considered to date from 1740–50. During the

1760s to 1790s Bilston produced great numbers of fine painted enamels.

Binche lace: pillow lace (q.v.) made with very fine thread and such a close texture that the pattern was almost lost. Gradually it became more open and eventually lost its delicacy.

Bing, Samuel: (1838–1905), proprietor of the shop 'La Maison de l'Art Nouveau', in Paris, selling and promoting interest in Japanese art and Art Nouveau (q.v.).

Bin label: large-sized pottery label, usually pierced with a hole for suspension from a hook or nail, for hanging beside a wine bin. Some date from the late 17th cent. and it has been suggested that they were made at one of the Lambeth potteries. Later examples originated in Staffordshire.

Birdcage (or **squirrel**): hinge device on the underside of table tops, permitting them to tip or revolve.

Bird fountain: wall bracket with a projecting socket for water, made in blue-printed, lustred, or enamelled earthenware, 18th and 19th cent.

Bird's-eye veneer: a veneer patterned with small spots, supposed to resemble birds' eyes, often found in the wood of the sugar maple. Used and much prized in America from the earliest to present times.

Birge, M. H., & Sons: firm established in 1834 in Buffalo, New York. It achieved one of the longest traditions among American wallpaper manufacturers specializing in a wide variety of papers, including complex panel designs.

Biscuit: a fired but unglazed pottery or porcelain, usually the latter. In porcelain, used as a modelling medium to resemble marble (see Derby porcelain).

Biscuit box: silver or electroplate (q.v.) box of rectangular, circular or oval form to contain biscuits, made from the late 18th cent.

Biscuit tin: tin container made in a variety of regular and novelty shapes and produced for the biscuit manufacturers. After 1860 the design was generally transfer-printed (q.v.) and, after 1875, printed by offset litho.

Bismuth: a metal added to harden pewter. Also called tinglass.

Bisque: see Biscuit.

'Black and White' wallpaper: modern name given to the 16th- and 17th-cent. letterpress-printed wallpaper, much of which was designed in imitation of the black-thread embroideries of the Tudor period.

Black Egyptian ware: see Basaltes.

Black-glazed pottery: red earthenware covered with a lustrous black or brownish-black glaze made in Staffordshire at Fenton Low by Whieldon (q.v.) and others; at Burslem by Thomas Holland (1748–1807), often erroneously described as the 'first' maker of 'shining black' ware, and his widow, Ann Holland; and in Shropshire at Jackfield.

Blackjack: leather tankard or jug, occasionally mounted with silver rim, of 17th and 18th cent. Certain examples bearing pretentious historical inscriptions should be viewed with scepticism.

Black-printing: described by William Evand in *The Art and History of the Potting Business* in 1846 as 'a term for applying impressions to glazed vessels, whether the colour be black, red or gold', it was extensively used by outside decorators in Staffordshire and the potteries of Liverpool, Yorkshire and the Tyne in the second half of the 18th cent. and first three decades of the 19th cent. Black was more extensively used than other colours, hence the term. (See also Transfer-printing.)

Black, Starr & Frost: trading name since 1962 of an American firm of jewellers and silversmiths founded in 1810. In the 19th cent. the firm imported jewellery from Europe, retailing it in its shop, which was known as 'The Diamond Palace of Broadway'.

Black-work: the name given to a type of Elizabethan embroidery worked in black silk on linen. It was used widely for both household articles and costume, particularly on long pillow-covers, bodices, coifs and nightcaps. Gold thread is often found in conjunction with black-work and coiling stem designs were most frequently used.

Elaborate diaper filling patterns, worked in black stitch, are a feature of this work, and the effect is often similar to the wood-block-printed lining papers of the period. Black-work is also found in Spain.

Bladed knop: a knop or protuberance on the stem of a drinking glass or other vessel of thin, sharp-edged flattened form, placed horizontally.

Blanc-de-Chine: the porcelain known as *blanc-de-Chine* was made at Tê-Hua in the Chinese Province of Fukien. This china, in which the white varies in colour from a deep ivory to the starkest bluish white, was first manufactured some time during the Ming dynasty (1368–1644). The factory specialized in figures of the numerous deities and sages of the Buddhist faith.

From about 1650 this factory began to make pieces that show European influence. A soldier, perhaps Dutch, dates from this time; another well-known figure of a man wearing a tri-corn hat is probably rather later. It has been pointed out that the inhabitants of Fukien Province are extremely superstitious, and it has been suggested that this may explain why there exist *blanc-de-Chine* groups and figures of Europeans placed in typically Chinese settings and attitudes. For example,

there is a group in which a European is seen standing on the head of a dragon, which symbolizes the attainment of the highest literary honours.

Tê-Hua porcelain was occasionally painted in China, but when coloured is found to have been decorated more often in Holland or Germany during the 18th cent.

Blazes: pattern formed on a glass vessel by cutting in deep relief a series of upright or slanting lines.

Bleeding bowl: see Cupping bowl.

Bleu céleste: a turquoise-blue ground used on Sèvres porcelain (q.v.) and introduced in 1752. Also known as *bleu turquin*.

Bleu-de-roi: Sèvres porcelain ground colour imitated at Worcester (q.v.) and contemporaneously at Derby (q.v.) at the end of the Chelsea-Derby period, consisting of a bright lapis-lazuli opaque enamel.

Bleu persan: semi-oriental type of decoration on pottery in which the design is painted in opaque white over a dark blue ground colour. Used in France at the Nevers factory (q.v.), and copied in England.

Blind printing: see Gauffrage.

Blister: American term to describe the marking, thought to resemble a blister, found in various woods, such as cedar, mahogany, pine, poplar and especially maple.

Block front: various types of American furniture – chests of drawers, chests-on-chests, knee-hole dressing-tables, slant-front desks, secretaries (q.v.), etc. – were made with block fronts in the late 18th cent. Thick boards, usually mahogany, for the fronts of the drawers and cabinets, are cut so that the centres recede in a flattened curve while the ends out-curve in a flattened bulge. At the top of the three curves, one concave and two convex, a shell is often carved or glued on. Should the piece be in two sections, often only the lower section is block fronted. The origin of block fronting is unknown; the development is believed to be American, evolved about 1760–80, by John Goddard (q.v.), of Newport, Rhode Island, perhaps with the aid of his associate, John Townsend (q.v.). They may have arrived at it by straightening the curves of the Dutch cabinet.

Block-printed wallpaper: most early wallpapers were printed by wood block, the engraving of which was a skilled craft owing its origin to the wood engravers of Medieval times. The size of block varied according to the size of design, but was usually governed by the ease with which the operator could handle the block. Hand-printed wallpaper is produced today according to traditional methods.

Block printing: a method of printing textiles. The colour is applied by means of wood upon which the design is cut in relief. A 'coppered' block is one in which the design is outlined with brass or copper strips driven edgewise into the block, the areas intended to print solid colour being filled with felt.

Blonde lace: a French pillow lace (q.v.), silk, made in the Arras, Lille and Chantilly regions from the 1740s, first in unbleached Chinese silk but soon in white and black. Had a ground of the Lille type, loosely twisted.

Bloom: an all-over film of opaque dullness occasionally found on the surface of flint glass (q.v.) both of English and Irish origin, although it is frequently associated with Irish glass. The effect is caused by the use of high-sulphur fuels in the lehr (q.v.). Bands of bloom may be found encircling hollow-ware (q.v.) a little distance below the rim; these are the results of re-heating at the furnace mouth. This bloom is not to be confused with the milkiness found inside old decanters.

Blowhole: a small hole pierced in hollow castings or seamed hollow members such as handles, finials (q.v.), etc., to allow escape of the air expanded by heat when soldering to the

main body. Silver tankards with this feature have long been mistakenly known as 'whistle' tankards, to be used for calling for another drink.

Blowing tube: forerunner of, and contemporary with, the bellows (q.v.) was a long metal tube widening from a mouthpiece and with a short projection at the base to raise it from the ground. The user blew down the mouthpiece.

Blown glass: see Free-blown glass.

Blown-moulded glass: see Mould-blown glass.

Blowpipe: long, hollow, iron tube used to hold a gather of molten glass.

'Blue-and-white' Chinese porcelain: decoration with painting in cobalt blue under the glaze has continued ever since its introduction. It is both attractive and economical, requiring one firing only. Some 14th-cent. wares depict plants and animals within floral scroll borders. The classic 15th-cent. Ming reigns of Hsüan Te and Ch'êng Hua produced perhaps the finest of all 'blue-and-white', with perfect forms, superb glaze, rich colour, and lively yet restrained painting of dragons and floral scrolls. A deep violet-blue was used in the Chia Ching period, and 16th-cent. painting is freely executed in 'outline and wash' technique. As well as the traditional subjects, ladies on garden terraces, playing boys, and animals in landscapes are now depicted. Much Ming porcelain now in European collections comes from the Near East or South-East Asia, whither it was exported in many styles and qualities. From about 1600 the East India Companies imported into Europe thin porcelain plates and bowls with indented edges, painted with emblems and figures in wide panelled borders. The 'Transitional' period wares of the mid-17th cent., e.g. cylindrical vases and bottles with tulip designs, bold landscapes and figure subjects, are often finely painted. The paste of K'ang Hsi period wares is fine and white, and for the best pieces a brilliant sapphire blue was used, applied in overlapping flat strokes, as on the famous 'prunus jars', with sprays of plum blossom reserved in white. Decorative vases and 'useful' wares are extremely various in shape and decoration. Landscapes and scenes from literature, with elegant ladies or huntsmen, are common, and a great variety of panelled, brocaded and bordered designs with flowers (aster and tiger-lily patterns, lotus, chrysanthemum, etc.), as well as the traditional animals and emblems. Ming reign marks were often used; that of K'ang Hsi rarely. The Yung Cheng and Ch'ien Lung periods produced little besides revivals of early Ming styles, and export wares of declining quality. Later 18th-cent. services made to European order ('Nankin china') are rather coarse, with thick glazes, and crowded designs of the 'willow-pattern' type.

Blue clay: more commonly known as ball clay (q.v.). A plastic clay quarried in Devon and Dorset, forming the basis of most earthenware bodies.

Blue-dash chargers: circular Delft ware (q.v.) dishes painted with various figural or floral subjects with blue strokes or dashes at the edge, ranging in date from 1614 to 1740 or later. The archaistic word 'charger' was applied to this purely decorative class of tin-glazed earthenware by E. A. Downman who collected them.

Blue glass: glass vessels tinted blue, which could be achieved by the addition of cobalt. In England blue glass scent bottles, snuff boxes and similar small articles were popular about 1770 and later, inspired by Sèvres porcelain (q.v.). These blue glass wares were made not only at Bristol but also in South Staffordshire and Birmingham among other centres, and the boxes, etc., were decorated in enamellers' workshops. Blue finger bowls were favoured about 1800. (See also Coloured glass.)

Blue John: also known as Derbyshire spar. A fluorspar of violet-blue colour, often with yellow veinings, much used in the second half of the 18th and in the 19th cent. for decorative purposes, such as on vases, urns, sometimes mounted in ormolu (q.v.), candlestick bases, etc.

Blue tint: the faint bluish hue present in the texture of some late Georgian flint glass. This has often been taken as a characteristic of Waterford glass (q.v.), but it is apparent not only in examples from Waterford but also in the productions of Stourbridge, Birmingham, Bristol, Scotland and elsewhere.

This peculiar depth of tone shows the glass to contain lead oxide prepared from Derbyshire mined lead, preferred at many glass houses because of the superior manipulative properties it gave to the molten metal. The Derby lead contained an impurity which caused the bluish tint. The Irish glass houses for the most part used lead oxide made by Wilson Patten, Bank Quay, Warrington, from Derbyshire lead. Not every consignment contained the blue-tingeing impurity, then known as Derby blue, so there was no consistency in the presence of Derby blue in flint glass during the period concerned and depth and tone of tint varied.

Blunderbuss: a short musket with large bore widening at the muzzle, designed to fire shot. Apparently introduced into England from the Continent in the middle of the 17th cent., it was used principally by civilians as a protection against thieves until well into the 19th. Many blunderbusses are equipped with a hinged spring bayonet, which is thrown forward into the fixed position when a catch is released.

Boarded chest: early, poor alternative to the framed or joined chest, the horizontal planks of wood forming the front and back being hammered to the vertical end pieces or flush with heavy corner stiles, and frequently reinforced with corner pieces of iron. As wood tends to shrink across the grain, the result was never satisfactory, and the horizontal planks usually show signs of splitting. Oak might be used, or planks of elm, large and comparatively little given to warping. The flush construction as contrasted with the loose panels of the mortice-and-tenon-jointed (q.v.) chest offered a smooth surface for covering with leather or hair cloth.

Boat bed (**gondola bed** or **lit en bateau**): bed with curved foot boards and boat-shaped outline, a type introduced in the French Empire (q.v.) period and adopted in the United States in the following decade.

Bobbin lace: alternative term for pillow lace (q.v.), but distinguished from bone lace (q.v.) in early inventories as being coarser, of thicker thread requiring large bobbins.

Bobbins: spools wound with thread for pillow laces (q.v.), a separate bobbin for each thread. English bobbins are distinctively ornamental, light and dainty for Honiton and Buckinghamshire lace, but often weighted with spangles, or beads, for the coarser laces.

Bobbin turning: one of the many varieties of wood turning popular in the 17th cent.

Bob clock pendulum: the earliest form of pendulum invented by Christiaan Huygens in 1657 and used with the verge escapement (q.v.). In England the pendulum rod was usually fixed to the end of the escape pallet arbor (q.v.), but on the Continent suspension was generally from a silk cord, the pendulum being actuated by a crutch. Regulation was by means of a fine thread cut on the lower end of the pendulum rod. The hole in the bob had a softwood core which 'took up' the threads of the rod.

Bocage: modelled foliage or tree backgrounds to porcelain or earthenware figures or groups, 18th and 19th cent. Made in Germany from *c.* 1740 and England from *c.* 1760.

Boccaro ware: a misnomer for Yi-hsing stoneware (q.v.).

Boch Bros: company founded in 1845 by a family of German potters, William, Anthony and Victor Boch at Greenpoint, Long Island, New York. They manufactured porcelain pitchers, mugs, vases, furniture knobs and funerary images until 1862, when the factory was purchased by Thomas C. Smith, who continued its production under the name Union Porcelain Works (q.v.).

Body: the composite materials of which potter's clay is made – the ware itself, usually pottery or stoneware; for porcelains the word paste is preferred (as hard-paste, soft-paste).

Boettger or **Böttger, Johann Friedrich:** (1682–1719), an alchemist in the service of Augustus the Strong, Elector of Saxony and King of Poland, whose early researches were concerned with a means of manufacturing gold. His efforts in this direction proving fruitless, he was employed on the problem of making porcelain. In fact, he discovered in 1710 a red stoneware 'which surpasses the hardness of porphyry'. Shortly afterwards he succeeded in replacing the red clay with white kaolin (see China clay). Thus he produced the first real porcelain to be made in Europe. As a result of his discovery the Royal Saxon Porcelain Manufacture was established at Meissen in 1710. (See also Meissen porcelain.)

Bog oak: dark-coloured wood, stained by immersion in peat bogs, used as an inlay (q.v.) and in the 19th cent. for entire pieces of furniture.

Bois durci: imitation ebony patented in France in 1855. The basic ingredient was sawdust, hardened by heat, and die-stamped into decorative shapes.

Bokhara or **Bokara rugs:** these rugs, known as 'Bokara', have long been popular in England. They are made by Turkestan tribes of which the Tekke is the most esteemed. The gules are well balanced and the side borders follow variations of the same motif. The end borders are usually latch hook in diamond formation, and conventional tree or life forms. The yarns are very fine, often knotted 300 to 400 to 6 sq cm (1 sq in) on a weft and warp usually of wool, but sometimes of fine hair. (See also Turkoman rugs.)

Bokhara work: the term is generally applied to the bright-coloured embroideries of Western Turkestan. Large floral sprays or a diapered ground filled with flowers are the most common patterns and diagonally laid Oriental stitch and chain stitch are most frequently used. Large coverlets and divan covers are most common and the finest date from the 18th cent.

Bolection moulding: a moulding of ogee (q.v.) section used as a projecting surround to door or wall panels.

Bolt-and-shutter device: a means of maintaining power in clocks. The shutters cover the winding squares so that the clock cannot be wound without pushing them aside. This action brings into play a small subsidiary force that keeps the clock going during the period of winding.

Bombé form: a term adopted from the French to describe a curved or swelling form. Late 18th-cent. commodes were frequently of *bombé* form.

Bonbonnières: small shaped boxes intended for sweetmeats made of gold, silver, porcelain or enamelled copper and made in various forms according to the fantasy of the designer.

Bone china: the standard English porcelain since 1800. It is basically hard-paste, modified by the addition of bone ash which may be as much as 40% of the ingredients of the bone-china body. Josiah Spode II is credited with stabilizing the proportions, although bone as an ingredient of porcelain was used at Bow (q.v.) from 1749, Lowestoft, Chelsea and Derby (q.v.) in the 18th cent. and is stated by Church to have been common knowledge among potters in Staffordshire in Spode's time.

Bone lace: a term sometimes specifically applied to gold and silver lace (q.v.) but more often also to all good quality pillow lace (q.v.), as distinct from needlepoint (q.v.). It has been variously argued that the name referred to the sheep's trotter bones sometimes used as early bobbins (q.v.) and to the bone pins used in place of metal pins to shape the pattern – fish bones on occasion. Metal pins were priced in 1543 at as much as 6s 8d a thousand. The term has been applied also to the ivory effects of Venetian raised point lace (q.v.). It was the accepted term until the early 18th cent. for much pillow lace and there are many records of its cost: such as 1s 4d a yard for narrow bone lace edging in 1594, and 2s 4d a yard in 1685.

Bonheur-du-jour: (*Fr.*) a small writing table usually on tall legs, and with a central drawer sometimes fitted to hold toilet accessories and bibelots (q.v.). It first appeared *c.* 1760.

Bonnet-scroll pediment: American term for the crowning feature of case furniture, a broken pediment with S-scrolls. Also known as a goose-neck, scrolled or swan-neck pediment. (See Broken pediment.)

Book rest: a stand used in Georgian libraries to support large books, consisting of a square or rectangular framework with cross bars, the upper bar being supported by a strut which was adjusted on a grooved base. This kind of stand was sometimes fitted into the top of a table.

Boreman, Zachariah: (1738–1810), a landscape painter on porcelain. He worked originally at Chelsea but moved to Derby about 1783, when he renewed a contract with Duesbury (q.v.) for three years at two guineas a week wage. He returned to London in 1794 and worked as an outside decorator at one of the London establishments. His work, executed in quiet tones, possesses a certain sober dignity. It was painted in the 18th-cent. watercolour technique of glazing local colours over a monochrome foundation.

Boston and Sandwich Glass Company: United States glasshouse (previously known as the Sandwich Manufacturing Co.) which was incorporated under its new name in 1826 by D. Jarves (q.v.). Produced some superb cameo-cut glass lamps and ornamental ware in the late 19th cent., especially Smith Bros (q.v.) vases and lampshades. Ceased production in 1888.

Boston rocker: the most popular of all rocking chairs in America. Apparently evolved from the Windsor rocker (see Windsor chair). Usually painted, it has curved arms, a tall spindle back, broad top rail generally showing stencilled designs: a kind of ornamental panel – and a 'rolling' seat, curved up at the back and down at the front.

Botanical flowers: a type of floral decoration inspired originally by Meissen porcelain and occurring on Chelsea porcelain, 1750–6 (from engravings in Philip Miller's *The Gardeners Dictionary*, 1724, issued in parts with numerous copperplate engravings from 1755); on Derby porcelain painted by William Pegg (1775–1851), early 19th cent.; on porcelain decorated at Yarmouth by William Absolon (q.v.); and by Thomas Pardoe (q.v.) on Swansea

porcelain. Pardoe's careful imitations of plants and flowers from Curtis's *Botanical Magazine* were probably due to the influence of Lewis Weston Dillwyn who was a keen botanist. Decorations from the same source are recorded on earthenware.

Bott, Thomas John: (1854–1932), son of noted Worcester (q.v.) artist, Thomas Bott who specialized in a Limoges enamel style of painting. He succeeded his father at the Worcester factory and subsequently worked independently and as art director at the Coalport (q.v.) porcelain works.

Bottengruber, Ignaz: (*fl. c.* 1720– *c.* 1736) an independent porcelain decorator of Breslau in Germany working between about 1720 and 1736, whose painting can be found on Vienna and Meissen (qq.v.) porcelain.

Bottle glass: glass of a greenish or brownish tone caused by an impurity in the silica used in its production.

Bottle tickets: contemporary term for decanter labels. These labels were intended to be hung by a chain on the neck of a decanter. The engraver Simon-François Ravenet (q.v.) was associated with a series of Battersea enamel (q.v.) bottle tickets depicting *putti* engaged on tasks associated with the production of the designated liquors. Bottle tickets were also made of silver, engraved or stamped with the name of a beverage. They were rarely made in England after 1860, when it was required by law that descriptions of the contents should appear on paper labels attached to the bottles.

Bouche: a notch cut in the upper edge of a shield to support a lance.

Boudoir clock: brass clock, engraved and gilded and often made with a strut or swivel foot so that the clock could be made to stand up or fold flat for travelling. Introduced in *c.* 1860, probably for a lady's bedroom or sitting room.

Boulle, André Charles: French cabinet maker. Born in Paris in 1642, the son of a carpenter, and died there in 1732. His training was various, and he appears to have worked at different times as a painter, architect, engraver and bronze worker, as well as an *ébéniste* (q.v.) of importance. He worked as an *artisan libre* from 1664 onwards, but in 1672 he was appointed *ébéniste du Roi* through the intervention of Colbert. From this time he worked continually for the Crown and established a workshop in which he employed about twenty assistants, who were constantly at work providing furniture for the new palace at Versailles.

He possessed a large collection of old master drawings from which he may easily have drawn inspiration for his mounts. His ingenuity as a designer was very great, as can be seen from a series of engravings which he published, and from a number of his drawings which still exist. But throughout his career his actual style changed very little. He never signed his work and his authenticated productions are very rare.

Boulle (or **buhl**) **marquetry:** the name given to the type of inlay evolved for use on furniture in the late 17th cent. by André Charles Boulle (q.v.).

The process involves glueing one or more thin layers of tortoiseshell to a similar number of brass. The design of the marquetry is set out on paper, which is pasted on the surface. The pattern is then cut out with a saw. The layers of brass and tortoiseshell are separated and can be made to form two distinct marquetries by combining the materials in opposite ways: either with the design formed by the brass on a ground of shell, known as *première partie* or first part, or the exact opposite, known as *contre-partie*, or counterpart, with the design in shell on a ground of brass. These two types of inlay can be glued on to a carcase in the form of a veneer. Often the two types are found side by side as part of the same design, to give contrast. Again, when pieces are made in pairs one may be veneered with *première partie* and the other with *contre-partie* marquetry.

The brass in the *première-partie*

marquetry was often engraved naturalistically, frequently very finely, and was sometimes combined with other substances, such as pewter, copper, mother-of-pearl and stained horn, to give contrasts and naturalistic effects to the design. Additional colour was also given by veneering the shell over coloured foil, usually red or green.

The carcases on to which Boulle marquetry is veneered are usually found to be of oak or deal, and the parts which are not covered are veneered with ebony, coromandel wood or purple wood, in order to tone with the shell of the inlay.

Boulle furniture is usually lavishly mounted with ormolu, to protect the corners and the more vulnerable parts of the inlay, but the mounts are frequently also adapted in a decorative manner to form hinges, lock plates and handles. It will be noticed that the ormolu is sometimes fully gilt, which provides a strong decorative contrast with the inlaid brass; equally, the bronze is sometimes left ungilt, and therefore harmonizes with the metal inlay to a greater extent.

Boulle furniture, so much in demand in the reign of Louis XIV, went out of fashion during most of that of his successor, but did not cease to be made, and the Boulle *atelier* continued to turn out pieces from time to time. They were therefore ready when, under Louis XVI, the taste for this type of furniture returned. At this period a very large number of pieces were made, often to the original designs.

Boullemier, Anton or Antonin: (*c.* 1840–1900), French porcelain painter, Sèvres (q.v.)-trained, who worked for Minton (q.v.) from 1872.

Boulton, Matthew: (1728–1809), a Birmingham manufacturer of small metal objects such as *étuis* (q.v.), snuff boxes, buckles, etc., who combined the functions of manufacturer and merchant. In 1761 he established the firm of Boulton and Fothergill which gradually extended its manufactures to include cut-steel jewellery, Sheffield plate (q.v.), silver and ormolu (q.v.). He was, in fact, the only manufacturer in England of ormolu and achieved a quality rivalling that of the finest Parisian work in this material. Robert Adam (q.v.) supplied designs for his ormolu and Sheffield plate.

Bourg-la-Reine: see Mennecy porcelain.

Bourne & Son: a firm of stoneware manufacturers, which continues to this day, founded by Joseph Bourne in 1812. He was the son of William Bourne, master potter of Belper, and factories at Belper and Denby were carried on by the family simultaneously until 1834 when the Belper works was discontinued and its materials and plant were transferred to Denby. A works at Codnor Park passed into Bourne's control in 1833 but also finally closed down and its plant and workpeople were brought to Denby in 1861. Similarly the Shipley Pottery, acquired in 1845, was absorbed in 1856. Marks: the name of the firm

J. BOURNE & SON
with
PATENTEES DENBY POTTERY
NEAR DERBY
arranged variously, or
BOURNE'S POTTERY BELPER
& DENBY DERBYSHIRE.

Excellent brown salt-glazed stonewares including hunting jugs with relief ornament and greyhound handles, and other ornamental wares were made.

Boutet, Nicholas-Noël: (1761–1833), founder and director of the Royal Arms Factory at Versailles, established in 1792. Boutet, who signed himself 'Directeur-Artiste', applied the massive Empire style of ornament to the presentation swords and firearms which were the main production of the factory. His finest work, dating from the Napoleonic period, achieves a luxury hardly paralleled in the history of firearms.

Boutique d'Or: a name given to the Paris 17th-cent. tapestry factory of De La Planche and Comans. These weavers had been brought from Brussels and Antwerp by Henry IV. The factory was noted for the silken texture of its products and the imposing formality of the borders used. The designers included Simon Vouet and Rubens. The factory was combined with the Gobelins (q.v.) in 1662.

Bow-back chair: see Windsor chair.

Bow front: in the second half of the 18th cent. in particular, case furniture designed with a convex front.

Bow porcelain: the early history of the factory is obscure. In 1744, Edward Heylin, and Thomas Frye took out a patent for the manufacture of 'a certain material' equal in beauty and quality to imported porcelain, from a recipe including a material called unaker, 'the produce of the Chirokee nation in America'. Doubt has been cast upon the workability of their specification, and no Bow porcelain of this early date has been identified with certainty.

Another patent was taken out by Frye alone in 1749 for a phosphatic porcelain including a percentage of bone ash or 'virgin earth' which accounts for the high phosphorous content of identified early Bow porcelain.

By 1750 the manufactory had been taken over by Weatherby & Crowther, merchants, under the name 'New Canton', but Frye remained as manager until 1759. Weatherby died in 1762, and in 1763 Crowther became bankrupt. The factory, however, continued in operation until 1776 when it was taken over by William Duesbury (q.v.) who closed it down and removed the moulds to Derby. Numerous factory and workmen's or repairers' marks have been recorded on identified Bow porcelain, but before *c.* 1760 wares can only be distinguished by qualities other than marks. The most generally recognized Bow marks after 1760 are an anchor and dagger in red or underglaze blue. Chaffers suggests that the dagger was adopted

BOX 43 **BRA**

because Weatherby and Crowther were freemen of the City of London. The manufacture of Bow porcelain may be divided into four periods; (1) before 1749; (2) from 1749 until 1755; (3) from 1755 until 1760, when the most valued and typical Bow qualities appeared; and (4) after 1760, when there was a general lowering of quality apart from modelling, and the work became imitative in character.

(1) The wares made, if made at all, under the patent of 1744 were non-phosphatic. A number of figures, on the evidence of style mannerisms, have been conjecturally attributed to this early period.

(2) From 1749 a creamy bone paste was produced, and wares were rather heavy in weight with an uneven glaze and of variable translucency. Plain white figures were made, and groups attributed on stylistic grounds to the 'Muses' modeller', often of women and children with round, doll-like heads and receding chins. These are generally treated with originality and painted sparingly with a limited palette of pigments. Useful wares followed Oriental porcelain shapes or contemporary silver, and were frequently decorated with versions of Chinese *famille rose* (q.v.) patterns; designs reminiscent of Japanese Kakiemon (q.v.); or with applied prunus sprays in relief on white wares.

(3) The distinctive qualities of Bow porcelain *c.* 1755–60 are a rather waxy glaze, sometimes slightly iridescent; the irregular spreading of the blue colour used for underglaze painting giving the surface a bluish tinge; and bright clear colouring with delicate flower painting. Figures display a liveliness of modelling and colour, in spite of strong Meissen influence. 'General Wolfe' and the 'Marquis of Granby' (*c.* 1759) are examples of the best and most original Bow style. Figures tend to be a little heavy for their size and are sometimes provided with a square hole in which a support for candles could be placed. Mound bases gave place about 1758–60 to four-footed Rococo scroll pedestals tricked out in crimson and purple. Useful wares were decorated in Oriental styles with Kakiemon patterns in red, blue and gold; with floral sprays dominated by two big peonies; or with 'botanical' flowers (q.v.). Mixed decorative styles were sometimes used containing motifs from East and West. Transfer-printed decorations in black or brick red are beautiful but uncommon.

(4) Bow figures of the last period retained something of the charms of the earlier work, but the paste was greyer and the decoration tended to become over-elaborate. Useful wares in this phase follow Meissen, Chelsea and Worcester styles and marks.

1750

1760   1770

Box chair: early panelled chair with arms and a high back and a box as the base. The seat was formed by a hinged lid. Box settles were made on the same principle.

Box inkstand: a rectangular inkstand of silver, pewter (q.v.) or brass with one or two wells, drawers beneath.

Bozetto: small scale sketch in terracotta, wax or some other suitable material, for sculpture.

Bracket: wall attachment of wood or metal which either supports an object, such as a clock, or from which an object is suspended.

Bracket clock: many clocks of the 17th and 18th cent. were provided with their own brackets, usually designed to harmonize with the case.

Only rarely have original brackets survived. They frequently contain a drawer to hold the winding key. Portable clocks are known as both mantel and bracket clocks.

Bracket foot: a foot supporting a piece of case furniture and attached directly to the under-framing. It consists of two pieces of wood, joined at the corner. The open side is generally cut out in a simple pattern. The corner end is sometimes straight, at other times curved in an ogee (q.v.) pattern.

Bradbury, Thomas, & Sons: English manufacturers of silver, Sheffield plate (q.v.), and, after 1840, electroplate (q.v.). The firm was founded in 1832 by Thomas Bradbury (1763–1838).

Bradwell Wood pottery: the traditional and generally accepted site in Staffordshire of Elers' (q.v.) factory. It was situated on a wooded ridge which separates Burslem from Newcastle-under-Lyme and this afforded some element of secrecy. Good red clay was abundant in the area, from which Elers made 'red china' teapots which gave him a national reputation.

This site has been frequently investigated but little of any value has ever been discovered. Shaw says that Enoch Wood (q.v.) and John Riley measured the oven in 1808 and came to the conclusion that it was unsuitable for salt-glazed stoneware which Elers was alleged to have introduced into Staffordshire. In a memorandum written in 1814 into Cox's *Magna Britannia and Hibernia*, Enoch Wood recorded his opinion that it had been 'built to fire red china only'. The site has been frequently explored since Enoch Wood's time by the Rheads, by Thomas Pape, and in 1955 by A. R. Mountford who discovered fragments of 'red china'. The site awaits more through excavation.

Braiding: embroidery executed by means of couched braid chiefly in designs of arabesques (q.v.) or continuous scrolls.

Bramah lock: the first lock to be operated by a small conveniently carried key, invented by Joseph Bramah in 1784. The key did not act directly upon the sliding bolt, but through the medium of the rotating barrel, thus anticipating Yale's cylindrical lock of 1848. Insertion of the key pushed back a number of sliding plates until notches at different positions came into line, allowing the barrel to be turned and the bolt withdrawn.

Brampton stoneware: brown stone wares made from early in the 18th cent. and throughout the 19th cent. The principal potter in 1800 is said to have been William Bromley who was succeeded by Robert Bambrigge & Co.

Six factories existed in Brampton early in the 19th cent.

The wares made at Brampton were, in the 19th cent., classed with – and are still when unmarked often mistaken for – Nottingham wares. They fall into two categories: one, of a fine chocolate colour similar to Belper wares, decorated with applied ornament; and two, wares varying in colour from buff to red of some brilliancy. This second group included toby jugs as well as tea and coffee pots, which were mostly made by Briddon or Oldfield c. 1835. A characteristic feature of Brampton wares is an internal green glaze which occurs on dated specimens from 1820 to 1894.
Marks:

S. & H. BRIDDON
(Samuel & Henry Briddon) c. 1848

OLDFIELD & CO. MAKERS
(Oldfield, Madin Wright, Hewitt & Company, or John Oldfield.)

J. OLDFIELD

OLDFIELD & CO.
CHESTERFIELD

Brandenbourgs: jewelled clasps, originally invented for masculine use in the latter half of the 17th cent. and quickly adopted by ladies for the ornamentation of their triangular bodice fronts. A series of these clasps in diminishing size were worn on the bodice, one set below the other. The popularity of this form of jewellery continued into the 18th cent.

Brander: a pierced metal plate, with a half-hoop handle by which it was suspended from a pot-hook. It was used principally in Scotland for the making of brander bannocks (oatmeal cakes).

Brandy bowl: two-handled silver bowl used for serving raisins in brandy, first made in the 17th cent.; popular in Holland and the Scandinavian countries.

Bras de lumière: see Wall-lights.

Bratina: a globular, covered cup with a contracted lip peculiar to Russia. It was a form of loving-cup, intimately associated with its owner and used at his funeral feast. Fine vessels were made of gold or silver; the peasant version was in wood.

Brazier: circular bowl with pierced plate in base for burning charcoal as heaters for kettles or dishes. European examples date from the Middle Ages. (See also Chafing stand.)

Breakfast table: a small, four-legged table with hinged flaps which could be extended on brackets. Examples of such tables were illustrated by Thomas Chippendale (q.v.) in the third edition of *The Gentleman and Cabinet-Maker's Director*, published in 1762.

Break-front bookcase (or **wing bookcase**): a bookcase in which the central section projects slightly beyond the side sections or 'wings', a form popular from the mid-18th cent.

Breloque: a small ornament attached to a watch-chain or châtelaine (q.v.).

Brescian steel: see Chiselled and cut steel.

Breton work: a type of embroidery derived from Breton peasant costume worked in coloured silks and gold thread, mainly in chain and satin stitch and used for the borders of garments, neck-tie ends and small articles such as book-markers.

Brewster chair: an early 17th-cent. Dutch type of American armchair made of turned posts and spindles. A handsomer variety of the Carver chair (q.v.). It has two tiers of four spindles in the back, a similar tier under the arms and, occasionally, two or more tiers under the seat at the sides. Usually of ash or maple with rush seats. Named after William Brewster, first leader of the Plymouth colony pilgrims, who is said to have brought one to America with him in 1620 in the *Mayflower*. Popular to the end of the 17th cent. Earliest surviving examples perhaps about 1650.

Brewster shape: oval, straight-sided teapot with lid set into an oval, vertical collar, made at the Wedgwood factory (q.v.) in the 1780s. This shape was popular at all potworks making wares in the Neoclassic style.

Briand, Thomas: (d. 1784), a chemist who demonstrated examples of a soft-paste porcelain before the Royal Society in 1742-3, and was part-proprietor of the Chelsea porcelain factory (q.v.) on its foundation. Later he worked at Champion's Bristol porcelain manufactory (q.v.) and some plaques in biscuit (q.v.) have been attributed to him.

Bridal fans: date from about 1720 until the end of the 18th cent. At first they were costly, designed and painted by master fanmakers. Souvenir copies by lesser hands were presented to the maids of honour and women guests. Other fans, with mounts hand-coloured over copies of a specially designed engraving, were sent as mementoes to a wider circle of friends. Marriage fans might be painted with scenes from the lives of the bride and groom, with their miniatures in ivory set into the guards (q.v.).

Brides: French term usually preferred to the English bars or ties, describing those parts of a piece of lace connecting and supporting the pattern where there was no net ground. Found mainly in needlepoint (q.v.) and mixed laces.

Bridge fluting: a decoration applied to drinking glasses, being an extension of faceting from the stem to bridge the junction of the bowl and the stem. This type of decoration was used in the second half of the 18th cent., and in the later examples extends over the lower part of the bowl. Also known as cresting.

Brigandine: a light, flexible body defence (armour), consisting of small, overlapping metal plates riveted to the interior of a canvas or leather jacket. It was usually covered with coloured silk or velvet, the rivet heads on the exterior being gilt to produce a decorative effect. The term first occurs at the end of the 14th cent., but the majority of surviving examples date from the 16th and early 17th cent.

The jack was a cheaper form of the brigandine, its plates, which were often of horn, being held in place by stitching.

Bright-cut engraving: a particular form of engraving on silverware and plate, popular about 1790, in which the metal is removed by bevelled cutting and the cut burnished, giving a jewel-like, faceted sparkle to the surface.

Brilliant cut: a form of diamond cutting introduced by Vincenzo Peruzzi at Venice about 1700. Diamonds cut in this way end in points both at the front and the back and have up to 58 facets, visible in open-claw settings.

Brinjal bowls: K'ang Hsi porcelain bowls with incised flower-sprays coloured yellow and green on an aubergine (derived from the same root as the Anglo-Indian word *brinjal*) purple ground, in glazes applied 'on the biscuit'.

Briolettes: drop-shaped gemstones cut with triangular facets.

Brisé fan: composed solely of sticks of slightly flexible ivory, tortoiseshell or horn, delicately pierced. The sticks were joined by ribbons of closely woven silk, apparently in one continuous length passing through the whole fan, but in reality consisting of many short lengths each separately attached to a fan stick. These leafless fans were introduced in the early 1680s and were fashionable from about 1715 until the end of the cent. The sticks were cut to wafer thinness, the upper part of each being saw-cut with designs so exquisite as to resemble the finest lace and enriched with burnished gilding. In the lower portion might be worked an armorial device. Equal care of craftsmanship was given to both sides of the fan. Another type of brisé fan was made from unperforated sticks which, overlapping, formed a plain field for decoration. Each side might be covered by an all-over painting in oils. The minuet fan is a type of brisé fan. By the end of the 18th cent. ivory and mother-of-pearl sticks were replaced by bone, scented sandal wood, laburnum wood and cut steel.

Brislington: a delftware manufactory flourished here from *c.* 1650 to 1750. (See Bristol delftware.)

Bristol delftware: a pottery at Brislington, near Bristol, was founded by Southwark potters *c.* 1650; it in turn colonized a factory in Bristol (Temple Pottery, 1683–1770, when delftware was abandoned). Others were St Mary Redcliffe's (*c.* 1700–77) and Limekiln Lane (*c.* 1700–54).

Early Bristol delftware is difficult to distinguish from Lambeth (q.v.) and the latter from that of Liverpool (q.v.). The Bristol glaze, however, often had a distinctive lavender-blue tone, and the early red (*c.* 1700) stands out in appreciable relief. The Bristol *bianco sopra bianco* (q.v.) borders usually include a cone motif and curved sprays of leaves. Characteristic Bristol shapes include a plate with straight sides forming an obtuse angle with the bottom; puzzle jugs (q.v.) with open-work necks formed by intersecting circles; flower-'bricks' pierced with a square hole at the top and mounted on small bracket feet, and 17th-cent. porringers having a circular handle with corrugations radiating from a central hole.

Bristol glass: Glasshouses were in existence in the city and port of Bristol in the 17th cent. By the early 18th cent. some fifteen are recorded, most of them making window glass or bottles. It was not until the mid-cent. that more sophisticated articles of good quality began to be made. In 1745 the Glass Excise Act placed a duty on glass which was levied by weight and seriously hampered the trade. Forms of decoration suited to lighter glass, such as engraving and enamelling began to flourish and it has been suggested that these circumstances caused the Bristol makers to produce coloured glass, a material with which their name has been linked ever since, although the production of such glass was by no means either wholly or mainly confined to Bristol. A rich deep blue was popular and also purple and green.

Among the articles made were fingerbowls, decanters, etc., and also scent bottles, étuis (q.v.), snuff boxes (q.v.) and other 'toys'. Opaque-white glass, made in competition with porcelain, was also produced at Bristol and various glassmakers in the city are recorded as having made it. Again, white glass was also made at other centres and particularly the snuff boxes and étuis, etc., of opaque glass were most probably made by the box makers of Birmingham and South Staffordshire. Of the larger articles, opaque white glass, not being suitable for tea or coffee services, was employed mainly for ornamental vases and beakers as well as tea caddies and candlesticks, the enamelled decoration resembling that applied to porcelain. (See also Opaque glass and Edkins, Michael.)

Bristol porcelain:
(1) A type of soft-paste porcelain, making use of soapstone quarried in Cornwall, was made between 1749 and 1752 by William Miller and Benjamin Lund at a glass house at Redcliffe Backs, Bristol, known, because owned until 1745 by William Lowdin, as Lowdin's China House. A few pieces survive: Chinese-copy figures, and more rarely sauceboats decorated with flowers. They may be marked BRISTOL, or BRISTOL 1750.

In 1752 the factory amalgamated with Worcester (q.v.), from which its products are no longer distinguishable.

(2) Hard-paste porcelain was made at Bristol for only eleven years between 1770 and 1781, first by William Cookworthy (q.v.), who moved his factory from Plymouth, later by Richard Champion (q.v.), his associate, who acquired his patent and bought his business in 1773. Cookworthy's patent soon expired, and when its renewal was contested by Wedgwood, Turner and others in Staffordshire, he retained the sole use of Cornish china clay and china stone in translucent wares, but being unsuccessful he was compelled to sell his patent and abandon porcelain manufacture in 1781. The patent was acquired by a company of Staffordshire potters who traded from New Hall, Shelton.

Marks: A cross, or a cross and a letter 'B' in blue enamel; or crossed swords with a cross in underglaze blue and blue enamel.

1770　　　　　　　1775

1776

1780

Richard Champion claimed that his hard-paste porcelain rivalled that of Meissen for strength, and Sèvres for elegance. He manufactured with it a variety of useful wares ranging from ungilded cottage china decorated with sprigs of blossom to elaborate services with initials for his friends or to special order. Elegant Sèvres-style cabarets (q.v.) were also made.

Teapots in the form of an inverted pear with double-curve handles are characteristic. Tightly bunched floral sprays, or sprays with angular spiky foliage recur. Typical colours are leaf green and clear deep red.

Sets of figures representing the *Seasons*, the *Elements* or *Venus and Adonis* decorated in the Sèvres style of Louis XVI period were made by Champion. Rockwork bases and a touch of sentiment are features of these wares.

Large hexagonal vases were decorated with masks and floral festoons in relief, and painted in colours.

Britannia metal: a trade name given to a tin-antimony-copper alloy, lending itself to mass production by spinning. Although the name was used before 1800 it rightfully should be named 'hard metal' until 10 August 1842 when the English patent No. 9441 was granted to Richard Ford Sturges for the name and composition of 'Britannia Metal'. Plating on Britannia metal was introduced in the early 1820s by Kirby, Smith & Co., Sheffield. A sheet of pure silver was laid on a flat surface and well heated. Molten Britannia metal was poured over this. When cold it was found to have picked up the silver. The two were then rolled into sheets as for plated copper. It superseded the use of pewter (q.v.) and was employed instead of copper in electroplating (q.v.). E.P.B.M. was the mark used to signify electroplated Britannia metal.

Britannia Standard: the Higher Standard for wrought silver plate, introduced in 1697 to prevent the melting down of coinage by silver smiths. It consists of 958 parts of fine silver in 1000 of base metal. So named from the mark of Britannia replacing the Sterling mark of a lion passant. In force till 1720, when Sterling (q.v.) or Old Standard was restored, the Higher being left as optional, which it still is.

Broad glass: flat sheet glass made by blowing a long bubble of metal into a cylindrical form, splitting the cylinder and re-heating it for flattening into a sheet. The technique was first developed in 12th-cent. Lorraine.

Broad Street glasshouse: glasshouse set up in London in 1575 by Giacomo Verzelini (q.v.) with the purpose of making glasses in the Venetian manner.

Broadsword: a sword with a straight double-edged blade. The term is applied chiefly to the basket-hilted cavalry sword of the 17th and 18th cent. It survived in the Scottish basket-hilted sword (q.v.), often erroneously called a claymore (q.v.).

Brocaded Imari: see Imari porcelain.

Broderie anglaise: a type of whitework embroidery (known also as Ayrshire, Eyelet, Madeira or Swisswork) in which open spaces are cut or punched with a stiletto. The edges of the holes are then overcast. The finest specimens of this type of work, which was used chiefly for sleeve frills, baby clothes and underwear, were produced in the late 18th or early 19th cent.

Broderie perse: see Cretonne appliqué.

Broken-arch clock cases: an arch terminating on either side with a horizontal projection. There are broken arch dials and cases. If a full semicircle, they are known as deep; if less, and this usually applies to the earliest, as shallow arches.

Broken pediment: Georgian cabinet makers frequently made use of architectural motifs in constructing bureau-bookcases and similar pieces. Of these, two forms of broken pediment in which the apex of the triangular cresting was absent, were popular: the angular form in which the two upper sides of the triangle remain straight, and the swan-neck in which these two sides are allowed to curve into an elegant scroll. (See also Bonnet-scroll pediment.)

Bronze: an alloy of copper and tin. The earliest metal to be used by man; the ease with which it can be cast, chiselled, chased and engraved and the fine patina (q.v.) it acquires with age have assured its popularity ever since.

Bronze disease: natural patina often of a soft and porous nature, formed on bronzes buried in the soil, tends to retain some saline constituents of the soil. These salts, together with the moisture in the atmosphere, may form bright-green spots, which are sometimes dry or moist, a condition called bronze disease. The disease, if not attended to, spreads quickly and has a destructive corrosive action.

Bronze doré: see Ormolu.

Bronzes d'ameublement: (*Fr.*), a term, with no exact English equivalent, describing lacquered, patinated or gilt-bronze furniture. It embraces such items as candelabra, candlesticks, wall lights, chandeliers, fire dogs, clock cases, mounts for furniture and porcelain, etc., whose manufacture was the particular province of the *fondeurs*, *ciseleurs* and *doreurs*.

Bronzes d'appliqué: see Ormolu.

Bronzing: the name of the metallic shading on some glass silhouettes. In some cases this was used with beautiful effect, particularly by John Miers, who used real gold. It was usually, though not exclusively, used on painted work.

Brownfield, William: (d. 1873), English potter and porcelain manufacturer at Cobridge in Staffordshire who made quality porcelain in the 1871–91 period.

Brown-Westhead, Moore & Co.: noted partnership working Ridgway's (q.v.) former Caulden Place Works at Hanley in the 1862–1905 period. A little-known firm closely rivalling the leading houses.

Brushing slide: some commodes (q.v.) and chests of drawers of the second half of the 18th cent. were equipped with a shelf above the top drawer which could be drawn out when needed for toilet purposes.

Brussels carpets: see Moquette.

Brussels lace: needlepoint and pillow laces (qq.v.). Needlepoint was made from 1720, but took second place to the pillow laces. The ground was a plain looped mesh and late in the century there was a tendency to restrict the slower needlepoint work to the pattern and introduce a pillow lace ground. Pillow laces included bride-linked tape lace of the 17th cent., (tape lace being bobbin lace in which the design is formed of a continuous lace twisted and stitched into place; bride is the network connecting the pattern in lace). Those were succeeded by grounded laces, the ground worked after the pattern, its hexagonal mesh consisting of two sides with four threads plaited four times and four sides of two threads twisted. Patterns in the mid-18th cent. included many Rococo-Oriental extravagancies. The Brussels *point plat appliqué* was a pillow lace of the late 18th cent. with a net ground supporting small sprigs worked separately.

Brussels tapestry: capital of Brabant and the Netherlands since 1483, Brussels became Europe's leading centre of tapestry weaving from about 1500, and retained its reputation throughout the 17th and 18th cent., though eclipsed by Louis XIV's Gobelins (q.v.) factory since 1670/80. Brussel's reputation was definitely sealed by Pope Leo X's order for the weaving of tapestries for the Sistine Chapel from Raphael's cartoons (about 1515). But as a tapestry designer Bernard van Orley and his school exercised a far greater influence at Brussels in the first half of the 16th cent. The *History of Jacob*, at Brussels, and the *Hunts of Maximilian* at the Louvre are superb examples of his style. Francis I of France, England's Henry VIII, and the Emperor Charles V of Austria all had recourse to Brussels for specially fine sets (the *Great Scipio*, *Story of Abraham*, now at Hampton Court, the *Conquest of Tunis*), and it was there also that the Duke of Marlborough ordered his set of *Victories* (*c.* 1712). Throughout the 16th, 17th and 18th cent. the Habsburgs were Brussels' chief patrons.

Among the many outstanding workshops, those of Van Aelst, de Pannemaker and Geubels should be mentioned for the 16th cent. Jan Raes, Martin Reymbouts and the Leyniers family excelled in the 17th. The large and extravagantly designed Baroque tapestries of that cent. were probably less popular in England than sets with subjects taken from Roman or Biblical history. Mythological subjects were also in great favour, especially those set in wooded landscapes and surrounded with rich floral borders. So, too, were *genre* and peasant subjects taken from paintings and designs after the second David Teniers. These so-called 'Teniers tapestries' were in vogue from the late 17th and all through the 18th cent. J. van der Borcht (senior, who also signed himself in the latinized form 'A. Castro'), J. de Vos, and various members of the Leyniers and van den Hecke families are names frequently met with on Brussels tapestries of this period.

The mark, a red shield between two B's (for Brussels, Brabant) is normally seen in the border of a Brussels tapestry after the Edict of 1528 which introduced trade marks.

BᗡB

Brustolon, Andrea: (b. 1622), Italian furniture maker and sculptor working in Venice from 1684 to 1696. His pieces are invariably elaborately carved.

Bruting: the grinding into shape of a rough diamond by rubbing it with another – the first step in grinding the precious stone.

Bucket-form bowl: bowl of a drinking glass in the form of a straight-sided bucket with horizontal base, a shape which continued in popularity from the 1730s until the early 19th cent.

Buckle-back: balloon-back (q.v.) with a carved cross rail resembling a buckle. A type of chair back popular in the 19th cent.

Buckler: in the 16th cent. the majority of shields were circular, one of the most popular types being the buckler (introduced as early as the 13th cent.), held in the left hand by means of a crossbar on the inside.

Bucks point lace: pillow lace (q.v.), mainly showing the influence of Lille (q.v.) and with much use of Lille's ground – *fond clair* (q.v.) – although often in company with *fond chant* (q.v.) and the soft Mechlin (q.v.) mesh. The patterns were lightened with attractive fillings and outlined with gimp, wide and flat. There was some direct copying of Mechlin.

Buckwheat celadon ware: see Tobi seiji.

Bud thumbpiece: a thumbpiece (q.v.) in the shape of two ovoids rising from a common stalk and resembling bursting buds found on 17th- and 18th-cent. pewter (q.v.) vessels.

Buen Retiro porcelain: porcelain was made at Buen Retiro, near Madrid, from 1759 until 1808, when the factory closed. The premises at Buen Retiro were set up by Charles III upon his succession to the throne of Spain, the purpose being to house his workmen and artists who had previously worked for him at Capo-di-Monte (q.v.), Naples. Buen Retiro porcelain was soft-paste of a creamy tone, the figure modelling reaching a high level of achievement, although examples are extremely rare.

Buffe: see Burgonet.

Buffet: term variously applied to open, doorless structures, of more than one tier (see also Court cupboard, Livery cupboard).

Bulb (or **melon bulb**): decorative swelling on the upright members of 16th- and 17th-cent. furniture, sometimes with carving.

Bullet knop: a knop or protuberance on the stem of a drinking glass or other vessel of small spherical form. Sometimes known as an olive button.

Bull's eye: popular American term for a smallish round mirror of concave or, more often, convex glass in an ornate round frame. With candle brackets attached to the frame, the type is generally known in America as a girandole mirror. Many of these bull's eye mirrors are of English or French rather than American make. They were highly fashionable about 1800–20.

Bun foot: a variation of the ball foot, in which the rounded form is slightly flattened at the top and bottom, introduced as a terminal support to cabinets or table legs in the mid-17th cent. (See also Ball foot.)

Bureau: desk with, except in the case of the *bureau-plat* (q.v.), a sloping hinged flap that opens to form a writing surface. The earliest examples date from the late 17th cent. In the United States the term also refers to a chest of drawers.

Bureau bookcase: a piece of cabinet furniture which came into use towards the mid-18th cent., consisting of an upper stage with shelves enclosed within doors, sometimes glazed, and below a slope-front desk which opens to reveal small drawers for writing materials in the interior. Below are long drawers.

Bueau-plat: (*Fr.*), a writing-table supported on tall legs with a flat top and drawers beneath. Began to appear in France towards the end of the 17th cent.

Bureau-toilette: (*Fr.*), a piece of furniture intended for the use of ladies, combining the functions of a toilet- and writing-table.

Burges, William: (1827–81), English architect, designer and craftsman of the Gothic Revival (q.v.). His designs to be executed in various materials demonstrate an admiration for Medieval techniques and forms of decoration. He rebuilt, decorated and furnished Cardiff Castle.

Burgonet: an open helmet, used chiefly by light-horsemen in the 16th and early 17th cent. It usually had a peak (fall) over the eyes and hinged cheek-pieces fastening under the chin. It was sometimes worn with a deep chin-piece (buffe).

Burl: see Burr.

Burmese glass: opaque glass shading from yellow to pink by the action of oxides of uranium and gold, with a glossy, or satin finish. Produced in a variety of table and decorative wares and popularized in England as Queen's Burmese following the presentation of a set to Queen Victoria in 1885.

Burne-Jones, Sir Edward Coley: (1833–98), English painter and designer of tapestries and stained glass for Morris, Marshall, Faulkner & Co. (q.v.).

Burnishing: polishing with a hand tool containing a hard, smooth stone or, in modern times, steel; used to remove planishing marks from the 'planishing teats' (q.v.) or hammer.

Burr: known as burl in the United States, it is a knot or growth in the wood of certain trees such as the oak, walnut, yew and maple. When sliced through, the beautifully patterned and grained wood is used as a veneer (q.v.).

Burt, John: (c. 1692–1745), American silversmith, of Boston, Mass., whose sons Benjamin, Samuel and William continued in his trade.

Bushire carpets: see Beshire carpets.

Bustelli, Franz Anton: (1723–63), a porcelain modeller employed at the Nymphenburg factory (q.v.) in Germany from 1754 to his death in 1763. His figures show great affinity of style with those of contemporary Bavarian sculptors. His was perhaps, the greatest creative genius in porcelain of the 18th cent. He recaptured the playful mood of the Rococo period (q.v.) in his figures, often rendered in pure white or in restrained colours. Among the finest of his models are those derived from the Italian *Commedia dell' Arte.*

Butler's finish: a matt finish on silver and electroplate (q.v.) patented in the United States in 1870. It was obtained by the application of acid or by rubbing with an abrasive material or sand-blasting.

Butler's sideboard: uniquely American piece, also known as a Salem secretary. It combines a glass-fronted china cupboard with drawers and a drop-fronted writing compartment.

Butler's tray: a tray mounted on legs or on a folding stand, in use throughout the 18th cent. The X-shaped folding stand was in general use from about 1750, the tray normally being rectangular and fitted with a gallery (q.v.). Oval trays were sometimes made in the later part of the cent.

Butterfly paperweight: a coloured butterfly occupies the centre of the paperweight. The insect can be poised over a flower, above a latticinio (q.v.), or other filigree (q.v.), ground. Butterflies, snakes, ducks and caterpillars rate as among the most valued subjects of all baccarat (q.v.) paperweights.

Butterfly table: drop-leaf table with swinging supports resembling butterfly wings. Believed to be uniquely American. The legs are raked and stretchered so that the wings can be pivoted in the stretchers (q.v.). They were made between 1700 and 1725, the earliest examples being usually of maple.

Butter knife: blunt knife in the shape of a scimitar of silver or electroplate (q.v.), introduced c. 1790.

Button upholstery: type of upholstery with deep-set buttons popular after 1840.

Bygones: any objects no longer in use, such as obsolete agricultural implements, old-fashioned spits (q.v.), fenders, bellows (q.v.), and so on.

Cabaret set: porcelain tea set for two people, provided with a porcelain tray. Sometimes the cups were placed immediately on the tray and the saucers dispensed with.

Cabasset: see Morion.

Cabbage-leaf jugs: there are two large jugs in Worcester Corporation Museum, moulded with overlapping leaves in relief, dated 1757, which were made at the Worcester porcelain factory. Worcester cabbage-leaf jugs have cylindrical necks (later ones sometimes with masks), and ovoid relief-ornamented bodies upon which the decoration was superimposed. This type of jug was imitated later at Lowestoft and Caughley (qq.v.) usually with the addition of a mask-lip spout.

Cabinet: piece of furniture with a door or doors, often with interior drawers, shelves or compartments. In the 17th cent. cabinets were sometimes mounted on stands and in the following cent. on bases with drawers.

Cabinet-makers: towards the end of the 17th cent., the joiner was replaced by the cabinet-maker as the supreme furniture craftsman. The new technique of veneering furniture, which was introduced into England at the return of Charles II, was probably taught to the English craftsmen by either Dutch or French cabinet-makers. The new craft found a firm footing and by the mid-18th cent. the work of the English cabinet-makers displayed a great technical excellence.

Cabochon: stones of rounded, natural form, polished but not cut.

Cabochon ornament: a carved ornament found on furniture of the middle years of the 18th cent. and particularly on the knees of chair legs, so named on account of its resemblance to the polished, rounded shape of an uncut gem. It is usually oval and surrounded by a scrolled leaf ornament.

Cabriole leg: a chair or table leg much favoured in the first half of the 18th cent. and based on a stylized hind leg of an animal. The leg curves outwards at the knee and inwards towards the foot in an elongated 'S' form and is tapered at the base. Sometimes the knee bears a carved shell ornament.

Cabriolet fan: fashionable from the 1770s until the 1790s and contemporary with medallion fans (q.v.). The name was derived from the wheels of a light-weight carriage of the period. The fan consisted not of a single broad leaf, but of two or three narrower, arc-shaped bands of silk or chicken skin (q.v.). The upper mount, measuring twice the depth of the others, might be painted with a scene including a cabriolet, its occupant being a portrait of the fan's owner. The sticks offered further scope for ornament, such as piercing and gilding, on the spaces visible between the bands. Tiny mirrors might be inset into the blades and a minute telescopic glass inserted into the stick pivot (q.v.).

Cadborough ware: red earthenware (q.v.), coated and streaked with a lead glaze (q.v.). It was introduced in 1790 by the Smith family of Rye, Sussex.

Caddy spoon: small spoon with short handle for measuring tea from the caddy. Made in numerous fancy forms, leaf, jockey cap, hand, etc., from about 1780 onwards.

Cadogan teapot: a pot or jug filled through a tube which extends from a hole in the base to within a few millimetres of inside of top, preventing spillage when pot is righted, said to have been named after the Hon. Mrs Cadogan, who brought to England an original Chinese teapot of this type. Presumably intended as hot-water pots, unsuitable for brewing tea. A Cadogan teapot is lidless and shaped like a Chinese peach-shaped wine pot. First made at Swinton, Yorkshire, about 1795, with a purple-brown 'Rockingham' (q.v.) glaze, Cadogan teapots became popular, and John Mortlock of Oxford Street, London, whose name, impressed, frequently occurs, bought and sold large quantities of them. In Staffordshire Cadogans were made by Davenport, Copelands (qq.v.) and other firms. Made at Rockingham from 1806–42.

Caen lace: pillow lace (q.v.) imitating the silk *blondes* of Chantilly (q.v.) from the mid-18th cent.

Cafaggiolo maiolica: tin-glazed earthenware made after 1500 under the patronage of a branch of the Medici family at their castle of Cafaggiolo, near Florence. During the Renaissance (q.v.), the art of the potter in Italy was encouraged by patronage and *maiolica* (q.v.) represents one of its supreme achievements. Work characteristically decorated in the *istoriate* style and with grotesques, allegories of love and subjects of a general religious nature, are depicted in a wide range of intense colours.

Café-au-lait glaze (or **t'zu Chin**): a warm brown glaze used on Chinese porcelain of the Ch'ing dynasty (q.v.), sometimes over-painted in *famille verte* (q.v.) enamels and sometimes as a monochrome.

Caffawa or **caffoys**: English 18th-cent. term for flock wallpapers simulating damask.

Caffiéri, Jacques: (1678–1755) French sculptor, one of the chief exponents of the Rococo style in France; he was employed extensively by the Crown at Versailles, Fontainebleau and elsewhere. He also occasionally worked as a portrait sculptor. He often signed his bronzes with his surname only, and his chief works are to be found at Versailles, the Louvre, Paris, and the Wallace Collection in London.

Cage-cup: see Diatreta vase.

Cage-work: type of silver decoration, a pierced and often chased outer layer enclosing a plain inner section, which is sometimes gilded. A technique of German origin.

Cake basket: a silver or plated circular or oval bowl for bread or fruit as well as cake, made from the 16th cent. onwards. By 1730 there was generally a centrally placed handle. The decoration was commonly pierced or chased to resemble basketry. American examples of the 18th cent. are rare.

Cake slice: silver implement with a flat, triangular blade originating in the mid-18th cent.

Calendar clock: a clock which indicates days, months or years. A simple calendar clock has to be reset

each month according to the numbers of days in the month. A perpetual calendar includes an additional train (q.v.).

Calibre cut: gemstones of small dimensions cut to special requirements.

Callot figures: miniature figures, usually amusing or grotesque, in porcelain or in silver or gold, enamelled or gem-set, are known as Callot figures. This is a reference to the French engraver Jacques Callot (*c.* 1592–1635), who specialized in vivid drawings of beggars and cut-throats and the swaggering characters of the Italian *Commedia dell'Arte*.

Caltrop: a four-spiked device so arranged that one spike always projects upwards. Used as a form of defence against cavalry attack as the horses were lamed by these implements placed in their path.

Cambrian pottery: see Swansea earthenware and porcelain.

Camel-back sofa: colloquial term for a sofa, with the top curved somewhat like the hump of a dromedary. They date from the late 18th cent.

Cameo: a gem or shell carved in relief in such a way that the contrasting colours of the material carved are exploited. The cameos cut by the Romans were much admired throughout the Middle Ages and the Renaissance (q.v.). The Neoclassical taste of the late 18th cent. brought a revival of interest in cameos. Cheaper materials began to be used in imitation of gems, such as the paste copies of antique cameos made by James Tassie (see Tassies) or the Wedgwood jasperware cameos. (See also Wedgwood, Josiah.)

Cameo glass: a relief carved in glass on the lapidary's wheel through a surface layer of white fused on to a darker ground. A Roman technique, it was imitated in England in the late 19th cent. by several Stourbridge firms and others.

Cameo incrustation: see Crystallo-Ceramie.

Campaign furniture: 18th- and 19th-cent. furniture with brass corners and recessed handles which was easily dismantled. It was used by the military.

Campana vase: a vase made in the Neoclassical (q.v.) style, during the first decades of the 19th cent. Possibly from *campana*, a church bell, hence bell-shaped.

Canapé: the French word for a conventional sofa. Evolved in France in many forms during the Louis XV period.

Candelabrum: branched candlestick (q.v.) of silver, plate (q.v.), ormolu (q.v.), porcelain, etc., plain or ornamented in the prevailing taste.

Candle box: a cylindrical or square box, of metal or wood, widely used in the Georgian period for storing candles.

Candle snuffer: candle-flame extinguishers were made either in the form of a conical hood with a handle or in pincer form. The latter resembled scissors with blunt blades and metal discs instead of points.

Candle stand: a portable stand (known also as a lampstand, *guéridon* (q.v.) or *torchère*) for a candlestick (q.v.), candelabrum (q.v.) or lamp. After 1660 the fashion arose of having two candle stands flanking a side table with a mirror on the wall above; the stands usually took the form of a baluster or twist-turned shaft, with a circular or octagonal top and a tripod base. At the end of the cent. more elaborate kinds, copying French stands, became fashionable, with vase-shaped tops and scrolled feet, all carved and gilded. Other examples were of simpler design, but had rich decoration in gesso (q.v.) or marquetry (q.v.). In the early Georgian period, when gilt stands followed architectural forms, the vase-shaped tops and baluster shafts were larger, and the feet curved outwards, replacing the scrolled French style. About 1750 stands became lighter and more delicate, many of them being enriched with Rococo decoration. There was a distinct change in design in the later 18th cent.: the traditional tripod continued, often in mahogany, with turned shaft and a bowl or vase top in the Classical taste; but a new type, which was originated by Adam (q.v.), consisted of three uprights, mounted on feet or a plinth, supporting usually a candelabrum, or with a flat top. Smaller examples of the latter type were made to stand on tables. A much smaller candle stand, popular after 1750, had a circular base and top, and sometimes an adjustable shaft.

Candlestick: metalwork, ceramic, glass or wood candleholder made in Europe since the Middle Ages. It reflects the current requirements and forms and styles of decoration.

Cane: name for the rods of coloured glass from which the patterns were formed in many types of paperweights.

Cane ware: a tan-coloured stoneware 'dry' body made by Josiah Wedgwood in 1770 by refining the red and buff clays used by local potters. Similar bodies were made by John Turner (q.v.) of Lane End, Staffordshire, Elijah Mayer and others. It was sometimes enamelled in blue and other colours. (See also 'Bamboo' ware.)

Cann: an American term for a silver drinking vessel, usually of one-pint capacity, like a mug.

Cannetille: coarse type of gold or imitation gold filigree (q.v.) popular in France and elsewhere from *c.* 1811 to 1850. Beads of coiled wire, pyramids and rosettes were favoured as motifs.

Canopy: raised covering of beds, thrones, etc., supported by posts or attached to the wall or ceiling. Also, the umbrella-shaped feature at the top and base of some chandeliers (q.v.).

Canted corner: bevelled or obliquely faced surface. Deriving from an architectural form, 18th cent. case furniture sometimes had canted corners.

Canteen: small individual silver set of knife, fork and spoon with beaker (q.v.) and condiment box, contained in shagreen (q.v.) case, used for travelling, dating from late 17th to early 18th cent. Also, large wooden boxes with fittings for table silver.

Canterbury: a term used to describe (1) a small music-stand with partitions for music-books, usually mounted on castors, and sometimes with small drawers, much used in the early 19th cent.; (2) a plate and cutlery stand particularly designed for supper parties in the later 18th cent., with divisions for cutlery and a semicircular end, on four turned legs.

(1)

Canton enamel: enamel ware on copper made for export to Europe at the Canton enamelling workshops, in China. Eighteenth-cent. pieces include teapots, teacaddies (q.v.), trays, bowls, etc. painted with flowering sprays or fruit and sometimes with European scenes.

Canton porcelain: the familiar name for a type of 19th-cent. Chinese porcelain exported to Europe, decorated with butterflies, flowers, etc., on a celadon-green ground. Canton was the principal port on the coast of China for trade with Europe in the 18th and 19th cent. Porcelain was brought to Canton by river from Ching-Tê-Chên. From the middle years of the 18th cent. increasing quantities of porcelain were sent unpainted and were decorated to order by artists in enamelling workshops at the port. (See also Canton enamel.)

Capacity mugs: measures: cylindrical mugs of a certified content, stamped with an excise mark, used in ale-houses, or by street hawkers and shopkeepers; and made in salt-glazed stoneware in London, Staffordshire and elsewhere from the end of the 17th cent., and in dipped, mocha (q.v.), and banded earthenware (q.v.) from the end of the 18th cent.

Capo-di-Monte porcelain: soft-paste porcelain was made at Capo-di-Monte, Naples, at a factory founded by the King of Naples in 1743. Examples are scarce. Decoration in relief and coloured was a characteristic of the factory but as the Doccia (q.v.) factory purchased numbers of the moulds in the early 19th cent. and used them, many reproductions exist; the copies made at Doccia are, however, of hard-paste porcelain. The factory was moved to Buen Retiro (q.v.), near Madrid in 1759, when the King of Naples also became King of Spain.

Capstan salt: a salt-cellar shaped like a ship's capstan.

Caqueteuse: a late 16th-cent. chair with tall narrow back and widely splayed arms and seat widening towards the front. It was introduced into Britain from France and the name is derived from the French word *caqueter*, to chatter.

Carat: measure of purity of gold (pure gold is 24 carats); also of weight for precious stones.

Carbuncle: a garnet cut *en cabochon*, that is, rounded and polished but unfaceted.

Carcase: the body of a piece of furniture upon which the veneer (q.v.) is applied.

Card case: small, generally highly decorated, rectangular box for visiting cards made in the 19th cent. of a variety of materials.

Card table: table originating in the 18th cent. designed specifically for card games. The most common type had a folding top which was covered in a material such as baize.

Bouillotte, a French card game, was played on a table with a marble top and metal gallery which had drawers and flat sliding shelves in the sides. The game of lanterloo was played on a 'loo table', which generally had a round top.

Cardinal's hat dish: a deep pewter (q.v.) dish with a broad rim.

Carlin, Martin: French cabinet-maker. Very little is known about the life of Carlin. His place and date of birth are unknown. He died in Paris in 1785. He is first mentioned in 1763 and became a *maître ébéniste* (see *Menuisiers Ebénistes, Corporation des*) in 1766. He worked for Queen Marie Antoinette and the Royal Family, but it is uncertain whether he received an official appointment with the *Garde Meuble* (q.v.).

Carlin was a most refined and delicate craftsman. He worked particularly in lacquer and with plaques of Sèvres porcelain (q.v.).

Carlton House table: a writing table of 'D' shape, the flat front containing drawers, the top surmounted by a border containing further drawers, crested by a brass gallery (q.v.). The term is contemporary and derives from the tradition that tables of this type were first supplied to the Prince of Wales, later George IV, for Carlton House. Many examples exist, dating from *c.* 1790 to *c.* 1820, usually of mahogany and sometimes satinwood.

Carré, Jean: (d. 1572) a glass-maker of Arras and Antwerp, who introduced Protestant emigrant glass-makers from Lorraine into England where they settled. He obtained a privilege from Queen Elizabeth I in 1567. In 1570 he set up a glass house in Crutched Friars in London, employing Italian workmen and producing glasses in the Venetian manner. He died in 1572. (See also Verzelini, Giacomo.)

Carriage clock: originally a clock designed for the rough coach and carriage travel of previous centuries. This type of clock was particularly popular in England in the late 19th cent. The case usually consists of a brass base having four vertical corner pillars holding mainly glass panels at the front, side and back.

Carriage glass: a footless drinking glass for serving travellers or riders.

Carriage lamp: glass-panelled oil lamp with a characteristic fuel reservoir in the form of a column and surmounted by a finial (q.v.), usually of brass.

Carrickmacross appliqué: similar to but not a real lace as the pattern was cut from cambric, applied to net and given needlepoint fillings (q.v.). It was first made in Ireland in the 1830s.

Carrickmacross guipure: similar to Carrickmacross appliqué (q.v.) but with needlepoint brides (q.v.) instead of net.

Carron: the Carron Ironworks, Falkirk, Scotland, opened in 1759 and was responsible for the making of much fireside equipment. Small andirons (q.v.) of early 19th-cent. pattern are found with the name of the firm cast on the fronts. Many of these have been re-cast from the original moulds, in the present cent., but it is stated that in these instances the name 'Carron' appears at the back of each piece.

Cartel clock: a mural clock, usually of somewhat flamboyant design. More often found in France than in England.

English are usually of carved wood, whereas the French are usually of cast brass or bronze and gilt.

Cartlidge, Charles, & Co.: founded in 1848 by Charles Cartlidge at Greenpoint, Long Island, former American agent for the English pottery of Ridgway (q.v.). Cartlidge manufactured porcelain tableware, buttons, hardware trimmings and parian ware (q.v.), and maintained a high reputation for his painted decoration and gilded trim. Because Cartlidge was more interested in artistic excellence than financial success, the factory was forced to cease operating in 1856.

Cartonnier: (*Fr.*), a piece of furniture intended to hold paper, made in various forms. Usually it stood at one end of a writing-table and was sometimes surmounted by a clock. Also known as a *serre-papier*.

Cartouche: a decorative framing or border device, or tablet, with scrolled edges. Used in wood and metalwork, it often bears an inscription or a coat of arms.

Carver: armchair in a set of dining-chairs.

Carver chair: an American early-17th-cent. Dutch type of arm chair made of turned posts and spindles. It has three rails and three spindles in the

back. Such chairs may be seen in 17th-cent. paintings of humble Dutch interiors, though the American example was probably derived from an English model. Usually of ash or maple, with rush seats. Named after John Carver, first governor of the Plymouth colony, who is said to have brought one to America with him in the *Mayflower*. Made until the end of the cent. Many examples survive, the earliest dating perhaps about 1650. (See also Brewster chair.)

Caryatid: strictly a female sculptured figure used as a support in place of a column, but frequently used to describe a figure of either sex employed in this manner as a decorative form. The term derives from the legend of the women of Carya, enslaved and immured for their betrayal of the Greeks to the Persians. (See also Atlanta.)

Cased glass: two or more layers of glass differing in colour; called overlay when design is cut through to body colour; popular Bohemian glass technique.

Casket: the earliest caskets likely to come the way of the collector are those made in Sicily during the 13th to 14th cent. They are constructed of ivory with brass mounts, and are believed to have been the work of Arabic craftsmen. The Near Eastern element in them can be seen, not in any constructional detail but in the painted ornament with which the finer examples were enriched. This ornament often introduces Cufic characters or amorphous scrollwork of Saracenic origin. Caskets or small coffers of the 15th cent. are far less rare than the earlier examples; there were two main types; those constructed entirely of iron and those of wood, sometimes covered with leather and always furnished with more or less elaborate bands of iron. Such caskets were made in France, the Low Countries, Germany, and Spain, and it is often difficult to be certain of the country of origin, especially of the earlier types. Subsequently, recognized national types emerge. One French type is entirely of iron with an arched lid. The earlier examples have applied Gothic tracery ornamentation, the later ones have a plain surface with either etched or damascened ornament (Fig. B). The Spanish type is of almost rectangular section with only slightly curved walls. It is of wood covered with one of more layers of tinned sheet iron, pierced with reticulated ornament. This type is provided with stout bands and an elaborate lock decorated with Gothic pinnacles.

The most common German type dates from the second half of the 16th cent. and shows no trace of the Gothic ornament which persisted so long into the 16th cent. in the locksmiths' workshops. It is rectangular in plan and is constructed of iron sheet sometimes enriched with mounts of gilt brass. The whole of the exterior surface is etched with floral scrolls or with hunting or allegorical subjects. The lock, which is accommodated on the underside of the lid, is of great elaboration, shooting as many as a dozen bolts. These coffers were made in Nuremberg and Augsburg but are never signed (Fig. C). On the other hand, the miniature caskets of gilt brass, sometimes enriched with silver and even enamel, and engraved instead of etched, are usually known as Michael Mann boxes because so many of them bear the signature, of a Nuremberg locksmith of that name (Fig. A).

Fine coffers of English manufacture do not appear before the second half of the 17th cent., when we find the very rare but incomparable works of the Bickfords (e.g. the jewel casket of Queen Mary II in the Victoria and Albert Museum) and the fairly common but extremely attractive caskets with fall fronts veneered with oyster marquetry (q.v.) and furnished with elaborate gilt brass hingework.

Fig. B

Fig. C

Cassel porcelain: table wares and figures of rather simple character often in blue-and-white were made at a porcelain factory at Cassel between c. 1680 and c. 1788, subsidized by the Landgrave of Hesse-Cassel. Between about 1770 and the close of the factory two marks were in use: an 'H.C.' in blue or a two-tailed heraldic lion from the arms of Hesse.

Cassone: the *cassone*, an Italian term for chest, was clearly one of the most popular pieces of furniture in 15th- and 16th-cent. Italy. It was also the most richly decorated, and, for this reason, perhaps, numerous examples have survived. It was used to hold linen or clothes and might also serve as a seat (with or without the upright back which made it into a *cassapanca*). *Cassoni* are frequently referred to as dowry chests, and although they were often made to hold the supply of linen which a bride took to her new home, there is no reason to suppose that the majority were intended for this purpose.

The earliest *cassoni* were probably very unpretentious, but a few of the early 15th-cent. examples which have survived are decorated with Gothic curvilinear carving or rough paintings of heraldic achievements. In the Renaissance period, great ingenuity was expended on their design and adornment. Some were decorated with gesso (q.v.) friezes of *putti* sporting on the front and sides and others were fashioned like antique sarcophagi, but

Fig. A

most seem to have been painted on the front (some were also painted inside the lid). Several highly able Florentine 15th-cent. painters, like the famous Master of the Jarves *cassoni*, seem to have specialized almost exclusively in the decoration of furniture of this type: and some more important artists, like Bartolomeo Montagna, occasionally turned their hands to this decorative work. In Florence paintings of battles and the triumphs of Roman generals were in particular demand, elsewhere religious and mythological scenes seem to have enjoyed great popularity but in Venice patterns of ornamental motifs were generally preferred. Intarsia (see Tarsia) views of real or imaginary architecture were also employed. In the 16th cent. the painted *cassone* seems to have gone out of fashion and most surviving examples from this period are simply carved with abstract decorations. A few later 16th-cent. *cassoni* are adorned with figures at the corners and low reliefs in the same style on the front.

Cast: a piece produced by pouring molten metal or other liquid matter into a previously modelled mould.

Castel Durante maiolica: tin-glazed earthenware made at Castel Durante (now Urbania) in Italy. Much Castel Durante ware of the 16th cent. is decorated with figure subjects from classical mythology in rich, full pigments.

Castellani, Fortunato Pio (1793–1856): a Roman jeweller of the mid-19th cent. who rediscovered the Etruscan secret of applying minute grains of gold to a gold base, producing a granulated ground. With his two sons, he produced in his workshop many fine pseudo-Greek pieces of jewellery.

Castelli maiolica: tin-glazed earthenware made near Teramo in the Abruzzi from the 16th cent. Castelli wares of late 17th-cent. date are often decorated with mythological or historical scenes in a subdued range of colours, dominated by a pale greyish-blue.

Caster: found singly or in a set of three, of silver, also occasionally of brass or pewter (q.v.), for sugar, pepper, and with unpierced cover for mustard. Late 17th-cent. form cylindrical. In the 18th cent. pear-shaped and later of vase form, polygonal or circular in outline.

Castleford pottery: at Whitwood Mere, David Dunderdale, an apprentice of the Leeds (q.v.) Pottery, established a factory *c.* 1790 for the manufacture of cream-coloured earthenware, Egyptian black and felspathic (q.v.) stoneware. From 1793 until 1821 when it closed down, it traded as David Dunderdale and Co. The most typical products were in unglazed stoneware with relief decorations in panels. Similar wares, with or without panels picked out in blue, were made elsewhere. The marks used were:

DD&Co.	DD&Co.	DD&Co.
CASTLEFORD	CASTLEFORD	CASTLEFORD
POTTERY	DD & CO.	POTTERY

In 1825 the factory was partly reopened by Asquith, Wood & Co. and from that time onwards was continued under various ownerships.

Castle Hedingham: pseudo-Medieval and Tudor pottery was made here by Edward Bingham (b. 1829). Sometimes mistaken for authentic 15th-, 16th- and 17th-cent. wares.

Castor or **caster:** wheel or roller attached to the underside of furniture at the corners to facilitate movement. First used in the 17th cent.

Castwork: decoration or parts of a silver vessel cast in a mould and soldered to the main body. Principally used for handles, feet, spouts and finials.

Cat: a stand used after about 1750 to warm plates in front of the fire; it had three arms and three feet of turned wood (or three legs of cabriole form). The turning was well ringed to provide sockets for plates of various sizes.

Catacomb glasses: fragments of gold-engraved glasses found in the Roman catacombs, being the bottoms of shallow bowls decorated with medallions of engraved gold leaf.

Caucasian rugs: rugs which come from the Caucasian Mountains between the Caspian and Black Seas. The designs show both Persian and Chinese influence, but retain strong characteristics of their own. The employment of the local highland wool, which is unsurpassed, combined with meticulous and regular weaving, has given these rugs lasting quality, and many examples of merit exist.

Among the earliest specimens are the famous Armenian Dragon rugs, woven in the 16th cent. The main motifs consist of conventional upright dragons, forming panels, flowering trees with birds, and often elephants and camels. A pleasing shade of soft rose relieved by dark blue or black are the predominant colours. The dragon design has influenced many later specimens.

A great similarity of design and the knotting, which is almost exclusively Ghiordes (q.v.), through Caucasia renders identification of each type difficult, if not impossible. It is mainly on quality that the rugs are classified.

The most prevalent motif is of jewel shapes, both diamond and octagonal in form, with use of latch hook in white or cream. The detail is generally of conventional small flowers, stars, squares and swastikas.

Caudle cup: silver, pewter (q.v.) or ceramic cup for drinking caudle, a hot, spiced beverage. They were made with one or two handles and a lid. Cups made for posset – milk curdled by liquor – were similar in form.

Caughley porcelain: Thomas Turner, previously at Worcester (q.v.) became the proprietor of the Caughley works which were near Broseley in Shropshire in 1772. These had been worked as an earthenware factory since 1754. Turner manufactured at Caughley a soapstone porcelain similar to that of Worcester but slightly different in colour and less well potted. In 1799 John Rose of Coalport (q.v.) purchased the factory and used it to produce biscuit porcelain (q.v.) which was glazed and decorated at Coalport. The factory closed in 1814. A number of marks were used, some clearly imitating those of other English and foreign factories. The most notable are the letters 'S' or 'C' in blue, or the word 'Salopian' in upper or lower case letters, impressed. The bulk of the factory's output of useful wares was decorated in blue and white, sometimes by transfer printing (q.v.), in the Worcester manner. Two patterns which were originated here, the 'Willow' (q.v.) and 'Broseley Dragon', attained great popularity and are known in numerous variations, produced by later Staffordshire and other earthenware factories. Gilding was combined with blue decoration at the end of the cent. A greyish and bright-purplish blue was used for decoration, lighter and brighter than that of Worcester. Shapes and patterns followed Worcester lines. Ambitious coloured decorations were produced.

Cauldron: (kettle), one of the oldest of all cooking utensils and recorded from the earliest times. They were first made of sheets of bronze, hammered to shape and riveted together; later they were of cast bronze. From the 16th cent. they were made of cast iron, and formed an important item of equipment. Small-sized cauldrons were known in some regions as 'crocks'.

Cauliflower ware: green and yellow glazed earthenware made in the form of cauliflowers, pineapples and other vegetables, by Whieldon (q.v.), Wedgwood (q.v.) and others from 1750 onwards; cauliflowers were also made in porcelain.

Causeuse: (*Fr.*) a large chair or small sofa to accommodate two persons. Roughly corresponds to the small English settee. Sometimes referred to as a love-seat.

Cavetto frieze: see Concave frieze.

Ceiler: the fabric covering hung over the Medieval bed, replaced in the 16th cent. by a wooden tester (q.v.) which formed the four-poster bed roof.

Celadon wares: Chinese porcelain wares with felspathic glaze (q.v.) of characteristic pale greyish- or bluish-green tone derived from iron; the name was apparently taken from the character Céladon in Honoré D'Urfé's early 17th-cent. pastoral romance *L'Astrée*, and not from *Saladin*, as sometimes supposed. Typical are the early Yüeh (q.v.) ware, and the much-exported Lung-chüan celadons of the Sung and Ming dynasties. Ch'ing dynasty celadons generally differ from those in their white porcelain body, even glaze and careful finish. But some Sung wares were skilfully copied, and the bluish, and lavender-toned Kuan and Ko (qq.v.) glazes, their crackle, and even their dark body, were reproduced. In 18th-cent. France the later celadons were sometimes mounted in ormolu (q.v.).

Celestial globe: a spherical model of the heavens. (See Terrestrial globe.)

Cellaret: the name given, generally after 1750, to a case on legs, or stand for wine bottles. Prior to that date, from the end of the 17th cent., the same kind of case was called a cellar. In the early 18th cent. cellarets, lined with lead and containing compartments for bottles, stood under side-tables. They were still made later in the cent. when sideboards, containing drawers fitted to hold bottles, came into general use. Sheraton (q.v.) classified the cellaret with the wine-cistern (q.v.) and sarcophagus, and distinguished them from the bottle case, which was for square bottles only.

Cellini, Benvenuto: (1500–71), a Renaissance goldsmith and sculptor whose literary work is a guide to the technical background and social standing of the members of his craft in the 16th cent.

Censer: covered bowl with suspension chains for burning incense in liturgical use. Made of precious or base metal, the latter mostly Medieval.

Centre-piece: a silver table centre being a late form of épergne, usually with one wirework or pierced central basket on high foliage or figure stem. Centre-pieces are found after 1800 in a wide range of decorative forms, sometimes with separate plinth or mirror plateau. (See also Epergne.)

Centre seconds clock: a clock or watch in which the seconds hand is placed on the same arbor (q.v.) as the hour and minute hands.

Centre table: a table, often circular, designed to be free standing. The earliest English examples were generally of gate-leg (q.v.) construction.

Century Guild: founded *c.* 1882, it existed until 1888 as a society to promote good craftsmanship and design. The central figure was A. H. Mackmurdo (q.v.).

Ceramic Art Co.: founded in 1889 at Trenton, New Jersey, the company produced both decorated and plain wares and brought the production of Belleek (q.v.) china to the highest state of perfection in the United States.

Chafing dish: container for hot charcoal on which dishes were placed to keep warm. They were made from the 17th cent. onwards in silver, copper and brass, some examples having a wooden handle. (See also Brazier.)

Chair-table: combined chair and table, the back of the chair tilting forward to form the table top. In the United States it is called a hutch table.

Chaise longue: day bed; a chair, with or without arms, the seat extending to support the legs.

Chalice: cup-shaped vessel used to contain wine in the celebration of the Mass. In England this term should be confined to Communion vessels made before the Reformation and the extension of the cup to the laity in the Church of England. In the 17th cent. the form was revived for a short period and never discontinued in Ireland. The essential form is that of a shallow hemispherical or conical bowl on high knopped stem and circular or polygonal foot (see Communion cup and Paten).

Chalk engraving: an etching technique used for making facsimiles of chalk drawings.

Chamber candlesticks: also known as flat candlesticks. Usually circular, flat base. Early examples have cast pear-shaped handles, later of scroll or ring form. Extinguishers fit in slots on sockets or handles. Late examples often with snuffers carried in opening in stem. Found from late 17th cent. onwards in silver, brass, plate (q.v.) and Britannia metal (q.v.).

Chamberlain, Robert: (*fl.* late 18th and early 19th cent.) in 1783 Robert Chamberlain, a painter at the Worcester porcelain (q.v.) factory, severed his connection and opened a factory of his own in Worcester in rivalry to the old company. It was at first a decorating business, but porcelain of a dense, hard kind was made from 1792, and later in a much improved paste. Robert Chamberlain had for partners his son Humphrey Chamberlain and Robert Nash. In 1840 Chamberlain's factory and the old company were amalgamated. In 1850 W. H. Kerr joined the firm which traded as Kerr & Binns in 1852. In 1862 the firm became the Royal Worcester Porcelain Co. Marks: Various marks were used,

H. Chamberlain
& Sons
Worcester
(incised)

Printed in red

Elaborately painted wares in a naturalistic style with lavish gilding and striking ground colours, their quality bore close comparison with the wares of the original Worcester factory.

Chamfer: a bevelled edge, or edge which has been smoothed off or cut away from the square.

Champion, Richard: (1743–91), porcelain manufacturer, Bristol; joined forces with Cookworthy (q.v.), c. 1770 and received from him a licence to manufacture under his hard-paste patent when he retired in 1772. In 1774 Cookworthy assigned his patent rights to Champion for a consideration and in 1775 Champion petitioned Parliament for an extension of the patent rights for a further 14 years. In this he was successful (in spite of the opposition of Josiah Wedgwood (q.v.)) but the business crippled him financially. By 1778 Champion's Bristol manufactory was in financial difficulties. In 1781 Champion sold the patent for the manufacture of hard-paste porcelain (q.v.) to a company in North Staffordshire (which became known as New Hall (q.v.)) and moved to the Potteries to supervise its manufacture.

Champlevé enamel: see Enamel.

Chandelier: hanging branched candleholder, the earliest examples dating from the Middle Ages. Glass chandeliers were first made in Venice and Bohemia in the late 17th cent. With the introduction of gas lighting in the mid-19th cent. they were known as gasoliers. Kerosene chandeliers were first made in the United States in the 1860s.

Chanfron: the plate defence for a horse's head, introduced early in the 12th cent. and remaining in use until well into the 17th.

Chantilly lace: pillow lace (q.v.), silk with *fond chant* (q.v.) ground and some use of *fond clair* (q.v.). (See Blonde lace.)

Chantilly porcelain: a porcelain factory was founded at Chantilly in France about 1725, as a result of the financial support and interest of the Prince de Condé, an enthusiastic collector of Arita porcelain (q.v.). The factory was closed in 1800. Soft-paste porcelain (q.v.) was made, and until about 1751 tin oxide was used in the glaze, which rendered it smooth and opaque, as against the usual transparent porcelain glaze. Much early Chantilly is decorated in the Kakiemon style (q.v.) and subsequently first Meissen and then Sevres (qq.v.) were freely copied. Decoration consisting of small blue flowers, known as the 'Chantilly sprig', was popular and much copied in England. The mark used was a hunting horn in red or blue.

Chapter ring: the applied circle, found in earlier clocks, upon which are engraved the hour numerals. Derives its name from the fact that hours are struck on a bell. Originally a clock served to rouse the sexton, who then struck the hour of the chapter, or religious office, on a bell.

Charge mark: mark struck on unfinished pieces of silver and gold in France after 1672. (See also Discharge mark.)

Charger: a large circular dish designed as a serving dish or for display. Silver examples are usually enriched by finely engraved or embossed armorials.

Chasing: (1) the *cire-perdue* (q.v.) process of casting metal leaves roughness and poor finish as well as often resulting in the loss of detail. It is therefore necessary to chase the rough-cast with steel chisels and gravers. The absence of such evidence of individual treatment of bronzes, for example, may be taken at best as a sign of a poor workshop production, at worst as a sign of modern after-casting. (2) the term chasing is also used to describe the relief decoration on silver, raised by the surface hammering of the metal. (See also Flat chasing.)

Châtelaine: a clasp or brooch, usually of silver, from which various small objects are suspended by means of a chain. Fastened at the waist, the châtelaine was originally worn by the mistress of the house, and keys, seals, watches, nutmeg-graters, quizzing-glasses and countless other articles are to be found attached to the ends of their chains. In the late 18th cent. Wedgwood (q.v.) jasper cameos (q.v.) were mounted as ornaments to châtelaines. Steel châtelaines were fashionable from 1845 to 1855 and again from the 1870s onwards.

Chaton: the enamel ornament of a ring.

Chausse: close-fitting armour for the legs and feet.

Cheesequake Pottery: stoneware (q.v.) based on English design and made on the Cheesequake Creek, New Jersey, during and after the American Revolution.

Cheese-scoop: introduced in late 18th cent. for serving cheese. Consists of a short, curved blade with silver shaft and ivory or wood handle. Later examples have silver handles conforming to table service patterns.

Chelsea Keramic Art Works: art pottery in Massachusetts owned by the Robertson family. Founded in 1866 for the production of brown earthenware (q.v.), the plant was enlarged and the new name adopted in 1872. The factory closed in 1888, but a new company, the Chelsea Pottery, was formed in 1891, successfully producing Oriental crackled (q.v.) and high-fired glazes (q.v.).

Chelsea porcelain: the Chelsea Works was probably founded about 1745 or shortly before. Until 1750 it is believed that Charles Gouyn, silversmith, was proprietor and chief manager of the factory. The name of Nicholas Sprimont first appears in connection with Chelsea in 1749 when he managed the factory for Sir Everard Fawkener, and on his death in 1758 became its owner. The factory changed hands in 1769, and again in 1770 when it was bought by William Duesbury (q.v.) and John Heath of Derby (q.v.). From this time until its closure in 1784 its products followed Derby rather than established Chelsea styles, and so this is known as the Chelsea-Derby period.

In 1784 the Chelsea workshops and ovens were demolished and many moulds destroyed. Some were removed to Derby.

Marks:

Incised

Chelfea 1745
Incised

Incised
1745–9

In under-
glaze blue
1749

In applied
relief
1750–3

1755   1765   1755   1760

1760   1760   1760   1765

Four clearly defined periods of Chelsea manufacture are recognized: Triangle 1745–9; Raised Anchor 1750–3; Red Anchor 1753–8; and Gold Anchor 1758–70. The earliest Chelsea group bears the mark of an incised triangle.

Work of the 'raised' (i.e. embossed) and 'red anchor' periods enjoys the highest esteem, in spite of its imperfections. This was made from a very fine soft paste which had the characteristic of forming transparent glass spots or 'moons' under firing. These can be seen when the ware is held up to the light. It was eliminated in the 'gold anchor' period (and in occasional perfect 'red anchor' pieces), but the ware also lost its celebrated creamy texture.

During Fawkener's ownership (c. 1749–58), Meissen (q.v.) styles were most often copied, though the colouring and quality of the china give the ware an original beauty. Colour washes were employed to give simple

effects in keeping with paste and form. Gilding (q.v.) was little used.

When Sprimont became owner, several changes occurred. Sprimont's is the 'gold anchor' period, the 'red anchor' being rarely used. Bone ash was introduced into the paste; Sèvres became the dominant influence; decoration became richer employing elaborate floral backgrounds; heavy gilding was used. Some fine ground colours were introduced, 'mazarine' (an uneven dark blue) and 'claret', as well as more flamboyant modelling. The resulting quality, though notable, was perhaps inferior to 'red anchor' Chelsea.

Under Duesbury the Chelsea and Derby styles gradually blended, the vigour of Chelsea being lost under Derby influence. It becomes difficult to distinguish between wares made at the two factories.

A considerable number of interesting miniature pieces, scent bottles (q.v.), flowers, seals, snuff boxes (q.v.), known as Chelsea Toys, have survived.

Subjects:

Triangle Period: Silver shapes predominate, with applied ornament, fluting and raised foliage and floral sprays. Painted subjects included Japanese patterns derived from Meissen examples. The apparently haphazard application of tiny flower sprigs or insects concealed imperfections of paste or glaze.

Not many Triangle figures are known. A notable class of uncoloured figures takes its name from the well-known 'Girl in a Swing' and is attributed on evidence of paste and style to the earliest Chelsea period.

Raised Anchor Period: Oriental influence via Meissen is strong in this phase of Chelsea. Decorations were applied with regard to the beauty of the paste and glaze. Figures in this period are very uncommon; outstanding are Italian *Commedia dell'Arte* figures and the tender earthenware-derived 'Nurse'; portrait busts, and models of birds.

Red Anchor Period: The finest of the Chelsea porcelains. Meissen, Chinese, and Japanese influences are strong. A version of botanical flowers, some adapted from Philip Miller's *Figures of*

Plants, was an outstanding decoration. Fantastic animal and vegetable shapes were used for tureens and dishes, and gaily coloured. Crimson monochrome landscapes and Aesop's Fables again appear. Other subjects of this mature Chelsea phase are naked children at play, birds, moulded scroll borders, Watteau subjects, and bouquets of flowers.

Splendid figures were made, some derived from Meissen.

Gold Anchor Period: Meissen influences yield to Sèvres, and the vigorous playfulness of the earlier phrases gives way to a new elegance and sophistication. New colours were adopted including a rich sonorous blue. Elaborate gilding became fashionable, subjects for decoration included groups after Teniers, exotic or naturalistic birds, chinoiseries, flowers and fruits.

Figures with elaborate and fulsome bocages (q.v.) are typical, usually with Rococo scroll bases.

Chenets: (*Fr.*), see Andirons.

Ch'êng Hua period: (1465–87), the rarest Chinese porcelains of this classic reign employ coloured enamels over sparing underglaze blue outlines ('*tou ts'ai*' enamels); and this style was much imitated from the 17th cent. The blue-and-white 'palace bowls' were more slightly potted and decorated than previously. The reign-mark is much used on later wares.

Chequer ornament: an inlaid pattern of small squares in light and dark woods, resembling a chess board, used as a decorative border especially on 16th- and 17th-cent. furniture.

Chesterfield: large overstuffed sofa popular in the 19th cent. Many examples have button upholstery (q.v.).

Chesterfield stoneware: brown stonewares characterized by relief decorations of hunting scenes or drinking bouts: J. Aiken (*A Description of the Country round Manchester*, 1795) noted the existence of three potworks making coarse earthenware in Chesterfield in 1795. In 1848 there were several potteries, chiefly for coarse brown and yellow stoneware.

Chestnut servers: these urn-shaped containers might be oval or round, their bodies raised from copper in two halves and vertically joined. From about 1800 to 1820 they were spun from Britannia metal (q.v.), from about 1820 they were spun from a special copper alloy. The vessel was supported on a spreading foot, round or square, and a short, slender stem. It usually had lion mask and ring handles of cast lead gilded and with a domed cover surmounted by a gilt acorn or other simple finial.

Chestnut servers were handed with coffee and contained Spanish chestnuts, boiled and then roasted. They were served hot, and were lifted from the server with a fork; their husks were removed at table and they were eaten with salt.

Chest-on-chest: see Tallboy.

Cheval glass: a larger type of toilet mirror in a frame with four legs; also known as a horse dressing-glass; dating from the end of the 18th cent. The rectangular mirror either pivoted on screws set in the uprights or moved up and down by means of a weight within the frame ('the same as a sash-window' – Sheraton). Turned uprights and stretchers (q.v.) were often found on these pieces about 1800.

Cheval screen: fire screen, often with a central panel of needlework, on four legs. The height of the panel was in some cases adjustable, as in a cheval glass (q.v.).

Chevron motif: a zig-zag pattern formed by inlay (q.v.) or a moulding, or architectural derivation, but also used as a decoration on furniture.

Chia Ching period: (1521–66), Ming reign noted for painted blue-and-white (q.v.) porcelain of rich violet tone, and the development of brilliantly coloured enamel painting, chiefly in red, green, yellow and turquoise. Coloured glazes, too, were used, sometimes in combination (e.g. yellow and green), covering incised designs 'on the biscuit' (q.v.). Heavily-potted blue-and-white jars and dishes were much exported to the Near East. The reign-mark was used in K'ang Hsi times.

Chia Ch'ing period: (1795–1820), in this period the later Ch'ien Lung (q.v.) porcelain continued to be made, but with poorer glaze and less lively drawing in enamelled wares. Iron-red enamelling was popular, and heavily potted wares with thick blue or celadon-green glazes may be mentioned.

Chichi rugs: Caucasian rugs bearing small jewel-like designs in the centre panel.

Chicken skin: fashionable 18th-cent. fan mounts were made of fine vellum known to fan makers as chicken skin. Actually it was prepared from the skins of newly born lambs so as to be exceptionally thin and supple. No grain is visible unless held to the light when a slightly mottled appearance may be detected.

Ch'ien Lung porcelain: (1736–95), in the Chinese porcelain made during this period the antiquarian tastes of the Emperor were reflected in continued borrowings from the classical styles and from foreign techniques. The *famille rose* style (q.v.) went on, but often with crowded effects of design and less harmonious combinations of colour. Strong yellow or pink grounds (q.v.) or a celadon ground may surround panels of delicate painting; and the rich effects of *cloisonné* enamel (see Enamel) were sometimes sought. Some of the monochrome wares continue very fine in colour, notably

the flambé copper-reds, and the soft, low-temperature enamels were much used as glazes. Shapes such as those in Figs. A and B are certainly not lacking in decided character. But the later wares of the reign undoubtedly show a marked decline in taste, inclining to fussiness and prettiness; and former standards were not to be recovered. Poorer quality materials, slack shapes, uninspired drawing and insipid colour are faults present to a greater or lesser degree in the wares of Ch'ien Lung's successors.

Fig. A   Fig. B

Chien ware: made in Fukien Province, China, during the Sung dynasty consisting principally of small conical tea-bowls. A very granular grey-black stoneware, with thick treacly-brown or black glaze, often streaked with fine golden lines ('hare's fur'), or spotted and dappled, and arrested above the foot. These effects result from the varied response of iron to kiln conditions. Known to the Japanese as '*temmoku*' ware. Other brown and black wares from Kiangsi, Honan, or Tz'u Chou (qq.v.) have a lighter body.

Chiffonier: low cupboard with shelves for books or china, Regency examples sometimes having grille-doors. After 1850 an upper section often incorporated a mirror.

Chill: earthenware oil lamp shaped like a large candlestick with a lipped cup large enough to hold two cups of 'train' (pilchard oil), used in Cornwall before candles. Sometimes known as 'stonen chill'.

Chiming clock: a clock which sounds at the quarters a chime on four or more bells in addition to striking the hour.

Chimney crane: known in Scotland as a 'Swey', this was a bracket of wrought-iron from which a cauldron (q.v.) or tea kettle was suspended. Cranes were of many types; large and small, simple and complicated. In the case of the latter the pot could be raised or lowered and swung to any position over the fire.

Chimney glass: a wide mirror above the chimney piece, usually consisting of three plates, two smaller ones flanking a larger one, introduced in the early 18th cent.

China cabinet: piece of furniture incorporating a glass-fronted cupboard, sometimes mounted on a base containing drawers or a cupboard with wooden doors.

China clay: a white burning refractory clay produced by the decomposition of felspathic rock, called by the Chinese *kaolin*, and quarried in Cornwall. It is an essential ingredient of hard-paste porcelain (q.v.), and English bone china (q.v.). The *unaker*, specified in the patent of Heylin and Frye (see Bow porcelain) in 1744, was American china clay.

Chinaman: an importer of Oriental porcelain; a pottery dealer; ('went to see a garden belonging to one Mr Bauldy, a china-man' – *Diary of Sylas Neville*, 20 September 1771).

China-stand: an ornamental stand for displaying china or flowers, introduced at the end of the 17th cent. and at first taking the form of a low pedestal on carved and scrolled feet, or of a vase on a plinth. In the early 18th cent. the form was sometimes that of a stool with cabriole legs (q.v.), in mahogany. More fanciful designs, in the Rococo taste, were evident after 1750, as in the 'Stonds for China Jarrs' presented in Chippendale's *Director*. In the Adam (q.v.) period some attractive stands for flower bowls resembled the contemporary candle stands (q.v.) with three uprights. Little four-legged stands with shelves were also made at this time for flowerpots.

China-stone: a fusible felspathic rock, known to the Chinese as *petuntse*, used in the manufacture of porcelain, and generally known in England as china-stone, or, because quarried in Cornwall, Cornish stone. Discovered in Cornwall before 1758 by W. Cookworthy (q.v.).

Chinese export porcelain: porcelain made in China specially for export to Europe. Although Chinese porcelain had always been eagerly sought after in foreign countries, it was not until the latter part of the 17th cent. that wares were made specifically for exportation. By the 18th cent., trade with the East was flourishing and among the particular types of porcelain made for this trade are plates with wide flat rims, teacups with saucers and sets of vases for the mantelpiece, known as *garniture de cheminée*. Sometimes these export pieces bear decorations derived from European sources, such as representations of contemporary European figures in landscapes or scenes from classical mythology. Sometimes dinner services, bearing the coat-of-arms of the European purchaser, were made specially to order, while others bear *famille rose* (q.v.) decoration. The so-called Jesuit porcelain also belongs to the export class. (See also Jesuit china and Armorial china.)

Chinese Imari: imitations of the Japanese export porcelain, with strong decoration in greyish underglaze blue and enamel colours, especially iron-red, and prominent gilding; made in the first half of the 18th cent.

Chinese Lowestoft: an incorrect name sometimes given to Chinese export porcelain (q.v.). (See also Lowestoft porcelain.)

Chinese-Turkestan rugs: in these rugs the influence of Chinese art is clearly defined in the use of such motifs as the plate medallion, cloudbands and lotus, pomegranate and peony, but in a subtle manner the rugs show Persian influence.

The stitching generally is not fine and the pile is short. The merit of these rugs is in the extremely varied and un-usual colouring, yellows, lacquer red, and blues, appearing in infinite variety.

The main types are from Khotan and Lashgar, and are often called Samarkand.

Ch'ing dynasty: dynasty of the Chinese Ch'ing Emperors covering the period 1644 to 1912.

Ching-tê-chên: great centre of the porcelain industry, in Kiangsi Prov-ince, China. Wares of all kinds have been made here in quantity since the 14th cent.

Chinkinbori: (*Japanese* = sunk gold engraving), an Oriental lacquer-work technique in which an incised design is made in the surface of the lacquer and gold is rubbed in.

Chinoiserie: a free rendering in western terms of what was thought to represent the Chinese style. Through-out the 17th cent., Chinese lacquered screens and furniture, as well as textiles and porcelain had excited European admiration. Towards the middle of the 18th cent. fashionable taste so concentrated on the Far East that a contemporary comment stated 'according to the present prevailing whim everything is Chinese or in the Chinese taste . . . chairs, tables, chimney-pieces, frames for looking-glasses, and even our most vulgar utensils are all reduced to this new-fangled standard.' This vogue resulted in such Chinese motifs as pagodas,

latticework and frets and figures of Chinamen appearing as decorative forms on furniture, overmantels and plasterwork, while textiles, porcelain, silver, etc. all bore witness to the enthusiasm. Based largely on romantic fancies, the style was an aspect of

Rococo (q.v.) taste and had declined in general favour by *c*. 1770.

Chinoiserie wallpapers: known in the 18th cent. as 'Mock India', these papers were imitations and variants of the beautiful painted Chinese wall-papers so popular during the 18th cent. A notable English example from Wotton-under-Edge (*c*. 1740) is to be seen in London's Victoria & Albert Museum. France and other European countries also made chinoiserie papers.

Chip-carving: lightly cut ('chipped') surface ornament, mostly of formal geometric character and including whorls and roundels (q.v.), chip-carving appears on woodwork of the Middle Ages. With other forms of carving, it continued as a decoration on oak furniture until a much later date, and enjoyed a renewed popu-larity at the end of the 19th cent. as decoration on small wooden articles.

Chippendale, Thomas: (1718–79), cabinet-maker and designer. Born at Otley, Yorkshire, it is known that he was in London by 1748, and shortly afterwards was established in St Martin's Lane where, at the sign of 'The Chair', he remained until his death. Twice he worked with partners, firstly with James Rannie and later with Thomas Haig (q.v.). He has attained a world-wide fame from his volume of designs, *The Gentleman and Cabinet Maker's Director*, which was first issued in 1754. The book was reprinted in 1755, and an enlarged edition appeared in parts between 1759 and 1762. (See Matthias Lock.)

Some of the furniture from Chippen-dale's workshop has been identified from bills that have been preserved.

The business in St Martin's Lane was continued on the death of Thomas Chippendale by his eldest son (also named Thomas) in partnership with Haig.

Chippendale, Thomas, the Young-er: (1749–1822), son of Thomas Chippendale (q.v.). He continued his father's business as a cabinet-maker in St Martin's Lane from 1779 until 1796, during which time he was in partner-ship with Thomas Haig (q.v.).

Chiselled and cut steel: the art of steel chiselling is a by-product of the locksmith's and gunsmith's trade. Small articles have been chiselled from iron or steel since the Middle Ages, but from the collector's point of view, four main groups can be recognized. Firstly, the articles made in the northern Italian city of Brescia in the 17th and 18th cent. These include snuff boxes, scissors, tweezers and thimbles usually chiselled and pierced with floral scrollwork interspersed with monsters, similar in design to the ornament familiar on Brescian-made firearms (Fig. A). The most distinguished Brescian artist, who usually signed his works, was Matteo Acqua Fresca (q.v.) (Fig. B). The second

Fig. A

Fig. B

group was produced in Paris by the same chisellers who decorated sword and gun furniture of the period of Louis XIV and Louis XV. Characteristic of their work are the châtelaines, étuis (qq.v.), shuttles and, more rarely, snuff boxes (q.v.), usually chiselled with classical figure subjects against a gilt stippled ground. Similar but somewhat coarser work was also produced in Germany. The third group was produced by the artists of the Imperial Russian small arms factory at Tula. The factory was founded by Peter the Great, and their work dates from the 18th cent. The artisans mastered not only the art of chiselling iron but also of encrusting it with various softer metals and of faceting it (cut steel). Besides smaller objects, such as candlesticks and caskets, the Tula factory

also turned out large pieces of furniture and even mantelpieces entirely constructed of cut and faceted steel. The last group is English and flourished at first about the middle of the 18th cent. in Woodstock in Oxfordshire and subsequently at Birmingham in the Soho works set up by Matthew Boulton (q.v.). The Woodstock cottage industry produced both chiselled and faceted steel but the Birmingham factory, which eventually put Woodstock out of business, concentrated on cut steel. They made sword hilts, buttons, châtelaines, buckles and cheap jewellery. Cut steel was used as a more durable alternative to marcasite (q.v.) in the late 18th and early 19th cent.

Chocolate muddler: American term for a long-handled spoon used for stirring chocolate.

Chocolate pot: the silver chocolate pot is of the same basic form as the coffee pot (q.v.), from which it can be distinguished by the detachable or sliding cover finial (q.v.) concealing the hole for insertion of the swizzle-stick to stir the chocolate. Many pieces must have been used indiscriminately for both liquids.

Chokusai, Miyagi: (b. 1877), prominent Japanese *netsuke* (q.v.) artist.

Chop dish: small, flat, two-handled, oblong silver or plate dish made from about 1750 to 1800.

Chopin: a Scottish measure (q.v.) containing one and a half Imperial pints.

Christening cup: cups, mugs and goblets, mainly of small proportions, were fashionable christening presents in the 19th cent. They were often engraved with the child's name and a date. In the United States similar small drinking vessels may be called orange juice cups. Spoons, often single or a set of apostle spoons (q.v.), were also regarded as suitable christening presents.

Chromolithograph: lithograph (q.v.) printed in several colours.

Chūban: medium-sized Japanese print, approx. 279 × 203 mm (11 × 8 in): a *chūban tate-ye* is a medium-sized vertical print and a *chūban yoko-ye* is an oblong print of the same size.

Chün ware: Sung (q.v.) stoneware, more or less porcellaneous, usually burnt buff at the foot, with thick, opalescent glaze ranging from pale lavender to deep blue, sometimes with crimson splashes; from Chün Chou (Honan Province). Frequent shapes are spreading bowls, two-handled jars, and flat dishes. There is also a green variety. Large flower pots and bulb bowls often have streaked 'flambé' glazes. 'Soft Chün' wares (Ma Chün) have a sandy buff body and soft crackled glaze. The similar stonewares of Canton and Yi-hsing are seldom earlier than the 17th cent.

Church fans: issued with the sanction of the Bishop of London from about 1730. They were decorated with Biblical subjects pointing a moral rather than illustrating a story. The soft colours of the painted mount were repeated on guards and blades (q.v.). Similar fans for chapel goers date from 1796.

Church plate: any metalwork vessel for liturgical use, such as a ciborium (q.v.) or censer (q.v.).

Ciborium: standing bowl and cover used to contain the Host, or in the Protestant church, for Communion bread. Some of the most important examples of Medieval goldsmiths' work take this form.

Cinquedea: a short sword, or large dagger, with a flat triangular blade some five fingers in width near the hilt (hence the name from the Italian *cinque dei*), and often elaborately etched and gilded. It was essentially a civilian weapon and was used chiefly in Italy in the late 15th and early 16th cent.

Cire-perdue: the 'lost-wax' method of casting, used for all bronze casting of any complication from ancient to modern times. Its processes are, briefly, this: the work is modelled on a clay core in wax of a thickness intended in the final bronze product. The finished wax model, to which vents and pouring channels are added, is then surrounded by an envelope of plaster and grog to form the mould. The whole is then baked in a kiln to harden the core and the mould and liquefy the wax, which runs out. Into the space vacated by the wax is poured the molten bronze. When this has cooled, the mould is broken off the bronze and the core removed by breaking it up. It is, of course, obvious that only one bronze can be cast from each wax model by this method. For each of the workshop productions of the Renaissance there must therefore have been a wax model first, and this explains the infinite slight variations in each example made after the master model produced by the head of the workshop. Moulds which may be taken apart in small sections are called piece-moulds, and have perhaps been known since the 16th cent. They were probably never used for bronze sculpture until the 19th cent., and the presence of small ridges, that are the result of the tiny gaps between each section of the mould, may be taken as the surest evidence of modern manufacture.

Ciselé: (*Fr.*), chiselled.

Cistern barometer: a barometer in which the lower open end of the vertical tube is placed below the level of the mercury in open reservoir. The earliest type.

Claire-de-lune glazes: porcelain glazes of shades of lavender blue obtained by adding small quantities of cobalt to clear glazes. Used on Chinese porcelain and with particular success under Yung Chêng and Ch'ien Lung (qq.v.). At this period also lavender-blue glazes were used in conjunction with crackling in imitation of Sung Kuan and Ko wares (qq.v.).

Claret ground: a ground colour used in porcelain decoration, introduced in England by Sprimont at the Chelsea porcelain factory (q.v.) in 1760; a fine crimson. It was imitated at Derby and Worcester (qq.v.), although the claret ground of Derby tended to a brownish hue and was less attractive in appearance. The fine claret colour of Worcester was produced perhaps, as suggested by W. B. Honey, with the help of migrant Chelsea craftsmen. Plymouth (q.v.) produced an unsuccessful claret-crimson.

Most of the 19th-cent. Staffordshire bone china (q.v.) houses of repute produced a more-or-less successful crimson ground colour, notably Copelands, and Mintons (qq.v.).

Claw foot: foot resembling an animal's claw, of Oriental derivation.

Claw setting: a means of setting a precious stone whereby the stone is secured by claws. Claw settings are either round or square, whereas coronet settings, in which the stone is similarly held in position, are round in form.

Claymore: from the Gaelic *claidheanh-mòr* (great sword). The Scottish two-hand sword introduced in the 16th cent. Of very large proportions, it usually had straight quillons (q.v.) inclining at a sharp angle towards the broad, straight blade. In the 17th cent. the quillons became curved and were supplemented by two (sometimes only one) large solid shells bent towards the hilt. Since the 19th cent. the term has been applied erroneously to the basket-hilted Scottish broadsword.

Clepsydra: a timekeeper motivated by water running either into or out from it. Water clocks are among the earliest forms of timekeeper known, preceding the discovery of the verge escapement (q.v.) and the weight as a motive power.

Clichy paperweights: Clichy, a suburb of Paris, was the home of a factory that made glass paperweights of most types. They were not dated but it is known that paperweights were made there from about 1849. They are found signed with an initial 'C', Clichy in full, CL and ICHY in separate canes (q.v.) or CHY. The presence of a rose in the pattern is an indication that a paperweight was made in Clichy, and the colours are often noticeably vivid.

Clobbering: badly applied fake overglaze enamel colours on porcelain, only partly obliterating the original underglaze or painting.

Clock frets: pierced metallic decorative pieces originally used to hide the balance in lantern clocks. Later, either in wood or metal, inserted into clock cases to facilitate the elimination of sound.

Clock plates, back, front, top and bottom: plates between which are pivoted the trains (q.v.) of a clock or watch. Early back plates in clocks were quite plain, except for the signature; later they began to be decorated, and the decoration became more and more ornate, reaching a peak in the first quarter of the 18th cent. From this point it declined until the last decade of this cent. saw the return of the plain back plate. These back plates are a useful guide to the date of a clock.

Cloisonné enamel: see Enamel.

Close helmet: a close-fitting, visored helmet completely enclosing the head. The term is now usually confined to the type of headpiece introduced early in the 16th cent. with the visor (q.v.) and chin-piece pivoting at the sides, as opposed to the armet (q.v.), which has hinged cheek-pieces fastening at the chin.

Close nailing: convex-headed nails of a darkish tint of brass hammered with great exactitude by the cofferer, head beside head, were used all around the edges of the leather-covered chest and in sufficient numbers over the body of the piece to avoid any loose flapping of the inelastic cover. Similar treatment was given to hair cloth. Brass nails, arranged in one or more lines, or to form a pattern, were used to secure the upholstery on chair seats and backs from a very early date.

Close stool: simple, box stool with a hinged lid, sometimes with a fabric covering, for sanitary use. It was fitted internally with a metal or ceramic chamberpot or basin. The earliest surviving examples date from the 16th cent. Also known as a necessary stool or night commode.

Clous d'or: see Piqué.

Club foot: the simplest terminal to a cabriole leg (q.v.) used on chairs, settees and tables from about 1705 and particularly in the 18th cent., resembling in shape the pad of an animal's foot.

Cluster-column leg: a chair leg in the form of pillars clustered together. In the mid-18th cent., and again in the 19th cent., a revival of the Gothic taste led to the use among furniture makers of Medieval forms such as tracery, clustered columns etc.

Clutha glass: deliberately bubbled and streaked glass, first made by James Couper & Son, Glasgow.

'Coaching glass': a 19th-cent. drinking cup without a foot which requires to be emptied at one draught.

Coade's stone: moulded architectural stoneware to imitate carved stone made by Batty Langley (q.v.) at Lambeth before 1738. About 1760 the Misses Coade set up a business under the name 'Coade's Lithodipyra, Terra Cotta, or Artificial Stone Manufactory'. A cousin of the Coades named Sealey joined the business in 1769, and the mark used was COADE & SEALEY, LAMBETH, impressed.

Statuary, busts, church monuments and furnishings, and ornamental architectural details were made. Well known artists and sculptors were employed.

The relief upon the pediment over the west portico of Greenwich Hospital, the rood screen of St George's Chapel, Windsor, and the statue of Britannia on the Nelson monument at Yarmouth were said to be the work of this firm.

When Sealey died the business passed through several hands, but continued until about 1840.

Coalbrookdale: see Coalport porcelain.

Coalbrookdale Co.: ironworks, founded in Shropshire in 1709. In the 19th cent. it was the largest and most important English manufacturer of ornamental cast and wrought ironwork, including furniture, railings, door furniture (q.v.), etc.

Coalport or **Coalbrookdale porcelain:** John Rose left the Caughley (q.v.) factory after a difference with Thomas Turner and started on his own first at Jackfield and then at

Coalport on the opposite bank of the river, c. 1796. He took over an opposition works started by his brother and then, in an attempt to recover lost business, purchased Turner's Caughley factory, after which biscuit (q.v.) china was made at Caughley and sent to Coalport for glazing and decoration. In 1814 the entire manufactory was removed to Coalport. John Rose bought the Cambrian Pottery at Swansea (q.v.) in 1820.

There have been a number of different proprietors of Coalport since 1862. Coalport china is now made at the Crescent Works, Stoke-on-Trent, by Coalport China Ltd.

Marks:

Early Coalport is indistinguishable from Caughley. From 1820 onwards the employment of Billingsley (q.v.) may have led to the use of the Nant-garw and Swansea formula and the product is extremely translucent. Bright flower painting, particularly roses, with modelled and applied decoration, is characteristic of the Coalport style up to 1850. At the same time models of Sèvres, Dresden and Chelsea (qq.v.) were not only imitated but skilfully faked at the Coalport factory. Less elaborate tea and tableware made from about mid-cent. onwards is lightly decorated and makes use of green and rose coloured grounds.

Coal vases: replaced coal scuttles in wealthy homes from 1840. They were intended to remain decorating the fireside and be filled from buckets, unlike scuttles which were carried into the cellar. The coal for the first time was concealed beneath an ornamental cover. Fearncombe of Wolverhampton displayed at the Great Exhibition a coal vase in the shape of a nautilus shell resting on coral, the cover handle representing a seahorse. Others were in the shape of miniature Gothic fonts and great tureens which the Jury's Report stated were 'ornamented in the Italian style and worthy of being imitated in silver'.

Coaster: a receptacle which came into use before 1750 for moving wine, beer and food on the dining-table; also variously known as a slider, decanter stand and beerwagon. For ease of movement, the coaster was normally fitted either with small wheels or with a baize-covered base, and the materials used in good examples included mahogany, lacquer, *papier maché* and silver. Examples in silver have pierced or solid sides and usually a turned wooden base. They occur in pairs, or sets of four or more. Beer wagons were sometimes made with special places for the jug and drinking vessels.

Cobb, John: in partnership with W. Vile (q.v.) cabinet-maker (q.v.) and upholster to George III. He continued to work until 1778.

Cobirons: these are similar to andirons (q.v.) but are usually quite plain in design and have rows of hooks on the standards on which spits could be placed. Some examples of cobirons have basket-like tops, and it has been suggested that they are 'cressets' for holding a light. They may have been intended for a cup used in basting meat.

Cochins: the small cartouches or vignettes (q.v.), named after their inventor, depicting contemporary events. Cochins were used decoratively on boxes and other *objets-de-vertu.*

Cock beading: a small moulding of half-round section applied to the edges of drawer fronts from *c.* 1730 to 1800

Cockpit Hill pottery: some slipwares were made at Cockpit Hill although the date of origin of this Derby pot-works is unknown. Some white cream jugs marked DERBY and dated 1750 were, however, probably made there. From the early 1750s until 1779 the proprietors were W. Butts, Thomas Rivett, John and Christopher Heath. It is likely that the factory closure was due to the Heaths' bankruptcy and that the stock was acquired by William Duesbury (q.v.) (see also Bow, Chelsea, Derby). The ware was of a Stafford-shire type and usually unmarked.

Cock's head hinge: twin-plate hinge of curvilinear shape, the finials (q.v.) formed as a cock's head. Frequently found on woodwork of the late 16th and first half of the 17th cent., held in position by handwrought iron nails, never by screws. (See also 'H' hinge.)

Coconut cup: standing cup with bowl and sometimes cover formed from the

nut with silver straps, lip and foot in the prevailing style of the period. Found from the Medieval period down to the 19th cent. In the 18th cent. a low form on small silver feet, also occurs.

Codnor Park stoneware: a potworks was established here in 1821 by William Burton for the manufacture of stoneware bottles from local clay, but closed in 1832 when Burton got into financial difficulties. Joseph Bourne (q.v.) of Denby re-opened the factory, which employed about 60 hands, in 1833, and continued to work it until 1861 when the workmen and plant were transferred to Denby.

Coffee, William: porcelain modeller, started in his trade at Coade's factory (q.v.) in Lambeth, but later found employment at the Derby porcelain (q.v.) factory, where he was working in 1794. In 1795 he is said to have gone to another and rather mysterious porcelain factory at Church Gresley, but returned to Derby. Subsequently he entered into partnership with a relative of Duesbury (q.v.) in a small china factory in Derby and, when the partnership was dissolved, commenced to make terra cotta (q.v.). Finally he emigrated to America. His own pro-ductions in terra cotta are said to have been stamped:

W. COFFEE DERBY

Coffee pot: although coffee was intro-duced into England as a beverage in the mid-17th cent., coffee pots were not made in quantity until after 1700. The most common form is cylindrical, broadening towards the base, with a domed, hinged lid. Late 18th-cent. examples may be baluster, pear, or urn shaped. They were made in silver, Sheffield plate (q.v.) and electroplate (q.v.) The handles are sometimes of wood.

Coffee spoon: introduced in the mid-19th cent., it was a reduced version of a teaspoon.

Coffer: term freely confused with chest. In strict definition a coffer was a chest or box covered in leather or some other material and banded with metalwork, but it seems likely that the term was not always precisely used. It may not be wrong to class as coffers various stoutly built or heavily ironed strong-chests and -boxes, even though they do not fulfil all the above requirements. Trussing coffers were furnished with lifting rings and shackles or other devices for transportation; but chests and coffers not intended for transport might be chained to the wall for security.

Coif: a close-fitting cap formed of one piece of embroidery seamed along the top of the head. These are often found unpicked or not made up, and are therefore difficult to recognize. The Elizabethan coifs were embroidered in coloured silks and metal thread, or in black silk, in patterns of coiling stems or less frequently with diaper patterns.

Coin glasses: wine glasses in which a coin is enclosed in the knopped stem. Examples exist from the late 17th and the 18th cent.

Cole, Sir Henry: (1808–82), English designer and founder in 1847 of Summerly's Art Manufactures (q.v.). He was one of the organizers of the Great Exhibition of 1851 and of the South Kensington (later Victoria and Albert) Museum.

Colfichet: the name given to small embroidered pictures, originating in Italy in the late 18th cent., worked in floss silks on paper so that each side was alike. They were used either as book-markers or placed between two sheets of glass.

Colichemarde: a modern term for a type of small sword blade which is wide near the hilt and narrows abruptly half way down. (See also Smallsword.)

Collar knop: see Merese knop.

Collar lace: early 17th-cent. term for imported Venetian point laces, simple and largely geometrical in vandyke outlines. A few designs are considered identifiable as English. (See also Venetian flat point, grounded point, raised point and rose point laces.)

Collas method: Mechanical means of making reproductions of sculpture and other objects in the round devised by the French inventor Achille Collas (1795–1859). After much experimentation he succeeded in 1836 in making a copy of the *Venus de Milo* in the Louvre two-fifths the size of the original. The machine he invented consists of a wooden structure with a soft-tipped arm, which is guided over the surface of the original. The movement of this member corresponds with that of the copying arm, which can be set to increase or diminish the movement and consequently the size of the copy, at the tip of which is a sharp point that cuts into a block of damp plaster. The plaster copy might be left in its natural state and sold at a reasonable price or a bronze cast made from it. The Parisian founders such as Barbedienne (q.v.) and Susse Frères (q.v.), who employed the Collas method, exported a number of bronze casts to Britain in the mid-19th cent.

Collcut, Thomas Edward: (1840–1924), English architect and furniture designer. A number of the pieces he designed were of ebonized wood (q.v.) with painted decoration, based on the Early English style. He executed a number of designs for Collinson & Lock (q.v.), and his art furniture was much imitated in the United States.

Collet setting: a method of setting precious stones in which the stone is enclosed in a band or ring of metal, foiled at the back to increase the intensity of the colour. Collet settings were usual until about the close of the 18th cent.

Collinson & Lock: a London firm of cabinet-makers from 1870–85, specializing in art furniture. Designers who worked for it included T. E. Collcutt (q.v.), E. W. Godwin (q.v.) and B. J. Talbert (q.v.).

Cologne ware: see Fulham stoneware.

Colonial style: American style in the decorative arts relating to the period from the early 17th cent. to 1789, when Federal government was established.

Coloured glass: glass tinted by the addition of natural or prepared metallic oxides. Turquoise-greens and -blues obtained from copper, greens from iron, blues from cobalt, browns and yellows from iron and antimony, purples from manganese were the principal colours used from the very early days of glass-making. Ruby glass was first invented by the German chemist Johann Kunckel in the late 17th cent. by the addition of gold chloride, although pink glass had been produced in the Middle Ages. The 19th cent. increased the range by making black glass with iron and manganese, among others, while new colours from titanium, selenium, nickel, etc., have been produced in modern times.

Coloured lithograph: lithograph (q.v.) printed in one or two neutral colours with other colours applied by hand.

Colour print: a woodcut (q.v.), lithograph (q.v.), etching (q.v.) or any other form of graphic art printed in colour, rather than hand coloured; the latter should be termed a coloured print. Basically the method is to prepare a number of blocks, plates or stones, ink them with different colours and print them one after the other on a single sheet of paper. An alternative method is to use a single plate or block, applying the ink by hand to the appropriate areas before printing. In the 19th cent., European artists were inspired by the Japanese *uki-ye* (q.v.) woodcuts. (See also Baxter prints.)

Colour-twist stem: a type of stem found on glass drinking vessels between 1755 and 1775, containing spirals of glass, opaque or transparent, either singly or in combinations. The colours favoured were blue, green or ruby, less frequently red, yellow, sapphire, black, and greyish blue.

Colt, Samuel: (1814–62), American firearms manufacturer. His first successful revolver (q.v.), the Walker Colt, was produced in 1847. He pioneered mass-production methods and the manufacture and use of interchangeable parts.

Columbian Art Pottery Co.: established at Trenton, New Jersey, in 1893, the year of the World's Columbian Exposition in Chicago, Illinois. The company produced domestic china, Belleek (q.v.) art wares and small porcelain trinkets.

Columbine cups: candidates for admission as Masters to the Nuremberg Goldsmiths' Guild were required to produce a standing-cup to a fixed design, based on the form of the columbine flower. The practice was introduced in the second half of the 16th cent. and probably continued until early in the 17th cent.

Comb: a ridge on the top of a helmet, a characteristic of the burgonet (q.v.) and the morion (q.v.).

Comb-back: chair back found especially on American Windsor chairs (q.v.) of the mid-18th cent. The spindles and curved top rail form a shape resembling a comb.

Comfit box: see Bonbonnières.

Cominazzo, Lazarino: (b. 1563), Italian barrelsmith, working in the small village of Gardone near Brescia about the middle of the 17th cent. His barrels were so strong, in spite of their thin walls, and so highly esteemed that they were exported for mounting all over Europe. The name was widely forged, both at the time and after his death.

Commode: French term for a low chest of drawers made in a wide variety of forms. The word was later adopted in Britain.

Communion cup: the Protestant equivalent of the chalice (q.v.). Introduced under Edward VI and continued as a basic form until the end of the 18th cent. Silver examples have a deep, beaker-shaped bowl, spool-shaped stem, with compressed central knop (q.v.) and circular foot. The accompanying paten (q.v.) usually fits the lip to form a cover.

Communion table: in churches the Post-Reformation Communion table replaced the Medieval altar. It was essentially similar to the domestic table of the time, supported on a developed framework with a leg at each corner and possibly others along the sides, and was usually of oak.

'Compagnie des Indes' china: Chinese porcelain imported into Europe by European trading companies such as the French *Compagnie des Indes* or the English East India Company.

Compagnie dessin: (*Fr.* = Company pattern), the French name for porcelain made to European order in the Far East and imported by the *Compagnie des Indes*, the French East India Company.

Compensation clock pendulum: a pendulum which provides for the compensation of the effects of heat and cold.

Comport: footed, high dish, a component part of a Victorian dessert service.

Compound-twist stem: a type of stem found on glass drinking vessels between 1760 and 1800, containing a

pair of air or enamel spiral formations, one within the other: a central spiral or (in enamel) a closely knotted central cable with another formation spiralling around it. This type has straight stems only.

Concave frieze or **cavetto:** a hollow moulding or frieze appearing as a feature of the cornice on late 17th-cent. case furniture.

Concertina construction: a modern term used to describe the way in which the framework of some 18th-cent. card tables and side tables are constructed, allowing the hinged top to be opened and to rest at the corners on the two extended legs, drawn into place on a jointed framework.

Confidante (**sociable** or **tête-à-tête**): an upholstered settee, common in the 19th cent. in Britain and the United States. Some were in the form of an 'S', others incorporated seats set at right angles to each other.

Conical bowl: see Straight-funnel bowl.

Conical clock pendulum: a pendulum that rotates in a circle, the point of suspension being the apex of the cone. Robert Hooke experimented with conical pendulums in 1666. Huygens also made experiments, but it is seldom found in practice.

Connecticut chest: a variety of chest made in the 17th and 18th cent. in Connecticut. Decorative chest, sometimes including one or two drawers, and ornamented with applied bosses and split spindles. The three front panels are carved in low relief with conventionalized flowers – the centre panel containing sunflowers and the side panels, tulips.

Console table: a type of side table permanently standing against a wall and often supported by bracket-shaped legs. About 1725, console tables, gessoed and gilt, were elaborately ornamented with masks, scrolls and foliage and frequently had marble tops.

Constitution mirror: a term widely used in America for a wall mirror with strings of leaves or flowers at the sides, a scrolled-arch top, and a fanciful finial (q.v.), generally an eagle. The frame is usually in walnut or mahogany and partly gilded.

Contour-framing: a means of decorating pottery in isolating an ornamental feature by means of a white or uncoloured border, being more or less parallel, and following its outline: a feature of Near Eastern Islamic pottery decoration from which it was derived via Italy and Holland. Recorded on an English late 16th-cent. tin-glazed earthenware vase.

Contre-partie: see Boulle marquetry.

Convertible furniture: piece of furniture serving more than one purpose, such as a chair table (q.v.), but in particular American patent furniture (q.v.) developed in the latter part of the 19th cent.

Convex frieze: a frieze or moulding of cushion-shaped section; a characteristic feature of the straight cornices of late 17th-cent. chests-on-stands and tallboys (q.v.).

Convex mirror: a circular mirror with a convex glass, first made in France in the 18th cent., but popular in Britain and the United States after 1800.

Cookworthy, William: (1705–80). born at Kingsbridge in South Devon, of humble parentage.

Cookworthy was a Quaker. After his wife's death in 1745, Cookworthy developed his researches into the secrets of porcelain-making. He journeyed to Cornwall many times, discovered the Cornish equivalents of kaolin and petuntse (see China clay and China-stone); and found a partner for his Plymouth hard-paste porcelain (q.v.) venture in Lord Camelford, whom he visited with the object of securing the mineral rights of his land. The first fired experiments in hard-paste were made in 1765, and in 1768 he was sufficiently confident to take out a patent and form a company for its manufacture. The venture was transferred to Bristol in 1770, and in 1774 the patent was bought by Champion.

Copeland: see Spode.

Copenhagen porcelain: soft-paste porcelain (q.v.) was made at Copenhagen at a factory started by Louis

Fournier, a previous modeller at Vincennes and Chantilly (q.v.), between 1759 and 1765, of which examples are rare. The more famous Royal factory, founded in 1774, produced a hard-paste porcelain as a result of the assistance of a previous Fürstenberg (q.v.) modeller and arcanist (q.v.), A. C. Lupau. The most famous production of the factory is the Flora Danica service, upon which work was started in 1789. The service was intended for the Empress Catherine II of Russia and numbered 1602 pieces, each decorated with a botanical painting of Danish flora. From 1775 onwards Copenhagen porcelain was marked with three horizontal wavy lines. The factory is still in existence.

Copland, H.: see Lock, Matthias.

Copper blank: paper-thin metal serving as a base or core to every enamel. Only when copper could be refined adequately and also adequate rolling machinery was available did this metal become a practicable, cheaper alternative to gold as a base for enamels. The metal was cut and shaped and, when necessary, jointed before being covered on all sides with enamel and set into metal mounts. Warping was minimized and the general effect improved on plaques and box-lids, etc., by making the blanks slightly convex, but in some scent bottles, bonbonnières (q.v.), etc., there was very considerable shaping, the blanks being cut with steel punches.

Copperplate engraving: see Line engraving.

Copperplate printing: a method of printing textiles whereby the colour is applied to the cloth by means of an engraved flat copperplate the full width of the fabric. Used in England c. 1760; introduced a monochrome, pictorial style of printing.

Copper-red porcelain glazes: when successful, the fugitive high-temperature copper-red is one of the most splendid glazes in Chinese porcelain. Fourteenth-cent. painted wares were often imperfect in colour, but both painted and colour-glazed wares succeeded brilliantly in the 15th cent. In later Ming times (q.v.) the iron-red enamel is more common. A triumphant revival was however achieved by the K'ang Hsi potters (q.v.). Justly famous are the brilliant *sang-de-boeuf*, or 'oxblood' monochromes (Chinese = lang yao); other shades are the ruby-red and cherry-red, and those of a paler or browner colour, e.g. the 'liver-red' and pale 'ashes of roses'. The apple-red and rare brownish pink 'peach-bloom' often show brown or green mottlings. Yung Chêng and Ch'ien Lung (qq.v.) pieces in general show more regular, even glazing and a neatly finished foot. Flambé (q.v.) effects or red streaked with purple or blue, become more common and are imitated in the flambé Canton stonewares. Nineteenth-cent. pieces are distinguishable by poorer shape and finish, especially of the foot. Painting in underglaze red, again popular from the K'ang Hsi period (q.v.), include more or less exact copies of the early Ming, especially in combination with underglaze blue.

Coquillage: from the French *coquille*, a shell-fish. An ornament in the form of a shell much favoured as an element of Rococo (q.v.) decoration on overmantels, furniture, silver, etc., in the mid-18th cent.

Corbould, G.: an outstanding designer and engraver of trade cards, operating in Lombard Street, London, during the 1750s and 1760s. Later work was signed 'Corbould & Jeffreys Foster Lane sculp'.

Corded quilting: see Quilts.

Cordial glass: during the 17th cent. cordials were taken from miniature wine-glasses measuring 10 to 15 cm (4 to 6 in) in height. A distinct type of glass, its bowl shorter, squarer, and of smaller rim diameter than a wine-glass bowl, it became fashionable from about 1720; (a) 1720–40: straight stem of normal length and diameter; (b) from 1735: the stem was lengthened, of extra thick diameter, and might be centrally knopped; (c) from 1740: the bowl was less capacious; (d) 1740–70: the flute cordial, often termed a ratafia glass.

Cordonnet: French term used in lace-making, usually preferred to the English gimp or trolly thread, to describe the more substantial outline often given to the solid pattern motif on a piece of lace. It might be composed of several threads whipped or buttonholed together, as in Venetian raised point lace (q.v.); or be one thread whipped or buttonholed, as in Alençon (q.v.); or be a different coarser thread, as in Mechlin lace (q.v.).

Cords: slight striae discernible to the fingers on the surface of glass.

Cork Glasshouse, later **Cork Glasshouse Company:** established in Hanover Street, Dublin, in 1793, as makers of plain and cut flint-glass and black bottles. The firm specialized in lightweight blown-moulded (q.v.) hollow-ware. Although heavily subsidized by the Dublin Society, receiving some £1600 in 1787 and £2304 in 1793, throughout its existence the Cork Glasshouse appears to have laboured under financial instability and ever-changing proprietorship. A newly patented Donaldson furnace was installed. This gave to flint-glass a clarity and brilliance never before achieved, and some outstanding handcut work was produced. The number of hand-cutters employed was such that they founded the Cork Glasscutter's Union.

In 1812 the firm, under the proprietorship of William Smith & Company, became the Cork Glasshouse Company. Pieces marked 'Cork Glass

Co.' date no earlier than this. In 1817 steam-power was installed in a final effort to survive against competition from the newly established Waterloo Glasshouse. A year later, however, the Glasshouse was closed.

Corkscrew thumbpiece: an American term for a thumbpiece (q.v.) of twisted shape derived from the Dutch form, used especially on New York tankards.

Cork Terrace Glasshouse: an Irish glasshouse established in 1819 by Edward and Richard Ronayne. The productive capacity was equal to that of Waterford, for when the firm closed in 1841 it was announced that they possessed tools and machines for forty glasscutters. They made all kinds of table glass as well as lustres and Grecian lamps, and were specialists in cut and engraved dessert services.

Corner chair: an armchair that could be placed in a corner. The arrangement of the legs is unusual, with one at each side, the third in the centre of the back and the fourth in the centre of the front. The chair back is generally only as high as the arm rest. The shape of the seat varies from a segment of a circle to an almost rectangular shape. Corner chairs were known in the 17th cent. and were sometimes called elbow chairs or roundabout chairs.

Corner cupboard: a triangular structure, fitting a corner, doored or open. The front is diagonal or curved and it is usually fitted with shelving. Small hanging corner cupboards, lacquered or veneered in burr (q.v.) walnut were popular in England in the first half of the 18th cent. and examples in mahogany were made throughout the cent. Known in France as *encoigneurs*, standing corner cupboards began to appear during the Louis XV period and were usually in pairs, often *en suite* with a secretaire or chest of drawers. They continued to be made right up to the Revolution.

Cornice: the projecting top course of a building or a piece of case furniture.

Coromandel lacquer: a variety of Oriental lacquer brought to England in the late 17th cent. in which the design was incised into the surface. Large folding screens or panels were imported and then cut up in England for making into looking-glass frames, door panels etc., so that the designs are often incomplete or appear upside down. (See also Bantam work.)

Costrel: a pilgrim's bottle; a bottle with ears or handles for suspension from a cord or sling.

Coteau enamel: see Enamel.

Cottage clocks: name now given to many small Connecticut spring clocks in wood cases; *c.* 1850–1900.

Cottage furniture: a term bearing particular reference to simple bedroom furniture made in the United States in the second part of the 19th cent. It is also used to describe some unstained and unpolished English furniture inspired by the Arts and Crafts Movement (q.v.).

Cottages: pottery cottages were used as night-light shields, pastille burners, and mantelpiece ornaments. The latter frequently represent the scenes of sensational crimes, such as the Red Barn at Polstead (Maria Marten) or Stanfield Hall (the Rush murders).

Couched work: embroidery in which the thread is laid on the material and held down by stitching.

Coudière: plate or hardened leather elbow cap, first incorporated in suits of armour of the late 14th cent. Knee plates are called '*grenouillières*'.

Counterguard: comprises those parts of a sword in addition to the quillons (q.v.) which are interposed between the hilt and the blade. It may take the form of a solid plate or a network of bars.

Counterproof: a print made from a damp impression and not a plate. It is much weaker than an ordinary impression and presents the subject in reverse. Artists usually made counterproofs in order to have a print in the same direction as the plate to assist them in making alterations to the plate.

Courtauld, Samuel: (1720–65), Huguenot silversmith working in London. He was apprenticed to his father, Augustin Courtauld II (*c.* 1686–1751), eventually taking over his business. He is principally known for his domestic silver in the Rococo (q.v.) style.

Court cupboard: from the French *court* meaning short. Introduced early in the 16th cent., probably for use in the dining parlour, existing examples are usually of oak but also of walnut. It usually consists of a stand in two or three stages, supported at the back corners by plain posts and at the front by bulbous columns of various forms. A central recessed cupboard with canted sides was sometimes contained in the upper part but it was also made as an open structure. (See also Livery cupboard.)

Courting mirror: small mirror, known in America, framed with mouldings and a cresting, the crested area often containing a painted picture or design. It was traditionally a courting gift in 18th-cent. New England. It is said that this type of mirror was derived from a Chinese example made for the export trade.

Cow milk jug: model of cow with mouth and tail forming spout and handle. Filled from an aperture in the back. An example, in silver, by John Schuppe, probably a Dutchman, dates from about 1755. Jugs in this form were also made in pottery in Staffordshire, South Wales, Yorkshire, and Scotland.

Cox, James: an 18th-cent. London clockmaker and jeweller. He opened an exhibition of clocks, singing birds and automata (q.v.) at Spring Gardens. According to one writer, 'The charge was half a guinea each person; a regulation providing for the presence of but a few visitors at a time was, needless to say, quite unnecessary'.

Cox made many elaborate and costly clocks for export to the East.

Cozzi porcelain: see Venice porcelain.

Crace & Son: founded in 1745, this was an English firm of manufacturers and decorators, later known as J. G. Crace & Sons. It was involved in the Chinoiserie (q.v.) decorations of the Royal Pavilion, Brighton, and in association with A. W. N. Pugin (q.v.) with the design of furniture, wallpaper and textiles in the 19th-cent. Gothic Revival style (q.v.).

Cracked ice pattern: a means of decoration resembling ice cracks, found on Bristol delftware (q.v.), *c.* 1770.

Crackle: a means of decorating porcelain by intentional or controlled 'crazing' (q.v.), used extensively by the Chinese potters but not known in Europe until the 19th cent. Used frequently by modern studio and artist potters.

Cradle pipe-tray: presentation piece of pottery for a newly-married couple. Slipware (q.v.) specimens are recorded from 1673 to 1839.

Cran: an iron trivet fitted over the fire for supporting a kettle, girdle-plate, etc.

Crane, Walter: (1845–1915), English designer, painter and writer who produced numerous designs for wall-papers and textiles.

Crayon engraving: a process in which etching (q.v.) and stipple engraving (q.v.) were combined to render the lines of a chalk drawing. Roulettes with heads designed to reproduce the grain of a chalk line were used to prepare the plate for biting with acid. After the plate had been etched, burin, dry-point and roulette were used direct on its surface. This process was much employed for the reproduction of Old Master drawings, mainly by artists who otherwise worked in stipple or mezzotint (q.v.).

Crazing: a fine network of cracks occurring in the glaze of earthenware (sometimes a long time after manufacture) due to the tension set up in the glaze because of unequal shrinkage of glaze and body. In decorative pottery the effect may not be unpleasant. (See also Crackle.)

Cream-coloured earthenware: a good quality lead-glazed earthenware with light body made of pale clay and usually containing calcined flint, perfected in Staffordshire about 1740–50. It began to oust other tablewares about 1760. It was made extensively in Staffordshire, Yorkshire and elsewhere, and enjoyed a world market in the late 18th and early 19th cent. It could be decorated with pierced, moulded, enamelled or printed designs.

Cream jug: small silver or plate (q.v.) jug introduced as part of the tea service in the early 18th cent. It varied in shape from a helmet form, to a low, four-legged form resembling a sauce boat (q.v.). It was decorated in accordance with contemporary taste.

Creamware: see Cream-coloured earthenware.

Credence (*It.* **credenza**): a term sometimes used for a side-table in a church on which the Elements were placed before Consecration. Such tables were sometimes of hutch-like formation, and the term credence has been loosely extended to cover other side-tables of more or less similar construction. In Italy, the *credenza* was a type of sideboard or buffet used as a serving-table on which silver might also be displayed. Fifteenth- and 16th-cent. *credenze* were either simple tables designed to stand by a wall or else long cupboards, sometimes with canted corners, the height of an ordinary dining-table. As they were normally covered with linen they were very simple in design and decoration. A recessed top story containing a cupboard was added to many *credenze* in the 16th cent. and this was usual in subsequent periods.

Creepers: these, in pairs, were small irons of similar shape to andirons (q.v.), between which they were placed in the hearth to bear the weight of the logs. Creepers were of very simple design, and they came into use when andirons grew elaborate and costly.

Cressent, Charles: (1683–1768), French cabinet-maker, the son of François Cressent, a sculptor, and grandson of a cabinet-maker. He studied under A. C. Boulle (q.v.) and became a member of the *Académie de Saint Luc* in Paris in 1714. In 1719 he married the daughter of Joseph Poitou, an *ébéniste* (q.v.) working for the Duc d'Orleans, and he also at this time was given commissions by the Regent. After this he seems officially to have abandoned sculpture for cabinet-making, but he was several times prosecuted by the *Corporations des Fondeurs* and *Doreurs* (qq.v.) for casting and gilding his own mounts. In 1723 he was actually forbidden by law to produce mounts not made by a qualified *fondeur*. This type of litigation was repeated from time to time throughout his life.

The Regent died in 1723 but Cressent continued service with his son Louis, Duc d'Orleans, as late as 1743, on the Duc's retirement from public life. With the profits from the sale of his furniture Cressent formed an impressive collection of works of art, which he three times tried unsuccessfully to sell owing to financial difficulties.

Towards the end of his life he used the stamp: C. CRESSENT, but it never appears on pieces of very great quality and should always be treated with suspicion in view of his fame in his lifetime and later. The identification of his work therefore depends almost entirely on documents and tradition.

Cresset: generally an iron basket affixed to a rod and designed to hold wood or other fuel for lighting purposes.

Cresting: shaped and sometimes perforated ornament on the top of a structure, such as the foliate cresting running round the covers of Medieval silver-gilt cups. (See also Cresting rail.)

Cresting rail: the top rail or horizontal on the back of a chair.

Cretonne appliqué or **Broderie perse:** was composed of groups of flowers, leaves, birds, etc., cut out from printed cotton and applied to a plain ground, usually black. The edges of the motifs were worked round in buttonhole or overcast stitches. Details, such as the veining of the leaves, or the centres of flowers, were picked out with embroidery in coloured silks.

Crewel-work: crewel-work is embroidery in thin worsteds, and is the term usually applied to the curtains and bed hangings of linen and cotton twill embroidered in coloured wools during the second half of the 17th cent.

This type of work is often called Jacobean embroidery. The designs were based on the printed cotton 'palampores' (chintz hangings) which were imported into England at that time. The 'Tree of Life', with waving stems of acanthus-like foliage rising from a hillocked ground, was the most popular pattern. The embroidery was either polychrome or worked entirely in shades of green which has often faded to a dull indigo. Coiling stems and an asparagus pattern are also found.

Cricket table: three-legged table of simple, often rough, construction.

Crimping: dents or flutes impressed by a tool, usually diagonal, used round the foot or at the base of the handle of a glass vessel.

Crinet: armour of overlapping scales for a horse's neck.

Crisselled glass: glass in which the ingredients are not correctly proportioned and an excess of alkali, for example, has resulted in a clouding of the material caused by a network of cracks. Such glass is described as being 'diseased' and ultimately crumbles. Some of the early glass vessels made by George Ravenscroft (q.v.) suffered from this defect.

Crochet: a brooch-like jewelled ornament fixed on a vertical pin, worn in the late 17th and 18th cent. and also known as a breast ornament. Contemporary sources refer to 'croshetts'.

Croft: a small writing cabinet of the late 18th cent. (named after its inventor), specially designed to be moved about easily in the library; it had many small drawers and an oval drop-leaf top.

Cromwellian chair: a modern term used to describe a chair with a leather seat and back; turned legs and stretchers, occasionally spiral turned. Generally ornamented with brass-headed tacks these chairs were made in the mid-17th cent. and have been much reproduced in modern times.

Cromwellian clock: see Lantern clock.

Cross-banded veneer or **cross-grained:** a characteristic decoration of a veneered surface in which a border of contrasting wood, cut across the grain, is applied to a piece of furniture. Narrow cross-bandings were frequently employed on walnut furniture, while in the later 18th cent. broad bandings in exotic woods were popular.

Crossbow: a bow mounted at right-angles upon a stock, which is grooved for the arrow (bolt), and fitted with a trigger-mechanism so that it can be discharged from the shoulder like a gun. The bow was made variously of wood, steel, or a composition of layers of wood, horn and sinew glued together; it could be spanned by hand, a stirrup at the end providing purchase for the foot by a forked lever, or by various forms of windlass. It was known in Europe as early as the 4th cent., but did not become popular until the 10th. Its use against Christians was prohibited by the Church in 1139, but despite this it was used extensively in warfare throughout the remainder of the Middle Ages. As a sporting weapon it has remained in use until the present, especially in Switzerland.

A light version of the crossbow fitted with a sling to fire bullets or stones, and known as a prodd or stone-bow, was much used from Medieval times onwards for shooting small game. It remained popular, particularly in Lancashire and East Anglia, until well into the 19th cent.

Cross-grained veneer: see Cross-banded veneer.

Crosshatching: shade or tone indicated in drawing, graphics and engraving on silver and glass by a system of crossing parallel lines.

Cross rail: a horizontal rail on a chair back.

Cross-stretcher: X-shaped stretcher (q.v.) in straight or curved lines. Sometimes found on side tables and chairs in the late 17th and early 18th cent.

Crouch ware: the early grey stoneware of Staffordshire with a ferruginous wash is probably the 'crouch' ware mentioned by Simeon Shaw (*History of the Staffordshire Potteries*, 1829) as the earliest Staffordshire salt-glazed pottery. The name perhaps came from the Derbyshire Crich clay.

Crown Derby porcelain: see Derby porcelain.

Crown glass: flat glass made by a process whereby a blown bubble was spread by rapid rotation on the rod into a flat sheet, leaving a bull's eye in the middle where the rod was attached. (See also Broad glass.)

Crown paperweight: a paperweight composed of coloured canes (q.v.) radiating in straight lines from the top.

Crown setting: a means of setting a precious stone whereby the stone is exposed (open setting) and held secure with rebated points.

Crozier: bishop's pastoral staff with a curved end resembling a shepherd's crook, often elaborately carved or decorated with precious stones.

Cruets: (1) the vessels containing the wine and water for use at the Eucharist. Sometimes wholly of silver, they are frequently of glass with silver mounts and follow the patterns prevalent in domestic plate; (2) bottles for condiments, contained in cruet frames. The first examples of silver frames date from Queen Anne. They were made with open rings and central or side handles to hold the sets of casters (q.v.) with or without glass oil and vinegar bottles. Later forms of the frames were oblong or boat-shaped, containing silver-mounted glass bottles, casters and mustard pot.

Crystal: strictly a clear, transparent variety of quartz, the term also is used to refer to the finest colourless or clear flint glass. The clear Venetian glass, first made perhaps before the 15th cent. was called *cristallo* from its resemblance to rock crystal.

Crystal ball clock: large clock designed to stand on a desk, invented in *c.* 1900, with a half-spherical front and back of glass forming a ball and often decorated with a surround of coloured pastes.

'Crystallo-ceramie': a process of enclosing cameos (q.v.), moulded in a porcellaneous material, representing Classical portraits, figures, etc., in deeply cut glass. The method was adopted by Apsley Pellatt (q.v.) from the French and was also known as 'Cameo incrustation'.

C-scroll: a term applied usually to the shape of a handle in form like the letter C; also called a single scroll.

(2)

Cuckoo clock: first made by Anton Ketterer of Schönwald in the Black Forest, Germany, its hours and half-hours are struck on a gong that signals the emergence of a wooden model of a cuckoo through a door at the top of the case.

Cuirassier armour: armour for the heavy cavalry of the first half of the 17th cent., consisting of a close helmet (q.v.) and defences covering the whole of the body down to the knees.

Cuir bouilli: (*Fr.*), leather which has been boiled in oil, moulded or stamped into shape and allowed to dry hard.

Cuisses: armour for the thighs, introduced in the mid-14th cent., of boiled leather and later of plate. Their use was continued in Europe until well into the 17th cent., by which time they were made of narrow plates connected by straps and sliding rivets.

Culet: the point of a brilliant cut (q.v.) diamond at the base of the stone, which is cut to form a horizontal facet.

Cullet: broken glass for remelting, included in the ingredients of the frit (q.v.) used in the manufacture of early soft-paste porcelain. Also used in making new glass, to promote fusion and improve the quality of the metal.

Cup-hilt rapier: in Southern Italy and particularly in Spain, in the second quarter of the 17th cent. the cup-hilt rapier came into fashion, the guard being formed by a circular bowl supplemented by straight quillons (q.v.) and a knuckle-guard. This type of rapier remained in use until the 18th cent.

Cupid's bow cresting: the top rail of a chair or settee in the form of a bow. Rococo (q.v.) chairs frequently had this form of top-rail, which was introduced about 1730.

Cupped top: yoke-rail (q.v.) with a semi-circular indentation.

Cupping-bowl: this term is popularly but incorrectly used for flat, shallow, circular bowls of silver with one flat, pierced and shaped handle. These were, in fact, a form of individual porringer (q.v.), by which name they

are always called in America. The covers of early skillets or saucepans are of the same basic form.

Curfew: a metal cover (*couvre-feu*) used to cover a fire when left unattended or to enable it to be kept alive during the night. Roughly in the shape of a quarter-sphere with a handle attached, the rare examples which are extant are of brass or copper, with embossed ornament.

Curl veneer: a veneer (q.v.) cut from just below a fork in the tree.

Curtain-holder: metalwork wall-fitting, made in pairs, to gather curtains in a loop at approximately dado level.

Cushion frieze: a frieze of convex or cushion-shaped form appearing as a feature of the cornice on late 17th-cent. case furniture.

Cushion knop: a large spherical knop or protuberance, flattened at the top and bottom, on the stem of a drinking glass.

Custodia: monstrance (q.v.) of elaborate architectural form, most common in Spain of the 15th and 16th cent.

Cut cardwork: a method of decorating silver in which flat sheet metal is cut into foliage and strap outline and soldered to the main surface to produce relief decoration. Of French origin, introduced in late 17th cent. and later built up in various planes to greater relief.

Cut glass: glass ground to a required pattern by means of a grindstone equipped with metal or stone disc. These discs are of varying size and can be changed at will according to the requirements of the design. For facet cutting an iron wheel fed with sand or emery is used. Cutting as a form of decoration on English glass was introduced in the early 18th cent. although few examples survive of earlier date than the mid-cent. Excise duties on glass imposed the need for light, thin vessels towards the later years of the cent., hampering the use of cutting as a decoration, but Irish glass of the period, not affected by the duties, was decorated with elaborately cut designs, and decanters, in particular, were treated in this manner.

Cutlass: a term first appearing in the 16th cent., denoting a short, single-edged sword, usually curved, the successor of the Medieval falchion (q.v.). In the 18th and early 19th cent. it was a standard naval weapon.

Cutlery stand: see Canterbury (2).

Cut steel: see Chiselled and cut steel.

Cut-work embroidery: suggested by drawn work (q.v.) but lighter and more conspicuously ornamental, as part of the fabric was cut away and the holes filled with geometrical patterns worked with needle and thread. At its most advanced, it consisted of buttonhole stitch, double loop, darning and knotting stitch. It was important in Elizabethan England.

Cycloidal cheeks: curves fitted to a pendulum clock to overcome circular error. It was found, however, that the errors they introduced were greater than those they eliminated, hence they were soon abandoned. Only found in the very earliest pendulum clocks.

Cylinder escapement: a type of watch escapement (q.v.). A form of this escapement was patented by Tompion (q.v.), Barlow and Haughton in 1695. but it was never developed. It remained for Tompion's successor, George Graham (q.v.), to perfect this escapement about 1725. Graham used it very extensively in his watches, and this greatly helped him to gain the reputation of being the best watchmaker of his day. As with the anchor escapement (q.v.), the pallets are in the same plane as the escape wheel. This escapement remained the best for watches until supplanted by the duplex and the lever escapements (qq.v.) about the end of the 18th cent.

Cylinder knop: a knop or protuberance in the form of a cylinder on the stem of a drinking glass, sometimes containing a tear or air bubble.

Cylinder-top desk: (*Fr. = bureau à cylindre*), a writing table, incorporating drawers and writing accessories, the functional part of which is closed by means of a curved panel fastened with a lock. It is usually supported on tall legs and differs from a roll-top desk (q.v.) in that the curved panel is in one piece and not slatted.

Cyma recta: a moulding composed of two curves, the upper of concave form.

Cyma reversa: a moulding composed of two curves, the lower of concave form.

Cyst: a round protuberance in the base of a wine-glass bowl.

Damascening: the art of encrusting the surface of iron, steel, brass or copper with gold or/and silver has been known and practised since Antiquity, especially in the Near East, but at no time in Europe has it flourished more than in Milan during the middle and second half of the 16th cent., where it was a by-product of the thriving armourers' trade. Thin iron sheets were embossed with subjects from Roman history or mythology against landscape backgrounds and damascened with gold and silver. The Milanese damascening of this period is of fine quality and bears comparison with the best Saracenic work. Damascened plaques were made in quantity to more or less standard shapes and were sold to cabinet-makers, who mounted them on ebony caskets, chests of drawers, and even large pieces such as tables and mirrors. Though the majority of the damascened ironwork encountered by the collector is likely to be of Milanese origin, there were highly competent damasceners at work elsewhere in Europe, in Augsburg and Nuremberg, in Paris and in other Italian cities. In the 17th cent. some fine damascencing was done on English sword and knife handles, probably by immigrant Italian artists. The art did not survive the 16th cent. in Italy. It was revived in Spain in the mid-19th cent. and by Elkington & Co. (q.v.) in England.

Damask: (1) a silk fabric used extensively in the 18th cent. for walls, curtains and upholstery. The matt and glossy one-colour design is formed by the manner of weaving. Later, other yarns (cotton, etc.) came to be used. (2) a type of wallpaper of similar visual effect, popular in Britain in the late 1870s and early 1880s.

Dandies' sticks: walking-sticks flaunted by early 19th-cent. dandies displayed knobs carved with heads of Moors, Turks or Chinese. These have been noted in mahogany, teak, ash, ironwood, snakewood, penang wood and blackthorn. Less expensively the heads might be in cast and gilded brass.

Dangle-spit: a non-mechanical type of spit for roasting meat over a fire which operated in the manner implied by its name. It hung downwards, twisting one way and another on a rope as the latter wound and unwound

itself, clockwise and anti-clockwise, sometimes with the aid of two weighted arms.

Dargastan rugs: both Dargastan and Derbend rugs come from the north-east Caucasus and resemble Shirvan rugs (q.v.).

Darly, Matthew: designer and engraver of furniture to the trade, produced trade cards of outstanding quality from about 1750 until the 1780s, the finest being in the Chinoiserie (q.v.) style in which he was a master designer. His own card, issued from 'the Acorn, facing Hungerford, Strand', shows him also to have been a maker of paper hangings. This card also states that he 'engraved Shopkeepers' Bills in greater variety and cheaper than any other Shop in Town'. The signature 'M. Darly Sculp' appears on 81 of the 200 plates in Thomas Chippendale's (q.v.) *Director*.

Date letter: the specific mark of a letter of the alphabet used on English silver at the various Assay Offices to distinguish the year of hall marking. There are no date letters on American silver.

The system was introduced in France in 1461 and adopted in England in 1478. Each Assay Office had its own cycle and forms of lettering.

Davenport: a small chest of drawers with a sloping top for writing, popular in the early 19th cent.; said to be named after a client of the firm of Gillow (q.v.) who claimed to have invented it. The term may also refer to a settee (q.v.) in the United States.

Davenport ware: John Davenport (*c.* 1766–1848) took over Brindley's established pottery works in 1793, and for some years continued to produce earthenware, in 1801 adding the manufacture of glass. In the early 19th cent. he began producing bone china (q.v.). He retired in 1832, the business being continued by his sons until 1887. Marks:

DAVENPORT   DAVENPORT
LONGPORT   LONGPORT
               STAFFORDSHIRE

Printed

Typical of the early earthenware were cream-coloured, painted and 'flown' blue (q.v.) decorated wares, and plates with openwork rims. Peasant-style painted designs were popular in the period 1815–35 and also monochrome landscapes on a coloured ground. Stone china (q.v.) with rich coloured and gold 'Imari' (q.v.) decoration followed the vogue of the 1830s.

Bone china varied in quality from a greyish body to a fine translucent white body with brilliant decoration of enamelled flowers, fruit, etc., in naturalistic designs. Tea and dessert sets were typical products, and designs often derived from Sèvres, Derby (qq.v.) and other factories. A 'cottage' style of decoration was used in the early days, but later a heavier, more ornate style with lavish gilding became general.

Davidson & Co.: a glass factory in County Durham producing, from the 1880s, articles of table glass in pressed, slag (qq.v.), 'Pearline' and 'Primrose' glass.

Davis, Alexander Jackson: American architect and designer working between 1849 and 1860. He is best known for his furniture in the Gothic style for Lyndhurst, New York (originally called Paulding Manor).

Davis, Greathead & Green: the first mechanized glasshouse founded in England (1809) in Stourbridge. Pressed glass was made from the 1830s. Later specialities were *millefiori* paperweights (q.v.), black flint and cased glass (q.v.), and many kinds of coloured glass.

Day bed: a couch that became fashionable during the Restoration, although it had been introduced at an earlier date. Usually made of walnut and sometimes of painted beech, the seat and back rest were often caned, while the uprights, stretchers (q.v.) and legs were turned and carved. The back rest could be adjusted for comfort.

Day-of-the-month clock: see Perpetual calendar clock.

Deacon's mark: from 1487 to 1681 the mark of the deacon of the guild was struck on Scottish gold and silver. The mark of the Assay Master was struck between 1681 and 1759, when this was replaced by a thistle. (See also Hallmark.)

Deadbeat escapement: a type of clock escapement (q.v.) invented by George Graham about 1715. Graham was the leading astronomical instrument-maker of his day, and from his close connection with astronomers was, doubtless, aware of their demand for still greater accuracy than could be attained with the anchor escapement (q.v.). The deadbeat escapement is an improvement on the anchor in that it eliminates the recoil, and remains steady at the end of each beat. It held the field for the most accurate escape for astronomical work for nearly two hundred years. It is still used today in high-grade clocks, both long-case and mantel (qq.v.).

Debased wriggling: zigzag pattern achieved mechanically on 19th-cent. pewter (q.v.) in imitation of 17th-cent. decoration.

Decalcomania: a process of transferring pictures from prepared paper to the surfaces of glass, porcelain, etc., popular about 1862–4.

Decanter: a decorative glass bottle used for serving wine and spirits. They became widely used in the 18th cent. Many different shapes were made in green, blue or plain glass, becoming more delicate in shape and style of decoration as the century progressed. Gilt, enamel or engraved ornamentation was used, often including the name of the intended contents. In early examples corks were used; glass stoppers became general in the mid-18th cent. Victorian decanters were more solid in appearance and were often of coloured glass (green, yellow, amethyst), moulded or cut with bold designs, and became highly ornate towards the end of the 19th cent.

Découpage: until the mid-1670s the mounts (q.v.) of folding fans were cut with open-work lace-like patterns copying the intricate designs of French and Flemish lace. The blades were in tortoiseshell elaborated to harmonize with the lace patterns and trimmed with gold and precious stones; or were in Levantine mother-of-pearl carved and engraved with mythological subjects.

Delamain, Henry: partner with Janssen and Brooks in the Battersea enamel (q.v.) venture. He left the firm soon after Brooks in 1754 and died in Dublin in 1757.

Delaunay, Nicolas: (d. 1727), French silversmith and medallist who worked for Louis XIV and Louis XV and produced domestic plate.

Delft: Delft, near Rotterdam, became the centre of the Dutch tin-glazed earthenware industry in the mid-17th cent. The blue-and-white wares were originally made as inexpensive reproductions of Chinese procelain. The trade grew and other styles were added, while an individual Delft style also began to emerge. Enamel colours began to be used in the 18th cent., but the industry then declined as a result of increasing production by European porcelain factories. The many Delft factories were known by their signs, including the Greek A, the Double Jug, the Rose, the Peacock and the Porcelain Bottle.

Delftware: English tin-glazed earthenware, made from the 16th to 18th cent., named after similar wares made at Delft. Main factories producing delftware were at Lambeth, Bristol, Liverpool (qq.v.), Glasgow, Dublin, and Limerick.

Delorme, Jean-Louis-Faizelot: French *ébéniste* (q.v.) who became a *maître-ébéniste* in 1763. He specialized in lacquer furniture, while his brother Adrien specialized in marquetry (q.v.).

Demidoff: St Petersburg firm of goldsmiths and silversmiths and craftsmen in malachite (q.v.).

Demi-parure: a small matching set of jewellery, consisting of brooch with earrings or necklace with earrings or other combination. (See also Parure.)

Denby: an English pottery company founded in 1809, trading until the 20th cent. as Joseph Bourne & Son. Typical products were light brown salt-glazed stoneware (q.v.) vessels for domestic use and, later, terra cotta (q.v.). The company is still in operation.

Dennison, Aaron L: (1812–85), the 'father of American watchmaking'. He invented the Dennison Standard Gauge in 1840, and in 1859 set up the American Watch Co. (later the American Waltham Watch Co.), which became the largest in the world. In 1870 he emigrated to England and set up the Dennison Watch Case Co. in London, which was in operation until 1967.

Dent, Edward John: (1790–1853), an English clockmaker who set up his own business in 1840, building up a fine reputation. He supplied the clock for the Royal Exchange in 1844 and won the contract for the clock at the Houses of Parliament. He died before completion, and the order was carried out by his stepson Frederick.

Dentil moulding: a cornice (q.v.) moulding made up of a row of rectangular, tooth-like forms, used on case furniture.

D'Entrecolles, Père François Xavier: a Jesuit missionary who went out to China in the year 1698. At a time when all the nations of Europe were trying actively to discover the secrets of porcelain manufacture he informed his compatriots of the methods of the Chinese potters. Two long letters, detailing with accuracy all that he had seen and heard, were written by him in 1712 and 1722, and published later in Paris. These documents are still the basis of much of our knowledge of porcelain-making in China. Pere D'Entrecolles died in Peking in 1741.

Derband rugs: see Dargastan rugs.

Derby porcelain: the date when porcelain was first made in Derby is not certainly known. André Planché

was making it by 1751 probably at Cockpit Hill, and the enameller William Duesbury (q.v.) is known to have decorated in London 'Darby' or 'Darbyshire figures'. A cream jug dated 1750 is believed to be the earliest dated specimen.

By 1756 a flourishing business had been built up and Duesbury and John Heath had become proprietors. In 1770 the Chelsea (q.v.) factory was acquired.

Heath failed financially in 1779 and in consequence Duesbury became sole owner. He died in 1786, his son of the same name continuing the factory until his death in 1796. In 1795 he had taken as partner Michael Kean who married his widow, and remained in control until 1811.

The works were bought in 1811 by Robert Bloor. He became insane in 1826, and the factory was managed until its closure in 1848 by James Thomason and Thomas Clarke.

The present Royal Crown Derby Porcelain Company was formed in 1876.

Marks:

1750   1780

1795   1830

Chelsea Derby

1760   1770–80   1784   1784–1810

1795–6   Imitation

The paste of the earliest phase of Derby porcelain was non-phosphatic, and the wares produced rather heavy and of a creamy warm white.

The next phase of Derby was characterized by the use of pale delicate colours, large flat flowers and scrolls picked out in colour or mounds with flowery reliefs. The figures themselves were generally of Meissen (q.v.) origin, Derby setting up claims to be 'the second Dresden'. At this period figures seemed to have had precedence over useful wares.

The third phase of Derby is distinguishable by the dirty patches (three or four) underneath the wares caused by the wads of clay upon which they were rested during firing. Wares of this kind are referred to frequently as belonging to the 'Patch' family. Figures become more sophisticated and static, rather larger in size, and tend to over-elaboration.

Useful wares were sometimes decorated with blue-and-white Chinese landscapes upon plates with lattice borders with floral intersections. Other Chinese decorations were in crimson and gold on underglaze blue. Transfer printing (q.v.) was rarely used.

More importance seems to have been attached to useful wares in the Chelsea-Derby period. A creamy bone paste was used, set off by vigorous shapes, Neoclassic in form, and decorations of aristocratic severity, of urns and swags.

Figure groups took on a note of sentiment and tended to fussiness in the leafy backgrounds. The dominant influence was Sèvres (q.v.). Biscuit-porcelain figures simulating marble statuary are typical of the Neoclassic style about 1780.

Ground colours used at Derby did not achieve the beauty of those of Chelsea, but ambitious painting was done by the notable decorators. Figure painting was done on straight-sided coffee cans intended for display rather than for use. Zachariah Boreman (q.v.) and 'Jockey' Hill executed landscapes in a style carried forward into the early 19th cent. by George Robertson and Jesse Mountford, and the two drawing masters, the brothers Brewer.

Showy 'Japans' became popular in the Bloor period with heavy colour and lavish gilding. The fruit and flower painting of the Steeles reached a high standard of accomplishment but lacked sensibility. Figures were re-issued from earlier moulds.

Derbyshire chair (or **Yorkshire chair**): a type of mid-17th-cent. oak chair with an open back of sturdy arched rails ornamented with carving.

Derbyshire pottery: extensive manufactures of pottery and porcelain have flourished in Derbyshire including slipwares at Bolsover and Tickenhall; brown salt-glazed stonewares (qq.v.) at Chesterfield, Brampton, Denby, Codnor Park and Belper (q.v.); cream-colour of Staffordshire type at Cockpit Hill (q.v.); and porcelain at Derby (q.v.).

Deruta maiolica: tin-glazed earthenware made at Deruta, near Perugia. Deruta lustered wares of the 16th cent. achieved fame, often employing a pale brassy yellow combined with blue.

Desk box: box with with a sloping lid for writing; 18th-cent. examples often veneered.

Dessert service: by the late 18th cent. knives, forks, spoons, as well as a number of small dishes, were being made in gold, silver or silver-gilt sets for the dessert course.

Deu-ddarn: a two-tiered cupboard, being a Welsh variety of the press cupboard (q.v.).

Deutsche Blumen: (*Ger.*), see German flowers.

Devonia lace: Honiton (q.v.) product of the 1870s, with flower petals raised in relief by tension on the threads.

Devonshire pottery: several important slipware potteries existed in North Devon, working from the early 17th cent. until the end of the Victorian era, notably at Barnstaple and Bideford.

Crude pottery made at Honiton gave place in the 20th cent. to 'art' pottery. At Bovey, pottery of Staffordshire type was, and is, made extensively. Important terra-cotta (q.v.) works flourished at Watcombe, near Torquay, in the second half of the 19th cent.

Diagonal barometer: a type in which the recording part of the tube is at an obtuse angle with the lower upright part, so that the possible variation of the mercury height may be spread over the inclined length of the tube, thus extending the reading scale.

Dial clock (or **English dial**): a spring-driven clock, the works mainly hidden behind a large, clear face with bold numerals. These clocks were designed to be functional rather than decorative, and are found in railway stations, schools and kitchens of the late Victorian era.

Diamanté: a white paste used to imitate diamonds.

Diamond cutting: glass vessels decorated with cutting in low relief were made in England in the mid-18th cent., a pattern of facets (q.v.) forming diamond shapes being popular. Later in the cent., deep grooves giving high convex raised diamonds were employed, particularly on Irish glass (See also Hobnail cutting.)

Diamond moulding: see Rib or diamond moulding.

Diamond ornament: the diamond or lozenge motif is frequently found carved on 17th-cent. furniture, on the backs of settles, the doors of press cupboards (q.v.) the panels of chests, etc. Much formal ornament was carved on furniture of this period and the diamond motif was particularly suitable, on account of its shape, for the decoration of upright panels. It was also used on silver.

Diamond-point engraving: engraved designs on glass vessels scratched with the point of a diamond. The technique is of ancient origin and was much practised in Europe from the 16th to the 18th cent., often by independent decorators outside the glasshouses, including amateurs.

Diaper pattern: a geometric pattern of repeated lozenge shapes formed by intersecting diagonal lines, found on marquetry (q.v.) silver, porcelain, wallpaper, etc., either as a background to other patterns or simply to fill a blank area.

Diatreta vase (or **cage cup**): a Roman technique for decorating glassware which had a short revival in the late 19th cent. The outer layer of a vase or cup was carved or cut away to leave a design in high relief.

Dieppe lace: pillow lace (q.v.) suggesting simplified Valenciennes lace (q.v.). (See Antwerp lace, Ave Maria lace.)

Dinanderie: small brassware made in or around the town of Dinant, in the Ardennes, near Liège. Whereas elsewhere bronze was mostly employed for the manufacture of domestic vessels, the presence of zinc deposits around Liège led the founders of the valley of the Meuse to adopt brass in preference. The town of Dinant became by the late Middle Ages so famous for its brassware that the name Dinanderie was used to describe the production of the whole region. Typical articles made were aquamanile (q.v.), basins, jugs, cooking vessels and candlesticks, many of them quite simple objects for domestic purposes. Among the more splendid achievements of the Mosan craftsmen may be mentioned lecterns and fonts. In 1466 the town of Dinant was sacked by Philippe le Bon, and as a result the brass-founders emigrated, partly to other towns in the valley of the Meuse, partly to France and England.

Dipped ware: an inexpensive type of pottery made from the mid-18th cent. in Fenton, Staffordshire, by Thomas Heath; in the 19th cent. its manufacture was widespread throughout the Staffordshire potteries and elsewhere. Three or four coloured slips were simultaneously applied to the biscuit (q.v.) in a rotating lathe, producing distinct patterns of stripes, dots, spirals, etc. William Evans, writing in 1846, described three types: (1) marbled slipware (q.v.), (2) 'Mocha' (q.v.) and (3) banded ware.

Directoire style: decorative style of the Directoire period, 1795–9, combining elements of the Louis XVI and Empire (q.v.) styles.

Dirk: Highland Scottish sheath-knife developed during the 17th cent. It has a short grip with a blade that is often cut down from a sword. The term may also refer to a dagger carried by naval officers.

Discharge mark: mark on French silver after 1681 indicating that the duty had been paid.

Discharge printing: a 'dyed' style of printing textiles, first used *c.* 1806, in which the fabric is first dyed a solid colour and then the design is printed as a chemical which bleaches out or discharges the colour, producing a white design on a dyed ground.

Dish cover: silver or plate (q.v.) cover for hot food, generally with a ring handle.

Dish cross: a silver or plated spirit-lamp stand with two adjustable arms revolving around the lamp with sliding feet. The lamp sometimes omitted and replaced by a pierced plate for use with separate lamp below. Found from about 1750–80.

Dish ring: also called 'potato ring'. Of Irish origin. Circular silver dish or bowl stand with straight or incurved sides usually pierced and chased with pastoral or Classical motifs. Found from about 1740 onwards, many dating from about 1770.

Dish strainer: see Mazarine.

Dish-top table: table with the surrounding rim slightly curved up. Rectangular tables on four legs and pedestal tables of the mid-18th cent. are found with dish tops.

Divan: couch without back or arms introduced in the United States in the 19th cent. and especially popular in Turkish-style interiors.

Dixon, Arthur S.: (1856–1929), English silversmith, metalworker and designer. His work is characterized by simplicity of outline and decoration.

Dixon, James, & Sons: English Sheffield platers, silversmiths and electro-platers, the firm founded in Sheffield in 1806 as Dixon & Smith. They were also makers of wares in Britannia metal (q.v.). In 1848 they acquired a licence to electro-plate (q.v.), experimenting with a technique of plating Britannia metal (E.P.B.M.). They made silver and plated wares for Summerley's Art Manufactures (q.v.) and were large-scale exporters in the 19th cent. to the United States.

Djoshagan rugs: Persian rugs generally of palmette or vase (qq.v.) designs. They are simpler than those of Ispahan or Tabriz (qq.v.), with blue or deep red predominating. Knot: Ghiordes (q.v.).

Doccia: an Italian factory founded by Ginori in 1735, making soft-paste, later hard-paste, porcelain (qq.v.). The factory specialized in making imitations of the products of other factories, notably Capo-di-Monte (q.v.), and in the late 19th cent. also produced earthenware, particularly copies of early Italian *maiolica* (q.v.). The mark of a star in blue, red, gold or impressed was used in the late 18th cent. and is very similar to the Nove (q.v.) mark.

'Doctor Syntax': fine underglaze blue transfer-prints (q.v.) representing the adventures of Doctor Syntax, used as decorations on tableware by James and Ralph Clews, Cobridge, *c.* 1821. Pottery figures were also popular. *The Tours of Dr Syntax in Search of the Picturesque* by Dr Combe, with illustrations by Thomas Rowlandson, published 1815–21, was a satire upon the writings of the Rev. William Gilpin.

Dog-collar: a type of necklet made popular by the Princess of Wales (later

Queen Alexandra) in the late 19th cent. Several rows of precious stones are joined, one above the other, to make a stiff, close-fitting collar.

Dole cupboard: the term strictly applies to hanging or other structures, open-shelved or doored and railed, used in the charitable dispensation of bread, etc., in churches and other institutions in the 16th and 17th cent.

Domed foot: foot of a vessel of glass, silver, etc., rising in the form of a dome to support the stem.

Donaldson, John: (1737–1801), enameller and miniaturist, John Donaldson was born in Edinburgh, and from an early age showed ability as a portraitist. When he came to London he became a member of the Incorporated Society of Artists and executed a considerable number of commissions as a miniaturist. In 1760 he was living in London. He became one of the most notable independent porcelain decorators, executing some work for Sprimont at Chelsea (q.v.), and some extremely fine Classical pictures on Worcester porcelain (q.v.) about 1770.

Donegal carpets: Alexander Morton organized the weaving of coarse knotted carpets in Donegal at the request of the Congested Districts Board in 1898. Hand-knotted carpets are still made there.

Don Pottery: John Green, manager of Swinton Old Pottery, started this factory *c.* 1790, which was probably rebuilt in 1800–1. In 1807 the firm was known as Greens, Clark & Co., and in 1822 as John William Green & Co. It remained with the Greens until the late 1830s when Samuel Barker of Mexborough took over. It traded from 1852 and 1893 when it was finally closed as Samuel Barker and Son. Good quality white and cream-coloured earthenware, green glazed wares, and much painted and transfer-printed pottery, as well as Egyptian black and other stonewares were manufactured. About 1812 some china of good quality is said to have been made.

Marks:

Painted

Impressed

Transfer-printed

Door furniture: finger plates, key escutcheons (q.v.) and door handles. The importance attached to harmony of design in the second half of the 18th cent. resulted in attention being paid not only to the decoration and furnishing of rooms, in order that the whole should present a harmonious appearance, but also to the door furniture. Robert Adam (q.v.) designed key escutcheons and door handles for execution in ormolu (q.v.), while door furniture of pottery was made in the 18th cent. by Wedgwood (q.v.) and others. In mid-Victorian times the manufacture of door furniture became a specialist branch of the pottery industry.

Doorstop: glass doorstops, or dumpies, were usually of green glass, sometimes enclosing air bubbles. Metal doorstops were made of cast iron or brass, commonly in the shape of bells or figures, some having long handles.

Doreurs, Corporation des: (*Fr.*), the craft guild in France responsible for gilding in all its forms. The organization was similar to that of the *menuisiers-ébénistes* (qq.v.).

Double barometer: a type in which the mercury column is divided into approximately two equal halves fixed vertically side by side and connected by a tube filled with a lighter fluid substance such as oil or air.

Double-bob clock pendulum: a spring-suspended type of pendulum appearing towards the latter part of the 18th cent., in which the rod carries two lenticular-shaped bobs.

Double chest: see Tallboy.

Double-scroll handle: a sinuous line of S-shape, or composed of reverse curves, employed especially in design of handles.

Doublet: a counterfeit gem of which the back consists of glass or paste (q.v.), covered with a thin layer of gemstone.

Doulton pottery and porcelain: John Doulton (1793–1873), was a skilled potter who served his time at the Fulham (q.v.) factory. In 1815 with John Watts he acquired an interest in a potworks in Vauxhall Walk, Lambeth, where they made bottles, mugs and jugs in salt-glazed stoneware with relief decorations of topers, windmills, hunting scenes, etc. The firm was known as Doulton & Watts and its business prospered. In 1820 the partners became owners of the factory and in 1826 moved to more spacious premises in Lambeth High Street.

Between 1820 and 1860 new factories were built to answer the requirements of the chemical industry; the demand for salt-glazed drain-pipes which resulted from agitation for healthier living and sanitation; and the demand for insulators, stoneware filters and terra cotta statuary and vases. The Reform Flasks (q.v.), with demi-effigies of prominent politicians were a popular feature following the Reform Bill of 1832.

John Watts retired from the business in 1854 and the firm became known henceforth as Doulton & Co.

In 1877 the earthenware factory of Pinder, Bourne & Co., Burslem, was acquired for the production of good class domestic pottery, and in 1884 a new wing was added to it for the manufacture of bone china (q.v.). This factory soon acquired a reputation and made distinctive contributions in the field of ceramic painting and decorative pottery and porcelain.

The subsequent history of Doulton's is one of constant development; of the acquisition of fresh factories for special purposes; of plant renewal and factory rebuilding; and finally of reorganization and regrouping in face of contemporary economic problems. Marks:

DOULTON LAMBETH

Before 1836

Outside the products of chemical, sanitary and other social science industries and the excellent tablewares which they make, the important products of Doulton's include:

(1) Lambeth: Relief decorated stoneware – toby jugs, bottles, character pieces (Nelson, etc.) in style with other contemporary stoneware manufactures of 1810–35, but rather more ambitious in character; these derive from the Fulham tradition. Salt-glazed stonewares with incised decorations by individual artists and craftsmen who were allowed to sign their pieces, *c.* 1870 onwards. The Barlow sisters did admirable free sketches on pots of animals and foliage. Painted naturalistic decoration was also popular.

Other types of salt-glazed stonewares, overloaded with carved decoration or ornamental excrescences in blue, purple or grey Rhenish styles. Also figures modelled in naturalistic style by Tinworth, Marshall, Broad, etc., ranging from miniatures a few inches in height to monumental statues, altarpieces, etc.

(2) Burslem: ordinary type China painting in a free, vignetted, naturalistic style.

Strong colour glaze effects were also used – *rouge flambé, sang de boeuf*, 'Sung' and 'veined Sung'. The Doulton naturalistic figure, toby jug and character jug were also made at Burslem.

Douters: scissor-like implements with flat, elliptical 'blades' for extinguishing candles. Not to be confused with snuffers (q.v.), which have a cutting edge. Douters are comparatively rare and not always recognized as such.

Dovetail hinge: a butterfly hinge, the leaves of which resemble two dovetails joined at the narrow part.

Dovetailing: a technique of the cabinet-maker (q.v.); a means of interlocking angles on carcases (q.v.) and drawers. The earliest method to be employed was the common or through dovetail. This was strong but had the disadvantage of showing the end grain on both sides of the angle and was consequently not satisfactory for holding a veneer (q.v.). Shortly before 1700 this method was replaced by the lap or stop dovetail which had the end grain on one side only, leaving the front quite clear for veneering.

Dowel: headless pin used in construction. Though, architecturally, dowels may be of other materials, wood is understood when speaking of furniture. Trenail (i.e. treenail) is another term for a wooden dowel.

Down-hearth: a slab of stone or metal raised slightly above the level of the floor of the room, forming the earliest and most simple type of fireplace. The first versions were centrally placed in a room, and smoke rose to escape through a louvre in the roof. The down-hearth built in one side of the room with a flue communicating with the outside has remained in use in cottages to this day.

Downing, Andrew Jackson: (1815–52), American architect and landscape gardener and writer on interior decoration. He analysed the 19th-cent. Revival styles, dividing their application between the various rooms of a house.

Dowry chest or **dower chest:** romantic term for any chest reserved for the trousseau and household linen of a bride-to-be.

Drake foot: see Duck foot.

Dram cup: a small two-handled shallow bowl, similar to a wine taster (q.v.), seldom made after the second decade of the 18th cent.

Dram glasses: known also as nips, joeys, ginettes, and gin glasses; 17th cent: small tumbler with four tiny feet;

1675–1750: cup-shaped bowl with short, heavy knop or moulded baluster; 1690–1710: straight-sided bowl of thick section on flattened spherical knop; 1710–50: short, plain stem on foot, attached directly to bowl; 1720–1850: short, drawn-stemmed trumpet-bowled: some early examples have folded feet.

Drape paper: a type of wallpaper introduced into America in about 1806 by the Frenchman Joseph Dufour (q.v.). Imitation velvet or silk was caught up at intervals by heavy cords and tassels.

Drawn stem: a type of stem found on glass drinking vessels from the late 17th cent. It consists of a plain knopped or baluster stem drawn directly from a gathering of metal at the base of the bowl.

Draw-leaf table (or **drawing table**): a type of table with extensions at either end in the form of leaves which could be drawn out when needed to increase the length of the table. This type of table, supported on turned legs with stretchers (q.v.), was in general use by the late 16th cent. and was made throughout the Stuart period. Most extant examples are of oak, but they were also made of walnut, ash or elm.

Drawn-work embroidery: forerunner of real lace. Made from linen with some threads drawn out and the remainder grouped and whipped over to form geometrical patterns.

Dredger: small, cylindrical pepperpot with side scroll handle of early 18th-cent. date. Also called 'kitchen pepper'.

Dresden 'lace': drawn work (q.v.) on muslin.

Dresden porcelain: see Meissen porcelain.

Dresser: a cupboard with open shelves in the upper part, usually with low galleries against which rested a row of plates. The lower part usually had drawers and cupboards and occasionally a hutch (q.v.).

Dresser, Dr Christopher: (1834–1904), English botanist, writer and designer of silver, metalwork, pottery, glass, textiles and wallpaper. He exerted a strong influence in the late 19th cent., advocating, and displaying in his own works, simplicity of form, functionalism, and controlled, though often exotic, ornament. His interest in Oriental art led him to visit Japan in 1876 and he later opened an Oriental warehouse in London. He also drew inspiration from ancient cultures. The firms for which he executed designs included Hukin & Heath (q.v.), James Dixon & Sons (q.v.), Elkington & Co. (q.v.), Coalbrookdale Co. (q.v.) and J. Couper & Sons. In 1880 he organized the Art Furniture Alliance.

Dressing box: a toilet box, fitted with a looking glass in the lid and compartments for toilet requisites. Small boxes of this type were known in the Elizabethan age, but more elaborate in form were those made with marquetry (q.v.) decoration, probably *en suite* (q.v.) with a marquetry dressing table, in the late 17th cent. They continued to be made in the 18th and 19th cent.

Dressing glass: see Toilet mirror.

Dressing table: lady's or gentleman's toilet table incorporating drawers and, in some examples, a mirror.

Drop front: see Fall front.

Drop handle: the characteristic handle used on furniture with drawers from about 1690 to 1720. Of brass, solid or hollow, this pendant handle hangs from a brass plate and should be attached to the drawer by wire pins. Sometimes known as tear drop or pear drop on account of its shape.

Drop-in seat: a type of upholstered chair seat supported on the seat frame but which can be independently removed. First introduced about 1710.

Drop knop: knop or protuberance on the stem of a drinking glass resembling in shape the frustum of an inverted cone. Usually plated half an inch to an inch above the foot.

Drop-leaf table: a table with one or two hinged leaves which can be raised or dropped by bringing swinging legs or supports into use. Many kinds of drop-leaf tables have special names, such as gate-leg (q.v.), Pembroke (q.v.), etc.

Drug jar: pot or jar intended for use on apothecaries' shelves. English 17th-cent. examples are of tin-glazed earthenware, early vessels being squat and cylindrical in shape, either plain or painted with simple designs or stripes in blue or manganese. Later 17th-cent. jars are taller and sometimes bear the name of the drug within a cartouche (q.v.). Polychrome designs of sprigs and foliage appear on 18th-cent. jars.

Drum: body of a flagon, tankard, etc.

Drum clock: the earliest type of table clock, in the shape of a drum, made from the early 16th cent.

Drum table (or **capstan table**): a round table with a deep frieze for drawers and a central support in tripod form, the legs having a pronounced curve outwards. Sometimes this table had a solid three-sided pedestal base or monopodium (q.v.), mounted on claw feet. Common in the early 19th cent., it was usually made of rosewood or mahogany.

'Drunken Parson' toby jug: a variety of toby jug (q.v.) representing a parson with his hat askew, his beer mug upturned in his hand and a drunken expression on his face.

Dry-point engraving: a process of engraving on a metal plate with a solid rod of steel shaped like a pencil which is drawn (not pushed like the burin) across the plate and throws up a rich burr. This burr is allowed to remain on the plate, holds the ink and imparts a velvety tone to the print but is soon worn down. Only the first fifty impressions, or even fewer, show the full effect. The first prints scratched in a manner similar to that of dry-point were made by the anonymous German *Master of the Amsterdam Cabinet* in about 1480. Dürer engraved three outstanding dry-point plates, and in Italy Andrea Meldolla (Schiavone) (d. 1582) used dry-point in conjunction with etching (q.v.). The process was brought to a high pitch of perfection by Rembrandt, who occasionally produced pure dry-points but more often used the dry-point pencil to finish his etchings. In the late 18th cent. dry-point was revived in England by Thomas Worlidge (1700–66) and Benjamin Wilson (1721–88): and in the early 19th cent. by David Wilkie (1785–1841), Edward Thomas Daniell (1804–42) and many others. It has been extensively used by modern etchers.

Dubois, Jacques and **Réné:** French cabinet-makers (q.v.). Jacques Dubois was born in Paris *c.* 1693, became a *maître-ébéniste* (see *Menuisiers-Ebénistes, Corporation des*) in 1742, and was elected a *juré* (see Stamps on French furniture) of the guild in 1762. He specialized in the use of lacquer, both Oriental and European, and died in 1763, the same year as Oeben (q.v.), whose stock he helped to value. He used the stamp:

IDUBOIS

After his death his widow carried on the business with the help of her sons, the most celebrated of whom was Réné (b. 1737), who always used his father's stamp. He became a *maître* in 1754, was much patronized by Marie Antoinette, both before and after she became Queen, and also by the Court and nobility. He worked mainly in the Louis XVI style and eventually abandoned cabinet-making for selling furniture. He died in 1799.

Duchesse: (*Fr.*), a type of *chaise longue* (q.v.) in which two *bergère* (q.v.) chairs face each other, connected by a stool in the middle. An example is illustrated by Hepplewhite in his *Cabinet Maker and Upholsterer's Guide*.

Duck-egg porcelain: a much sought after variety of Swansea soft-paste porcelain (q.v.) showing a greenish translucency, made about 1816–17.

Duck foot: an American colloquial term for the three-toed club or Dutch foot, mostly found in Delaware River Valley furniture. Also called drake foot and web foot.

Duesbury, William (1725–86), independent porcelain decorator in London 1751–3 (his account book has been preserved and published). He obtained controlling interests in various porcelain factories in England: Derby (q.v.) 1756–86, possibly Longton Hall (q.v.) about 1760, Bow (q.v.) in 1763, and Chelsea (q.v.) 1770–84. His son, William Duesbury II (1763–96/7) owned the Derby factory from 1786 until his death.

Dufour, Joseph & Co.: a wallpaper manufacturing company established in Paris in 1807, later known as Dufour-Leroy. The firm produced drape (q.v.) and scenic papers, a great many of which were exported to America.

Dumb waiter: a dining-room stand. An English invention of the early 18th cent., with normally three circular trays, increasing in size towards the bottom, supported on a shaft with a tripod base. This established design gave way to more elaborate versions at the end of the cent.: four-legged supports and rectangular trays are found and other quite different kinds consisted of square or circular tables with special compartments for bottles, plates, etc. In America a special type, known as the 'Lazy Susan', was used for condiments on early 19th-cent. dining tables.

Dummy-board figure or **companion board:** figure painted in oils on board up to life size and cut out as a profile, popular as a form of decoration in Britain in the late 17th and early 18th cent. It stood upright and was often one of a pair.

Du Paquier, Claudius Innocentius: (d. 1751), founder of the Vienna porcelain (q.v.) factory. He appears to have been conducting experiments in Vienna as early as 1716, and was granted a monopoly in 1718. Successful production at the factory does not seem to have begun until 1719, after the arrival of Samuel Stölzel who had been kiln-master at the Meissen factory (q.v.). Du Paquier suffered from recurring financial difficulties and relinquished his factory to the State in 1744. He remained at the factory as manager and died in 1751.

Duplex escapement: a type of escapement (q.v.) of which the invention is usually attributed to Pierre LeRoy of Paris, about 1750. The escape wheel has two sets of teeth, one long and pointed, the other short and triangular and rising from the plane of the escape wheel. The long teeth escape through a small notch in the balance staff, which also carries a long arm by which the impulse is given through the short triangular teeth.

Dust board: a wooden partition between the drawers on a chest of drawers. This refinement in construction was introduced by the cabinet-maker (q.v.) and is not found in pieces made by the joiner (q.v.) in pre-Restoration times. It was a protection against dust and theft. In 18th-cent. furniture, the dust board is usually made of deal with a rail of oak or mahogany in front.

Dutch Colonial style: Baroque (q.v.) style of the Dutch settlers who colonized New Amsterdam (later part of New York State).

Dutch lace: pillow lace (q.v.) made from the 1660s, tightly woven and solid looking, often with closely grouped scrolls suggesting heavy flower heads. The grounds included the *cinq trous*. Huguenot refugees brought to Dutch lace something of the old Valenciennes (q.v.) style.

Dutch metal: alloy of copper and zinc used in place of gold-leaf in decoration.

Dutch oven: a curved, open-fronted oven, usually raised on legs, placed before the fire. Dutch ovens were made of sheet-iron on brass and reflected heat on to the joint of meat, which hung from a hook in the hood. Used from the 16th cent.

Dutch striking clock: one which strikes the repetition of the hour at the half-hour on a different toned bell.

Duty mark: sovereign's head mark, the English equivalent of the French charge and discharge marks (qq.v.) indicating that the duty on gold or silver had been paid. In use between 1784 and 1890.

Duty stamp on wallpaper: by an Act of Queen Anne (1712) every square yard of wallpaper 'printed painted or stained' was subject to a tax of 1d, increased two years later to 1½d; the excise officer had to stamp the paper with the appropriate stamp and attended the factories regularly for this purpose. The duty was repealed in 1836.

Dwight, John: (1633–1703), an English potter, who commenced experiments in the art of pottery (possibly in Lancashire) using local clays found in the Kennel pits at Haigh near Wigan. His first patent for making 'transparent earthenware commonly called porcellane or china' was granted for 14 years from April 1671, in which year he probably moved to Fulham. In 1676 he was in partnership in a 'Pottworks' at Fulham, with Windsor Sandys of St Martin's-in-the-Fields, and agreed to supply the Glass Sellers' Company with bottles. Sandys' name is omitted from the subsequent

agreement of 1677. In 1684 he took out a further patent which was the subject of lawsuits in 1693 and 1697 for infringement by potters in London, Southampton, Nottingham and Staffordshire. (See also Fulham stoneware.)

Dyottville Glass Works: an American glass factory founded in 1771 at Kensington, Pennsylvania, and taken over by T. W. Dyott in 1831. Products were coloured and pictorial glasses, bottles and tableware.

Eagle, American: the Seal of the United States, adopted in 1786, represents the American bald eagle with wings outspread. This emblem quickly became popular as a furniture ornament – carved (free or engaged), inlaid or painted – replacing the fanciful phoenix which had been used since the mid-18th cent.

Ear-dagger: a dagger with a pommel formed by two flattened discs set at an angle and resembling ears. This type of dagger is of Near Eastern origin and when found in Europe is usually Venetian or Spanish.

East, Edward: (1602–97), an English clock- and watchmaker of high repute. Clockmaker to Charles I and Charles II, he made the only known long-case night clock (q.v.).

Easter egg: see Fabergé, Peter Carl.

East India Company china: Chinese porcelain imported into Europe by European trading companies such as the East India Company or the French *Compagnie des Indes.*

Eastlake, Charles Lock: (1836–1906), influential English architect and designer and author of *Hints on Household Taste in Furniture, Upholstery & Other Details.* It was published in

London in 1868 and in Boston in 1872, giving impetus to the Art movement and advocating sparsely decorated, functional furniture. His theories found greatest acceptance in the United States where, in the 1870s and 1880s, a style of furniture based on the examples of the English Gothic was known as the Eastlake style. Herter Bros (q.v.) were manufacturers of furniture in the Eastlake style.

Ébéniste: the French term for a cabinet-maker (q.v.) concerned in making veneered furniture as distinct from a *menuisier* (q.v.), who specialized in carved or turned decoration. The word derives from the ebony (*ébène*) to be found on the earliest veneered furniture in France.

Ebonize: the staining of wood, such as pear wood or, in America, maple, to look like ebony. Much practised in the late 17th and 19th cent.

Echinus moulding: a moulding of quarter round section.

Ecuelle: a French form of shallow, circular soup bowl and cover occasionally also found in English silver. It has flat handles at the sides and a circular dish stand. Late 17th to mid-18th cent.

Edkins, Michael: Michael Edkins was a painter of pottery and of white and coloured glass. He received the freedom of the city of Bristol on 21 February 1756, but prior to that time is said to have served an apprenticeship in Birmingham. In 1755 he married Elizabeth, daughter of William James, a glassmaker, and it is not unexpected that he should have turned his hand to decorating that ware. He would seem to have started to paint glass soon after 1760, and to have continued at least until 1787,

probably in a freelance capacity for several firms.

The glass decorated by Michael Edkins is unsigned, and much that is claimed as his is the subject of dispute. W. A. Thorpe wrote (*English Glass*, 1949, page 206) that 'Edkins is known for his characteristic perched birds and his intense curly flower-bunches'.

Edouart, Augustin: (1789–1861), silhouettist of French origin who worked in England and America.

Egg, Durs: the first of a family of gunmakers of Swiss extraction, working in London in the late 18th and first half of the 19th cent. He was a noted maker of high quality flintlock duelling pistols and received the Royal Warrant of the Prince Regent, later George IV. His productions are highly efficient but devoid of ornament.

Egg-and-dart ornament: a border ornament composed of alternating ovolos (q.v.) and arrowheads. Of Classical origin, this motif was used by furniture makers, goldsmiths, etc., from the late 16th cent. onwards.

Egg-and-tongue ornament: repeat ornament of alternated ovolo and tongue-like motifs of Classical origin, it was first adopted during the Renaissance and was much used by architects and craftsmen from the 17th cent.

Eggshell porcelain: porcelain of extreme thinness, first made in China (hard paste). Thin bodied white bowls of Yung ho (1403–24), with faint incised or slip-painted designs, were copied in the K'ang Hsi (q.v.) period. (See *Famille rose*.) Some modern Japanese porcelains are eggshell thin. Some English factories in the 19th cent., such as Mintons, Belleek (qq.v.) and others, emulated this Chinese porcelain and produced wares of extreme thinness, finished on the lathe.

Egyptian black: the popular name in Staffordshire for the 'dry' black

stoneware named by Josiah Wedgwood 'basaltes' (q.v.). Also called
black Egyptian.

Elbow chair: see Carver.

Electric lamp: in 1879 the American,
Thomas Alva Edison, invented the
electric light bulb and domestic
lighting by electricity soon became a
practicality. Oil-light fittings were
adapted and transformed and new
designs devised. L. C. Tiffany (q.v.)
was one of the most imaginative
designers to apply the decorative style
of Art Nouveau (q.v.) to lamps.

Electro-gilding: a process invented
c. 1840 for gilding a metal surface by
electrical deposition. The process was
patented in 1845 and quickly replaced
mercury gilding. (See also Electroplate.)

Electroplate: The coating of a base
metal with silver or gold by electrical
deposition. The base metal object to
be plated is the cathode; the anode is
pure silver or gold. Both are placed in a
solution of potassium cyanide, through
which the electric current passes,
transferring the silver or gold on to the
base metal object. British electroplated articles are marked E.P.B.M.
for electroplated Britannia metal (q.v.)
E.P.G.S. for electroplated German
silver (q.v.); E.P.N.S. for electroplated
nickel silver (q.v.). American electroplate is often marked in four grades
determined by the quantity of silver
used: Standard Plate, Extra Plate,
Double Plate and Triple Plate.

In 1840 the electroplate process was
patented by Elkington & Co. (q.v.). In
the United States the first successful
electroplater was J. O. Mead (q.v.) in
1845. In Britain and the United States
electroplating had supplanted the work
of the Sheffield platers and Britannia
metal manufacturers by 1850.

Electrotype: a copy achieved by
electrical deposition. It was used to
make facsimiles of antique and new
objects. A metal cast was made of the
object to be copied and from this a
negative mould. The metal, usually
copper, was transferred by electrical

deposition on to this. The process was
developed in the 1830s and exploited
commercially by Elkington & Co.
(q.v.). (See also Electroplate.)

Elers, David (1656–1742); **Elers,
John Philip** (1664–1738): brothers
from Danzig, originally silversmiths,
who came to England in the 1680s and
set up as potters. David Elers was
born in Amsterdam. He started making
pottery at Fulham about 1690, and in
1693 he was cited, with others, for an
infringement of John Dwight's (q.v.)
patent. He appears to have worked a
potworks at Vauxhall from 1693 until
1700 and kept a shop in the Poultry,
London. In 1700 the two Elers became
bankrupt. David Elers subsequently
continued as a merchant.

John Philip Elers is rather more fully
documented. With his brother he was
associated in the manufacture of
'brown muggs and theapotts' in
England from about 1690, and was
cited by Dwight for an infringement
of his patent and for enticing from his
service a workman named John
Chandler. The brothers then opened
the factory at Vauxhall, which was in
operation until the Elers' bankruptcy.
Many red teapots were made there.

About 1693 one or both of the Elers
came to North Staffordshire and
started to make red teapots. It is unlikely in view of the continuity of the
London factory that both brothers
would venture north, and as David
Elers is known to have kept a shop in
the Poultry it seems likely that it was
John Philip Elers who started up in
Staffordshire, probably in their joint
names. It was at Bradwell Wood that
Elers made 'Red China'. Simeon
Shaw mentioned two sites, Bradwell
Hall and Dimsdale Hall. This Staffordshire venture lasted five years.

There is no evidence that the Elers
made salt-glazed stoneware other than
'brown muggs' or that they introduced the salt-glazing technique into
Staffordshire. They were justly famous
for red stonewares which vary in
colour from a rich red-brown to
vermilion, are close in texture, and are
thinly potted and fine in workmanship.
The precision finish of the Elers
products was a portent of industrial

standards set up by Josiah Wedgwood sixty years later. The Elers decorations comprised beautifully spaced plum blossom springs in relief; countersunk relief chinoiseries, and moulds of merry-andrews (clowns) and wyverns (birds).
Marks:

None of the Elers' ware was marked in an identifiable manner. Imitation Chinese marks were stamped underneath their products, but the square stamps enclosing English initials written pseudo-Chinese fashion occur only on later Elers-type red pottery, some probably by Greatbach for Wedgwood (who produced a jasper cameo medallion of J. P. Elers.)

Elkington & Co.: a firm founded in Birmingham by the partnership of George Richards Elkington (1800–65) and his cousin, Henry Elkington (*c.* 1810–52), which began in 1824. They were the pioneers and patent holders in 1840 of the process of electroplating (q.v.). In 1841 they took out a patent covering the electrotype (q.v.) process. From 1842 until 1864 the Birmingham branch traded under the name of Elkington, Mason & Co. The London branch, opened in 1829, traded as Elkington & Co. after 1848. Their techniques and stylistic innovations were widely followed in Britain and the United States.

Ell: the ell (*Fr. aune*) is the measure used for tapestry. The English ell is 1.14 m (45 in), the Flemish (*el*) 0.69 m

(27 in), the French 1.187 m (46¾ in). Thus 12 Flemish ells are approximately 7 French, or a square French ell equals 3 square Flemish ells.

Ellicott, John: (1706–72), London clockmaker of eminence and fellow of the Royal Society. The inventor of the Ellicott clock pendulum (q.v.).

Ellicott clock pendulum: a type of pendulum invented in 1752, utilizing the principle of the difference in the expansion between steel and brass. The heavy bob is carried on two angular hinged supports. As the length of the pendulum rod changes with the temperature, the vertical arms of the support are raised or depressed, giving a complementary movement to the horizontal arms carrying the heavy bob.

Email ombrant: an illusionist style of decoration on pottery, like lithophane (q.v.), but the intaglio (q.v.) decoration was filled with coloured transparent glaze (usually green) which produced a monochrome picture in a variety of tones.

Embossed wallpapers: known in the 18th cent. as 'Stamp'd' or 'Embost' wallpapers. Description given to an after process involving the use of block or roller under pressure which gives to the paper an embossed finish resembling leather, textiles or plaster. Embossing was practised at an early date although it is not known when it was first introduced (see 'Stucco' wallpapers). In 1829 the device for embossing and twilling papers was patented in England by Tom Cobb.

Embossing: a general term to describe reliefwork on metal. Strictly applicable only to work hammered on the reverse side (*repoussé*) but extended to cover any technical method resulting in relief.

Embroidered pictures: a great variety of embroidered pictures is found in England from the mid-17th cent. onwards. Pictorial compositions as part of the decoration of a cushion or valance are not uncommon earlier, but it was not until about 1640 that the fashion for working purely decorative pictures as an end in itself was evolved. Subjects from the Old Testament were most popular, also allegorical figures of the Virtues, Vices or the Senses, or a King and a Queen. Stumpwork (q.v.) was the most popular medium for pictures during the second half of the 17th cent., but beadwork (q.v.) was also employed.

The pictures of the early 18th cent. are generally worked on canvas and pastoral or 'chinoiserie' (q.v.) subjects are most common. During the second half of the 18th cent. subjects were mostly taken from popular paintings or engravings. The designs were either printed or drawn on the material. Portions of the background and the faces and hands of the figures were painted in watercolours and the rest of the design worked in coloured silks. Other pictures were worked in black silk, or even hair, in fine stitches, to simulate etchings. Simple landscape subjects or portraits of eminent people are most common.

Empire style: style current in France in the early 19th cent., during the period of the first Empire. It was a style based on Classical forms, overlaid with Egyptian motifs, and characterized by the use of gilt ornament on furniture and decorative features such as the Napoleonic N, laurel wreaths, sphinxes and swans.

Enamel: a form of glass which, when heated, may be applied by fusion to a metallic surface. When colourless this is known as flux. Enamel may be translucent or opaque; opalescent enamel is the term most frequently used to describe the milky semi-transparency which is obtainable by a careful mixture of both.

Painted enamels: opaque enamel on a metal base, fired to achieve a smooth glossy surface which was then decorated with the brush in variously coloured enamel pastes, each colour being fixed by a separate firing. In England, painted enamel was made at the Battersea factory (q.v.) and in South Staffordshire in the second half of the 18th and in the 19th cent.

In the 19th cent. the Swiss perfected the technique of painting extremely highly finished scenes and pictures in enamel on a prepared *fondant* ground. Very often a coating of counter-enamel is applied on the reverse side of the painted surface to counteract any stress which may be brought about in the firing.

En plein enamelling: the enamelling most typical of the Louis XV and Louis XVI periods is known as *en plein*, which indicates that the colour has been applied directly on the body of the object and not on *plaquettes* introduced at a later stage. The gold ground or field is prepared by being carved into and engraved to form a sunken bed, sometimes on several levels, to receive the enamel, the top layer of which should be flush with the gold surrounding surface. This operation is also known as *basse-taille* or *sur fond reservé* enamelling.

Cloisonné: one of the most ancient forms of enamelling involving the use of a network of raised metal enclosures, or *cloisons*, which is applied to the object chosen. The enamel is poured into these *cloisons*, the metal tops of which remain exposed, allowing the different colours in each one to be distinctly shown.

Champlevé enamelling: grooves, often in very graceful linear designs, are carved in the metal which is to be treated, and these are filled with enamel, which is polished down so that the top surface is exactly level with the surrounding metal. This inlaid enamel is thus, as the name of this technique implies, a raised field.

Plique à jour enamelling: the name given to the vivid stained-glass effects obtained when an object consists of an unbacked honeycomb of cells, each filled with translucent enamel through which the light passes freely.

En ronde bosse enamelling: the term applied to the opaque enamel, generally white, covering subjects carved in the round.

Coteau enamelling: a complicated process invented by Jean Coteau, the 18th-cent. Geneva craftsman, for which he used different coloured *motifs*, including red and green *paillons* as well as the more conventional gold variety against *bleu de Roi* translucent backgrounds, giving a vivid effect of relief.

En résille sur verre: a technique requiring great skill, practised in France for a very short period in the second quarter of the 17th cent. Miniature cases were enriched in this manner, whereby the design was cut or engraved on a medallion of blue or green glass, the hollows thus formed lined with thin gold and filled with powdered enamel, which would fuse at a low temperature.

Enamel colours: low-firing over-glaze ceramic pigments derived from metallic oxides such as copper, manganese, iron or antimony used singly, or combined with an opaque white and lead, zinc or some special flux, were extensively used from the middle of the 18th cent. A fine pink, crimson or crimson-purple was obtained from gold. During the 17th cent. a cheap form of enamelling was introduced in England and on the Continent in which brass was used as a base. The enamel was of the *champlevé* type, but instead of the depressions for the enamel being cut out by hand they were cast in one with the object. Such a method was unsuited for the production of small or fine objects, but it was applied to quite a variety of brassware, including andirons (q.v.), candlesticks (q.v.), stirrups and horse harness, and sword hilts. English enamelled brassware of this type usually goes by the name of 'Surrey' enamel, but there are no grounds for thinking that such articles were produced in the county of Surrey. Similar objects were made on the Continent; amongst the Continental items not made in England are small caskets and knife handles. The place of manufacture is not known, but it may have been in the Meuse region. (See also Enamel.)

Enamelled glass: glass painted in fusible colours or enamels, being metallic oxides mixed with fluxes and painted on in an oily medium. The painted glass is then fired in a muffle-kiln, the colours softening and adhering to the surface. The technique is of ancient origin and was re-discovered by Venetian craftsmen perhaps in the 15th cent. Much German glass of the late 16th and 17th cent. is decorated with vigorous enamelled painting and sometimes with unfired oil or lacquer colours. In England the practice was not adopted before the second half of the 18th cent. (See Beilby, William.)

En arbelette: (*Fr.*), an expression used for shapes and forms which have a double curve similar to that of a stone-bow.

Enarmes: the straps by which a shield was attached to the left arm of the wearer as a defensive weapon.

En camaieu: (*Fr.*), monochrome painting in several tones on porcelain pottery.

Encaustic tiles: the word encaustic, meaning baked or burnt, is frequently applied to Medieval inlaid tiles and the imitations made in the 19th cent.; and in consequence identified not with the firing process but erroneously with the technique of manufacture. Wedgwood (q.v.) decorated some of his black basaltes (q.v.) with white and red encaustic enamels after the style of Greek vases, and in 1769 he took out a patent for 'ornamenting earthen and porcelaine ware with an encaustic gold bronze, together with a peculiar species of encaustic painting in various colours in imitation of the antient Etruscan and Roman earthenware'.

Enclosed overlay paperweight: see Overlay paperweight.

Encoigneur: see Corner-cupboard.

Encrusted paperweights: see Sulphides.

End-boards: solid boards, often carved in profile, forming the supports of a Gothic stool or chest. Stools with the seat supported on two vertical end-boards were still made in the middle of the 16th cent. After this date, stools were constructed with joined frames consisting of frieze rail, legs and stretchers (q.v.).

End-of-day glass: small articles (e.g. bottles, jars, ornaments, bells) made by glass-workers over and above their normal production, in their own time.

Endive marquetry: see Seaweed marquetry.

En esclavage: (*Fr.*), a type of necklace consisting of strands which start and finish together but separate in the centre.

Engine-turning: (1) decorative process involving the turning of an unfired pot in the leather-hard state, upon a specially designed lathe having an eccentric motion to produce geometrical, diced, fluted or similar patterns. Used from *c.* 1764–5, by Wedgwood and other later potters. (2) the application of similar designs by mechanical means – also on a lathe – to metal articles. Mainly used on gold or silver snuff boxes (q.v.), étuis (q.v.) and watch-cases.

English dial: see Dial clock.

English four-glass clock: a small table clock in a wooden case with glass panels at the sides, back and top, introduced in the mid-19th cent.

English plate: a term used by Sheffield platers (see also Sheffield plate) to distinguish ware in which the silver was plated on copper from that plated on white alloy such as German silver (see Nickel silver).

English regulator clock: a long-case clock designed for highly accurate performance, with temperature compensated pendulum, jewelled pivots, etc. Introduced in the mid-18th cent.

Engobe: a thin coating or layer of clay applied to pottery in the liquid form of slip (q.v.).

Engraving: (1) a print on paper obtained by a process of incising lines into a metal plate with a burin or graver. (2) decoration of a metal object which involves incising the surface with a cutting tool. It is the normal method of rendering inscriptions and armorials and has been used at all periods for every variety of ornament. Sometimes combined with flat chasing (q.v.). (See also Bright-cut engraving).

En plein enamel: see Enamel.

En résille enamel: see Enamel.

En ronde bosse enamel: see Enamel.

Enseigne: see Hat badge.

En suite: (*Fr.*), to match; in a set.

Entrée dish: a covered dish of silver or plate (q.v.), early examples usually circular or polygonal. Later chiefly of oblong form or occasionally oval. The covers may have detachable handles, enabling their use as separate dishes. Later examples have silver or plated heater stands *en suite* (q.v.).

Epergne: a silver or porcelain table centrepiece of elaborate design incorporating numerous dishes for fruit or sweetmeats. Early examples also fitted with candle-branches, casters and other accessories. Rococo models were sometimes festooned with floral, pierced and boat-shaped forms, Chinese pagodas, and Classical temples. (See also Centre-piece.)

Equation clock dial: a dial that records both Solar and Mean time.

Equation kidney device: a kidney-shaped cam (q.v.), invented by Christiaan Huygens in 1695, which made possible the transformation of simple forward rotary motion on a clock into a backward or forward motion, varying daily, both in direction and amount, necessary to indicate the daily difference between Solar and Mean Time.

Erect thumbpiece: a tall, solid thumbpiece (q.v.) found on early 17th-cent. pewter (q.v.) flagons. A lighter, curving form is found on certain Scottish measures, notably tappit hens (q.v.).

Esari rugs: Turkoman rugs in which the octagonal gule (see Turkoman rugs) is usually enclosed by bands forming a distinct diamond design.

Escapement: the means, or device, by which the power of a time-piece is allowed to escape, and is transmitted to the pendulum or balance. Hundreds of types have been invented, but only a very few are in general use. The anchor or recoil escapement (q.v.) and the dead beat (q.v.) are types used in the majority of pendulum clocks; the lever escapement, the cylinder (q.v.), duplex (q.v.) and other types were used in watches. Great mechanical ingenuity has been shown by inventors in designing escapements. These technical features are of special importance in the study of watches.

Escape wheel: the final wheel of the time train (q.v.) of a clock or watch which gives impulse to the pendulum or balance. Often shortened to 'scape wheel.

Escritoire: see Scrutoire.

Escutcheon: a shield with a coat of arms. An escutcheon plate is the metal surround of a keyhole.

Espagnolette: (*Fr.*), a decorative motif popularized by the engravings of Gillot and Watteau, consisting of a female head surrounded by a large stiff lace collar of a type worn in Spain in the 17th cent. It was used frequently in the early 18th cent. as a mounted decoration for furniture.

Etagère: (*Fr.*), a small work-table consisting usually of shelves or trays set one above the other. The word is of 19th-cent. origin, the ordinary term used earlier being *table à ouvrage*. It was also called a whatnot.

Etched metalwork: the art of etching is believed to have originated in the process of ornamenting armour with acid etching first introduced in the second half of the 15th cent. In the 16th cent. small objects of iron, brass, copper, and even silver, were commonly decorated with etched ornament. This technique of ornament was particularly popular in Germany in the second half of the 16th cent., and was applied to a great variety of objects. In the case of small articles, such as cutlery, tools, watch cases, locks and scientific instruments, panels of Moresque ornament were used, the larger surfaces available on caskets or clock-cases were decorated with figure subjects. The finest etched ornament is to be found on the various tools, instruments and articles of military equipment made for the Saxon Court. Whether these were produced in

Dresden or obtained from Nuremberg or Augsburg, is uncertain. The etched ironwork of Nuremberg and Augsburg had an importance comparable with that of the damascened (q.v.) panels made in Milan. Etched ornament is also found on French and Italian lock-smiths' work but it does not approach the quality achieved by the German craftsmen.

Etching: a print made by covering a metal plate of copper or steel with a wax coat, drawing the design with a needle, and 'biting' the plate by immersion in a weak acid solution, generally nitric. When inked, the bitten lines hold the ink as the plate is wiped, and when an impression is taken the design is transferred, in reverse, to the paper. (See also Etched metalwork.)

Eternity ring: a ring in the form of a plain circle symbolizing eternity, often set with a single row of stones.

Etruria: in 1766 Josiah Wedgwood (q.v.) purchased the Ridge House Estate in Staffordshire and planned to build a new pottery, a house for himself, and a village for his workpeople. He appointed Joseph Pickford of Derby as his architect and the factory and Etruria Hall were completed by 1770.

Étui: small case usually of tapering form fitted with scissors, bodkin, snuff-spoon, etc., for ladies' use, made in a variety of materials, including gold, silver, pinchbeck (q.v.), enamel (q.v.), porcelain, etc.

European-style decoration: in the 18th cent. Chinese porcelains were enamelled to order with European heraldic emblems, and with many designs from European prints. K'ang Hsi blue-and-white and *famille verte* (q.v.) examples are uncommon, but subjects skilfully drawn in black or sepia, or with *famille rose* (q.v.) colour-ing, shortly became popular, and often show an amusing naïvety of inter-pretation. Large punch-bowls with ships, hunting scenes, etc., were favourites. Later wares exhibit the hybrid style of 'mandarin china'.

There are some close copies of European porcelain; and Chinese porcelain was also decorated in Holland or England, sometimes in Oriental style. (See also Chinese export porcelain.)

Ewer and dish or **basin:** used for finger-washing at table. Extant examples of silver from early 16th cent. onwards. Dishes were made usually circular or occasionally oval. Ewers were of various form, chiefly vase- or helmet-shape. Important pieces of decorative plate displayed the highest standards of ornament and design of their periods. Less important examples were made in other materials.

Exc. or **Excud.:** short for excudit or excuderunt. Means 'printed by' or 'engraved and printed by'. Sometimes seen on bird prints.

Exeter carpets: Claude Passavant, a native of Basel, and successful wool merchant and manufacturer at Exeter, started the subsidiary enterprise of making expensive hand-knotted car-pets. He bought up Parisot's equip-ment in 1755 (see Fulham carpets) and took many of his men to Exeter. In 1758 he was a competitor for the Royal Society of Arts prize and gained an award. A beautifully made and excellently designed carpet by him in the Victoria and Albert Museum is marked 'Exon 1757' and may be the prize-winning piece. Another dated 1758 is at Petworth. Giuseppe Baretti, secretary of the Royal Academy, wrote a favourable account of his factory in 1760 and reported on his success; but his carpets, which were more expensive than Moorfields (q.v.) are extremely rare.

Eyles, Henry: designer and manufacturer of English furniture in the mid-19th cent., established in Bath. His work is recognized by exaggerated, carved decoration.

Fabergé: born in 1846, Peter Carl Fabergé, a Russian descended from a Huguenot family in Picardy, was a jeweller who brought about an extraordinary revolution in taste in the final decade of the cent. In brief, he declared that valuable materials were of little importance where the craftsmanship was wanting. He delighted in overcoming technical problems and revived the four-colour gold processes of the 18th cent. as well as the forgotten art of translucent enamelling on a prepared *guilloché* (q.v.) field. He often designed, and always scrutinized at every stage, each piece made by his five hundred or so highly skilled craftsmen working in St Petersburg and Moscow. These pieces were of great variety and ranged from boxes, clocks and miniature frames to automatic toys and bell-pushes.

His work in every type of semi-precious stone remains unsurpassed, and his lively animal studies and miniature flowers, usually in rock crystal pots which are carved to appear as though they were half filled with water, are eagerly collected. Gold and silver cigarette cases by Fabergé display a seemliness of style and a precision of hinging rarely attained before or since. Apart from his completely original work, he enjoyed designing *pastiches* of earlier manners.

Fabergé is perhaps most celebrated for his fantastic procession of Easter Eggs, each with its own concealed surprise, made annually for the Tsar, his greatest patron, to present to the Tsarina. The House of Fabergé had an elaborate but easily understood system of signing the objects it produced. The firm ceased operating with the Revolution, and in 1920 Carl Fabergé himself died an exile in Switzerland.

'Fable' painter: an unidentified Chelsea artist, working *c.* 1750–5, who decorated tablewares with illustrations derived from the folio edition of *Aesop's Fables* (1687) by Francis Barlow. J. L. Dixon suggests there have been as many as three 'Fable' painters of whom one was J. H. O'Neale (q.v.).

Fabric paper: a type of wallpaper that imitates the texture of gold, silk, chintz, etc. Until the 1870s these papers were hand made, then machine-operated rotary brushes were introduced. Flowered silk designs were popular but the quality declined by the mid-19th cent. At the end of the Victorian period, satin papers, polished by rubbing with French chalk, were considered a major triumph.

Facet: one of the small surfaces of a cut gemstone or of other ground material such as glass, steel, etc., that has been cut into a series of faces set at an angle to each other.

Facet-cut stem: stem of a drinking glass, usually drawn (q.v.), decorated with cutting in the form of diamond or hexagonal facets (q.v.). A type of decoration popular in the second half of the 18th cent.

Façon de Venise: glassware made in the Venetian style by or under the direction of Venetian craftsmen living in other countries, from the 16th cent. The term is used also for 19th-cent. glass inspired by early Venetian designs.

Faenza maiolica: tin-glazed earthenware made at Faenza in Italy from the later 15th cent., the early wares often decorated in sombre colours with foliage of pronounced Gothic character. A speciality of Faenza at this period were devotional figures imitating enamelled terra cotta (q.v.). The Renaissance wares of the 16th cent. show a full range of colour, but towards the end of the cent. slighter painting and more subdued colouring reflects the interest in the cool blue-and-white Chinese porcelain that was reaching Europe in increased quantities.

Faience: a French word describing tin-glazed earthenware. Adopted in England in the 19th cent. to describe the larger units employed in architectural ceramics, and also for underglaze-decorated earthenware.

Faience fine: fine cream-coloured or white earthenware.

Faience Manufacturing Co.: Established in 1880 at Greenpoint, New York, this factory produced hard-paste porcelain (q.v.) under the name Royal Crown. Edward Lycett, a noted china painter, was superintendent and principal decorator.

'Fair Hebe' jug: a jug in the form of a tree with spreading base modelled in relief with figures of seated girl to whom a youth is offering a nest full of eggs, above which (on a paper) are the words 'FAIR HEBE' on one side; on the other a man holding a glass above which occur the words 'A BUMPER'. Sometimes signed 'Voyez 1788'.

A blue-and-white version has also the impressed mark ASTBURY (q.v.). The mark R.M.A. (Richard Meir Astbury) has been recorded. Modelled by John Voyez (q.v.).

Fairings: small porcelain groups sold at country fairs in the 19th cent. They were made mainly in Germany for the British market. They illustrated various situations connected with politics, animals, family and married life.

Falchion: a short, curved, single-edged sword, known as early as the 12th cent. The Medieval form had a broad, cleaver-like blade.

Fall: see under Burgonet.

Fall front: hinged, usually sloping, front of a bureau (q.v.) or writing desk supported on sliding rails or brackets to form a writing surface. Also called a drop front.

Falling table: see Drop-leaf table.

False bob pendulum: see Mock pendulum.

Famille jaune: see *Famille verte*.

Famille noire: Chinese porcelain of the K'ang Hsi period (q.v.) enamelled in *famille verte* (q.v.) style, generally 'on the biscuit', with dry black ground colour, made lustrous by a covering of green glaze. The large vases with superb floral designs have fetched great sums, encouraging forgeries and skilful redecoration of old pieces. Cups and bowls are less rare. A few marked examples are of the Yung Chêng period (q.v.).

Famille rose: a class of Chinese enamelled porcelain wares characteristic of the reigns of Yung Chêng and Ch'ien Lung (qq.v.) named after the prominent rose-pink introduced from Europe. The rose, blue and yellow were often thickened with opaque white. A new delicate painting style began to oust that of the *famille verte* (q.v.) about 1720, and was applied especially to plates, bowls and cups and saucers of 'eggshell' thin porcelain. The 'ruby-black' variety is coloured deep rose-pink on the reverse. Frequently painted subjects are scenes with ladies and children, birds or flowers, often framed in elaborate diapered borders. Pieces with European figure subjects, often imitated from engravings, were made to order for export. Many Ch'ien Lung and later wares employ the *famille rose* enamels, but with diminishing delicacy and taste.

Famille verte: a large family of Chinese porcelain wares of the K'ang Hsi period (q.v.) painted in a harmonious palette of brilliant green and red, yellow, aubergine-purple and violet-blue enamels, the strong iron-red being almost as characteristic as the green. The blue enamel replaces the underglaze blue of the late Ming (q.v.) and 17th-cent. 'five-colour' palette. The full range of colours were not always used. To heighten the effect, gilding was sometimes added. The paste of these wares is fine, white and excellently potted, and a great variety of plant, landscape, animal, and romantic or historical figure subjects, as well as emblematic designs and elaborate borders and panel work, were employed in their decoration. The best examples exhibit superb painting on the finest materials, but others were only sketchily executed. A more delicate style appears towards the end of the reign, e.g. on the Imperial 'birthday' plates, foreshadowing the *famille rose* (q.v.) wares. The rarer examples with yellow or black grounds are known as *famille jaune* and *famille noire* (q.v.), and there are wares with celadon or coffee-brown grounds, or in the 'powdered blue' surround. Imitations of Japanese 'Imari' porcelains (q.v.) should also be mentioned.

Fan-back chair: see Windsor chair.

Fan blade: the lower ornamental part of an inner stick of a fan. Known also as a brin.

Fancy chair: an American term for almost any variety of decorative occasional chair, generally light in weight, painted, and with a cane seat.

Fan guard: the two outer sticks of a fan between which the mount (q.v.) is folded. The guard consists of three sections, the handle end, the shoulder which extends to the lower edge of the mount, and the guard proper.

Fan mounts: known also as leaves, unite and cover the upper part of the sticks of folding fans, and might consist of vellum, chicken skin (q.v.), silk, lace or paper. The mount was usually double so that each side of the fan could display ornament.

Fan pivot: a pin or rivet passing through the handle end of the fan sticks joining them together to swing on a pivot. On fine fans the pivot was set with jewels such as diamonds, pearls, rubies, sapphires, opals. Less costly gems were also used. In quizzing fans (q.v.) a tiny spy glass also swung at the pivot. The metal loop for the attachment of a ribbon or cord was introduced after 1816. Such a loop might be added to an earlier fan.

Fan sticks: the principal parts of a fan extending from the pivot (q.v.) to the perimeter of the mount. As a rule early Charles II sticks were deeply shouldered and widely spaced and sparsely decorated: later they touched. In this detail period characteristics overlapped and hybrid varieties are numerous. In the early 18th cent. they became straight without a visible shoulder, with ornament still complete on each stick and never carried over from one stick to another. Several designs might ornament the sticks of a single fan. As the cent. advanced fans became more and more elaborately decorated with carving, painting, staining, gilding and piercing, the design being carried out on two, three or four sticks and finally across the entire fan.

Farthingale chair: a type of chair evolved during the reign of James I to accommodate the farthingale or hooped dress, with a comparatively wide and high seat and no arms. It was usually upholstered in Turkey work (q.v.) or velvet.

Fausse-montre: (*Fr.*), a sham watch sometimes worn to balance the real watch on what was known as the Macaroni or hookless châtelaine (q.v.), fashionable at the end of the 18th cent. These hookless châtelaines were of gold, with two ends hanging down, from which a watch and a *fausse-montre* could be suspended.

Fauteuil: a French armchair, less embracing in form than the *bergère* (q.v.), as the sides are not upholstered.

Favrile glass: a type of iridescent glass made in America from 1880 by Louis Comfort Tiffany (q.v.). It was later produced elsewhere.

Fazackerley flowers: delftware (q.v.) decorated with bold floral ornament in polychrome – green, dark blue, brick red and bright yellow – has been identified as of Liverpool origin, on the traditional evidence supplied by a mug with the initials and date 'T.F. 1757' said to have been made by Thomas Shaw of Liverpool for Thomas Fazackerley.

Feather banding: see Herring-bone banding.

Feather-edge ornament: decoration of edge of silver spoon and fork handles with chased, slanting lines. (See also Table service.)

Feather fans: an early Victorian vogue. These fans, painted and embroidered with feathers, with pierced sticks (q.v.) of ivory, were imported from China and sold in England at about twenty shillings each.

Federal style: a term often used in America to describe furniture made in the United States between 1789 and 1830, the early days of the Republic. It includes works showing Hepplewhite, Sheraton, Directoire and early Empire influence.

Fede ring: a ring in the form of a band terminating in joined hands, often holding a heart or a precious stone.

Feeding cup: small, plain, saucepan-like cup with one or two handles and curved or straight spout designed for child or invalid feeding. Found from mid-17th cent. onwards. Also called 'Spout-cup'.

Felletin tapestry: see under Aubusson tapestry.

Felspar china: a felspathic china made by the younger Josiah Spode (q.v.) *c.* 1820, marked 'Felspar Porcelain' within a wreath beneath the name SPODE, transfer-printed (q.v.) in purple.

Felspathic glazes: those containing felspar rock, an essential ingredient of porcelain glazes; but used also on stonewares.

'Female archer': subject of 'Pratt' type (q.v.) jugs and earthenware figures intended as satire upon the smart archery parties popular in 'high' society, 1800–50. Sometimes known as the Fair Toxophilite.

Fender: low, solid or pierced, metal-work guard in front of a hearth to protect the flooring from sparks. Introduced in the late 18th cent.

Fenton, Christopher Weber: In 1947, the producer of the first parian ware (q.v.) in America, and his company in Vermont became the largest manufacturing organization of this ware in the States, both copying English designs and creating several purely American pieces. The factory closed for financial reasons in 1858.

Feraghan carpets: Persian carpets woven with a Sehna (q.v.) knot, which have enjoyed great popularity in this country, and vary slightly in the treatment of the traditional Herat (q.v.) design.

Ferronière: a narrow chain or band encircling the forehead, Renaissance-style. It was worn in the late Georgian and early Victorian period, particularly 1837–44.

Ferrule: cap fitted over the end of a walking-stick to strengthen it and to prevent the wood or cane from splitting. Also the strengthening ring by which the head is attached to the stick.

Festoon (or **swag**): Renaissance ornament, popular thereafter in various forms, consisting of looped flowers, or fruit, and leaves.

Fetter chain: a chain worn as an ornament with long-shaped links.

Fiddle back: chair back with the central splat (q.v.) in the form of a violin.

Fiddle pattern spoons: see Table services.

Fiddler jug: a rare type of early toby jug (q.v.) representing a seated figure playing the fiddle, probably made by Astbury (q.v.). (See also Midshipmen jugs.)

Fielded panel: a raised panel with bevelled edges found on drawer fronts of 17th-cent. oak dressers, etc.

Fielding, S., & Co.: a pottery works in Staffordshire founded in 1870 that produced terra cotta and tin-glazed earthenware (qq.v.) for domestic use. In 1880s 'majolica argenta' – a white-glazed ware decorated with bright colours and raised designs – was introduced. Marks vary; examples are FIELDING (impressed) and SF & Co.

Figure: the natural pattern in a wood. The introduction of the use of veneers (q.v.) in cabinet-making made it possible to exploit the full figure and texture of woods such as walnut, mahogany, yew, elm, mulberry, laburnun and many others.

Figure jugs: see Toby jugs.

Filigree: ornament in metalwork, resembling lace, made from fine wirework. It was popular in the 17th cent. and again in the 19th when many of the articles thus decorated were imported.

Filigree paper work: throughout the 18th cent. filigree was a popular amateur ornament for small cabinets, calling for neat fingers and considerable patience.

The ornament entirely covered the main panels of the cabinet, creating pictorial designs and arabesque (q.v.) patterns in an effect of metal filigree. This was achieved solely with tiny rolls of paper arranged so that they projected edgeways from their background. To complete the effect, they were gilded or coloured on their exposed edges.

Fillet: a narrow strip of wood, especially between mouldings or the flutes of a column.

Fillings: a term used in lace-making, synonymous with the French term *à jours*, to describe the fancy open stitches introduced in the pattern spaces in both needlepoint and pillow laces (qq.v.).

Fine drawings: a term used in lace-making, synonymous with French *point de raccroc*, to describe the delicate work of joining lengths of lace net.

Finial: an ornamental projection or knob. Found on furniture, sometimes carved in the form of an antique vase with drapery or an acorn, forming a decorative motif on the top of such pieces as knife case (q.v.) or pole-screens. Similarly used by the goldsmith in a variety of forms such as human figures on covered cups and spoons or in the more familiar urn, acorn or pineapple shape on sugar casters, coffee pots (q.v.), etc.

Fireback: a slab of cast-iron, sometimes referred to as a 'reredos', standing at the back of the fireplace, protecting the wall and reflecting the heat of the burning fuel. Firebacks were made by the simple means of pouring the molten metal on to a prepared bed of sand in which a pattern had been impressed. The patterns were carved in wood, and were either of a full-sized design or in the form of single ornaments which were composed into a whole to suit the taste of the maker or his client.

The iron firebacks of Sussex are the best-known English ones, but many were imported from Holland late in the 17th cent. and onwards. It is often difficult to determine the origin of one from another; the firebacks with scenes from the Bible or mythological subjects are usually said to have been of Dutch make, but these were copied in England and there is no certainty on the point. In Holland the castings were made thinner than in England, but this feature also was adopted here. The earliest English firebacks were of a wide, low shape, but by the mid-17th cent. tall ones, of 'tombstone' style, were introduced.

Fire dogs: see Andirons.

Fire forks: an instrument made of wrought-iron, some 1 m (4 ft) or more in length in order that the user would be away from the heat when moving burning logs in the hearth. Usually it had two stout prongs, but some examples have a spike at one side about three-quarters of the way down from the handle. The fire fork was the forerunner of the poker, and it went out of general use when coal replaced wood.

Fire irons: set of implements for the fire, comprising tongs, a poker and shovel. In the 18th cent. they were generally of burnished iron or steel and were often made to match the fender (q.v.). Later sets often included a hearth brush.

Fire mark: stain on silver caused by annealing (q.v.). It may be removed by polishing or filing. Also, cast-iron badge issued by fire insurance companies in Britain and the United States.

Fire-polishing: reheating of finished glassware at the furnace mouth to obliterate marks left by tools and produce a smooth, even surface.

Fire screen: an adjustable screen made from the end of the 17th cent. to give protection from the intense heat of large open fires. Two main kinds were used. (a) Pole screen: with the screen on an upright supported on a tripod base; (b) horse or cheval screen (q.v.) – two uprights, each on two legs, enclosing a panel. Elaborate carving and gilding of the crests was often found until the end of the 18th cent., when lighter and simpler screens were in vogue. Needlework was the popular material for the panel.

Firing glass: also known as hammering glass. Used for thumping the table as a form of acclamation when drinking toasts, etc. The glass was necessarily heavy, with drawn bowl on thick stem and heavy, flat foot.

Fisher, Alexander: (1864–1936), English painter, sculptor and craftsman best known for his enamelwork. In 1896 he was appointed head of the enamelling section of the Central School of Arts and Crafts in London. His silver with Celtic-inspired decoration excited a strong influence on the design of Cymric and his technique of giving enamels a base of foil was much copied.

Fish knife and fork: introduced in the early 19th cent. to avoid contaminating the taste of fish with steel of an ordinary knife. (Stainless steel was not invented until the 20th cent.) The knife has a blunt blade.

Flag finial: finial (q.v.) carved in the form of flame, found especially on 18th-cent. American furniture.

Flagon: large vessel for serving wine or other liquors. Pear-shaped and cylindrical bodies occur contemporaneously at most periods and are always closely related in form and decoration to tankards. Except for ecclesiastical use, the flagon is rare after the 18th cent.

Flag seat: an American term sometimes used to describe a chair seat woven of rush.

Flambé glazes: glazes found on Chinese ceramics in which kiln conditions produce variegated colour effects, e.g. on some Chün porcelain (q.v.) wares of the Sung dynasty, the 18th-cent. copper-red wares, and on Canton stonewares. This effect was copied in the late 19th cent. by artist potters in Europe and America.

Flanders chest: chest with elaborate carved decoration imported into Britain from the Netherlands in the 16th and 17th cent.

Flashed glass: glass with a 'flash' of colour, made by dipping the newly blown but cooled glass shape in molten coloured glass. This was then sometimes decorated by cutting or etching. The technique was widely used in the 19th cent. to produce inexpensive decorative glassware.

Flat chasing: surface decoration in low relief on precious metal, produced by hammering with small blunt tools. The characteristic feature of the process is that no metal is removed.

Flat cutting: see Panel cutting.

Flat-iron: sad-irons, as they are called in the United States, were used from the 15th cent. onwards for pressing clothes. They are generally of cast iron and they were heated against the bars of a stove, by an iron block heated at the stove and inserted in a box body or by hot embers placed in a similar cavity.

Flattened knop: see Annulated knop.

Flatware: metal articles of flattened form, especially spoons, forks and other gold, silver and plated eating and serving implements.

Flaxman, John, R. A.: (1755–1826), born at York, son of a moulder of plaster casts, with premises in Covent Garden, London. He exhibited models at the Free Society of Artists in 1767 and 1769, and in 1770 won a silver medal at the Royal Academy. From 1775 until 1787 he modelled reliefs for Wedgwood's jasper wares such as the well known 'Dancing Hours' and 'Apotheosis of Homer', and figures. He spent seven years in Italy from 1787, studying art, and while there he executed designs for Dante's *Divina Commedia* (1797), Homer (1793) and Aeschylus (1795), marble groups of 'The Fury of Athamas' and 'Cephalus and Aurora', and works for Wedgwood (q.v.). He also designed presentation and domestic silver for Rundell (q.v.). He was elected R. A. in 1800, and Professor of Sculpture to the Royal Academy in 1810.

Flemish tapestry: the term Flemish or Netherlands tapestry, as distinct from French, is only applicable after the fall of the Burgundian dukes in 1477 (for earlier tapestry see Franco-Burgundian). Flanders, Brabant and Hainault, which included the famous tapestry cities of Tournai, the ruined Arras, and the rising Brussels, were then ruled for the Habsburgs by Mary, Governess of the Netherlands, and in 1515 came under Charles V's empire. The Netherlands and France grew further and further apart, and Flemish tapestry became distinct in style and workmanship from French.

Brussels (q.v.) was already in the first decade of the 16th cent. the leading tapestry city, but there were also Bruges, Antwerp, Tournai (q.v.), Oudenarde and Enghien. The late Medieval period was famous for its religious tapestries, finely woven with much silk and lavish use of gold and silver thread; many were made on a very large scale. Brussels was certainly the principal centre for these, but some were probably made at Bruges. Antwerp, a great seaport, was also a principal market, but tapestries were made there, and the 1544 laws prohibited its use of the Brussels mark

(though not wholly successfully). Antwerp catered especially for foreign markets in the 17th and 18th cent., England included (see Wauters family). Tournai, with high-warp looms, continued to produce pastoral and other subjects in Late Gothic style, which are often mistaken for French weaving. Its decline in the 16th cent. was rapid, and indeed the terrible religious wars severely affected the Flemish looms. The revival inaugurated by the Archduke Albert and Isabella in 1606 was furthered by the renown of Rubens and Jordaens, who both designed celebrated tapestries, and by the Exhibition Gallery established at Brussels in 1655.

Meanwhile at Oudenarde and Enghien a steady stream of less pretentious tapestries were woven and the former remained famous for its *verdures* (q.v.), adapting its style in the latter part of the 17th cent. to landscape *verdures*, which were popular throughout the 18th cent. During the 16th, 17th and 18th cent. the most widely commercialized tapestry was Flemish. It included many different qualities and never ceased to produce masterpieces under special patronage. From Flemish cities weavers were recruited for the several dozen factories that rose and fell in almost every European country.

Flight and Barr; Flight, Barr and Barr: see Worcester porcelain.

Flint glass: now termed lead crystal, flint glass was developed by George Ravenscroft (q.v.), who was granted a seven-year patent (No. 176) in May 1674, to make a glass in which the silica was derived from calcined flints. In 1675 he first used lead oxide as a flux in place of vegetable potash. This produced a glass denser, heavier, softer, and with greater refractive brilliance than anything previously made. Flint-glass vessels, if flicked with a finger, emit a resonant tone.

Flintlock gun: a type of gun lock developed from the snaphaunce (q.v.) in the first quarter of the 17th cent. It is fitted with a pan (holding priming powder round the touch-hole), with a hinged cover from which rises a flat steel. When the gun is discharged, a specially shaped flint, held in the jaws of a spring-operated cock, strikes the steel, throwing it and the pan cover back, and at the same time sending a shower of sparks into the priming.

In its earliest form this lock had a horizontal scear, the tip of which projected through the lockplate and engaged with a projection on the heel of the cock, holding the latter back until released by the trigger. There was no half-cock (safety position), although on English locks this was provided by a dog catch, a small pivoted hook which engaged in a notch at the rear of the cock. The flintlock proper, with a vertical scear engaging in one of two notches in an internal tumbler, giving respectively half- and full-cock, appears to have been invented in France about 1610–15, possibly by Marin le Bourgeoys of Lisieux (d. 1634). This form became increasingly popular and virtually superseded all others in the second half of the 17th cent., remaining in use until well into the 19th. A special type of flintlock used in Spain and Southern

Italy was the *miquelet*, which had an external mainspring and a scear operating through the lockplate.

Flitcroft, Henry: (1697–1769), described by George Vertue, the engraver: 'Mr Flitcroft was a Joyner – now Architect'. He became a protégé of the Earl of Burlington (q.v.) and was among those early 18th-cent. Palladian (q.v.) architects who were interested in the furnishing of their buildings.

Flock paper: a type of wallpaper in which powdered wool is applied to the paper on which the design is first printed, painted or stencilled with a slow-drying adhesive. The process was known to Antiquity and especially associated with early cloth-workers. At the 1862 International Exhibition flock-upon-flock was shown, the design standing out in heavy relief.

Flock prints: known in French as *empreintes veloutées* and occasionally referred to as *samt-teigdrucke*. They were printed from ordinary black-line wood-blocks on which a glutinous ink or paste had been used. Before the ink dried the impression was sprinkled with powdered colour which gave it a velvety surface.

Flowered glasses: trade name for wine glasses engraved with naturalistic flowers on the bowl, popular in the mid-18th cent.

Flower stand: see China-stand.

Flown blue decoration: a method of decorating porcelain with an under-glaze transfer-printed effect in which the design melts into the surrounding glaze with a kind of coloured halo, caused by firing in an atmosphere containing volatile chlorides. Flown blue effects were popular in mid-Victorian times. Other colours, such as brown, green and yellow are subject to the same treatment but have been little used.

Flushed glass: glass with a slight 'flush' of colour produced by coating the newly blown glass with coloured glass dust and firing. An Art Nouveau (q.v.) technique.

Flute glass: a drinking glass with a tall, deep conical bowl, popular in the Netherlands in the 17th cent.

Fluting: a decorative form consisting of parallel concave channels found on Classical columns, used in close repeated formation as a border or body ornament. Found extensively on bodies of silver cups, tankards and other vessels in late 17th cent. alternating with gadroons (q.v.) to form corrugated surface. Also used as a decorative motif on furniture, particularly in the last quarter of the 18th cent. (See also Reeding.)

Fob: a decorative attachment to a pocket watch, or the pocket in which it is carried, or a lady's small pendant watch.

Foil: a thin sheet of metal placed behind a gem in a collet setting (q.v.) to strengthen its colour.

Folded foot: the foot of a drinking glass where the rim has been folded under while hot, forming a selvage and giving extra strength to a part most likely to become chipped in use.

Folding table: 'folding' tables appear in inventories of the 14th cent. but it is not known for what purpose they were used. The folding table had one fixed and one hinged leaf and when closed, the table had the hinged leaf resting on the fixed top. In modern usage a folding table is sometimes incorrectly described as a credence (q.v.) table.

Foliot: the earliest form of controller in a mechanical clock. Always found with a verge escapement (q.v.). The balance wheel and, especially later, the pendulum so improved time-keeping that it is very rare to find a clock with its original foliot.

Folwell, John: (fl. 1775) Philadelphia master cabinet-maker of the Chippendale school. Just before the Revolution, Folwell solicited subscriptions for his proposed book of American furniture drawings, entitled *The Gentleman and Cabinet-maker's Assistant.* In consequence, he is sometimes called 'the Chippendale of America'.

Fond chant: (*Fr.*), a term used to describe a six-pointed star lace ground found in so-called *point de Paris* lace (q.v.), English Midland laces, and trolly lace, Chantilly lace (qq.v.), etc.

Fond clair: (*Fr.*), a term used in lace-making, synonymous with *fond simple*, to describe the mesh ground found in Lille lace (q.v.), with four sides formed of two twisted threads and two sides of crossed threads. This sometimes suggests diamond rather than hexagonal meshes, depending on the tightness of the work.

Fondeurs, Corporation des: (*Fr.*), the craft guild in France responsible for casting and chasing metal, either for sculpture, furniture or *bronzes d'ameublement* (q.v.). It was organized similarly to those of the *menuisiers-ébénistes* (q.v.) and *doreurs* (q.v.).

Food warmer: a composite article of pottery or porcelain, usually from 229 to 305 mm (9 in to 12 in) high, consisting of a hollow pedestal into which a covered bowl with a projecting flange nests. Within the pedestal, which has an arched opening at the bottom on one side, there is a cup or container (godet) which fits into a raised verge on the base. Food warmers were made in delftware, salt-glazed stoneware (qq.v.), and earthenware, at Leeds, Swansea and in Staffordshire, 18th and 19th cent.

Footing: upper edge of a piece of lace.

Footman: the name given to a four-legged trivet (q.v.) made to stand in front of the fire in the sitting room or parlour. They were made of wrought iron or brass, or partly of each, and commonly had front legs of cabriole design. The top was often pierced with a central hole so that it could be carried. The footman dates from the second half of the 18th cent. onwards.

Forestier, Étienne Jean and **Pierre Auguste** (1755–1838): French sculptors, brothers, the sons of Étienne Forestier (c. 1712–68). All three were *fondeurs-ciseleurs* (bronze casters – see *Fondeurs, Corporation des*), and after the father's death his widow carried on the business with her two sons. Their names constantly occur in the Royal accounts, and they are known to have worked at Versailles and Compiègne, and for the Prince de Condé. After the Revolution, Pierre Auguste established a successful workshop, supplying furniture, *bronzes d'ameublement* (q.v.), etc.

Forestville Hardware & Clock Co.: a clock-making concern operating in Bristol, Connecticut, from 1852, reputed to have produced 100,000 clocks a year.

Forestville Manufacturing Co.: a clock-making concern allied to the above, specializing in eight- and thirty-hour marine clocks, from 1835 to 1853.

Fork: the three-pronged fork came into use in the late 17th cent. and the four-pronged fork in the mid-18th cent. The earliest recorded English two-pronged fork dates from 1632.

Form watch: a watch made in some form that departs from the standard of the period, e.g. book, cruciform, skull, dog, etc. These are found in the 17th cent. Later, at the end of the 18th, there are lyres, mandolines, baskets of flowers, fruit, etc.

Forte: the strong portion of the sword blade, usually about one-third, nearest the hilt.

Fortin barometer: a type in which the level of the cistern is adjusted to a fixed pointer before a reading by difference is taken, thus eliminating capacity error.

Foster, Edward: (1762–1867), English silhouettist working after 1811. His silhouettes are often signed.

Foules point d'or: see Piqué.

Francis ware: japanned tinware made and decorated by Henry and Thomas Francis of Philadelphia between about 1832 and 1845.

Franco-Burgundian tapestry: the great development of Medieval tapestry seems to have taken place in the 14th cent., principally in France at Paris and Arras. But the Hundred Years War drove the French Court from Paris to the Loire, and it was the Dukes of Burgundy who patronized the 15th-cent. florescence of tapestry. Apart from the *Apocalypse* tapestries at Angers, woven by Nicolas Bataille of Paris (c. 1375–80), and the *Nine Worthies* at the Cloisters, New York, scarcely a 14th-cent. piece is known. Even 15th-cent. tapestries are rare, but the *Clovis* set at Rheims, the *Caesar* set at Berne, and *Alexander* in the Palazzo Doria, Rome, are eloquent remains of famous hangings which figured in inventories and chroniclers' accounts of marriages or court festivities. The Burgundian dukes fostered the arts and raised tapestry to the level of diplomatic gifts as highly prized as gold.

Philip the Good inherited Flanders, Artois and Hainault (1384), which included Arras and Tournai, the two great tapestry cities of the 15th cent. With Charles the Bold's defeat and death in 1477, French and Flemish tapestries diverged as different schools.

Frankenthal porcelain: a factory was established at Frankenthal, near Mannheim in Germany in 1755 by Paul-Anton Hannong under the protection of the Elector Palatine. Hannong had made hard-paste porcelain (q.v.) at his factory at Strasbourg but the French authorities obliged him to cease his activities in view of the monopoly held by Vincennes (see Sèvres porcelain), and he consequently moved to Frankenthal. Frankenthal porcelain figures often have rich, pierced, scrolled Rococo bases and sometimes include trellis work, a style which is connected with the modeller J. F. Luck (1758–64). Tablewares belonging to the period up to 1775, in which the best achievements of the factory were reached, are sometimes decorated in the Meissen (q.v.) manner and sometimes with elaborate figure subjects. Trellis and diaper patterns were popular and cabaret sets (q.v.) were a favourite form. The factory closed in 1799. The marks varied, showing Hannong's initials until 1756 and thereafter a quartering from the arms of the Palatinate, occasionally also the lion from the same arms. The initials of the Elector Carl Theodor, with or without crown, appear after 1762, all in underglaze blue.

Franklin clock: a type of wooden movement shelf clock made (1825–30) by Silas Hoadley of Plymouth, Connecticut, and called by him 'Franklin'. It is perhaps the earliest instance that a clock was given a specific (model) name by a maker. This movement is practically an inverted form of the movement then being made by Terry (q.v.) and others.

Franklin stove: small cast-iron stove designed by Benjamin Franklin (1706–90) in 1742 and the subject of frequent improvements. It could be carried from room to room and connected to an existing fireplace flue. Its importance was that it was a method of creating a heat source in, rather than at the edge of, a room.

Free-blown glass: glass formed by blowing and manipulation with hand tools, without the aid of moulds; also called hand blown and off-hand blown.

Freedom box: small circular or oblong box, silver-gilt or gold, presented with a script conferring the freedom of a town. Particularly popular in Ireland from the late 18th to the early 19th cent.

'French' chair: a high-backed, elaborately carved arm chair which came into fashion shortly after the Restoration. These chairs were richly upholstered and were made *en suite* (q.v.) with stools. Although walnut was more usually employed, they were also made of beech and gilt. In the mid-18th cent. mahogany chairs with upholstered seats and backs and padded arms were also described as 'French'.

French jet: black glass, used in inexpensive costume jewellery as a substitute for real jet.

French polish: a coating of transparent gum applied to the surface of furniture to produce a permanently glazed effect. Introduced in the late 18th cent., it did not become popular until the 19th.

Fret: a metal or wooden plate in a striking clock, pierced, usually decoratively, to allow the sound to escape. Also the pierced ornamental sides and back of a lantern clock.

Fretwork: two forms of fretwork were frequently used decoratively on mid-18th cent. furniture: (a) open-fretted galleries (q.v.) appear on tea-tables or on stands made in the Chinese taste;

(b) geometrical fretwork patterns were also used on chair legs or friezes, carved or applied, inspired by the Chinese or the Gothic taste.

Frieze: an architectural term describing the decorative band placed immediately below a cornice.

Also used to describe the band below the cornice on a piece of furniture.

Frieze rail: horizontal member supporting the surface of, for example, a table.

Friggers: a colloquialism used to describe the innumerable minor articles made of glass, of which the principal purposes were to delight and surprise the recipient and beholder, and to exhibit the prowess of the maker. Into this category fall such objects as hand bells, flasks, rolling pins, walking sticks, tobacco pipes, swords, sceptres, crowns and hats.

Less common than the above are model ships with rigging and crew, birds on perches, fox hunts with hounds in full cry, and similar tours de force. The latter were perhaps made as suitable table decorations at hunt breakfasts.

Friggers were made both at Bristol and at Nailsea (qq.v.) as they were at all the other glassworks in England. Unless such pieces bear a signature or other mark of identification, there is seldom any way by which the productions of one place can be distinguished from those of another. (See also End-of-day glass.)

Frit: a calcined mixture of sand and fluxes ready to be melted in a crucible to form glass.

Frodsham, Charles: (1810–71), the son and apprentice of W. J. Frodsham who was Master of the Clockmakers' Company from 1836 to 1837. Charles Frodsham experimented with the compensation balance (q.v.) and balance spring, and wrote several technical papers.

Frog: a sleeve-like device, normally of leather, used to attach the sword to the belt. Usually the scabbard was thrust through the sleeve and a stud on its throat engaged in a hole in the frog.

'Frog' service: a celebrated service of cream-coloured earthenware manufactured by Josiah Wedgwood (q.v.) in 1773 for Empress Catherine of Russia. Each piece of this enormous service was painted at Chelsea with individual landscapes and mansions of England, and a leaf border with the crest of a green frog in purple-black. The service was so named because it was intended for the Grenouille Palace.

There were more than 900 pieces: the ware cost £51 8s 4d: the decorations nearly £2450: Josiah Wedgwood received for it £3000.

It is now in the Hermitage, Leningrad.

Fromanteel family: London clockmakers of repute, the various members of the family being active between 1625 and 1725.

Froment-Meurice, François-Désiré: (1802–55), a French jeweller and goldsmith, said to be the greatest of his age, specializing mainly (though not entirely) in work in the Medieval and Renaissance styles, and in the use of the human figure in his work.

Frosting: a rough or matt white surface on silverware produced by acid fuming or scratch brushing. Not found before the early 19th cent., principally used on ornamental and figure work on silver centre-pieces (q.v.).

Fruit paperweight: glass paperweight (q.v.) containing canes (q.v.) so arranged as to represent fruit.

Frye, Thomas: (1710–62), born in Ireland near Dublin, studied art and came to London about 1729. He painted portraits in oils and became proficient as a miniature painter. Became interested in the idea of manufacturing porcelain and in 1744 took out a patent with Edward Heylyn. Frye patented another porcelain formula in 1749. He became manager of the Bow (q.v.) factory but retired in 1759 when his health gave way. He toured in Wales for a time and then settled in London as a mezzotint (q.v.) engraver.

Fuddling cup: a cup with a number of conjoined compartments communicating internally, made in *sgraffiato* (q.v.) slipware at Donyat and Crock Street, Somerset. Dates recorded from 1697 to 1770. Similar vessels were made in tin-glazed earthenware at Bristol (q.v.). Earliest dated piece 1633.

Fukien porcelain: see Blanc-de-Chine.

Fulda faience: made at Fulda, in Germany, *c.* 1741–58.

Fulda porcelain: a factory was founded at Fulda in Germany in 1764 under a privilege from the Prince-Bishop of Fulda, Heinrich von Bibra, and continued until 1790. Examples of Fulda porcelain are rare and both the tablewares and the figures are of high quality. The body is hard paste (q.v.). The mark varies. From about 1765 to 1780 a cross, taken from the arms of the city, was used, principally on figures, while again from 1765 to about 1788, two 'Fs', linked to form an 'H', below a crown, appear. Between 1788 and 1790 a crowned 'A' is occasionally found.

Fulham carpets: Peter Parisot, an ex-Capuchin monk from Lorraine, procured the patronage of the Duke of Cumberland for a carpet-knotting factory in Fulham. He is supposed to have employed as many as a hundred workmen, many from the Savonnerie

(q.v.), but owing to extravagances he was forced to sell up within five years (1755). A portrait of the Duke, dated 1755, is probably his work, and pile fire-screens are occasionally found.

Fulham stoneware: John Dwight (q.v.) of Fulham took out a patent in 1671 for the manufacture of 'transparent earthenware' and stoneware, then sometimes known as Cologne ware. After Dwight's death the works remained in the family for many years. In 1862 the factory came into the possession of Messrs MacIntosh & Clements: in 1864 it was disposed of to a Mr Bailey. It is still in existence as the Fulham Pottery and Cheavin Filter Co.
Marks:

Fulham
Pottery

This mark is found on a flask of brown-glazed stoneware decorated with a watch, *c.* 1811, in the British Museum. No other marks are known to have been used.

John Dwight contributed to the progress of pottery manufacture in England. He was the first maker of a semi-translucent stoneware, the link between earthenware and the fine porcelain produced later. He also made a successful copy of Cologne ware, a greyish durable earthenware used for pots, mugs, etc., imported from Germany in great quantities. Many such articles for domestic use, in various qualities, were made at Fulham in the 17th and 18th cent.

Some beautifully modelled statues and busts in salt-glazed stoneware were made by Dwight. Red ware of the Elers (q.v.) type was probably also made at Fulham. Between 1693 and 1696 Dwight instituted several lawsuits to defend his patent rights for the manufacture of this and other types of ware. The brothers Elers were cited in one of these cases.

In the 18th cent. only the coarser wares were produced, beer jugs, tankards for the most part crudely decorated with reliefs of convivial and other subjects, and later marked with name of owner or inn for which they were intended.

Fundame: a Japanese lacquer-work technique in which powdered gold is worked to a matt surface.

Funnel bowl: bowl shaped in the form of a funnel found on baluster-stemmed drinking glasses of the late 17th and 18th cent.

Fürstenberg porcelain: a factory was founded at Fürstenberg in Germany in 1747 by Duke Carl I of Brunswick, although porcelain was not made before 1753. Some of the early tablewares were modelled with Rococo patterns in relief in order to hide faults in the body and glaze. L. V. Gerverot, who had formerly worked with Wedgwood (q.v.), became manager in 1795. Classical figures after bronzes were produced, as well as copies of Wedgwood's jasper and black basaltes (q.v.) ware. The factory still exists. The mark used was an 'F' in blue.

Fusee: a conically shaped and spirally grooved pulley which, utilizing the principle of the lever, equalizes the pull of the mainspring of a clock or watch on the train. This has generally been attributed to Jacob the Czech, of Prague, based on the earliest known survival in a clock by him, owned by the Society of Antiquaries of London, dated 1525.

Gadroon: a border ornament composed of radiating lobes of either curved or straight form. Used on oak furniture in the late Elizabethan and Jacobean period and on mahogany in the mid-18th cent. Also a familiar ornament on the rims and feet of silver cups and other vessels and on the borders of silver plates and dishes from the late 17th cent. onwards.

Gale, William, & Son: New York silversmiths, eventually absorbed by Reed & Barton (q.v.). Their 381-piece dinner-service, presented to Commodore Matthew Calbraith Perry in 1855, represents the height of the 19th-cent. Rococo style in the United States.

Gallé, Emile: (1846–1904), French glassmaker of Nancy whose glass reveals a Japanese inspiration in the use of natural floral motifs. Gallé abandoned symmetry and Classical proportions and sought an association with carved stone by means of using opaque coloured glass and crazings and irregularities in the material.

Gallery: in furniture, a raised border of, for example, a table top, often in the form of a miniature balustrade. A comparable feature may occur at the edge of silver or plated trays.

Gallipot: originally, pots brought in galleys; subsequently applied to pottery glazed with tin enamel, especially a small, glazed earthenware pot such as was used by apothecaries for ointments.

Galloons: the plain, ribbon-like outer border of a tapestry. The factory and weaver's mark, when used, are woven into the galloon.

Gally paving tiles: glazed tiles, usually earthenware covered with tin glaze used for wall decorations: the name was derived from imported wares brought from the Mediterranean in galleys.

Gambeson: quilted garment worn under a suit of armour, especially in the 12th and 13th cents. It was the foot soldier's only protection.

Garde Meuble de la Couronne: (*Fr.*), the department which dealt with all matters connected with the furnishing of the Royal palaces in France. It was established by Louis XIV in 1663, and survived until the end of the monarchy. Very fortunately, its records exist more or less intact.

The first inventory of furniture belonging to the Crown was completed in 1673 and has been published in full by M. Emile Molinier, but the most important item among the records is the *Journal*, instituted in 1685 and continuing until 1784. In it every piece acquired for the Crown was scrupulously entered and given a number, with dates of delivery, the name of the maker, costs and measurements, eventual destination in the Royal palaces, and a full description. The numbers often correspond with those painted on the backs of existing pieces (see Inventory numbers), and these can be thus identified fairly closely from the descriptions and measurements.

The *Journal* consists in all of eighteen volumes and 3600 pages, of which only a small proportion is missing. After 1784 a new system of recording was introduced, but the same numbers were preserved, and these, in fact, continued to be used until well into the 19th cent.

Garden carpets: Persian carpets, showing formal designs with figures and animals.

Gardner's porcelain: an Englishman, Francis Gardner (d. 1796), founded a factory in Moscow in 1758. His factory produced some well-known figures of Russian peasants. Some of Gardner's wares bear a mark resembling the Meissen mark of the Marcolini period. (See also Meissen porcelain.)

Garnish: a household set of plates and dishes.

Garniture de cheminée: set of five porcelain or faience (qq.v.)´vases consisting of two trumpet-shaped beakers (q.v.) and three covered vases, usually of baluster shape, a combination originating in China, whence it was adopted by most European faience and porcelain factories. Also made of silver in late 17th-cent. England, France or Holland, but few examples survive.

Garrard & Co.: London silversmiths and jewellers founded in the 18th cent. In 1830 they succeeded Rundell, Bridge & Rundell (q.v.) as the Royal Goldsmiths. They were leading makers

of domestic silver and presentation pieces in the Victorian period.

Gasolier: see Chandelier.

Gate-leg table: an oval or round table in oak or, more rarely, walnut, originally known as a 'falling' table on account of the two hinged leaves which hang down beside the frame and can be raised and supported on two, and sometimes four, gate supports. The leg turning used was very varied. These tables became particularly fashionable in the late 17th cent. Gate-leg tables made to fold completely flat are known but the more usual construction had a rigid central panel. (See also Drop-leaf table.)

Gather: a blob of molten metal (q.v.) on the end of a glassblower's blowpipe ready for blowing.

Gaudreau, Antoine Robert: French cabinet-maker. One of the most celebrated of the known *ébénistes* (q.v.) of the Louis XV period. He was born *c.* 1680, and was in the Royal service from 1726.

Gaudy Dutch: the popular American name for a gaily decorated Staffordshire pottery produced *c.* 1810–30 for the American trade.

Gaudy Welsh: also known as Gaudy Ironstone. A popular American name for pottery wares (*c.* 1830–45 and 1850–65) made in Swansea for the American trade.

Gauffrage: blind printing, producing an embossed effect without colour, and used in Japan from the late 18th cent. as a technique in making prints.

Gauntlet: hand armour, introduced at the beginning of the 14th cent. Early examples are of leather covered with leather scales or mail (q.v.); later ones consist of a single plate covering the hand and wrist, and scales covering the fingers. These were eventually articulated to the hand plate. Knobs attached to the knuckles are termed 'gadlings'. A gauntlet for duelling was devised in the early 17th cent.

Gemellion: this term describes one of a pair of basins used for the liturgical washing of the hands at the Mass. Though the ornament found on them is in most cases of secular character, their use seems to have been mainly ecclesiastical. One was provided with a spout at the side and served as a ewer for pouring water, while the other without spout received it. The gemellion was one of the standard productions of the enamelling shops at Limoges, and the majority of those known are decorated with Limoges enamel. They date from the 13th and 14th cent.

Genoa lace: gold and silver plaited border laces were made at Genoa in the 16th cent. Pillow lace (q.v.) was perhaps developed here or alternatively in Flanders.

Georgette: popular name for a snuff box made in the style of Jean George, the Paris mid-18th-cent. goldsmith.

Georgian style: a style associated with works of art made during the reigns of the three Georges up to the time when the illness of George III made it necessary for the Prince of Wales to become Regent (1811).

Gera porcelain: see Limbach porcelain.

Germain, Thomas: (1673–1748), French Rococo silversmith, the eldest son of Pierre Germain (1645–84), a silversmith in the service of Louis XIV. After studying and working in Italy, he returned to Paris about 1706 and executed various ecclesiastical commissions. In 1723, having become a master in 1720, he was appointed silversmith to Louis XV, for whose coronation in 1722 he made a silver-gilt sun for Rheims Cathedral. In 1726 he supplied a fifty-one piece toilet service (q.v.) for Marie Leczinska, wife of Louis XV, and he later executed other commissions for the French and other European Courts. Little of his work survived the Revolution. His son, François Thomas Germain (1726–91), became Royal silversmith in 1748 and he also worked for the Royal Courts of Russia and Portugal.

'German Flowers' (Deutsche Blumen): contemporary name for naturalistically painted flowers, introduced as porcelain decoration at Meissen (q.v.) about 1740. *Ombrierte Deutsche Blumen*, flowers with shadows, are a variation. Later the treatment became freer, and smaller flowers, arranged in sprays or bouquets, were scattered over the whole surface until, under classical influence, they were confined between conventional rims and borders.

German silver: see Nickel silver.

Gesso: a composition of parchment, size and whiting applied to furniture as a medium for carving and gilding. A pattern in low relief is carved in the thickness of the whiting ground and the background stamped or punched to give a matt effect, the whole surface being then gilded. Gesso work is found on table tops, mirror frames and stands dating from the late 17th and throughout the first half of the 18th cent.

Ghiordes knot: used in Oriental carpets from Djoshagan (q.v.), Herez and Kurdistan, and sometimes from Tabriz, Shiraz and Herat (qq.v.). These last also use the Sehna knot (q.v.).

Ghiordes rugs: the finest of Turkish rugs. The knot is usually Turkish; yarns are very fine, warp and weft often being of silk. The colours are very varied, while the borders usually consist of bold conventional floral designs, beautifully treated.

Gibbons, Grinling: (1648–1720), carver and designer of Dutch birth and English domicile. His work, of distinctive character, included the carving in wood of picture frames with profuse and naturalistic foliage, fruit swags, birds and shells. Arnold Quellin (1609–68), was probably responsible for the best of the sculptures executed in his studio.

Gilding: various relatively impermanent forms of gilding were employed on salt-glazed stoneware, earthenware, porcelain and glass in the 18th cent., by means of an emulsion composed of linseed oil and mastic, japanners' size, amber varnish, or honey. These were fixed by firing at an extremely low temperature. Honey gilding was used at the Chelsea and Worcester porcelain (qq.v.) factories. It was rather dull in appearance but could be applied with enough thickness to allow for chasing (q.v.). It was much more durable than size gilding.

The principal types of gilding on furniture are oil gilding and water gilding. With the former process a mordant of solidified linseed oil combined with either white lead and verdigris or with yellow ochre or raw sienna is painted on to the ground. This may be of gesso (q.v.) or of white lead or red ochre powdered and combined with oil. The mordant must acquire a tacky consistency before the gold leaf is laid on.

With water gilding, the ground is always gesso and the mordant usually of parchment size. The gold leaf, which can be applied in more than one coat, is laid on when the mordant is wet. Water gilding, unlike oil gilding, may be burnished, and it is the more complicated and expensive process. It is also the least durable.

Gilding became common on English furniture after the Restoration and following the French example. The ground is often tooled or punched. Silvering, which is cheaper than gilding, came into fashion at the same period.

Before the invention of electrogilding (q.v.), metalwork was fire gilded. Powdered gold was combined with mercury and applied to the object. During firing, the mercury evaporated leaving the gold adhering to the metal. (See also Ormolu.) Parcel gilding is a term meaning partial gilding.

Giles, James: (1718–80), an enameller of Bow, Worcester (qq.v.) and other porcelains from before 1760 until *c.* 1780. Many unusual styles of decoration came from his workshop. He was apprenticed to a jeweller, before becoming a ceramic artist. By 1760 he was well established and advertising that he was prepared to 'procure and paint for any person Worcester porcelain to any or in any pattern', and in 1771 hired a room in Cockspur Street from which he advertised wares 'curiously enamelled in figures, birds and flowers' and ornamented with mazarine blue and gold.

The gilding on wares decorated in Giles's workshop is said to have been thick and crudely chased.

Various styles of enamelling have been ascribed to him: the dishevelled birds, Chelsea landscapes drawn in black and coloured in green, some Chelsea fruit painting, etc.

He was financially embarrassed in 1777 and appealed to Duesbury (q.v.) for a loan, and when he ultimately failed Duesbury took on his premises and stock.

Chaffers suggested that the red seal mark occurring over the Worcester crescent in underglaze blue may be an indication of his work. Honey suggested that the dagger and another mark on Bow was Giles's sign.

Gillow, Robert: an 18th-cent. joiner of Lancaster to whom George Hepplewhite (q.v.) was apprenticed in his youth. Robert Gillow's firm opened a branch in Oxford St to which furniture from the workshops in Lancaster was sent. Some 18th-cent. pieces made by Gillow and all those he made after 1820 were stamped 'Gillow's' or

'Gillow's, Lancaster'. His son Richard, who died in 1811, became his father's partner in 1757. The firm continues as Waring & Gillow.

Gimson, Ernest William: (1864–1919), an English architect and furniture designer and a founder in 1890 of Kenton & Co. (q.v.). He carried the principles of William Morris (q.v.) into workshop practice, reviving and preserving traditional English designs and standards of craftsmanship. In 1893 he moved to the Cotswolds with Sidney and Ernest Barnsley (q.v.), establishing a workshop there.

Ginette: see Dram glasses.

Gin glass: see Dram glasses.

Giobu: Japanese lacquer-work technique in which irregular pieces of foil are mixed with lacquer, giving a mottled effect.

Girandole: (1) a carved and gilt candle sconce (see Sconce) of asymmetrical design, sometimes enclosing a looking-glass as a back plate. About 1750 girandoles provided some of the most lively interpretations of the Rococo (q.v.) fashion. (2) a type of earring in which three pendent stones hang from a large central stone, worn in the late 17th and 18th cent. (3) a type of American wall clock designed by Lemuel Curtis dating from c. 1820.

Girdle: the term used to describe the line dividing the crown and the base of a faceted gem stone.

Girdle plate: a Scottish flat iron sheet on which oatcakes were baked.

'Girl-in-a-swing' family: a group of porcelain figures manufactured at Chelsea c. 1751; so named from a figure of a girl in a swing in the Victoria and Albert Museum, London. The figures are of primitive simplicity and show some affinity to Staffordshire wares of similar date.

Gisarme: see Pole-arms.

Giuliano, Carlo: an Italian goldsmith and jeweller working in London from the 1860s, specializing in elaborately enamelled and gem-set jewellery in the Classical, Renaissance and other styles. Most of his work bears the initials C.G. He was succeeded in his business by his sons, A. and C. Giuliano.

Glaive: see Pole-arms.

Glasgow School: a style of architecture, interior design, furniture, metalwork, jewellery and textiles developed in the 1890s and 1900s. It was an independent expression of Art Nouveau (q.v.) and closely associated with the Glasgow School of Art and the designer C. R. Mackintosh (q.v.).

Glass bottle seals: the circular glass seals found on glass bottles were almost certainly impressed with an original intaglio (q.v.) made of brass. This was made either by a professional engraver working on his own behalf or at the glassworks itself. No name of any craftsman connected with this particular branch of the art of die-sinking has been recorded, and the makers of these seals, as most of the makers of more elaborate desk seals, have remained anonymous.

Glass bottle seals fall into three categories, whether they bear dates or not, and may be conveniently classified as: armorial, name or initial, and 'others', the last including merchant's marks, Masonic signs and the names of houses.

Glass pictures: see Back-painting, Under-glass painting, Mirror painting, Gold-glass engraving, *Verre églomisé* and Glass silhouettes.

Glass silhouettes: silhouettes painted on to glass by one of the following methods: (a) *Verre églomisé* (q.v.) and gold-glass engraving. Silhouettes of this kind were produced by the Parisian artist A. Forberger (1762–1865), who backed his portraits with gold leaf or blue wax and often gave them floral borders, and W. A. Spornberg, a Swede, who worked at the end of the 18th cent. in Bath, and whose profiles are backed with red pigment and usually surrounded by a geometrical border. (b) Painting on to the reverse side of flat or convex glass. This was a common form of silhouette painting, and one capable of giving very effective results, particularly on those painted on convex glass, mounted over white backgrounds on to which their shadows could be thrown. Work of this kind was painted by Walter Jorden (late 18th cent.), Isabella Beetham, Charles Rosenberg (1745–1844), W. Rought (early 19th cent.), and many others.

Several silhouettists, among them John Miers, mounted their ordinary painted work beneath convex glass with *églomisé* borders and Mrs Beetham often combined *églomisé* mounts with portraits in plain black painted on the underside of the same glass. At least one silhouette in a glass millefiori paperweight (q.v.) is on record.

Glass walking sticks: chest-high shepherd's crook walking sticks in pale green bottle-glass were made in the late 18th cent.; few remain. Early 19th-cent. walking sticks were tapered at the ferrule end; later examples appear to have been simply rounded off. Those with shepherd's crook heads, measuring about 91 cm (3 ft) in length, were merely sheared off with a cold iron. These were intended for decorating the walls of cottage parlours. The majority are enriched with coloured spirals, those in red, white and blue being particularly numerous. These interior threads on genuine examples cause very slight ridges on the surface of the glass. In others the coloured threads are spiralled around the surface of the sticks.

Glastonbury chair: a type of chair with X-supports and elbowed arms linking seat and top of back. The name derives from an example at Wells, supposedly associated with the last Abbot of Glastonbury. Examples of similar construction have been made or embellished at various, including modern, periods. (See also X-chair.)

Glaze: the application of a glassy material to earthenware or porcelain renders it impervious to liquids and smooth to the touch. Glazes may be dull or matt or brilliant, translucent or opaque, or they may be shot through with brilliant colour. They may be hard and resistant to a knife edge or they may be soft and easily scratched.

Glaze has been applied by dusting powdered lead ore upon the ware, throwing common salt into the kiln so that it volatilizes and forms a thin film of salt-glaze, or by dipping in a liquid glaze solution.

Lead glazes were general until the end of the 19th cent. except for salt-glazed stoneware and hard-paste porcelain. John Rose invented a leadless glaze for porcelain in 1820 which was awarded the Isis gold medal of the Society of Arts, and Job Meigh a leadless glaze for red earthenware in 1822.

'Goat and Bee' jug: a jug decorated in relief with goats and a bee, incised in the base with the word Chelsea, a triangle, and a date, generally 1745, which is regarded as an important documentary piece in respect of the Chelsea factory. A specimen dated 1743 has been recorded.

The shape is known in variations and unmarked, and was derived from a silver prototype. Goat and Bee jugs were made at Coalport, *c.* 1850.

Gobelins, Manufacture Royale des: (*Fr.*), the State-supported organization founded in 1667 by Letters Patent at Gobelins, France, through the inspiration of Colbert, Louis XIV's finance minister. It was designed to provide, apart from tapestry, all products of the luxury arts, including furniture, and its first great task was the equipment of the interior of the Palace of Versailles. It owed its success and great reputation to the energies of the first director, Charles Lebrun (q.v.), who made it the foundation stone of the organized applied arts in France.

For the weaving of tapestries, there were ateliers of both high- and low-warp (qq.v.) weavers; no expense was spared, and all the tapestry was the property of the King. Within twenty years Lebrun and his designers had created several new styles of tapestry and made the Gobelins renowned for sumptuous quality and originality. The different series of *Portières*, the *Seasons and Elements*, the *Months or Maison Royales* and the *History of the King* were novel and wonderful achievements. By 1694 one hundred sets (880 pieces) had been woven, mostly with gold. After Louis XIV's declining later years, the Regency and Louis XV styles were reflected at the Gobelins. In 1730 Oudry became director, and though he over-emphasized pictorial effects, his *Chasses de Louis XV* was a masterpiece. As at Beauvais (q.v.), his style gave place to that of Boucher. In the latter part of the 18th cent. Neilson, who was Scotch by birth, was the most influential weaver. Until then no Gobelins tapestry could be bought from the factory, being reserved exclusively·for royal and diplomatic use. France's financial embarrassments led to Neilson's taking special orders from abroad, and the sets of tapestry with furniture to match, as at Osterley, were the result. The classicism of the late 18th cent. did not interpret well in tapestry, and it is difficult to see the 19th cent. as anything but a steady decline.

Goblet: a drinking glass with the bowl supported on a tall stem.

Godet: a cup.

Goddard, John: (1723/4–85), the originator, perhaps together with his brother-in-law, John Townsend (q.v.), of block-front (q.v.) and shell-carved cabinet furniture. Widely reckoned the foremost Rhode Island furniture-maker of his day. Apprenticed to Job Townsend, of Newport, whose daughter he married. His sons, Stephen and Thomas Goddard, became first-class cabinet-makers.

Godwin, Edward William: (1836–86), an English architect and designer of furniture, wallpapers and textiles. He set up practice in Bristol in 1854 and moved to London in 1865. A leading exponent of the Japanese style, his designs for angular ebonized furniture were much imitated in Britain and the United States.

Gold and silver lace: plaited border laces of gold and silver wire, exported from Genoa as early as the 16th cent.

Gold-glass engraving: a technique involving the engraving of a picture on the back of a piece of glass (usually a goblet or some similar container) through a layer of gold leaf previously attached to it. Sometimes colour was added from behind. Usually a second piece of glass was used to seal this engraving from behind although this was more often omitted in later work intended purely as pictures and not as incidental decorations for glass vessels. Many such pictures were made in Italy in the 14th cent. From this technique was developed *verre églomisé* and under-glass painting (qq.v.).

Gold ground: a descriptive term for porcelain made in Europe in the first quarter of the 19th cent., in which large areas of the piece have been gilt.

Gold leaf: gold beaten into very thin sheets.

Goldsmiths and Silversmiths Co. Ltd: London firm of retail goldsmiths, silversmiths and jewellers, founded about 1881. In 1952 it amalgamated with Garrard & Co. (q.v.).

Gombron ware: in the early part of the 17th cent. the English East India Company established a factory at the port of Gombron, in the Persian Gulf. As a result of this, native Persian ware and Chinese porcelain imported into England from this source were referred to indiscriminately as Gombron ware. As late as the 1770s Horace Walpole wrote of 'two basins of most ancient Gombron china', which may have been either Persian or Chinese. The modern name of the port is Bandar Abbas.

Gong: a spirally wound steel wire on which the hours are struck. First used instead of a bell in the last quarter of the 18th cent.

Goodison, Benjamin: (d. 1767), a well-known 18th-cent. cabinet-maker who supplied furniture to royal order and whose workshop was in Long Acre.

Goose-neck pediment: see Broken pediment.

Gorget: close-fitting armour of mail or plate protecting the throat and upper part of the chest.

Gorham Manufacturing Co.: trading name between 1865 and 1961 of silver and electroplate manufacturers and retailers of Providence, Rhode Island, now known as Gorham Corporation. They employed the English designers Thomas Pairpoint and A. J. Barrett and were among the first in the United States to adopt mass-production methods of silver manufacture. In the late 19th cent. William C. Codman produced a number of Art Nouveau (q.v.) pieces, using the trade name of Martelé.

Goss, William Henry: (1833–1906), a pottery and porcelain manufacturer now best known for his small cream-glazed souvenir pieces with town crests, etc., made from about 1880. Goss also made domestic ware, portrait figures, ornaments, brooches, etc.

Gotch: East Anglian word for a large stoneware jug.

Gotha porcelain: a factory was founded at Gotha in Thuringia in 1757. The finest wares date from 1772 when vases in the Classical taste, biscuit figures, etc., were produced. The first factory mark was an 'R' (for Rotberg, the name of the original proprietor) which appears to have been used from *c.* 1770–83 or later, followed by 'R – g' between 1783 and 1805, and then onwards a 'G' or 'Gotha'.

Gothic armour: a modern term for the style of plate armour, characterized by slender elegant lines, and decorated with cusped borders and shell-like rippling, developed particularly in Germany in the 15th cent. The term is extended to cover the 15th-cent. Italian style, which was rounder in form than the German, and usually had smooth, plain surfaces.

Gothic Revival: a style in the decorative arts that started in Britain and spread to the United States in the mid-19th cent. Principally, it was a reflection of the enthusiasm of A. W. N. Pugin (q.v.) for the 14th-cent. forms of decoration, codified by Owen Jones (q.v.) in *The Grammar of Ornament* of 1856.

Gothic style: the word Gothic was first used by Italian art critics in the Renaissance (q.v.) to describe a style which they thought owed its origin to the Goths, the vanquishers of the Roman Empire. In fact the style was first developed in Northern France in the 12th cent., involving, in architecture, the use of pointed arches, flying buttresses, rib-vaults and stone tracery in windows, arcading, canopies, etc. The new style quickly spread across Europe and remained dominant until the 15th cent. in the South and the 16th cent. in the North. Characteristic decorative motifs such as tracery, cusping, finials (q.v.), trefoils, etc., all found in Gothic buildings, appear similarly on Medieval woodwork, metalwork, etc.

Gothic wallpapers: style of design favoured, if not innovated, by Horace Walpole for Strawberry Hill. Inspired by certain features of Medieval architecture. Wallpapers of similar inspiration were also popular during the Gothic Revival of the 19th cent.

Gotzkowsky, Johann Ernst: see Berlin porcelain.

Gouge work: a form of decoration used extensively on oak furniture in the 17th cent. in which the pattern is scooped out by a semi-circular gouge.

Gourd cup: a tall silver cup made in the 16th and 17th cent. in a form reminiscent of a gourd, supported sometimes on a stem in the shape of twisted trees. They were first made in Germany.

Gouthière, Pierre: (1732–*c.* 1813), French sculptor, the most celebrated of the later 18th-cent. *fondeurs-ciseleurs-doreurs* (fire metalworkers). He is known to have been in Paris by 1758, where he became a *maître-doreur*. He made the mounts for furniture by J. H. Riesener (q.v.) and was employed by the Crown between 1769 and 1777, but after the latter date his name disappears from the Royal accounts. Gouthière's signed works are exceedingly rare and can be supplemented by a few that can be identified by documents. Almost all bronzes of any quality of the Louis XVI period have been attributed to him, and it is only recently that the increased study of the Royal accounts have revealed the names of other *ciseleurs-doreurs*.

Grace cup: another name for a small wine cup (q.v.).

Graham, George: London clockmaker who made an important contribution towards accurate timekeeping by his invention of the deadbeat escapement (q.v.). Active between 1713–51.

Grandfather chair: see Wing chair.

Grandfather clock: properly known as a long-case clock (q.v.). Came into existence directly after the invention of the anchor escapement (q.v.), 1670. The narrow arc of swing of this escapement made possible the enclosing of the weights and pendulum in a narrow trunk. When the term 'grandfather clock' first came into use is uncertain, but Barham uses the term in his *Ingoldsby Legends*, which date from about 1835.

Grandmother clock: a small long-case clock, not exceeding 2 m (6 ft 6 in) in height.

Grand Rapids furniture: mass-produced furniture manufactured in Michigan. From 1870 imitations – or caricatures – of furniture in the prevailing styles were produced there by firms such as Berkey & Gay.

Grand Sonnerie: a system of clock striking whereby the hour and the quarter are struck at each quarter. The earliest known example is the movement with the silent escapement made by Tompion about 1676–80. This system of striking was rendered possible by the invention by Edward Barlow, in 1676, of the rack and snail method of striking (q.v.).

Granite ware: hard, durable and cheap white earthenware, made extensively for the American market in the middle of the 19th cent.

Graver: tool used to engrave metal.

Grease pan: the circular dish beneath the nozzle of a candlestick into which grease from the burning candle might drip. Grease pans on glass chandeliers were of moulded pattern with plain edges in the early examples, but by 1750 were of extravagant shapes. The latter were elaborately cut and their pointed rims were drilled and hung with drops.

Greatbach, William: (1735–1813), modeller and potter, son of a farmer at Berryhill; worked for Whieldon and came into contact with Josiah Wedgwood (qq.v.); manufactured biscuit (q.v.) pottery, particularly fruit and pineapple wares, to be sent to Wedgwood's factory to glaze. At Lane Delph 1760–70, his cream-coloured teapots decorated with black transfer prints of 'The Prodigal Son' (engraved by Radford) are well known. He was ruined by a bad debt; worked for other potters, producing a good 'china' glaze for the Baddeleys of Shelton; in 1788 employed by the Turners of Lane End (see Turner, John); and from 1788–1807 worked for the Wedgwood factory receiving a pension for life on his retirement. A teapot in the British Museum bears his name. He also used the Chinese Seal mark.

Greek lace: a name given to drawn- and cut-work embroidery (qq.v.), often combined with geometrical needle point or pillow lace (qq.v.). When the British occupied the Ionian Isles they brought home great quantities, but much of it was imported from Italy while the Isles belonged to Venice.

Greene glasses: drinking glasses of the type ordered between 1666 and 1673 by the London firm of glass-sellers, John Greene and Michael

Measey, from the Venetian maker, Morelli. The original drawings sent with the orders survive and provide a record of the taste of the period. Mainly illustrating simple shapes, they include short-stemmed wine glasses with conical bowl, some with a flat base, tumblers and winged goblets.

Greener, Henry, & Co.: an English glass factory in Sunderland, founded in 1850. Pressed glass (q.v.), (usually marked on the base with a lion facing left, bearing a halbred) was the main product; stippled lacy glass (q.v.) was made from 1869. Slag glass (q.v.) was marketed under the names of Opal, Malachite and Black Majolica.

Greenwich armour: armour made in the only English royal workshop, founded at Southwark by Henry VIII in 1519, and subsequently removed to Greenwich Palace, where it remained until closed in about 1637. It was staffed largely by foreign workmen, of whom one of the most important was Jacob Halder, master workman, 1576–1607. He was almost certainly responsible for an album of drawings of armours made at Greenwich, now in the Victoria & Albert Museum, which has made possible the identification of a number of surviving suits, several of which are in the Tower of London.

Greenwood Pottery Co.: a company established in 1861 at Trenton, New Jersey, under the name of Stephens, Tams & Co. The name was changed to Greenwood in 1868. The factory produced porcelain hardware trimmings and electrical supplies as well as tableware, and copies of Royal Worcester porcelain featured extensive use of silver and gold enamel. The mark was a printed G.P.Co.

Grendy, Giles: (1693–1780): a successful joiner and chairmaker who exported much of his furniture. He became Master of the Worshipful Company of Joiners of the City of London in 1766.

Grenouillière: see Coudière.

Greybeard: a large earthenware spirit jar or jug; a Bellarmine (q.v.).

Possibly named from the greyish stoneware from which it was made and the fact that it was usually decorated with a bearded relief mask. 'We will give a cup of distilled waters . . . and ye may keep for the purpose the grounds of the last greybeard.' – Sir Walter Scott, *The Monastery*, 1820.

Grey hen: stoneware liquor bottle.

Greyhound jugs: pottery jugs with greyhound handles and relief decorations of sporting subjects.

Gridiron: a grid placed over the centre of the fire for cooking, comprising a number of parallel bars, on which meat, etc. rested during the process. Early gridirons were of simple pattern and made of wrought iron. Later ones sometimes had the bars channelled and leading to a trough at the front, which had a spout for pouring out the gravy and fat collected in it.

Gridiron pendulum: a type of pendulum invented about 1725 by John Harrison, a carpenter born in 1693 at Soulby in Yorkshire. Sometimes attributed jointly to him and his brother James. Harrison discovered that brass and steel have an expansion ratio of 3:2. This property is utilized in this pendulum, with its alternate rods of brass and steel. One side only is required, the other rods being put in for balance and symmetry.

Gros-point embroidery: a type of embroidery worked on a woven canvas in a cross stitch.

Grossbreitenbach porcelain: see Limbach porcelain.

Grotesque: type of ornament deriving from the decoration of Ancient Roman buildings. It consisted of a combination of human, animal and floral elements and it was used after 1500, when the Roman buildings were excavated.

Ground: a term used in lace-making, synonymous with the French *fond* or *réseau*, and basically meaning any background to a lace pattern, but usually restricted to a mesh or net so that grounded laces (q.v.) are contrasted with those where brides (q.v.) support the pattern. Some grounds are best known by their French names. (See *Fond chant, Fond clair*.)

Ground colours: areas of coloured glaze on porcelain or enamels, providing a background to painted or gilt decoration, often in reserved panels.

Grounded laces: laces with meshed backgrounds to their patterns, allowing more freedom of design than the alternative linking of brides (q.v.) found in early needlepoints (q.v.). The mesh might be made along with the pattern as in, for example, Valenciennes (q.v.); it might be worked around the pattern afterwards as in Brussels *point d'Angleterre* (q.v.); or worked first and the pattern put into it as in Alençon (q.v.); or worked separately with completed pattern units attached to it as in Brussels *point plat appliqué* (see Brussels lace). The grounds are considerable aids in identifying old laces since in pillow laces (q.v.) the tiny hexagons or lozenges are composed of different numbers of threads variously twisted and plaited.

Grounded wallpapers: the overall application of colour to the paper before printing. A hand process up to recent times, including various types, polished, lustred (with the use of mica), metallic, flock, etc.

Grubbe plates: four plates presented to the Victoria and Albert Museum, London, by Mrs Dora Grubbe, a descendent of James Giles (q.v.), the independent London porcelain decorator; used as a means of identifying wares decorated in Giles's workshop either by himself or his assistants.

Grueby Faience Co.: an American art-pottery works established in Boston, Massachusetts, in 1894 by William H. Grueby. Inspired by the work of the French potter Auguste Delaherche, the characteristic leaf-shaped forms were covered with a matt glaze, generally dark green, developed by Grueby. Tiles and plaques were derived from Hispano-Moresque and Della Robbia styles. Production ceased early in the 20th cent.

Guard chain: a long chain hung round the neck to support keys or toilet requirements.

Gubbio maiolica: tin-glazed earthenware made at the workshop of Giorgio Andreoli at Gubbio, in the duchy of Urbino. This workshop was famous in the 16th cent. for its lustre wares and particularly for its ruby-coloured pigment.

Guéridon or **Guéridon table:** (*Fr.*), a small piece of furniture, usually circular, intended to support some form of light. In the 17th cent. in France it sometimes took the form of a Negro figure ('blackamoor') holding a tray. Subsequently the term was extended to cover almost any form of small table on which candelabra, etc., might be placed. (See Candle stand.)

Guernsey measure: a baluster-shaped pewter (q.v.) measure, encircled by two broad bands, and having a heart-shaped lid and twin acorn thumb-piece (q.v.); peculiar to Guernsey, C.I.

Guilloche: a border moulding composed of interlaced ribbon often enclosing foliate rosettes. This form of ornament appears especially on furniture and metalwork, from the 16th to the 18th cent.

Guilloché: (*Fr.*), engine-turned (q.v.).

Guimard, Hector: (1867–1942), French architect, designer and decorator and a protagonist of the Art Nouveau (q.v.) style in France. He is best known for his entrances in metalwork for the Paris Métro, designed in 1900.

Guipure: confusing term for needlepoint or pillow lace (qq.v.) without grounds (q.v.) supported by brides (q.v.).

Guipure d'Art: a type of embroidery worked in white thread on a netted foundation in the manner of 16th-cent. lacis (q.v.) and often classified as lace.

Gumley, John: d. *c.* 1729), looking-glass maker at Lambeth and cabinet-maker to George I. Some knowledge of Gumley's activities has been gained from frequent notices in the press of his day. His glasshouse was set up in 1705 and in the following year his showroom over the New Exchange received a commendation from the pen of Richard Steele. A looking-glass with the name *Gumley* carved on a small gilt plaque is at Hampton Court Palace and another with *John Gumley, 1703*, is at Chatsworth. He was in partnership with James Moore and would seem to have died some time before 1729, in which year accounts were rendered by Mrs Elizabeth Gumley & Co.

Gunner's stiletto: a stiletto (q.v.) with a scale on the blade for converting weight of gunshot into diameter of bore.

Gwa: Japanese term meaning picture or drawing; drew (at the end of an artist's signature).

Gwim, James: originally a coach-painter in Kildare, who worked for Stephen Theodor Janssen (q.v.) at the Battersea enamel factory (q.v.). His designs for enamels included one of Britannia encouraging the Linen Manufacture in Ireland, engraved by Ravenet, and he was probably responsible for others in similar vein, such as Britannia encouraging the Arts and Sciences and Hibernia receiving the apple from Paris.

Hadley, H.: maker of fine quality holster pistols in the third quarter of the 18th cent. His productions were furnished with silver mounts of unusual richness. He followed the Hispanicizing fashion in his barrel design.

Hadley chest: an American type of chest found in and around Hadley, Massachusetts. A characteristic New England dowry chest (q.v.) of 1690–1710. Its distinctive feature is the incised carving of tulips, vines and leaves which cover the entire front.

Hague, The, porcelain: hard-paste porcelain (q.v.) was made at The Hague in Holland from about 1776 with the help of German workmen, while a certain amount of decorating of pieces made elsewhere was also done at the factory. A stork in blue, either under or over the glaze appears as a mark. Tournai porcelain (q.v.) was sometimes decorated at The Hague and such pieces are found with the stork in blue over the glaze.

Haig, Thomas: cabinet-maker, in partnership with Thomas Chippendale (q.v.) from 1771 to 1779 and then with the latter's son, Thomas Chippendale the younger (q.v.), until 1796.

Hair jewellery: in the Victorian era in Britain hair jewellery was frequently worn in remembrance of a loved one or as a token of sentiment. Complete pieces were made of woven hair, or a lock of hair was mounted in a brooch or other item of jewellery. Hair jewellery was also popular in America in the 1850s and 1860s. Some was made in homes, hospitals and prisons, and much, especially the tubular knotted type seemingly of horsehair, came from Germany.

Halberd: see Pole-arms.

Half-armour: a light armour covering the whole body excepting the legs, and often also excluding the arms.

Half-hunter watch: a pocket watch with a hinged lid in which is a glazed window, so that the hands may be seen without opening the lid. A development of the 'hunter' watch said to have been initiated by Napoleon Bonaparte, and for this reason this type of watch is sometimes referred to as a Napoleon watch.

Halfpenny, William and John: father and son who were both architects and designers and whose publications, such as *Rural Architecture in the Chinese taste* (1751–2) and *New Designs for Chinese Temples* (1752), disseminated the new light, exotic taste. They are concerned principally with building and garden architecture, but the latter includes some designs for chairs.

Half-seconds pendulum: a type of pendulum 249 mm (9.8 in) in length, beating twice a second. This is the longest pendulum normally found on verge escapement (q.v.) clocks.

Half-tester: see Tester.

Hall, John: engraver, apprenticed in 1754 to Stephen Theodor Janssen (q.v.) at the Battersea enamel factory (q.v.).

Hall chair: plain, un-upholstered chair, introduced in the early 18th cent. 'for the use of servants and strangers waiting on business', according to Sheraton (q.v.). Some examples have a coat of arms on the back.

Hallmark: strictly speaking, the distinguishing mark of the Hall or Assay Office at which a piece of silver so marked is assayed, e.g. Leopard's head for London, Crown for Sheffield, etc. Used generally in the plural to denote the whole group of marks employed, viz. hall, maker's (q.v.), standard, and date-letter (q.v.). There are no hallmarks on American silver.

Hamadan rugs: Hamadan is the marketing centre for Kurdish rugs, and they are often known by this name. Heavy, long pile of great durability, rather coarse in stitch but well coloured, designs often embellished with animal figures.

Hampshire, Isle of Wight: 'lace' made in running stitch on machine-made net.

Hampshire Pottery: an American pottery established in 1871 at Keene, New Hampshire, making a variety of useful and ornamental wares, including souvenirs, often with black transfer printing (q.v.). *Maiolica* (q.v.) was also produced. Mark: HAMPSHIRE/POTTERY with signature of J. S. Taft, the proprietor.

Hanap: the Medieval name for 'standing-cup' (q.v.).

Hancock, Charles Frederick: English silversmith and jeweller who worked with Storr & Mortimer before founding his own firm in the 1840s. He competed with Garrard & Co. (q.v.) and Hunt & Roskell (q.v.) for commissions for display and presentation pieces.

Hancock, Robert: (1729/30–1816), engraver; son of John Hancock;

apprenticed to George Anderton, Birmington, 1746; working at York House, Battersea (q.v.), 1753 as engraver for enamels. Probably at Bow (q.v.) 1756 for a brief period before moving to Worcester (q.v.) where he served as engraver, becoming partner in the business 1772–4. Hancock joined Turner at the Caughley (q.v.) factory 1775. He was at Oldbury 1780 (and possibly did some engraving for Bilston (q.v.) enamels); Tividale, nr Dudley 1781; Birmingham 1791; Bristol 1796; and London 1808. Died 14 October 1816 and was buried at Brislington, Bristol.
Marks:

R . Hancock fecit

RH . Worcester

RH Worcester

R . H . f .

Hand-blown glass: see Free-blown glass.

Hand-coolers: semi-precious stones carved in the form of eggs, and of a similar size, for the purpose expressed in their name. Highly polished agates, marbles, and interesting pieces of Blue John (q.v.) were favourite materials chosen for these attractive objects.

Hand gun: the earliest form of hand firearm, introduced early in the 14th cent. It consisted simply of a tubular barrel attached to a long wooden stock designed to be held under the arm, and ignited at the touch-hole by hand.

Handkerchief ring: a small gold ring worn on the little finger in the 1870s, connected by a chain to a larger ring which held a handkerchief.

Handkerchief table: an American term for a single-leaf table with leaf and top triangular in shape. Closed,

the table fits in a corner; opened, it is a small square.

Han dynasty: dynasty of the Chinese Han Emperors covering the period 206 B.C. to A.D. 220. Earthenware found in Han tombs indicates that the skilful potter had mastered techniques of wide artistic possibilities, notably that of glazing. Vessels were still following metal forms, decorated with bands in moulded relief. A green or brown 'lead' glaze was applied to a reddish earthenware, but some grey earthenwares were left unglazed. Even more important was the discovery at this time of felspathic-glazed (q.v.) stoneware. The hard impervious body with its semi-transparent olive-brown glaze, containing felspar rock, foreshadows the invention of porcelain.

Hanger: (1) a light, curved, single-edged civilian sword used by horsemen and sailors in the 17th and 18th cent. The term when first used appears to be synonymous with falchion (q.v.) and cutlass (q.v.); (2) the triangular buckled sling attached to the belt, in which a rapier was carried in the late 16th and early 17th cent.

Harache, Pierre: the first of the Huguenot goldsmiths seeking refuge in London from persecution to gain admittance to the Goldsmiths' Company (1682) and the right to have his wares assayed by the Company.

Hardman, John, & Co.: Birmingham firm producing church plate (q.v.) and furnishings, founded in 1838 by John Hardman (1811–67) and A. W. N. Pugin (q.v.), who was the principal designer. Their early manufactures were in the Gothic Revival (q.v.) style.

Hard-paste porcelain: true porcelain manufactured from china clay and china stone, glazed with china stone made fusible with a flux. It shows a shining fracture when broken and is completely vitrified and dense. Chinese porcelain is hard-paste. The secret of its manufacture was discovered c. 1708 by the Meissen arcanist (q.v.) J. F. Boettger (q.v.) and it was subsequently made in several Continental factories, but in England only three factories made it, Plymouth, Bristol, and New Hall (qq.v.) in its early days. New Hall advertised its product as 'Real China'.

Harrison, John: a carpenter's son, born in Yorkshire in 1693, who won a Government award, offered in 1714, for the invention of a marine chronometer. A London clockmaker of eminence, he invented the gridiron pendulum (q.v.).

Harvard chair: American chair with three legs, made of turned members.

Hash dish: 18th- or 19th-cent. circular dish of silver plate (q.v.) with straight sides, close-fitting cover and loop or drop-ring handles. Similar to, and probably used also as, a vegetable dish. Often found with open-frame stand and spirit lamp.

Hashira-e: Japanese print of long, narrow format; a 'pillar picture'.

Hasp: a hinged strap used with a pin or lock to secure a door or chest.

Hat badge: originally derived from Medieval pilgrim signs, enamelled and jewelled badges were worn by men during the Renaissance. Antique cameos (q.v.), mounted in contemporary settings reveal the Humanist interests of the age. Many hat badges have mythological themes, while religious subjects usually include the figure of a patron saint.

Hatching: shade or tone indicated by a system of parallel lines. (See Cross hatching.)

Haviland: a family of porcelain manufacturers of Limoges, established there since mid-19th cent. Noted for production of tableware; strong ties with America.

Haystack: more properly Haycock, which it resembles. An Irish pewter (q.v.) tavern measure, made chiefly in Cork.

Heading sword: an executioner's sword, usually with a plain cruciform hilt long enough to be used with two hands, and a broad, straight, two-edged blade with a rounded or squared point. It was employed on the Continent, and especially in Germany, from the 16th to the early 19th cent.

Heal, Sir Ambrose: (1872–1959), from 1896 the designer of all the furniture for the family firm of Heal & Son, which was founded in 1810. He became chairman in 1913. His early designs reflect the influence of the Arts and Crafts Movement (q.v.).

Helm: a large headpiece or helmet, covering the entire head and face and reaching nearly to the shoulders, introduced at the end of the 12th cent.

The top was at first flat but by the middle of the 13th cent. had become conical, giving an improved glancing surface. Later it was usually bolted or chained to the breast and back.

Hen dish: oval, basket-shaped egg dish with cover in the form of a sitting hen.

Henri Deux ware: often called St-Porchaire ware. English earthenware of the mid-19th cent., decorated with a complicated pattern of clay inlays after the manner of 16th-cent. work at St-Porchaire, near Poitou. A notable exponent of the technique was Charles Toft at Mintons (q.v.).

Hepplewhite, George: (d. 1786), cabinet-maker (q.v.), whose pattern book *The Cabinet-maker and Upholsterers' Guide* published in 1788, after his death, has made him known to posterity. Hepplewhite interpreted the new Classical style inspired by Robert Adam (q.v.) and many of the designs in his pattern book are for inlaid furniture. As a working cabinet-maker he does not appear to have enjoyed any fame in his lifetime.

Herat carpets: fine quality Oriental carpets. The design most closely associated with them is a close conventionalized all-over effect, with a recurring leaf or 'fish' motif and small rosettes. This is copied throughout Persia; ground shade is usually dark blue, and a distinguishing feature of fine specimens is a soft green border. Knot: Ghiordes or Sehna (qq.v.).

Herculaneum: a potworks near the site of the present Herculaneum Dock in Liverpool was founded by Richard Abbey & Graham in 1793. It was sold to Worthington, Humble & Holland three years later. The company was enlarged in 1806 and continued to operate until 1833 when the partnership was dissolved and the property sold to Ambrose Lace and others for £25,000. Lace leased the premises to Thomas Case, gentleman, and John Mort, potter, who operated until 1836. Subsequently the firm traded as Mort and Simpson until the works were closed down in 1841. Apart from the Herculaneum Pottery the company was also in occupation of an earthenware factory on the Sankey Canal, St Helens. The products of the factory included blue-printed earthenware, cream-coloured stoneware jugs, drab stoneware, busts, earthenware figures, and, from 1801, porcelain of the Staffordshire type.

Herold, Johann Gregor: (1696–1775), trained as a miniature and enamel painter. Herold was put in artistic direction of the Meissen porcelain factory (q.v.) in 1720 and was formally appointed director and arcanist (q.v.) in 1731, which he remained until his retirement in 1765. He himself decorated Meissen porcelain and was responsible for the introduction, about 1725, of scenes, painted in brilliant colours, containing pseudo-Chinese figures framed in scrollwork in gold and sometimes lustre.

Herringbone banding: a decorative veneer (q.v.) border much used on walnut furniture of the late 17th and early 18th cent. consisting of two narrow strips of veneer laid together diagonally forming a pattern resembling a herringbone or feather and contrasting in design with the surface veneer on the piece. Drawer fronts, table tops, bureau flaps and similar fields were frequently bordered with a herringbone banding or cross banding (q.v.) or with both. Also known as feather banding.

Herringbone fringe: see Blazes.

Herter Bros.: leading New York firm of decorators and furniture manufacturers. It was founded in the 1860s by Gustave Herter (d. 1880), who was joined by his younger half-brother, Christian Herter (1840–83). The latter took over the firm in 1870. In the 1870s and 1880s it specialized in creating interiors and designing furniture in the Japanese taste, inspired by the example of E. W. Godwin (q.v.). In 1882 Christian Herter designed a Japanese parlour for the William H. Vanderbilt house in New York.

Heywood, Higginbottom & Smith: for a time one of the largest British wallpaper manufacturing companies. Their greatest achievement was the development in the 1870s of the 'sanitary process', by which engraved rollers pressed the design on to the paper with oil colours, producing for the first time a washable wallpaper.

'H' hinge: like the cock's head hinge (q.v.), an early external type of hinge in the form of the letter 'H' extensively used on cupboards of the 16th and 17th cent. Good-quality hinges of these two varieties have stop-chamfered edges and were originally held fast by hand-wrought nails, never by screws.

Highboy or **high chest of drawers:** an American tall chest of drawers mounted on a commode (q.v.) or lowboy (q.v.) sometimes topped with a broken-arch pediment usually heightened with finials (q.v.). Characteristically plain in New England; highly carved and ornamented in Philadelphia. The earlier examples are sometimes japanned (see Japan work) in a manner popular in England in the late 17th cent. Mid-18th cent. pieces are of mahogany, white walnut or walnut, while towards 1775 maple was also used.

High-warp tapestry: tapestry woven on an upright loom. In the Middle Ages such tapestry was considered superior. It is slower to make, but the work can be more exact and it allows for subtler effects of texture. The weaver sits at his upright loom, divides his warp with his left hand with the aid of leashes, and inserts his coloured wefts in accordance with his cartoon, which is placed behind him. He works with the back side of the tapestry towards him and he can see the face by means of a mirror. For closer inspection he need only move round to the front of the loom. (See also Low-warp tapestry.)

Hila rugs: Caucasian rugs, frequently with a small centre medallion with matching corner-pieces, the subsidiary design being a clearly defined cone. Ice-blue is the distinguishing shade.

Hipped knee: an ornamental treatment of the knee of a cabriole leg (q.v.) sometimes found on good quality chairs and settees of the first half of the 18th cent. in which the carving on the knee is extended on to the seat rail above.

Hiramakiyé (*Japanese* = flat-sown picture), a Japanese lacquer-work technique involving a flat decoration on the lacquer surface.

Hiramé: (*Japanese* = flat aspect), a Japanese lacquer-work technique in which small pieces of gold or silver leaf are placed on the lacquered surface, fairly wide apart but evenly spread and covered with layers of clear lacquer.

Hispano-Moresque maiolica: tin-glazed earthenware made in Spain by Moorish craftsmen first at Granada and later from about the end of the 14th cent. for some 300 years in the workshops of the Manises in Valencia. The ware is decorated with metallic lustre pigments made from oxides of silver and copper, probably originally invented in Persia.

Hitchcock chair: an American adaptation of an English late 18th-cent. painted and stencilled chair. It has round-turned legs, raked, and an oval-turned 'pillow-back' top rail. Almost always painted black with stencillings of fruits and flowers in gold or colours. Named after Lambert Hitchcock, of Hitchcockville, Connecticut, who made this type of chair in quantity from about 1820 to 1850.

Hobbs, Brockunier & Co.: an American glassworks, established about 1844 in Virginia. Pioneers of many art glass techniques, including Peach Blow (Coral), spangled and crackle glass (qq.v.), and other new forms between 1882 and 1891.

Hobnail cutting: a method of decorating glass vessels by cutting or grinding in deep relief to form a pattern of large diamonds, each with a flat point incised with a simple cross. Late 18th and early 19th-cent. Irish and English glass vessels were frequently decorated with this doubly cut diamond pattern.

Hobnail glass: also called dewdrop glass, a type of glass made in America at the end of the 19th cent. by Hobbs, Brockunier & Co. (q.v.), for bottles, tableware, etc. The technique involved hand shaping and raised decoration.

Höchst porcelain: hard-paste porcelain (q.v.) was made at Höchst-on-Main, Germany, from the year 1750, at a factory which had been founded four years earlier for the purpose of making faience (q.v.). At first the new venture experienced financial difficulties but was subsidised by the Elector of Mainz in 1765. The factory closed in 1798. The early wares follow the Meissen (q.v.) example, a rich lilac being much favoured with gilding in the borders. Höchst figures from about 1765 often have a grassy-mound base. J. P. Melchior became chief modeller in 1767, much of his work being in the Classical style. The mark used is the wheel of Mainz, either incised or in colour, above or below the glaze.

Holdship, Richard and **Josiah:** engravers and part-proprietors of the original porcelain works at Worcester (q.v.), from 1751 until 1759. Richard Holdship went to Derby (q.v.), and in 1764 offered to impart information concerning the Worcester porcelain formula, and to teach 'Printing in Enamell and Blew'.

Some Worcester engravings carry a rebus design of R H in monogram and an anchor.

H Worcester

H Worcester

H Worcester

These marks are traditionally regarded as those of Holdship who was believed to have been in charge of the printing department. This mark however may stand for Robert Hancock (q.v.) who later added his name in full because the monogram was confused with that of Holdship. Much confusion has arisen from the initials of Hancock and R. Holdship being the same. The monogram with the reversed 'R' has been described as RJH and believed to represent Richard and Josiah Holdship.

Holland, Henry: (1746–1806), an architect of influence whose work for the Prince of Wales at Carlton House, and for Samuel Whitbread at Southill made him famous. He designed the interiors and the furniture at Southill in a combined Louis XIV and Graeco-Roman style.

Holland & Sons: London furniture manufacturers, founded in the 18th cent. They continued to make furniture in the 18th-cent. styles throughout the Victorian period, specializing in floral marquetry (q.v.), and they supplied furniture for Queen Victoria's residences – Osborne, Balmoral and Sandringham. They also produced furniture in the Victorian eclectic style, employing designers such as B. J. Talbert (q.v.).

Hollie-work: a type of white-work embroidery popular during the Georgian period, particularly for babies' clothes and bonnets. It was worked on fine linen, lawn or cambric in white thread. Delicate openwork patterns, worked without any foundation in the manner of needlepoint lace (q.v.), were inserted into holes cut in the material, which were previously edged with buttonhole stitch. Alternatively, the threads of the ground material were drawn out one way only and the pattern worked on the remaining threads.

Hollins, Samuel: (1748–1820), son of Richard Hollins of Far Green, Hanley; manufacturer of earthenware and 'red china' (q.v.) at a factory on the Caulden Canal, Vale Pleasant, Shelton, from c. 1780 until c. 1815. He was one of the original partners in the New Hall porcelain factory (q.v.) which traded as Hollins, Warburton & Co., and by a codicil to his will dated 27 April 1820 he left his interest in the Company (valued at his death £5975), to his son Thomas Hollins of Cheetham Hill, Manchester.

About 1815 he must have made over his earthenware business to Matthew

Mare, his son-in-law (who manufactured earthenware on the Cauldon Canal and is listed in Parson and Bradshaw's *Directory*, 1818).

Samuel Hollins made excellent unglazed dark green and dark red stonewares with relief decoration.

Hollow cutting: a method of decorating glass vessels by means of cutting or grinding a pattern with a convex-edged wheel, producing shallow concavities in the glass.

A pattern of 'hollow diamonds', consisting of intersecting cavities was much used on mid-18th-cent. wares, but many variants of cut motifs were employed.

Hollow stem: a type of stem found on drinking glasses in the late 18th cent. in the form of a hollow cylinder, sometimes, though rarely, knopped.

Hollow ware: a general term for vessels designed to hold liquids.

Holy-water bucket: the receptacle for the holy water sprinkled in the *asperges* at the beginning of the Mass. Early examples are normally straight sided, polygonal or cylindrical, and occasionally waisted; the bombé-vase shape came into fashion in the 17th cent. Handles were occasionally terminated with dragon heads. In the 19th cent. A. W. N. Pugin (q.v.) made designs for holy-water buckets in a Gothic Revival (q.v.) style.

Honan wares: black- and brown-glazed Chinese porcelain wares of the Sung dynasty (q.v.), probably made in Honan Province.

Honey gilding: see Gilding.

Honeysuckle motif: see Anthemion.

Honiton lace: pillow lace (q.v.), the best and the first made in England, described as bone lace (q.v.) in about 1620 in Westcote's *View of Devonshire* and continuing until about 1725. Suggestive of *point d'Angleterre* (q.v.) with the ground worked round the pattern, but with less attractive pattern shapes. Honiton net, made

from costly Antwerp thread, and of excellent quality, was an important product in the 18th cent. Honiton *appliqué* lace was made with motifs of pillow lace applied to this net ground but the net was soon machine-made, with the flower motifs reduced to meaningless ugly shapes. Late in the 19th cent. Honiton made a tape pillow lace with brides (q.v.), sometimes in needlepoint (q.v.), instead of a mesh ground, and also Devonia lace (q.v.).

Hood: the upper removable portion of a long-case clock (q.v.). In all, except very early cases, it draws forward.

Hoof foot: a foot in the form of a hoof appears on early examples of walnut chairs made with the cabriole leg (q.v.) between about 1695 and 1720. A simpler terminal, which retained its popularity for a longer period was the club foot (q.v.), introduced shortly after the first appearance of the hoof foot.

Hoop-back chair: see Windsor chair.

Hope, Thomas: (1769–1831), a wealthy connoisseur and collector of antique sculpture and pottery, whose writings on architecture, furniture and costume are a guide to Regency taste. His book of designs, recording the furniture made for his house, Deepdene, in Surrey, entitled *Household Furniture and Interior Decoration*, was published in 1807.

Horn mark: a mark used on porcelain at the Chantilly factory and imitated at Worcester and Caughley (qq.v.).

Horse brass: brass horse-furniture attached to the harness. Horse brasses may derive from the heraldic devices applied to Medieval horse armour, later examples being presented as prizes or bought as charms. In the 1840s and 1850s, when casting and stamping had replaced hammering as the principal methods of manufacture, there was a fashion for commemorative and portrait brasses. After 1870, mass production caused a decline in quality, and since that time numerous copies, which are comparatively valueless, have been made of the earlier types.

Horse dressing-glass: see Cheval glass.

Horseshoe-back chair: American name for a hoop-back Windsor chair (q.v.).

Horta, Victor: (1861–1947), Belgian Art Nouveau (q.v.) architect and designer. Furniture and interiors designed by him are characterized by sinuous, 'growing' forms deriving from the stems and roots of plants and executed in pale woods.

Hoso-ye: small vertical narrow Japanese print about 35 mm × 17 mm (12 in × 6 in).

Hour circle: see Chapter ring.

Hsüan Tê period: (1426–35), classic reign for blue-and-white Chinese porcelains of very fine, richly glazed material. A certain rhythmic vitality is found alike in the contours of vessels and in their painted lotus scrolls, flying dragons, etc. Blackish spots sometimes mottle the cobalt pigment. Underglaze copper-red painting, white wares with faint incised or slip designs (*an hua*), blue or red monochromes, and the use of yellow enamel grounds, are found. Later times (especially the 18th cent.) 'borrowed' the reign-mark, and also made admirable copies of the wares.

Hukin & Heath: Birmingham silver and electro-plate (q.v.) manufacturers from 1879 to 1953. They also made electro-types (q.v.). C. Dresser (q.v.) was associated with the firm as artistic director.

Hull, Belle Vue Pottery: a potworks was started here in 1802 by James and Jeremiah Smith, Job Ridgway of Shelton and Josiah Hipwood. In 1806 the factory passed to Job and George Ridgway who, after working it for a few years, closed it down. In 1825 William Bell purchased the pottery and used it until 1840. Much creamware, usually painted or transfer-printed in blue or brown with landscapes, etc. was exported to Germany. The factory was a large one with a depot in Hamburg. The following marks were used:

Impressed

Transfer-printed

Hunt & Roskell: London silver and electro-plate (q.v.) manufacturers and retailers founded about 1840 by John Mortimer and Samuel Hunt. After 1843 the name became Hunt & Roskell and as such they traded until about 1940. Like Garrard & Co. (q.v.), they produced a number of display and presentation pieces in the mid-Victorian period as well as domestic wares.

Hunt board: a high sideboard originating in the southern states of America in the second part of the 18th cent. Refreshments were laid out on it for hunters to stand and eat from after a day's sport.

Hunter: a type of pocket watch with a hinged cover over the face, made throughout the 19th cent.

Hunting carpets: Persian carpets with elaborate hunting scenes, realistically depicted.

Hunting sword: a short, light sabre (q.v.) with a straight or very slightly curved blade and usually no knuckle-bow. Originally designed to be worn while hunting, as its name implies; it was often affected by high-ranking officers during the 18th cent.

Husk ornament: an ornamental motif resembling the husk of a wheat ear used by architects and craftsmen in the Adam (q.v.) period. Festooned husks and pendent husks in diminishing size appear, for example, carved on chair backs of the period, as a decorative inlay on cabinet furniture, or applied and chased on silverware such as sugar vases or sauce boats. (See Bell flower ornament.)

Hutch: enclosed structure, often raised on uprights, or an enclosed structure of more than one tier. The name derives from Fr. *huche*, a chest, but the significance of hutch was much wider. Food-hutch, often confused with dole cupboard (q.v.), is a name given to a hutch with perforated panels.

Hutton, William, & Sons: Birmingham manufacturers of silver, Sheffield plate (q.v.), pewter (q.v.) and Britannia metal (q.v.) wares. They undertook commissions for trophies and presentation pieces as well as domestic articles, especially flatware (q.v.). The firm was founded in 1800.

Ice glass: glass to which an appearance of cracked ice has been given by means of plunging the hot glass in water and later reheating it. This method of decorating glass was used in Venice in the 16th cent. and subsequently by Venetian workmen who set up glasshouses elsewhere.

Ice pail: see Wine cooler.

Ichimai-ye: single-sheet Japanese prints.

Ilmenau porcelain: see Limbach porcelain.

Image toys: contemporary designation of mid-18th-cent. Staffordshire pottery figures.

Imari porcelain: a familiar name for the porcelains exported by Japan from Arita in the province of Hizan during the first half of the 18th cent. 'Brocaded Imari' in blue, red and gold were the inspiration of later English china and earthenware patterns made at Derby, Worcester, Spode, Mintons and Mason's (qq.v.). These were generally known as 'Japans'.

Imp.: short for *impressit, impresserunt* or *imprimé*, in which case it means printed by; or for *imprimerie* – printing establishment or works.

Impasto ware: a type of English stoneware (q.v.) made by Doulton (q.v.) from about 1879, on which the decoration is formed by thick layers of coloured slips, giving a raised effect to the pattern.

Imperial Russian service: see 'Frog' service.

Impression: a term applied to any print made from a metal plate, wood block or stone.

Ince, William and Mayhew, John: (active 1759–1803), cabinet-makers (q.v.), who published a series of some 100 furniture designs, entitled the *Universal System of Household Furniture.* They appeared between 1759 and 1762.

Incense boat: the vessel in which the incense is carried before it is placed in the censer (q.v.) to burn. Normally it is a fairly simple boat-shaped vessel, and it was occasionally made to match a censer. Made of precious or base metal, or of semi-precious stone mounted in metal.

Inc., incid., incidit: engraved.

Incise carving: see Scratch carving.

Incised decoration on pottery: decoration cut into the paste or body with a sharp pointed instrument. Much used by country potters for names, inscriptions and dates. (See also Sgraffiato.)

Incised stem: a type of stem found on drinking glasses in the late 17th and 18th cent. ornamented with spiral grooving.

Independent decorators: in the 18th and early 19th cent. porcelain was often bought 'in the white' for decoration by outside enamellers and gilders. This practice was much developed in Germany where these independent decorators were known as *Hausmaler.* In England the most notable were Giles, Duesbury, Baxter (qq.v.) (who embellished Coalport china), T. M. Randall & R. Robins (who, from Spa Fields, London, decorated Swansea, Nantgarw and Coalport for London dealers).

Salt-glazed stoneware (q.v,) was similarly decorated by Duesbury, and cream-coloured ware (q.v.) by Mrs Warburton at Cobridge, Robinson & Rhodes at Leeds, and Absolon (q.v.) at Yarmouth.

Other English outside decorators were Fidèle Duvivier, Allen of Lowestoft, John Cutts & Sons of Shelton.

Indian mask: a mask with a plumed head-dress used as a decorative motif on crestings (q.v.), particularly of mirrors, at the end of the 17th cent., and more popularly, during the earlier years of the 18th cent.

'India' wallpapers: 18th-cent. name given to many articles imported from the Far East, including paper-hangings specially made for the European market.

'India' ware: the term in general use in England during the 18th cent. for imported Chinese porcelain. It gained currency owing to the fact that the East India Company held a monopoly of trade with the East. It sold the goods it imported by auction at India House, London. This building in the City was demolished in 1861.

Inlaid tiles: a process of inlaying was used by Medieval potters for decorating paving tiles (Cleeve Abbey, Westminster Abbey) and by Sussex potters, *c.* 1790–1850, for useful and ornamental wares. The decoration was formed by impressing the body with punches or with printers' types, and filling in with clay of a contrasting colour, usually white on red.

Inlay: furniture decoration consisting of surface ornament formed by insetting separate pieces of differently coloured woods, or bone, ivory, shell, etc., in a recessed ground. Inlay was popular as a decoration on chair-backs, chests, table friezes, etc., between 1550 and 1650, and should not be confused with marquetry (q.v.).

Inro: a seal-case worn with conventional dress in Japan at the end of a cord to which various necessities were attached. It was convenient thus to carry everyday objects as the dress included no pockets. The seal case was a small box of one or more sections fitted together, and lacquered or carved and held shut by a cord holder which could be slid down the cord. Early examples are of lacquered wood, sometimes with additions of ivory or shell. The shape is fairly constant but the number of compartments varies from one to five. Though intended at first for seals, these compartments came to be used for medicines and sundry needs. Slight variations of form and arrangement occur, as, for example, when the cases are enclosed in a surrounding sheath. Like netsuke (q.v.), this art was described in a book known as the *Soken Kisho* of 1781. The inro was seldom signed in the 18th cent. but was increasingly signed in the 19th. The lacquer used is the natural gum of a sumach tree, mixed with various pigments and with gold and silver. Raised designs were produced by building up with gesso (q.v.) and other compositions.

Intaglio: a carved pattern or design hollowed out from the surface of a gem or of rock crystal or glass.

Intarsia: see Tarsia.

Invar: an alloy of nickel and steel, produced from 1898 and used for pendulums.

Inventory numbers: these are often found painted or branded on furniture made for the Crown or Royal Family of France. They frequently refer to the *Journal du Garde Meuble de la Couronne*, which has survived intact for some periods between the late 17th cent. and the Revolution. (See *Garde Meuble . . .*)

Iridescent glass: glass made from the 1880s with a prismatic, mirror-like film achieved by metallic vapours, oxides or acids. Much used in Art Nouveau (q.v.) period.

Iron red: a red pigment made from an oxide of iron; used to decorate ceramics.

Ironstone china: a hard, durable white earthenware alleged to contain slag of ironstone as one of its ingredients, patented by Charles James Mason in 1831. The patent specification was false and unworkable. Other firms have used the name, notably Ridgway & Morley and Geo. L. Ashworth & Bros.

Ishi-zuri: Japanese term for a stone-print.

Isleworth earthenware: pottery was made at a factory established about 1760 by Joseph Shore. It closed down about 1825.

'Welsh' wares, useful domestic articles decorated with zigzag patterns in brown and yellow slip (q.v.), were probably the main products of the factory.

Red, green and buff terra cotta (q.v.) teapots and ornamental pieces with relief decoration and of 19th-cent. manufacture, marked 'S. & G', have been wrongly ascribed to this factory. Its mark was:

S & G

Isnik pottery: Turkish earthenware made at Isnik in Anatolia. The industry flourished in the second half of the 16th cent. when the Ottoman Empire included Asia Minor, Syria, North Africa and a large part of south-eastern Europe. The earthenware is white, covered with a clear alkaline glaze. Pigments used include rich blues, greens and reds. Designs are composed of formal flower motifs within scrolled borders. The name 'Rhodian ware' is erroneously given to this pottery.

Ispahan carpets: Persian carpets or rugs, often employing medallion or vase designs (see Vase carpets) in a wide range of colours, the composition being very well balanced.

Italian comedy figures: the Catalogue of the Chelsea porcelain factory (q.v.) (1755) refers to 'Figures of the Italian Theatre'. These subjects from the Italian *Commedia dell' Arte* were frequently copied by the porcelain modellers of Bow (q.v.) and Chelsea from Meissen (q.v.) adaptations of Callot and other designs in Luigi Riccoboni's *Histoire du Théâtre Italien* (1728). Some became extremely popular; Pierrot, Harlequin and Columbine; Pantaloon; the Captain, the Doctor and the Advocate; Isabella and Cynthio.

The better known reappeared in Staffordshire salt-glaze.

Ives, Joseph: (1782–1862), in business from 1812 producing tall, wooden-movement clocks, Joseph Ives invented and patented the mirror clock and roller pinions. He went to Brooklyn, New York, in 1825, where he produced the famous wagon-spring clock (q.v.). In 1830 Ives found himself in financial difficulties and was bailed out by Birge.

Jack: a mechanically operated figure that strikes a bell on the outside of a clock. In the first instance jacks were of carved wood, a well-known example, dating probably from the 15th cent., being *Jack the Smiter* at Southwold, Suffolk. Jacks of a later date, on smaller portable clocks and on wall clocks, were made of metal.

In the 19th cent. a French writer carefully traced the origin of the word to its being a corruption of *Jacquemart:* the name of a 15th-cent. clockmaker of Lille, France. Others have contended that it is an abbreviation of *Jaccomarchiadus:* a man in armour. In spite of this academic dispute, it seems hardly necessary to look farther than the still current and expressive name *Jack* for any man whose actual patronymic is unknown. These lifelike and nearly lifesize figures were doubtless the recipients of this commonly used name, as they had none of their own.

Jack: see Brigandine.

Jack, George: (1855–1932), American architect and furniture designer who settled in England and worked with Philip Webb (q.v.), taking over his practice in 1900. In about 1880 he became the principal furniture designer of Morris & Co. (q.v.), where he encouraged the production of expensive walnut and mahogany pieces in traditional styles.

Jackfield earthenware: earthenware is said to have been made at Jackfield in the 16th cent., but nothing is known with certainty until Richard Thursfield from Stoke began to manufacture there at the beginning of the 18th cent. He was succeeded by his son who carried on the business until about 1780, when it was taken over by John Rose from Coalport.

No marked examples are known, but there is reason to believe that a type of black-glazed red earthenware, usually decorated with oil-painting over the glaze, was made here from about 1760–75. But this kind of ware was produced in some quantity throughout Staffordshire at that time, so that no pieces can definitely be attributed to Jackfield.

Jackson & Graham: London firm of cabinet-makers (q.v.), founded in 1840 and eventually taken over by Collinson & Lock (q.v.). It specialized in expensive and elaborately decorated furniture, often with floral marquetry (q.v.).

Jacob, Georges: (1739–1814), French cabinet-maker (q.v.), *maître-ébéniste* in 1765. An originator of the French Neoclassical (q.v.) style, he executed a number of Royal commissions and specialized in the design and production of chairs. In his later work he introduced Etruscan and Greco-Roman elements. His early work is often stamped

G ◆ I A C O B

Jacobean embroidery: see Crewel-work.

Jacobite glasses: propaganda glasses bearing emblems and mottoes of a cryptic character associated with the Jacobite cause. Most common is the six-petalled Jacobite rose with one or two buds: the rose is said to represent the House of Stuart, the small bud the Old Pretender, the large bud on the right being added later, either in honour of Prince Charles Edward's arrival in Scotland or after James's proposal to 'abdicate' in favour of his son. Other Jacobite emblems include a stricken and burgeoning oak, oak leaf, bee, butterfly, sunflower, etc. (See also Jacobite pottery.)

Jacobite pottery: occasional inscriptions and emblems on salt-glazed stoneware, earthenware and Jackfield ware (q.v.) indicate Jacobite sympathies. Portraits of Bonnie Prince Charlie are not uncommon on salt-glazed stonewares. Inscriptions and emblems on contemporary glass (such as 'May the tenant be ready when the steward comes', a stricken and burgeoning oak, oak leaf, bee, butterfly, jay, Jacob's Ladder foliage, carnation, fritillary, thistle, triple ostrich plume, and the six-petalled rose of the House of Stuart with one or two buds – all of which are considered Jacobite emblems) have few echoes on pottery.

Jacquard loom: see Moquette.

Jacquet-Droz family: Swiss family of watch and automaton makers established in Geneva from early 18th cent. by Pierre Jacquet-Droz. The family produced ornate musical snuff boxes, singing bird watches and precision watches throughout the 18th and 19th cent.

Jamnitzer, Wenzel: (1508–85), Austrian silversmith in the service of the Habsburgs. He and his brother Alberich are especially known for their cast ornament of natural objects.

Janssen, Stephen Theodore: Lord Mayor of London in 1754 and later City Chamberlain. A merchant stationer, considerable patron of the arts and friend of artists and engravers, he launched the painted-enamel enterprise at York House, Battersea (q.v.), in 1753, his associates being the engraver John Brooks and the potter Henry Delamain (q.v.). Was declared bankrupt in 1756, and there is no evidence of his having had any further connection with the painted-enamel trade. Before he died in 1776 he had succeeded to his father's baronetcy and was again a wealthy and influential man. (See also Battersea enamel.)

Japanese lacquer print: see Urushi-ye.

Japanese print: was discovered by Europeans soon after the opening up of the country to foreign visitors in 1854, and considerable impetus was given to the formation of collections later in the century by the enthusiasm of the French Impressionists and their protagonists, who found much that appealed to their aesthetic senses, ever tuned to receive the new, the adventurous, the unacademic, in the calculated design and arbitrary use of form and colour, of the Japanese print designers. The most immediately attractive of these exotic engravings were the colour-prints of the late 18th cent., but it was not long before the origin of these gay pictures was traced back to black outline prints of the 17th cent.

Indeed, the earliest wood engravings made in Japan belong to a very remote period. Some can reliably be given to the 8th cent. and, as wood engravings are still being published in Japan. The term 'Japanese print' might embrace everything from the crude Buddhistic cuts of an almost legendary antiquity to the pseudo-Picasso abstractions of post-war Tokyo artists. Specifically, however, the term is usually held to apply to the productions of a certain school of mainly Yedo artists, the Ukiyo-ye, which arose in the mid-17th cent. and whose work was virtually ended by the time of the Restoration in 1868.

Japanned metal ware: see Pontypool.

Japan pattern: rich, formal design normally incorporating underglaze (q.v.) blue with overglaze (q.v.) red and green enamels and gilding (q.v.). These patterns are normally associated with the Derby (q.v.) factories but most porcelain manufacturers used these colourful designs which were universally popular in the 19th cent.

Japan patterns: a loose term covering a wide variety of patterns and styles derived from Oriental sources, employed in decorating English porcelain in the 18th and 19th cent., including Chinese *famille verte* and *famille rose* patterns (qq.v.); the Imari (q.v.) of Arita with showy floral or brocaded effects in underglaze (q.v.) blue and enamel colours with added gilding; and patterns in the Kakiemon style (q.v.) enamelled in turquoise, red, green, yellow and blue.

The Japans became very popular in the 1820s, and were extensively used at Derby (q.v.), and in Staffordshire on bone china made by Spode (q.v.), Minton (q.v.) and Davenport (q.v.), as well as for decorating stone or ironstone china.

Japan work: japanned or lacquered furniture began to enjoy a considerable vogue in the late 17th cent. As early as 1661 Pepys recorded seeing 'two very fine chests covered with gold and Indian varnish'. Lacquer work was originally imported from the East, and was known variously as Indian, Chinese or Japanese, but the best kind was made in Japan, and was called 'fine' or 'right' Japan, to distinguish it from substitutes. Most of the genuine Japanese work was brought to England by the Dutch, but the English East India Company handled Chinese and Indian varieties, which had a ready sale in the home market and went under the general name of 'Indian' goods (and were sold in 'Indian' shops). So great was the demand for these goods that some English merchants exported patterns and models of all kinds of furniture to be copied and lacquered by native workmen, who could thus manufacture English-style furniture. The completed goods were reimported and sold at home. But meanwhile an English japan industry had sprung up. In 1688 Stalker and Parker published their *Treatise of Japanning and Varnishing*, and in 1693 a company was formed with the title of 'The Patentees

for Lacquering after the Manner of Japan'. Naturally, the home producers of japan disliked the practice of sending goods abroad to be lacquered, and so did other cabinet-makers (q.v.), who looked upon it as unfair competition. In 1701 the London cabinet-makers, joiners (q.v.) and japanners petitioned Parliament to put a stop to it, and an Act was passed imposing heavier duties on all imported lacquer. Thus from that date nearly all japan work was home-made. It was very popular until about 1740, and much of it was exported. The colours used were bright ones, often scarlet, yellow, etc., and carried out Eastern designs, but English work lacked the high quality of the true Oriental variety. In fact, inferior work was merely varnished. It was usually applied on a background of deal for carcases, or of beech for chairs. Good-class work often had a smooth-grained, veneered surface as a basis. Normally, designs were raised on the surface, but a rare form of lacquer work, known as Bantam work (q.v.), used incised designs. Cabinets, chairs, bureaux, screens, clock cases and mirrors were among the more usual pieces for japanning. There was a revival of this fashion in the later 18th cent.

Japonisme: at the International Exhibition of 1862 in London, and at the Paris Exhibition of 1867, there were a number of Japanese exhibits. Encouraged by J. M. Whistler and E. W. Godwin (q.v.) in particular, there was a vogue for collecting blue-and-white porcelain, Oriental lacquerwork and Japanese prints and the introduction of Oriental elements into

European decorative art. *Japonisme* was a feature of the Aesthetic Movement (q.v.).

Japy Frères: company established *c.* 1770 by Frédéric Japy (1749–1812) at Beaucourt in the French Jura mountains. Specialized in machinemade brass movements, drum clocks and watches. Products stamped JAPY.

Jardinière: a container for flowers. Made in metal, earthenware or wood, dating from the early 19th cent.

Jarves, Deming: (1790–1869), an American glassmaker from Boston, Massachusetts who founded the New England Glass Company (q.v.) in 1818. He left to found the Boston and Sandwich Glass Company (q.v.) in 1826; in 1837, he founded the Mount Washington Glass Works (q.v.) and in 1858 the Cape Cod Glass Co.

Jaseron chain: a thin Venetian gold chain from which a cross or a pendant was suspended, fashionable between 1804 and 1811.

Jasper: a fine close-grained stoneware body of unusual composition including in its ingredients barytes and barium-carbonate, dense and hard enough to stand polishing on a lapidary's wheel and capable of being stained throughout its substance with metallic oxides to fine shades of blue and lavender, sage and olive green, lilac, ochreous yellow (a rare tint) and a peculiarly velvety black. It was the culmination in 1774 of an extended series of experiments by Wedgwood (q.v.) 'over a long period of time'. Wedgwood himself described it as 'white porcelain *bisque* of exquisite beauty and delicacy'. To be distinguished from the less valuable 'Jasper dip' (q.v.).

Jasper dip: coloured solution applied to white jasper body by dipping; name also of ware made of white jasper covered with a surface colouring.

Jaune jonquille: (*Fr.*), a daffodil yellow enamel ground used on Sèvres porcelain (q.v.) and introduced in 1753. The tone is deeper and warmer than that of the yellow ground porcelain made earlier at Meissen (q.v.).

Jeannest, Pierre-Emile: (1813–57), French designer of silver and ceramics noted for his work for Elkington & Co. (q.v.). He also executed designs for Mintons (q.v.).

Jekyll, Thomas: (1827–81), English architect and designer, at first much influenced by the Japanese taste (see Japonisme). He is particularly known for his designs for metalwork carried out by Barnard, Bishop & Barnard (q.v.), for whom he designed a cast-iron pavilion in the Japanese style for the Philadelphia Centennial Exhibition of 1876.

Jelliff, John: (1813–90), American furniture-maker of Newark, New Jersey. He worked in many of the 19th-cent. Revival styles.

Jelly glass: tall glass with a handle intended for jelly, custard or sillabub. Jelly glasses were much in use in the 18th cent. when it was customary to serve an elaborate dessert, the jelly glasses set on glass salvers with baluster or moulded pedestal (q.v.) stems, arranged in tiers of two or three laden salvers.

Jennens & Bettridge: foremost English manufacturers of *papier mâché* (q.v.) in Birmingham between 1816 and 1864. They made articles ranging from substantial pieces of furniture to small decorative objects for the dressing-table and desk, setting the fashions in decoration. Their wares are generally stamped with their name, which became Bettridge & Co. in the 1860s.

Jensen, Gerreit: (known also as Garrett or Gerrard Johnson) cabinet-maker and 'glasse-seller', who supplied much furniture to the Royal Household from 1680. A tall mirror at Hampton Court tallies with the description on his bill rendered in 1699, and it is assumed that Jensen had the monopoly of supplying overmantel mirrors and pier-glasses to the royal palaces during the reign of William and Mary. The date of his birth is unknown, but his will was dated 1715 and he retired from business in that year. His furniture was often japanned inlaid or decorated with marquetry (q.v.).

Jersey measure: a plain baluster-shaped pewter measure, with lid and thumbpiece as in a Guernsey measure; peculiar to Jersey, C.I.

Jesuit china: Chinese porcelain wares of the first half of the 18th cent. painted with Christian subjects supplied by Jesuit missionaries, principally in black monochrome or *famille rose* (q.v.) enamels.

Jet-enamelled ware: one of the most celebrated productions of the Worcester porcelain (q.v.) factory in the 18th cent. consisting of wares transfer-printed in black. Giles (q.v.) purchased 'jet-enamelled' services from Worcester in 1769.

Jewel ornament: ornament with raised devices distantly suggestive of gem-stones, often combined with raised mouldings arranged in geometrical designs. This type of ornament is found carved in relief or applied on early and mid-17th-cent. furniture.

Joey: see Dram glass.

Johnson, Thomas: London designer and wood-carver in the Rococo (q.v.) style. He published a volume entitled *Twelve Girandoles* in 1755, and a more ambitious work, *One Hundred and Fifty New Designs*, between 1756 and 1758.

Joined furniture: term used in describing furniture made with mortice and tenon joints (q.v.) and fixed with pegs.

Joiner: craftsman in early periods responsible for making house fitments as well as furniture. From the 15th cent., in the making of furniture, the joiner used the panel construction in place of thick boards, whereby the panel was held in position in a framework of stiles and rails (qq.v.). This rendered the furniture less cumbersome and more elegant in design. For the framing of the panels the joiner used the mortice and tenon joint (q.v.). Throughout the 16th and for a large part of the 17th cent., the joiner remained the chief maker of furniture, to be replaced in the reign of Charles II by the cabinet-maker (q.v.). From this period the joiner confined himself to the making of bedsteads and 'wainscot' furniture, so called, as they were made from imported oak. Wainscot furniture was not veneered (q.v.) in the manner of the fashionable products of the cabinet-maker but in form followed the prevailing taste of the day.

Joint stool: 16th- and 17th-cent. stool used at the dining table. Of joined construction, it has a rectangular seat and four turned legs and stretchers (q.v.).

Jones, George: (d. 1893), Staffordshire potter who worked at Mintons (q.v.). In 1861 established the Trent Pottery at Stoke-in-Trent, trading from 1873 as George Jones & Sons. Made white, transfer-printed (q.v.) and ornamental earthenware with pâte-sur-pâte (q.v.) decoration.

Jones, Owen: (1809–74), English architect and ornamental designer. By his example and the publication of *The Grammar of Ornament*, he exercised a great influence on English wallpaper, carpets and furniture.

Joney or joney grig: a dialect term for a pottery chimney ornament in the form of a dog. A well-known

Burslem pottery in the 19th cent. was known as a 'doll and jona' (figure and dog) works.

Joubert, Gilles: (1689–1775), French *maître-ébéniste* in the Régence (q.v.) period, and in 1758 *ébéniste* (q.v.) *ordinaire* of the *Garde Meuble de la Couronne* (q.v.).

Jugendstil: general term for German and Austrian design in Art Nouveau (q.v.) style 1896–*c.* 1900, named after theoretical magazine, *Jugend*, published in Munich from 1896 with contributions from O. Eckmann.

Jump, Joseph: (d. 1899), son of Richard Thomas Jump, who had joined Vulliamy (q.v.) in 1812, Joseph Jump was himself apprenticed to Vulliamy in 1827, remaining with him until the latter's death in 1854, after which he worked in Bond Street and Pall Mall, London.

Ju ware: rare Chinese porcelain Imperial ware of the early 12th cent., with buff body and crackled lavender-blue glaze.

Kabistan rugs: considered the finest of the Caucasian rugs (q.v.), these are from the Baku district, and include the Kuba and Hila (q.v.) rugs. The design of the Kuba consists often of independent flower heads, palmettes and eight-pointed stars, with well-balanced borders carrying the same motifs. Some early examples show an elongated panel with interlocking tree forms.

Kaendler (or **Kändler**) **J. J.:** (1706–75), appointed as chief modeller at the Meissen porcelain (q.v.) factory in 1731, Kaendler was the first to recognize the sculptural possibilities of hard-paste porcelain (q.v.), the secret of whose manufacture had so recently been discovered at the factory, and to exploit its natural qualities. His figures from the Italian *Commedia dell' Arte* (q.v.) seem to dance on the shelves of china cabinets, and his fashionable ladies to swing their crinolines in rhythmic movements, anticipating Mozart's minuets. Even conventional tableware takes a share in plastic decoration, and the 'Swan Service', which Kaendler modelled for Count Brühl (1737–41), reveals his creative genius in the many variations on the theme of swans. Kaendler's birds were all studied from nature, since Augustus the Strong kept a large collection of domestic and rare specimens at the Moritzburg.

Kakemono: Japanese hanging picture, rolled up when stored.

Kakemono-ye: Japanese prints in the form of hanging pictures, usually about 660–700 × 254–300 mm (26–28 × 10–12 in).

Kakiemon style: a name given to a distinctive asymmetrical style of enamel decoration on Japanese porcelain, extensively imitated or copied in 18th cent. by German, French and English porcelain factories. In England porcelain painters at Bow, Chelsea and Worcester used the Kakiemon style, copied either directly from Japanese wares, or indirectly from Meissen copies or adaptations. Named after the Japanese potter Kakiemon (1596–1666), who used enamel colours at Arita.

K'ang Hsi porcelain: Chinese porcelain made in the reign of the Emperor K'ang Hsi (1662–1722). The nobility and elegance of the K'ang Hsi style is exemplified in Fig. A and in the forms of the 'rouleau' and 'trumpet' vases of Figs B and D. The ware now used was a refined white porcelain, thinly and evenly glazed and with a meticulous finish, showing painted decoration to great advantage. For the best of the very numerous blue-and-white (q.v.) wares a brilliant sapphire blue was preferred, and designs, first drawn in outline and then washed in boldly in broad tones, are more precisely executed than hitherto. We find ambitious landscapes or figure subjects. On some pieces there is also painting in copper-red or a partial blue, celadon-green or golden-brown glaze. For enamelled wares, the brilliant *famille verte* (q.v.) palette soon replaced the Ming 'five-colour' style (see Wu Ts'ai.) The rare vases with black or yellow ground (*famille noire*, *famille jaune*) are generally enamelled 'on the biscuit' i.e. without intervening glaze, and this attractive technique distinguishes a whole *famille verte* group, which specially includes accessories for the tea table, study or studio. The third main group of K'ang Hsi wares are those with monochrome glazes, among them the sang-de-boeuf and peach-bloom red (see Copper-red porcelain glazes) and other high-temperature colours, blues, celadon-green, white, brown and mirror-black – as well as many others. The beautiful *blanc-de-chine* porcelain (q.v.) of Fukien (q.v.) and the unglazed red stoneware of Yi-hsing (q.v.) also flourished at this time.

Fig. A   Fig. B

Fig. C   Fig. D   Fig. E

Kaolin: see China clay.

Kas: a Dutch form of wardrobe made in the Hudson and Delaware River valleys in America between about 1675–1750; a large clothes cupboard with panelled doors, large mouldings, overhanging cornice and, usually, ball-front feet. Often painted with decorative designs.

Kasak rugs: Caucasian rugs bearing panelled designs of bold character and in striking colours. They are deep pile rugs and have a character entirely their own. Strong deep red, clear yellow and blue are the predominant colours. Woven with extra weft threads, the pile lies flat and is very strong.

Kat stitch: a term used in lace-making to describe a *fond chant* ground (q.v.) but frequently found in Bedfordshire lace and given legendary association with Katherine of Aragon.

Kauffman, Angelica: (1741–1807), painter, born in Switzerland. She worked in London between *c.* 1766 and 1782. In 1781 she married the Italian painter, Antonio Zucchi with whom she had worked while she was in England. She was employed by Robert Adam (q.v.) on interior decoration and also painted furniture.

Keeper ring: a rather heavy gold ring bearing chased decoration (see Chasing).

Kelsterbach porcelain: hard-paste porcelain (q.v.) was made at the factory of the Landgrave of Hesse-Darmstadt, Ludwig VIII, from 1761–8 by the arcanist (q.v.) C. D. Busch. The factory was later re-opened in 1789 with the help of another arcanist and remained in existence until 1802. The earlier wares were not marked, the crowned monogram 'HD' appearing on the wares of 1799–1802 and occasionally on those of 1766 to 1768.

Kent, William: (1686–1748), an architect who also planned the land-scaping of gardens, painted pictures and was one of the first of his profession to lavish as much care on the interior decoration and furnishing of a house as he did on the building itself. He was an exponent of the Palladian style, and his name has been given to the mirrors with frames of architectural type that were fashionable in the years 1730–40.

Kent & Parr: Staffordshire potters working at Burslem *c.* 1880–94, making earthenware figures, hens on nests, dogs, etc.

Kenton & Co.: venture lasting from 1890 to 1892 founded by S. Barnsley (q.v.), E. W. Gimson (q.v.), W. R. Lethaby (q.v.) and others, to combine the efforts of furniture designers and makers.

Kerman rugs: this district of Persia has produced many rugs of merit and was particularly popular with the American and European market *c.* 1870. Medallion and tree designs are popular, introducing floral effects in graceful intertwining vines. The yarn used is rather soft. Fine examples are known as Kerman Laver rugs. The colours, beautifully toned, are particularly suitable for English furnishings. Knot: Sehna (q.v.).

Kerr & Binns: see Worcester.

Keshan carpets: Persian carpets in which medallion and prayer designs predominate, woven in wool or silk; they are orthodox in conception, and are notable for the use of ivory as a ground shade; the most favoured colours are rich tones of red or blue. The famous Polonaise rugs, remarkable for the use of gold and silver thread as a base and the unusual colour effects in pastel greens and browns, were probably woven in Keshan. It is thought that they were woven as gifts for foreign monarchs by the order of Shah Abbas. Fine Keshan carpets sometimes combine the medallion with the floral and tree motif. Knot: usually Sehna (q.v.).

Kettle stand (also **urn stand** and **teapot stand**): a special stand that was introduced with tea-drinking in the later 17th cent., of two main kinds. (a) A small table, tripod or four-legged, with a gallery (q.v.) round the top. Slender four-legged tables were common in the later part of the 18th cent., nearly always with a slide for the teapot. (b) A box-like arrangement set on four legs; the box was usually lined with metal, and had an opening in one side for the kettle spout, as well as a slide for the teapot. Another version of the box type had a three-sided enclosure with a metal-lined drawer. The two main types of stand persisted until the end of the 18th cent., when they were superseded by occasional tables.

Kettle-tilter: (Idle-back, Lazy-back, Handy-maid), a simple device of wrought iron for tilting the kettle when water was wanted from it. Not only was there no need to soil the hand by touching a smoke-blackened kettle, but the handle of the tilter projected outside the fireplace, was cool and there would be no risk from scalding steam or water. The kettle was suspended over the fire in the tilter, which in turn hung from a pothook or cran (q.v.).

Kew Blas glass: type of iridescent Art Nouveau (q.v.) glass patented in 1893, characterized by contrasting colours of green, cream and tan with a sharp pattern and a sheen.

Key pattern: repetitive pattern made up of straight lines joined at right angles at alternate ends and used as a border ornament by architects and craftsmen during the Neoclassical (q.v.) period. Deriving from classical Greek architecture, it appears for example, as a decorative border on furniture, silver and porcelain. Also known as Greek fret.

Khorassan carpets: Persian carpets in which the yarn is generally softer; the stitch is fine and the general effect is more splendid than in Feraghan (q.v.) carpets, but they are not so durable. Knot: usually Sehna (q.v.).

Kick: the pyramidal dent found in the bases of many pre-1760 glass decanters (q.v.), bowls, and bottles.

Kidderminster rugs: Kidderminster in Worcestershire is probably the oldest centre of rug production in England, the early pieces being smooth-faced and without a true pile, that is to say, a cheap form of carpeting. Kidderminster carpets were often mentioned in inventories; for example, '4 carpets of Kidderminster stuff', in the Countess of Leicester's inventory,

1634. Two-ply or double-cloth carpets were made there from 1735, when Pearsall and Brown built their factory. But in 1753 Brussels carpets or moquette (q.v.) were introduced by Brown in rivalry with Wilton (q.v.). A thousand looms were at work in 1807, rising to 2020 in 1838. Jacquard looms were introduced about 1825, and the use of jute rather earlier.

Kidney dagger: a type of dagger with a guard formed by two lobate protuberances. It was probably from the kidney dagger that the Scottish dirk (q.v.) developed in the 17th cent.

Kidney table: introduced in the mid-18th cent., tables with kidney-shaped tops were usually designed as kneehole writing tables (q.v.), with two tiers of drawers, or as work tables (q.v.). Also known as a horseshoe table.

Kilmarnock carpets: double-cloth carpeting was made in Kilmarnock from 1778 and three-ply was perfected in 1824.

Kiln: oven used to fire body and glaze of hard-paste porcelain (q.v.) at about 1200–1400°C. (grand feu.)

Kiln waster: porcelain spoilt in the kiln, and therefore thrown away as useless. Kiln wasters discovered in excavation provide good evidence of factory production.

King's pattern spoons: see Table services.

Kinji: (*Japanese* = gold ground), a Japanese lacquer-work technique in which powdered gold is worked into the lacquer surface and then burnished.

'Kinuta' celadon ware: see Lung-chüan celadon ware.

Kirchner, Johann Gottlob: modeller at the Meissen porcelain factory from 1727–8 and 1730–3, where he was responsible for some of the large figures and animals required by Augustus the Strong for the decoration of the Japanese Palace.

Kirikane: (*Japanese* = cut gold), a Japanese lacquer-work technique in which cut squares of gold leaf are embedded in the lacquer.

Kirk, Samuel, & Son: trading name 1846–61 and 1868–96 of the oldest surviving silversmiths in the United States. Samuel Kirk (1793–1872), the founder, opened a shop in Baltimore in 1815, and it was he who introduced the repoussé (q.v.), or Baltimore, style of ornament into American silver. In the 19th cent. the firm received a number of important commissions for trophies and presentation pieces.

Kir-Shehr rugs: Turkish rugs (q.v.) with typical designs. The Mihrab is usually filled with an angular tree, border and panel are conventional, while the colours are bright and virile, varying reds being a feature of the weave. Warp and weft are usually wool.

Kit Cat glass: a baluster wine glass of the first quarter of the 18th cent. with tall stem and bowl curving outwards at the rim, known by this name on account of its appearance in a picture by Kneller of the members of the Kit Cat Club.

Kloster Veilsdorf porcelain: hard-paste porcelain (q.v.) was made at Kloster Veilsdorf in Thuringia from 1760, when a factory was set up under the protection of Prince Friedrich Wilhelm Eugen of Hilburghausen.

The monogram 'CV' (for Closter Veilsdorf) in underglaze blue was used in various forms as a mark. (See also under Limbach porcelain for other Thuringian factories.)

Knee-hole table: a table fitted with drawers and an arched apron piece (q.v.) in the centre. Walnut tables of this type made at the end of the 17th and early 18th cent. could be used as dressing or writing tables, the arched apron allowing comfortable space for the knees of the sitter. Dressing tables of knee-hole form containing a row of small drawers on either side, on plain bracket feet (q.v.) and a recessed cupboard within the arched knee-hole were also popular in the early 18th cent. Some examples in mahogany dating from the mid cent. have tops which can be raised to reveal a fitted interior. Library tables of knee-hole type with end pedestals containing drawers and a space in the centre were popular from the mid-18th cent.

Knibb, Joseph: a London clock-maker, active *c.* 1650–1711.

Knife case: a container for knives, and other cutlery, introduced in the 17th cent. for use in dinning rooms. Two distinct varieties appeared: (a) until the later 18th cent. the usual shape was a box with a sloping top and convex front: the interior had divisions for the cutlery. Walnut, shagreen (q.v.) and later mahogany, some-times inlaid, were the main materials; (b) this was succeeded by the graceful vase-shaped case the top of which was raised and lowered on a central stem around which the knife partitions were arranged; this type was designed to stand on pedestal or at each end of the sideboard. Straight-sided cases were favoured in the early 19th cent. They were often made in pairs.

Knife rest: a support for a knife at table used from the 18th cent. They were of two varieties: cross-ends joined from their centres by a short rod, and solid or pierced triangular ends joined from each angle by short rods.

Knife tray: 19th-cent. American rectangular tray with high, sloping sides for knives. It has a central division incorporating a handle.

Knole sofa: upholstered settee (q.v.) with arms that may be lowered or raised, deriving from an early 17th-cent. model at Knole, in Kent. There are many 19th-cent. copies or versions of the original.

Knop: swelling member on a shaft, pillar, or stem of cup or goblet; a knob. Many differently shaped knops are found on stemmed drinking glasses (see Ball, Cushion, Merese knop, etc.).

Knopped stem: a type of stem found on 18th-cent. drinking glasses com-posed of a varying number of knops (q.v.) or knobs.

Knotted lace: made in 16th-cent. Italy with short lengths of thread or thin cord. When longer threads were introduced bobbins (q.v.) were de-veloped to carry them, first of lead then of wood or bone and the threads were twisted and plaited.

Knotted pile carpets: when carpets first came to Europe from the Near East in the 15th and 16th cent. they were used as covers for tables, cup-boards and chests, or were placed before the altar in church or chapel. Only kings and the higher nobility used floor carpets. A small number of knotted pile carpets in imitation of Oriental ones were made in Europe. English examples date from the 16th and early 17th cent. Some of the patterns follow Turkish models, others are like contemporary English em-broideries. In France, at the Savon-nerie (q.v.), a Western style of carpet was created which was taken up by different countries when floor carpets became more general in the 18th cent.

Knox, Archibald: (1864–1933), English designer and craftsman in silver and pewter (q.v.) and of jewellery. Many of his designs inspired by Celtic art were executed for Liberty & Co. (q.v.).

Knurling: a short fluting of irregular outline used as a decoration on silver or plate in the mid-18th cent. for borders and on handles.

Knurl toe: see Scroll foot.

Kny, Frederick: most distinguished engraver on glass in the 1860s to 1870s and prominent for the rest of the 19th century, Kny, a Bohemian immigrant, worked briefly for James Powell & Sons (q.v.) and then established his own workshop at Thomas Webb & Sons (q.v.). His most famous wheel-engraved piece, the Elgin Claret Jug, made in 1873 and exhibited in Paris in 1878, reflects the Classical influence on much of his work.

Kny, Ludwig: (d. 1937), distinguished etcher, engraver and designer, Ludwig inherited the decorating business of his father, Frederick Kny (q.v.).

Kōban-ye: a Japanese print being a size smaller than the chūban (q.v.), about 20 × 18 cm (8 × 7 in).

Koehler, Florence: (1861–1944), American artist-craftsman; leader of craft-revival movement in the United States and remembered, in particular for her jewellery.

Köpping, Karl: (1848–1914), foremost German *Jugendstil* (q.v.) glass artist who specialized in fragile ornamental glassware in iridescent glass.

Ko ware: crackled Sung celadon (q.v.) ware of Kuan (q.v.) type.

Krater: two-handled Greek vessel of vase shape.

Kretschmer, F.: engraver and enameller who worked as part of the Woodall (q.v.) team of Thomas Webb & Sons (q.v.). Particularly noted for his decoration of plaques and vases in the Chinese style.

Kuan ware: rare Chinese celadon (q.v.) of the Sung (q.v.) dynasty, patronized by the Emperor, with dark grey porcellaneous body and thick, often crackled glaze of pale greyish blue or greyish green colour, suggesting marble or jade; made at Hangchow (Chekiang Province) from the 12th cent. Creditable imitations were made during the 18th cent.

Kuba rugs: see Kabistan rugs.

Kula rugs: Turkish rugs (q.v.), less varied in colour than other Turkish types, and the panels of the Mihrab are usually fully patterned. Borders are popular with repeating floral miniature motifs.

Kurdish rugs: Nomadic tribes wove these rugs. The designs are often bold and the colours limited. The yarns employed are generally coarse, but the effects are pleasing and the wearing quality excellent, often found in long runners. One of the outstanding types is the Bidjar, probably the heaviest of all Oriental rugs. Woven on a twofold warp, designs are various, often including a bold medallion and corner-pieces on a plain field, the borders in the Herat (q.v.) manner.

Kurlbaum & Schwartz: founded in 1851 by Charles Kurlbaum and John T. Schwarz at Philadelphia, Pennsylvania, the factory produced true or hard-paste porcelain (q.v.) closely resembling French porcelain.

Kü Yüeh Hsüan ware: a group of 18th-cent. Chinese porcelain wares of Imperial quality, carefully painted with flower and landscape subjects in coloured enamels, principally of the *famille rose* (q.v.), sometimes with coloured grounds. They are often inscribed with a poem. The title more properly belongs to some later painted glass vessels.

Kwachō-ye: Japanese bird and flower pictures.

Labelled furniture: furniture bearing the paper label of a cabinet-maker.

Lace glass: see Vetro di trina.

Lachenal, Edmond: (b. 1855) French artist-potter active in Paris in the late 19th cent.

Lacis: French term for darned patterns on netting in vogue in 16th-cent. Italy, a direct preliminary to pillow lace (q.v.).

Lacquer work: see Japan work.

Lacy glass: American term for type of pressed glass made *c.* 1828–40 bearing intricate relief designs on a finely stippled, lace-like background. Lacy glass is brilliant and sparkling. Salts, dishes and plates, and more rarely, bases of lamps and candlesticks were made in this technique.

Ladder-back chair: a mid-18th-cent. mahogany chair, the back composed of curved horizontal rails, frequently pierced. A similar type of back had been known in the late Stuart period.

Ladik box rugs: Turkish rugs (q.v.) which follow the Ghiordes (q.v.) design very closely, though the use of Rhodian lily motifs is a distinguishing feature.

Lalique, René: (1860–1945), a French jeweller, silversmith and glassmaker who produced moulded, pressed and engraved glass, often favouring massive bowls and vases. As a decorative artist he produced figures and panels for furniture, decorated with foliate and animal motifs in rich profusion. He achieved prominence through his work shown in the Paris salon in 1894.

Lambeth delftware: certain kinds of delftware and *maiolica* (qq.v.), the earliest known pieces being of the late 16th cent., are designated 'Lambeth', although this type of pottery was made not only in the factories there but also at other works in Vauxhall, Aldgate and Southwark, and possibly in other riverside boroughs. Work from the various factories of this group cannot be assigned to individual potteries, and some is in fact difficult to distinguish from Dutch tin-glazed wares of the early period. Lambeth ware was produced over two centuries, and examples have principally come to light in excavations in the City of London.

In 1571 two potters from Antwerp, Andries and Janson, settled at Aldgate. Earliest examples of English tin-glazed ware date from about this time, not all of these being derived from the Dutch tradition, although many potters from Holland certainly came to London in the late 16th and early 17th cent.

From the early 17th cent. Italian, Dutch and Chinese styles of decoration are common. Some are initialled for their owners, the letters usually being placed in triangle-form, and many bear the arms of London livery companies. Designs, usually in bright, thick *maiolica* colours include stylized fruit and foliage, star-shaped flowers, birds and sphinxes, and, towards the end of the 17th cent., portraits of kings, family groups, biblical subjects, inn signs and verses or inscriptions appear more frequently and colours become more various. Chinese subjects were copied from imported oriental wares and often greatly improved upon by simplification and freedom of treatment. Articles for domestic use formed a large part of the manufacture of the potteries; these included tiles, plates, mugs, jars, jugs, wine bottles, posset pots, punch bowls, wall pockets and plaques.

The Lambeth ware factories were still in existence at the beginning of the 19th cent. They were in decline, however, in 1800 and as regards work after that date no examples of decorated wares are known.

As no marks were used on these wares, their origin is ascertained by comparison with delftware known to be from Holland, inscriptions on various commemorative pieces, and names of owners sometimes incorporated in the design. In articles made at a later date, a more distinctively English form of decoration is apparent.

These later productions are sometimes difficult to distinguish from contemporary Liverpool and Bristol tin-glazed earthenware; in general, Lambeth potters produced a neatly drawn design and more finished effect, but often lacked the vigour and individuality of the best examples from Bristol.

The glaze on early Lambeth pottery is usually white. In later pieces a blue-green tint becomes apparent, fairly easily distinguishable from the bluish-purple of Bristol (q.v.) glaze.

Lambeth faience: English earthenware made at the Doulton (q.v.) workshop in London from 1873.

Lambrequin: (*Fr.*), a short piece of hanging drapery, often imitated in metal or wood for decorative purposes.

Lamerie, Paul de: (1688–1751), the foremost member of the second generation of Huguenot goldsmiths working in London. Born in Liège, he was apprenticed to Pierre Platel (q.v.). His earliest recorded work dates from 1711–12. He enjoyed the patronage of the leading nobility but not, curiously enough, of the Crown. One of the most prolific goldsmiths of his time, his main achievement was the popularization of the French Rococo (q.v.) manner in English silver.

Lance: see Pole-arms.

Lancet clock: design of late 18th and early 19th cent., in which a bracket clock (q.v.) has a pointed 'Gothic' top.

Langley, Batty and **Thomas:** two brothers who were authors of a pattern book, published in 1740 called a *Treasury of Designs*. It included designs for furniture which could be treated in an architectural manner according to the precepts of Palladian (q.v.) taste although some of the designs indicate the acceptance of the new Rococo (q.v.) spirit that was shortly to become popular.

Lang yao: see Copper-red porcelain glazes.

Lantern clock: a clock of typically English design evolved in the early part of the 17th cent., and persisting especially in the provinces, until well into the 18th cent. Erroneously called a Cromwellian clock. Much copied today. All original lantern clocks are weight driven and, with the rarest exceptions, never exceed a thirty-hour going period.

Latten: a yellow alloy of copper and zinc not unlike brass, used especially in the Middle Ages.

Lattice work: a form of decorative work popular on mahogany furniture of the mid-18th cent. Chippendale's *Director* (1754) contained designs for a 'Chinese Chair' and a 'Gothick Chair' which include open lattice work on the legs and stretchers (q.v.) in the appropriate spirit. Chairs in the Chinese taste were also made with the back splat of lattice work, or with lattice work filling the space between the arm and the seat in the case of armchairs.

Latticinio decoration: a type of decoration on glass which came into use in the second quarter of the 16th cent. in Venice and remained fashionable for a long time afterwards. It involved the use of opaque white or coloured threads of glass drawn together with tools into a network and melted into the surfaces of the clear glass vessel which was then blown and manipulated. Although the technique was of Venetian origin, it was also used by Italian workmen and their pupils at glasshouses set up elsewhere in Europe.

Lava glass: see Slag glass.

Laver rugs: see Kerman rugs.

Law, Thomas: (1717–75), Sheffield cutler and an early manufacturer of

Sheffield plate (q.v.). His wares are generally marked. The business was carried on by his son.

Lazulite: a blue-tinted parian ware (q.v.). .

Lazy Susan: an American·type of dumb waiter (q.v.) used for condiments in the early 19th cent.

Lead glass: glass containing lead as a flux. (See also Flint glass.)

Lebrun, Charles: (1619–90), principal artistic advisor to Louis XIV and founder and director of the Académie Royale des Beaux-Arts in Paris. He was appointed painter to the King in 1662 and director of the Gobelins (q.v.) and Savonnerie (q.v.) manufactories in the following year, contributing many designs.

Le Compte, Père Louis: a Jesuit missionary who published in Amsterdam in 1697 *Memoirs and Observations made in a late Journey through China.* The book was issued in translation in London in the same year. Le Compte devotes several pages to porcelain and mentions that blue-and-white was the principal product. He adds that the European merchants foolishly bought anything that the Chinese were willing to sell.

Leeds earthenware: the Old Pottery at Hunslet (as distinct from the later factories of Hunslet Hall and Rothwell in the same district) was established about 1760 by two brothers named Green. The factory was sold in 1825 to Samuel Wainwright and was known for a time as S. Wainwright & Co. Subsequently it was the Leeds Pottery Co. and Warburton, Britton & Co. It closed in 1878.
Marks:
Some comparatively modern Leeds productions are marked 'Leeds Pottery' (impressed). The wares which sometimes make use of old patterns and old moulds are easily distinguishable from earlier pieces, for the mark is impressed in very even lettering and has none of the irregularity of the type used in marking earlier pieces.

Impressed

Impressed *c.* 1864

Early earthenware made at Leeds is notable for its colour, a rich cream with a deep fine glaze, sometimes of a slightly greenish tinge rather more hard and brilliant than Wedgwood (q.v.) but less even. Queensware (q.v.) of this sort was made in quantity in many Staffordshire potteries at about this time, but that made at Leeds has a particularly delicate and highly-finished appearance. From about 1780 until 1820 it formed the largest part of the production of the factory and was exported to several European countries. Pierced (q.v.) or basket work was popular and made with great skill.

Plates bordered with · interwoven twigs, all fashioned by hand; centre-pieces (q.v.) of complex design and making use of figures; dishes with twisted handles; small, well-modelled figures; all these are characteristic subjects in Leeds creamware. Transfer-printing was also used to decorate some pieces. Red, black, lilac and green were colours most frequently used, together with the underglaze blue popular throughout Staffordshire at that time. Enamelled decoration was usually in subdued colours.

Certain types of agate wares (q.v.) were made, often having reserved panels painted with flowers.

At a later date, the factory also produced Egyptian black (q.v.) and lustred wares, and a white ware with a bluish glaze. (See also Wedgwood, Josiah.)

Leeds horse: large pottery model of a horse on a rectangular plinth made specially at Leeds, and probably used as the sign of a horse leech.

Left-hand dagger: a dagger used in conjunction with the sword in 16th- and early 17th-cent. fencing. It usually had quillons (q.v.), often strongly arched to entangle an opponent's sword blade, and a side-ring, but a special form, with a triangular knuckle-guard, was used in Spain during the last three quarters of the 17th cent. in conjunction with the cup-hilt rapier (q.v.).

Legras: French glasshouse founded in 1864 by Auguste Legras at St-Denis, near Paris. Noted for ornamental ware in Art Nouveau (q.v.) style and enamelled cameo (qq.v.) vases.

Lehr: the heated chamber or tunnel, sometimes known as a 'leer', in which glass, whether hand-made or machine-made, was toughened by annealing (q.v.).

Leleu, Jean-François: (1729–1807), French *maître-ébéniste*, trained under J. F. Oeben (q.v.), after whose death in 1763 he hoped to be chosen to take over the direction of the workshop. Oeben's widow's choice, however, fell on Riesener (q.v.), whom she married. Leleu then opened his own workshop and received several Court commissions. He used the stamp:

J·F·LELEU

Lenox, Walter Scott: (1859–1920), by 1887 Lenox was art director for Ott & Brewer (q.v.) of Trenton, New Jersey. With Jonathan Coxon he established the Ceramic Art Co. (q.v.) in 1889 for the production of Belleek (q.v.) wares, in the interests of which they imported two craftsmen from Ireland.

Lenticle: the glass let into the door of a long-case clock to allow the motion of the pendulum bob to be seen.

Leontine chain: a long gold chain worn in the 19th cent., to which a watch was attached.

Leopardware: see Tigerware.

Lessore, Emile: (1840–1908) porcelain decorator born in France, who worked initially at the Sèvres (q.v.) factory and then at Mintons (q.v.) from 1858, before joining Josiah Wedgwood & Sons (q.v.).

Lethaby, William Richard: (1857–1911), English architect and designer of metalwork, ceramics and, in particular, furniture. He was a founder of the Art Workers' Guild (q.v.) and of Kenton & Co. (q.v.) and principal of the Central School of Arts and Crafts. He is noted for his unpolished furniture in the Arts and Crafts (q.v.) manner with the occasional use of inlaid decoration. He designed a number of pieces for Morris & Co. (q.v.).

Léveillé, Ernest: (*fl.* 1885–1900) French Art Nouveau (q.v.) glass artist, working in Paris. Pupil of E. Rousseau (1827–91).

Lever escapement: a type of watch escapement (q.v.) invented about 1758 by Thomas Mudge (q.v.) and incorporated in a watch given by George III

to Queen Charlotte. Mudge only made one or two other examples and does not seem to have realized the importance of his invention, which lies in the fact that the balance is free from interference for the greater part of its swing, thus leaving it free to perform its true function as controller. From the beginning of the second quarter of the 19th cent., the lever escapement, in one of its many forms, became the standard escapement for watches and still is so today. Before that date, despite the appearance of the cylinder, duplex (qq.v.) and lever escapements, the standard watch escapement was the verge (q.v.).

Lever lock: the earliest was patented in 1778 by Robert Barron, its mechanism a system of fixed wards in combination with two pivoting or lifting tumblers which he termed levers, held in position by a steel spring. Attached to the tumblers were stumps or studs which retained the bolt in its locked position. Only its own individually made key, cut in steps of different radii, corresponded with the varying lifts of the two tumblers, so that the latter were raised to the exact height to bring the studs into line with the slot in the bolt, and thus allow the top step of the key to act upon the stump and unlock it. Any attempt to pick the lock was frustrated by a number of upper transverse notches in the bolt. This rendered it impossible to tell when the tumblers had been lifted correctly. From this developed, in the early 1800s, the ordinary lever lock.

Libbey Glass Company: an American glasshouse founded in 1888 in Toledo, Ohio, by Edward Libbey (d. 1925) which employed workers from the defunct New England Glass Co. (q.v.). Particularly noted for its cut glass (q.v.).

Liberty & Co.: English retail firm established in 1875 by Arthur Lasenby Liberty, formerly manager of the London Oriental warehouse, Farmer & Rogers in Regent Street. In the 1880s, the firm commissioned a range of fabrics and goods harmonizing with Art Nouveau (q.v.) decorative schemes which in their turn established the Italian term for Art Nouveau, *Stile Liberty*. Liberty imported Eastern, Egyptian and Moorish furniture and commissioned furniture from designers involved in the Arts and Crafts Movement (q.v.). The firm also sold and popularized art pottery (q.v.) and entered its first silver mark, *Ly & Co.*, at Goldsmiths' Hall in 1894, which was probably intended for use on Japanese and other manufactured silver. Cymric was the trade name for a range of silver and jewellery launched by Liberty & Co. in 1899, its design being of Celtic inspiration.

Library steps: found in libraries of large houses after about the middle of the 18th cent., and of two main kinds: (a) the fixed pair of steps, some with hand-rails, and (b) the folding steps, sometimes ingeniously fitted into other pieces of furniture, such as chairs, stools and tables.

Lighthouse clock: an American shelf or mantel clock designed by Simon Willard (q.v.) about 1800. The case is judged to have been modelled after the lighthouse on Eddystone Rock in the English Channel. Miller declares that 'because of mechanical difficulties . . . very few were made'.

Lille lace: pillow lace (q.v.) very popular in later 18th-cent. England, made sometimes in black, but never as a dress lace. Its somewhat meagre patterns were heavily outlined in flat glossy trolly thread and set in a plain *fond clair* (q.v.) mesh.

Limbach porcelain: the Limbach porcelain factory in Thuringia was one of seven owned by members of the Greiner family, being founded by Gotthelf Greiner in 1772. The rather stiff, crude little figures modelled at Limbach, with scroll bases, are the most interesting of the factory's productions. Other Thuringian factories established or acquired by the Greiners include Wallendorf, founded in 1764 by Gotthelf Greiner and his cousin; Ilmenau, founded in 1777 and acquired by the Greiners in 1786; Gross-breitenbach, founded in 1778 and bought by Gotthelf Greiner in 1782; Gera, started in 1779 and taken over by the Greiners in the following year; and Rauenstein, founded by the Greiners in 1783. These Greiner factories and others in Thuringia produced utilitarian rather than decorative porcelain and were basically commercial enterprises, unlike the famous German factories that depended upon noble patronage. They used local china clay and sandstone containing quartz, and fuel was available cheaply from the Thuringian forests. The wares were inexpensive and intended for the country markets.

Between about 1772 and 1787 Limbach used a monogram formed by a 'B' within an 'L' or interlaced 'Ls', and at the same period also interlaced 'Ls' over a star imitating the Meissen (q.v.) mark of the Marcolini period. Wallendorf used a 'W' written in two ways, one version, appearing between 1764 and 1787, closely approximating to the crossed swords of Meissen. Ilmenau, from about 1792 onwards used a dotted 'i' in blue and Gera a 'G' or the name Gera from about 1779. Rauenstein employed an ' R' over a star or 'R-n' from 1783 onwards. A clover-leaf mark was also used at the Greiners' factories from 1786 to 1792.

Limehouse: a London porcelain factory of short duration was situated here, near Dick Shore, as early as 1746 (*Daily Advertiser*, 1 January 1747), but was in difficulties in 1748 (*Daily Advertiser*, 3 June 1748) and probably wound up shortly after.

Limoges enamel: the town of Limoges in France was a principal centre of enamelling (see Enamel) in the Middle Ages. The art of the 12th-cent. goldsmith developed opaque *champlevé* enamel in place of the earlier translucent *cloisonné* in gold. Apart from the great centres on the Rhine and the Meuse, a regular industry, of which products were distributed all over Europe, was developed at Limoges. Numerous enamelled pieces used in the ritual of the Church were made and have been preserved in abbeys and cathedrals. Secular enamelled jewellery was also made in large quantities but little has survived. In the early 16th cent. the Limoges enamelling workshops regained their dominant position, using another technique, that of painted enamel on a copper base. No other Renaissance (q.v.) workshops could seriously rival those of Limoges in the production of sumptuously painted enamels in polychrome, often bright with gold. The sources of the designs used on these painted enamels were contemporary German, Italian and French engravings. The art was revived briefly in about 1820. (See also Enamel.)

Lincoln rocker: American mid-19th-cent. rocking chair with an upholstered seat and back and upholstered pads on the arms, which generally have pierced decoration.

Line engraving: often called copper-plate engraving; it was the favourite method of book illustration in the 17th and 18th cent. The design is incised by means of a burin, and a more formal effect than etching is produced. Colour could be added by selective inking of the one plate or by printing from several different plates, but neither method was as much used in books as hand colouring.

Linenfold carving: a carved ornament suggested by folded linen, first found in England late in the 15th cent., very popular in the first half of the 16th, but not very often used in the later years of the century. Of Flemish origin, linenfold carving, sometimes described as parchment pattern, was used as a panel decoration principally on walls, but also on chests, chair backs, etc. Sometimes the folds were ogee-shaped at top and bottom, or plain, and a later pattern includes carved tassels and other emblems.

Linen press: a standing cupboard for storing linen, or a frame with a wooden spiral screw for pressing linen between two boards, dating from the 17th cent.

Ling lung: pierced openwork, as found on some 17th- to 18th-cent. Chinese blue-and-white porcelain (q.v.) bowls, and on elaborate vases of Ch'ien Lung (q.v.) and later date.

Lining papers: the 16th and 17th cent. saw a great variety of these papers, usually printed in black ink on self-coloured paper. Designs were floral, heraldic and conventional, and while generally produced specifically for lining boxes, coffers, etc., were sometimes used as wallpapers, particularly those designs capable of 'repeat'.

Linnell, John: (d. 1796), English cabinet-maker (q.v.) and carver, many of whose designs for mirrors and other furnishings have been preserved and are in the Victoria and Albert Museum. He worked in the period 1760–90, and his designs are in the Palladian, Rococo and Neoclassical (q.v.) styles.

Linoleum: material for floors and table tops devised by Frederick Walton and patented by him in 1860, with improvements in 1863. Its basic components were ground cork and linseed oil.

Linthorpe pottery: established in 1879 near Middlesbrough, Yorkshire, by John Harrison with initial designs provided by Dr Christopher Dresser (q.v.), some reminiscent of Pre-Columbian American pottery. The pottery closed in 1889.

Lion mask: an ornamental motif of Classical inspiration used by furniture-makers, silversmiths, etc., in the first half of the 18th cent. and during the Regency period.

Lion's paw foot: a foot carved in the form of a lion's paw sometimes found on carved and gilt armchairs of the late 17th cent. Lion's paw feet formed popular terminals to cabriole legs (q.v.) on early 18th-cent. chairs and side tables but were not a feature of Rococo (q.v.) taste. The fashion returned during the Regency, when lion's paw feet appear sometimes on the front legs only, or on both front and back legs of chairs. Lion's paw feet were used also by silversmiths and appear, for example, as supports to late 17th-cent. wine cisterns (q.v.).

Lithograph: a print made by what its inventor, A. Senefelder (1771–1834), c. 1797, called 'chemical printing', based on the principle that oil and water do not mix. It was a single-plane process. The design was drawn with a special crayon on calcareous limestone, and a film of water passed over the surface. When greasy ink on the roller passed over the stone, the water repelled it, but the crayoned surface took it up, and an impression could be taken.

The process was first used for the production of ceramic transfers in 1839. Francis Morley, used this technique at Shelton, in the 1840s. Some of the lithographic stones have survived.

The first litho-transfers were made in 1863 and submitted to Josiah Wedgwood & Sons, Etruria, but they were extremely crude.

In the 1890s several firms experimented with litho-transfers, but little progress was made until the invention of duplex paper.

Lithophane: a porcelain or bone-china (qq.v.) transparency moulded thinly in *intaglio* (q.v.) to produce monochrome illusionist pictures (portraits, figure groups, landscapes) by transmitted light. The process was invented in 1827 by Baron de Bourgoing, and used by Minton's, Copeland's (qq.v.), and Grainger, Lee & Co. of Worcester. Lithophanes are sometimes called transparencies.

Littler, William: (1724–84), salt-glazed stoneware (q.v.) manufacturer, in partnership with Aaron Wood at Brownhills, and porcelain manufacturer at Longton Hall trading as Littler and Co. from 1752 until 1760. Later manager to the firm of Baddeley & Fletcher at Shelton.

Liverpool delftware and porcelain:
(1) Delftware: it is said that the manufacture of delftware (q.v.) in Liverpool began about 1710 when some potters from Southwark settled in the district, but potteries certainly existed in the city at an earlier date and some faience bowls painted with ships and inscriptions and made early in the 17th cent. are attributed to Liverpool. By 1780 the manufacture of delftware had almost ceased and many of the best potters had departed to work in Staffordshire.

Little is known of individual potteries in Liverpool, marks are rare, and only certain features common to wares from the district single them out for identification.

The date at which the manufacture of porcelain began in the Liverpool factories (of which there were about a dozen in 1760) is also uncertain; it is likely that potteries already producing delftware turned to porcelain manufacture to compete with the Staffordshire firms.

The industry in Liverpool was in decline in 1780–90, but some cream and white wares were produced after that period.

About 1750, John Sadler, another Liverpool potter, introduced (possibly invented) transfer-printing (q.v.). In partnership with Guy Green he developed the process with such success that wares were imported from other parts of the country to be decorated at Liverpool in this way. A large export trade, mainly to America, grew up and by 1760 articles of all kinds both useful and decorative came in a steady flow from the factories.

Punch-bowls, made largely for ships and often bearing the name of the vessel and paintings of ships or marine subjects, form a large class of Liverpool ware. Many are very attractive, but some later examples are of enormous size and grotesque design. A characteristic example of the earlier type is in the Liverpool Museum, dated 1760 and inscribed 'Success to the Monmouth'.

Flower painting of a bold and rather crude type is seen at its most distinctive on a mug made for a man named Fazackerley in 1757, and this kind of decoration, making use of *bianco sopra bianco* (q.v.), is known by his name. (See Fazackerley flowers.)

Vases and jugs (especially ones of large size with curved sides), wall-pockets, trinket trays, and 'bricks' (rectangular flower vases), were all made in quantity in Liverpool.

A large and attractive class of earthenware consists of tiles printed with such subjects as actors and actresses of the day, etc., usually in black or red but occasionally in polychrome.

Chinese subjects popular in the 18th cent. were used at Liverpool as elsewhere, usually on a plain cream ware, painted or printed in blue under the glaze. In articles decorated in polychrome, a greyish-green, purple, bright blue and reddish-brown were much employed. The 'Fazackerley' design of a flower in the shape of a Tudor rose, outlined in *bianco*, is distinguishable with certainty as Liverpool, and is found on a considerable number of plates and dishes. Armorial designs were often used, as were river-scenes and marine views. Flower decorations in reserved panels on a mottled ground of blue or purple were copied from imported Oriental wares.

With the popularity of transfer-printing, a fashion grew up for reproducing illustrations from contemporary books, prints and paintings of the period. These are often well engraved and usually printed on plain cream wares in monochrome. Subjects from Hogarth and his school are characteristic.

Marks are almost unknown: a prunus blossom on the base of articles decorated in the Chinese manner is sometimes found, but this was also used at Bristol and, less frequently, at Lambeth. Numerals occur on various types of delftware; the numbers used are said to be higher at Liverpool than at either Bristol or Lambeth. A border of reddish-brown on plates is reputed to be a Liverpool characteristic.

(2) Porcelain: a considerable variety of porcelain is attributed to the Liverpool factories, some of which seems to have been experimental and some of good quality and pleasing design. None can be assigned to individual factories,

and it is possible that some pieces attributed to Liverpool may have been of Staffordshire manufacture.

The paste used is soft, heavy and somewhat coarse, with a bluish glaze often deepening in colour at the base of the article. Some pieces are reminiscent of Worcester, especially in their shape. Tall jugs and coffee pots, and barrel-shaped mugs, are especially characteristic.

The flower decoration used is similar to that found on Liverpool earthenware, and is usually in rather bright colours with the flowers outlined in black. Transfer-printing is of rather indifferent quality; it is often found in a dark shade of red which seems to be peculiar to Liverpool wares.

Livery cupboard: the 'cup-board' was originally the board upon which the cups were displayed. In its early stages it was an open structure fitted with shelves normally two or three in number. Before the end of the 15th cent. the space on the central board or shelf was sometimes enclosed by panels at the side and doors in front. Contemporary inventories refer to livery cupboards and court cupboards (q.v.). Some modern authorities identify livery cupboards with those open structures not containing an enclosed compartment, and others with the type fitted with a doored enclosure. The term 'livery' refers to the ration of food and drink dispensed in large households for the night and eaten in the bedchamber. For this reason livery cupboards are often listed in bedroom inventories. A form of hanging cupboard enclosed by two pierced doors, each with two rows of turned balusters, dating from the early 17th cent. is also known as a livery cupboard. By the 1660s the livery cupboard was outmoded.

Lobby chest: defined by Sheraton as 'a kind of half chest of drawers, adapted for the use of a small study, lobby, etc.', with a sliding writing surface.

Lobing: see Gadroon and Knurling.

'Lobster-tail' helmet: a modern term for a form of burgonet (q.v.) worn by cavalry in the 17th cent. It had a laminated tail, hinged cheek-pieces and a peak (often pivoted), with one or more bars extending from it over the face. The English form with three bars was the characteristic helmet of the Civil War.

Lock, Matthias: English carver and designer who published a number of books of furniture designs between the years 1740 and 1769. He collaborated with H. Copland, and modern research has led to the conclusion that these two men were responsible for many of the plates in Thomas Chippendale's *Director* for which Chippendale earned so much fame. He promoted the Rococo (q.v.) in England, later adopting a Neoclassical (q.v.) style. (See also Chippendale, Thomas.)

Locke, Joseph: (1846–1936), British painter, etcher, engraver and sculptor on glass, and a prolific inventor. A major technician in the art of cameo cutting, his masterpiece was the medal-winning second copy of the Portland vase (q.v.). In 1882, Locke emigrated to the United States where, as designer for the New England Glass Co. (q.v.), he developed Amberina, agata and pomona glass (qq.v.).

Locking plate: a clock plate with notches set at increasing intervals around its circumference, which allows the striking train (q.v.) to sound the correct number of blows before the locking arm falls into a notch and stops the train.

Lock-plate: (a) flat plate attached by screws, usually to the side of a firearm at the breech end of the barrel, to which the moving parts which provide ignition are attached; (b) the background to which all the pins and stumps of a lock are riveted and over which the cover is fixed; (c) plate protecting a keyhole or front-plate of a lock.

Long-case clock: the correct horological term for a grandfather or grandmother clock.

'Long Elizas': curiously elongated renderings of Chinese women occurring upon Worcester porcelain (q.v.) in the 1760s. The name is an anglicized version of the Dutch *Lange Lyzen*.

Long pillow covers: long pillow covers, or 'pillow beres', to give them their contemporary name, unlike cushion covers, were always worked on linen and were used in the bedroom. The most usual size for Elizabethan examples was about 890 × 510 mm (35 × 20 in), and the back of the cover, which was left plain, has rarely survived. All-over patterns of the coiling stem type were most popular and black-work (q.v.) was frequently employed. In the late 17th and early 18th cent. pillow covers embroidered entirely in yellow silk are often found; also examples quilted in white linen thread or cotton.

Longton Hall porcelain: little is known of the history of Longton Hall, the first porcelain factory in Staffordshire. It is believed to have been established about 1750 and certainly before October 1751. It was first worked independently by William Jenkinson, but in 1751 in partnership with William Littler (q.v.) and Aaron Wedgwood. From 1752 until 1760 the style of the firm was Littler and Co. William Duesbury (q.v.) appears to have had some associations with the factory. Evidently the story of this factory is still far from complete.
Marks:

In blue

Crossed 'L's' appear in several forms and these may stand for Littler, Longton. Marks are usually in blue under the glaze.

The name of Wm. Littler is associated with that of the factory almost from its foundation: his work there included much which seems to have been experimental. A deep blue glaze seen on some wares is supposed to have been his invention.

Two types of porcelain are attributable to Longton Hall. The more usual is a crude rather heavy porcelain of peculiar translucency for its thickness, the body appearing a pale green or blue with 'moons' of white when seen by transmitted light. The basic colour is a cold glassy white in natural light.

The wares include leaf dishes similar to those made in Staffordshire saltglazed stoneware (qq.v.), various articles in fruit and vegetable form often with twig-handles painted green, vases and basketwork dishes. Plates and dishes with moulded borders are frequent.

Decoration is in bright and rather crude colours, notably a deep underglaze blue, yellowish-green, dull pink and a rather thick red. Gilding (q.v.) was used sparingly.

The second Longton Hall type is a rather finer porcelain, in imitation of Meissen (q.v.), often making use of the same subjects: vases decorated with applied double flowers, plates painted with birds, and bouquets of flowers, etc. There is some similarity to Chelsea (q.v.) in many of the pieces, but most are of inferior quality.

Figures were made at Longton Hall probably from its inception. It is now known, as the result of recent excavations on the site, that the 'Snowman' (q.v.) type of figure was made here. Later figures have the merits of vigorous execution and individuality, but are usually roughly modelled and give the appearance of being unfinished. Scrolled bases picked out in red are a distinguishing characteristic of these figures, together with the Longton Hall palette of yellows, blues and deep red.

Lonhuda Pottery: American art pottery established at Steubenville,

Ohio, in 1892 by William A. Long for the production of underglazing (q.v.) decorated art pottery (q.v.). Shapes derived from American Indian pottery. The company was bought in 1895 by Samuel A. Weller, who introduced art pottery to Zanesville (q.v.), Ohio.

Loop-back chair: American term for a type of Windsor chair (q.v.).

Looped pile carpet: a carpet woven in loops, in the manner of velvet, which are afterwards cut.

Loopings or **draggings:** decorative device achieved by the glassblower in applying glass threads of contrasting colours to the body of the glassware, which are then dragged upward by a tool and embedded. The technique has been used since ancient times.

Lotus ornament: a decorative motif, intended to represent the lotus, inspired by the interest in Egyptian art prevalent during the Napoleonic wars. The campaign in Egypt provoked the general popularity of Egyptian forms and motifs and the lotus, as well as representations of the sphinx, etc. appeared on furniture, silver, etc., in the first decade of the 19th cent.

Louisiana Porcelain Works: established in 1880 at New Orleans, Louisiana, the factory produced a general line of porcelain in imitation of Limoges (q.v.), utilizing French workers and materials. All wares were sold undecorated.

Lovebird thumbpiece: a thumbpiece (q.v.), representing twin birds, their beaks jointed, surmounted by a volute (q.v.), found on pewter (q.v.) tankards.

Love seat: an upholstered settee intended for two persons. (See Causeuse.)

Loving cup: a drinking vessel with two handles, originally used for toasting. General term for twin-handled cups.

Lowboy: a piece of American furniture inspired by the English flat-top dressing table with drawers, yet in its final development, similar to a French commode. Lowboys date from the 18th cent., New England examples being attractively simple and those from Philadelphia much carved and ornamented. Known in the 18th cent. as dressing tables, chamber tables or low chests of drawers, lowboys were often made as companion pieces to highboys (q.v.).

'Lowdin's' Bristol: see Bristol porcelain.

Lowestoft porcelain: a factory manufacturing soft-paste porcelain (q.v.) was established in Bell Lane (now Crown Street), Lowestoft, in 1757. The original partners were Robert Browne, Philip Walker, Obed. Aldred, and John Hickman. The firm lasted until 1802 and produced unpretentious coloured and blue-and-white ware of attractive quality. Contrary to many ancient claims, hard-paste porcelain (q.v.) was never made here.

No mark was consistently used, but numerals up to 28 often in underglaze blue inside the footring are found on some pieces. Factory marks of Worcester, Meissen and other factories were sometimes imitated.

Many pieces made at this factory are dated or inscribed and a fairly complete sequence from the earliest to the last years of the factory can be established. Tea caddies, inkstands, and other small pieces intended for visitors were often lettered 'A Trifle from Lowestoft'. Dates from 1761 until 1795.

The Lowestoft porcelain paste was very similar to that of Bow (q.v.), although the glaze was generally thinner and rather absorbent. Patches of discoloration are to be found on Lowestoft tea cups.

Tablewares and numerous small articles were most frequently decorated in underglaze blue, the colour being usually darker than that of Bow or Worcester (q.v.). Porcelain moulded in relief was made in some quantity and can be identified from surviving moulds. A wickerwork design of rough character was much used. Openwork baskets and cabbage-leaf jugs were also made.

Oriental designs of figures in landscapes or flowers are common; marine views and inscriptions were popular, some being in distinctive colours, for the most part bright browns and reds. A similarity to delftware of the period is sometimes noticeable.

In the later articles the designs become more elaborate, Chinese influence being dominant. Commemorative pieces such as punch bowls (q.v.), jugs, and plaques, often inscribed and frequently painted with local views, were made. Among other pieces there are mugs with double-twisted handles; teapots of globular form and toy tea services. Recently a few figures have come to light, but no larger groups.

Low-warp tapestry: tapestry woven on a horizontal loom. The weaver controls his warp with treadles, leaving his hands free and is therefore able to work more quickly than the high-warp (q.v.) weaver. The cartoon is placed under the horizontal warp, requiring it to be drawn in reverse. At the Gobelins (q.v.) where both low-warp and high-warp weaving were employed, it was reckoned that at least a third more low-warp tapestry could be woven in a given time.

Lozenge ornament: see Diamond ornament.

Ludwigsburg porcelain: hard-paste porcelain (q.v.) was made at the ducal factory at Ludwigsburg, near Stuttgart, in 1758–9 under Duke Carl Eugen. The factory itself had been founded at an earlier date for the manufacture of faience. The porcelain was brownish-grey in colour and consequently somewhat inferior for tablewares. The body was, however, admirable for figure modelling and the figures produced are the most sought after of the factory's productions. Of these, those modelled by the Court sculptor J. C. W. Beyer, appointed chief modeller in 1764, are masterly in their combination of Rococo (q.v.) elements and Classical (q.v.) tendencies. The factory was closed in 1824, but it had already begun to fail after the death of the Duke in 1793. The early mark consists of interlaced 'Cs', with or without a crown, replaced by the stag's horns from the arms of Württemberg about 1793.

Lug: an ear (Scots); the handle of a quaich (q.v.).

Lunar clock dial: a dial which shows the lunar periods.

Lund's Bristol: see Bristol porcelain.

Lunette ornament: formal carving composed of semicircles, variously filled and embellished, frequently disposed in a repeat band.

This type of ornament is frequently found on oak furniture of the first half of the 17th cent. The fan-shaped or lunette motif was also used on late 18th-cent. furniture, either painted or inlaid.

Lung-chüan celadon ware: this centre for celadon wares (q.v.) in Chekiang Province, China, flourished during the Sung dynasty (q.v.). The greyish-white porcellaneous body often appears brown where exposed raw to the fire. The characteristic glaze is thick, smooth and translucent, varying principally between a cool greyish and deep grassy green, the colour being derived from iron. Best known are the stoutly potted, large, heavy dishes, jars and vases exported in quantity throughout the Near and Far East. Finer wares are various in shape, often with freely carved or incised designs, or decoration impressed from moulds of fishes, dragons or plants, sometimes left unglazed and burnt an attractive red. The Kinuta celadon, a subdued bluish green in colour, is of outstanding quality. Another type with brown spots is the Japanese *tobi seiji* (q.v.). Early Ming (q.v.) celadons are similar, but often more elaborately decorated. Quality then declined rapidly.

Lustre: this term is now used to describe a vase with everted rim from which hang cut-glass drops. At one period it was used to describe a chandelier, and in 1739 Jerom Johnson the glass-seller, advertised for sale 'the most magnificent lustre that was ever made in England'.

The vase lustre was made in pairs, and came into vogue in the middle of the 19th cent. The most esteemed were of ruby or green glass with an overlay of white, and decoration, in addition to the cutting, in the form of painted flowers or miniature portraits in colours, and gilding (q.v.). They were made in Bohemia (now Czechoslovakia), but considerable numbers were manufactured in England, at Stourbridge and elsewhere. Wedgwood's (q.v.) jasper (q.v.) ware was used for embellishing lustres.

Lustre decoration: decoration on pottery or porcelain by means of thin films of metal. Josiah Wedgwood (q.v.) experimented with lustre decoration from about 1790 and his successors made commercial use of silver, pink (gold) and 'moonlight' lustre from about 1805. John Hancock claimed to be the first to produce lustre effects in Staffordshire while employed by Henry Daniel & John Brown, enamellers of Hanley (*Staffordshire Mercury*, 1846). Hancock sold the recipe to various persons for small sums of money and its use soon became widespread. The earliest commercial use of silver lustre is stated to have taken place at Wolfe's factory in Stoke. Others had also had a hand in its early development and application. Various methods of application were used: pencilled, 'resist', banded, or in conjunction with transfer-printing and enamelling (qq.v.). It enjoyed popularity in Staffordshire from about 1805 until 1875. Burgess, Dale & Goddard did an extensive trade in lustre wares with America in the 1850s. The subjects used for lustre decoration cover the whole field of public and domestic life, religious, political, sporting, travel and sensational events – the humours of every day life accompanied sometimes by pious quatrains, or sentimental and licentious doggerel. W. de Morgan (q.v.) revived the technique in the early 1870s, producing examples in the Pre-Raphaelite style.

Lutz, Nicholas: (*fl.* 2nd half of 19th cent.) French glass artist, leading craftsman of period in *latticinio* (q.v.) and *vetro di trina* (q.v.) techniques. Emigrated to the United States where he worked in a number of American glasshouses.

Lycett, Edward: foremost American china decorator. Trained in Staffordshire, England, Lycett arrived in New York City in *c.* 1861 and established an extensive decorating business. In 1884 Lycett joined the Faience Manufacturing Co. (q.v.) where, under his direction, a fine grade of porcelain in the Moorish style was produced.

Lyre-back chair: a late 18th-cent. chair of a design favoured by Robert Adam (q.v.) and Duncan Phyfe (q.v.). The splat (q.v.) contained in a square back, is carved in the shape of a lyre with metal strings.

McCabe: English firm famed for its fine watches and clocks, especially in India, and its duplex escapements (q.v.). Operated from 1838 to 1883 from Cornhill, London.

Macdonald, Frances: (1874–1921), Glasgow School (q.v.) designer and metalworker who collaborated with her sister, M. Macdonald (q.v.), and later with her husband, J. H. McNair (q.v.).

Macdonald, Margaret: (1865–1933), Glasgow School (q.v.) designer, metal- and needleworker, sister of F. Macdonald and wife of C. R. Mackintosh (qq.v.).

Mace: civic, university or state emblem of authority derived from Medieval war weapon. Usually sur- mounted by Royal arms and crown. Silver examples date from 15th cent. onwards.

Macer Pottery Co.: established in 1868 at Trenton, New Jersey, the factory claims to have produced the first porcelain in the United States.

Machine-cut silhouette: silhouette produced by a mechanical profile machine, of which there were many forms. Such work may usually be distinguished by a certain hardness and lack of freedom in its outlines. There were, however, a few machine- cutters who produced commendable work. One such was Mrs Sarah Harrington (fl. 1775), whose shades are full of vivacity. On the whole machine-cutting is the most debased form of the art of the silhouette.

Machine-printed wallpaper: the first successful wallpaper printing machine was in operation in England about 1840. Based on calico-printing principles, it was dependent on the invention and supply of paper in 'continuous' lengths.

Mackintosh, Charles Rennie: (1868–1928), Scottish architect, de- signer and decorator and central figure of the Glasgow School (q.v.). His first designs for furniture date from the early 1890s and in 1896 he submitted the successful design for the building and furnishing of the Glasgow School of Art. He created a style that com- bined balance with asymmetry, ex- aggerated lines, as in his chair backs, with gentle curves. He was to exert a strong influence on the development of the Vienna Secessionists—the Austrian version of Art Nouveau (q.v.). He was married to M. Macdonald (q.v.).

Mackmurdo, Arthur Heygate: (1851–1942), English architect and designer and founder of the Century Guild (q.v.) and its publication, *The Hobby Horse*. He was a close follower of William Morris (q.v.) but at the same time developed a personal, and in- fluential, style in his designs for textiles and wallpaper, furniture and metalwork based on plant forms. His ideas were adopted first by the designers associated with the Aesthetic Movement (q.v.) and later by Art Nouveau (q.v.) designers and artists.

McLaughlin, Mary Louise: late 19th-cent. exponent of art pottery (q.v.) decoration in Cincinnati.

McNair, J. Herbert: late 19th-cent. Scottish architect and associate and follower of C. R. Mackintosh (q.v.).

He designed furniture in the Glasgow School (q.v.) style and was married to F. Macdonald (q.v.).

Maidenhead spoon: a spoon with a finial (q.v.) in the form of a female bust traditionally representing the Virgin Mary.

Mail: armour made of interlinked rings which, on most European examples, are riveted. It was known in Europe at least as early as the 2nd cent. B.C., and was the normal defence during the early Middle Ages. It was relegated to a subordinate role with the general adoption of plate armour in the 14th cent., but nevertheless remained in common use until well into the 17th.

Main-gauche dagger: see Left-hand dagger.

Maintaining power: a device used in weight clocks and in clocks and watches fitted with a fusee (q.v.), whereby a subsidiary force is brought into play to keep the clock going while it is being wound. In early clocks the winding squares were often covered by shutters, which, when pulled aside, brought into operation the maintaining power, thus ensuring its use.

Maiolica (and **Majolica**): the name given to tin-glazed earthenware made in Spain and Italy from the 14th cent., being the Italian form of the place-name Majorca, whence ships engaged in transporting Valencian lustred pottery from Spain traded. First applied to Spanish lustred wares, the term was gradually extended to cover Italian lustred wares executed in the Spanish technique, and ultimately to any kind of earthenware with painted decoration on tin glaze. The technique of the Italian *maiolica* potter is described in *The Three Books of the Potters Art* by Cipriano Piccolpasso, *c.* 1556, translated by Bernard Rackham and A. van de Put. Should not be confused with Majolica – the name given by Victorian potters to earthenware decorated with coloured glazes, introduced at Mintons (q.v.) about 1850. Used extensively for decorative pottery, domestic wares, architectural pottery intended for facing pillars, walls, staircases, balconies, and flower-pots and umbrella stands.

Majorelle, Louis: (1859–1926), French cabinet-maker (q.v.) in Nancy. Much influenced by E. Gallé (q.v.), he was, from about 1890, a leading designer of furniture in the Art Nouveau (q.v.) style. From 1900 he was also an important and prolific manufacturer of furniture, producing, among much else, mounts for A. Daum's glass.

Maker's mark: the distinguishing mark of the individual goldsmith, device or initials struck on every piece of plate (q.v.) from his workshop. First enforced in London in 1363.

Malachite: a name given to a parian ware (q.v.), coloured to resemble the green of malachite stone.

Malling jugs: English tin-glazed pottery jugs splashed or mottled with metallic oxides in imitation of Rhenish Tigerwares (q.v.), and similarly mounted. Dates recorded from 1549 until 1618. Some of these wares have been attributed to a Sandwich-Maidstone potter, working *c.* 1582, and derive their name from a specimen formerly in West Malling church, Kent. Also called Tigerware or Leopardware.

Maltese lace: pillow lace (q.v.) made from 1833, the designs including 'wheat grains' grouped in fours to make Maltese crosses.

Manchette: a cuff-bracelet worn in the 19th cent.

Manchu dynasty: dynasty of the Ch'ing emperors in China (1644–1912).

Mandarin china: Chinese porcelain wares imported during the second half of the 18th cent. and later, with predominantly pink, red and gold enamelling of floral or figure subjects, often framed in underglaze blue scrollwork; frequently with undulating glaze.

Manière criblée: prints in the *manière criblée*, sometimes called 'dotted prints', are taken from a metal plate engraved in the same manner as a white-line woodcut. The name is derived from the groups of dots made on the plate with a punch to break up otherwise black areas of background. Prints of this type were made in the late 15th and early 16th cent., especially in Florence. The method was revived in England towards the end of the 18th cent.

Mannerist style: an international style which emerged in the second decade of the 16th cent. as a reaction against the harmony and order of the Renaissance (q.v.). Embraced by the French court at Fontainebleau, where Italian artists were employed in the decoration of the Palace, the style spread throughout Europe as a Court art characterized by anti-naturalism and an intellectual approach to form. There were many local variations to suit local requirements but the same rejection of the Classical spirit, involving a disregard of naturalistic forms, is everywhere apparent.

Mannheim gold: an alloy of copper, zinc and tin.

Mansell, Sir Robert: a financier who organized the English glass industry in the first half of the 17th cent., and who eventually controlled glasshouses all over the country. He imported skilled workers from Murano, and successfully made mirror glass.

Mantel clock: see Bracket clock.

Manton brothers: the foremost London gunmakers of the first quarter of the 19th cent. The two brothers, John and Joseph, vied with each other for supremacy. John, the elder, was more popular with the Royal family but Joseph was the greater. At the height of his career, he was unequalled and his name lives on as one of the most famous gunmakers of all time.

Manwaring, Robert: cabinet- and chair-maker. Published *The Cabinet* *and Chair Maker's Real Friend and Companion* in 1765 and *The Chair-Maker's Guide* in 1762.

Mappin & Webb Ltd.: Sheffield firm of cutlers and silversmiths which in the mid-19th cent. had a London showroom specializing in electroplated (q.v.) wares and luxury items.

Marbled ware: a slipware (q.v.) decorated by working together various coloured slips with a wire comb and sponge in emulation of marbled papers or natural stones. Common on Staffordshire, Swansea, Leeds and Don pottery in the 18th cent.

Marbled earthenwares had been made in China during the T'ang and Sung dynasties (q.v.), produced either by rolling together differently coloured clays or by manipulating a coloured slip on the surface.

Marcasite: iron pyrites, faceted in the manner of precious stones, made by mechanical process. Widely used by jewellery makers from the 18th cent. onwards.

Marcolini, Count Camillo: (1739–1814), appointed director of the Meissen porcelain (q.v.) factory in 1774, where he remained for forty years. The period of his directorship is known as the Marcolini period, the wares being marked during this time with crossed swords and an underglaze blue star between the hilts.

Marcotte, Léon: (*c*. 1825–*c*. 1886/7), French cabinet-maker (q.v.) who emigrated to New York in 1854. In 1861 he founded Marcotte & Co., becoming a leading decorator and exponent of the Rococo (q.v.) Revival style.

Marieberg porcelain: porcelain was made at Marieberg, near Stockholm, from 1758. The factory was directed by a Frenchman who had previously worked at Mennecy (q.v.). It was closed in 1788. The mark until 1769 was the monogram MB, either incised, in blue or in red.

Marine barometer: a type in which part of the bore in the vertical tube is constricted in order to minimize a movement of level in the vertical tube by reason of the ship's motion. This type was also capable of plugging when not in use.

Markwick family: an eminent London family of clockmakers, the various members being active between 1666 and 1805.

Marlborough leg: a straight, tapered leg of square section, sometimes supported on a plinth, used by cabinet-makers (q.v.) in the second half of the 18th cent. The origin of the term is obscure but it may have been invented in compliment to the fourth Duke of Marlborough to whom Ince and Mayhew (q.v.) dedicated their *Universal System of Household Furniture*.

Marot, Daniel: (1663–1752), a Huguenot refugee who became Minister of Works to William of Orange. He visited England from 1694 to 1697 and again in 1698 and worked at Hampton Court. His designs for furniture and silver and for the interiors of rooms were influential in Holland and England.

Marouflage: a scarlet cloth backing to pierced lock plates.

Marquetry: (*Fr.*), *Marqueterie* from *Marqueter*, to spot, speckle, variegate. Ornamental veneer (q.v.) of wood or other materials in which veneers of various coloured woods were cut into delicate patterns and fitted together on to a prepared carcase. The practice of decorating case furniture and tables with marquetry was introduced from Holland in *c.* 1675. At first English cabinet-makers (q.v.) followed the Flemish fashion and used bird, flower and foliage designs, sometimes introducing bone and ivory. The colours toned to darker or golden shades by 1690 and later arabesques (q.v.) became popular. This phase of the fashion did not survive the early 18th cent. but marquetry once again enjoyed a period of favour in the last quarter of the 18th cent. and again in the 19th cent. with the Revival styles.

Marquise: (*Fr.*), a small sofa also known as a causeuse (q.v.). English settees of this type are sometimes known as love seats (q.v.).

Marquise ring: a ring of oval form, pointed at each extremity.

Marrow spoon: long, narrow-bowled spoon, usually double-ended with two widths of bowl for eating bone-marrow. Alternative version has normal tablespoon bowl and marrow bowl in place of handle. Found from early 18th cent. onwards.

Marsh (d. 1810) **and Tatham** (1763–1818): principal cabinet-makers (q.v.) to the Prince of Wales, future George IV, with whom the architect and designer Henry Holland (q.v.) was closely associated.

Martha Gunn: toby jug modelled in the likeness of Martha Gunn (1727–1815), the Brighton bathing-woman.

Martha Washington chair: slender mid-18th-cent. armchair with tapered outlines; a 'lady's chair', with upholstered, low, shallow seat and high back, usually with serpentine cresting. So named in America because Martha Washington is supposed to have used a chair of this type at Mount Vernon.

Martha Washington mirror: walnut or mahogany wall mirror, Georgian style (q.v.), with handsome gilded mouldings, strings of leaves, fruits or flowers down the sides, a scroll top and a bird finial (q.v.). The base is cut in a series of bold curves. Made in

America from about 1760 to 1800, and known there by this name, because Martha Washington is supposed to have used one at Mount Vernon. (Also known in America as a Constitution mirror.)

Martha Washington sewing table: oval box-form sewing table with rounded ends and hinged top. Fitted with drawers and sewing material compartments, it is an American variant of an English late-18th-cent. type. So named in America because Martha Washington is supposed to have used one at Mount Vernon.

Martin Bros: association of four brothers, led by Robert Wallace Martin, formed in 1873 to produce salt-glazed stoneware (q.v.), first in London and then at Southall, Middlesex. The decoration and shape often show Oriental influence and products include jugs and jars made in the shapes of grotesque faces and masks.

Mary Gregory glass: generic term, named after an artist at the Boston & Sandwich Glass Co. (q.v.) in the third quarter of the 19th cent., for clear and coloured glass painted in white enamel with figures of children.

Mason's bone china: Miles Mason, after some years of experimental potting in Liverpool and in Fenton started to make porcelain at a factory in Market Street, Fenton, in 1800. In 1807 he moved to the Minerva works, Fenton, where he continued to make porcelain and bone china (qq.v.) in conjunction with his eldest son, William Mason. When he retired in 1813 the business was continued by G. M. and C. J. Mason, the other son, William, having taken over a separate factory. George Miles Mason withdrew from the business about 1829, leaving Charles James Mason to continue on his own account, or for a short period in partnership with Faraday until he became bankrupt in 1848. Charles James Mason started up again at the Daisy Bank, Longton, in 1851, exhibited at the great Exhibition in that year but closed down in 1854.

Marks:

Transfer-printed

Variations in crown

Transfer-printed

Early types of porcelain made by Miles Mason were of an extremely hard consistency and rather opaque; a translucent bone paste was also made. Blue printed decorations were popular, and painted landscapes, Chinese subjects and border patterns in the Regency style.

G. M. and C. J. Mason made showy Imari (q.v.) patterns with massed effects of colour and gold, often rather crudely applied. Very large pieces were made in ironstone china, including fireplaces, bedposts, vases five feet high, some in a revived Rococo (q.v.) style, others with pseudo-Chinese decorations. Blue-printed earthenware was extensively made.

Massachusetts shelf clock: a type made by the Willards (q.v.) and others, mainly in Massachusetts. Also called half-clock, box-on-box, or case-on-case, eight-day brass movements, timepieces or occasionally striking clocks. c. 1800–30. Rare.

Matchlock: the earliest form of mechanical ignition for a gun, introduced late in the 15th cent., in which an arm holding a lighted match (cord made of tow soaked in a solution of saltpetre) is brought into contact with priming powder at the touch-hole by pressure on a trigger. Despite the invention of the wheel- and flintlocks (qq.v.), it remained in use for military purposes, on account of its cheapness, until the end of the 17th cent.

Matt glaze: a glaze with a dull, non-reflecting surface.

Matting: a dull, roughened surface produced on silverware by repeated punching with a burred tool. Much used in mid-17th cent. on tankard and cup bodies and in the 19th cent. as a background for chased ornament.

Mauchline woodware: decorated boxes and small wooden keepsakes, usually of sycamore, made in or near Mauchline, in Scotland. The snuff boxes (q.v.) and tea caddies (q.v.) characteristically had integral wooden hinges. In the 19th cent. the principal forms of decoration were pen-and-ink work, varnished transfers and fern silhouettes made with sprayed paint.

Maximilian armour: a modern term for the style of fluted armour that came into use in Italy and, more particularly, in Germany during the reign of the Emperor Maximilian I

(1494–1519). It is rarely found after c. 1540, but examples dating from as late as c. 1560–70 are occasionally encountered.

Mayhew, Thomas: see Ince and Mayhew.

Mazarin blue: a dark rich blue frequently used for the decoration of porcelain, less frequently for earthenware. The origin of the name is unknown, but thought to be an attributed use of the name Cardinal Giulio Mazarin (1602–61) jurisprudent, diplomat and cardinal, or the Duchesse de Mazarin (died 1699). The name is mentioned in the 1756 catalogue of the Chelsea porcelain (q.v.) factory.

Mazarine: pierced, flat silver straining plate for use especially with fish dishes.

Mazer: Medieval drinking bowl formed from a turned section of maple burr, mounted with silver rim and occasionally straps, usually gilt. Large standing examples on high feet found in Scotland and a few in England. Rare after the 16th cent.

Mead, John O.: Philadelphia manufacturer of wares in Britannia metal (q.v.) and gilder by the mercury process. In the mid-19th cent. he went to Birmingham to learn to electroplate (q.v.) and on returning set up as the first successful electroplater in the United States.

Meakin, J. & G. Ltd.: a Staffordshire pottery firm originally based at Longton which transferred to Hanley in 1848. Specialized in earthenware and granite ware (q.v.) for the American market, decorated in the style of French porcelain.

Meander ornament: a repetitive pattern consisting of straight lines intersecting at right-angles used as a border ornament. Also known as key pattern (q.v.).

Measure: a vessel of a standard liquid capacity, used in taverns for serving into drinking vessels.

Meat fork: used at the fireside when cooking. It usually had two prongs and hardly differed from a toasting fork.

Mechanical birds: among the most popular of all automata were birds, from the duck of Vaucanson (q.v.) onwards. Marie-Antoinette, Queen of France, possessed a life-sized canary in a cage, the underneath of which showed the dial of a clock. The bird sang realistically. Catherine II, Empress of Russia, was presented in 1780 with a large caged mechanical peacock made by James Cox (q.v.). On the smallest scale were the singing birds fitted into snuff boxes (q.v.). These were quite invisible until on the pressure of a button, they sprang up, moved their heads, wings and tails, and sang. They were, understandably, highly popular and expensive. Many were mounted in gold boxes, set with precious stones and contained a musical-box movement as well. The Jacquet-Droz (q.v.) and the Rochat brothers are among the best known makers of these remarkable *tours-de-force*, which date from the late 18th and early 19th cent. Even more remarkable are watches with singing birds and gold pistols from the mouths of which tiny birds emerge and sing when the triggers are pressed.

Mechanical pictures: framed pictures (landscapes, seascapes, etc.) in which figures, animals, windmills and water were all operated mechanically.

Mechlin lace: pillow lace (q.v.), much imported to England, although it must be remembered that all Flemish laces until the 17th cent. were called Mechlin in England. Queen Anne, who prohibited imports of French lace, allowed those from the Low Countries. The earliest that can be identified, however, dates only to the 1720s. Handsome Rococo (q.v.) patterns were used, outlined in a separate, heavier flat thread, the pattern and ground being made together in one operation. The ground was the familiar hexagonal mesh in which four sides were of two threads twisted and two sides were of four threads plaited three times. Structurally this was nearly the same as the Brussels ground but the effect was altogether less stiff and angular. Other grounds were sometimes used such as the *œil de perdrix* (q.v.). The spotted patterns of the 1770s onwards consisted of rows of small sprays and the mesh was also variously spotted, the whole effect being subdued and soft. Some lace in Mechlin style was made in Denmark in the 18th and early 19th cent.

Medallion design carpets: Persian carpets often included the medallion motif, common in all Eastern decoration. The Ardebil carpet in the Victoria and Albert Museum is considered the finest example of this type.

Medallion fans: fashionable from the 1770s to the 1790s. The mount of finely woven silk was painted all over with a light coloured ground. Upon this three medallion subjects were painted: the central one might be elliptical, rectangular or round, its smooth symmetry often emphasized by a flanking pair of small vignettes or medallions depicting associated subjects. These were the work of expert miniature decorators: the detail was displayed quite as finely as on the more costly chicken skin (q.v.). The background was ornamented with minor motifs, scrollwork, sequins, cut steel and other beads. The silk might be mounted on fine gauze.

Medallion fans with their narrower sticks of mother-of-pearl superseded mounts with all-over paintings, but although handsome they are not to be compared with the regal fans of the previous hundred years. Late in the period tiny Wedgwood jasper cameos (q.v.) were set in the sticks, many of which were richly overlaid with embossed gold or silver work, often in the form of a cartouche (q.v.) extending over six or eight sticks.

Medici porcelain: the first successful attempt to produce soft-paste porcelain (q.v.) in Europe was made at Florence about 1560, under the patronage of Francesco de' Medici. Inspired by the contemporary blue-and-white Ming (q.v.) ware, an artificial porcelain was produced for a short time only, which contained some kaolin, the pure infusable clay used in China, mixed with powdered glass and frit (q.v.).

Medici porcelain, proudly marked with the cupola of the cathedral and the 'F' of Florence, is decorated in underglaze blue of varying intensity, which melts into the glaze.

Meeks, Joseph, & Sons: New York firm of cabinet-makers (q.v.) with a branch in New Orleans from early in the 19th cent. It was founded in 1797. Before closing in 1868, it produced good-quality furniture in most of the 19th-cent. Revival styles.

Meerschaum: magnesium silicate, first discovered by the Black Sea and thought to be petrified sea foam (*Ger.: Meerschaum*). It was used in the manufacture of pipes, the greyish material turning amber when stained by tobacco smoke.

Meigh, Charles: (fl. mid-19th cent.) Staffordshire potter who succeeded his father at Old Hall Works, Hanley, in 1835. The firm produced a wide range of earthenware for table or toilet use, vases, figures, groups and busts in parian ware (q.v.) and stoneware (q.v.) jugs with architectural detail in the Gothic style.

Mei p'ing: Chinese porcelain 'prunus' vase, with small mouth to hold one spray of plum-blossom.

Meissen (or **Dresden**) **porcelain:** the foundation of the Meissen factory (near Dresden), 1710, marks the actual beginning of porcelain making in Europe, where its commercial value to an impecunious Court was immediately recognized. J. F. Boettger (q.v.), an alchemist in the service of August the Strong, Elector of Saxony and King of Poland, discovered a red stoneware 'which surpasses the hardness of porphyry', as he reported to the King in March 1709. During the following year this red stoneware was offered for sale at the Leipzig Easter Fair. Almost immediately rival factories appeared, one at Plaue on the Havel, where a Prussian minister found red clay on his estate, another at Potsdam, encouraged by the King of Prussia himself. But neither of these factories was progressive, whereas Boettger succeeded in replacing the red clay with white kaolin (see China clay). Thus he produced the first real porcelain in Europe, called Boettger ware, after the inventor, and sold at the Leipzig Fair from 1713 onwards. Above the entrance to Boettger's laboratory, where the King had virutally kept him a prisoner, there is a significant inscription 'God, our maker, has turned a goldmaker into a potter'.

The earliest tableware made at the Meissen factory followed the shape of contemporary silver and the first modeller, Johann Jacob Irminger, was a Court silversmith. Some of this porcelain is decorated with applied floral motives, some with enamel, gilding or lustre colour, which is a pale mother-of-pearl coating obtained from gold, the outcome of another of Boettger's experiments. The earliest figures show dependence upon ivory statuettes and ivory carvers are known to have found employment at the Meissen factory. A figure of the King himself, in heroic attitude, made first in red Boettger ware and later in white with enamel colouring, belongs to this period, and is attributed to the Saxon ivory carver, Johann Christoph von Lücke. With the rediscovery of underglaze blue at Meissen, the first factory marks were introduced. A pseudo-Chinese sign of square shape is the earliest mark recorded followed by the so-called Caduceus, in turn replaced by the letters K P M (Königliche Porzellan Manufaktur), until in 1724, the crossed swords, taken from the King's arms, were permanently adopted.

Special commissions executed for the King himself bear his initials A R (Augustus Rex) in underglaze blue. Incised signs are usually factory assembly marks for the convenience of workmen or repairers (q.v.).

Meanwhile Johann Gregor Herold, a miniature and enamel painter, who had been in charge of the artistic direction of the factory in 1720, experimented with colours and, among others, produced a clear yellow ground which found the King's special favour, since it recalled the Imperial colour of China. Herold's Chinoiserie (q.v.) subjects, based upon engravings, became an established fashion as a means of enamelled decoration, followed in the later 1730s by harbour views with figures which reveal the influence of Delft. In spite of the complete anonymity which Herold insisted upon, it is sometimes possible to trace the style of individual artists such as C K. Hunger and A. F. von Löwenfinck since they were able to sign work done elsewhere, when visiting other factories. Such moving about by porcelain workers was often caused by financial gains resulting from the disclosure of technical secrets. Painted porcelain was more costly than whiteware and outside painters, called *Hausmaler* or independent decorators (q.v.), often executed private orders upon request. The Meissen factory suffered from such competition, and introduced measures to prevent the further sale of undecorated porcelain, unless imperfect or of a discontinued pattern. But we may be glad that the competition existed, for some of the *Hausmaler*, mainly those centred at Augsburg and Dresden, display an originality of design which would have been difficult to attain under the levelling influence of Herold's strong personality.

With the employment at Meissen of Johann Gottlob Kirchner (q.v.) in 1727, the great period of porcelain sculpture begins. Misled at first by his ambitious Royal patron, who commissioned large-scale statues for the Japanese Palace, Kirchner modelled figures which did not obey the innate laws of the new material. His powerful fantastic animals, in white, are again more distinctive as remarkable *tours de force* rather than as cabinet pieces for the porcelain collector.

J. J. Kaendler (q.v.), who was appointed as chief modeller in 1731, was the first to recognize the possibilities of the new material, and to exploit its inherent qualities. His Italian *Commedia dell' Arte* figures seem to dance on the shelves of china cabinets. Even conventional tableware takes a share in plastic decoration, and the Swan Service which Kaendler modelled for Count Brühl reveals his creative genius in the many variations on the theme of swans. Kaendler's birds were all studied from nature, since Augustus the Strong kept a large collection of domestic and rare specimens at Dresden.

Meissen figures and groups served often as table decoration, replacing earlier ones of wax or sugar. The themes are suggested by Court amusements from theatrical characters performing with Baroque (q.v.) exuberance, to disguised princesses and shepherds of sophisticated elegance. Mythological and allegorical subjects are never absent: river gods, seasons, continents or the arts, all richly endowed with the graces of 18th-cent. society. Watteau scenes begin to appear on Meissen porcelain about 1738–40. At that time the King's daughter Maria Amalia Christina married Charles IV, King of Naples, and the famous service with green monochrome Watteau decoration made as a wedding gift, established the new fashion. The increased demand for French engravings as sources of designs was satisfied by J. C. Huet, brother of the painter, who became the factory agent in Paris. Kaendler himself visited Paris in 1749, when French influence gained in intensity at Meissen. Elongated figures, painted in soft colours, turn into pleasing conservation pieces and an air of sentimentality prevails, replacing the whimsical mood and vigour of the earlier days. Kaendler was assisted by a few gifted modellers, and Peter Reinicke as well as Johann Friedrich Eberlein deserve special credit. Friedrich Elias Meyer, appointed after Eberlein's serious illness in 1748, belonged to a younger generation. Meyer's figures are recognizable by their small heads and slender proportions, to which richly moulded and gilt scroll bases lend additional height.

With the outbreak of the Seven Years' War in 1756, the Meissen fac-

tory suffered a heavy blow. The Prussians occupied the town and the King fled to Warsaw. Frederick the Great had thirty boxes of porcelain despatched to Potsdam and placed further orders for table services and snuff boxes with the factory, some of which were copied later on at the Berlin factory (q.v.). After the war, Meissen never regained its former unchallenged lead. A Neoclassical phase followed, known as the Academic period, during which the wares were marked with the usual crossed swords with a small dot between the hilts (1763–74). During the directorship of Count Camillo Marcolini which immediately followed (1774–1814) the mark was the crossed swords with a star between the hilts. In the 19th cent. the factory made many debased versions of earlier wares. These are now commonly described as 'Dresden' to differentiate them from the original wares, usually known as Meissen porcelain.
Marks:

Meissonier, Juste-Aurèle: (c. 1693–1750), French designer, architect and craftsman, the initiator of the Rococo (q.v.) style in the decorative arts. In 1726 he was appointed *Dessinateur du Cabinet* to Louis XV, and he produced several influential pattern books.

Melon bulb: the swollen member on legs or posts of furniture. An exaggeration of the knop (q.v.), it attained full development in the Elizabethan period, becoming less globular in the early 17th cent.

Memento mori: see Mourning jewellery.

Mendlesham chair: a variety of Windsor chair (q.v.), being of stick construction, with turned legs and solid elm seats. This type of chair was traditionally first made by Daniel Day of Mendlesham in Suffolk. In examples of fine quality, the backs are decorated with inlay.

Mêne, Pierre-Jules: (1810–79), French *animalier* (q.v.) sculptor who established his own foundry in 1838. Many copies of his work have appeared since his death, including a series made at Coalbrookdale.

Mennecy porcelain: soft-paste porcelain (q.v.) was made at Mennecy, Ile-de-France, between 1734 and 1785 (the factory being transferred to Bourg-la-Reine in 1773). The Mennecy factory imitated St Cloud and Chantilly (qq.v.) at first, soon attaining great technical skill. Kakiemon patterns (q.v.) were used in the early period but the mature style of Mennecy was chiefly inspired by that of Vincennes (see Sèvres porcelain). Tea ware, coffee pots, vases and flower pots were made in quantity. Some figures were produced but soft paste did not lend itself easily to moulding in the round, and there was danger of collapse in the kiln during the firing. The mark 'DV' appears on some pieces.

Menuisier: (*Fr.*), the term corresponds roughly to the English 'carpenter' or 'joiner'. In France, as far as furniture was concerned, the *menuisiers* were responsible for making chairs, beds and other furniture made from plain or carved woods, as distinct from veneered pieces which were the province of the *ébénistes* (q.v.). Although permitted by guild regulations to work in both techniques, they seldom did so.

Menuisiers-Ebénistes, Corporation des: (*Fr.*), the craft guild in

France that embraced all craftsmen engaged in making wood furniture. An apprentice began his training at the age of fourteen with a *maître-ébéniste* or *maître-menuisier*, lasting for six years. This period was followed by a further three to six years of training, known as *compagnonage*. During this latter time, the young man was paid for the work he did. After the *compagnonage*, he was ready to become a *maître* or master of the guild. After 1751, a *maître* was also required to stamp the furniture he sold. The maintenance of standards was in the hands of a *syndic* and six *jurés*. All pieces of furniture approved by the *jurés* were stamped with the monogram J.M.E. (*Juré* or *jurande des menuisiers-ébénistes*).

Mercury clock pendulum: a type of pendulum invented in 1726 by George Graham, who had previously experimented with brass and steel without conclusive results. The bob of the pendulum consists of a jar containing mercury. As the temperature changes the length of the pendulum rod, the level of the mercury in the jar alters in the inverse sense, thus keeping constant the centre of oscillation of the pendulum. Still in use today in high-grade clocks.

Mercury gilding: see Gilding.

Mercury-twist stem: a type of stem found on drinking glasses between about 1745 and 1765 containing air-twists of exceptionally large diameter spiralling down the centre in close coils, or a pair of corkscrew threads.

Merese knop: a knop or protuberance in the stem of a drinking glass or other glass vessel of sharp-edged, flattened form, resembling a button, and connecting bowl and stem or placed between the foot and the stem of a stemmed vessel. Also known as a collar knop.

Meriden Britannia Co.: American firm founded in 1852 by the amalgamation of several Britannia metalware (q.v.) manufacturers in Meriden, Connecticut. By 1855 it was producing electroplated flatware (q.v.) and hollow ware (q.v.) and it also made elaborate exhibition pieces. In 1898 the firm became part of the International Silver Co.

Merryman plates: an inscription, variously spelt, extended over a set of six octagonal plates made in tin-glazed earthenware in London from last quarter of 17th cent. until *c.* 1750 (dates recorded range from 1684–1742). The uncertain orthography was taken by W. B. Honey as an indication of manufacture by a Dutch potter working in England, if not of actual Dutch manufacture. Louis Gautier claimed the plates for a Dutch potter working in England named James de Pauw. Prof. F. H. Garner regards them as English. The rhyme reads '(a) What is a mery man? (b) Let him doe all what he kan (c) To entertayne his gess (d) With wyne and mery jests (e) But if his wyfe doth frown (f) All meryment goos downe.' Other rhymes extended over a series of plates are recorded, such as the 'Servant and Grace' series. The 'Servant' series (dated examples 1711) has the following rhyme: '(a) I am a servant unto all, (b) Both rich and poor, grate and small, (c) Who uses me with diligence (d) Will be on me at small expense. (e) But when by servants I am ended, (f) My grate fault is I can't be mended'. The 'Grace' extended over a series of six plates, dated 1697, reads '(a) When thou sit down to meat, (b) Give thanks before thou eat, (c) Be sure that thou conceive (d) The mercies thou receive, (e) That such favours may be (f) Repeated unto thee'.

Metal: the substance of glass, either molten or hard in the form of finished ware.

Metal spinning: a process used in the mass production of metal hollow-ware (q.v.) by which a thin metal sheet is pressed against a wooden core in a spinning lathe to be forced into shape.

Metropolitan slipware: the name given to a class of red earthenware decorated with white trailed slip, most of which has been found in the London area and probably originated there; characterized by commonplace shapes and inexpertly applied inscriptions often of a puritan religious character. Examples dated from 1638 to 1659 are recorded. Articles made include jugs, mugs, bowls, chamber pots. There are numerous examples in the British Museum. A chamber pot in Hanley Museum is lettered, 'Earth I am et tes most tru disdan me not for so are you.'

Meuble à hauteur d'appui: (*Fr.*), a term used extensively at all periods in France to describe any low bookcase or cupboard, usually between three and four feet high.

Meuble d'entre deux: (*Fr.*), a term used in the 18th cent. in France to describe a type of furniture consisting of a cupboard or chest of drawers flanked at each side by a set of shelves. Sometimes these are enclosed by a curved door forming a small cupboard.

Mezzotint: engraving distinguished by dark tones, obtained by roughening the plate all over to produce a black and then smoothing where required for lighter tones. The engraver therefore works from black to white and in tone rather than line. This is the process par excellence for reproducing paintings in monochrome, and so it was used throughout the 18th cent. It is a process that lends itself to hand colouring, and it was often applied over an aquatint (q.v.) ground.

Midband: an American term to describe a moulded band slightly below centre of a silver tankard which strengthened and decorated it. Introduced in Boston in first quarter of 18th cent. Also used on large two-handled covered cups about 1740.

Midshipmen jug: an early variety of toby jug (q.v.), somewhat crude in potting and glazing. Jugs of this pattern are from 165 to 215 mm (6½–8½ in) high and are thought to have been made by Astbury. (See Astbury-type ware.) The fiddler jugs (q.v.) also belong to this early group.

Mihrab design: see Turkish rugs.

Milan lace: pillow lace (q.v.). James I specifically prohibited the import of 'all lace of Millan and of Millan fashion'. In the later work identified today the pattern was worked first and the ground put round it at all angles.

Milk glass or **milk-white glass:** opaque white glass made in imitation of Chinese porcelain, produced by mixing oxide of tin with the body. This material was known to English glass-makers in the late 17th cent. and after a brief eclipse in the early 18th cent., seems to have regained popularity about 1730. From then until *c.* 1770, jars, beakers, tea caddies, candlesticks, etc., were decorated in fine enamel colours.

Millefiori glass: glass decorated by means of sections of rod bearing floral designs embedded in clear glass. The technique, employed at Venice in the 16th cent. was of Roman inspiration.

Millefiori paperweight: the first *millefiori* (*It.*: thousand flowers) paperweights were made in Venice. The St Louis factory (q.v.) in Paris made them in 1845. In the next year they were made at Baccarat (q.v.), and before long they were produced at Clichy (q.v.).

Mille fleurs: (*Fr.* a thousand flowers) decoration occurring on Chinese porcelain with panels of growing plants reserved on a flower-covered ground: employed from the Ch'ien Lung period (q.v.).

Mille fleurs field: a design used on Medieval and 16th-cent. tapestries employing scattered flowers and leaves as a background to scenes of Medieval life.

Millegrain setting: a means of setting a gemstone whereby the stone is held in a mount ornamented with a band of very small beads of metal.

Miller, Abraham: noted American potter from Philadelphia, Pennsylvania, who experimented with the production of porcelain (q.v.) as early as 1824.

Millington & Astbury: established by Richard Millington and John Astbury at Trenton, New Jersey, in the 1850s for the manufacture of porcelain (q.v.), the company was purchased by Thomas Maddock & Co., who continued the business into the 20th cent.

Ming dynasty: dynasty of the Chinese Ming Emperors covering the period 1368–1644. The dynasty, which began by overthrowing the Mongols, gave strong patronage to the porcelain (q.v.) industry, and in place of the variety of Sung wares (q.v.) and glazes, developed a more or less standardized porcelain body as a vehicle for brilliantly coloured decoration. Its animated character and lively forms may be seen in Figs. A–D. Ming glazes tend to be thick and 'fat'. Always popular, painting in underglaze (q.v.) blue was at its finest in the Hsüan Tê and Ch'êng Hua periods (qq.v.), since regarded as classic for perfection of material and harmonious proportion of forms and decoration. During the latter period painting in coloured enamels is found in the delicate *tou ts'ai* class (q.v.). In the 16th cent. the 'red and green' family became conspicuous; but the Chia Ching and Wan Li (qq.v.) periods are further noted for many rich combinations of enamels, including those with yellow and turquoise. A rich violet-blue distinguishes the best blue-and-white of Chia Ching (Fig. C). The Wan Li *wu ts'ai*, or five-colour decoration, remained prominent. In the decoration of Ming porcelain much use was made of scrolling floral designs, flying dragons and phoenixes taken from silk brocades and such pictorial subjects as landscapes with animals and garden terrace scenes with children. In later periods their execution becomes careless and little of note emerges after Wan Li. Exports of blue-and-white were very considerable, however, and the crisp porcelains brought to Europe from

1600 and boldly-painted 'Transitional' wares may be very pleasing. These are not uncommon but the finer Ming wares are almost as rare as the Sung.

Fig. A

Fig. B

Fig. C   Fig. D

Miniature automata: not content with models a foot or so in height, craftsmen, principally Swiss, set to work to make miniature automata (q.v.). They made snuff boxes and watches with disappearing singing birds; boxes with magicians who held up inscribed plaques with answers to questions that were put to them; and other boxes in which landscape and other scenes surprisingly came to life on pressing a button. Watches were made with miniature jacks that struck miniature bells; others showed moving figures that danced to the music of a minute musical-box within the case. One can only marvel at the ingenuity and skill of the designers and makers – and, at the same time, envy those fortunate possessors of these extreme rarities. (See also Jacks.)

Minton Hollins & Co.: leading English tile manufactory established as a branch of Mintons (q.v.) under M. D. Hollins who was a partner in the main firm from 1845.

Mintons porcelain: founded by Thomas Minton in 1793, in partnership with William Pownall and Joseph Poulson. Minton had previously worked as an engraver, and for Spode. After Poulson's death in 1808 Thomas Minton continued the business on his own account and in 1817 he took his sons into partnership and traded as Thomas Minton & Sons. After Thomas Minton's death the firm was continued by Herbert Minton and John Boyle until 1841. During this period tiles and buttons were manufactured under patents of Samuel Wright 1830 and Richard Prosser 1840. Michael Daintry Hollins became a partner in 1845 and the style of the firm was Minton & Marks:

Hollins, or Minton Hollins & Co. (q.v.), and so continued until the tile business was separated from the china and earthenware trade in 1868. Herbert Minton died in 1858 and his nephew Colin Minton Campbell became head of the firm which was known as Minton & Co. In 1873 it became Mintons Ltd.

Early earthenware made at the Stoke factory is usually white decorated in blue, often in a pseudo-Chinese manner. These productions were of good quality and careful finish, owing much to Thomas Minton's early experience at Spode's. In 1798 porcelain manufacture was started but at first did not prove profitable, and was

Transfer-printed
1800–36

Printed or
impressed
after 1851

MINTONS B B *New Stone*

Impressed
20th-century

Impressed

MINTON

Impressed 1861 onwards

Transfer-printed
M – 1822–30
M & Co – 1841–4
M & H – 1845–68

Transfer-printed

1822–36

Transfer-printed
1860–80

Transfer-printed

**SOLAR
MINTON
ENGLAND**

Transfer-printed
uranium glaze
1918

MINTONS (DATE MARKS)

1842–1850

1851–1859

1860–1868

1869–1877

1878–1886

1887–1895

1896–1904

1905–1913

1914–1922

1923–1931

1932–1940

From 1824 onwards marks, as above impressed in the paste, were used on china and sometimes on earthenware to denote years of manufacture.

not made in any quantity until about 1825 when artists from the Derby (q.v.) factory brought new talent to Mintons. The body of the porcelain is from that time of a lighter and purer colour, and the glaze finer.

Some delightful patterns, evidently the work of one artist, are characterized by flecks, dots, circles, used to texture patterns of original and sometimes fantastic character.

Table wares feature consistently among Minton productions. Early pieces have a mark which is sometimes confused with Sèvres (q.v.). Dark blue grounds, medallions of flowers, Chinese landscapes and much gilding (q.v.) are all characteristics, but painting of finely engraved shells and similar subjects occur on early pieces.

Parian (q.v.) was made from 1845; majolica glazes (see *Maiolica*) were introduced in 1850 and used for table wares, toilet wares, figures and architectural faience (q.v.). M.-L. Solon (q.v.) brought to the factory the *pâte-sur-pâte* technique (q.v.).

In 1869 the firm engaged William Stephen Coleman, under whose direction Mintons Art-Pottery Studio was established in 1871 in Kensington, London. The Studio products usually have a printed mark, Mintons Art-Pottery Studio Kensington Gore, as well as the factory marks.

Minuet fan: see Brisé fan.

Miotti glasshouse: Venetian glasshouse established at Murano, Venice, by the Miotti family in the early 17th cent. It at first specialized in Aventurine glass (q.v.), later in opaque white glass (q.v.).

Miquelet: see Flint-lock gun.

Mirror cutting: see Table cutting.

Mirror painting: a type of glass picture in which the glass was first coated at the back with an amalgam of tin and mercury to make it into a mirror. The parts to be painted were then scraped away and painted in as required. Such paintings were often made in China, where the technique is thought to have been introduced by Jesuit missionaries. Vauxhall bevelled plate glass was exported to China for this purpose in the 18th cent. (See also Under-painting and Vauxhall Glasshouse.)

Mirror stand: an adjustable mirror mounted on a shaft and tripod base, resembling a pole screen; popular at the end of the 18th cent.

Mission style: simple, often mass-produced, furniture made in the United States in the late 19th cent.

Mitchell & Rammelsberg: large American firm of furniture manufacturers in Cincinnati, founded in 1836 or 1844. Their productions were mainly in the 19th-cent. Revival styles, but they also made some furniture that is close in style to the work of B. J. Talbert (q.v.).

Mitre cutting: a method of decorating glass vessels by means of cutting or grinding a pattern with a V-edged grinding wheel of about 60 degrees. Many cut motifs were used on 18th-cent. glass, based on panel, hollow (qq.v.) or mitre cutting. About 1800 the double-mitre wheel was introduced and cutting in deep relief in complicated diamond forms, etc., became fashionable.

Mitre joint: employed by joiners (q.v.) to unite the mouldings framing a panel in which the two edges are cut at an angle of 45 degrees.

Mixed-twist stem: a type of stem found on drinking glasses between about 1750 and 1770 including a combination of air-twist and opaque-white twist (qq.v.) in a single stem.

Mocha ware: a form of 'dipped' pottery decorated with coloured bands into which tree, moss or fern-like effects have been introduced by means of a diffusing agent, a drop of which 'ramifies' the coloured bands to produce the pattern. 'Mocha' occurs under the heading 'Dipped' pottery (q.v.) in the working-price list appended to *The Declaration . . . Chamber of Commerce* for the Potteries, June 1836.

Undoubtedly many pottery firms whose names were appended to the list were making it.

The process was used from about 1780 until 1914, chiefly for ale, shrimp and nut measures, less frequently for kitchen and table wares.

Mock pendulum: a swinging bob attached to the escape arbor (q.v.), which shows through a slot in the dial plate of a clock. Only used in clocks with the verge escapement (q.v.). Sometimes called a false bob.

Modes: see Fillings.

Modillion: projecting bracket in the pediment (q.v.) or below the cornice (q.v.) found on furniture of architectural character.

Moiré wallpapers: printed or embossed wallpapers imitating watered-silk effects.

Mokumé: (*Japanese* = wood aspect). Japanese lacquer-work technique involving an imitation of wood graining.

Monopodium: single-legged table, such as some console tables (q.v.).

Monotype: glass plates painted with oil colour instead of ink yield a single impression which is called a monotype. This process was occasionally used by G. B. Castiglione (1616–70), William Blake (1757–1827) and Edgar Degas (1834–1917). It has been further developed by a few modern artists.

Monstrance: vessel in which the Host is displayed, varying in size according to its use, i.e. whether it was primarily for use on an altar or intended to be carried in procession. Frequently enriched with enamelling and precious stones, they are among the most magnificent pieces of Church plate (q.v.).

Monteith: large silver bowl with indentations in the rim designed to hold the stems of wine glasses while the bowls were cooled in water or ice. They were introduced in the late 17th cent. Later examples with detachable rims were intended as punch bowls. The name is said to be derived from that of a Scottish adventurer who wore a cloak with a scalloped edge.

Month clock: a clock that goes for a period of one month with one winding. The usual period is 32 days.

Moon dial: see Lunar dial.

Moonlight lustre: a marbled lustre effect, used as a decoration on earthenware, produced by mixing gold, pink, grey and other colouring stains, used by the Wedgwood factory (q.v.), early 19th cent., and the Turners of Lane End, Staffordshire (see Turner, John).

Moons: small areas of greater translucency observable by transmitted light in some early porcelains such as Chelsea, the cause of which is not known for certain.

Moore Bros.: manufactures of porcelain at St Mary's Works, Longton, from 1872 to 1905 whose characteristic motifs were raised floral designs and hops.

Moore, James: (? 1670–1726), cabinet-maker in partnership with John Gumley from 1714. Moore is known to have made much furniture decorated with gilt gesso (q.v.), on some of which his name is incised. He was concerned in the furnishing of Blenheim, and it is assumed that some gilt pier glasses (q.v.) and tables there were made and supplied by him.

Moorfields carpets: Thomas Moore of Moorfields successfully competed for a Royal Society of Arts award in 1757. An account of his workshop, where hand-knotted carpets of the highest quality were produced, was given by Lady Mary Coke in 1768. A carpet was then being woven for Lord Coventry at a cost of 140 gns. Moore was extensively used by the architect Robert Adam (q.v.), and a number of his carpets have survived in beautiful condition, as well as Adam's designs for them at the Soane Museum. A carpet at Syon House is inscribed 'by

Thos. Moore 1769'. There are two at Osterley, made about 1775 and 1778; and Chippendale (q.v.) recommended him to Sir Edward Knatchbull in 1778, who paid him £57 for a carpet for Mersham le Hatch. Moore's carpets in Neoclassical designs were sumptuous additions to the houses they furnished.

Moquette: woven on the principle of velvet, but in coarser wool and linen materials, moquette is allied with plushes and Utrecht velvet as an upholstery or carpeting material. Tournai seems to have been its chief centre in the Middle Ages. It was much used in the 16th to 18th cent. Abbeville was the chief centre of production in France from 1667. Antwerp, Amsterdam, Utrecht and Leyden and Thuringia, in Germany, were other centres of production. Known as 'Brussels carpet' in England, it was made at Norwich and Bradford besides Kidderminster and Wilton. The use of the Jacquard loom greatly increased and cheapened production in the early 19th cent.

Morel-Ladeuil, Léonard: (1820–88), French metalwork designer who settled in England in 1859. He produced a great number of designs for Elkington & Co. (q.v.), including those for some of their most important exhibition and presentation pieces.

Moresque ornament: a linear ornament consisting of formal scrollwork and foliage, of Near Eastern derivation, found as a border decoration engraved on 16th-cent. plate (q.v.).

Morgan, William de: (1839-1917), art potter most closely associated with the Arts and Crafts Movement (q.v.). He started a small pottery in Chelsea in 1872, moving to Merton Abbey in 1882 but returning to Fulham 1888-1907 in partnership with Halsey Ricardo. He produced Moorish and Gubbio lustres (q.v.) on a variety of ornamental vases, tiles and dishes decorated in greens and blues with animal, birds, flowers and fishes.

Morion: an open helmet much used by foot-soldiers in the second half of the 16th cent. Contemporary texts mention two forms: (a) the Spanish morion, called a cabasset by many modern writers, with a pear-shaped, pointed skull and a narrow, flat brim; (b) the comb morion, with high comb and a curved brim peaked before and behind. The modern term peaked morion refers to an intermediate type with a curved brim, and a pointed apex terminating in a small stalk.

Morris, William: (1834–96), English painter, writer, designer, printer and craftsman. He rejected the growing use of machine-made objects and originated the handicraft revival which inspired the Arts and Crafts Movement (q.v.). In 1861, he formed the firm of Morris, Marshall, Faulkner & Co., which became Morris & Co. (q.v.) in 1874. It specialized in designs for furniture, ceramics and textiles. He produced forty-four designs for printed fabrics, the first to be put on the market being *Tulip* in 1875, the last, *Compton* in 1896. All his designs were printed by woodblock, the majority in vegetable dyes. He designed a number of machine-woven carpets in the 1870s and in 1879 embarked on the weaving of the hand-knotted Hammersmith carpets and rugs. (See also Morris carpets.)

Morris & Co.: firm which in 1874 succeeded Morris, Marshall, Faulkner & Co., which had been founded in 1861 by William Morris (q.v.), P. Webb (q.v.) and others. It specialized in textiles, stained glass, ceramics and furniture. After 1890 it produced some reproduction furniture. Morris was the sole proprietor and the designers who worked for the firm included Webb, W. A. S. Benson (q.v.), and George Jack (q.v.).

Morris carpets: the first carpets woven by William Morris were made about 1878 at Hammersmith (mark: hammer, river and letter M) and from 1881 at Merton Abbey. The later two- and three-ply carpets were woven for Morris & Co. at Heckmondwike, Yorks.

Morse: a clasp for fastening a cope, occasionally made of gold or silver and decorated with jewels.

Mortars: in Antiquity mortars were usually made of stone or heavy pottery; during the Middle Ages they were normally cast in bronze. Their use was widespread, both in the apothecaries' laboratories for the grinding and pounding of chemicals and at home for the pounding of condiments and spices. In the painter's studio they might also have been found for the pulverization of pigments. From the 14th cent. onwards mortars survive in considerable numbers, especially from Flanders and England and later from Germany and Italy. With the exception of Italy, they seem to be mainly the work of the bell foundries, and because the alloy used is so often close to that employed by these foundries, they are normally made of bell metal (q.v.). They often bear inscriptions in raised lettering, usually pious in intention or giving the owner's or maker's name as well as the date of production. Many 19th-cent. aftercasts (q.v.) were made, usually of very crude quality and slurred definition. Mortars of the 14th and 15th cent. are rare, the bulk being of the 16th and 17th cent.

Mortice-and-tenon joint: the mortice is a cavity, usually rectangular, and the tenon is shaped to fill the cavity exactly. The tenon was held fast by a peg. This was the principle joint used by the joiner in furniture making and was introduced in the 16th cent.

Mortice lock: a lock concealed from view by the use of a hole cut into the door edge. In most early mortice locks only the brass knob remained visible, the keyhole masked by a swinging escutcheon. Decoration might be added in the form of an ornamental end-piece matching the adjoining striking plate: this might be engraved, pierced, or cast and chased, often displaying the owner's coat of arms or cypher.

A new style of lock furniture associated with mortice locks was introduced during the mid-1760s. Robert Adam (q.v.), writing to Sir Rowland Wynn in 1767, observed that 'Bent the locksmith is making lock furniture after a new pattern'. This set consisted of an expansive back-plate of chased and gilt cast brass, in scrollwork designs symmetrically arranged with festoons of husks (q.v.) centering on the door knob and flanked with a keyhole escutcheon and a matching dummy escutcheon. The centre rosette and the escutcheon harmonized with the knob. In some instances the dummy was replaced by a small knob operating a night latch.

Mortlake tapestry: Charles I, as Prince of Wales and later King, took an active interest in the Mortlake factory, which worked for the Court and rivalled the Paris factory set up by Henry IV, on whose charter it was modelled. Already active in 1620, Mortlake enjoyed a very high reputation in Europe until checked by the Civil Wars in the 1640s, which also caused the sale abroad of most of its finest works. Prince Charles's purchase of the seven extant cartoons of the *Acts of the Apostles* by Raphael for £300 in 1623 at Genoa undoubtedly did much to enhance Mortlake's name. Other notable subjects woven were *The Months* and *Vulcan and Venus* (based on 16th-cent. originals), *Playing Boys* and *Hero and Leander*, designed by Francis Cleyn, who was brought from Rostock as chief designer. Sir Francis Crane was in charge until 1636, and was succeeded by Sir Sackville Crowe at the Restoration. Rather later Verrio succeeded Cleyn. Among the fifty weavers from the Netherlands, Philippe de Maecht was the most notable. A few good sets were woven under

Charles II from the old cartoons, but the more elaborate and beautiful borders were abandoned and a decline rapidly set in. Lord Ralph Montague became Master of the Great Wardrobe and acquired Mortlake in the 1670s. Soon the Great Wardrobe, established at Hatton Garden in 1679, incorporated the best weavers from Mortlake. Francis Poyntz, last technical director of Mortlake, who wove the *Battle of Solebay* (Hampton Court), worked there as manager (1667–85) as did Stephen Demay and Thomas Poyntz. The Mortlake mark, red cross on white shield, continued to be used, as it resembled the Arms of the City of London. Some weavers left Mortlake to set up independently, as William Benood in Lambeth (*c.* 1670), who signed a *Horses* set at the Victoria and Albert Museum. In 1685 the Great Wardrobe was moved to Soho (q.v.) and Mortlake was finally wound up about the year 1700.

Mortuary chair: a mid-17th cent. chair with scrolled back, the rails bearing in the centre a carved representation of a bearded head, traditionally thought to refer to Charles I.

Mosaic: this term is usually applied to the decoration of a wall or panel with a design made up of small fragments of stones or coloured glass fixed to the surface with cement or special adhesive. The best-known form of mosaic, usually called Roman or Byzantine mosaic, is formed of small cubes or *tesserae* of coloured stone and glass. The Romans also developed a second technique of mosaic, using, instead of cubes, various-sized segments cut into shapes so as to form a design or picture when joined together. This technique may be regarded as the forerunner of *pietra dura* (q.v.).

Mosaic jewellery: made in Italy in the early 19th cent. and bought by English travellers as souvenir jewellery. Also imported, unmounted, for setting by jewellery manufacturers. Designed as small medallions which were generally framed in gold and made up into necklaces, bracelets, clasps and earrings.

Moscow porcelain: see Gardner's porcelain.

Moss agate glass: coloured glass powders are trapped internally in the glass body in random patterns to simulate the mineral, moss agate.

Mother-of-pearl glass, pearl satin glass or **pearl ware:** pattern-moulded (q.v.) opaque glass patented in 1885 and covered with a layer of transparent colour to bring out the design. The whole is sometimes covered with transparent crystal plating and satin finished.

Mould-blown glass: glass made by blowing a gather (q.v.) of metal (q.v.) into a mould, a technique known to the Romans who used clay moulds. Techniques introduced in the 19th cent. opened up new possibilities. Of these, one-piece moulds were used during the earlier part of the cent. for shaping inexpensive hollow ware (q.v.). A quick-setting flint glass was evolved as the molten glass solidified rapidly on the surface of the mould. Glass made by this process has a slightly pebbly appearance caused by contact with the mould. Two-piece open-and-shut moulds were invented in 1802 by Charles Chubsee of Stourbridge. Glass blown into such a mould could be shaped and decorated with diamonds and other motifs in deep relief. Patterns followed those worked on free-blown glass (q.v.) by the wheel-cutters. From 1825 the long accepted geometrical designs met active competition in the form of Baroque (q.v.) scrolls, fan patterns and arch patterns. The three-pieced mould, with one fixed and two hinged sections, each cut with an intaglio pattern (q.v.), dates from about 1830. When the glass was inflated within the mould, the blowing force caused the joints to open slightly, thus producing tiny ridges on the surface of the glass or a slight break in the pattern. Mould marks are no more than slightly convex swellings on the surface of the glass in no way resembling the hair lines or threads on pressed glass (q.v.), which are so sharply defined that they appear to have been applied. The number of marks indicates the number of pieces forming the mould. From 1835 blown-moulded glass was finished by fire polishing.

Moulded glass: glass blown in a mould for pattern and given partial or final body shape by the mould; generally called blown moulded.

Moulded pedestal stem: a type of shouldered stem found on drinking glasses from about 1705 to 1750, also known erroneously as a 'Silesian' stem. The earlier examples are four-sided and ribbed. Later the stem became reeded or polygonal and was often twisted spirally. Candlesticks, sweetmeat and dessert salvers also were made with shouldered stems during the second half of the 18th cent.

Mount Mellick embroidery: a type of whitework, first introduced about 1830 at Mountmellick in Queen's County, Ireland, and revived as a local industry in the 1880s by a Mrs Millner. It was worked on a stout white satin jean in white knitting cotton which gave a raised effect to the work. The designs were naturalistic, passion flowers, blackberry sprays, oak leaves and acorns being the most favoured patterns. Many designs for this type of work were issued by Weldon's and other publishers in the late 1880s and 1890s.

Mount Washington Glass Works & Co.: advertising itself as the 'Headquarters in America for Art Glass Wares', the Company was founded in South Boston, Massachusetts, by Jarves (q.v.) in 1837. In 1869, the owner, William Libbey, moved the works to New Bedford, where in 1894,

the Company merged with the Pairpoint Manufacturing Co. (q.v.). Award-winning productions include cut crystal, opal and pressed (qq.v.) table ware and lamps, but the firm is justifiably most famous for its art glass (q.v.).

Mourning fan: fan painted in black and grey overlaid with white. The ivory sticks were stained brown to unify the general tone and might be burnished with a simple design of silver blending with the grey of the mount. Solomon receiving the Queen of Sheba was a frequent subject late in the 15th cent.

Mourning jewellery: mourning jewellery became particularly fashionable in the second half of the 18th cent. Oval frames were favoured, of varying size according to the ultimate destination of the jewel, i.e., ring, pendant, locket or bracelet slide. These frames were set with enamels or miniature paintings of funerary urns on plinths, by which stood the bereaved under the shadow of weeping willow trees. The back of the frame was filled with an appropriate design, often a monogram of the deceased's initials executed in a lock of hair. Such jewellery was usually inexpensive; a thin gold frame was set with, at the most, seed-pearl or diamond sparks. Earlier mourning jewellery of the 16th and 17th cent. of which comparatively few examples remain, was of a more gloomy kind, including coffin-shaped pendants in gold or enamelled gold and enamelled jewels bearing such devices as skulls and crossbones.

Moustache cup: a cup with a screen or arrangement to protect the moustache from moisture when drinking, popular in Victorian times, introduced by Harvey Adams and Co., china and earthenware manufacturers, of Longton, Staffordshire.

Moustache spoon: silver or electroplate (q.v.) spoon patented by E. B. A. Mitcheson of Philadelphia in 1875. There were left- and right-handed versions, with a guard covering one side.

Moustiers faience: Moustiers, in Provence, was a centre of the faience (q.v.) trade in the 18th cent. The best period, before 1750, saw the use of Baroque (q.v.) ornamental designs in blue monochrome or in soft high-temperature colours.

Movement: the 'works' of a clock or watch.

'Mr and Mrs Caudle': relief decoration on brown stoneware spirit flasks, made about 1846 by Doulton of Lambeth (q.v.), and based upon Douglas Jerrold's *Punch* papers ('Mrs Caudle's Curtain Lectures'). One side shows 'Mr and Mrs Caudle in Bed', the other 'Miss Prettyman'.

Moyr Smith, John: English painter and designer and author of an influential pattern book entitled *Ornamental Interiors, Ancient and Modern*, published in 1887. It described and illustrated some of the most up-to-date decorative schemes. He also worked for Mintons (q.v.), designing transfer-printed (q.v.) tiles.

Mudge, Thomas: London clock-maker who first invented the lever escapement (q.v.) about 1758. He was active between 1740 and 1794.

Muffineer: alternative name for a caster (q.v.), usually given to those examples with low, slightly domed covers. The derivation presumably indicated their use for sprinkling salt on muffins.

Muffle kiln: kiln used for low-temperature porcelain or enamel firing (*petit feu*) of about 700–900° C. The porcelain piece is enclosed in an inner chamber called 'muffle', out of contact with flames or smoke, hence the name. It is used to fuse enamel painting into the glaze of faience (q.v.) and porcelain (q.v.) in general.

Mulberry spoon: see Straining spoon.

Mule chest: a mid-17th-cent. chest, usually of oak or walnut, with a drawer, or two drawers side by side at the bottom. This type of chest was the forerunner of the chest of drawers.

Mull: Scottish snuff mulls (the Scottish pronunciation of 'mill') vary a great deal within the limits imposed by their form. They are natural horns, sometimes twisted at the tapering end. The open aperture is surmounted by a decorative hinged lid often set with semi-precious stones. The local cairngorm, a pale topaz, is the most usually found. Dr Mott observes in his edition of *Dekker's Gull's Hornbook* that 'The Scotch mull, or sneeshing mull, was often accompanied by a spoon and hare's foot attached by chain, the one for applying the snuff to the nose, the other for wiping the upper lip.'

Müller, Karl: German sculptor, educated in Paris and employed as a modeller and designer by the Union Porcelain Works (q.v.). He designed exhibition pieces for the Philadelphia Centennial Exposition of 1876.

Multiple knops: knops or protuberances of a single shape repeated on the stem of a drinking glass or other glass vessel.

Muntin: upright (other than an outermost upright) connecting the upper and lower stretchers (q.v.) of a wooden framework. An instance is the bearer between the doors of the lower stage of a press-cupboard (q.v.); the number of muntins depend on the nature of the structure. (See also Stile.)

Mural clock: a clock made to hang on the wall.

Murray, James: James Murray founded his business at Cornhill, London, in *c.* 1814, and became a celebrated chronometer-maker and watchmaker..He was succeeded by his two sons, James and John.

Mushroom knop: a knop or protuberance on the stem of a drinking glass or other glass vessel of mushroom form, usually associated with incurved and funnel bowls.

Mushroom paperweight: a paperweight in which the canes (q.v.) are bunched together and raised in a sheaf from the bottom. Usually surrounded by a ring of lacework at the foot.

Musical clocks: the first mechanical music was performed upon cymbals or bells, and was a part of the display of some of the elaborate clocks made on the Continent of Europe from the 14th cent. onwards. By the time of Queen Elizabeth I the mechanical principle had been extended to the operation of organs. There exists a description of a most complicated clock that was sent as a gift from the English sovereign to the Sultan of Turkey in 1593. This clock incorporated both carillon and organ, either of which could be played by hand or be set to operate when the clock struck the hour.

In the 18th cent. and later, large bracket clocks and grandfather clocks (qq.v.) were made with music on bells to be played each hour. They usually have a choice of tunes, which could be changed by moving a pointer on a dial on the face. A musical movement was constructed also that operated a small bellows and worked a miniature organ. With the introduction of the comb this, too, was adapted to become part of a clock.

Among the more prominent English makers of musical clocks were: Charles Clay, who exhibited a bell and organ clock to Queen Caroline in 1736; Markwick Markham; Christopher Pinchbeck (q.v.), inventor of the gilt metal which bears his name and a famed clock-maker; and James Cox (q.v.), who exhibited to the public musical clocks and watches, along with other mechanical *objets d'art*, in the last half of the 18th cent. The list of Continental makers should not omit Father Primitivus Niemecz, who made three famous clocks for the Hungarian Prince Esterhazy. These had music especially composed or arranged for them by Joseph Haydn.

Musical watches: the addition of the playing of music to the normal performance of a pocket timekeeper grew from the repeater mechanism, which was a necessity for telling the time in the dark before the use of luminous composition or the invention of electric light. The hour was repeated on one or more tiny bells upon pressing a button, and very little adaptation of the basic mechanism was needed. With more bells, and more pins to hit the hammers, more notes could be played to form a simple melody.

With the advent of the steel comb a much greater compass of notes could be achieved with no increase in the size of the apparatus.

Musket: a military match- or wheel-lock (qq.v.) firearm introduced in the third quarter of the 16th cent. It was heavier than the arquebus (q.v.), and consequently was usually fired from a forked rest. After the introduction of the flintlock (q.v.) the term was used loosely to describe any portable firearm larger than a pistol.

Musketoon: a short, heavy flintlock (q.v.) gun with a large bore, generally used for discharging shot.

Mutchkin: a Scottish wine measure containing 426 ml ($\frac{3}{4}$ pint).

Nail-head decoration: a carved decoration in the form of a series of small squares, each containing a raised point resembling a nail head, used on furniture from the Middle Ages to the 17th cent.

Nailsea glass: the brownish-green glass speckled with white, with which the name of Nailsea, near Bristol, is associated, was used on occasions for the making of wine-bottles, and sealed examples exist. Some specimens are inscribed with initials, the date, and the name of a town. Glasses of this type were not exclusive to the West-country manufacture, and were probably also made in Scotland. Many novelty items were made as love or friendship tokens.

'Nankin' china: Chinese blue-and-white porcelain (q.v.) of the late 18th and 19th cent. which was shipped from Nanking.

Nankin yellow: lustrous pale golden brown glaze used as a decoration on

Chinese porcelain in association with K'ang Hsi (q.v.) underglaze (q.v.) blue painting, especially in export wares for the Near East.

Nantgarw porcelain: William Billingsley (q.v.), who had been a well-known flower-painter at Derby, founded the factory in November 1813, in partnership with his son-in-law, Samuel Walker. After exhausting his capital, William Weston Young advanced sums amounting to nearly £600 and eventually became partner in the venture. This proved inadequate and the three partners appealed for financial assistance to the Government with the result that their endeavours were brought to the notice of L. W. Dillwyn who arranged for the transference of the business to the Cambrian factory at Swansea.

Billingsley stayed at Swansea until 1816 when he returned to Nantgarw, there to be rejoined by Walker in 1817. With new capital supplied by W. W. Young and some country gentlemen, the Nantgarw concern was operated until the end of 1819, but, their capital exhausted, Billingsley and Walker were compelled to vacate Nantgarw in the spring of 1820. In November the moulds and plant, with some decorated and a lot of undecorated china, were offered for sale and taken over by Young, who became sole proprietor. No further ware was made, although much of the undecorated porcelain was painted by Pardoe (q.v.). Further sales took place in 1821 and 1822 when it was said that Rose of Coalport (q.v.) bought up the plant and moulds. Marks:

NANT GARW
C.W.

Billingsley himself decorated some of the Nantgarw products: he was assisted by his daughter and two other women. Billingsley also employed flower painters.

A much larger proportion of Nantgarw porcelain was sent undecorated to London to various independent enamellers. This was more ambitiously decorated and is usually fairly easily distinguishable from the simpler local designs used at Nantgarw.

During its short life the Nantgarw factory produced some fine porcelain of quite exceptional translucency. Billingsley himself compared it to that of Sèvres (q.v.), and the decoration used was often in the French manner. Extremely white and at times almost glasslike, the porcelain unfortunately did not always stand firing and much was lost in the kiln. These losses led to the financial difficulties that eventually forced Billingsley to leave Nantgarw. He was never successful in finding a soft paste of comparable quality which could be fired reliably.

Few shapes were made at Nantgarw and these are generally simple in character. Table wares comprising tea and dessert services were the chief productions of the factory. A distinguishing feature of the plates was a fine embossed scroll and flower pattern, although, of course, plain shaped plates were also used.

Less frequent are such decorative pieces as spill holders, taper stands, specimen and cabinet cups and saucers, pen trays and pot-pourri vases.

Nashiji: (*Japanese* = pear ground), a Japanese lacquer-work technique in which gold dust is sprinkled on the lacquer and then polished like aventurine (q.v.). Various forms, e.g. *Muranashiji* in which the gold is spread in irregular patches.

National League of Mineral Painters: national association of ceramic clubs and professional china decorators established in the United States in 1892. The organization was founded to provide a closer relationship between china decorators and to develop a national school of ceramic art. A national exhibition was conducted each year. Founded by Mrs S. S. Frackelton of Milwaukee, Wisconsin.

National Watch Co.: founded in 1864 at Elgin, Illinois, the firm took the name Elgin National Watch Co. in 1874.

Nautilus cup: ceremonial drinking vessel incorporating a nautilus shell as the bowl, made in the 16th and 17th cent. principally in Italy, Germany, Austria and the Netherlands.

Neale, James, Earthenware Manufactory: James Neale took over the factory in Hanley in 1778. Robert Wilson was made a partner in 1786 and for a time the firm was known as Neale & Wilson. In 1817, when John Wilson, a descendant of · Robert Wilson, became bankrupt, the factory passed to other hands.
Marks:

NEALE & Co

NEALE & CO

NEALE

NEALE & CO

G

NEALE & WILSON

Impressed

The firm made good quality cream-coloured wares, blue-painted and lustred table ware, jasper, black Egyptian (qq.v.), marbled vases etc.; many pieces in close imitation of Wedgwood (q.v.). Designs from Wedgwood were not infrequently copied, and Classical shapes and decoration figured largely in work from the pottery.

Figures are often of considerable merit. Usually small in size, they are modelled, and coloured in · a neat restrained manner (a turquoise blue is notable for its frequent use) in fine, clear enamels. The figures were generally made for easy delivery from moulds, and were sometimes gilded.

Nécessaire: a container for miscellaneous small tools and instruments designed for various purposes. Included among 18th-cent. toilet and household equipment are such items as toothpicks, tweezers, earpicks and tongue scrapers. Queen Elizabeth was reputedly never without her ruby- and diamond-studded earpick on state occasions.

The more conventional implements to be found in *nécessaires* and *étuis* (q.v.) include snuffing spoons, pencils, funnels for powders, scent bottles, scissors and other sewing and manicure instruments, and very often ivory tablets for notes and prescriptions.

The *nécessaires* themselves are made in the same variety of materials as snuff boxes (q.v.). They were still being produced in the 19th cent.

Needlepoint lace: the ultimate development from cut work (q.v.) with threads tacked on to a parchment pattern as the basis for stitches worked with a needle and a single thread. An outline was drawn on parchment stitched to two thicknesses of linen and this outline covered with threads exactly tack-stitched in position about every 6 mm ($\frac{1}{4}$ in). This outline was buttonholed over closely to form the cordonnet (q.v.) and on this the lace was created, the solid areas of pattern – *toilé* (q.v.) – in close rows of buttonhole stitch and these linked and supported by connecting buttonholed brides (q.v.) or a regular mesh ground of buttonholed or looped stitches. It must be emphasized that a single thread on a needle was used throughout so that there could be no plaiting or weaving effects such as characterized pillow lace (q.v.). The lace was released from the parchment by cutting between the layers of linen.

Needlework cabinets: 'A coffer maid in broderie upon reid satine' was listed among Elizabeth I's movables in 1561. This was a forerunner of innumerable examples characteristic of English needlework around the mid-17th cent. Every well-to-do young lady then embroidered a set of satin pieces for mounting on a little wooden cabinet fitted either with doors or with a fall-front to allow access to jewellery drawers and toilet compartments. In some examples the interior above the drawers consisted of a little well surrounded by lidded boxes for toilet accessories and ornamented with pieces of the still-novel looking-glass and perhaps carpeted with a hand-coloured print. But the major work went into the exterior mountings, usually embroidered on the narrow rich satin, then newly available, that allowed the embroidery to break away from the customary ground-covering tent stitch into speedier ornament that left some of the ground visible.

Most often the main embroidery was scenic, such as one of a few favourite scriptural scenes – the story of Rebecca, or Jephthah and his daughter. Always the tendency was to crowd the scene with fascinating, disproportionate detail in the Elizabethan manner. Often some of the main figures were padded and stitched separately, their faces and hands of wood, silk covered, their clothes exquisitely wrought with minute lace stitches and decked out in all the trinket ornaments that age has rendered somewhat tawdry. Beads and coral, feathers and tinsel, were freely used in what was then termed raised work but has become known as stump work.

Needlework carpets: in the 16th and early 17th cent. Oriental carpets were much copied in Europe in cross and tent stitch on canvas. This was quite suitable for use on tables and cupboards, for which they were intended. There is a good collection in the National Museum, Zürich, and some superb English examples in the Victoria and Albert Museum. In the 18th cent. they were again in favour, but the designs were now purely European, with lavish floral patterns for the floor of boudoir or drawing-room. Many of these carpets have survived in England, but they are rarely found in good condition, as they wear easily. Their beauty depends as much on the brilliant dyes used as on the design. The fashion continued into the 19th cent., but these pieces can be recognized by design and colour. Italian carpets embroidered entirely in silk are occasionally seen.

Nef: a vessel shaped like a ship and made in the later Middle Ages; some served as ceremonial salts. In 1392 a nef on wheels was recorded in the Papal collection. In the 16th cent. ornaments, jugs and cups were made in the same form, notably in Germany and Switzerland. Many were very elaborate and accurate models, richly enamelled and peopled with little figures of sailors. There are in existence a number of 19th-cent. copies.

Neoclassicism: revival of Classical forms and motifs following the excavations of Classical remains at Herculaneum and Pompeii which were begun in 1738. The momentum came from France in the mid-18th cent. and spread to the rest of Europe and the United States, gradually superseding the Rococo (q.v.). It persisted into the second decade of the 19th cent. In Britain it is particularly associated with the work of Robert Adam (q.v.).

Netsuke: the conventional dress of Japan had no pockets so it was convenient to carry necessities attached to a cord, at the end of which was a toggle to be pushed through the belt to hold the objects secure. This toggle was called a *netsuke* (= end attachment) and was carved to represent various subjects. The early history of *netsuke* is very obscure. The earliest book that discusses them seriously was the *Soken Kisho*, published in 1781. This book mentions about fifty carvers' names and discusses their work, with illustrations. Early examples are generally of ivory and are not signed by the maker. By the end of the 18th cent. more artists took up the profession of *netsuke* carving and then began the great era of this art, when artists became better known and took to signing their work. At first the *netsuke* were simple and bold in design, but towards the middle of the 19th cent. the designs became more naturalistic and intricate, while at the end of the century the simple rotundity of the piece was sometimes sacrificed to the fashion for detail. After the revolution of 1868, European dress gradually came into favour and the need for *netsuke* declined. They were then made for export to the European collector. There have been well over 2000 makers who signed their works. Artists chose their own art-names of two syllables, sometimes followed by the name of the studio. The characters were written either in block letters (*Kaisoh*) or in cursory script (*Sosho*).

Neuber, Johann Christian: (1736–1808), the maker of extremely beautiful and original snuff boxes (q.v.) in hard-stones. Usually round or oval, these boxes would consist entirely of small-shaped panels of different stones selected for their colour and translucence or opacity, held by a finely wrought gold webbing. The inlay work is of a uniformly high order, the whole surface being absolutely smooth, and the gentle harmonies of tone and colour combine happily with the different patterns, which almost invariably radiate boldly from the centre. Many boxes were composed of stones specially chosen for their local interest; numbers would be engraved on the slender gold skeleton mount, each referring to a particular little stone panel. Inside these boxes, which were known as *Stein Kabinetts Tabatieren*, a book serving as a key should be found listing in full the names of the various specimens numbered on the box.

Sometimes these numbered lists would be hidden within a secret compartment or drawer, which springs open when a particular part of the box is pressed. Miniatures or carved or engraved gem stones are usually set in the centre of the lids. Neuber by no means restricted his expression to boxes

alone, and the laborious technique, which was his life work, was used very successfully in the designing of *carnets*, *étuis* (q.v.), *châtelaines* (q.v.) and centre-pieces (q.v.) as well as a table and even an elaborate fireplace.

Nevers faience: the chief Nevers pottery was founded early in the 17th cent. by Italian potters. The decoration employed was akin to the pictorial style used rather earlier at Urbino (see Urbino *maiolica*). Chinese themes became popular later in the century, the wares were often painted in blue and manganese purple. At the same time a technique was adopted of painting in opaque white and colours on a deep blue enamel ground known as *bleu persan* (q.v.). By the 18th cent., only cheap, popular wares were produced.

Nevers glass: see Verre de Nevers.

Neville, George: introduced the art of painting on papier mâché (q.v.) 'on the black' (on a black ground) in 1831 while employed by Jennens and Bettridge (q.v.). His signature flower was a blue convolvulus, one petal turned over in contrasting colour. In 1846, he set up with a partner and died a wealthy man in 1887.

New Canton: see Bow porcelain.

Newcastle-under-Lyme earthenware: famous for its clay pipes in the 17th cent., notably those made by Charles Riggs (d. 1676). From about 1730 until 1754 Samuel Bell (d. 1754) and Joseph Wilson made brown glazed Astbury-type (q.v.) teapots at a potworks in Lower Street. The names of thirty potters are given in the Newcastle Poll Lists between 1774 and 1792. In 1873 the names of forty potters are listed. In the closing years of the 18th cent. J. Bulkeley and William Bent manufactured in Newcastle, but dissolved the partnership in November 1797. Robert Bath, variously described as earthenware manufacturer, saggar maker and licensed retailer of beer and tobacco, had a potworks at Halmerend near Newcastle but became bankrupt in 1840.

New England armchair: an American version of the hoop-back Windsor chair (q.v.) in which the hoop includes the arms so that one continuous binding encloses all the spindles of the back.

New England Glass Co.: originally the Boston Porcelain & Glass Manufacturing Co. established in 1814 at East Cambridge, Massachusetts, the firm was incorporated by Jarves (q.v.) and his associates as the New England Glass Co. in 1818. Major productions throughout the firm's distinguished career were cut (q.v.) and blown glass; pressed (q.v.) wares from the mid-1820s onwards and the highly successful amberina (q.v.) glass of the 1880s.

New England Pottery Co.: founded in 1854 by Frederick Meagher at Boston, Massachusetts, the Company was producing parian ware (q.v.) and porcelain (q.v.) by 1862.

New Hall porcelain: in 1780 Richard Champion (q.v.) approached Josiah Wedgwood (q.v.), seeking his advice and assistance in disposing of his patent for the manufacture of hard-paste porcelain (q.v.). The outcome was the formation of a company comprising master potters of repute which operated first of all in Tunstall at the factory of Anthony Keeling, purchasing Champion's patent and beginning the manufacture of hard-paste porcelain in 1781.

A dispute arose among the partners shortly after the enterprise was launched, and Keeling and Turner withdrew. Champion also, having obtained the position of Deputy Paymaster of the Forces, went to London in 1782. The business was transferred to Shelton. Samuel Hollins, Peter Warburton, John Daniel and William Clowes, who were their partners, purchased the New Hall Estate on behalf of the Company.

Samuel Hollins died in 1820 and John Daniel in 1821. Daniel's place as manager was taken by John Tittensor who managed the business until it finally closed down in 1835. In 1831 the estate and factory were offered for sale. In 1832 they were announced to be let, but the business was not finally wound up until the sale of manufactured stock in 1835.

As well as earthenware, two grades of porcelain were made at this factory: hard-paste porcelain until about 1810, and bone china (q.v.) subsequently. The firm also traded in potters' materials, being able to supply Cornish clay and Cornish stone for local use.

The 'sprigged muslin' type of pattern is chiefly associated with New Hall, but elaborate painted and gilded wares were produced, with Chinoiseries (q.v.) and picturesque printed landscapes washed over in crude bright colours. Fancy jugs with relief hunting scenes were made as well as chimney ornaments, although the latter have never been identified. The Neoclassical (q.v.) style is evident in some of the handles, but not stressed. A distinctive silver-shape teapot is peculiar to this factory.

Little has been recorded about the personnel of this factory.

Marks:

Pattern numbers prefaced by a letter 'N' or 'No' in cursive style occur on hard-paste porcelain: a double circle enclosing the words 'New Hall' on bone china. Earthenware is usually unmarked.

Initials and pattern number printed before 1812; circular mark transfer-printed 1812–35.

New Hampshire box: rectangular wooden box, usually with stencilled decoration, made in New Hampshire from the mid-19th cent.

New Haven Clock Co.: founded in 1853 at New Haven, Connecticut, the firm made movements (q.v.) in the first instance for the Jerome Manufacturing Co. Its own clocks date from 1896 and were made with both one- and eight-day brass movements.

Newport School: group of 18th-cent. cabinet-makers (q.v.) working in the Baroque (q.v.) style at Newport, Rhode Island. The craftsmen included John Goddard (q.v.) and members of the Townsend (q.v.) family.

Nickel silver: also known as German silver. A silver-coloured alloy of copper, zinc and nickel. Electroplated (q.v.) nickel silver is often stamped E.P.N.S.

Niderviller porcelain: hard-paste porcelain (q.v.) was first produced at Niderviller in 1765 at a factory established in 1754 for the manufacture of faience (q.v.). In 1770 the factory passed to the Comte de Custine and in the early 19th cent. changed hands again. It has continued working to the present day. Niderviller figures are of a quality to rival Sèvres (q.v.) and include such genre subjects as the *Cries of Paris*. Porcelain flowers were made. The monogram of the Comte de Custine, formed by interlaced 'Cs' was used as a mark between 1770 and 1793.

Niello: a black alloy containing lead inlaid decoratively on silver. Much practised in the 19th cent. in Tula, Russia. (See also Tula work.)

Night clock: a clock that shows the time by night, usually by means of a light shining through a pierced dial.

Night table: a pot cupboard which replaced the close-chair (q.v.) after 1750; sometimes also fitted as a washing-stand (q.v.). Among the features commonly found on these pieces may be noted a drawer under the cupboard, a tambour front (q.v.) and a tray top. Some night tables were given a triangular shape to fit into a corner.

Night-Watchman jug: a variety of toby jug (q.v.) representing a seated figure holding a hat and a lantern.

Nip: see Dram glass.

Nishiki-ye: Japanese brocade pictures, colour-prints.

Nock, Henry: London gunmaker (1741–1804), best known as the maker of a seven-barrelled carbine, intended for use in the tops of ships. He received the Royal Warrant of George III and was a large-scale manufacturer of service arms.

Noggin: a small drinking vessel. Noggin-bottle, a small bottle holding a quantity of liquor, usually 142 ml (a ¼ pint).

Nonsuch chest: chest, dating from the second half of the 16th cent., decorated with an inlaid design representing an ideal building resembling the Palace of Nonsuch, near Cheam, built for Henry VIII. Such architectural motifs were much favoured by Renaissance taste and many such chests were made in Germany and Flanders.

Northern celadon: Chinese Sung (q.v.) wares probably from Honan Province, with grey porcellaneous body burnt brown where exposed, and usually a glazed base. The glaze is often glassy and olive-green to brown in tone. They include beautifully shaped bowls, pear-shaped vases, and small shallow dishes superbly carved with plant forms or free designs incised with a comb.

Northwood, John: (1836/7–1902), outstanding figure in the history of English glassmaking, Northwood produced the most famous piece of

modern cameo glass (q.v.), the Portland Vase (q.v.) replica. He established the successful J. & J. Northwood Decorating Works in c. 1861 and
as art director of Stevens & Williams
Ltd (q.v.), he trained a famous team
producing cameo glass.

Norton, Captain John: established
one of the earliest potteries in Vermont
in 1793. Succeeded by his son Lyman,
in 1823 and by his grandson, Julius, in
1840. Under Julius Norton the firm
entered into brief partnership (1845–7)
with Christopher W. Fenton who
introduced Rockingham ware (q.v.)
and yellow ware (q.v.) to the range of
pottery. The firm finally closed in
1894.

Norwich carpets: Norwich carpets
are mentioned in 17th-cent. inventories. Possibly Turkey-work (q.v.)
was made there as well as cloth
carpeting and moquette (q.v.).

Nottingham earthenware: pottery
was made in Nottingham from the
13th cent. and its production continued
along characteristic lines until about
1800. The manufactories making
Nottingham wares are unidentified,
but occasionally the name of the potter
appears on the article. James Morley,
one of the defendants in the action for
protection of his patents brought by
Dwight of Fulham (q.v.) late in the
17th cent., certainly worked here as
did other members of the Morley
family. The name of William Lockett
is found on pieces made about 1755,
and William Woodward is listed as a
maker of slipware (q.v.) in the 18th
cent. As Nottingham began to decline
as a centre for pottery, neighbouring
towns (Denby, Chesterfield and Swinton among others) began to produce
wares similar in style. The last
authenticated piece from Nottingham
is dated 1799.
  Earliest pieces made in Nottingham
were of lead-glazed earthenware.
Many-handled tygs (q.v.) date from the
16th cent. It is believed that stoneware
began to be made in the second half of
the 17th cent. About 1690 the most
productive period in Nottingham
began. The ferruginous clay which

overlaid a very hard body gave a rich
brown colour and a faint metallic
lustre to the surface of the wares. The
grain of this surface is much finer than
that of other stonewares of the period,
and the pieces are light and usually
very thin. Posset pots, some teapots
(now rarely seen), mugs and small jugs
were made in Nottingham. The decoration often consists only of lines incised round the piece; formal flowers,
sometimes reserved in a lighter colour,
or alternately painted in slip of a
darker colour, bands of roughened
clay, small stamped patterns and,
more ambitiously, the piercing of an
outer layer of clay (called 'carving')
were all common forms of decoration.
Inscriptions were often incised. Very
much later some designs in relief were
produced in the Fulham (q.v.) manner,
but these entirely lack the charm of the
simpler designs.
  Nottingham wares are nearly always
distinguishable from other stonewares
made at rival factories by their superior
design and finish. Nowhere at this
period were salt-glazed (q.v.) articles
made with such precision and sureness
of touch.
  'Nottingham' is sometimes marked,
often as part of an inscription or in
shortened form – a jug in the Victoria
and Albert Museum is marked
'Nott. 1703'.

Novelty clock: any of many types
which, in addition to indicating time,
has some unusual feature or that
indicates time in a peculiar way. Most
clocks in this group were made after
1850; many are now rare and are of
interest to collectors for their peculiar
features. Most were inexpensive when
originally manufactured; some were
made to be sold as souvenirs, or to be
used for advertising purposes and
might be made in the shape of flowers,
animals or globes. Many sorts of
novelty alarm clocks were made –
some that lighted a lamp or fired a
powder charge at the pre-set time.
Other novelties had the conventional
pendulum replaced by swinging figures
or flying balls.

Nove porcelain: soft-paste porcelain
(q.v.) was made from about 1752 at the

Nove factory, Venice, which had originally been established about 1728 for the purpose of manufacturing faience (q.v.). The factory remained in existence until about 1835, the mark being an eight-pointed star in red and gold.

Nozzle: the socket in which the candle is held on candlesticks (q.v.), wall-lights (q.v.) and chandeliers (q.v.).

Nulling: see Knurling.

Nuremberg egg: a misnomer applied to early South German watches. Arose from the misreading and mistranslation of *Uhrlein* into *Eierlein* (little clocks into little eggs). These early watches were usually drum shaped.

Nymphenburg porcelain: hard-paste porcelain (q.v.) was first made with the assistance of the arcanist (q.v.) J. J. Ringler in 1753. The factory at that time was situated at Neudeck but was moved in 1761 to a building in the palace grounds of Nymphenburg. From 1755 to 1767 the factory was under the patronage of Prince Max III Joseph of Bavaria and Count Sigismund von Haimhausen. It was during this early period that the most famous wares of the factory were produced. Later in the century it became the property of the Elector Palatine and ultimately of the State. In the latter part of the 19th cent. it was leased to a private company and still exists today. The table wares of the early period are decorated in an imaginative Rococo (q.v.) style, or with flowers, fruit, or landscapes in the manner of Meissen (q.v.). The most renowned wares of the factory are the figures modelled by Franz Anton Bustelli (q.v.) who was chief modeller at the factory from 1754 until his death in 1763. His figures capture the playful mood of the Rococo period, sometimes rendered in pure white and sometimes in restrained colours, exploiting to the full a capricious and lively spirit. His work is closely akin to that of the contemporary Bavarian wood sculptors and displays a masterly linear rhythm. Some of Bustelli's models seem to have been reassembled by a 'repairer'

(P. A. Seefried) after his death, while the modern factory has made copies in pure white porcelain of some of the early models. Bustelli's successor, D. Auliczek, continued along established lines, but showed his originality by modelling animal groups of a type not hitherto attempted. In 1797, J. P. Melchior, formerly at Hoechst (q.v.) and Frankenthal (q.v.) came to Nymphenburg, where, following the taste of the time, he modelled his sensitive portrait busts and medallions in biscuit (q.v.). The Nymphenburg mark, the shield from the arms of Bavaria, is usually shown upon the base, impressed as part of the decoration.

Nyon porcelain: a factory was founded at Nyon, near Geneva, in 1780 and existed until 1813. Current French fashions were closely adhered to and many of the wares bear floral decoration.

Oban: Japanese print of full-size, 381 × 254 mm (15 × 10 in).

Obsidian: a dark-coloured volcanic rock of glassy consistency, usually containing dark green flecks. Parian ware (q.v.), by 1850 made by many firms in Staffordshire and generally referred to as Statuary Porcelain, imitated obsidian.

Occasional table: modern term to describe the small table, intended to serve various purposes, first introduced shortly after the Restoration and popular, in different forms, throughout the 18th cent.

Oeben, Jean François: (*c.* 1720–63), French cabinet-maker, the son of a postmaster at Ebern in Franconia. He married in Paris in 1749, but we do not know the date of his arrival there from Germany. He entered the workshop of C.-J. Boulle, son of A.-C. Boulle (q.v.), in 1751, and on the latter's death in 1754 Oeben succeeded him as *ébéniste* (q.v.) *du Roi* and was granted lodgings at the Gobelins (q.v.), whence he moved in 1756 to the Arsenal.

While working for Boulle, he was also employed by Madame de Pompadour and others, and after his move to the Gobelins he began in 1760 his most celebrated work – the monumental *Bureau du Roi Louis XV*, which, however, was not completed until after his death. Riesener (q.v.) who was one of his assistants, succeeding him at the Arsenal, together with Leleu (q.v.).

Oeben also collaborated with Carlin (q.v.) and P. Caffiéri (q.v.). He died bankrupt in Paris, where his widow carried on the business until 1767, when she married Riesener, who then carried on the business in his own name.

Oeben only became a *maître-ébéniste* in 1761 under special circumstances, having worked for the Crown for so long. His stamp on furniture is therefore rare, and when found it is more probable that the piece was made by Riesener before he took over the business, as Madame Oeben continued her husband's stamp while running the workshop herself.

After Cressent (q.v.) and Gaudreau (q.v.), Oeben is the most celebrated *ébéniste* of Louis XV's reign. He specialized in elaborately planned pieces, fitted with secret drawers and complicated locking devices, but, owing to the amount of furniture which must necessarily have left his workshop unstamped, his work cannot easily be identified.

Oeil-de-perdrix: (*Fr.*), literally, partridge eye: (1) a decoration in enamel colours, used on porcelain, consisting of an even ground of small circles usually upon a coloured background; (2) a term used in lace-making, synonymous with *réseau rosacé* and *fond de neige* or snowflake ground, to describe the most effective of the grounds used in Argentella needlepoint lace and also pillow laces of Valenciennes and some Binche and early Mechlin (qq.v.). Each of the irregular spidery meshes had a dot in it.

Ogee: in the shape of a double curve, the lower part being concave and the upper convex.

Ogee bowl: a popular shape of bowl found on mid- to late 18th-cent. drinking glasses in which the bowl rises from the stem in a gentle 'S' curve. Double- and triple-ogee bowls, formed by two or three curves, were particularly favoured for sweetmeat glasses.

Ogee-pattern wallpapers: geometrical device based on circles much favoured by wallpaper designers.

Ohio Valley China Co.: established in 1890 at Wheeling, West Virginia, the factory produced a general line of porcelain table wares, figures and cuspidors (spittoons). Shortly after 1893, the factory was closed for a few years and then reopened for the production of sanitary wares until 1900, when the factory ceased operation.

Oil gilding: gilding on porcelain or glass applied by means of japanner's size, used in the 18th cent. before the method of firing gold became known.

Oilspot glaze: some of the Chinese wares bearing so-called Honan brown and black glazes of the Sung (q.v.) dynasty bear attractive silvery spots, caused by precipitated iron crystals.

O'Neale, Jeffrey Hamet: (1734–1801), O'Neale, miniaturist, book illustrator and ceramic artist, was born in Ireland, worked at Chelsea soon after 1752 and later for Worcester and Josiah Wedgwood (qq.v.) as an outside decorator. From the latter he received three guineas a week which Wedgwood considered excessive, although he acknowledged that 'O'Neale works quick' (1771). In 1765 he was a member of the Incorporated Society of Artists. Animals, illustrations from the Fables of Aesop and figures in landscape were among the subjects he used. It has been suggested that he also worked for James Giles (q.v.) of Kentish Town, London. Signed Worcester pieces are to be found in the British Museum.

O.N.P

O.N.P. is also found on Worcester and Chelsea porcelain.

One-and-a-quarter-seconds clock pendulum: a type of pendulum 1.55 m (5 ft 1 in) long. When the improved performance of the seconds pendulum (q.v.) and anchor escapement (q.v.) were realized, attempts were made to increase this by using longer pendulums. William Clement first made clocks with $1\frac{1}{4}$ seconds pendulums. The seconds dial of a clock originally so made should have four divisions between each 5-second interval on the seconds dial. Sometimes clocks have their escapements and pendulums altered from 1 second to $1\frac{1}{2}$ seconds in order to enhance their value. These will generally have their old seconds dials with five divisions. The base of a $1\frac{1}{4}$ seconds clock should have a door to allow access to the bob (q.v.).

Oneida: American company founded within a farming community at Oneida Lake, New York State, in 1848 and lasting until 1881. At first it manufactured silver and cutlery, turning to other forms of metalwork in the 1850s and '60s, and also to the manufacture of silk.

On-glaze decoration: decoration applied to glazed pottery or porcelain after the ware has been glazed and fired; literally, decorated on top of the glaze.

Onslow pattern spoons: see Table services.

'Onyx' glass: glass of several colours mingled before the formation of the vessel in imitation of onyx. A Roman technique, revived in Renaissance (q.v.) times, particularly in Venice and Germany.

Opalescent enamel: see Enamel.

Opal glass: glass rendered semi-opaque or of an opalescent 'milk-and-water' colour, an effect which could be obtained by the addition of the ashes of calcined bones. Late 18th- and early 19th-cent. country-market glass table wares included sugar basins, milk jugs and vases of opal white glass, often painted in unfired colours.

Opaque china: trade name for a fine white porcellaneous earthenware used by Swansea, Ridgway & Morley and others.

Opaque enamel: see Enamel.

Opaque glass: glass rendered opaque-white by the addition of tin oxide, or arsenic or the ashes of calcined bones. Venetian Renaissance glass vessels were decorated with threads of opaque-white, known as latticinio (q.v.) work, while opaque-white glass alone is also known to have been made in Venice in the latter part of the 15th century. Opaque-white glass aroused particular interest on account of its resemblance to porcelain and it is recorded that this type of glass was included in orders placed by English merchants with Venetian glassblowers in the second half of the 17th cent. At this period there was in England, as elsewhere, an enthusiasm for Chinese porcelain. It is possible that some surviving examples of this date may have been made in England. In general, however, English opaque-white glass belongs in date to the second half of the 18th cent. and was made not only at Bristol, as is so commonly thought, but at many other glasshouses in the country. The wares, which include sets of vases, tea caddies, candlesticks, etc., and snuff boxes and other 'toys', were decorated with enamel painting in the manner of porcelain, which was now being made for the first time in England, and doubtless the close similarity of the two materials encouraged the making of opaque-white glass. A forerunner of art glass (q.v.), it was always popular. (See Bristol glass and Edkins, Michael.)

Opaque-twist stem: a type of stem found on drinking glasses in the second half of the 18th cent. containing spirals of dense-textured white enamel, varying from fine hairs to broad solid tapes; single or compound in more than a hundred variations: (a) straight stem with single twist; (b) with shoulder or central knop and single twist, usually multiple spiral; (c) straight stem with compound twist (q.v.) – the most common type – from 1760; (d) with knops in various positions, shoulder, central base, or any two or all three, with compound-twist, from 1760.

Opus Anglicanum: the name given to English ecclesiastical embroidery of the 13th and 14th cent. The art of embroidery had flourished in England from Saxon times, but it reached its highest peak of excellence in the 13th cent., and was known all over Europe as *opus anglicanum*. The figures and other details are mostly worked in fine split stitch with backgrounds of couched work (q.v.). A great deal of *opus anglicanum* was exported to the Continent, where some of it still remains. Towards the middle of the 14th cent. the standard of both design and execution began to decline.

'Orange-jumper': local subject on Yorkshire cream-coloured earthenware (q.v.) made at the Don pottery, *c.* 1808, depicting a coarse-featured local horse-breaker who acted as messenger for Lord Milton in the 1807 election. He is clothed in orange, the 'colour' of Lord Milton.

Ormolu: the term 'ormolu' (from the Fr. *or moulu*) is used to describe decorative objects and furniture mounts of the 18th and 19th cent., cast in bronze or brass and gilt. Though cast and gilt bronze was by no means an innovation in the 18th cent., it was used in France to an extent that could not be paralleled in previous epochs. Similar work was done in Germany, England, and elsewhere, but the fineness of design and perfection of finish of the French artists was never equalled. The main volume of production was of furniture mounts, but vases, candlesticks (q.v.), chandeliers (q.v.), andirons (q.v.), inkstands and clock cases were also made.

These objects were cast, chiselled, and finally fire-gilt. True ormolu should be distinguished from cheaper objects cast in the same moulds and from the same metal, which were roughly finished and lacquered instead of being chiselled and fire-gilt. Ormolu of the Régence (q.v.) and Louis XV periods was never so finely finished as that of the Louis XVI and Empire (q.v.) periods. During the first half of the cent. French furniture was very lavishly decorated with ormolu, and the effect was achieved by mass of ornaments rather than by detail. Later, when marquetry (q.v.) and parquetry (q.v.) were going out of fashion, we find less florid mounts against a background of figured mahogany, a setting which showed them off to the maximum advantage. In the Empire period the ormolu mounts played, if possible, an even more important role, and furniture was constructed as a vehicle for the display of fine ormolu. Such was the detail of the chiselling put into good work, that it was hardly less expensive than similar articles made of silver gilt.

After the restoration in France we find a deterioration in standards of production, and the large-scale re-production of earlier styles, but throughout the 19th cent. there were still craftsmen who could turn out very fine work in this medium, and it is extremely difficult to distinguish between 18th-cent. ormolu and the best of the 19th-cent. reproductions.

In England the Birmingham firm of Boulton & Fothergill produced ormolu vases, candlesticks and perfume-burners (q.v.) during the 1760s and '70s. The finish was never up to the highest French standards but the designs, furnished by the Adam brothers, were of great elegance and fitness for purpose. There was no great demand for furniture mounts in England, but some houses of the second half of the 18th cent. still retain their ormolu door furniture made by Boulton after Adam designs.

Orris lace: see Arras lace.

Orrery: see Planetarium.

Osler, F. & C.: Birmingham firm founded in 1807, with a branch in London, which specialized in the production of large-scale glass fabrications. The centre-piece at the Great Exhibition of 1851 was Osler's three-tiered clear glass fountain.

Ostensory: see Monstrance.

Ostrich-egg cup: sometime supposed to be the eggs of griffins or phoenixes, ostrich eggs were often mounted as cups (and occasionally made into flasks) in the 16th cent. and later. Many surviving specimens are German.

Ott & Brewer (Etruria Pottery): established in 1863 by Bloor, Ott & Booth at Trenton, New Jersey. In 1865 John Hart Brewer bought the interest of Bloor, who subsequently moved to East Liverpool, Ohio, changing the firm's name to Ott & Brewer. The production from 1863 to 1875 was limited to granite ware (q.v.) and cream-coloured wares (q.v.). In 1875 parian ware (q.v.) was introduced consisting largely of busts and figures. The first Belleek (q.v.) ware manufactured in America was produced by Ott & Brewer in 1882. Workers from Belleek, Ireland, were persuaded to work in the United States and direct the Belleek production for Ott & Brewer. Henry Saunders directed the production of *pâte-sur-pâte* (q.v.). In 1871, the firm was reorganized with special emphasis on production for exhibition and display. Isaac Broome's works featured a series of original parian designs. Throughout its history Ott & Brewer remained one of the largest ceramic producers in Trenton, and the firm was finally dissolved in 1893.

Ottoman: upholstered seat, originating in Turkey, introduced into Britain and the United States in the early 19th cent. It occurred in a wide variety of forms and was often covered with cushions. An essential feature of Turkish-style interior decoration in the late 19th cent.

Ottweiler porcelain: a factory was started at Ottweiler, Nassau-Saarbrücken in 1763 for Prince Wilhelm Heinrich of Nassau-Saarbrücken. It existed until 1797, making hard-paste porcelain (q.v.) in its earlier years and latterly only earthenware (q.v.). The table wares are sometimes decorated with mythological or figure subjects framed in Rococo (q.v.) scroll-work, and pear-shaped jugs reflect a taste for French forms. Figures were made, and the French modeller Paul-Louis Cyfflé worked here about 1765. The mark in use from 1763 to about 1775 is the 'NS' of Nassau-Saarbrücken in blue or gold and occasionally incised.

Oude Amstel porcelain: see Weesp porcelain.

Oude Loosdrecht porcelain: see Weesp porcelain.

Overdoors: (*sopraporte*) carvings, paintings on wood or canvas or painted or printed papers suitable for the decoration of the space between the top of a door and cornice (q.v.). A speciality of the wallpaper maker in England, France and America during the 18th cent. Similar decorative panels were made to fit empty chimney-pieces in summer months.

Overglaze: decoration applied to porcelain or pottery above the glaze.

Overlay paperweight: the coating of the exposed surfaces of a paperweight with one or more layers of white or coloured glass. The finish is then cut to leave windows (see Punty mark), through which the interior of the paperweight is visible. Very rarely, after the above process, the weight is further encased in clear glass. Such a paperweight is known as an enclosed overlay.

Overmantel: an ornamental mirror over a mantelpiece.

Over-upholstered seat: a chair seat in which the upholstery is carried over the seat rail and secured beneath it.

Ovolo base: hollow-ware (q.v.) having a base formed by a plain projecting quarter-curve or moulding. Pewter (q.v.) flagons of the 17th cent. are found with this type of base.

Ovolo moulding: (1) a small oval convex moulding chiefly used in repetition, sometimes with egg and dart (q.v.) enrichment, as 16th-cent.

border ornament. Some use also made of the ornament, revived in the 19th cent., on plate (q.v.); (2) a continuous moulding of convex profile, also known as a lip moulding, applied by the cabinet-maker (q.v.) in the early 18th cent. to the top edges of chests of drawers, stands, tables, etc.

Owen, George: (d. 1917): Worcester (q.v.) craftsman-designer famous for his reticulated or pierced designs. Examples are normally signed but other firms produced inferior essays in Owen's style.

Owl jugs: jugs with detachable heads made in slipware (q.v.) in Staffordshire in the late 17th and early 18th cent., and white salt-glazed stoneware (q.v.) from 1730 to 1770, sometimes with brown slip enrichment.

Ox-blood glaze: see Copper-red glazes.

Oxbow or **oxbow front:** an American term used to describe the curved form, resembling a bow, and the reverse of a serpentine curve, often employed by Boston and other New England cabinet-makers (q.v.) in the late 18th cent. Chests of drawers and other types of case furniture of the finest quality were designed with oxbow fronts.

Oyster veneer: a type of veneer (q.v.) in which the wood is cut from small branches and laid together to form a surface pattern resembling a series of oysters placed next to each other. This oyster veneering was used on cabinet doors and drawer fronts during the late 17th cent. and derives from a Dutch fashion. The woods used included walnut, olive, laburnum and kingwood.

Pad foot: a simple terminal to a cabriole (q.v.) leg used on chairs, settees (q.v.) and tables from about 1705, resembling in shape the club foot (q.v.) but resting on a small disc.

Pagoda wallpapers: Chinese wallpapers.

Paillon: small decorative spangle in gold, silver or colours cut into a formal shape and set in translucent enamel (q.v.) on boxes, *étuis* (q.v.), etc.

Painted silhouettes: these were produced in a number of techniques on various materials, ranging from paper to glass. (See Glass silhouettes.)

Painted wallpapers: probably used in England as early as the end of the 15th cent. Painting of *'trompe l'œil'* was undertaken by 18th-cent. paperhanging makers (q.v.), frequently after the plain paper had been hung.

Pairpoint Manufacturing Co.: firm of electroplaters (q.v.) established at New Bedford, Massachusetts, in 1880. From its inception it provided its neighbours, the Mount Washington Glass Works & Co. (q.v.), and also Harry & Alfred Smith, with mounts and holders for their glasswares. In 1894 the Pairpoint and Mount Washington companies merged and in 1900 became the Pairpoint Corporation.

Paktong: an alloy of copper, nickel and zinc, of whitish colour, resembling silver when polished. Grates, candlesticks and other domestic appliances were made of this metal in the last third of the 18th cent. The name is derived from the Chinese, who used the metal for hinges and furniture mounts. It is also known as tutenag, which, properly speaking, is zinc without admixture of other metals.

Palace letters: these, with inventory numbers (q.v.), are often painted or branded on French furniture and occasionally stamped on *bronzes d'ameublement* (q.v.), made for the French Crown. On veneered furniture they are usually to be found on the carcase (q.v.) at the back or under marble slabs, but in the case of chairs and joined furniture generally, they are often in the under parts and sometimes on the bottom of the upholstered seats. They almost always take the form of the initial letter or letters of the palace

concerned beneath a crown. Thus F =
Fontainebleau; CT = Château de
Trianon; W (two Vs) = Versailles;
S.C. = Saint Cloud; etc. Like inventory numbers, their existence on
furniture of any date is worth careful
investigation.

Palissy ware: lead-glazed pottery
made by Bernard Palissy (d. 1590),
born at Agen and long resident at
Saintes in France, consisting of dishes
either decorated with casts from
nature or fishes, reptiles and other
creatures, moulded with Renaissance
ornament or figure subjects, covered
with coloured glazes. His methods
were adopted by other potters, particularly at Avon, near Fontainebleau.
In England, lead-glazed earthenware
dishes were made in imitation of
Palissy ware and there are known
examples dated between 1633 and
1697.

Palladian style: a style of architecture based upon the principles
followed by the Italian architect
Palladio in Italy in the 16th cent. In
England, a small group of connoisseurs, led by the Earl of Burlington and
the architect William Kent (qq.v.)
encouraged a revival of this style in the
first half of the 18th cent. The rigid
principles of Classical proportion,
involving the use of Classical forms and
motifs, were applied not only to
buildings but to their interior decoration and to furniture. Furniture
made in the Palladian style was consequently of architectural character,
lavishly carved and frequently gilded,
making use of pediments, heavy
cornices, swags of fruit or flowers,
masks, lions' paws, etc.

Pallets: the parts of the escapement
(q.v.) of a clock against which the
teeth of the escape wheel push, giving
impulse to the pendulum or balance.

Palmer, Thomas J.: in 1887, Palmer
took out a patent in England for
embossing pulp on a paper-making
machine. He also produced an inexpensive relief wallpaper known as
Anaglypta.

Palmette: a decorative motif deriving
from a branched palm tree, a popular
ornamental form in the late 18th cent.

Pancheon: a large shallow bowl with
sloping sides used for settling milk.

Panel: compartment usually rectangular, and sunk or raised from the
surface of its framework. Panel is the
filling of such framework, whereas
panelling refers to the framework and
its filling.

Panel cutting: a method of decorating glass vessels by means of cutting
or grinding a pattern on the flat edge
of a grinding wheel. Also known as
flat cutting, many variants of cut
motifs are found on 18th-cent. glass.

Panelled construction: until the
15th cent., furniture in England was
made of heavy boards. A new method
was then introduced by the joiners
(q.v.) involving the use of panels held
in a framework of stiles and rails
(qq.v.). Panelled construction rendered furniture less clumsy and
provided new possibilities for design.

Pap boat: small, shallow oval bowl
with tapering lip or spout at one end
for feeding infants. Surviving silver
examples date from early 18th cent.
onwards, but they were also made of
other materials. Sometimes known as
a pap dish.

Paperhanging maker: 17th- and
18th-cent. term describing the maker
of wallpaper, superseded by 'paper-
stainer' until 'wallpaper manufacturer'
became generally used within the
present century.

Paperweight: heavy bun-shaped
piece of clear glass containing within it
a pattern or design of coloured glass
representing flowers, fruit, butterflies,
etc. Cone-shaped examples of light
green glass sometimes contain vases of
flowers. Originating in Venice in the
19th cent., the art of making glass
paperweights was perfected at the St
Louis glassworks in France and at the
French factories at Baccarat and

Clichy. French paperweights were copied widely in England. The glass-making centres of Stourbridge and Bristol produced examples. The White-friars Glassworks in London and George Bacchus and Son in Birmingham also made paperweights. The successful sale of French paperweights imported into America induced manufacturers there to produce their own wares. The factories of Deeming Jarves (q.v.) at Sandwich, Cape Cod, opened in 1825, and at East Cambridge and South Boston, in Massachusetts, opened in 1818 and 1837, produced designs in the French manner and evolved original models.

Papier mâché: a material composed of paper, reduced to a fibrous pulp, with chalk and sand and shaped by being pressed into boxwood moulds, was made in England in the mid-18th cent. An improved composition of ground rags, glue, flour and water was patented in 1786 by Obadiah Westwood of Birmingham. A real advance in technique was made by Henry Clay of Birmingham, who, in 1772, patented a process for making a tough, heat- and moisture-resisting material which could be oven-japanned to acquire a surface finish as lustrous as Oriental lacquer. It was made from sheets of paper having a porous texture, saturated with a solution of flour and glue. Any number of sheets of paper could be applied, attached by glue and dried between each addition. When the correct thickness was reached, the shape was taken from the mould and planed and filed. Decoration was painted in colour, gold or bronze over the dried and varnished object and covered with a coat of shellac. The piece was then hardened in a japanning oven and rubbed with oil to obtain a polish. Trays, boxes, tea caddies (q.v.) and coasters (q.v.) were among the many objects made.

Pappenheimer: a heavy rapier with a form of swept hilt (q.v.) incorporating two large perforated shells. It was used during the first half of the 17th cent. and was named after the celebrated Imperialist general of the Thirty Years' War, Gottfried Heinrich,

Count von Pappenheim (d. 1632). Sometimes referred to as a Walloon sword.

Papworth, John Buonarotti: (1775–1847), an architect whose popularity and versatility were such that he did not confine his attention solely to buildings. He painted in water-colours, and designed book illustrations, furniture, silverware and gardens. He designed a glass throne for the Shah of Persia, and is considered to have been responsible for the introduction of chandeliers composed of long 'prism' drops arranged in concentric rings. Many of these were made by John Blades, of 5 Ludgate Hill, London, for whose business premises Papworth designed the front.

Parcel-gilt: descriptive of plate (q.v.) decorated by the partial application of gilding (q.v.).

Pardoe, Thomas: (1770–1823), an artist who worked for the Derby, Worcester and Swansea (qq.v.) porcelain factories from about 1785 until 1809, when he removed to Bristol and worked as an independent enameller until 1821. Thereafter he decorated porcelain at Nantgarw (q.v.). Principally a flower painter, much of his work is found on all the above porcelains and also on Coalport (q.v.). Plates copied from botanical magazines were seen in his earliest work. Later his painting is inclined to be careless. His signature in gold is quite often found on various pieces.

Pardoe, Fecit Bristol.

His son, W. H. Pardoe, opened the earthenware manufactory at Nantgarw in 1833.

Pargeter, Philip: (1826–1906), a partner of Hodgetts, Richardson and Pargeter from 1863 to 1869, Pargeter became proprietor of the Red House Glassworks from 1872.

Parian ware: a special kind of biscuit porcelain (q.v.) used for statuary and intended to replace the famous Derby biscuit porcelain. It was stated in the *Art Union*, Vol 10, 1848, to have been invented at Copeland & Garretts, Stoke-on-Trent, about 1845, with the active encouragement of Thomas Battam (1810–64) who was art director. Elsewhere Spencer Garrett is credited with its invention, which was disputed, however, by John Mountford, by Minton (q.v.), and by T. & R. Boote. John Mountford stated (*Staffordshire Advertiser*, 20 September 1851) 'I am prepared to prove that in the latter part of 1845 I discovered that material known as "statuary porcelain", that I gave to Mr S. Garrett (then of the firm of Messrs Copeland & Garrett) the receipt for its production'. John Mountford was then employed at the Copeland factory. T. & R. Boote claimed that Thomas L. Boote first made the body in 1841, 'when learning the art of pottery with Mr E. Jones, and he produced a further specimen from the same receipt in the year 1842 when with Mr Maddock'. Mintons claimed they produced it in 1845. By 1846 it was in commercial production and by 1850 numerous firms were making the body. Wedgwoods called their parian Carrara. Until about 1849–50 the body was generally known in the trade as Statuary Porcelain. Parian tinted to various shades was popular in 1870s and 1880s.

Parison: a glassblower's term for an inflated, unformed gather (q.v.) of metal (q.v.).

Parisot carpet: floor carpets produced at the first carpet mill in England, which started production in 1747 in Paddington, London; these carpets were imported by the United States after 1790.

Parquetry: (*Fr. parqueterie*, from *parqueter*, to inlay), a form of surface decoration or veneer (q.v.) in which the pattern formed is geometrical. Parquetry was first used in England in the second half of the 17th cent. It was popular in France and Italy in the 18th cent.

'Parson and Clerk': a figure group produced in earthenware showing a drunken parson being conducted home by his clerk, after a night's carousal; first made by Enoch Wood (q.v.) *c.* 1790 as a sequel to the 'Vicar and Moses'. This popular satire on the squarson (= parson who was also the squire of his parish) type of incumbent was also used with appropriate verses as a transfer-print on cream-coloured earthenware (qq.v.) in Staffordshire and Leeds. The design was possibly suggested by the fourth plate, 'Night', in Hogarth's series 'Four Times of Day' (engraved and dated 25 March 1738) which shows a reveller being led home after celebrating Restoration Day.

Parting-shards: bits of fired pottery used to separate pots after they have been glazed to prevent them sticking together: 'Their flat ware though it be leaded, having only parting-shards i.e. thin bits of old pots put between them, to keep them from *sticking* together.' (R. Plot, *Natural History of Staffordshire*, 1686.)

Partizan: see under Pole-arms.

Parure: a full set of matching jewellery including a necklace, brooch, earrings and bracelet.

Passglas: (*Ger.*), a German glass beaker encircled by a notched spiral thread dividing it into equal parts so that the glass could be passed from guest to guest allowing each his allotted share.

Paste jewellery: jewellery made with coloured glass, used to reproduce precious stones. Paste gems have been known since Roman times, usually with coloured foil placed beneath in order to enhance their appearance. Colourless paste is practically a modern invention, worn as a substitute rather than as an imitation of precious stones.

Pastille burners: box-like containers, often made in the shape of cottages, summerhouses and churches, with detachable perforated roofs for burning cassolette perfumes, made in china and earthenware in the 18th and 19th cent. but very popular 1820–50.

Cassolette perfumes consist of finely powdered willow-wood charcoal, benzoin, fragrant oils and gum arabic.

Patch family: porcelain figures made at Chelsea and Derby (qq.v.), so named from the presence of three or four dark unglazed patches left on the under surface by the pads or wads of clay upon which the wares were rested during the glost-firing (firing glazed wares).

Patchwork quilts: in England patchwork quilts did not originate until the 18th cent., and most surviving examples date from the end of the 18th or the early 19th cent. Most patchwork patterns were geometrical or formal, such as the 'Honeycomb', which was composed entirely of hexagons, and was the most popular design. Other patterns, such as the 'Shell' and various 'Feather' patterns, were taken from traditional quilting designs. True patchwork consists of a mosaic of fragments of materials sewn edge to edge, but some so-called 'patchwork' quilts are, in fact, applied work (q.v.), as, for example, are those quilts where floral motifs are cut out from chintzes and applied to the ground of the quilt.

American patchwork quilts of the 18th and 19th cent. show an amazing variety of patterns of much greater elaboration than English examples. There are over three hundred named designs, many of them with a religious origin. One of the most striking and commonest traditional patterns is the 'Star of Bethlehem', an eight-pointed star worked either as a single central motif surrounded by smaller stars, or as a number of small stars of equal size regularly arranged on a white ground. Other quilts were made with applied coloured patches on white grounds that were elaborately quilted with geometrical, feather or floral designs.

Pâte-de-verre: (*Fr.* glass paste), moulded glass made of actual glass of various colours, powdered and mixed and re-fired. The technique was used in ancient Egypt and has been adopted in modern times in France.

Paten: small circular plate for the wafer or Protestant Communion bread, Medieval examples have a shaped central depression and a broad flat rim. The depression is engraved with appropriate religious subjects and, in the case of the finest examples, also enriched with translucent enamel. Elizabethan paten covers fit the chalice (q.v.) and have a flat seal foot. Later examples follow this pattern until the Gothic Revival. Small circular footed waiters or tazze (q.v.) should not be confused with ecclesiastical pieces.

Patent furniture: mid-19th-cent. American furniture incorporating mechanisms for adjusting or converting the piece, e.g. platform-rocker, piano-bed. The term embraces various types of invalids' chairs.

Patera: an ornamental motif, of Classical origin, based on the saucer used in sacrificial libations, of round or oval form. The patera was frequently used for decorative purposes on furniture of the Adam (q.v.) period and during the early years of the 19th cent., either carved or painted. It also appears on metalwork.

Pâte-sur-pâte: painstaking method of building up by hand a white design in slip (q.v.) over a tinted parian (q.v.) ground. Introduced into England by Solon of Mintons (q.v.) in 1870.

Patina: on furniture, woodwork and metalwork, patina is the undisturbed surface, heightened by centuries of polishing and usage, or by the presence of oxide produced naturally on the surface of metal.

Pattern-moulded glass: term used to differentiate glass moulded for pattern or decoration only, in a small-dip or part-size piece-mould and then expanded, from that blown in a full-size mould.

Pattern number: identifying number placed on stock designs, mainly table wares, to help in the reordering and identifying of the design by recourse to the factory pattern books.

Paul Pry: model for pottery figures and toby jugs based upon the meddlesome hero of John Poole's comedy of that name, 1825.

Pavé setting: a means of setting jewellery, popular in the late 18th and 19th cent., in which the ornament is paved with clusters of stones touching each other and held in position by grains of metal.

Paw foot: a terminal to a cabriole leg (q.v.) carved in the form of a lion's paw used on tables and chairs in the mid-18th cent. and particularly on those pieces inspired by the designs of William Kent (q.v.).

Pax: a tablet with a projecting handle behind, used in the Eucharist when it is kissed by the celebrant, the other priests and, very occasionally, the communicants. It is usually decorated on the front with a sacred symbol, a scene from the Gospel (usually the Crucifixion) or the lives of the saints, engraved, nielloed or enamelled.

Paysage wallpapers: see Scenic wallpapers.

Peachbloom glazes: see Copper-red porcelain glazes.

Peach blow, peach glass, coral or **wild rose glass:** patented in 1886, the glass is cased (q.v.) or solid, shading from burgundy or pink to yellow or white with a satin or glossy finish and enamel or gilded (qq.v.) decoration.

Peaked morion: see Morion.

Pearce, Daniel: (1817–1907), British glass designer and decorator and a partner of Dobson & Pearce, later Philips & Pearce. As head of the design department at Thomas Webb & Sons (q.v.) from 1884, Pearce designed and made cameo (q.v.) pieces showing perfect linear control and carved detail.

Pear-drop moulding: a moulding, found below a plain cornice on late 18th-cent. bookcases, carved in a repetitive design of inverted pear-shaped forms.

'Pearl' ware: white earthenware containing a larger proportion of flint and white clay than cream-coloured earthenware (q.v.); made by Josiah Wedgwood 1779 but not much used by him. Also a dry body made by Chetham & Woolley, Lane End, c. 1795 and used like jasper (q.v.) for the manufacture of ornaments.

Pear shape: a term used to describe a curved or pyriform shape in hollow-ware (q.v.).

Pebbled vases: vases with marbled surface (see Agate ware).

Péché mortel: (*Fr.*), a couch made up of a stool and an easy chair, similar to a duchesse (q.v.). Chippendale (q.v.) illustrated designs for these couches in the third edition of his *Director*.

Pedestal table: a round-topped table supported by a central pillar on a tripod base, the legs being of cabriole form (q.v.), ending in club or claw-and-ball feet (qq.v.). Pedestal tables were used for general purposes and varied in the degree of carving applied to the base and legs. They were first introduced about 1730 and remained popular throughout the cent.

Pediment: architecturally, the triangular end to a roof. During the 18th cent. pediments sometimes surmounted the cornices of bookcases, cabinets, etc. (See also Broken pediment.)

Peever: a piece of slate or stone used in the game of hopscotch; also a disc of pottery, so used, coloured and lettered with the name of the owner. Made at Alloa and elsewhere in Scotland in the 19th cent.

Pegged chests: occasionally a chest is noted that can be dismantled for travelling or store by removing wooden pegs in the manner of many early table trestles. Some are authentic, but most surviving chests are 19th cent. and not Medieval.

Pegged construction: furniture made by joiners (q.v.) constructed with mortice and tenon joints (q.v.), the tenon being held in the mortice by a square peg, riven or split from green wood.

'Peggy Plumper': crude decoration sometimes appearing on earthenware, showing Peggy Plumper sparring with Sammy Spar for mastership of bed and board, accompanied by a long rhyme 'about wearing the breeches'.

Peg tankard: rare form of 17th-cent. silver tankard, the interior fitted with a vertical row of small studs to measure drinking.

Peking bowls: Chinese porcelain bowls of Ch'ien Lung (q.v.) or later date, with painted *famille rose* (q.v.) medallions reserved on a single-coloured ground covered with engraved scrollwork; said to have been sent as yearly tribute to the Emperor at Peking.

Pellatt, Apsley: (1791–1823), glass-maker, whose father of the same name founded the Falcon Glasshouse in Southwark, London, in the late 18th cent. Apsley Pellat patented a novel form of cameo, being a relief moulded in a porcellaneous material enclosed in deeply cut glass, which he called 'crystallo-ceramie' (q.v.) or 'cameo incrustations'. He was the original director of Apsley Pellatt & Co. whose noted productions include crystallo-ceramic ware, crackle, engraved and cut crystal glass (qq.v.), the latter winning a prize medal in 1851.

Pembroke table: a small table with short drop leaves supported on swinging wooden brackets. The term Pembroke is first used in England in the 1760s. Although Chippendale (q.v.) lists tables of this description as 'breakfast tables' in the *Director*, he used the term on bills. Sheraton popularized the type of table and claimed that it was named after the lady who first ordered it. It was particularly popular in the late 18th-cent. period and Hepplewhite (q.v.) also suggested designs for it.

Pendant: particularly fashionable as a necklace ornament in the mid-19th cent., often in the Greek and Etruscan styles, with medallions or a locket enclosing a lock of hair.

Pendeloque: a gemstone of drop-shape, faceted and used as a pendant.

Pendent husks: see Husk ornament.

Pennsylvania Dutch: the name applied to German settlers in Pennsylvania. Their furniture and crafts have many distinctive qualities since they assimilate English and German peasant styles. Their cabinet-makers (q.v.) worked in soft woods which they painted and often decorated with floral patterns and other motifs from the vocabulary of peasant design.

Penny bank: earthenware money-box in the form of a house or chest of drawers.

Penwork: technique for the decoration of furniture and small wooden items, popular in the early 19th cent. The intention was generally to imitate the appearance of marquetry (q.v.).

Percussion lock: a form of ignition for a firearm, involving the use of a detonating compound. The first patent for a lock of this type was taken out in 1807 by the Rev. Alexander Forsyth (d. 1843). As put on the market, this had a small, flask-shaped magazine that could be rotated on a central spindle, and contained detonating powder in the lower end and a spring-loaded striker in the upper. By turning the magazine through 180 degrees a small amount of powder was deposited in a recess in the central spindle, connecting through a channel to the touch-hole; when the magazine was returned to the normal position this powder was detonated by the striker, which was itself struck by a hammer-like cock.

Improvements made on the Forsyth lock included the pellet- or pill-lock, in which the detonating powder was replaced by a pellet, sometimes enclosed in a paper cap; and the tube-lock, which used a tubular metal primer held by a spring clip. All types were superseded by the percussion-cap system, apparently invented between 1818 and 1820, in which a thimble-shaped copper cap containing detonating powder was placed on a hollow nipple communicating with the chamber, and fired by the action of the cock. Many flintlock guns (q.v.) were converted to this system, which remained in use until the second half of the 19th cent.

Pergolesi, Michele Angelo: Italian painter employed by Adam (q.v.). He was in England from *c.* 1758. Between 1777 and 1801 he published his *Original Designs* for painted furniture.

Perpetual calendar clock: clock including a calendar, which corrects itself for the short months, and, more exceptionally, for leap year. The mechanism consists of a slotted wheel revolving once a year (or four years) with slots of varying length which control the movement of a lever, allowing it to pass one or more teeth of the calendar wheel at a time.

Perry, Edward: an important manufacturer of *papier mâché* (q.v.) who started in Queen Street, Wolverhampton, later moving to Paul Street. The Wolverhampton *Directory*, 1829, described him as 'Manufacturer of Fine Paper Goods and Fancy Pontypool (q.v.) Work'.

Persian carpets: the Persian carpet at its best is worthy to be ranked among the great examples of creative art. Springing naturally from a luxury-loving and refined civilization, and finding at hand an unsurpassed quality of wool from the highlands of Persia, combined with a natural feeling for colour and form in all classes of its people, it is not surprising that many of these lovely pieces are so beautiful. There are secrets of dyeing: the ability to use brilliant colours impervious to strong sunlight and time alike, yet applied without damage to the sometimes delicate fabric. The apogee of Persian craftmanship seems to have been reached during the reigns of Tashmak (1524–77) and Shah Abbas (1588–1629), and it is in this period that a number of the most famous carpets now existing were woven, usually under royal decree or patronage, and irrespective of cost. The famous Ardebil carpet from the Mosque of Sheik Safi and now in the Victoria and Albert Museum, London, for instance, was largely the work of one man, who started his labours on this one carpet as a young weaver and finished it as an old man of over seventy, weaving into the cartouche (q.v.):

> I have no refuge in the world, other than thy threshold,
> My head no protection other than this porchway.
> The Work of the slave of the Holy Place, Maksud of Kashan in the year 946.

Petit-point embroidery: a type of embroidery worked on a woven canvas in a tent stitch or slanting stitch. The technique, which combined rich and pictorial effects, had rarely been used in the Middle Ages but was characteristic of post-Renaissance secular embroidery all over Europe. It was much used for cushion and chair covers.

Petits patrons: see Cartoons.

Petronel: a large pistol, or short arquebus (q.v.), fitted with a match- or wheel-lock (q.v.) and used in the late 16th and early 17th cent. It had a curved stock, which was rested against the chest when fired.

Petuntse: fusible feldspathic ingredient of hard-paste porcelain (q.v.). (See also China-stone.)

Pew group: figure group representing a man and woman (more rarely two men and a woman) seated upon a high-backed settle; made in white salt-glazed stoneware (q.v.), Staffordshire, about 1730–40; more rarely in earthenware (q.v.). The name was probably derived from Sir Arthur Church's description in *English Earthenware* 1884 – 'a man and a woman . . . are seated on a high-backed bench or pew'.

Pewter: an alloy, chiefly of tin, with varying proportions of copper, lead, antimony or bismuth.

Phoenix Pottery Co.: in 1872 the factory at Phoenixville, Pennsylvania, was leased to W. A. H. Schreiber and J. F. Betz. Until it closed in 1899 the factory manufactured parian ware and lithophanes (qq.v.).

Phyfe, Duncan: (1768–1854), New York master cabinet-maker. Born in Scotland, he went in his early 'teens to Albany, New York, and there became apprenticed to a cabinet-maker. In 1790, aged twenty-one, he arrived in New York City, where shortly he set up a shop and made fine quality furniture in the Sheraton and Directoire styles (qq.v.). Phyfe's work possesses grace of line, refinement of proportion and delicacy of ornament – reeding, fluting, cameo-carving – which lend it both elegance and distinction. Among his chairs, sofas and tables he produced so many little masterpieces incorporating the lyre motif that he is now considered the chief American exponent of this decorative form. Phyfe's individuality again stands out in his Empire-style (q.v.) furniture. He was so successful, that at one time he employed a hundred workmen; eventually his work suffered from his success. He retired from business in 1847.

Picot: (*Fr.*), a term used in lacemaking to describe the purl or tiny loop ornamenting bride or cordonnet (qq.v.).

Pictorial lace: made in the mid-17th cent. and resembling the raised embroidery now known as stump-work (q.v.) and with similar use of raised canopies, loose hangings, beads, seed pearls, and disproportionate details to fill in the background.

Pie-crust table: a round tilt-top table on a tripod base popular in the mid-18th cent. The top has a scalloped edge finished with a carved moulding which is suggestive of the notched rim of a pie crust. The tripod consists of three cabriole legs (q.v.) terminating generally in claw and ball feet.

Pie-crust ware: pottery pie dishes of buff stoneware with covers simulating pastry were made during the flour tax by the firms of Wedgwood, Turner (qq.v.), etc. ('After Brummel's retirement, viz., in July 1800, the scarcity was so great that the consumption of flour for pastry was prohibited in the Royal Household, rice being used instead; the distiller left off malting, hackney coach fares were raised 25 per cent, and Wedgwood made dishes to represent pie-crust.' Capt. Jeffs, *Life of George Brummel* Esq. 1844, Vol 1, p. 49.) 'About 1780 he (Turner) discovered a vein of fine clay . . . at Green Dock . . . From this he obtained all his supplies for manufacturing his . . . *Stone Ware Pottery* of a cane colour . . . some of them represent different kinds of pastry . . .' (Simeon Shaw, *History of the Staffordshire Potteries*, 1829, pp. 172–3).

Pied de biche spoon (**hind's hoof spoon**): see Trefid spoon.

Pierced earthenware: earthenware (q.v.) decorated by hand-piercing the walls in the leather-hard state with punches shaped like leaves, hearts, trefoils, quatrefoils, etc., arranged to form intricated lacelike designs. It was extensively employed at Leeds, where the designs were executed with remarkable precision and delicacy. The process was also used by Wedgwood (q.v.) and others in Staffordshire.

Pier glass: a tall, narrow mirror, usually made to match a pier table (q.v.) or commode (q.v.), to hang on the wall space between windows, in elaborately carved and gilded frames, popular throughout the 18th cent.

Pier table: a table designed to stand against the pier, the part of the wall between the windows. The pier table was often placed below a looking glass or pier glass (q.v.). Early 18th-cent. examples were often of gesso (q.v.) while those designed in the latter part of the cent. were lightly constructed, sometimes with marble tops or veneered in satinwood. At this period they were often semi-elliptical or D-shaped.

Pietra dura: the Italian term for those stones (literally 'hard stones') which are roughly classed as semiprecious in English: i.e. such stones as are composed mainly of silicates in contrast to 'soft' stones, such as limestone and most marbles, which have a large proportion of calcium in their composition. Much used for table tops, altar frontals, and decorative cabinets from the 16th cent.

Piggin: a small milk pail.

Pike: see under Pole-arms.

Pilaster wallpaper: a richly patterned paper suitable for use in elaborate schemes of panelling. Sets of papers containing units of the complete scheme were made in France and in England during the early part of the 19th cent.

Pilchard pots: earthenware pots made in North Devon, South Wales, and Cornwall for the West Country fishermen, and known by size as 'gallons', 'bussas', 'great crocks', etc.

Pilgrim bottle: in the Middle Ages a leather bottle, sometimes with metal mounts, used for carrying water. It was of flattened form with a loop on each side through which suspension cords were passed. A few early examples have survived in silver (e.g. French bottle in All Souls College, Oxford) but many more in earthenware. The type is also known in the rare Medici porcelain (q.v.). Pilgrim bottles of exceptionally large size were made of silver in the late 17th and early 18th cent. These seem to have been intended for display as sideboard plate only.

Pilgrim furniture: a general term used in America to describe the New England furniture made during the 17th cent. for the Puritans, the 'Pilgrims'. (See Brewster chair, Carver chair, Hadley chest.)

Pilgrims' badges: cast from lead, these badges were distributed at the shrines of Medieval Europe to pilgrims, and were worn in the hat or on the person as evidence that the pilgrimage had been completed. These little objects, worthless in themselves, usually bore some allusion to the saint at whose shrine they were received. The best-known pilgrims' sign is the shell of St James of Compostella in Spain. The most popular English shrine was that of St Thomas at Canterbury. Pilgrims' signs, being made of lead, bear a superficial resemblance to the notorious class of fake lead medallions and amulets of the Middle Ages, made in London about the end of the 19th cent., and commonly known after their inventors as 'Billies and Charles' (q.v.). The lettering of any inscription on a putative pilgrims' sign should be examined with care, as it is in this feature that the fakers betrayed themselves.

Pilkington's Tile & Pottery Co.: a Lancashire pottery established in 1892 at Clifton Junction for the manufacture of tiles.

Pillar-and-scroll clock: an American shelf or mantel clock by Eli Terry

(q.v.). The wooden works are housed in a vertical rectangular case with a scrolled-arch top, small, round pillars at the sides, and delicately small feet. Also known as a 'Terry' clock.

Pillow lace: the most usual name for laces made with bobbins (q.v.) as distinct from needlepoint laces (q.v.) although those too were worked on cushions. Padded boards were used at first.

Pill slabs: apothecaries' pill slabs were made in tin-glazed earthenware at Lambeth, and were decorated frequently with the arms of the Apothecaries' Company, or those of the City of London.

Pinchbeck: an alloy of copper and zinc similar to brass but containing a higher percentage of copper. Invented by the London watchmaker, Christopher Pinchbeck (q.v.) (d. 1732). Finished with gilding, it was much used in the 18th cent. for watchcases, *étuis* (q.v.), etc. and had the advantage that when the gilding was worn, the metal did not show a different colour.

Pinchbeck, Christopher, Snr and **Jnr:** London clockmakers, the father being active between 1695 and 1732 and the son between 1735 and 1783.

Pineapple cups: standing covered cups in the shape of stylized pineapples, were distinctive products of Germany (called *Ananaspokal*), where they were made in the 16th and 17th cent. Some stand as much as 762 mm (30 in) in height.

Pineapple ware: see Cauliflower ware.

Pin-hinge: method of hinging, as found on 13th-cent. chests, the lid being pinned through the rear stiles (q.v.) and pendent side-rails (q.v.) of the lid.

Pin locks: these were usually in oak, the flat bolt passing completely through the locks, one end expanded to engage in the jamb socket, the other shaped to form a handle. Three recesses were sunk into the top edge into which loose pins fell from above when the key was removed, thus holding the pin immovable. Pin locks were opened by inserting a wooden key into an aperture immediately above the bolt handle, and lifting it slightly. Projections on its upper surface raised the locking pins so that the bolt might be withdrawn from its socket.

Pinxton porcelain: a small porcelain factory was established at Pinxton about 1796 by William Billingsley and John Coke. Billingsley left the concern in 1801 and his partner Coke carried on the works until they were sold to a landscape painter named John Cutts in 1804. The factory is believed to have been closed about 1812.
Marks:

Billingsley himself decorated some of the wares. He brought to Pinxton from Derby a staff of workmen, and the soft-paste porcelain (q.v.) produced while the factory was under his management was made to his own formula: it is of that peculiarly translucent quality characteristic of Swansea and Nant-garw (qq.v.). Simple shapes were decorated in the Derby manner, not, however, making use of the raised flowers and leaves characteristic of Derby (q.v.). The best known designs from Pinxton are those using only a small sprig – a cornflower or forget-me-not – on a white ground. Plates and dishes were most often edged with gold, or with a dark red or blue.

Landscapes washed with a yellow-green colour are fairly common. Ground colours are exceedingly rare on most flower decorated pieces, but occasionally a canary-yellow is seen. Billingsley left the factory, taking his recipes for soft-paste porcelains with him; and thereafter a much coarser and more opaque type of ware was made, not unlike Derby of a poor quality.

Pipe-clay: a fine white clay used in the manufacture of tobacco-pipes. According to Dr Pococke, pipe-clay was imported into Staffordshire from Poole, Dorset, but earlier local white firing clays were used by the Newcastle-under-Lyme pipe-makers.

Pipe kiln: a tubular wrought-iron frame with a handle at the top and feet at each end. Clay 'churchwarden' pipes were placed in the kiln in order to clean them when they had become foul, and the pipe-kiln and its contents were then put into an oven. It is said that in country districts the local baker performed this task.

Pipe rack: a stand for clay pipes. Of the various wooden kinds in use in the 18th cent. one can distinguish (a) the stand of candlestick form with a tiny circular tray on the stem, pierced with holes for holding the pipes, and (b) the wall rack, either an open frame with notched sides so that the pipes could lie across or a board with shelves from which the pipes hung down. In addition to these, metal pipe-kilns (q.v.) were widely used for the purpose from the 17th cent.

Pipe tray: a long and narrow wooden tray with partitions for 'churchwarden' pipes, in use throughout the Georgian period.

Pipkin: small metal earthenware vessel, like a saucepan with spout and turned wooden handle, for warming brandy.

Piqué: tortoiseshell inlaid or overlaid with cut sheet or pinhead in gold or silver. Boxes of all descriptions, fans, bodkin-cases, games counters, *étuis* (q.v.), shuttles and many such small articles of tortoiseshell are found, decorated with gold or silver piqué. The gold points, or *clous d'or*, as they are called, are known as *piqué point*, and the inlaid strips *piqué posé*. Tiny points tracing the design are described as *foules point d'or*.

Piraube, Bertrand: one of the foremost gunmakers at the Court of Louis XIV. He was granted a *logement* in the Galerie du Louvre in 1670 and produced some of the finest presentation firearms for the French king.

Pirlie-pig: earthenware money-box. 'Pig' is a North Country word for an earthen jar: 'pirlie' is a diminutive indicating something of slight value.

'Pisan' armour: a misleading modern term for a type of late 16th-cent. armour, apparently produced chiefly in Milan and Brescia. Its chief characteristic consists of bands of coarsely etched decoration of confused design.

Pistol handle: the characteristic 18th-cent. knife handle was of pistol shape. Porcelain or stoneware were

fashionable materials but silver was the most usual for all except the cheaper grades, which were made of horn or wood.

Planetarium: a representation of the chief celestial bodies, sun, moon, earth and planets, which, when put into action, usually by turning a handle (although some are driven by clocks), shows the relative motion of these bodies. More usually called 'Orreries' after Richard Boyle, 4th Earl of Orrery, in the mistaken belief that the first of these was made for him. The first was made by Tompion and Graham (qq.v.) for Prince Eugene in about 1705.

Planishing: giving a smooth surface to a sheet of metal by hammering with an oval-faced punch, originally called a planishing teast.

Planter jug: see Sailor jug.

Plaquette: plaquettes are found cast in lead and silver as well as in bronze, and were used to decorate household utensils and furniture from the 15th cent. onwards. They have also been collected for their own sakes by connoisseurs since the 16th cent., and formed part of collectors' cabinets, together with medals, intaglios and cameos (q.v.). It is not always easy to distinguish between medals and plaquettes, but basically the medal has an obverse and a reverse and is circular, whereas the plaquette is one-sided and square, oblong or oval. More precisely, the medal is commemorative or historical in character, bearing on its obverse the portrait of a notable personage, usually surrounded by an inscription, while plaquettes are purely decorative in intention, with mythological, historical or religious subjects depicted. Plaquettes belong to the category of reproducible objects, and one may almost speak of different 'states', as in the case of prints. In each reproduction it tends to lose some of its definition, and poorer, often modern, copies show little of the sharpness and individual chasing that characterize the first few to leave the artist's workshop. Plaquettes are more closely connected with painting than with sculpture, and their composition can be related to the various Renaissance (q.v.) schools of painting – and especially to the engravings which gained in popularity during the 16th cent. They were mostly issued from the schools of bronze casters, beginning with Donatello's in the 15th cent.

Plaquettes of religious subjects were made north of the Alps from the 15th cent. onwards, and in the early 16th cent., under Italian influence, secular subjects began to be produced in southern Germany, especially Nuremberg, in the Vischer school and by Peter Flötner, who is not known to have worked in the round at all. Plaquettes never attained the popularity in the Netherlands and in France which they enjoyed in Italy and Germany.

Plaster silhouette: silhouette (q.v.) painted on slabs of plaster, often with beer as a medium. Plaster was at one time a common background, its snowy depth giving the greatest possible contrast and sharpness to the black of the shade or silhouette. Probably the greatest master of this type of silhouette was John Miers (1758–1821).

Plate: the generic term for wrought silver or gold. Later applied by transference to the imitative wares of Sheffield and to electro-plate (q.v.).

Plateau: a flat plinth or stand for a centre-piece (q.v.), usually of silver, with mirror centre. Principally of early 19th-cent. date. Large examples are sometimes many feet in length and consist of numerous sections in order to run the full length of a dining table.

Plated Amberina glass: glass patented in 1886 with pattern-moulded (q.v.) vertical ribs (q.v.) on the surface. It has a creamy opal lining and shades from yellow to red. (See also Amberina.)

Platel, Pierre: (d. 1719), Huguenot silversmith, a freeman of the Gold-

smiths' Company in London in 1699. Paul de Lamerie (q.v.) was apprenticed to him in 1703.

Plate lock: lock in which the working parts are exposed and riveted to a heavy hatchet-shaped plate of wrought iron fixed flat against the door. The iron bolt worked in slides and engaged in a striking plate fitted to the door jamb. The visible working parts might display some decoration. By utilizing only the minimum number of parts, at a time when iron and steel were highly expensive, plate locks were made at comparatively low cost. Antique plate locks are of iron, made close-textured by hammering: the Victorian type have cast or rolled iron plates.

Plate mark: the name given to the indentation made by the edges of the plate on a print. This mark forms the frame of an etching or line engraving (qq.v.) but is rarely visible on woodcuts or lithographs (qq.v.). Impressions of etchings or engravings cut within the plate mark are said to be clipped and are of considerably less value than those on which the mark is to be seen.

Plate-pail: a mahogany container with handle for carrying plates from kitchen to dining-room, often a long journey, in large houses in the 18th cent.; of various shapes, generally circular with one section left open for ease of access.

Plate-warmer: this stood before the fire in kitchen, living-room, or dining-room, to heat the plates preparatory to the serving of a meal. Several types of plate-warmer have been recorded; all date from the 18th and 19th cent., and the surviving examples are not numerous. One variety is in the form of a wrought-iron revolving stand on a tripod base with upright bars to hold the plates in position. Another kind is similar to a Dutch oven (q.v.), and has a handle so that the whole apparatus, complete with warmed plates, might be brought from the fireside to the table. A third type is the cat: an ingenious arrangement of three turned wood or metal rods, arranged cross-wise to form a double-ended tripod that could stand either way up.

Plinth: architecturally, the square base of a column. Also the base or foundation supporting a piece of sculpture, a porcelain figure, a piece of cabinet furniture, etc.

Plique à jour enamel: see Enamel.

Plymouth earthenware: coarse earthenware (brown and yellow) was manufactured here in the 18th cent., but gave way about 1810 to the production of painted or printed cream colour. In 1815 three factories were operating in Plymouth.

The Plymouth Pottery Company founded by William Alsop made common blue transfer-printed white earthenware.

Jewitt gives its mark as 'P. P. Coy. L, Stone China' with the addition of the Royal Arms.

Plymouth porcelain: this, the first English factory to make hard-paste porcelain (q.v.), was established in 1768 by William Cookworthy (q.v.), who in that year patented his formula for the manufacture of hard-paste. He was aided in the founding of the works in Coxside, Plymouth, by a company of Quakers; in 1770 the factory was moved to Bristol, and in 1773 the patent rights were sold to Champion (q.v.) who assumed control of the business. The factory was known as the Bristol China Manufactory (see Bristol porcelain). In 1775, in the face of intense opposition from potters in Staffordshire under Wedgwood's (q.v.) leadership, Champion obtained a modified renewal of the patent, but, crippled financially, was compelled to sell out to a company of potters in Staffordshire in 1781.

Marks:

A number of different marks were used, and some of these were certainly employed after the factory had been moved to Bristol.

$$2\!\!\!\perp$$

Tablewares, figures and statuettes, vases and other ornamental pieces were made at Plymouth. Early porcelain was often decorated in Oriental styles in underglaze (q.v.) blue. Applied decoration in relief was used for shell and rock-work pieces such as salt cellars, small dishes, etc., these proving very popular. Sets of the 'Seasons' and the well-known 'Continents' are typical of the figures produced at Plymouth and later at Bristol.

Much of the early porcelain made at Plymouth is clearly of an experimental nature. Flaws, firecracks and discolorations are common, and a smoky tint affects nearly all the colours used. The glaze is rather thick and dull in appearance. In pieces decorated in underglaze blue the blue is of a greyish tone, often according pleasantly with the body of the ware which is semi-translucent and has a grey, faintly brown tint by transmitted light.

Figures made at an early date at Longton Hall (q.v.) clearly served as models for those made later at Plymouth. The resemblance is so marked that it has been suggested that Cookworthy acquired some of the actual moulds used there when the Longton Hall factory closed down.

Generally there is little originality in forms of decoration, and most designs are derivative, Derby and Worcester (qq.v.) influences being apparent in many cases. Work in the Sèvres (q.v.) style by Soqui (q.v.) is of a higher quality, some of his birds and landscapes being very well executed.

Figures have scrolled, hollow bases, picked out in dull crimson.

Transfer-printing (q.v.) is extremely rare and does not seem to have been used with any success.

Plywood: laminated wood consisting of two or more veneers (q.v.) glued together with the grain running in different directions.

Point d'Angleterre à brides: (*Fr.*) pillow lace (q.v.), variant of point d'Angleterre lace (q.v.), the meshed ground supplemented by *brides picotées* (see Brides and Picot).

Point d'Angleterre lace: this is not an English lace but is a pillow lace (q.v.) made in Brussels. English dealers so named it in 1662 when the import of Flemish lace into England and France was prohibited. It is the loveliest of Brussels laces, distinguished by the raised rib of plaited threads outlining leaves, etc., in a pattern which was loosely woven and edged elsewhere with rows of open stitches. The ground was worked after the pattern and was the Brussels hexagonal mesh, sometimes accompanied by the snowflake ground associated with Valenciennes lace (q.v.).

Point de France lace: a needlepoint lace (q.v.). Some collectors limit the term to French raised bride-linked (see Brides) laces in contrast to grounded needlepoints made in the 18th cent. Designs were more flowing than in the raised Venetian needlepoints (q.v.). The term is more usually accepted in its original usage for the lace made at a number of towns in France where the craft was established in 1665 with state support, under Venetian tutelage, including especially Alençon (q.v.).

Point de Paris lace: pillow lace (q.v.) believed to be the first made in France, but there is no proof that this had any association with a coarse type of lace now sold by that name.

Point lace: all French laces, including pillow laces (q.v.), so that it is impossible to reserve the term for needlepoints (q.v.).

Points d'esprit: (*Fr.*), a term used in lace-making to describe small square dots scattered over a mesh ground, as in Lille lace (q.v.).

Poissardes: (*Fr.*), long earrings fashionable about 1800 in France.

Pole arms: a modern term denoting any type of cutting or thrusting weapon mounted on a long handle. They can be divided into the following classes: (a) thrusting weapons, including the spear in all its forms; the horseman's lance, at first simply a long spear, but later fitted with a large metal guard for the hand (vamplate); the pike, a long spear, often measuring as much as 7 m (22 ft) in the 16th and 17th cent., when it was used by the infantry to form a 'hedge' against cavalry; the partizan, which had a long triangular head, usually with two pointed lugs (q.v.) at the base; (b) percussion weapons, consisting mainly of the various forms of club (including the horseman's mace), the axe and the hammer, the last two often having a sharply pointed fluke at the rear of the head; (c) weapons designed for cutting and for thrusting, including the halberd, which had a flat axe blade balanced by a fluke and a long, sharp spike above; the bill and the gisarme each with a cutting edge curving up to form a short hook, a fluke at the rear and a spike above; and the glaive, with a large cleaver- or scythe-shaped blade.

Pole screen: see Fire screen.

Pomander: from the French *pomme d'ambre*. Small box usually of precious metal for sweet-smelling spices carried to ward off infections. Formed as segmented spheres, skulls, fruits or other fancies. Used up till the 17th cent. Partially superseded by vinaigrettes (q.v.).

Pomona glass: colourless glass patented *c.* 1884–8 with staining or tinting and usually a garland of flowers against an etched (q.v.) ground.

Pompadours: the name given to fine fans dating from the reigns of the first two Georges (1714–60). These were radiant with burnished gilding, set with flashing jewels and glowing with paintings copied from or resembling the works of Boucher and Watteau.

Pontil: see Punty.

Pontil mark: see Punty mark.

Pontipool: the industrial japanners of Birmingham and South Staffordshire found it convenient to market their japanned metal under the name of 'Fancy Pontipool Ware', the spelling serving to distinguish it from the Allgood japanned ware. (See also Pontypool ware and Allgood family.)

Pontypool ware: the name given to japanned ware made by the Allgood family (q.v.) at Pontypool, Monmouthshire. Their many agents sold Allgood productions as 'Pontypool Japan' and their London agent, Edward Binyon, Fenchurch Street, London, advertised in 1783 that his was 'The Original Warehouse for the Real Ponty-pool Japann'd Ware'. The terms 'Pontypool' and 'Pontipool' (q.v.) distinquished japanning on metal from japanned wood and Clay's japanned paper ware dating from 1772. (See Papier mâché.)

The craft of japanning, or lacquering was first practised in England during the reign of Charles II, when the increasing demand for Oriental lacquer stimulated efforts at imitation, at first on wood, then on metal. Japanners on metal are recorded at Bilston in Staffordshire whence the trade spread to Wolverhampton. The Pontypool workshop was founded in 1722 and closed in 1822. (See also Japan work.)

Pope and Devil cup: reversible bell-shaped cup showing the Pope in his triple tiara when held one way up, and the Devil when reversed. Sometimes inscribed 'When Pope absolves, the Devil smiles'. Late 18th cent.

Poppy (popey) head: decorative finial (q.v.) of a bench- or desk-end, as in Medieval ecclesiastical woodwork. Plant and floral forms are numerous; human heads, figures, birds, beasts and other devices are also found.

Porcelain: a word loosely applied in the 17th and 18th cent. to white wares

with Oriental designs attempting to simulate imported Oriental porcelain, such as delftware, stoneware (qq.v.), etc. Imported Chinese red teapots were called red porcelain, a name which clung to Elers-type red teapots (see Elers, David and John Philip) and other wares throughout the 18th cent.

The term has been used more narrowly and correctly since the 18th cent. to describe translucent wares made in emulation of Chinese and Continental porcelain, but only three factories certainly made true (that is hard-paste (q.v.)) porcelain in England, namely Plymouth, Bristol and New Hall (qq.v.).

The fine porcelains of the 18th cent. were soft-paste (q.v.), either glass, or bone, or soapstone (q.v.).

The standard bone china (q.v.), produced since the time of Spode (q.v.), is a hybrid porcelain with heavy percentage of bone ash in the ingredients.

Porcelain transparencies: see Lithophane.

Porphyry ware: a red-stained parian ware (q.v.) said to resemble porphyry.

Porringer: two-handled bowl of pewter (q.v.), silver or Sheffield plate (q.v.) with or without cover for porridge, caudle, posset or other concoctions. Surviving examples date from the first half of the 17th cent. and last into the 19th. Shallow bowls with flat handles commonly called cupping- (q.v.) or bleeding-bowls, were in fact small porringers.

Portable barometer: a type in which the cistern or siphon can be entirely enclosed, and in which the mercury can be plugged in the vertical tube.

Portland House: Wedgwood (q.v.) and Bentley's showroom in Greek Street (No. 12) was given this name. It was opened in June 1774, and the cream-ware service made for the Empress of Russia was placed on exhibition. In 1791 one of the best copies of the Portland vase (q.v.), after having been shown to Queen Charlotte, was placed on view there.

Portland vase: a cameo glass vase traditionally but erroneously stated to have contained the ashes of Alexander Severus and his mother, and to have come from his sepulchre at Monte del Grano: probably made at Alexandria *c.* 50 B.C. Before 1642 it passed into the possession of the Barberini family from whom it was purchased by Sir William Hamilton in 1770, who sold it to the Duchess of Portland. Lent to the British Museum in 1810 but smashed by an 'inebriated neurotic' named Lloyd in 1845 and restored with the aid of Wedgwood's copy. Put up for sale at Christie's 1929 but withdrawn when the bidding reached £29,000. Purchased by the British Museum in 1946.

Josiah Wedgwood (q.v.) copied the Portland Vase 1786–90, his copy being pronounced accurate in effect and detail by Sir Joshua Reynolds P.R.A. The first edition comprised 29 specimens. William Webber was chiefly responsible for the modelling. There were several subsequent editions, the 1839 being notable because the nude figures are 'decently' draped; the Bellows edition was issued for an American firm in 1909; an ordinary jasper (q.v.) Portland Vase has been issued from 1880 onwards. The finest 19th-cent. edition is that undercut and polished by John Northwood of Stourbridge (q.v.) for Wedgwood's in 1877–80, limited to 15 copies, cipher signed N above the Wedgwood impress mark.

Portmanteau: a term introduced about the mid-16th cent., applied to a case specifically for horse travel yet large enough for bulky clothing. In 1611, for instance, Cotgrave noted 'a portmantue with chaine and locke' and in the 1620s the Howard Accounts refer to a leather portmanteau priced 10s 1d. There are numerous references to portmanteau saddles, even to portmanteau horses, in the 17th and 18th cent. Thus the *London Gazette* referred to 'a coloured leather Portmantle Saddle'. Such a saddle, according to Randall Holme, had 'a Cantle behind the seat to keep the Portmantle . . . off the Rider's back'.

Portobello ware: pottery made at Tunstall, Staffordshire, *c.* 1830, in imitation of banded and Pratt ware (q.v.) pottery made at Portobello in Scotland.

Portuguese bulb: a simple, baluster-turned (q.v.) chair leg in the form of an inverted pear, used on late 17th-cent. chairs, when the Restoration fashion for more elaborately turned legs had abated.

Posset pot or **posset-cup:** straight-sided or bell-shaped vessel with multiple loop handles and spouts, generally covered with a slanting or dome-shaped lid, and occasionally 'crowned' with an elaborate knob and series of handles. Used for carrying or drinking posset, made in the 17th and 18th cent. in slipwares, delftware, stoneware, (qq.v.), etc. A favourite inscription on Staffordshire slipware specimens was 'The best is not too good for you'. Two-handled bowls of silver are also known as posset pots. Also called a spout cup and caudle cup (qq.v.). (See also Porringer.)

Posy ring: a ring with a motto engraved on the inside.

Pot: a term used in the 17th cent. apparently to designate any type of open helmet. Modern writers usually confine it to the large, wide-brimmed variety used by 17th-cent. pikemen.

Potato ring: see Dish ring.

Pot belly measure: a Scottish pewter tavern measure with broad belly and narrowing neck.

Pot board: an open shelf or board forming the lower stage of a 17th-cent. court or livery cupboard (qq.v.).

Pot hook (cottrall, jib crook, hanger, tramelle or **hake):** a wrought-iron (q.v.) device that was in use from Medieval times for suspending a pot over the fire. By means of a ratchet it could be adjusted for height. In Scotland the same means was attained by using a chain and hook, known as a 'jumping rope'.

Potiche: large, broad-mouthed Chinese porcelain (q.v.) jar of baluster shape, with cover; favoured from Ming (q.v.) times.

Potichomanie: 19th-cent. French fashion for decorating glass vases to resemble porcelain or pottery (qq.v.).

Pot lace: see Antwerp lace.

Pot lids: decorative earthenware lids covering containers of bear-grease and other toilet preparations and, later, preserves. Over 300 designs produced from the mid-19th cent. in decorated underglaze (q.v.) with polychrome transfer-printed (q.v.) engravings, notably by J. Austin of the firm F. & R. Pratt & Co. (qq.v.).

Potters of Darwen: first British firm successfully to use machinery for producing wallpapers on a commercial scale.

Pottery: opaque fired earthenware.

Pottery moulds: the introduction of porous plaster-of-Paris moulds as a means of making pottery made possible a wide variety of shapes of irregular form and decoration.

Some form of mould had been in use in Staffordshire for a long period, probably 'formers' made of wood, fired clay (pitcher moulds) or alabaster. Metal moulds were used for fine sprig decorations.

The porous plaster mould was adopted *c.* 1745, and the process was to cut a model or block in alabaster, make impressions from it in clay, assemble them and fire them to form 'pitcher' moulds from which working moulds in plaster could be run off as required. Later a model was made in clay, 'blocked and cased' by the mould-maker from which working moulds were prepared.

Many old moulds exist, some dated and inscribed, thus affording valuable evidence of factory or individual style.

Pottle pot: quart pot.

Pounce box or **pot:** baluster or vase-shaped bottle for sprinkling powdered pumice (pounce) on writing paper. Indistinguishable from a sandbox (q.v.).

Pouncing: producing a powdered effect on a metal surface.

Powder blue glaze: a mottled glaze used on Chinese porcelain of the K'ang Hsi (q.v.) period, when it was sometimes enriched with gilded (q.v.) designs (often since restored) or used as a surround for underglaze (q.v.) painting. A rich blue, granulated ground-colour was also used by the Worcester (q.v.) porcelain factory. The effect was achieved by blowing powdered pigment on to the surface of the ware, prepared with a coating of oil.

Powder flask: flask for carrying the black powder used for charging muzzle-loading guns. It was made in a variety of different shapes and was usually fitted with some kind of measuring device. A smaller flask was often carried for the finer powder used in priming. The more elaborate example was customarily made *en suite* (q.v.) with a firearm and was decorated with inlaid bone or silver, corresponding to the decoration on the gun. Powder flasks were also made of metal.

Powell, James & Sons: the only late 19th-cent. company to revive the tradition of hand-blown glass, emphasizing shape rather than decoration. The firm achieved an excellent reputation for diamond-point engraving (q.v.), pure jewel-like colours and for stained glass.

Prairie School: group of designers and decorators, including Frank Lloyd Wright (1867–1959), based in Chicago, who in the 1880s and '90s had a continuing interest in the Arts and Crafts Movement (q.v.).

Pratt ware: earthenwares made at the end of the 18th and beginning of the 19th cent., decorated with a distinctive palette of high temperature colours, including a drab blue, yellow, ochre, dirty orange, dull green, brown, etc. Relief decorations are common. Figures also were decorated in this range of pigments. This type of ware is usually associated with Felix Pratt of Fenton, and the name 'Pratt' is occasionally found on them, but it is unlikely that the earlier pieces were made by Felix Pratt, who was not born until 1780 and died in 1859. William Pratt (1753–99) and his wife Ellen Edwards (1760–1815) who succeeded him, may have been responsible for some of these wares which are, how-ever, known to have been made by potters in other parts of England and Scotland over a long period of time. Pratt ware is particularly associated with pot lids, decorated with poly-chrome printing by the engraver Jesse Austin (q.v.) and also with Greek Revival vases.

Prayer rugs: Oriental rugs, bearing as central feature the 'Mihrab', a design derived from the traditional form of niche or chamber that shows the direction of Mecca in the Muslim mosque.

Preissler, Daniel: see Schwarzlot decoration.

Première partie: (*Fr.*), see Boulle marquetry.

Press cupboards: during the 16th cent. there were several kinds of cup-board. A press cupboard was entirely closed, with small cupboards in the upper stage and a large cupboard below. (See also Court cupboard.)

Pressed glass: glass pressed mechani-cally in moulds. Molten glass is dropped into a patterned mould, a plunger is rammed into the mould, forcing the glass into all parts and impressing the pattern upon it. The plunger has a smooth surface so that the inside of the piece is smooth in contrast to blown moulded glass. The method originated in the United States in about 1827 and is sometimes wrongly known in America as 'Sandwich glass' from the famous factory at Sandwich, Massa-chusetts, where it was first produced on a large scale. By 1828, many

American glasshouses were producing pressed glass which also formed an important part of English production of the second quarter of the cent. and revolutionized the industry in its ability to produce cheap glassware.

Pricket candlestick: the earliest form of candlestick in which the candle was stuck on a metal spike, usually iron, projecting from the wax-pan.

The socket type, in which the candle was held in a cup or socket, did not become usual until the 14th cent., though it was certainly known much earlier.

Pricking: delicate needlepoint engraving used principally for decorating silver with armorials and inscriptions in 16th to 17th cent. and also to a limited extent with naturalistic decoration on a small scale.

Prie Dieu chair: (*Fr.*), a chair with a tall back and low seat intended for prayer.

Prince Hal jug: a variety of toby jug (q.v.), being one of Ralph Wood's later models, dating from *c.* 1775.

Prince's metal: a brass alloy evolved in the 1670s and tinged to the colour of gold. It was named after Prince Rupert (1619–82). The metal was heated until slightly red and laid to pickle in a diluted spirit of vitriol. After removing dirt and scale by washing, it was immersed for a moment in *aquafortis* (nitric acid), dried, and burnished with a blood stone. It does not tarnish.

Printies: circular or oval concavities cut into glass vessels to form a decorative motif. Sometimes they cover the entire surface of the vessel, or two or three rows encircle the body of a decanter, jug, rummer (q.v.) or bowl.

Print rooms: rooms decorated by means of pasting prints on to the wallpaper, framed in paper. This type of mural decoration became fashionable in the Regency period and the Duke of Wellington made his own print room at Stratfield Saye.

Prismatic cutting: a method of cutting glass vessels in deep relief in a pattern of horizontal prisms adapted to curved surfaces. Popular as a means of decorative cutting in the first half of the 19th cent. and sometimes known as step cutting.

Provenance: the ownership pedigree of an object.

Prunts: applied blobs of glass tooled or moulded into various forms and applied to the stem or bowl of a drinking vessel.

Pugin, Augustus Welby: (1812–52), English architect, also a designer of furniture, silver, textiles, stained glass and jewellery. The main instigator of the revival of church embroidery in England, Pugin designed the wallpapers for the new Houses of Parliament and several important English houses of the early Victorian period.

Pulse watch: see Stop watch.

Punch: a die for striking the maker's touch or other identification or decorative designs into metal.

Punch bowl: large circular bowl made in silver, tin-enamelled earthenware, salt-glazed stoneware (q.v.) or porcelain (q.v.), ranging in size from 284 ml (½ pint) to 14 l (12 quarts), used for serving punch. Silver examples are with or without drop-ring handles and were used contemporaneously with Monteiths (q.v.) from the 17th cent. onwards.

Punched work: elementary form of embossing metal, struck with blunt punches grouped to form primitive floral designs, principally used on mid-17th-cent. silver.

Punch kettle: a vessel like a gigantic teapot used *c.* 1750 for blending, carrying and serving hot punch.

Punto in aria embroidery: Italian term meaning stitch in the air, and used to describe a very early form of lace, the cutwork (q.v.) fabric reduced to a strip supporting the needlepoint (q.v.) work. The transformation was complete when the line of fabric was replaced by threads laid over the pattern drawn on parchment.

Punty mark (or **pontil mark**): a scar left on blown glass when the punty (q.v.) is broken off. Generally found on the base of a glass. From about 1760 these marks were usually ground and polished into a smooth depression and this was invariably the case on fine glass from about 1780.

Punty (or **pontil**) **rod:** a long iron rod attached to one end of blown glass to hold the vessel during the finishing processes after removal from the blowpipe.

Puritan furniture: a term sometimes used in America to describe the simple, functional, 17th-cent. New England furniture of the early Puritans (see Pilgrim furniture).

Puritan spoon: a mid-17th-cent. spoon with flat stem, straight top edge and nearly oval bowl, the earliest form of English flat-stemmed spoon.

Purled ornament: all-over diaper moulding with small round or oval compartments found on glass vessels.

Puzzle fans: evolved in the mid-18th cent. by John Cock, London. Instead of two subjects back and front, four pictures were displayed according to the way in which the fan was manipulated. These fans had more blades than was usual as they needed to be strung in such a way that only half of each was visible at one time.

Puzzle jug: a pitcher or jug made from the Middle Ages and particularly in the late 17th and early 18th cent. Made in earthenware, stoneware or delftware (qq.v.) usually with a capacious globular body and pierced, cylindrical neck offering a challenge to the uninitiated drinker: 'From Mother Earth I take my birth/ Am made a joke for man;/ And am here filled with good cheer/ Come taste it if you can', or 'Here gentlemen come try your skill/ I'll hold a wager if you will;/ That you drink not this liquor all/ Without you spill or let some fall'.

The rim of the neck usually consisted of a hollow tube connected with the inside by the hollow tubular handle, and this rim tube generally issued into a number of spouts or apertures, frequently three but sometimes five or even seven. Almost invariably there was a hidden hole underneath the top of the handle. To meet the challenge the drinker had to block all the openings with his finger-tips except the one from which he intended to imbibe the contents, and drain the jug by suction. Commonly made in the 17th and 18th cent., particularly at Liverpool. Prof. Garner points out that the perforations and proportion of neck to body in delftware offers a clue to origin; those made at Liverpool generally being pierced with 4 hearts and ellipses arranged circularly; those of Bristol with intersecting circles; and those of Lambeth with narrow necks.

Pyx: a small vessel, usually a cylindrical silver box, in which the Sacrament is carried to the sick. They were frequently richly decorated. Many Medieval examples survive of Limoges enamel (q.v.).

Quaich or **quaigh:** Scottish drinking bowl, originally of wood in stave formation, later silver-mounted and then entirely of silver or pewter (q.v.). Shallow circular form on rim foot with two or three flat handles or lugs (q.v.). Found from early 17th cent. onwards.

Quail patterns: sometimes called partridge patterns. A pattern used for the decoration of porcelain on the Continent and in England based on the example of Japanese Kakiemon (q.v.) porcelain, incorporating, with foliage and rocks, a pair of quails. In England, used on Bow, Chelsea and Worcester porcelain (qq.v.), on delftware (q.v.) of the 18th cent. and on earthenware of the 20th cent., where it has been adapted as an underglaze transfer-print (qq.v.) in blue.

Quare, Daniel: (1648–1724), London clockmaker, active between 1674 and 1724, who invented repeating watch (q.v.) c. 1680.

Quatrecouleurs: the art of combining various colours of gold. The colour of gold is determined by the nature of the alloy. If copper is added to the pure gold, the result will be a red gold, if silver is added a green gold is obtained, and so on. Many subtle effects are possible as the balance of the alloy is varied.

Quatrefoil knop: a knop or protuberance on the stem of a drinking glass or other glass vessel of short form, pressed into four wings by vertical depressions, the metal being drawn out with pincers.

Queen's Burmese glass: British version of American Burmese glass produced under licence from 1886 by T. Webb & Sons (q.v.).

Queen's pattern: a counterchanging pattern consisting of alternate radiating whirling bands of red-on-white and white-on-blue ornament with gilded (q.v.) embellishments used at the Worcester porcelain (q.v.) factory from c. 1770 onwards, and continued into the Flight and Barr, and Chamberlain periods. Used also to describe 19th-cent. British silver flatware (q.v.) pattern.

Also known as the 'Catherine wheel', 'Whorl', or 'Spiral' pattern.

Queensware: the name given by Josiah Wedgwood (q.v.) in 1765 to his perfected cream-coloured earthenware (q.v.), after he had obtained for it the royal patronage and title 'Potter to the Queen', the Queen being his patroness, Queen Charlotte; subsequently adopted for this staple product of the earthenware industry throughout Staffordshire.

Quilling (or **pinched trailing**): an American term for a ribbon of glass applied decoratively to glassware and pinched into pleats. Found in particular on small bottles made at Nailsea (q.v.) in the 19th cent.

Quillon dagger: a type of dagger with a cruciform hilt.

Quillons: the cross-guard of a sword or dagger.

Quillwork or paper filigree: this is made of paper strips about 3 mm ($\frac{1}{8}$ in) wide, fluted, twisted, or rolled into tight little scrolls which are then arranged in designs closely resembling mosaic work. Coloured paper is used, or white may be painted or gilded at the edge; when gilding is used the effect is that of gold filigree; sometimes motifs are outlined in silver wire, and the work resembles silver filigree. The flutes and scrolls are pasted by one edge to a background of paper, silk or wood, and are combined with other substances to form elaborate designs.

Quilts: coverlets with a layer of wool, flock or down between two pieces of material with lines of stitching, usually back-stitch passing through the three layers. In England, quilting is a traditional craft, and it reached the height of its popularity and excellence in the 17th and 18th cent. During the first half of the 17th cent. quilted doublets and breeches were worn, and during the 18th cent. quilted satin petticoats were fashionable. Quilted bed coverlets were made in great numbers from the late 17th cent. onwards. In addition to the pattern formed by the quilting stitch, which was sometimes purely geometrical, sometimes of elaborate floral arabesques, the quilts were often further ornamented by embroidery in coloured silks. In the late 17th and early 18th cent. coverlets and pillow-cases were often quilted entirely in yellow silk. Others had a small quilted diaper background with floral or Chinoiserie (q.v.) motifs embroidered in coloured silks.

Another type is 'corded' quilting (often known as Italian quilting, although there is no evidence to support an Italian origin). This type

of quilting, employed for decorative rather than utilitarian purposes, was extremely popular in England during the 18th cent. Two layers of material, usually fine white linen, were sewn together in an elaborate design, often of scrolled arabesques (q.v.), worked by means of two parallel rows of stitching about a quarter of an inch apart. A cord was then inserted between the two rows of stitching through small holes cut in the back of the material. Quilting was also practised in most European countries, notably Sicily and Portugal, and in Oriental countries, particularly India and Persia. (See also Patchwork quilts.)

Quizzing fans: an amusing notion dating from the mid-18th cent. These fans were provided with peep-holes covered with transparent material: when open the fan showed a series of perforations around its upper border. Behind such a fan a woman could present a modest pose, yet miss nothing of the risqué plays of the time. In late examples a quizzing glass was fitted above the pivot.

Rabbet or **rebate:** a groove cut lengthwise in a piece of wood into which the edge of a board can fit. In furniture made by a joiner (q.v.), the bottom boards of drawers were nailed to the sides whereas cabinet-makers (q.v.) used the method of fitting bottom boards into a rabbet cut into the drawer sides.

Rack-and-snail striking: a system of clock striking invented in 1676 by Edward Booth or Barlow (1636–1716) which, except for turret clocks, has practically superseded the locking plate in Britain. This type of striking made repeating clocks possible.

Rail: the horizontal section of a framework holding a panel. Joined furniture of the 16th and 17th cent. was constructed on the panel system, involving the use of rails as horizontal members and stiles (q.v.) as vertical members of the framework. (See also Panelled construction.)

Raised work: see Stump work.

Raising: the normal technique of forming a hollow vessel from sheet silver by successive rows of hammering on a wood block, stretching and curving the metal. The silver, hardened by the hammering, is annealed (q.v.)

or softened by repeatedly being raised to red-hot heat as required.

Ramponneau: (*Fr.*), *Tabatière à la ramponneau* indicates a box designed in the form of a barrel.

Ramsey, David: an Edinburgh and London clockmaker and the first Master of the Clockmakers' Company. Active between 1590 and 1655.

Ram's head motif: a decorative form representing a ram's head mask, of Classical derivation and much used by Robert Adam (q.v.), both as an architectural motif and in his designs for furniture and metalwork. With the general adoption of forms and motifs inspired by the Classical revival, the ram's head mask was used on silverware, porcelain, etc.

Randolph, Benjamin: (d. 1792), an American cabinet-maker (q.v.) who shares with Thomas Affleck (q.v.) the reputation of being the leading exponent of the Philadelphia Chippendale school. He owned considerable property and is believed to have had the largest cabinet-making shop in Philadelphia. It has been said that no other American cabinet-maker mastered the true spirit of the Rococo more completely or came closer to the English tradition than Randolph.

Rapier: a sword with a long straight blade, introduced in the 16th cent. It was at first designed for thrusting and cutting, but as the science of fencing developed, emphasis was laid increasingly on the former. It was primarily a civilian weapon and in the 16th and 17th cent. was usually used in conjunction with a dagger or a cloak held in the left hand.

Rasp: a grater. Ivory tobacco-rasps are quite common.

Ratafia glass: a cordial glass of flute form, dating from the second half of the 18th cent.

Rat-tail spoon: the principal form of the late 17th- to early 18th-cent. spoon, distinguished by a tapering rib running down the back of the bowl.

Rattan furniture: chairs with seats and backs, often of elaborate form, made of rattan palm, especially popular in the United States in the late 19th cent.

Rauenstein porcelain: see Limbach porcelain.

Raven, Samuel: a Birmingham decorator of *papier-mâché* (q.v.) snuff-box (q.v.) lids, cigar cases, and card cases from about 1818 until the early 1840s. His pictures were copied from well-known engravings.

Ravenet, Simon-François: (1706–74), French engraver who was a pupil of Jacques-Philippe le Bas. From le Bas he learned the technique of first etching his subject and then afterwards deepening the lines with a graver. This was precisely what was required for perfecting the method of decorating enamels by means of transfer-printing (q.v.) invented by John Brooks at the enamel factory at York House, Battersea (q.v.). Ravenet came to London before 1750 and at once attracted notice. Over forty plates, besides smaller pieces representing cupids, decorative borders, etc. used on Battersea enamels, can be ascribed to Ravenet on the evidence of a peculiarly flowing line and graceful rendering of drapery. The subjects include royal portraits and others of famous contemporary figures, Classical and mythological subjects.

Ravenscroft, George: (1618–81), a glassmaker employed in 1673 by the Glass Sellers' Company to research into an improved means of making glass. It appears that Ravenscroft used ground silica from English flints, replacing the imported Venetian pebbles, and alkali in the form of potash. Early experiments indicated that too great a quantity of potash was included, as the vessels made revealed a fine network of cracks, known as 'crisselling' (q.v.). As a remedy, a proportion of oxide of lead replaced the excessive admixture of alkali. The new material came to be known as 'glass-of-lead' or 'flint glass' (q.v.). It was heavier and more brilliant in light-dispersing qualities than the thin Venetian crystal which had hitherto been made in England or imported from Venice and made possible decoration by means of cutting and engraving which became popular in the 18th cent. Ravenscroft was granted a patent for his invention in 1673 and became official glass-maker to the Glass Sellers' Company in the following year, there being two glasshouses, one at Henley-on-Thames, intended for experiment, and the other in the Savoy in London. The defect causing crisselling had been remedied by 1676, when Ravenscroft arranged with the company that his glasses should bear as his seal a raven's head. Ravenscroft retired in 1678.

Raven's head seal: see Ravenscroft, George.

Reading or cock-fighting chair: combined chair and reading stand dating from the early 18th cent. The reader faced backwards, his arms supported on the continuous yoke rail (q.v.).

Recessed carving: a type of carving on furniture much used by provincial joiners (q.v.) in the 17th cent. in which the background is removed, leaving the pattern raised and exposed. The background was usually stippled or punched to give it an uneven surface and to create a contrast with the plain pattern. This method of decoration is also known as sunk carving.

Recoil escapement: see Anchor escapement.

Red china or **'porcelain':** fine red stoneware of the type introduced into Staffordshire by Elers (q.v.), made from about 1693 until end of 18th cent. A similar body was made by Josiah Wedgwood (q.v.) which he called Rosso Antico, but Wedgwood was aware that it differed little from wares then in current production in Staffordshire. He wrote to Bentley, 3 March 1776, 'I am afraid we shall never be able to make the Rosso Antico otherwise than to put you in mind of a red-Pot-Teapot'. The inspiration came from the unglazed red stoneware body of Yi-hsing (q.v.) teapots which were exported from China with tea after the mid-17th cent.

Redgrave, Richard: (1804–88), English painter and designer, best known for his silver and glass designs for Summerly's Art Manufactures (q.v.). He became director of the South Kensington (later Victoria and Albert) Museum.

Redware: pottery first produced in the late 1600s in the American colonies and continued well into the 19th cent. The clay used was identical to that used in red brick and roof tiles, the colour coming from traces of iron oxide.

Reed & Barton: trading name of a firm in Taunton, Massachusetts, specializing after 1848 in electroplated (q.v.) wares. In the 1890s it started to supply the renewed demand for articles in Sterling (q.v.) silver.

Reed-and-tie moulding: an ornament composed of contiguous parallel convex mouldings bound together by straps simulating ribbons. (See also Reeding and Fluting.)

Reeding: similar to fluting (q.v.) but with the ornament in relief. A decorative motif used by furniture makers and silversmiths as well as architects, derived from the Classical column.

Reed-top writing box: whereas a large desk might open with a solid cylinder lid, a writing box might have the space-saving opening associated with tambour tables. In this the rounded top could be pushed out of sight inside the box, being constructed of lengths of thin moulded beading glued side by side on to a back of strong canvas, pliable enough to move in curved runners.

Refectory table: popular modern term for a long table of the type in use from the Middle Ages until the Restoration.

Reform flasks: brown salt-glazed stoneware (q.v.) spirit flasks made by Doulton (Lambeth), Stephen Green (Lambeth), Oldfield (Chesterfield), and Joseph Thompson (Wooden Box Pottery, Hartshorne), in the form of prominent politicians and royalty, at the time of the Reform Bill, 1832. Personalities portrayed included William IV, Queen Adelaide, Lord Grey, O'Connell, Brougham, Richard Cobden, and Lord John Russell.

DANIEL.O'CONNELL

Regard ring: 19th-cent. ring set with jewels of varying types, whose initial letters spell a word. Fashionable tokens of friendship and sentiment.

Régence style: (*Fr.*), Philippe d'Orléans was Regent during the minority of Louis XV from 1715 to 1723. It was during this period that the Régence style, a transitional phase between Baroque and Rococo (qq.v.), was developed.

Regency style: style of decorative art, the term particularly referring to furniture, in Britain during the regency of George, Prince of Wales (later George IV), from 1811 to 1820. It may also be used to describe pieces of a slightly earlier date. It is associated, in particular, with the work and designs of Thomas Hope (q.v.), who popularized Egyptian ornament in Britain, and a severe form of Neoclassicism (q.v.) inspired by the French Empire style (q.v.).

Regent china: a translucent china body, resembling that of Nantgarw (q.v.) but harder, introduced in 1811 for occasional use during the Regency at Chamberlain's Worcester (q.v.) factory and marked specially:

Chamberlains
Regent China
Worcester
E 155
New Bond Street
London

Reggivaso: (*Ital.*), a vase stand, a purely decorative piece of furniture which enjoyed wide-spread popularity in the 18th cent. *Reggivasi* were made in the form of putti, satyrs, chained negro slaves or blackamoor page-boys and are often minor works of sculpture of great charm. A superb example by Andrea Brustolon (q.v.) in the Palazzo Rezzonico at Venice is made in the form of a group of river gods holding trays for the porcelain vases.

Registration number: from January 1884, protected designs or shapes were given a number which appears on the ware. These numbers were normally prefixed with the abbreviated registry mark (q.v.).

Registry mark: appearing on English earthenwares in two cycles, 1842–67 and 1868–83. A lozenge with code letters and numerals assigned by the Registration of Designs Office.

Regulator: a high-grade long-case clock with compensation pendulum (q.v.) and possibly other refinements, such as roller bearings and jewelling. The hour is frequently read off a disc revolving behind the dial proper and showing through an aperture.

Relief: a design or ornamentation is said to be in relief when it is raised above the surface of the surrounding ground.

Relief decoration on porcelain or pottery: there are various ways of producing relief decoration: by free-hand modelling, free-incising or piercing or, more frequently, by pressing soft clay in plaster moulds; also by impressing the surface of soft clay objects with cut metal stamps. Occasionally separately moulded low reliefs are applied to the surface.

Reliquary: the vessel in which a relic or relics of the saints are kept. Reliquaries have been made in a great variety of patterns, offering the maximum scope for the invention of the goldsmith. Early examples were generally of architectural design, and those in the form of limbs and busts were also made as early as the 11th cent., and held their popularity for some five hundred years. They were frequently enriched with precious stones, which have in some instances (the bust of St Agatha at Catania) been so richly augmented by the offerings of the pious that the original work is now practically obscured.

Remarque proof: a print on which the engraver or etcher has added a little sketch or token in the margin as a sign of state (q.v.). This practice of marking prints was fashionable in the late 19th cent.

Renaissance: a revival in Europe of Classical ideals in literature, painting and architecture, which marked the end of the Middle Ages and the abandonment of Gothic forms. The movement began in Italy in the 15th cent., spreading quickly throughout Western Europe and making itself felt in England by the early 16th cent.

Rent table: table resembling a drum table (q.v.) with a pedestal base and drawers in the frieze (q.v.) marked with letters of the alphabet or days of the week.

Repairer (or **bossierer**): workman responsible for assembling the pottery or porcelain clay impressions of figures from moulds, attaching heads, limbs, etc., and finishing the figure which was usually modelled from a block made by another artist. Incised and impressed marks on figures and groups often refer to these repairers.

Repeat design: a characteristic of most wallpaper designs which enables these to be repeated when the sheets or lengths are placed in juxtaposition. English makers understood this principle as early as the 16th cent., and the idea probably goes back farther than this in textile production.

Repeater: a clock or watch on which the hours, and generally also the quarters, and in rare cases the five minutes and even the minutes, can be made to strike at will by the pulling of a cord, the pressing of a knob, etc. Repeating clocks were common until the end of the first quarter of the 19th cent.; thereafter the repeating mechanism was more usually found in watches.

Repoussé: (*Fr.*), a term used to describe embossed work. It refers to the technique of producing a design in relief on a ductile material, such as silver, copper or iron, by hammering the reverse side. A block of pitch was used to support the metal while it was being hammered. It was often finished with chasing (q.v.).

Réseau: (*Fr.*), see Ground.

Resht patchwork: a type of mosaic patchwork (q.v.) produced at Resht, Persia, during the 18th and 19th cent. for covers and prayer-rugs. The designs are inlaid in coloured felts with outlines and details worked in coloured silks in chain stitch and couched work (q.v.). Inferior examples are often not true patchwork, as the small pieces are applied to the ground and not inlaid. A similar type of work was produced in Ispahan.

Resist printing: (1) an ancient 'dyed' style of printing textiles in which the fabric is printed in the desired design with a substance which protects those areas of the cloth from the action of the dye. The patterns are usually white on a dyed ground, often indigo blue. (2) Pottery was also decorated by a resist process, a method generally used with silver lustre, fashionable in England from 1810–c. 1840. The decoration is painted upon the glazed surface of the ware in a 'resist', covered with metallic solution and fired, the infusible resist portion firing away during the process, leaving a white decoration reserved against a bright metallic background.

Reticella: a type of Italian needle-point lace (q.v.). Many English white-work samplers of the second half of the 17th cent. are of cut- and open-work with designs taken from Italian *reticella*.

Reticulated pattern: a pattern in diamond-like formation or resembling network. Glassware decorated with a moulded pattern of this form is said to be reticulated.

Revere, Paul: (1735–1818), silver-smith of Boston, Massachusetts, trained by his father who was a Huguenot who emigrated from Guernsey. He made copper and brass wares and domestic silver in the Rococo (q.v.) and Neoclassical (q.v.) styles and employed a number of workshop assistants. An American patriot, he took part in the Boston Tea Party in 1773 and in 1775 made his famous ride from Boston to Lexington to warn that the British were on the march.

Revolver: a firearm with a series of revolving chambers which come before the firing mechanism in turn. Early experiments with guns of this type date from the 16th cent., but the first commercially successful revolver was not introduced until 1818. In the 1830s Samuel Colt (q.v.) perfected his version which, with improvements, was manufactured until 1941.

Rhenish stoneware: German salt-glazed stoneware (q.v.), made mainly in Cologne, Siegburg and Raeren, frequently imported into England in the 16th cent., many pieces being mounted with Elizabethan silver or silver-gilt neckbands, covers, handles and footrims.

Rhenish tigerware: mottled brown salt-glazed stoneware (q.v.) made in Germany and imported into England in the 16th cent. German jugs of this material were mounted in England in silver-gilt.

Rhinoceros vase: a large, ungainly, covered porcelain perfume jar sur-mounted by a rhinoceros, made for Earl Fitzwilliam, Marquis of Rocking-ham, at Swinton, c. 1826. It was decorated with scenes from *Don Quixote* and its panels were embroidered with flowers and grapes.

Rhodian ware: see Isnik pottery.

Ribband-back chair: a mahogany chair, the splat carved in the form of knotted ribbons and bows in a manner highly expressive of Rococo (q.v.) taste. Ornament inspired by ribbons had been used on chair backs in France earlier in the 18th cent. Chippendale (q.v.) included designs for 'ribband-back' chairs in *The Gentleman and Cabinet-Maker's Director* which he published in 1754.

Ribbon work: embroidery in fine, narrow silk ribbons often combined with chenille thread and aerophane, a kind of muslin gauze. This type of work originated in the third quarter of the 18th cent. and was popular in both England and France, particularly for dress trimmings, bags and other small articles.

Rib or **diamond moulding:** a pattern consisting of straight or twisted lines forming diamonds or ribs impressed upon the surface of a glass vessel or dish.

Rice-grain decoration: a decoration used on Chinese porcelain in which small perforations in the body are filled with transparent glaze; a technique adopted from Persian pottery, popular during the 18th cent.

Rice, Harris & Sons: English glasshouse operating from Birmingham which, from 1848, made opaline wares,

a wide range of coloured wares and some of the earliest British pressed glass.

Richardson, Benjamin: (1802–87), called the 'father of the Glass Trade', because of the fame of his apprentices, his enthusiastic, wide-ranging patronage and his experimentation in decorative techniques. After managing Thomas Hawkes & Co., he founded his own successful firm Witt & B. & J. Richardson & Co. which by 1851, at the Great Exhibition, recorded 278 items in current production.

Richardson, Henry Hobson: (1836–86), American architect and designer of furniture in an architectural style that owed much to the influence of B. J. Talbert (q.v.) and C. Eastlake (q.v.). His practice was in Boston, Massachusetts.

Ricketts glassworks: wine-bottles with seals are sometimes found bearing the mark shown in Fig. A in raised letters round the base.

Fig. A

The Ricketts family were prominent in the business life of the city of Bristol between 1750 and 1850, and one or another of them was connected with such varied occupations as porter-brewing, tobacco, banking, and the manufacture of glass. Jacob Wilcox Ricketts and his brother, Richard Ricketts, were partners with John Wadham and David Evans, successively, in the Phoenix Glasshouse, Temple Gate, which was renowned for good quality cut glass comparable with that made in London and Stourbridge.

In 1811, Jacob Wilcox Ricketts and his third son, Henry, together with two partners, purchased a glassworks known as the Soapboilers' Glasshouse, in Cheese Lane, St Philip's, Bristol. They continued to make cut glass at the Phoenix factory, and made bottles in their newly acquired premises, both trading under the name of Henry Ricketts and Co. After various changes in the structure of the business, it was closed finally in 1923.

Ridgway earthenware and porcelain: the family of Ridgway had extensive connections in the potteries from the end of the 18th cent. In 1792 Job Ridgway and his brother George acquired the Bell Bank Works at Hanley, Staffordshire, and the partnership continued until 1802, when Job Ridgway established a separate factory at Cauldon Place. Job's two sons, John and William Ridgway, succeeded their uncle at the Bell Bank. In 1830 John Ridgway left to follow his father at the Cauldon works, while his brother William carried on and extended the Bell Bank.

Several other firms came under William Ridgway's, and his son E. J. Ridgway's, ownership, including those formerly owned by George and Thomas Taylor, Elijah Mayer, Palmer and Wilson, Toft and May, and Hicks,

Meigh and Johnson. The whole concern, known as W. Ridgway & Son, was dissolved in 1854, and shortly afterwards the Bell works were purchased by Joseph Clementson.

John Ridgway owned the Cauldron works until 1859; later they were taken over by Brown, Westhead, Moore & Co.

Marks:

Transfer-printed
1814–30

In the various factories owned by the Ridgways all kinds of pottery and porcelain were made. In the time of Job Ridgway, blue-printed wares were produced, and also a type of porcelain akin to Swansea (q.v.). Bone china (q.v.) of excellent quality was made at the Cauldon factory in the first half of the 19th cent.; designs used at the end of this period are very similar to those of Mintons (q.v.) with whom Ridgway's seem to have been in competition.

William Ridgway's son, E. J. Ridgway, is noted for his introduction of jasper (q.v.) wares which were manufactured with considerable success in the early and mid-19th cent. Stoneware (q.v.) articles of excellent design and finish were also made. The Ridgways pioneered several decorative processes, including the application of photography.

Riesener, Jean-Henri: (1734–1806), the most famous *ébéniste* (q.v.) of the 18th cent. in France. He was born at Gladbeck, near Essen, but it is not known when he came to Paris. He entered Oeben's (q.v.) workshop at the Gobelins (q.v.) about 1754, and moved with him to the Arsenal. At Oeben's death he was selected by the widow to take over the workshop, and he married her in 1768, the year when he became a *maître-ébéniste*. In 1769 Riesener completed the great *Bureau du Roi Louis XV*, which his predecessor had left unfinished (see Oeben). In 1774 he succeeded Joubert (q.v.) as *ébéniste du Roi*, and for ten years enjoyed the patronage of the Crown to a hitherto unprecedented degree, as expenditure during that decade was higher than it had ever been.

After 1784 his prosperity began to decline and he was made drastically to reduce his prices by the Treasury. It was at this time that Beneman (q.v.) to a certain extent succeeded him in the favour of the Court. Queen Marie Antoinette, however, seems to have remained faithful to Riesener through- out, for she continued to order furni- ture from him right up to the Revo- lution.

He continued in business during and after the Revolution but never actually reinstated himself. He seems to have retired in 1801.

J·H·RIESENER

Riesener's stamp appears frequently on furniture of all kinds in the Louis XVI period, but it is probable that works bearing Oeben's stamp may also be by him, and made while he was working for Madame Oeben before their marriage.

He was the most versatile, and be- came the most accomplished, *ébéniste* of the time and certainly deserved the success he obtained. His work covers nearly all types of furniture in use, and he specialized in highly elaborate mar- quetry (q.v.), mostly in geometrical designs.

Rigaree trail: a process of glass- blowing in which applied threads of glass are attached to a vessel and melted in to give a more or less smooth surface; such threads can be tooled in parallel vertical lines to form tiny contiguous ribs, which are pro- duced by the edge of a small metal wheel.

Rim lock: the mechanism is entirely closed within a rectangular metal case and attached to the inner surface of a door. In addition to the locking bolt, such a lock might have an independent smaller knob operating a spring catch to prevent the lock from being opened from the outside. Both of these entered the striking plate screwed upon the jamb.

Rising hood long-case clocks: the earliest form of long-case clock with a rising hood, made before the door was introduced in the front. The hood slides up on grooves in the back-board (q.v.) and is held in place by a catch, thus allowing access to the dial. As clocks increased in height, the rising hood became impracticable, and the draw-forward type of door was intro- duced.

Rising sun ornament: a fan-shaped ornament of semi-circular form, carved to suggest the rays of a rising sun, used as a decorative motif on late 18th-cent. American case furniture. The term 'setting sun' is also sometimes used. It was so often the only decoration on New England highboys (q.v.) that its presence generally indicates the New England origin of the piece. James (later President) Madison recalled that when the Constitution of the United States was finally adopted after much contention, Benjamin Franklin pointed to a decoration of this type painted on the back of the chairman's chair and said he had looked at it many times during the sessions 'with- out being able to tell whether it was rising or setting, but now I . . . know that it is a rising . . . sun'. .

Riven wood: this was much used in early strong chests, saving labour although wasting wood, and ensuring enduring work, little subject to warping and splitting that would render a plate chest useless. The tree trunk was split or riven along the natural growth lines of dense, non-cellular tissue radiating from the tree centre. These rays show a relief on old, weathered, riven timber, and probably suggested the early linenfold (q.v.) patterns.

Rivière: a long necklace consisting of gemstones, very often of diamonds, worn in the first quarter of the 19th cent

Robinson & Leadbetter: leading Staffordshire manufacturers of mass-produced parian ware (q.v.) figures and groups in the 1864 to 1924 period.

Rocaille: see Rococo.

Rockingham earthenware and porcelain: the Swinton Old Works or the Rockingham Works was founded at Swinton in Yorkshire about 1745 by Edward Butler. William Malpas made white and brown wares there in 1765 and later, in the early 1780s, Thomas Bingley and Co. made various types of earthenware. From 1785 until 1806 the factory was linked to Leeds, first as Greens, Bingley and Co. (1785–1800) and then as Greens, Hartley & Co. (1800–06). Its wares are probably inseparable from those of Leeds or Staffordshire (qq.v.). In 1806 William Brameld (1772–1813), took over, trading as Brameld & Co. and when he died his three sons continued the factory, producing earthenware of all kinds, including the well-known manganese-brown Rockingham glaze (q.v.) and the equally celebrated Cadogan teapot (q.v.). About 1820 they started to make bone china (q.v.) of the Staffordshire type, got into financial difficulties, and in 1826 became bankrupt. An appeal was made to Earl Fitzwilliam who granted financial resources and the right to use the griffin passant crest as a trade mark. From 1820 until 1842 excellent china was made, usually in a florid, Rococo (q.v.) taste.
Marks:

Painted in red

Impressed

None of the earthenware known to have been made at Rockingham before 1765 has been identified but after that date a brown stoneware (q.v.), often indistinguishable from that made at Nottingham (q.v.), was produced. Wares manufactured in the early years of the Brameld family's ownership are similar to Leeds (q.v.); creamware (q.v.), stonewares including black basaltes (q.v.), marbled and 'tortoise-shell' articles, were all made. From 1820 the characteristic types of Rockingham porcelain were manufactured. Decoration is often extravagant, including much gilding (q.v.) and flowers modelled in full relief. The simpler wares include some biscuit (q.v.) figures and table wares decorated with flowers on a pale green ground. Dinner and dessert services were made to order and in 1832 a most ambitious dinner service was made for William IV, decorated with views of castles and country seats.

Rockingham glaze: a lustrous, purple-brown lead glaze (stained with manganese oxide) made at the Rockingham factory, Swinton, from *c.* 1806, and in Staffordshire.

Rockingham ware: white earthenware covered with Rockingham glaze (q.v.) obtained from an admixture of manganese oxide. Originating in the Rockingham (q.v.) factory, it was subsequently used for a wide range of ornamental wares. Considerably developed in the United States, it became one of the most widely used types of American ceramic. The principal centre was East Liverpool, Ohio. In contrast with English Rockingham, the American ware was usually given a deliberately brown and yellow mottled appearance.

Rococo: the word derives from the French *rocaille*, a term used to describe a style of decorative art first evolved in France about 1700. Shortly before the middle of the 18th cent. the fashion for Rococo was adopted in England and in the United States in the 1760s to '80s. An imaginative and vivacious style, it combined with fantasy and charm motifs based on shell and rock forms, foliage and flowers, 'C' scrolls and tortuous curves. There was a revival of the style on both sides of the Atlantic in the mid-19th cent.

Roemer (or **römer**): a drinking vessel usually of pale green glass, consisting of a hemispherical bowl on a hollow stem with applied prunts (q.v.) and usually a hollow conical foot. The roemer is of German Medieval derivation and became the traditional Rhenish wine glass, which is still made today. The form was adopted both in England and in the Netherlands in the last quarter of the 17th cent.

Roentgen, David: (1743–1807), French cabinet-maker (q.v.). Born near Frankfurt, son of the cabinet-maker Abraham Roentgen, whose workshop at Neuwied on the Rhine he took over in 1772 and developed considerably. He first came to Paris in 1774 and received patronage from Queen Marie Antoinette. This established his reputation which, by the time of his second visit in 1779, had increased considerably, and he established a depot in Paris for selling furniture, as he did also in Berlin and Vienna. He travelled widely and visited Italy, Flanders and Russia, where he sold a great deal of furniture to the Empress Catherine II.

In 1780 he was compelled to become a *maître-ébéniste* in Paris, using the stamp, DAVID, and in 1791 was made Court furnisher to King Frederick William II at Berlin. He was ruined by the Revolution and his depot in Paris was confiscated. His workshop at Neuwied was also overrun by Republican troops. He returned there in 1802, however.

Roentgen specialized in furniture veneered with extremely elaborate pictorial marquetry (q.v.) and fitted with complicated mechanical devices, concealing secret drawers and multiple locks. His furniture was mostly made outside France and is seldom stamped.

Rogin: a Japanese lacquer-work technique, involving the use of powdered silver, burnished, on a lacquer ground.

Rohlfs, Charles: (1853–1936), furniture maker with a workshop employing no more than eight men in Buffalo, New York. His work is highly original, demonstrating the influence of the Arts and Crafts (q.v.) tradition in its construction and of Art Nouveau (q.v.) in its decoration.

Roiro: a Japanese lacquer-work technique. A black lacquer with a high polish. Also called 'mirror black'.

Rolled paper work: decorative treatment of furniture, boxes, etc., consisting of rolled card arranged in patterns. It was especially popular in the early 19th cent.

Rolling pins: the glass rolling pins that have survived are sufficient in number to prove they must have been made in quantity. Popular opinion states that they were made in the Bristol or the Nailsea glassworks (qq.v.), and that they all date from the first years of the 19th cent. or earlier. There is no doubt that a proportion of them actually did come from the West Country, but in the majority of instances it is impossible to say where they were made or at what date. They were normally intended to be sold cheaply at markets and fairs, and others, gilded, enamelled or painted with amorous pledges and biblical quotations, were intended for personal presentation.

There would seem to be little doubt that these articles were designed for use as rolling pins, although it is doubtful if many of them were actually put to use in pastry making. It is much more likely that they were hung on a farmhouse or cottage wall for decoration or as a reminder of the giver.

Roll or **piece of wallpaper:** early paper-hangings consisted of a number of sheets (generally a dozen) joined together end to end. Each sheet was roughly 57 cm (22½ in) wide by 89 cm (35 in) long (double demy), giving a length of about 11 m (12 yds). Today the British Standards Institution length of a piece of wallpaper is 10.5 m (11½ yds).

Roll-top desk: (*Fr. bureau à cylindre*); similar to a cylinder-top desk (q.v.) but the writing table and fittings are enclosed by a curved slatted panel. The French term is the same for both types of desk.

Roman strike: a system of clock striking devised by Joseph Knibb (q.v.) in the latter part of the 17th cent. to reduce the power needed, in spring-driven eight-day and month clocks especially, to drive the striking train. The hours are struck on two different-toned bells, one striking up to III and the other once for V, and twice for X. In clocks so made the IIII is usually marked IV. Sometimes found also in long-case clocks.

Rondel-dagger: a type of dagger with a disc-shaped guard and pommel.

Rookwood Pottery: established in Cincinnati, Ohio, in 1880 by Mrs Maria Longworth Nichols (later Mrs Bellamy Storer). From 1883 to 1913 the pottery was under the management of William Watts Taylor, who took over the ownership in 1889. It was declared bankrupt in 1941. One of the first successful art potteries (q.v.) in the United States, much of its early decoration is characterized by asymmetrical arrangements of flowers in the Japanese manner painted under the glaze (q.v.) in coloured slip (q.v.) on a dark ground. Among its prominent decorators were Albert R. Valentien and Kataso Shirayamadani.

Roycroft shops: a craft community founded by Elbert Hubbard (1865–1915) in 1895 at East Aurora, New York. They made Mission style (q.v.) furniture and traditional and rural pieces of various forms.

Rörstrand pottery: produced at Rörstrand in Sweden at the factory founded in 1726 and still in existence.

Rose, John: (*c.* 1772–1841), founder of the Coalport (q.v.) porcelain fac-

tory. Rose purchased the Caughley (q.v.) factory in 1799, and the moulds and stocks of Swansea and Nantgarw (qq.v.) 1822–3. He was awarded the 'Isis' Gold Medal of the Society of Arts for a leadless felspathic glaze (q.v.) in 1820 which was commemorated by one of the Coalport factory marks. The business was continued after his death by his nephew, William F. Rose (d. 1864).

Rose cutting: a method of cutting gemstones, used from the mid-17th cent., in which the stone has a flat base and is pointed on top, with usually twenty-four facets (q.v.).

Rose du Barry: a popular misnomer for the coloured ground used on Sèvres (q.v.) porcelain and properly known as rose Pompadour (q.v.).

Rose-engine-turning: basketwork patterns produced on pottery and porcelain on the engine-lathe.

Rose Pompadour: a ground colour introduced on Sèvres porcelain (q.v.) in 1757. The claret ground found in Chelsea porcelain (q.v.) is believed to have been an imitation, introduced in 1760. An advertisement of 1768 cited by J. E. Nightingale (*Contributions towards the History of Early English Porcelain from Contemporary Sources*, Salisbury, 1881), mentioning 'Mazareau and Pompadour Sets' probably refers to this colour. Coalport (q.v.) produced a rose Pompadour in the 19th cent.

Rosso Antico: the name given by Josiah Wedgwood (q.v.) to his red stoneware, which was a variation on the 'red porcelain' introduced into Staffordshire by Elers (q.v.): 'We shall never be able to make the Rosso Antico otherwise than to put you in mind of a red-Pot-Teapot.' (Wedgwood to Bentley, 3 March 1776). (*Letters of Wedgwood*, 1903.)

Rotterham & Son: Coventry firm who exhibited the only display of machine-made British watches at the Great Exhibition of 1851.

Roubiliac, Louis-François: (1695–1762), son of a banker in Lyons; studied under the sculptor to the King of Saxony, Balthasar Permoser; returned to France and worked with Nicholas Coustou in Paris; came to England in 1720 and worked here for the rest of his life, leaving only for a brief visit to Rome in 1752. He enjoyed the esteem of Walpole and became the most celebrated sculptor in England, his statue of Handel making him popular. Other and perhaps better works are his George I in Golden Square, and the Nightingale monument in Westminster Abbey.

His connection with the Chelsea porcelain (q.v.) factory has been the subject of considerable speculation. He belonged to the Soho circle of French expatriates, and Nicholas Sprimont (see Chelsea porcelain) was godfather of his daughter. The white royal busts have been attributed to him, as also have three large figures representing the senses of 'Sight', 'Smell' and 'Truth'.

Rouen faience: tin-glazed (q.v.) earthenware made at Rouen. This type of earthenware was made in France as early as the 14th cent., but the technique did not enjoy a wide use until Italian potters migrated to France in the 16th cent. and set up *maiolica* (q.v.) potteries at Rouen and elsewhere. The Rouen potteries achieved fame in the reign of Louis XIV, when faience (q.v.) was produced, decorated in blue or in blue with red or orange, with formal scrollwork designs. 18th-cent. wares have a wider range of colours and show the influence of Chinese *famille verte* (q.v.) porcelain.

Rouen porcelain: Louis Poterat, a faience (q.v.) manufacturer, was granted a monopoly for the making of porcelain (q.v.) in 1673. Few pieces are known. The body is a white vitreous frit (q.v.) porcelain with a yellowish surface, similar to that made somewhat later at St Cloud (q.v.). Porcelain was made only on a very small scale at Rouen and the factory does not appear to have continued after 1700.

Rouge de fer: (*Fr.*), iron-red enamel colour used on Chinese porcelain, particularly in Ming (q.v.) times, while it is also prominent on K'ang Hsi *famille vert* (q.v.) pieces and appears on *famille rose* (q.v.) wares, and as a monochrome glaze from Yung Cheng (q.v.).

Roundabout chair: see Corner chair.

Roundel: circular ornament enclosing sundry formal devices on Medieval and later woodwork; also human heads as in romayne work.

Round-funnel bowl: bowl of a drinking glass in the form of a round funnel, popular in the later 17th cent. Until about 1690 the bowl was long in proportion to the stem but by the early 18th cent. the bowl was less deep.

Round Glass House: the first flint glasshouse to be established in Ireland during the early 1690s by Captain Philip Roche. It continued to operate until 1755. The Round House appears to have been a highly flourishing business until the export of glass from Ireland was prohibited under the Excise Act of 1745. This prohibition was directly responsible for the glasshouse closing down ten years later and from then until 1764 no fine flint glass appears to have been made in Ireland. At this time an already existing bottle-house at Marlborough Green, Dublin, was enlarged to produce flint glass. When, in 1780, import restrictions were removed, several well-equipped glasshouses were established in Ireland, notably at Waterford, Belfast, Dublin and Cork. (See also Waterford glass and Cork Glasshouse.)

Roux, Alexander: (d. 1881), New York furniture maker, born in France. From 1847 to 1848 he worked in partnership with his brother, Frederick. His firm continued until 1898, producing pieces in the 19th-cent. Revival styles.

Royal clock pendulum: see Seconds clock pendulum.

'Ruby-back' decoration: see *Famille rose.*

Rummer: a short-stemmed drinking glass with capacious thinly blown ovoid bowl and small foot, popular in the late 18th and early 19th cent. Later examples are of heavier metal (q.v.) and stand on a square base. They were used in particular for hot toddy which was a fashionable drink in the Regency.

Rundell, Bridge & Rundell: London firm of silversmiths and jewellers between 1805 and 1842. Royal goldsmiths to George III, to the Prince Regent and later to him as George IV. Designers employed by them include J. Flaxman (q.v.) and A. W. N. Pugin (q.v.), and Paul Storr (q.v.) also worked for them. Throughout the early part of the 19th cent. they were arbiters of taste and had representatives in many European capitals.

Runner: alternative term, used in America, for the rocker of a rocking chair.

Ryijy rugs: Finnish rugs made in the old Norse tradition of knotted pile technique, which may go back to the Danish Bronze Age quite independently of Near Eastern influence. Although derived from Norway and Sweden, in the 16th cent. Finnish pile weaving already enjoyed a special reputation. Made primarily for bed coverings, sleigh rugs, or horse cloths, they have a very long knotted pile, but the ground texture of wool or linen is not thick and there are usually ten to twenty shoots of weft between the rows of knots. The knotting technique is also curious and varied. Made on a narrow loom, two widths were joined together, but a wide loom was also used. Patterns vary from plain-colour weavings and geometric motives to simple floral patterns. It was customary for a girl to make a rug for her dowry and many such pieces are dated, though few after 1860. The making of these exceptionally attractive rugs has been revived in the present cent.

Sabeji: (*Japanese* = rust ground), Japanese lacquer-work technique intended to produce a surface in imitation of old iron, etc.

Sabre: a heavy, curved, single-edged sword used chiefly by cavalry from the late 16th cent. onwards.

Sabre leg: a term used to describe a sharply curving chair or settee leg of rectangular section in the Classical style which prevailed in the late 18th and early 19th cent. Also called a scimitar or Waterloo leg.

Saddle seat: some late 18th-cent. chairs have a gently curving seat sloping down in the centre which is described colloquially as a saddle seat. A slightly different form is found on Windsor chairs (q.v.) where the centre of the wooden seat is shaped to resemble a saddle.

Sadler & Green: John Sadler (1720–89, son of Adam Sadler, a printer in New Market, Liverpool) invented a process by means of which pottery, already glazed (q.v.), could be decorated with designs first engraved in copper plates, thence transferred to paper and finally on to the wares. The colours were then fired in a muffle kiln (q.v.) for fixing. This method of transfer-printing (q.v.) made possible the accurate reproduction of complex designs. Guy Green was Sadler's partner from 1763 in an extensive business carried on in Harrington Street from the middle of the 18th cent.

It is said that the process was actually invented by Sadler about 1750; not until 1756 was a form of patent contemplated (but never finalized as Sadler and Green decided to keep the invention secret).

The firm is believed to have manufactured pottery, but its wares have not been identified with certainty. They decorated large quantities of Staffordshire and Liverpool earthenware (q.v.); Wedgwood's Queen's ware (qq.v.) was sent regularly to them for printing. They also printed porcelain for Longton Hall (q.v.). Oriental patterns, portraits, illustrations from Aesop, tiles showing figures of actors and actresses – all these were printed at the factory. Much of the earlier work was in black, or black and red; later brick red was also used.

Sadler retired about 1770, and Green continued the business until 1799. Marks:

SADLER   1756
SADLER & GREEN

Sadware: pewterers' term for flatware, namely plates, dishes and chargers as opposed to hollow-ware (q.v.).

Sailor jug: a variety of toby jug (q.v.) representing a Jack Tar of the period seated on a sea chest with the usual jug, glass and pipe, and on some models, an anchor at his feet.

St Cloud porcelain: faience (q.v.) had been made at St Cloud, near Versailles, before the 1670s, by Pierre Chicanneau, who is thought to have invented a type of soft-paste porcelain (q.v.). Little is known of the discovery but the porcelain factory was said to be safely established by 1700, the early wares being of excellent quality with a clear, warm glaze. Oriental shapes were eagerly copied and many pieces were decorated in the Kakiemon style (q.v.). The factory closed in 1773.

St Louis glassworks: the St Louis glassworks in France was founded in the second half of the 18th cent. and became a close competitor of the Baccarat (q.v.) factory. The first dated paperweights (q.v.) were made at the St Louis works in 1845. They were of *millefiori* (q.v.) pattern. Paperweights are known with the letters 'SL'; sometimes with the 'S' reversed.

St Petersburg porcelain: St Petersburg was the Russian Imperial factory, and although experiments appear to have been undertaken earlier in the cent., no examples of porcelain (q.v.) made before 1762 exist.

Salamander: a bar of wrought iron with a thick round or oblong piece at one end; somewhat like a long-handled shovel in appearance. The larger end was heated until it became red hot and then held near bread, cake, etc., in order to brown it.

Salem rocker: a type of rocking chair made at Salem, Massachusetts, in the early 19th cent. It is similar to the Boston rocker (q.v.) but with a lower back.

Salem secretary: an American Classical-style (q.v.) bureau with a china cabinet as the upper part. There is generally a double-doored centre part with a drawer that pulls out to serve as desk and flanking single-door sections.

Salem snowflake: an American term for a six-pointed punched decoration resembling a star or a snowflake found as background carving on Salem furniture.

Sallet: the characteristic helmet of the 15th cent., usually worn with a deep chin-piece (bevor). Its form generally follows that of the modern sou'wester, although it comes well down over the face, either having a movable visor, or a vision slit in its forward edge. The German type usually has a long, graceful, pointed tail, often laminated. The barbute (q.v.) is one of the forms of this helmet.

Salor rugs: Turkestan rugs similar in texture to Bokhara rugs (q.v.), but the octagonal gule (see Turkoman rugs) is more pronounced and the red is usually slightly brighter than in the Tekke.

Salt-glazed stoneware: stoneware in which the glaze is formed by throwing salt into the kiln when it reaches the maximum temperature of 1200–1300° C. The salt decomposes, forming sodium oxide and hydrochloric acid, the former combining with the alumina and silica of the surface of the wares to form a thin coating of glaze.

Chief centres of salt-glazed stoneware manufacture were Fulham and Lambeth, Nottingham and Staffordshire. Gradually superseded by creamware (q.v.).

Salt kit: dome-topped ovoid jar surmounted by a knob and loop handle with a wide circular aperture at one side; used for storing salt, etc.

Salver: a flat, circular plate for presenting other vessels. Early examples of silver have a central spreading foot and are often erroneously called tazzas (q.v.). From about 1725 salvers were supported on small feet. Oval and polygonal forms are also found, with chased or plain centres. Early pieces have plain moulded borders, followed by shell and scroll, pierced, beaded or gadrooned patterns (qq.v.).

Samarkand rugs: see Chinese Turkestan rugs.

Samenuri: Japanese term to describe the decorative use on inro (q.v.), etc., of fish-skin applied to the object; comparable to shagreen (q.v.).

Sampler: an embroidered panel originally intended as a reference sheet of stitches and patterns and later as an exercise for a beginner. The earliest surviving English samplers date from the first half of the 17th cent. and are worked on loosely woven linen in coloured silks and metal thread. They are generally shorter than those of the second half of the cent. Geometrical designs were used, together with animals, birds and floral motifs. In the second half of the cent., the samplers are long and narrow, on finer linen, and the patterns formally arranged in horizontal rows, worked in pale-coloured silks. Another common type is the white-work sampler of cut- (q.v.) and open-work. By the 18th cent. the sampler had become a child's exercise. They are generally squarer in shape and are usually signed and dated. The alphabet, texts and mottoes are commonly included and the colours are generally brighter.

Samson porcelain: this Paris porcelain factory is well known for clever copies of Meissen (q.v.) figures and old armorial Chinese porcelain, which have been made there for more than a cent. The coats of arms are often those of Great Britain or of France, or of some famous person. Examined closely, these copies should not deceive the collector. Samson's productions sometimes bear a simulated Chinese 'seal' mark or a disguised 'S' beneath the base in red. The factory specialized in reproductions of old porcelain of almost every kind.

Sand blast: a method of obtaining a matt finish on glass or metal by directing a jet of sand by means of compressed air or steam.

Sandbox: baluster or vase-shaped pot used for sprinkling sand on wet ink. Found as part of inkstands or separately (see also Pouncebox).

Sand casting: method of hollow casting, until the 1880s more popular than the cire perdue (q.v.) process for the casting of metalwork. A plaster cast is first made from the original clay or wax model and from this are made negative moulds of manageable sections in a mixture of sand and clay. The two sides of each section are then packed tightly into frames which exactly fit together. Into the empty space is inserted an iron rod and round this more of the sand and clay mixture. This new model is then removed and a layer equivalent to the intended thickness of the metal cast scraped away to form the core of the mould. The molten metal is poured into the space between the sand core and the sand mould. With the sand-casting method evidence of the joins, often accomplished by means of a system of flanges with corresponding grooves firmly united by screws, must be removed by careful chasing (q.v.).

Sand-dredger: see Sandbox.

Sanderson, Arthur, & Sons: a wallpaper manufacturing firm first established in 1860, the firm moved to Berners Street in the West End of London in 1864, where it still is.

Sand glass (or **hour glass**): an early form of measuring time by the period required for a given quantity of fine sand to pass from one bulb of the glass to the other, through a fine neck. Often found in sets of four, the glasses recording the four quarters of the hour. In genuine early examples the two bowls are separate and joined by an applied band. Invention attributed to 8th-cent. monk at Chartres in France.

Sand-grain aquatint: a sand-grain aquatint is obtained from a plate which has been pulled through the press with a piece of sand paper to roughen its surface.

Sang-de-boeuf glaze: see Copper-red porcelain glazes.

Saruk, Sarug, or **Sarouk carpets:** these Persian carpets woven in Saruk from the mid-19th cent. follow closely the tradition of the Keshan carpets (q.v.), often using the Herat (q.v.) motifs and medallion designs. The construction is sturdy, closely knotted deep pile. Knot: Sehna (q.v.).

Saryk rugs: Turkestan rugs, generally not so fine in texture as Bokhara rugs (q.v.), but bearing a similar design.
These Bokhara types are woven as prayer rugs and also as fine camel bags.

Satin glass: generic term for acid-finished coloured wares having a coloured matt outer layer and, usually, an opal lining.

Satsuma ware: pottery made at Satsuma, on the island of Kyushu, Japan. The wares date back to the early part of the 17th cent. Late 18th-cent. Satsuma includes cream-coloured wares (q.v.) decorated with enamel colours and gilding (q.v.) giving brocade effect. Much was produced for export in the 19th cent., very elaborately decorated.

Sauce boat: silver, Sheffield plate (q.v.) or ceramic container with a boat-shaped body. Early examples often have two spouts and an arch handle or two loop handles.

Sautoir: a long gold necklace often consisting of linked chains set with semi-precious stones or plaques of enamelled gold, and sometimes ending in two tassels. Fashionable in the 1890s.

Savery, William: (1721–87), renowned cabinet-maker of Philadelphia, whose work ranged from simple rush-bottom chairs to elegantly carved highboys (q.v.) in the Chippendale (q.v.) manner.

Savona maiolica: tin-glazed earthenware (q.v.) made in the 17th and 18th cent. at Savona, Italy. 17th-cent. wares were largely decorated in blue-and-white which had become the contemporary fashion, reflecting the interest in Chinese blue-and-white porcelain (q.v.). Later painting was generally in polychrome.

Savonnerie carpets: knotted pile carpets in the Turkish manner were first successfully made in France by Pierre Dupont, whom Henry IV installed in the Louvre in 1606. In

1627 the old soap works on the Quai de Chaillot, called the Savonnerie, were acquired and Dupont's partner, Simon Lourdet, began work there with orphan children as apprentices. The Louvre and Savonnerie workshops flourished, particularly under Louis XIV. Pierre Dupont died in 1644 (he wrote a treatise on carpet-making, *La Stromatourgie*) and was succeeded by his son, who removed to the Savonnerie in 1672. During the 18th cent. work continued steadily at the Savonnerie, although many of the workmen emigrated. Not till 1768 were Savonnerie carpets available to private individuals, but prices were very high and few pieces sold.

Under Napoleon the looms were kept busy. The Savonnerie was amalgamated with the Gobelins (q.v.) in 1825, where some looms are still at work. It was the Savonnerie which set the standard for European hand-knotted carpets and created a style which was copied far afield. The description 'Savonnerie carpet' has been widely applied to similar products from other European factories.

Sawbuck table: an American table with an X-shaped frame, either plain or scrolled. Often found in rural New England; Pennsylvania German examples are common.

Scagliola: (*It.*) a technique used for the imitation of marble and especially of Florentine mosaic. The term *scagliola* derives from the name of the special plaster or gesso (q.v.), made of pulverized selenite, which is of extremely fine quality, and takes a very high polish. Two processes were developed for the imitation of Florentine mosiac. The first consisted in painting on the wet gesso ground, fixing the colours by heat and then polishing the surface until it resembled a mosaic of *pietre dure* (q.v.). The second consisted in inlaying coloured plasters in the surface of the *scagliola* panel. This latter process was first developed in Northern Italy during the 16th cent. 'and reached its apogee at Florence during the mid-18th cent.

Scale ground (or **scale pattern**): a distinctive Worcester porcelain (q.v.) decoration, sometimes referred to as 'fish-scale' design, but possibly derived from Meissen (q.v.) 'Mosaik' border. Used at Worcester as early as 1761 in pink, and in 1763 in blue. The Chelsea (q.v.) *Catalogue* 1756 frequently cites wares decorated with 'Mosaic Border'. The motif was used on furniture and silver in the first half of the 18th cent., also for frets on clock cases.

Scalloping: a rim outline formed by a series of semi-circles. Sweetmeat glasses of mid-18th-cent. date were cut round the rim in this manner and were described in contemporary references as 'scaloped' and 'corner'd trim'.

Sceaux porcelain: a factory at Sceaux (Seine) was founded about 1735 but production was very limited in the early years on account of the monopoly held by the royal factory of Sèvres (q.v.). In 1775 the Duc de Penthièvre, High Admiral of France, became the patron of the factory and porcelain was produced with greater freedom – by now in the Louis Seize style. The factory closed in 1794. Its output closely resembles that of Mennecy (q.v.). Rare pieces bear an anchor mark.

Scenic wallpapers: exemplified in their most attractive form by the French panoramic types sometimes known as paysage or landscape papers. Among the first of these to be produced was *Vues de Suisse*, by Jean Zuber, in 1804.

Schaper (or **Schapper**), **Johann:** (1621–70), a German painter of stained window-glass who worked at Nuremberg and finding insufficient opportunity for decorating window glass, turned his attention to the decoration of pottery and glass vessels. He painted mainly in black, known as *Schwarzlot* (q.v.), sometimes using touches of red and gold. Glass beakers and goblets were painted in a similar manner by his followers.

Schiavona: a basket-hilted sword with a straight, two-edged blade, used during the late 17th cent. by the Slavonic troops (*schiavoni*) in the employ of Venice. It is often erroneously described as the prototype of the Scottish basket-hilted broadsword.

Schmelzglas: (*Ger.*), see Agate glass.

Schwarzlot: (*Ger.*), black monochrome decoration, sometimes heightened with iron-red or gold. This technique, originating with Dutch glass-decorators and Nuremberg glass and faience (q.v.) painters, was probably first applied to porcelain (q.v.) by Daniel Preissler (1636–1733), of Bohemia, whence it became characteristic for the decoration of Du Paquier porcelain, executed by Jacobus Helchis and others. (See Vienna porcelain).

'Scimitar' blade: 18th-cent. knife blades were frequently curved in a so-called 'scimitar' form, both the knife and the fork being mounted on 'pistol' handles (q.v.).

Scissor-work silhouette: silhouettes cut freehand from paper. Although this technique is not capable of giving such great refinements of finish as any of the painting methods employed, it is nevertheless capable of giving very striking effects of a different kind. Its most notable quality is the uncompromising sharpness given to the outlines of its subjects. It is possible for a cutter, by holding several thicknesses of paper together, to cut as many duplicates at the same time, thus giving several 'originals'. The most prolific cutter of all was A. Edouart. Other noteworthy cutters

were Francis Torond, 'Master' William James Hubard (1807–62), who achieved fame as a prodigy, and the ill-fated Major John André (1751–80), who was hanged by the Americans as a spy in the Civil War. One method of cutting was to cut out the portrait as a hollow from a piece of white paper and then mount it over a piece of black paper or material.

Sconce: a general name for a wall-light consisting of a back-plate and either a tray or branched candle-holders. Metal seems to have been the chief material from later Medieval times until the end of the 17th cent. when looking-glass became fashionable for back-plates. The use of looking-glass meant that sconces tended to follow the same decorative trends as contemporary mirrors but metal back-plates continued to be made and for a period after 1725 there was a preference for carved and gilt wood and gesso-work, often without looking-glass. About 1750 sconces provided some of the freest interpretations of the asymmetrical Rococo, either with looking-glass in a scrolled frame or in carved and gilt wood only; Chinese features were often blended with the Rococo (q.v.). In contrast, the sconces of the Adam (q.v.) period had delicate Classical (q.v.) ornament in gilt wood or in composition, built up round a wire frame. Cut-glass sconces were in vogue at the end of the 18th cent.

Scoop pattern: popular term for a band or other disposition of fluted ornament, gouged in the wood, the flute having a rounded top and sometimes a base. A motif of Renaissance origin, its use was widespread (see also Fluting).

Scorper: small chisel for engraving silver with blades of various shapes.

Scotch carpets: double-cloth or ply weavings for the floor, also known as Kidderminster (q.v.) or Ingrain.

Scotch pebble jewellery: made in Scotland of local stones and set in silver or gold mounts using pitch or shellac. The most popular designs were brooches made in the shape of thistles, shields, hoofs, buckles and crests.

Scotia moulding: concave moulding of half round section, being the reverse of an astragal (q.v.).

Scott, Isaac E.: (1845–1920), American furniture maker, born in Philadelphia but working in Chicago by 1873. He later worked in New York and Boston. His finely made pieces, often with carving and inlaid decoration, generally reflect the influence of B. J. Talbert (q.v.).

Scratch-blue ware: a class of white salt-glazed stoneware (q.v.) decorated with floral, bird or other ornament and inscriptions incised upon the wares in the unfired 'green state'; into which a mixture of clay and cobalt (the exact proportions of which were determined by experiments made by Gordon Forsyth *c.* 1922), was rubbed. Specimens dating from 1724–76 are recorded. The majority of the dated pieces were made from 1745–55, many by Enoch Booth (fl. mid-18th cent.) who was a master potter at Tunstall, Staffordshire.

Scratch-brown ware: a type of salt-glazed stoneware (q.v.) decorated with incisions into which brown pigment or clay was introduced. Specimens dated 1723–4. Used on settles of 'Pew' Groups (q.v.) *c.* 1730–40. Superseded by scratch-blue ware (q.v.).

Scratch carving: a cheap method of carving used on 16th- and 17th-cent. joined furniture in which the design is formed by a single outline scratched on the surface of the wood. Also known as incise carving. Chip and recessed carving (qq.v.) were other contemporary methods of carving on furniture.

Scratch-cross family: a group of porcelain wares, marked with an incised cross or one or two knife incisions on the inner surface of the footring, including pear-shaped jugs and cylindrical mugs, regarded by Bernard Rackham as indications of an experimental early Worcester paste (*Catalogue, Herbert Allen Collection of English Porcelain*, 1923). George Savage says they are probably workmen's marks and states that they also occur on 'indubitable Bow mugs' (*18th century English Porcelain*, 1952). F. A. Barrett records them as occurring possibly on Liverpool and Bristol porcelain (qq.v.) also (*Worcester Porcelain*, 1953).

Screen writing tables: late 18th-cent. devices by Gillow and others with adjustable screens of pleated silk.

Scrimshaw: objects fashioned from whales' teeth or whalebone by seamen. They are often etched with decoration of a patriotic, commemorative or dedicatory nature. Scrimshaw includes items that were for immediate use on board, such as busks and bodkins, as well as small decorative objects.

Scriptor: see Scrutoire.

Scroll-back chair: chair back curving backwards in a scroll at the top.

Scroll foot: a fashionable terminal to a chair leg in the mid-18th cent., in which the foot is in the form of a carved scroll. Designs for chairs with scroll feet were included in the third edition of Chippendale's (q.v.) *Director* where they were described as 'French' chairs. Also known as a knurl foot.

Scroll salt (or **spool salt**): a form of salt cellar popular in Lambeth delft-ware (q.v.) of the 17th cent. based upon a silver proto-type. F. H. Garner says the three projecting arms were used 'to support a napkin'. Penzer (discussing silver) says the arms were used to 'provide a stand for a flat porcelain fruit bowl'.

Scrutoire or **escritoire:** an early writing cabinet consisting of an upper part of drawers and pigeon holes, enclosed by a let-down front which provided a writing surface when lowered, and a lower part formed by either a chest of drawers or a stand with legs and stretchers. This type of writing cabinet, also known as a scriptor, was made in the late 17th cent., usually of walnut. The disadvantage of having to remove the writing materials before the front could be closed led to the introduction of the bureau writing cabinet or bureau bookcase (q.v.), as it is now termed. This had a shallow cupboard enclosed by two doors for the upper stage and a bureau (q.v.) for the lower. The bureau bookcase became fashionable during the reign of William III and has never lost its popularity.

Sculpture d'appartement: (*Fr.*) a term often applied to the pairs, or groups, of figures, usually rather larger than small bronzes and made for the decoration of the great French *salons* and galleries of the time of Louis XIV. They were normally enriched by much gilding and the use of coloured marbles.

Sealed glasses: George Ravenscroft (q.v.) who invented a new type of flint glass in 1673, obtained permission from the Glass Sellers' Company in 1676 to mark his vessels with a seal bearing his device, a raven's head. Shortly afterwards other glasshouses also began using seals on their glasses and this practice seems to have been common until about 1684, even on glasses containing no lead.

Seal-top spoon: the most common surviving form of early spoon with flat seal-like finial placed on a short turned baluster of oval, circular or polygonal section, and with hexagonal stem. Examples range from the 15th to the late 17th cent.

Seat rails: the horizontal members framing the seat of a chair.

Seaweed marquetry: a form of marquetry (q.v.) employing a complicated foliate design resembling flowing sprays of seaweed. This type of marquetry was used particularly on English and Dutch clock cases but also on cabinets and table tops about 1700.

Seconds clock pendulum: a type of pendulum 99.4 cm (39.14 in) in length. Those of longer length were made practical by the invention of the anchor escapement (q.v.). The vastly improved timekeeping resulting from the adoption of the seconds pendulum and the anchor escapement in the early 1760s caused it to be called the Royal pendulum.

Secretaire bookcase: a piece of furniture that came into use in the mid-18th cent. It consists of an upper stage with shelves, usually with glazed doors, and below a desk closed by a drop front which falls down to reveal a writing table and small drawers. The drop front is usually supported in its horizontal position by counterweights within the carcase (q.v.), but occasionally by struts. Beneath is a cupboard with shelves or long drawers.

Secretary: a modern term used in America for an enclosed writing desk with a cabinet section above that can be used for the storage of books or china (See Bureau bookcase.)

Sedan clock: a large-dialled travelling watch some 10 to 15 cm (4 to 6 in) in diameter, with bow for hanging in a sedan chair or couch c. 1750–c. 1800. Usually has a small watch type of movement behind the much larger dial and a wooden or metal case.

Sedding, John Dando: (1838–91) English architect of silver, embroidery and wallpaper, who was among the first to join the Art Workers' Guild (q.v.).

Seddon, John Pollard: (1827–1906), English architect and designer of furniture and ceramics. His most famous piece was designed for Morris, Marshall, Faulkner & Co. and had painted decoration by William Morris (q.v.), Sir E. Burne-Jones (q.v.) and others depicting the honeymoon of King René.

Seeds: a term used to describe the minute air bubbles sometimes found in glass, indicating that the glasshouse could not raise the furnace temperature high enough to eliminate all air bubbles trapped among the raw materials.

Sehna knot: a knot used in Persian carpets from Sehna, Ispahan, Tabriz (also the Ghiordes knot), Saruk, Serebend, Feraghan, Kerman, Shiraz and Herat (qq.v.).

Sehna or **Sennah rugs:** the Sehna knot (q.v.), generally described as Persian, is named after this weave. Finely woven Persian rugs in small Herat (q.v.) and cone designs, although lighter in colouring and general effect. These rugs are of real merit and can be distinguished by the very short upstanding pile. Main production was prayer rugs but kelims were also made.

Self-winding watch: see Automatic winding watch.

Semi-china, semi-porcelain: durable porcellaneous earthenware: stone china (q.v.).

Sepia aquatint: an aquatint (q.v.) printed in brownish ink.

Serebend rugs: Persian rugs bearing a cone design usually on red or blue field, the border following Herat (q.v.) influence; the sehna knot (q.v.) is used. Fine examples are known as Mir.

Serpentine front: cabinet furniture, such as sideboards or chests of drawers, of the second half of the 18th cent., was sometimes constructed with the front of undulating form, consisting of a convex, flanked by two concave curves.

Serre-papier (Fr.), see Cartonnier.

Settee: a seat for two or more with back and arms, introduced in the late 17th cent. Upholstered or caned, they sometimes have the appearance of individual seats joined together.

Settle: long, backed seat with boxed base, or on legs, and at each end sidepieces or arms. Fixed or movable, the settle represents a stage preceding the settee (q.v.), a derivative of the chair. Some quite late settles have one end scrolled like a sofa-head. Some, mostly country-made, settles have a storage press in the back, such being loosely known as a bacon cupboard.

Sévigné bow: a brooch in the form of a bow, worn in front of the bodice, popular in the 18th cent. Sometimes several bows of graduated size were worn on the corsage, in which case they were known as Brandenbourgs (q.v.).

Sèvres porcelain: soft-paste porcelain (q.v.) was first made in 1738 at a factory at Vincennes, installed in an abandoned royal palace. In 1756, the factory was transferred to Sèvres where it flourishes to this day. A monopoly, protecting the factory from competition, allowed Vincennes exclusive rights in the making of porcelain and in decorating it with figure subjects and gilding. This monopoly forbade the engagement of Vincennes workmen elsewhere and provided for the punishment of deserters. As further protection, a factory mark, consisting of the royal cypher, two crossed 'Ls', was introduced in 1753 and a date letter (q.v.) added at the same time. Thereafter the name *Manufacture Royale de Porcelaine*, was assumed, well before the time (1759) when the King finally bought the concern.

A new hard-paste porcelain (q.v.), made concurrently with soft-paste, was made from 1769, marked with a crowned version of the crossed 'Ls' and named *Porcelaine Royale* to distinguish it from the *Porcelaine de France*.

The earliest Vincennes, unmarked as yet, includes jardinières (q.v.), jugs, ice-pails and trays of simple shape. Among the factory's first achievements are decorations in blue monochrome with flesh tones added, and the earliest of the many famous ground colours, a dark and sometimes mottled *gros bleu*. Occasionally gold decoration is used alone, but more frequently in combination with *gros bleu* grounds and reserved panels, which are painted with figures and birds in landscapes or with silhouetted birds among blossoms. As yet, there are few figures, but the modelling of naturalistic flowers proved to be the factory's greatest success. Biscuit (q.v.) porcelain, as a medium for figure modelling, was first men-

tioned in 1753, and soon began to displace glazed and coloured figures. The influence of Boucher upon early biscuit groups of children and pastorals is felt strongly until the sculptor E. M. Falconet entered the factory. During his nine years at Sèvres, Falconet created models which were entirely original and belong to the best in the factory's history. The most characteristic of all Sèvres wares are those decorated with paintings enclosed in panels, reserved upon various coloured grounds, each shade in succession a triumph: turquoise in 1752, yellow the following year, pea-green in 1756 and the pink known as rose Pompadour (q.v.) a year later.

Finally, the strong, even *bleu-de-roi* (q.v.), of such unequalled brilliance that an all-over pattern called *oeil-de-Perdrix* (q.v.), consisting of tiny gilt dots within rings and white circlets, was often applied to soften the effect. Festoons of flowers were also popular. Landscape and figure decorations, which are frequently signed at Sèvres, tend to become more sumptuous than they had been on early Vincennes porcelain.

The Revolution of 1789 finally put an end to any restrictions on the production of other factories, but Sèvres survived in spite of the financial difficulties. The 19th cent. saw the introduction of new colours and technical innovations such as *pâte-sur-pâte* (q.v.), but artistically there was a rapid decline. The factory is still working.

Marks:

Sewing table: a small table with drawers and, frequently, a cloth bag to hold the sewing. This type of table was introduced in the late 18th cent. (See also Work table.)

Sgraffiato (or sgraffito): a means of decorating pottery by cutting away, incising or scratching with a pointed instrument through a coating of slip (q.v.) to expose the colour of the underlying body. A technique popularly used in Devonshire, Somerset, South Wales, Staffordshire and Sussex, 17th to 19th cent.

Shade silhouette: a silhouette portrait in which the face is painted in black. Ideally, the whole portrait should be in black, but sometimes clothes, nosegays or other details are inserted in colour, but the face itself must have no detail at all apart from that of its outline. J. Buncombe, who practised from *c.* 1745 to *c.* 1825 at Newport, Isle of Wight, painted fine shades of soldiers in which the uniforms are shown in colour and in great detail. Edward Foster of Derby often painted faces in brown, blue or some other colour, and unless details are shown in the faces, such may also be termed shades.

Shagreen: skin of various animals but especially shark skin often dyed green. Used from the 17th cent. onwards for covering cases for cutlery, scientific and medical instruments and domestic articles, especially tea caddies (q.v.).

Shaker furniture: a whole range of furniture – chairs, tables, chests of drawers – made in America by early 19th-cent. Shakers, a celibate religious sect. This furniture while provincial, is so simple, well proportioned and soundly constructed, that it is much prized today. Usually in pine, maple, walnut or fruit woods, a characteristic piece is a slat-backed chair designed to be hung from a peg on the wall.

Shearer, Thomas: English furniture designer, contemporary of Hepplewhite and Sheraton, whose work first appeared in the 1788 *Cabinet-Maker's London Book of Prices*. The sideboard, usually made in the Classical style, appeared first in his book of designs.

Sheep's-head clock: an English lantern clock in which the chapter ring extends appreciably beyond the rectangular frame of the front dial plate. Made from *c.* 1650.

Sheffield plate: the earliest and most effective substitute for wrought silver. Invented by Thomas Bolsover about

1743. Composed of copper ingot fused to a thinner one of silver and rolled to requisite thickness, the metals remaining in the same relative proportions when rolled. First used for buttons and other small articles, but from about 1765 onwards a serious rival to silver in every type of vessel.

Until the 1790s copper was silver-plated in the actual factories in which the ware was fabricated. Afterwards plating became a specialist trade, being made and stocked in three standard qualities, according to the thickness of the silver. This was sold to the plate-workers.

A 3.6 kg (8 lb) copper ingot alloyed with about $\frac{1}{8}$ its weight in brass, and measuring 20 to 25 cm (8 to 10 in) long by about 8 cm (3 in) wide and 5 cm (2 in) thick, was smoothed and cleaned on the upper and lower surfaces. At first this was done by hand-filing; from about 1820 by steam-driven planing machines.

An ingot of silver was rolled to the required thickness, as needed for varying qualities of metal, the lowest weighing 25 g (16 pennyweights), to cover one face of the copper. This was increased to as much as 227 g (8 oz) for the very rich plating used before the introduction of silver mountings and for the lavishly engraved work from 1820. The coating of silver required to be more than a mere film, otherwise it discoloured when heated by the soldering iron. A rectangle of silver plate, flawless in texture and unpitted, measuring about 3 mm ($\frac{1}{8}$ in) less each way than the surface of the copper ingot, was cleaned on one side. The two bright surfaces were then placed together and bedded by placing a heavy iron upon the silver and striking it with a sledge-hammer until every part of the two surfaces was in close contact.

A heavily whitewashed piece of thick sheet copper was placed over the silver and firmly bound to the ingot with iron wires, burnt borax and water being applied to the edges of the silver to act as a flux. The ingot was now placed in an oven containing a charcoal fire and its door pierced with a small hole through which the plater could observe its progress. A bright line encircling the edges of the silver told him when fusion had taken place. He immediately removed the ingot and plunged it into diluted spirits of salt. After cutting the wires the ingot was compressed in a rolling machine, repeated annealing (q.v.) being required as it was gradually converted into sheets of specified width and gauge. These sheets, of perfectly united silver and copper were not silvered on both sides until the early 1770s.

Sheldon tapestry: tapestry weaving was undoubtedly practised in England in Medieval times, but mostly on a small scale for armorial pieces or coarse *verdures* (q.v.). Finer pieces may have been worked but cannot now be identified. The weavers' main occupation was certainly repairing the innumerable tapestries which were in constant use, and in need of cleaning and restoration. Flemish, Dutch and French weavers settled in England in the 16th cent. William Sheldon (*fl.* 1750) claimed his factory, set up under the Flemish-trained Richard Hyckes in about 1560, was the first in England. This cannot be strictly accurate, but Sheldon's workshops at Barcheston in Warwickshire and Bordesley in Worcestershire are certainly the first about which anything definite is known and whose productions can be identified. The tapestry maps of local counties are known from fragments bought from his house at Weston by Horace Walpole in 1781; they bear a date 1588. These and another set woven at least a generation later can be seen at the Victoria and Albert Museum. Other hangings are known as well as cushion covers, which were much used in the days of hard oak benches; also small cushions, book-bindings and glove gauntlets. Sheldon tapestry is rather coarse and shows analogies in style with the carved wooden fireplaces of Elizabethan and Jacobean country houses. To furnish these it was singularly appropriate and this little weaving enterprise flourished until the founding of Mortlake (q.v.).

Shelf clock: free standing clock designed for standing on a shelf, mantel or bracket. (See bracket clock.)

Shell ornament: a motif in general decorative use during the first three quarters of the 18th cent. A simple shell is sometimes found carved on the knees of early 18th-cent. chairs, while more elaborate forms appear on furniture of the second quarter of the cent. Freer and more imaginative versions of the shell motif were used on silverware, furniture, porcelain, metalwork, etc., during the mid-18th cent. (See also Rococo.)

Shell thumbpiece: a thumbpiece (q.v.) formed of a ribbed or plain scallop shell, found on tankards, etc.

Shepherd's crook arm: chair or settee (q.v.) arm of elegantly curving shape, the end in the form of a shepherd's crook, fashionable during the first three decades of the 18th cent. Also known as a scroll-over arm.

Sheraton, Thomas: (1751–1806), a drawing-master and designer who supplied designs to cabinet-makers (q.v.). Sheraton was a journeyman cabinet-maker in his youth but does not appear to have owned a workshop in London or to have been a practical cabinet-maker. He published *The Cabinet-Maker and Upholsterer's Drawing Book* in four parts between 1791 and 1794. He favoured light, delicate furniture, including painted work and for his finest pieces he recommended satinwood. He also advised other tropical woods, popular about 1800, for the best apartments of the house. His designs were more inventive than those of Hepplewhite (q.v.).

Sherratt, Obadiah and **Martha:** started to manufacture pottery figures and toys in Hot Lane, Burslem, about 1815, but moved to Waterloo Road in 1828. On Sherratt's death the business was continued by his son Hamlet until about 1846, and subsequently by his widow Martha (née Vernon, b. 1784). The firm closed down between 1851 and 1860.

Sherratt's figures are never marked and include bull-baiting groups, 'The Death of Munrow' and 'Polito's Menagerie'.

Shield-back chair: a late 18th-cent. chair, the uprights and cresting carved in form of a shield, containing a carved and pierced splat (q.v.). Chairs of this type were included in Hepplewhite's (q.v.) *Cabinet-makers' and Upholsterers' Guide* published in 1788.

Shield toby jug: an early variety of toby jug (q.v.), so called because a shield is found at the left-hand side with the words impressed 'It's all out then fill him again'. Probably made by Ralph Wood (q.v.), there are perhaps not more than a dozen examples of this model known. They are well potted, with fine thin glazing and invariably have a Roman nose.

Ship's bell clock: simple clock made from *c.* 1850 with a lever escapement (q.v.) and striking work. Usually fitted in a circular brass case with a back flange for screwing to the bulkhead.

Shiraz rugs: Persian rugs woven by Kashkai nomads, bearing designs of a conventional Moslem character, related in style to Caucasian types. Diamond medallions predominate, while cone designs and latch hooks are also used. The term Mecca is often used to describe pieces of outstanding merit. Knot: Ghiordes or Sehna (qq.v.).

Shirvan rugs: Caucasian rugs, similar in design to the Hila rugs (q.v.) but generally coarser in quality and lacking the detail of the former. Crude animal forms are often introduced.

Shouldered stem: see Moulded pedestal stem.

Shrinkage: the contracting of porcelain after firing by about one-seventh of the size of the mould.

Shu fu ('Privy Council' or 'Central Palace') ware: Chinese Yüan dynasty (q.v.) porcelain of Ching-tê-chên with slightly opaque, bluish-tinged glaze covering moulded relief designs of flying cranes, lotus sprays, and the characters '*shu fu*'. The term '*shu fu*' indicates official use.

Siegburg stoneware: stoneware, made of creamy white clay, usually unglazed but sometimes covered with a colourless salt-glaze (q.v.), made at Siegburg, near Bonn in Germany from the Middle Ages. The potteries came to an end with the sack of the town by the Swedes in 1632.

Sign-post barometer: see Diagonal barometer.

Silesian stem: see Moulded pedestal stem.

Silhouette: the name usually given collectively to shades and profiles. It is derived from that of Étienne de Silhouette (1709-69), the parsimonious finance minister of Louis XV. He was an amateur cutter of shades.

Silver, Arthur: (1852-96), English designer and craftsman who founded the Silver Studios in 1880 which continued in active production until 1965. Designed fabrics and wallpapers for most of the leading firms of the day.

Silver gilt: silver with an applied surface of gold. Traditional technique known as fire, water, mercury or wash gilding consists of painting on an amalgam of mercury and gold. The former is driven off with heat and the gold combines with the silver. Modern method of electro-gilding employs the use of electric current in a bath of gold solution, producing a deposition of the latter as in electroplating (q.v.). (See also Gilding.)

Silveria glass: type of glass invented by the son of Northwood (q.v.) in which silver foil was sealed between two layers of glass.

Simple clock pendulum: a theoretical conception consisting of a weight or mass suspended by a weightless thread.

Singeries: ornament representing monkeys (*singes*) in the role of people. Popular in the period of the Rococo (q.v.).

Single-twist stem: a type of stem found on drinking glasses in the second half of the 18th cent. containing air, enamel, or coloured thread spiralling around a clear glass centre, or a pair of reciprocal spirals.

Siphon barometer: a type in which the reservoir is situated in the return section of a J-shaped tube.

Skeleton clock: an uncased clock produced commercially from the early 19th cent. and usually protected by a glass dome or shade, designed to display its mechanism and construction.

Skeleton clock dial: one in which the metal is cut away from the applied chapter ring, leaving only the numerals, minutes and interhorary marks.

Skillet (**posnet** or **pipkin**): Medieval skillets were shaped like cauldrons, and it was not until the 16th cent. that this ancestor of the modern saucepan became recognizable. These later skillets had no feet, but were made with the sides sloping outwards so that the circumference of the top was greater than that of the base. The handle was popularly used for advertising the name of the maker or for the spreading of texts such as 'Ye Wages of Sin is Death'. They were of earthenware or sometimes bronze. Examples in silver, supported on three feet for heating gruel or other liquids date from the 17th cent. They have covers of flat cap form with flat pierced handles resembling cupping-bowls.

Skirt base: a wide, spreading base sometimes found on late 17th-cent. pewter flagons.

Slag glass: opaque glass, veined and streaked like marble, often dark purple, its main constituent being waste slag from blast furnaces. Known also as 'End of Day' glass or vitro-porcelain.

Slat-back chair: a simple, late 17th-cent. chair with a back of horizontal slats. This type of chair is said to be a precursor of the late 18th-cent. ladder-back chair (q.v.).

Sleepy Hollow chair: a type of chair with a semi-circular arched back and continuous arms and yoke rail popular in the United States in the mid-19th cent. The name derives from *The Legend of Sleepy Hollow* by Washington Irving.

Slip: clay reduced to a liquid batter, used for making, coating, or decorating pottery; 'these (clays) mixed with water they make into a consistence thinner than a syrup, so that being put into a bucket it will run out through a quill; this they call slip, and is a substance wherewith they paint their wares.'

Slipper chair: a type of 18th-cent. American chair with a low seat and high back. In the 19th cent. some models were ornamented in the style of the revived Rococo (q.v.).

Slip-top spoon: early form with hexagonal stem with sloping or bevelled end. Examples occur from Medieval period until mid-17th cent.

Slipware: earthenware decorated with white or coloured slip (q.v.). (See also Combed ware and Sgraffiato.)

Smallsword: a light civilian sword with a simple hilt, often richly decorated, which succeeded the rapier (q.v.) in the third quarter of the 17th cent., with the beginnings of fencing as it is known today. The slender blade, although designed principally for thrusting, was at first double-edged, but from *c.* 1700 one of hollow triangular section became almost universal. The modern term *colichemarde* is often used to designate a blade which is wide near the hilt and narrows suddenly halfway along. The smallsword remained in active use until the end of the 18th cent., and still survives in the sword worn with modern court dress.

Smalt (smalts): the deep blue of cobalt oxide, also sometimes known as smales. Used in the preparation of enamel colours for the decoration of pottery and porcelain.

Smith, George: early 19th-cent. cabinet-maker (q.v.) and designer. Published the *Cabinet-maker's and Upholsterer's Guide* in 1828.

Smith, S., & Son: London makers of highly complicated watches and timepieces for observatory use. Forerunners of the present-day Smith's Industries Ltd.

Smith Brothers: family of British glass decorators (father and sons), who emigrated to the United States *c.* 1855. Worked first for the Boston and Sandwich Glass Company (q.v.) and then for the Mount Washington Glass Works (q.v.). Founded their own premises in New Bedford *c.* 1875.

Snaphaunce: the earliest form of the flintlock (q.v.), introduced apparently in the middle of the 16th cent. It is regarded by many writers as a distinct type, its chief difference from the flintlock being that the pan is fitted with a separate sliding cover opened, when the steel is knocked back by the cock, by the action of a cam. Most surviving examples date within the 17th cent.

Snowman figures: porcelain (q.v.) figures heavily glazed with a thick, opaque, glassy glaze (q.v.), obscuring the modelling, sometimes identified as the production of an experimental porcelain factory at Newcastle-under-Lyme, but now known to be the production of Longton Hall (q.v.). The figures include birds, animals and *Commedia dell' Arte* characters.

Snuff box: a box to contain snuff found in great variety of forms from late 17th cent. onwards, in solid gold, silver and wood, tortoiseshell and other materials mounted with silver, enamels (q.v.), etc.

Snuffer stand: upright container on stem and moulded base into which candle-snuffers (q.v.) fit. Introduced in late 17th cent., but superseded by trays in the early 18th.

Snuffer tray: oblong or oval tray with or without small feet and scroll or ring handle at side for holding candle-snuffers (q.v.). Not to be confused with spoon trays (q.v.).

Snufftaker: standing toby jug formed as an ugly man taking a pinch of snuff, usually with a deep purple-brown lustrous Rockingham glaze (q.v.).

Soap box: spherical box of silver, pewter (q.v.) or brass for soap, standing on a moulded base with screw-on or hinged, pierced or plain cover. Can be mistaken for pounce- or sand-box (q.v.), but the spherical form appears to have been peculiar to soap box.

Soapstone, soap-rock or **steatite:** soapstone was first used as an ingredient of the English soft-paste porcelain (q.v.) paste at a Bristol factory, and was adopted as the basis of early Worcester (q.v.) porcelain. Benjamin Lund, the Bristol Quaker brass-founder, was licensed to quarry soaprock or soapstone at Gew Graze near Mullion, 7 March 1748. Soapstone was also used for carving, notably in China.

Sociable: see Confidante.

Soda-lime glass: traditionally glass made with lime and some form of soda ash, for which in 1864, William Leighton substituted bicarbonate of soda, thereby producing a clearer, more brilliant glass which almost rivalled lead or flint glass (q.v.) in quality and cost one third to produce.

Sofa table: a rectangular table, sometimes with two front drawers in the apron and hinged leaves at each end; the under-frame of two legs at each end, or graceful bracket supports connected by a stretcher. This type of table was made in the late 18th cent. and was extremely popular in the Regency (q.v.) period. It was intended for the use of ladies seated at a sofa.

Soft-ground etching: an etching (q.v.) which relies on the softening of the ground of the plate by grease. Over this is laid a sheet of paper on which the drawing is made. When the paper is removed the ground adheres where the pencil has done its work.

Soft-paste porcelain: porcelain which is both softer as a material than true or hard-paste porcelain (q.v.), and less refractory and therefore requiring a less intense heat to fuse it. It differs also from hard-paste in that the glaze of hard-paste is closely allied to the nature of the body and may be fired with it, whereas soft-paste porcelain is given a lead glaze which is fired at a second (glost) firing at a lower temperature in the glost-oven. Use confined to small objects. Alternatively, sometimes used as a slip (q.v.) to cover hard-paste porcelain bodies.

Soho tapestry: when the Great Wardrobe moved to Great Queen Street, Soho, in 1685, the tapestry factory at Mortlake (q.v.) was virtually abandoned and Soho became the centre of production, most workshops apparently having some connection with the Wardrobe. From 1689–1727 the leading figure was John Vanderbank. *Chinoiserie* (q.v.) tapestries 'in the Indian manner' on brown grounds were very much in vogue. He was succeeded by Paul Saunders (active as late as 1758, d. 1772), known for his romantic landscapes. Joshua Morris wove Arabesques (q.v.) (or grotesque) sets designed by Adrian de Clermont, a French immigrant. These tapestries, entirely in keeping with early 18th-cent. taste, are perhaps the most distinguished contribution of the period. Bradshaw, who was connected with Morris at Soho, wove tapestries after pictures by Watteau and Pater. In general, a great deal of tapestry seems to have been woven under William and Mary, Queen Anne, and George I and II.

A new company, The Soho Tapestry Works, was founded in 1890 in Poland Street on the site of the original 18th-cent. works.

Solon, M.-L.: (1835–1913), French porcelain modeller and decorator who trained at the Sèvres (q.v.) factory and who is noted for his contribution to the *pâte-sur-pâte* (q.v.) technique. His son, Léon Solon, became the art director and chief designer at Mintons (q.v.).

Soqui (or **Lequoi**), **Saqui:** Monsieur Soqui, a bird-painter alleged to have come from the Sèvres porcelain factory (q.v.), was described as an 'excellent painter and enameller'. He worked at the Plymouth and Bristol porcelain factories (qq.v.) showing a special interest in exotic birds painted in strong colours with thick stippling against a pale ground.

Soufflé dish: silver or plated cylindrical bowl with liner, usually two-handled, to hold soufflés, introduced in early 19th cent.

Soumac rugs: Caucasian rugs in a tapestry weave with conventional designs. Large octagonal and star panels; colourings are mainly a deep copper and blue.

Southern Porcelain Manufacturing Co.: founded in 1856 at Kaolin, South Carolina, by William H. Farrar of the United States Pottery Co. of Bennington, Vermont. In 1857 Jones, formerly the chief modeller with Charles Cartlidge & Co. (q.v.), assumed management and succeeded in producing porcelain (q.v.). The pottery works continued in operation until the start of the Civil War, when the finer grades were discontinued and the factory limited its production to porcelain telegraph insulators. In 1864 the factory was destroyed by fire.

South Staffordshire enamels: painted enamels appear to have been produced in South Staffordshire – and in particular at Bilston and Wednesbury – shortly after the establishment of the enamel factory at Battersea (q.v.) in 1753 and at a rather later date, in Birmingham. Snuff boxes (q.v.), scent bottles, étuis (q.v.), wine labels, candlesticks (q.v.) and tapersticks (q.v.), etc., were produced in large quantities, the examples from the mid-18th cent. decorated with pastoral scenes, portraits or flowers and insects on a white ground. From about 1760, coloured grounds were introduced. Towards the end of the cent. and until about 1830, when the industry appears to have died out owing to lack of interest from foreign markets, cheaper wares such as buttons, summarily painted patchboxes and similar small articles were made.

Southwark delftware: see Lambeth delftware.

Sowerby's Ellison Glassworks: with the other Tyneside firms of Henry Greener & Co. and Davidson & Co. (qq.v.), this was one of the three most important manufacturers of pressed glass (q.v.) in England, its wares often being marked with a peacock's head.

Soy frame: silver or plated oblong or oval stand with ring frame for holding soy or sauce bottles. Introduced in late 18th cent. Found *en suite* (q.v.) with larger cruet (q.v.) frames.

Spade foot: a rectangular foot of tapered form found on late 18th-cent. furniture. Also known as a therm, or thermed, foot.

Spandrel: space between the curve of an arch and the frame in which it is contained.

Spangled glass: a type of glass patented in 1883 whereby mica particles were embedded in glass with an additional layer of coloured glass, to achieve a glittering, spangled effect.

Spängler, Jean Jacques: son of the director of the Zürich porcelain (q.v.) factory, at which factory he learnt the craft of ceramic modelling. In 1790 Spängler signed an agreement to work at Derby (q.v.) for three years, but appears to have been of a restless temperament, and after attempting to return to the Continent in 1792 was arrested and imprisoned at Ramsgate. He returned for a short time to Derby afterwards, but little more is known of him. A few Derby models can be attributed to Spängler with certainty.

Spanish foot: a scroll form with curving vertical ribs, often used as the terminal for a chair or settee (q.v.) in the late 17th cent.

Spanish morion: see Morion.

Spanish point lace: the name Spanish point was variously applied to loosely woven gold and silver lace (q.v.), much imported from Italy; to a raised needlepoint lace (q.v.) resembling the Venetian (q.v.), similarly imported, and to silk laces mainly from Chantilly (q.v.) and Bayeux, until Spain made her own.

Spatter: a cheerful range of pottery, with sponged colour and painted designs, made c. 1820–50 in Staffordshire for the American market.

Spelter: a base metal used in the 19th cent. for producing cheap and inferior decorative objects.

Spice box: a general name for caskets (q.v.) of indeterminate purpose of the early 17th cent., usually of shell outline with scallop lid and shell or snail feet. Later applied to oval caskets of the Charles II period which may also have served as tobacco boxes. An 18th-cent. version has centrally hinged twin lids with or without a detachable nutmeg grater in the centre.

Spinario: figure of boy made in pottery and porcelain, extracting a thorn from his foot, copied from a statue in the Capitoline Museum, Rome.

Spit: a metal bar with which meat was pierced and placed on cobirons (q.v.) before the fire for roasting; as the bar was rotated, all sides of the meat received the heat equally. The spit had prongs in the centre, and a grooved pulley at one end to connect by chain or rope to some sort of motive power, human, animal or mechanical. This motive power, if human or animal, was termed a 'turnspit', and if mechanical a 'jack'. Illustrations in early manuscripts show that boys were employed as turnspits, and by the 16th cent. spit-jacks were in use. These latter were made of brass and iron, and were driven by large weights of stone or metal, which descended slowly into pits dug for the purpose to increase the length of fall. Like the weights of a clock, once they had completely run down they were wound up again. Another mechanical method of turning the spit was by a fan fitted in the mouth of the chimney, which was operated by the rising draught. A further method was the employment of dogs, specially trained for the purpose, which were confined in a small treadmill fixed to the wall of the kitchen. At the end of the 18th cent., spring-driven jacks were in use, and culminated in the neat bottle-jack, brass-cased and driven by clockwork.

When not in use the spits were kept in the spit-rack: a row of hooks at either end of the space above the fireplace.

Splat: the vertical central section contained within the uprights of a chair back.

Splayed leg: outward-sloping leg. The back legs of chairs are frequently splayed to increase stability.

Splint: an American term for a seat made of thin interlaced hickory or oak strips. Much used in early American chairs, stools and settees (q.v.) of simple type. Still popular today in the kitchen.

Split-turned ornament: oak furniture of the mid-17th cent. was often ornamented with simply turned balusters, split in half and applied. Split balusters applied in this manner were frequently used decoratively in conjunction with applied jewel or lozenge ornament (see Diamond ornament).

Spode, Josiah: the Spode factory was founded by Josiah Spode (1733–97) in 1770; first apprenticed to Whieldon (q.v.) of Fenton in 1749, he became manager of the works owned by Turner and Bankes at Stoke at the age of twenty-nine. On the death of Bankes in 1770, Spode took over the factory on mortgage. By 1776 he was making earthenware (q.v.) in his own name, trade was increasing, and he was engaged on extensive pioneer work to improve his productions. He died in 1797, leaving a prosperous business to his son, Josiah Spode II (1754–1827). A grandson of the founder, Josiah Spode III, succeeded him, and the factory was carried on under his ownership until his death in 1829. The firm was bought from his executors in 1833 by Wm. Taylor Copeland, already a partner in the business in the time of the third Josiah Spode. During the period 1833–1847 the title was Copeland & Garrett. Thereafter, and up to the present day, the firm has been known by Copeland's name alone – sometimes as Copeland, late Spode – and is still owned by descendants of Wm. Taylor Copeland. The first Josiah Spode inherited a tradition of earthenware manufacture to which he adhered in the early years of his ownership of the factory; the favourite Oriental designs were used and improved, the transfer-printing (q.v.) in blue underglaze (q.v.) being especially successful. His work to improve the quality of transfer-printing greatly affected the future use of this process. In later patterns much of the transfer-print is left unpainted, only small portions of the design being enamelled afterwards. He also made jasper, black Egyptian (qq.v.) and black-printed wares of good quality.

Josiah Spode soon turned to the manufacture of porcelain (q.v.). After the expiry date of Cookworthy's (q.v.) patent for making porcelain from Cornish china-clay and china-stone, Spode took his basic recipe (on which he had been experimenting for several years), adding to it calcinated bone, which combination of ingredients produced a bone-china (q.v.) of fine quality, transparent and durable. This bone-china was to become the basic formula for china made by future generations of potters, and still remains a standard for present-day manufacturers. His son is credited with the introduction of Spode felspar and stone-china, the former akin to porcelain in its hard transparent body.

In the first half of the 19th cent. the Spode and Mintons factories were rivals in both artistry and output.

Early earthenware is usually easily distinguishable, as is most Spode work, and pieces were almost invariably marked from 1800 onwards. Some reproductions of Meissen and early Worcester (qq.v.) have had their marks removed by grinding, but identification is still possible: Spode's paste was considerably softer than that of Meissen, and the colours used in Worcester reproductions are on the whole brighter than those of the originals. Chelsea (q.v.) colours and types of design were used from time to time.

In the early years, the most popular Spode pieces were in the Chinese style. The peacock pattern and other designs originating in *famille rose* (q.v.) porcelains were also highly successful.

In porcelain, plates and dishes of unusual form were made as a departure from the circular and oval shapes traditionally used. Ground colours – dark blues, reds, yellow, green and lavender amongst others – of very rich appearance are characteristic, and most often found in conjunction with motifs of flowers and fruit, birds, etc. Designs became more ambitious and the demand for extravagant decoration grew. Gilding was profuse and stippled while solid gold grounds were frequent. Designs reminiscent of Sèvres (q.v.)

and other Continental porcelain were much used.

At the same time a form of decoration traditionally English is found; landscapes were painted in panels surrounded by coloured borders, garlands of flowers, etc., some of these pieces being extremely effective.

Marks:

Printed in purple

SPODE

Printed in blue   in red

COPELAND
& GARRETT

Sponged ware (or **spatter ware**): a crude, easily-recognized, peasant style of decoration on pottery achieved by free painting and by dabbing the ware with a sponge impregnated with pigment.

Spool turning: a form of repeat decoration on the members of chairs, beds and tables popular in the United States in the mid-19th cent. It was derived from 16th- and 17th-cent. bobbin turning (q.v.). Furniture with spool turning was sometimes referred to as Jenny Lind furniture after the famous Swedish singer who toured the United States in 1850.

Spoon-back chair: an American term describing a chair with a back, curved like a spoon, conforming to the human back. Common in early 17th cent.

Spoon tray: small oval or oblong dish of early 18th-cent. date used for holding teaspoons in the absence of saucers. Continued to be used, even after the saucer came into general use in the mid-18th cent.

Spout cup: popular in the early 18th cent. and later; a feeding-cup, generally with bulbous body and domed cover; handle generally at right angle to spout, and spout of duck-neck shape, close to body. Used for feeding children and invalids.

Sprayed leaf thumbpiece: a thin, wide fan-shaped thumbpiece (q.v.) with deeply-gouged lines radiating from the foot in a leaf pattern.

Sprigged decoration: application of relief ornament to pottery or porcelain, often in a contrasting colour by 'sprigging', or attaching small pads of clay, from a metal or hard-plaster mould to the surface of a vessel with slip (q.v.), as on jasper ware (q.v.).

Sprimont, Nicholas: (1716-70), born at Liège, nephew of the silversmith Nicholas Joseph Sprimont, to whom he served an apprenticeship. Came to England where he appears to have worked as a silversmith. In 1745 became factory manager and part proprietor with Charles Gouyn and Thomas Briand (d. 1784) of the Chelsea porcelain (q.v.) factory. After breaking with his partners he obtained for Chelsea the secret patronage of William Augustus, Duke of Cumberland, second son of George II.

Spur marks: rough marks formed by spurs or stilts upon which glazed pottery or porcelain wares are supported during the firing process. These are distinct from and smaller than the marks left by the bit-stones used earlier.

Squire jug: a variety of toby jug (q.v.) representing a country squire, seated corner-wise in an armchair, usually with a green or blue coat and brown hat and breeches.

Stackfreed: 16th-cent. South German device of unknown origin found in very early watches, whereby a roller attached to a strong spring bears against a shaped snail or cam, the radius of which decreases. The friction on the pivots of the snail and roller decreases as the spring is allowed to approach the centre of revolution of the snail; as the main spring is unwound and loses power the braking action of the roller decreases, tending to keep constant the force exerted by the spring on the watch movement. The principle of the lever underlies this as in the fusee (q.v.). Both methods are found in the early 16th cent., but the fusee ultimately supplanted the stackfreed everywhere.

Staffordshire dogs: chimney ornaments, made in Staffordshire and elsewhere in England from *c.* 1850, usually in pairs and often in the form of a King Charles spaniel seated without a stand or plinth.

Stake: an iron tongue or anvil, on which hollow-ware (q.v.) is formed. Many kinds of stakes are used, shaped for certain purposes, such as to give an inward curve, a flat surface, etc.

Stalker and Parker: The authors of a treatise on japanning, published in 1688, which did much to encourage the art among amateur enthusiasts, known as the *Treatise of Japanning and Varnishing, Being a compleat Discovery of those Arts. With the best way of making all sorts of Varnish for Japan . . . The Method of Guilding, Burnishing, and Lackering . . . Also Rules for Counterfeiting Tortoise-shell, and Marble . . . Together with Above an Hundred distinct Patterns of Japan-work, in Imitation of the Indians for Tables, Stands, Frames, Cabinets, Boxes, etc.* (See also Japan work.)

Stamped gold: thin gold sheet stamped into a required form and used for making cheap jewellery mounts towards the end of the 18th and in the 19th cent.

Stamped work: relief ornament produced on metal by hammering from reverse of the sheet into an intaglio-cut die. Commonly used in 16th cent. for strapwork and ovolo (qq.v.) borders on silverware, and occasionally for larger surface patterns. In late 18th cent. developed on a commercial scale with large dies at Sheffield and Birmingham for candlesticks (q.v.), dish-borders, etc.

Stamps on French furniture: various names and letters are often found stamped on French furniture made in the 18th cent. or later. The most important of these is the stamp (*estampille*), giving the name and often the initials of the *ébéniste* (q.v.) who made the piece of furniture. After 1751, it was compulsory according to guild regulations to strike a stamp on all work, unless the craftsman happened to be working for the Crown. Before 1751 *estampilles* are very rarely found.

These stamps are a most important means of identifying the makers of individual pieces of furniture, but it must be borne in mind that sometimes they only refer to the repairer of a piece as distinct from its original maker. Thus some pieces bear more than one *estampille*, and it is often doubtful which *ébéniste* was the actual maker.

The *estampille* is of roughly uniform size and format, usually incorporating the *ébéniste*'s name and initials, but sometimes the surname only. They are usually found in an inconspicuous place on the carcase (q.v.) of the piece, on the bottom or top rails (q.v.) front or back, under marble tops, etc. Very occasionally they appear on the surface of the veneer (q.v.) and sometimes panels of marquetry (q.v.) are signed in full by their makers.

Another important stamp to be found on French furniture after 1751 is that of the *jurés*. It consists of a monogram incorporating the letters JME (*juré* or *jurande des menuisiers-ébénistes*), and its presence implies that the piece concerned has passed the standard required by the *jurés* of the guild (see *Menuisiers-Ebénistes, Corporation des*).

In addition to the *estampille* and the *juré*'s stamp, furniture made for the Crown sometimes, though by no means always, bears the stamp of the

Garde Meuble de la Couronne (q.v.). Inventory numbers and palace letters (q.v.) are usually painted or branded, but seldom stamped, on furniture.

In the 18th cent. *bronzes d'ameublement* (q.v.) are very rarely stamped, but sometimes they do bear signatures. Jacques Caffiéri frequently signed his work with his surname. Inventory numbers and palace letters are even rarer, but they do occasionally occur on bronzes, and where they can be checked with existing documents they are found to be of 18th-cent. origin.

Standing cup: large ceremonial or decorative cup on high stem and foot, found in every variety of style and decoration down to the end of the 17th cent., after which it is replaced by the two-handled cup on low foot without stem. Examples without covers have probably lost them in the past.

Standing salt: a standing salt of precious metal was the focal point of the Medieval banquet high table. Many forms have survived. Elizabethan examples of pedestal- or bell-form are richly decorated. Early 17th-cent. models have 'steeple' finials (q.v.) to cover. A later cylindrical type has scroll supports on the upper rim.

Standish: an inkstand formed by a rectangular flat plate standing upon four feet, and having a curved edge. Upon the plate stand ink-well, dredger, etc., and there is usually a drawer beneath for quills.

State: a term with reference to prints. Each time there is any addition made to a plate, or lithographic stone, between printings, the new form becomes a new 'state' of the print.

Statuary porcelain: the original name of Parian ware (q.v.) used by Copeland (q.v.).

Steatite: see Soapstone.

Steele (or **Steel**), **Thomas** (1772–1850), a porcelain decorator who worked at the Derby (q.v.) factory in a careful, highly coloured style. He painted fruit and for a time appears to have worked at Swinton (Rockingham (q.v.) factory), later in Staffordshire for Davenports (q.v.) and from 1825 to 1843 for Mintons (q.v.).

Steel engraving: a process of engraving (q.v.), starting soon after 1800, upon steel rather than on copper plates. More impressions could be taken from a steel than from a copper plate. This was, however, such a mechanical process, where the actual engravers were treated merely as hands, that it fell into disfavour. Very few steel engravings were issued coloured.

Steen: originally an earthen vessel with two ears to hold liquids, later used for bread, meat or fish.

Steeple cup: a popular term for a particular form of standing cup (q.v.), surmounted by an obelisk or pyramid finial (q.v.), found in the reign of James I and early years of Charles I.

Stencilled wallpaper: one of the earliest forms of wallpaper and a ready means of repeating the design automatically over large surfaces. Stencilling (q.v.) was common during the 17th cent. as a means of adding colours to a block-printed (q.v.) outline.

Stencilling: a technique of applying colour with a brush through openings cut in heavy waterproof paper, used in the decoration of furniture, tôle (q.v.) and textiles. Most surviving examples date from the first half of the 19th cent.

Step: a term used to describe a flattened glass button connecting the stem of a rummer (q.v.) with its foot.

Step cutting: see Prismatic cutting.

Stepped lid: term indicating the elevations on the lid of a vessel, e.g. a tankard, as 'single-stepped' or 'double-stepped'.

'Step' toby jug: probably the first toby jug (q.v.) to be modelled at a date not later than 1750. It is thought that this variety of toby jug, representing a seated figure holding a pipe may have been modelled by Aaron Wood (see Wood, Enoch). It is sometimes known as a 'Twyford' jug and the potting and glazing is rather more crude than is the case with later models.

Sterling mark: from 1554, English Sterling Standard (q.v.) silver was marked with a lion passant. In Scotland, a thistle mark was introduced for the same purpose in 1759.

Sterling Standard: the normal standard for wrought plate in the British Isles. Established in London in 1300 and in force till 1696. Then replaced by Britannia Standard (q.v.) till 1720, when Sterling was restored as legal. Consists of 925 parts of fine metal in 1000 of wrought metal.

Stevengraph: the trade name for small, multi-coloured silk pictures woven on a modified Jacquard loom from 1863 by the Coventry firm of Thomas Stevens.

Stevens, Alfred: (1817–75), English painter, sculptor and designer of metalwork. In 1845 he was appointed to a post at the Government School of Design, and in 1851 a number of his designs for fire-irons, fenders (q.v.), etc., manufactured by H. E. Hoole & Co., of Sheffield, were shown at the Great Exhibition. For Thomas Bradbury & Sons (q.v.) he made designs for silver and electroplate (q.v.).

Stevens & Williams Ltd.: Joseph Silvers Williams-Thomas took over the old Brierly Hill Glassworks at Stowbridge in 1847 and made his award-winning firm synonymous with the success of John Northwood cameo glassware (q.v.), making Northwood art director in 1882.

'Stick' chair: see Windsor chair.

Stickley, Gustav: (1857–1942), American furniture designer and manufacturer of Mission-style (q.v.) furniture. In 1898 he founded the Craftsman Workshop at Eastwood, New York. His plain, undecorated furniture, sometimes with revealed construction, was popular in the first decade of the 20th cent. In his magazine, *Craftsman*, first published in 1901, he stated that his intention was 'to make furniture which would be simple, durable, comfortable and fitted for the place it was to occupy and the work it had to do'. His brothers, George and Albert, were furniture manufacturers at Grand Rapids.

Stickwork: known as inlaid turnery from the 1830s, although no inlay was used. This type of ornamental woodwork appears to have been evolved at Tonbridge early in the 18th cent. Fillets of various softly coloured native woods were coated with adhesive and pressed together longitudinally, to build up a variegated block. At first such blocks were shaped by the turner into chessmen, backgammon men and table skittles, all favourite indoor games of the period. Stickwork continued as a substantial manufacture until mid-Victorian days, and was made also in London.

Stiegel-type glassware: glassware produced in America at Stiegel's Manheim glasshouses. H. W. Stiegel (1729–85) was born in Cologne and his family settled in America in 1750. In 1763, having visited Europe, he brought back English and German glassmakers and set up his factory in Pennsylvania.

He produced vessels in lead metal, especially cylindrical tumblers engraved in the German manner and much coloured glass moulded with network. Over-rapid expansion led to financial failure and Stiegel was imprisoned for debt in 1774; his factories subsequently closed.

Stile: in construction, the outermost upright section of a framing as a muntin (q.v.) is the inner section.

Stiletto: a variant of the quillon-dagger (q.v.), first introduced in the 16th cent., with a stiff, narrow blade designed for stabbing only.

Stipple engraving: an engraving (q.v.) technique simulating tone, the design being engraved by means of grouped and graded dots. The invention of stipple engraving with a diamond point on glass vessels is attributed to Frans Greenwood (1680–1761), a native of Rotterdam, who used it as a medium of pictorial work. Many of his stipple designs on wine glasses bear his signature and dates ranging from 1722 to 1755.

Stirrup cup: handleless and footless drinking cup in the form of a fox's or greyhound's mask used at the meet and introduced in the second half of the 18th cent. Made in silver and also in earthenware by Whieldon (q.v.) and others and in soft-paste or bone porcelain at Chelsea, Derby, Rockingham and Coalport (qq.v.).

Stirrup guard: a form of knuckle-bow on a sword which resembles half of a stirrup.

Stock lock: a plate lock (q.v.) let into a rectangular block of oak and thereby attached to the door by bolts or rivets, later by screws. The mechanism in some stock locks was covered with an iron plate decorated with pierced designs, usually trefoil or cinque-foil, with a matching plate covering the wooden block. From the mid-18th cent. the mechanism was almost invariably covered with a solid iron plate.

Stomacher: the breast-piece of 15th- to 18th-cent. European female dress which was usually embroidered or jewelled. In some cases the stomacher formed part of the corset, when laced at the back, but when the corset was laced at the front the stomacher was made as a separate piece and pinned over the corset lacing. Few stomachers earlier than the 18th cent. have survived. The basic V-shape of the stomacher, tapering to a point at the bottom, varied with successive changes in fashion until it died out with the introduction of the Empire style of dress. Continental examples are often elaborately shaped at the lower end and French examples are usually more ornate than those of English origin. The stomacher returned to fashion at the end of the 19th cent. when it was often part of a parure (q.v.) of diamond jewellery.

Stone-bow: see under Cross-bow.

Stone china: a hard white earthenware containing china-stone (q.v.) made as a cheap substitute for porcelain (q.v.) in Staffordshire from c. 1805 and said to have been introduced by Josiah Spode II (see Spode, Josiah).

Stones: red and black specks within the fabric of early flint glass (q.v.), the result of imperfect fusion between oxide of lead and silica.

Stoneware: pottery using refractory clays which, fired at 1200–1400° C, vitrify without collapsing. The opaque dense body is impermeable to liquids and suited to engine-turned decoration.

Stoning: polishing silver with an emery stone.

Stop watch: one in which the seconds hand can be stopped or restarted at will without stopping the whole movement as in the earliest stop watches, c. 1680–90. They were used by doctors and were called 'pulse watches'.

Storr, Paul: (1771–1844), a London goldsmith working between 1797 and 1821, who is generally considered to be the creator of the Regency style (q.v.) in silver. Working for Benjamin Smith and subsequently for the Royal goldsmiths, Rundell, Bridge & Rundell (q.v.), he is believed to have been responsible for the design and execution of the great series of silver vessels ordered by the Prince Regent and known as the Grand Service. In 1819 he set up on his own account but did not succeed in retaining the royal custom.

Straight-funnel bowl: the bowl of a drinking glass of straight-sided form shaped like the frustum of an inverted cone.

Straining spoon: spoon with pierced bowl, found either in large sizes for gravy or similar use or in teaspoon size with thin, tapering stem and pricket top, used for skimming leaves from teacups. Their purpose as tea-strainers is exemplified by their conjunction with teaspoons in fitted tea caddies (q.v.).

Strapwork ornament: an arrangement of interlaced ribbon and scroll-work, sometimes mixed with foliage and flowers. This type of ornament originated in the Netherlands in the second half of the 16th cent. It appears carved on oak furniture of the period and engraved or repoussé (q.v.) on silver and metalwork. In the late 17th cent., a more delicate form of foliate strapwork, based on the designs of the French engraver, Jean Bérain was included in the characteristic repertoire of Baroque (q.v.) ornament.

Strasbourg faience: the Strasbourg factory was founded in 1721 by Charles-François Hannong, the earliest productions being blue and white, with Baroque borders. Paul-Anton Hannong took over the factory from his father and experimented successfully in the manufacture of porcelain (q.v.). The monopoly granted to Vincennes (see Sèvres porcelain) compelled him to cease and in 1755 he started a porcelain factory at Frankenthal (q.v.). The faience (q.v.) factory at Strasbourg was continued by his son, Joseph-Adam Hannong.

Strass: a form of white paste, closely resembling a diamond in effect, called after the inventor, G. F. Strass (1700–73), a Viennese, who came to Paris as a jeweller in 1724. It contains a high percentage of lead, hence more closely resembling a natural diamond when faceted.

Strawberry diamond cutting: a method of decorating glass vessels by cutting or grinding in deep relief to form a pattern of large diamonds, each flattened at the point and cut with numerous very fine relief diamonds. A type of decoration appearing on Irish and English glass in the late 18th and early 19th cent.

Strawberry dish: a name given to small saucer-like silver dishes of 17th- and early 18th-cent. date, the early examples with punched decoration, the latter with fluted borders. Probably used for a variety of purposes.

Straw-work: a method of decorating furniture, particularly smaller pieces such as mirror frames, with tiny strips of bleached and coloured straws to form landscapes, geometrical patterns, etc. This craft came to England from the Continent towards the end of the 17th cent. and was centred at Dunstable.

Stretcher: a horizontal member of various forms connecting chair or table legs. Stretchers on late 17th-cent. chairs were often elaborately carved, while those on mid-18th-cent. examples in the Chinese taste were sometimes of lattice work (q.v.).

Striae: undulating markings sometimes apparent in glass, perfectly vitrified and transparent, showing the metal to be of uneven composition because it has been insufficiently molten before working.

Strike-silent: any mechanism that stops at will the striking or chiming of a clock. The early forms had a pin showing through the dial, attached to a lever, and had the dial marked 'N' and 'S' (Not and Strike). Later a subsidiary dial appeared for this purpose.

Striking plate: the metal plate fixed to a door frame into which the bolt of a lock is shot by the key. The plate has a lip on which the bolt strikes.

Stringing: a line or lines of inlay (q.v.) used as a decorative border on furniture. In the late 18th cent. it was the practice to apply stringing of contrasting woods or, in the early 19th cent. of brass.

Stucco wallpaper: wallpaper imitating the effect of stone or plaster. During the 18th cent. the term was generally descriptive of papier mâché (q.v.) with which industry the paper-hanging maker (q.v.) was then closely associated.

Stuck shank: a stem of a glass vessel made from a separate gather (q.v.) of metal (q.v.) welded to the base of the bowl.

Stump: a circular pin within the case of a lock to guide the different working parts. In lever locks (q.v.) it works in the gating, that is, a slot cut in the lever.

Stump legs: plain turned legs of 'stump' shape, common as the back legs of North Country chairs from *c.* 1725 until the end of the cent. This type of leg was found to increase the strength of the chair.

Stump-top spoon: 17th-cent. form with octagonal stem swelling at the end and diminishing to a flattened point. Also known as a Puritan spoon.

Stump work (or **raised work**): raised embroidery, in which portions of the design were padded to give a three-dimensional effect, was widely used in England from about 1625 to the end of the cent. to decorate caskets, mirror frames and book bindings and for embroidered pictures. The type of work originated from the raised ecclesiastical embroideries of the 15th and 16th cent. in Italy and Germany, and was used earlier for church work in England. Scenes from the Old Testament, the Judgment of Paris, and other mythological subjects, or representations of a King and a Queen were most popular. The interspaces of the designs were filled with quaint beasts, birds and sprigs of flowers.

Sucket fork: silver two-pronged fork with flat stem, a spoon at other end, used for eating crystallized fruit.

Suffolk lace: pillow lace (q.v.), simple and less expert than the Midlands lace and with similar indications of Lille (q.v.) inspiration. Coloured worsted lace was also made.

Sugar basket: pierced or plain silver vases or boat-shape baskets were made from about 1760 onwards. The pierced examples usually have a swing handle and glass liner and were often made with matching cream basket.

Sugar tongs: appearing in the late 17th cent., they were of scissor construction or, later, of spring form.

Sulphides: the earliest glass paper-weights (q.v.) to achieve notice were the type known as sulphides, or encrusted cameos (q.v.). They comprise a plaque, made of unglazed white china with modelling in relief, embedded in glass. The process resulted in the china plaque appearing to be silver in colour. They were made at all three of the French paperweight factories and in England, with success, by Apsley Pellatt (q.v.).

Sulphur-tint aquatint: sulphur-tint aquatints (q.v.) are produced by dusting powdered sulphur above a layer of oil on the surface of the aquatint plate. Particles of the sulphur corrode the plate in a delicate grain which gives the appearance of a colour wash to the prints.

Sumi-ye: Japanese ink-pictures, i.e. printed in black only.

Summerly's Art Manufactures: an organization established in 1847 by H. Cole (q.v.) with the aim of improving public taste and persuading artists, designers and manufacturers to choose practical decoration appropriate to the use of the article. The project ceased in 1851.

Sunderland ware: several manufactories of a coarse type of cream-coloured earthenware (q.v.), for the most part transfer-printed (q.v.) and frequently pink-lustred and designed as commemorative ware, existed in the Sunderland area in the late 18th and the 19th cent. The following are the best known of these firms:

North Hylton Pottery, Sunderland: founded by Christopher Thompson and John Maling in 1762. Later the firm was known as Dixon, Austin & Co., and subsequently as Dixon, Phillips & Co. (owners of the Garrison Pottery in the same district). Similar pottery was made at Liverpool, Bristol and Staffordshire.
Marks:

DIXON & CO.
DIXON, AUSTIN & CO.
SUNDERLAND
(Impressed)

Wares decorated with transfer-prints (Wear Bridge), sentimental inscriptions and splashes of pink lustre were popular.

Ford Pottery, South Hylton, Sunderland: the pottery was founded in 1800 and was owned by John Dawson & Co. The Dawson family worked it until 1864 when it closed down.
Mark:

DAWSON (impressed)

Wear Pottery, Sunderland: founded in 1803 by Brunton & Co., and known soon after by the name of Samuel Moore and Co. Popular subjects – views, commemorative inscription etc. – decorate their wares.
Marks:

MOORE & CO.
SOUTHWICK
MOORE & CO. (impressed)

Southwick Pottery, Sunderland: in 1789 the pottery was owned by Anthony Scott, owner of another pottery at Newbottle. Combed slip-ware (q.v.) was included in the productions of this factory. Mark:

SCOTT (impressed)

(See also Lustre decoration.)

Sun-flash horse brass: a face piece, extremely popular in Kent, was originally a disc of latten (q.v.) with its centre hand-raised into a high dome or boss and encircled with a wide, flat rim. This extended almost across the horse's face and weighed about six ounces. In rolled brass the outer rim might be serrated. In some examples of the 1850s–80s the flat rim was pierced with twelve triangular rays extending outward to the rim which, from the early 1870s, might be encircled with drilled perforations. The entire brass, including dome and perforations, might be stamped from 1880. Sometimes the dome might be surrounded by a series of concentric circles in relief, number and width varying. A splash of colour might be given from the mid-1890s by fitting into the raised centre a boss of coloured glass or enamelled china: colours noted include yellow, green, dark blue, red, ringed red, white, blue. A series of uncommon rectangular sun flashes had incurved clipped corners and a central dome against a plain ground: others were shield-shape. Some late cast examples display the sun flash against a wide and elaborately patterned rim.

Sung dynasty: dynasty of the Chinese Sung Emperors covering the period 960 to 1279. During this period, pottery of some of the most beautiful shapes and glazes was produced. It excelled particularly in felspathic stonewares of a more or less porcellaneous nature, characteristic of which are the Lung-Chüan and Northern celadons (qq.v.) with their serene forms and soft jade-green depths of colour. Also of this kind are the rare Imperial Kuan or Ko (Fig. c) and Ju wares (qq.v.) and the opalescent blue and purple Chün (q.v.). Very attractive, too, are the brown and black glazes of Honan and Tz'ǔ Chou in the north (qq.v.) and the Chien ware (q.v.) tea bowls from southerly Fukien. All the above owe their colour principally to the presence of iron under varied kiln conditions. Among the vigorously shaped stonewares of Tz'ŭ Chou are those with skilfully carved decoration relieving white, brown or green glazes (Fig. A); and on others bold floral painting in brown now makes its appearance. Delightful incised designs of plants and animals are also a feature of much Sung pottery and especially of the superb creamy-white Ting (q.v.) and bluish *ying ch'ing* porcelains (q.v.). Typical of Sung forms are the small-footed bowl, two-handled jar, *mei p'ing* vase (q.v.) and graceful bottle shown in Figs. A, B and D. Large dishes, jars and bowls are found especially among the celadons exported in quantity throughout the Near and Far East.

Fig. A   Fig. B

Fig. C   Fig. D

Sunk carving: see Recessed carving.

Sunray clock: a type developed in the late 17th cent. at the time of the cult of the 'Roi Soleil', Louis XIV. A central circular dial with carved wooden sun's rays emanating therefrom. Much copied today. Original clocks have the rays of hand-carved wood.

Supper set: a series of four open dishes, which fit into each other around a central circular covered tureen or dish. Made of silver, Sheffield plate (q.v.) or porcelain (q.v.).

Sur fond reservé enamel: see Enamel.

Surimono: a Japanese term meaning literally 'printed things', especially prints used for greetings or to mark special occasions.

Surrey enamel: see Enamel.

Suspension: technical term referring to the method by which the pendulum of a clock is supported.

Susse Frères: firm of French bronze founders, noted for their castings of the works of Mêne (q.v.) and other *animalier* (q.v.) sculptors. Their casts are often stamped with the name 'SUSSE'.

Sussex chair: a type of traditional, rural English chair with a rush seat, produced in various forms by Morris, Marshall, Faulkner & Co. after 1865.

Sussex pig: pottery jug with a loose head used as a cup, enabling the user to drink a hogshead of liquor without disquieting after-effects. Peculiar to the Sussex factory of Cadborough, Rye, 19th cent.

Sussex slipware: crude types of slipware (q.v.) were made at various places in Sussex – Brede, Chailey, Rye, Winston, Dicker and Burgess Hill amongst them – in the late 18th and early 19th cent. Articles for domestic use such as jugs, plates and flasks formed the chief of their productions.

A better-finished and more interesting variety of slipware was produced at this period in Rye, Chailey and Brede, and also at Bethersden in Kent. This was made by inlaying with white clay incised or stamped designs (often inscriptions first impressed with printer's type) on the body of the ware. Formal patterns, foliage, stars, etc., are found on articles made in this way. At Burgess Hill an agate ware (q.v.) was made.

Sussex wares are often distinctive by reason of a streaked glaze used with pleasant effect on many pieces. A glaze speckled with manganese is also common. Jugs in the form of a pig, the head forming a lid or cover, and flat pocket flasks, seem to be peculiar to the Sussex potteries.

The Rye pottery, still in existence at the present time, made some interesting pieces in a red ware in the 19th cent. These were experimental and not made commercially.

Swag: a festoon of flowers, fruits and leaves used as a decorative motif in the late 17th and early 18th cent. During the Neoclassical (q.v.) period of the late 18th cent., swags of husks or drapery were used.

Swagger sticks: short canes, slender, varnished and decorated with cords and tassels, carried during the early Georgian period, continuing until early in the 19th cent. An eyelet hole was bored through the stick and threaded with a woven silk cord looped so that it could be swung from the wrist.

Swan-necked pediment: see Broken pediment.

Swansea earthenware and porcelain: the Cambrian Pottery at Swansea was founded about 1764. William Coles is believed to have been the proprietor during the early period. Coles died *c.* 1778–9 leaving the pottery to his three sons. Coarse red wares were manufactured in the early days. By 1790 John Coles was joined by George Haynes and the firm became Coles & Haynes.

In 1802 William Dillwyn purchased the lease of the pottery on behalf of his son, Lewis Weston Dillwyn. Haynes remained as manager, the firm being Haynes, Dillwyn & Co. In 1817 another company was formed which rented the Cambrian Works from Dillwyn, and traded as T. & J. Bevington & Co. or Bevington, Roby & Co. Their lease expired in 1824 when the potworks reverted to Dillwyn, who in 1831 took his son Lewis L. Dillwyn into partnership.

David Evans and a man named Glasson took over the pottery in 1850. The works were closed down in 1870 and later dismantled.

Marks:

SWANSEA DILLWYN & Co

SWANSEA

SWANSEA

Swansea   *Swansea*

**Pardoe
Cardiff**

The Swansea factory in its early years made wares similar to those produced in Staffordshire at the period – cream-wares, blue-printed, black basaltes, marbled wares and articles decorated with enamels and with lustre (qq.v.).

In 1814 Billingsley (q.v.) and Walker, then occupying the factory at Nantgarw (q.v.), joined Dillwyn at Swansea with the intention of collaborating in the production of a porcelain (q.v.) stronger in body and less subject to flaws in firing than that previously made at Nantgarw to Billingsley's formula. After experiments lasting nearly two years, a more stable composition was produced and manufactured commercially until September 1817. There are at least three distinct varieties of this paste, the most successful being that known as 'duck-egg' because of its greenish translucency by transmitted light. Later a more opaque type of porcelain was made; this had a yellowish tinge and a thin, rather dull, glaze. A third type is much harder, white and glassy in appearance.

After 1817 a porcelain incorporating soapstone (q.v.) and much inferior to the earlier kinds was made.

Porcelain made during Billingsley's period at Swansea is sometimes hard to distinguish from Nantgarw. The shapes and designs used at Swansea were often more ambitious, and in the period 1814–17 many of the productions owe much to French porcelain of the period. Designs taken from natural history, particularly flowers reproduced from rather stiff botanical prints or in sprays or scattered groups, are characteristic of Swansea. Thomas Pardoe (q.v.) and William Pollard were probably the most influential decorators at the factory.

Table ware, and especially plates, form the largest part of existing Swansea pieces.

Fakes are not uncommon – some marked with a Swansea mark – and were usually made in France.

'Swatow' ware: porcelains with thick, 'fat' glaze and roughly-finished, glazed, gritty base, made in southern China and probably exported from Swatow, especially to Japan and Java. Dishes, with wild, powerful painting in red, green and turquoise enamels and similar underglaze (q.v.) blue wares date from the late 16th to 17th cent.; also celadon (q.v.), light brown and pale blue monochromes with white slip flowers.

Sweetmeat basket: small oval or circular silver basket introduced about 1740, found separately or on *épergne* (q.v.) branches. Early examples mostly pierced with cast floral borders. Later ones solid and decorated with engravings (q.v.).

Sweetmeat glass: glass supported on a stem with a shallow bowl, examples from the second quarter of the 18th cent. often being decorated with shallow cutting or slicing. Referred to in the 18th cent. as 'desart glasses', they were intended, with jelly glasses, to be served on glass salvers arranged

in a tier, thus providing the elaborate display required for dessert. (See also Jelly glass.)

Swelling knop: a slight protuberance on the stem of a drinking glass, containing an air tear.

Swept-hilt rapier: a modern term for the type of rapier (q.v.) hilt, introduced in the 16th cent., in which the guard consists of a complicated series of curved bars.

Swing-leg table: a term used in America to describe a hinged-leaf table with a swinging rather than a gate leg. (See also Drop-leaf table.)

Swinton: see Rockingham porcelain.

Swirl paperweight: familiar name for a paperweight (q.v.) composed of coloured canes (q.v.) radiating spirally from the top.

Sword stick: a walking stick concealing a sharp, rapier-like steel blade. Sword sticks date from the 1730s and continued in production until the late 19th cent.

Synchronome clock: an electric master clock patented in 1895.

Tabernacle mirror: an American term generally applied to the late 18th-cent. mirror with flat cornice under which is a row of gilt balls above a scene painted on glass; columns at sides.

Table-chair, -bench: correct term for the misnamed monk's chair, or bench.

TAB   273   **TAL**

The term chair-table is also used. Convertible chair, the back pivoted to form a table top when dropped across the uprights. Though the type existed in pre-Reformation times, most surviving examples date from the 17th cent. and can have no monastic association in England. The device was convenient in saving space and furniture.

Table clock: a clock in a metal case with a horizontal dial, designed to be placed on a table and viewed from above. They were made mainly in Germany from the late 16th to the early 18th cent. The term is also used to describe bracket (q.v.) and mantel clocks.

Table cutting: a method of cutting gemstones in common use before the invention of rose cutting (q.v.) in the mid-17th cent., whereby the stone was ground to have a flat horizontal facet (q.v.) on top. Also known as mirror cutting.

Table services: matching sets of spoons, forks and other table ware. Complete extant services of silver are very rare before the end of the 17th cent. and are not common until the mid-18th. The main patterns are:

Feather-edged: found in the second half of the 18th cent. The stems bear a narrow border fluting, resembling the edge of a feather.

Fiddle pattern: the stems are shaped with a broad upper section and notched shoulders at the bowl end, resembling slightly the basic form of a violin. This pattern was introduced in the early nineteenth cent. Sometimes they are found plain, or with threaded edges, and sometimes with stamped shells on the top.

Hanoverian: the stems have a central longitudinal ridge on the front and upcurved ends. This pattern was the most usual from c. 1720–40.

King's pattern: an early 19th-cent. pattern, with shaped stems and waisted hourglass tops, decorated with scrolls, shells and foliage.

Old English pattern: a perfectly plain form with flat stems spreading slightly to the rounded ends. This pattern was in common use from the mid-18th cent. onwards. Scottish and Irish varieties often have more pointed stems.

Onslow pattern: a rare mid-18th-cent. design in which the upper third of the stems are decorated with radiating fluting and cast and applied cork-screw-like scroll tops.

Queen's pattern: this is a less elaborate form of King's pattern, the decoration struck only on the upper surface of the stem and without a shell on the bowl.

Tabouret: (*Fr.*), a stool.

Tabriz carpets: Tabriz, the capital of ancient Persia, was one of the principal centres of carpet weaving. Both the carpets and the rugs bear more realistic types of decoration than those characteristic of Ispahan (q.v.). The greatest of the 'Hunting' carpets (q.v.) were woven at Tabriz, while other motifs include court figures and animals and birds, although the medallion motif on a plain ground was also popular. Silk is often used in fine specimens, either for contrasting effect with wool, or sometimes alone.

Taft and Co., Messrs: a factory established in 1871 in Keene, New Hampshire, to produce stoneware, redware and *maiolica* (qq.v.).

Taille d'épargne: a jewellery-decorating technique in which engraved designs are filled with enamel. It was used in the 19th cent. in England and America.

Takamakiyé: (*Japanese* = raised sown picture). A Japanese lacquerwork technique whereby the design is in high relief, modelled in composition, and is then lacquered in the desired colours.

Talavera maiolica: tin-glazed (q.v.) earthenware made at Talavera in Spain. Towards the end of the 16th cent. the pottery at Talavera began to replace those of Valencia (see Hispano-Moresque *maiolica*). Blue-and-white and polychrome wares were made, closely influenced by the Italian potteries.

Talbert, Bruce J.: (1838–81), an English architect and prolific designer of furniture, silver, textiles and wall-papers. His style was characterized by sharply delineated outlines and was strongly influenced by Japanese art forms. His publications *Gothic Forms* (1867) and *Examples of Ancient and Modern Furniture* (1876) were pleas for rationalism, solidity and fitness for purpose, and his designs were widely imitated throughout the late 1870s and 1880s.

Tale glass: a second-quality metal (q.v.) taken from the top of the pot, and sold more cheaply than the lower, finer metal.

Tallboy: a double chest of drawers, also known in the 18th cent. as a 'chest-upon-chest'. This piece of cabinet furniture was first made early in the 18th cent. and derived from Dutch example. Early tallboys stand on plain bracket feet, while the ogee (q.v.) bracket foot became popular towards the mid-cent. The tallboy was a development from the earlier 'chest on stand' and continued in use throughout the cent., to be gradually replaced by the wardrobe.

Tall clock: an American term for a long-case clock (q.v.), also described as a hall or floor clock.

Tallow cutting: a method of cutting gemstones in which the stones are rounded in form with a flat top.

Tambour front: a curved sliding top fitted to writing desks, fashionable in the late 18th cent.

Tambour work: a form of chain-stitch embroidery worked with a steel hook, popular in England and France during the late 18th and early 19th cent. The name originated from the way the fabric to be embroidered was stretched over a round frame in the manner of a drum skin.

Tang: the narrow portion of the sword blade which passes into the hilt.

T'ang dynasty: dynasty of the Chinese T'ang Emperors covering the period 618 to 906. This period was the golden age of China, great in literature and painting, and receptive and fertile in its contacts with the outside world. T'ang pottery conveys an unmistak-able vitality and refinement, expressed in beautifully proportioned forms and a disciplined use of rich colour. The

lead glaze was now revived, and applied over a fine white earthenware in green, golden-yellow and blue colourings of great brilliance, which were often splashed on or mottled together or used to enliven designs incised into the surface. Designs were also impressed from moulds. Favoured subjects were stylized flowers and birds, also the palmette and vine which, like some forms, were derived from Hellen-istic sources. Among the tomb figures of the time are models of calm, smiling ladies, dancers, ferocious warriors and mythical monsters, and horses and camels with their riders and atten-dants, showing the most sensitive observation in their modelling. Some unglazed earthenwares were painted 'cold', usually over a white 'slip' (q.v.) of clay, which enhanced the colours. Apart from these, and the refined pale-green Yüeh ware (q.v.) the chief glory of T'ang potters was their invention of translucent white porcelain. General indications of T'ang date are flat bases, and glazes which stop well short of the foot.

Tan-ye: Japanese prints coloured by hand with tan, a red-lead pigment.

Tanzaku: Japanese narrow vertical prints, inscribed with verses, about 355 × 152 mm (14 × 6 in).

Tao Kuang period: (1821–50), characteristic Chinese porcelain wares of this reign are those minutely painted in *famille rose* (q.v.) style, employing low-toned enamels, and *graviata*, coloured grounds. *Tou ts'ai* (q.v.) decoration was also popular. The body is coarser than in 18th-cent. wares, and the glaze has an oily sheen.

Taper box: a small, cylindrical silver or silver-plate box with a handle and a hole in the lid, made to contain a coiled sealing-wax taper. Found from about 1700 onwards. (See also Waxjack.)

Taperstick: small version of contemporary candlestick to hold sealing taper. Found both in vertical form and with flat base similar to chamber candlestick (q.v.). Extant from late 17th cent. onwards. In 18th cent. found as central fitting to inkstands.

Tappit hen: a Scottish pewter (q.v.) measure, a 'hen with a top to it' (fanciful). The true tappit hen holds 1 pint Scots (equals 3 pints English), but the term is usually applied to all capacities.

Tarsia: (*It.*), a form of wood inlay or marquetry (q.v.) widely used in Italy but most notably in Lombardy and Tuscany. Tarsia or intarsia decoration, made up of polygonal *tesserae* of wood, bone, metal and mother-of-pearl arranged in geometrical patterns, was very popular in Lombardy and Venetia in the 15th cent. and much used for the decoration of cassoni (q.v.). The art of pictorial tarsia was brought to a high level of excellence at Florence in the 15th cent. by a number of craftsmen, of whom Francesco di Giovanni, called il Francione, was, according to Vasari, the most highly esteemed. In the 15th and subsequent cent. tarsia was much used for the decoration of both ecclesiastical and domestic furniture. Panels representing views of real or imaginary architecture were popular on cassoni in the late 15th and 16th cent., but during the 17th cent. abstract designs seem to have been preferred. In the 18th cent. tarsia was applied to tables and chests of drawers, usually in patterns of flowers and ribbons.

Tartanware: wooden items, such as small boxes, decorated with Scottish clan tartans. This was hand painted in the 1820s, later mechanically printed paper was stuck on to the object. This ware was particularly popular after 1852, when Queen Victoria acquired Balmoral Castle, in Scotland.

Tassies: (1) replicas of intaglios (q.v.) or glass paste impressions worn as jewellery and named after James Tassie, who settled in London in 1766, where he became famous for these cast gems. (2) Scots for a drinking cup (*Fr. tasse*).

Tate-ye: Japanese prints; upright pictures.

Tazza: (*It.* Cf. *Fr. tasse; Scottish tassie*); wine cup with shallow circular bowl. The name, correctly applied to such pieces of 16th to 17th cent., has become erroneously extended to cover flat dishes and salvers on central foot. Its derivation is clear, however, and can have no connotation with the latter pieces.

Tea caddy: a container for storing tea. 'Caddy' is a corruption of *kati*, a Malay measure of weight of just over one pound. The custom of locking up the family's tea in a box continued long after tea had ceased to be an expensive luxury; caddies, therefore, were invariably provided with locks, and were either divided into small compartments or were fitted with tea canisters (q.v.) for the different kinds of tea. A great variety of materials was used in their construction, including woods of all kinds and *papier mâché* (q.v.). There was also considerable diversity in shape, from rectangular (Fig. A) to square and octagonal (Fig. B); vase and pear (Fig. C) forms were introduced after 1750.

Fig. A

Fig. B

Fig. C

Tea canister: the container for tea in the caddy (if the latter were not already divided into compartments);

made of glass, metal or earthenware; usually bottle-shaped until *c.* 1750, and vase-shaped later.

Teapot stand: see Kettle stand.

Teapoy: until early in the 19th cent. the tea chest stood loosely upon a small tripod table with an octagonal tray top. *Simmonds' Dictionary of Trade*, 1850, defined a teapoy as 'an ornamental pedestal table with lifting top, for holding tea'. The tea canister (q.v.) is often wrongly termed a teapoy.

Tear-drop handle: see Drop handle.

Tears: bubbles of air enclosed within the stems of drinking vessels for decorative purposes. From 1715 to about 1760 clusters of spherical or comma-shaped tears appeared in bowl-base, knop (q.v.) and finial (q.v.).

Tebo: probably the French name Thibaud anglicized. Very little is known about this craftsman who has been the subject of speculation. A 'Mr Teboe, jeweller' is recorded as living at Fetter Lane, London, in 1747, (*Daily Advertiser*, 13 November 1747). There is evidence of a repairer (q.v.) at the Bow porcelain (q.v.) factory from about 1750 who signed his work

T°. Sometime between 1760 and 1768 the same workman was at Worcester (q.v.), and his mark also occurs on Plymouth porcelain (q.v.) of the Cookworthy (q.v.) period. From about 1775 Mr Tebo was working for Josiah Wedgwood (q.v.) who formed a poor opinion of his ability. Subsequently he went to Dublin and passed into obscurity.

Tê-Hua porcelain: see Blanc-de-Chine.

Temmoku: Japanese porcelain with lustrous brown or black glaze, influenced by Chinese Sung (q.v.) wares from Fukien province, made first in the Seto area, then in Mino province and elsewhere. Also the Japanese name for the original Sung ware.

Tenon: see Mortice-and-tenon joint.

Terra cotta: red biscuit earthenware varying in colours according to firing, from pink to purple-red.

Terrestrial globe: a spherical model of the earth. The suggestion that the world was, in fact, round was expressed in world models at an early date and a famous example is the globe made in 1492 by Martin Behaim. In the 18th cent., globes were considered a valuable addition to a library. They were sometimes made in pairs consisting of a terrestrial globe and a celestial globe, showing a spherical map of the heavens. The parts of the globe are, first, the sphere, constructed of wood, plaster or metal, such as copper or brass. The meridian is a flat graduated hoop of metal or wood which encircles the orb and into which the poles of the axis are set, permitting rotation. This meridian, borne on a short column, can be turned to raise or lower the poles. The framework of the stand carries on its upper surface, surrounding the globe, the horizon, on which is presented a perpetual calendar with day of the month, the sun's place in the zodiac, the points of the compass and fixed feasts and winds. A mariner's compass was often introduced on the stand. The surface details were printed on paper, pasted on to the orb. While a pillared stand, with the globe set into the encircling horizon, was the chief method of presentation, the sickle-shaped support, consisting of a brass half circle mounted on a turned column and base, was later common, especially for small globes. The style of the stand varied with furniture fashions.

Terret: these horse brasses, more correctly termed fly terrets, are also known as swingers and flyers. The terret is a vertical ring set between the horse's ears and in which swings a brass with both faces finished and polished. Such brasses are smaller in diameter than the ordinary horse brass.

Terry, Eli: (1772–1852), an American clockmaker, the first to introduce mass production of clocks into the United States. He invented and perfected the wooden movement (q.v.) in the shelf clock (q.v.) and was a master of difficult horological principles, taking out eight patents from 1797–1845. He specialized in tall, shelf, tower and regulator clocks with brass and wooden movements. His success in Connecticut encouraged a large influx of clockmakers and many new factories were started.

Tester: a wooden canopy over a four-poster bed. In the late 17th cent. posts, back and tester were covered with costly material and the corners of the tester were sometimes surmounted by plumes of feathers. At this period a new type of bedstead without footposts was introduced, known as a 'half-tester'. Mid-18th-cent. mahogany four-posters allow the posts and carved cornice (q.v.) of the tester to be exposed, while Regency fashions encouraged the French taste for high-domed canopies.

Tête-à-tête: an alternative name for a *confidante* (q.v.).

'Thin man' toby jug: a variety of early toby jug (q.v.), perhaps made by Whieldon (q.v.) or by Ralph Wood (q.v.), Senior. The figure represents a thin man holding a pipe and mug of beer and the glazing and modelling are not entirely assured.

Thistle bowl: bowl of a drinking glass of thistle form in which the bottom or lower part is a solid or a hollow sphere of glass.

Thistle cup: an exclusively Scottish silver cup, dating from *c.* 1690 to the early 18th cent., rather like a teacup, with single S-shaped handle, and everted lip. Principal decoration is calyx-like arrangement of *appliqué* lobes rising from foot towards waist, and waist is also encircled by fillet. The handle is sometimes enhanced with beaded ornament.

Thomas, Seth: (1785–1859), a Connecticut clockmaker who worked with Eli Terry (q.v.) on an order for 4000 clocks, and later with Silas Hoadley on thirty-hour wooden movements (q.v.).

Thomire, Pierre Philippe: (1751–1843), a French bronze artist. In 1783 he entered service at Sèvres (q.v.), making bronze mounts for porcelain, and from 1784 he was frequently employed by the *Garde Meuble de la Couronne* (q.v.) to make bronze mounts for furniture.

Thonet, Michael: (1796–1871), a furniture designer and craftsman who experimented with lamination and steaming techniques and patented the bentwood (q.v.) process in France, England and Belgium in 1841. He moved to Vienna in 1842 and entered into partnership with Carl Leistler, a Viennese cabinet-maker (q.v.), with whom he made furniture for the Liechtenstein Palace. Thonet established his own company in 1849 and in 1853 took his five sons into the

business, calling the firm Thonet Brothers (*Gebrüder Thonet, Thonet Frères*). Different styles and shapes were developed in bentwood; best known are the cane-seated chair and rocking chair which were mass produced and sold in great numbers all over Europe and America. The firm is still in operation.

Threading: one or two narrow lines engraved as a border on silver spoon and fork stems and other small pieces.

Thread setting: the setting of a gemstone in which the stone is surrounded by a thin strip of gold.

Three-piece glasses: drinking glasses in which the bowl, stem, and foot are made separately and welded together.

Thumbpiece (or **billet**): the projecting part above the hinge of a covered vessel whereby the cover might easily be opened with the thumb. Found in a great variety of forms on flagons and tankards of silver, pewter (q.v.), etc.

Thuringian porcelain: see under Limbach porcelain.

Tic-tac escapement: a type of escapement (q.v.) found in some clocks in the late 17th cent. A modified form of the anchor escapement (q.v.).

Tidal clock dial: a dial that indicates daily the time of high tide at any given port. Not found on Continental clocks. The earliest English dials were made for London, and show high tide at noon and full moon at 3 o'clock. Since the 24-hour cycle is completed each lunation, by having two circles, one fixed and marked 1–29½ (the days of the lunation) and the other movable, marked 1–12 twice over, the daily times of high tide for that port will be shown.

Tiffany, Louis Comfort: (1848–1933), an American designer in the Art Nouveau (q.v.) style, self-styled 'William Morris of America'. Son of C. L. Tiffany, founder of Tiffany and Co. (q.v.). Experimented with different glass techniques. Patented Favrile glass (q.v.) in 1880; founded the Tiffany Glass and Decorating Co. in 1890. His aim was to improve standards of everyday design, thereby abandoning the accepted ideals in his exploitation of the organic formation and fusible properties of the metal (q.v.) itself. Tiffany later worked in bronze, incorporating glass, as e.g. in his lamps, as an art-jewellery designer, and as a potter. He was art director of Tiffany and Co. from 1902.

Tiffany and Co.: a New York jewellery company established in 1834 by Charles L. Tiffany (d. 1902). A branch opened in Paris in 1850. Gained a reputation for fine jewellery and silver in innovatory styles, often influenced by eastern designs.

Tiger-eye glaze: a black and brown glaze which contains golden crystals, produced from 1884 at the Rookwood Pottery (q.v.).

Tigerware jug: a big-bellied pitcher with a cylindrical neck made in German salt-glazed stoneware (q.v.), with surface patterned to resemble tiger or leopard skin, imported into England in the 16th cent. Examples are found mounted with Elizabethan silver or gilt with embossed and engraved neckbands, covers, handles and footrims. Imitated in English tin-enamelled earthenware. (See Malling jug.)

Tiles: much used as ornamental features in rooms, round fireplaces, etc., from the mid-19th cent. Various techniques of manufacture and decoration were used, e.g. encaustic, lustre, *maiolica* (qq.v.), etc., and many artists – William Morris (q.v.), William de Morgan (q.v.), Burne-Jones, Rossetti and others – decorated tiles by hand.

Tills: forerunners of the fitted tray in a modern trunk. Inside many 17th-cent. chests a small tray was fitted on the right near the lid. Sometimes it was itself lidded, the lid hinged into the framework of the chest; sometimes it was locked and occasionally had a false-bottomed hiding place. Catherine of Aragon in 1534 had 'one cofar having four tilles therein, the fore-front of every one of them gilte'. The lidded box-like tills in a chest might be called drawing chests or drawers, although the chest of drawers, as a considerable piece of bedroom furniture and as distinct from a cabinet of tiny drawers, was evolved only in the 17th cent. Thus, in 1599, Minshen referred to 'a great chest or standard with drawing chests or boxes in it'.

Ting: the small three-footed Chinese cauldron used as an incense burner.

Tin glaze: a lead glaze, used as a decoration on pottery and made opaque by the addition of tin ashes. Sometimes called tin enamel. Used in England from *c.* 1570 until the early 19th cent.

Ting (or Ting-chou) ware: light, fine-grained, creamy-white porcelain of the Sung dynasty (q.v.), with ivory-toned glaze often running into gummy drops; from Ting Chou (Chihli Province). Common forms are shallow-lobed bowls and rimless dishes. The finest examples have decoration of plants or flowers, fish, swimming ducks, etc., freely incised under the glaze. Designs were also impressed from moulds. Ting-type wares were also made elsewhere, and at later dates – for example, the 'Kiangnan Ting' of South China, with softer, sandy body and crackled (q.v.) glaze, probably of the Ming dynasty and later. Eighteenth-cent. imitations of Ting at Ching-tê-Chên do not resemble it in quality.

Tint: a residual colour tinge apparent in glass and inherent in the ingredients from which the metal (q.v.) is composed.

Tinted aquatint: an aquatint (q.v.) washed over by hand with a water-colour tint.

Tinted lithograph: a lithograph (q.v.) which has undergone two printings, the key in black, followed by a printed tint.

Tinted lithograph, coloured: a lithograph (q.v.), printed in black with a monochrome mechanical print, other colours being applied by hand.

Toad mugs: commonly made in the North of England in the 19th cent., but also more rarely elsewhere. They consisted of drinking mugs with a large toad inside which can be seen only when the pot is emptied, causing surprise and consternation because of folk superstitions concerning the use of toad poison. The inscription 'Tho' malt and venom seem united . . .' is not uncommon.

Toaster: these were either standing toasters or the familiar fork, and were used for the toasting of both bread and meat. The fork almost always has three prongs. A variation of it is the toastholder, which has two short up-curved arms at the end of a long handle.

Standing toasters are rare and vary much in design. Some have simple tripod bases and central pillars with turned finials (q.v.). On each pillar is a bell-shaped fitting with three prongs

for holding the food to be toasted, and these are adjustable for height. Others are either in the form of a circular trivet (q.v.) with a three-pronged fork, or stand on the ground like a table toastrack.

Toasting glass: a drinking glass with a tall stem drawn to a diameter of 3 to 6 mm ($\frac{1}{8}$ to $\frac{1}{4}$ in).

Toastmaster's glass: a drinking glass with a thick bowl designed to magnify its capacity, on a tall stem. Short, deceptive glasses, known as sham drams, were used by tavern keepers in the late 18th and first half of the 19th cent.

Tobi seiji: ('buckwheat celadon'), Japanese ceramics of Kamakura period (1185–1333) that imitated brown-spotted Lung-chuan celadon (q.v.) wares.

Toby Fillpot: nickname of a noted toper, Harry Elwes, who, through contemporary engravings, served as model for the original toby jug (q.v.).

Toby jug: a jug in the form of a man holding a mug of beer and a clay pipe, adapted from an engraving issued by Carrington Bowles with the verses of a song *The Metamorphosis, or Toby Reduc'd*, said to have been translated from the Italian by the Rev. Francis Fawkes. The brim of the three-corner hat formed the lip of the jug, and the crown a detachable cover or cup. Female toby jugs are known, as well as other variants.

Made by Ralph Wood, James Neale (qq.v.), Lakin & Poole, Spode (q.v.), Davenport (q.v.) and others in Staffordshire, Yorkshire and other areas.

Variants include: Toby Fillpot (q.v.), Admiral Howe (q.v.), The Black Man, Martha Gunn, The Gin Woman, The Parson, The Welsh Country Gentleman, The Convict, The Hearty Good Fellow, The Snuff Taker, The Planter, Punch (19th cent.), John Bull (19th cent.), Pickwick (19th cent.), Shield Toby, Bluff King Hal, The Collier, The Thin Man (q.v.), The Farrier, The Unfrocked Parson (sometimes called Dr Johnson), The Night Watchman, The Sailor, Paul Pry (19th cent.), The Royal Bargeman, The Fiddler, Judy (19th cent.), The Woodman (19th cent.).

Toddy-lifter: a pipette with bulbous or decanter-shaped body for lifting hot toddy from bowl to drinking glass, used in the first half of the 19th cent.

Toft, Charles: (1831–1909), an English potter who worked at the Kerr and Binns factory at Worcester, Minton, and Wedgwood (qq.v.). At Minton, he specialized in the making of Henri Deux ware (q.v.). He established his own factory at Stoke-on-Trent in 1889.

Toft, Thomas: a name occurring on numerous large round slipware (q.v.) dishes and more rarely on hollow-ware (q.v.). It is not known for certain whether the name is that of maker or recipient, but it would seem that the traditional view that Thomas Toft made these pieces is justified for it is unlikely that any collector would have wished to have 35 or more such outsize dishes, some even decorated with the same subjects. The Royal Arms occur on Toft dishes at least five times.

There are numerous references to Thomas Toft in Stoke-on-Trent parish registers. He died a pauper in 1689. There are 35 large dishes, 2 jugs and a posset-pot (q.v.) recorded with Thomas Toft's name. They are decorated with 'trailed slip' (q.v.), the dishes having trellis rim borders interrupted by

panels enclosing the name. More rarely a border of fleur-de-lis or heads was used. The centre decorations comprised the Royal Arms (incorrectly rendered), Arms of the Cordwainers' Company, the Boscobel Oak, Pelican-in-her-Piety, lions rampant, double-headed eagles, figures of cavaliers and ladies, a man smoking, and foliage. Dated examples are known between 1671 and 1689.

Variations in letter 'A' in Toft signature

Togidashi: (*Japanese* = polishing out), Japanese lacquer work technique in which the design is made in colours and then rubbed down to an absolutely even surface, which gives a watercolour effect.

Toilé: (*Fr.*), a term used in lace-making, in preference to the English clothwork or mat, to describe the solid part of the pattern. In needlepoint lace (q.v.) it was composed of rows of stitches, buttonhole or loop. In pillow lace (q.v.) the multiple threads achieved an effect of weaving.

Toilet mirror (or **dressing glass**): a small mirror designed to stand on a table or, in early examples, to hang on the wall. This kind of mirror was a luxury in the Medieval and Tudor periods, and did not begin to come into wider use until the late 17th cent. Post-Restoration mirrors were usually square in shape, and frequently had their frames decorated with stump-work; they stood by means of a strut or hung by a ring. By about 1700 oblong mirrors with arched tops, in narrower moulded frames, veneered or japanned, had begun to replace the square shape. In the 18th cent. several changes occurred. Shortly after 1700 appeared the mirror supported by screws in uprights mounted on a box stand; the box was often in the

form of a flap or desk above a drawer which contained the many toilet requisites of the time; the mirror had a pronounced arched heading at first, and the front of the box was sometimes serpentine in form. The older type of strut support, without the box stand, continued to be made, however, and occasionally a stand with small trestle feet was found. By 1750 mahogany was in general use for toilet mirrors, though some in the Chinese style were gilt or japanned. Simpler designs were introduced in the Neoclassical period; mirror frames, in mahogany or satin-

wood, were often of oval or shield shape, and the uprights were curved to correspond. The stand was also a simpler arrangement, as toilet articles were now placed in the table on which the mirror stood. At the very end of the cent. and later, a wide oblong mirror was fashionable, and was usually swung on turned uprights. Mahogany and rosewood, often decorated with stringing (q.v.), were the chief woods for such mirrors at this time.

Toilet service: silver, or silver-mounted ebony or tortoise-shell sets of toilet boxes, vases, mirror, candlesticks, brushes, etc., of great magnificence introduced after the Restoration and lasting into the late 18th cent. Later replaced by wooden dressing chests with silver-mounted glass fittings.

Tôle: tin-plated sheet iron with japanned, painted or stencilled deco-ration (*Fr. tôle peinte*). Made chiefly by the Allgood family (q.v.) firm at Pontypool (q.v.) from the 1730s, it was popular until the late 19th cent. In America it was made mainly in Pennsylvania.

Tombac: a white alloy of copper and zinc used in the 18th cent. for buttons, snuff boxes and toys (q.v.).

Tompion, Thomas: (1639–1713), the most famous of Restoration clock-makers, described by a contemporary as 'a person deservedly famous for his excellent skill in making watches and clocks, and not less curious and dexterous in constructing and hand-working of other nice mechanical instruments'. He introduced into his clocks many refinements such as perpetual calendar (q.v.) work and elaborate repeating and astronimical work, and made two clocks for Greenwich Observatory.

Torchère: see Candle stand.

Torsion clock: an American clock with a unique striking system, prob-ably patented in 1829 by Aaron D. Crane.

Tortoiseshell ware: cream earthenware (q.v.) covered with a lead glaze stained with mottlings of blue, brown and green from oxides of cobalt, manganese, and copper. Made by Whieldon (q.v.) and other potters, c. 1750.

Torus moulding: a large convex moulding of semi-circular section.

Touch: the pewterer's trade mark. From the late Middle Ages it was obligatory for a London pewterer to mark his wares with a mark or touch which he had registered at Pewterers' Hall. The Great Fire of 1666 destroyed Pewterers' Hall and with it the touch-plates. The system was revived in 1668 when all pewterers were required to restrike upon a new plate, and it continued into the beginning of the 19th cent. No date letter appears on pewter (q.v.), but other marks, including quality marks, excise marks, etc., and what are erroneously called 'hallmarks' (q.v.) were applied. The latter were small punches, usually four, resembling those used on silver. One usually contained the maker's initials. These marks had no authority in law or craft regulations.

Touch-plate: a flat sheet of soft pewter (q.v.) for recording pewterers' touches (q.v.).

Touchstone: a piece of polished 'stone' on which a piece of silver of known quality could be rubbed to compare its mark with that of a piece being assayed.

Tourbillon: a watch in which the escapement (q.v.) is mounted on a revolving carriage, which carries it round. Invented by A. L. Breguet in 1801 to avoid positional error.

Tournai porcelain: soft-paste porcelain (q.v.) was made at Tournai in Belgium from 1751 and the following year the factory became known as the *Manufacture Imperiale et Royale*. Wares were made in the manner of Sèvres (q.v.) and principally biscuit (q.v.) figures were produced, some of which were copied at Derby (q.v.). In the 19th cent. much early Sèvres, Chelsea (q.v.) and Worcester porcelain (q.v.) was copied. The mark of crossed swords with four small crosses, one in each angle, is found in various colours.

Tournai tapestry: tapestries were woven in Tournai, Belgium, from the 14th cent., and rivalled the industry in Arras (q.v.), replacing it as the main manufactory for the Court of Burgundy in the mid-15th cent. Industry declined from the 16th cent. due mainly to political insecurity.

Tou ts'ai ('contrasting colour') enamels: delicate, sparing designs on

Robert Lucas, London, c. 1640

William Eden, London, 1690

James Tisoe, London, 1734

Adam Tait, Edinburgh, 1747

Bush & Perkins, Bristol, c. 1775

Chinese porcelain in underglaze (q.v.) blue, set off by transparent enamel colours, chiefly red, yellow and green; their jewel-like quality was perfected under Ch'êng Hua (1465–87). Deceptive imitations and new-style wares were made under Yung Chêng and Ch'ien Lung; and again revived under Tao Kuang (1821–50).

Townsend, John: renowned cabinet-maker (q.v.) of Newport, Rhode Island (b. 1733). He made excellent block-front (q.v.) furniture and is believed to have been associated with his brother-in-law, John Goddard (q.v.), in originating this form. Outstanding member of a famous furniture-making family, which included his father, Job, several brothers, sons and nephews. Some scholars think the Townsends deserve most of the credit now given to John Goddard for originating block-front furniture.

Toys: an 18th-cent. term to describe small objects of metal, enamel, glass, porcelain, etc. such as scent bottles, patch boxes, étuis (q.v.) châtelaines (q.v.) or seals.

Trade card: 18th-cent. trade cards were usually printed from an engraved or etched copper plate with a highly ornamental border, enclosing the tradesman's name and address and a list of his chief productions. The border might also display a selection of fashionable goods then in demand. Cleverly designed and skilfully engraved by etching or line-engraving (qq.v.) on improved copper, the majority were the work of specialists who, like Matthew Darly (q.v.), and William and Cluer Dicey, advertised themselves as 'Engravers of Shopkeepers Bills' who made 'Shop-keepers Bills curiously engrav'd on Copper Plates'.

Trailed slip: a clay slip (q.v.) used for coating or decorating pottery and applied by trailing it from a spouted or tubular vessel.

Trailing: a technique of the glassblower in which threads of glass are attached to the surface of a glass vessel and melted in. Ribbed surfaces may be produced by means of trailed threads melted in the body of the metal, or the threads may be pinched to form a wavy pattern.

Trailing, pinched: a technique of the glassblower in which applied threads of glass, melted into the body of a vessel, are pinched into a wavy formation.

Trail ornament: a border pattern consisting of formal leaf spray or tendril in a running design. Carved vine trails appear, for example, on 17th-cent. oak furniture, while the early 19th-cent. goldsmiths favoured bands of chased ivy trails as a decorative motif. It was, in fact, an ornamental form used in various ways at widely different periods.

Train: a series of wheel and pinions geared together, forming the mechanism of a clock or watch. There are going, striking, chiming, musical, astronomical trains, etc.

Transfer-printing: the application of decorations from engraved copper plates to pottery, porcelain or enamels by means of bats of gelatine (bat-printing (q.v.)) or later (c. 1800) by paper tissues, first practised on enamel wares at Battersea (q.v.); was effected over-glaze at the Bow (1756) and Worcester (1756–7) porcelain (qq.v.) factories by Robert Hancock (q.v.), and at Liverpool by J. Sadler (q.v.) c. 1756. Printing in blue under-glaze (q.v.) was practised at Worcester c. 1759 and popularized during Hancock's employment at Caughley (q.v.) 1775, and adopted soon after at Liverpool, Lowestoft, Bristol and in Staffordshire.

Other colours were used during the 19th cent. including pink, puce, orange-brown and green. Gold-printing was patented by Peter Warburton in 1810. Multi-colour and block-printing were used from the 1840s in Staffordshire, having been perfected by Messrs F. and R. Pratt and Co. (See also Black-printing.)

Translucent enamel: see Enamel.

Transparencies, pinprick pictures, etc.: a coloured print mounted on a board and pasted over a transformation scene which will show through when the print is held before a strong light. The best-known Victorian series of transparencies are Spooner's *Transformations* and Morgan's *Improved Protean Scenery*, both of which appeared in the late 1830s and the 1840s.

Pinprick pictures were a more simple variant since a coloured print was perforated with a number of small holes and, hence, when held to the light the print would appear to be illuminated. Coloured paper would sometimes be fastened behind the print to change, for instance, sunlight into moonlight, or to show a church in the daytime illuminated at night when held up to the light. An elaboration of this was the making of small transparent slides, which were placed in a box and viewed through peepholes. By raising lids in the box at the top or at the back, the print could be transformed.

The transparency was not a Victorian invention but, like so many other peculiarities, achieved its greatest popularity in Victorian times. The classic book on the subject is *An Essay on Transparent Prints* by Edward Orme (1807). This is illustrated and tells how to construct a transparency.

Treasury inkstand: a four-footed oblong box, with double lid centrally hinged, containing four compartments for writing accessories. So called from an example in the Government department of that name.

Treen: old adjectival form of tree meaning wooden. Now used for a variety of wooden articles, mainly small and of almost any period, such as bowls, Welsh love-spoons, staybusks, boxes, pepper-mills, etc.

Trefid (or **trifid**) **spoon:** also known by the French term, *Pied de biche*. Late 17th-cent. spoon with flat stem widening to a lobed outline at the top, split by two cuts forming three sections suggestive of a cleft hoof. The ends sometimes curve upwards.

Normally found with rat-tailed (q.v.) bowls.

Trembleuse: a saucer with a raised ring, usually decoratively pierced, which holds the cup in place. Made in porcelain (q.v.), silver and *maiolica* (q.v.) in the early to mid-18th cent.

Trencher salt: small individual salt-cellar with solid sides lying flat on the table. Earliest examples date from about 1630. The standard form of table salt till about 1725. Of circular, oval, square or polygonal form with oval or circular well.

Trenton: in New Jersey, established as a pottery centre after William Taylor and Henry Speeler set up a factory there in 1852 for the manufacture of Rockingham and yellow ware (qq.v.). Called the 'Staffordshire of America'.

Trestle table: a long table supported on free-standing trestles. This type of table was in use for dining in the Middle Ages until well into the 16th cent., when a table supported on a joined frame was used.

Tricoteuse: (*Fr.*), a term probably of 19th-cent. origin, applied to a small work table surrounded by a gallery, part of which can be lowered to contain sewing materials. Made from the 18th cent.

Tridarn: a Welsh variety of the press cupboard (q.v.) made in three stages, the two lower enclosed and the top open.

Triple reed dish: a dish having a rim with multiple mouldings around the edge.

Tripod table: see Pedestal table.

Trivet: strictly a three-legged stand on which utensils might rest before the fire, but the word is used to cover many types of stand. The trivets of the 17th and 18th cent. were usually circular and of wrought iron (q.v.); sometimes they had a projecting handle. Later versions, also on three legs, were of an oblong shape with one end curved and fitted with a handle, while the far end had curved projections to fit over the fire-bar of a grate. Others dispensed with legs, and were made to hang on the front of a stove; of this last type many were made in the 19th cent. of cast iron (q.v.) with pierced brass tops.

Trolly lace: pillow lace (q.v.), coarse, made especially in the 18th cent. in Devonshire, with heavily outlined patterns in a *fond chant* ground (q.v.).

Trolly thread: gimp outlining the pattern in Lille lace (q.v.).

Trompe l'oeil: the use of light and shade, perspective and foreshortening that occurs in many forms of art to give a three-dimensional effect and the illusion of reality. Examples may be found in marquetry, wallpaper, etc., as well as in painting.

Trumpet bowl: bowl of a drinking glass of waisted incurving form, merging into a drawn stem (q.v.).

Trussing coffers: a frequent term for leather-covered travelling chests.

Tschinke: a light wheel-lock gun, generally rifled, used for bird-shooting in the area of Germanic culture during the 17th cent. The butt usually takes a sharp downward curve while the lock has an external mainspring.

Tsuikoku: (*Japanese* = heaped black), a Japanese lacquer-work technique in which a deep surface of solid black lacquer is prepared. The design is then carved in the lacquer.

Tsuishu: (*Japanese* = heaped red), a Japanese lacquer-work technique in which a deep surface of solid red lacquer is made, of several layers, and the design is carved in the lacquer.

Tubular chiming clock: a chiming clock invented *c.* 1870 in which tubes are employed in place of bells, gongs or rods.

Tuckaway table: an American hinged-leaf gate-leg table (q.v.).

Tucker Porcelain Factory: a factory established in 1826 at Philadelphia by William S. Tucker, producing both plain white and decorated porcelain of excellent quality. After Tucker's death in 1832 the business was carried on by his partner Joseph Hemphill until 1838, when the factory closed. It was the first large-scale manufactory in the United States and played an important role in the subsequent development of the ceramic industry.

Tudor style: the Tudor period lasted from 1485 to 1603; during this time, both architecture and the decorative arts gradually discarded the Gothic (q.v.) tradition of the Middle Ages and adopted the new modes of expression fashionable in Renaissance Italy.

Tula work: a particular type of silverwork, decorated with niello (q.v.) and sometimes partly gilt, to which the town of Tula in central Russia has given its name, although, in fact, such work was not only made at Tula. Snuff boxes (q.v.) and similar small articles were decorated in this manner with figure subjects, floral or geometrical ornament. Most examples are of no earlier date than the beginning of the 19th cent., although the art of decorating in silver with niello has a longer history in Russia. Tula was also a centre of the iron and steel industry and Peter the Great established a small arms factory there in 1705. (See also Chiselled steel.)

Tulip (or **pear**): a pewter tankard or mug with body of bulbous form.

Tulip ornament: a formal ornament which appeared frequently in the second half of the 17th cent. in a variety of forms. Tulips were painted on tin-glazed (q.v.) earthenware, carved on oak furniture and both chased and embossed on silverware. An intense interest in horticulture, which had already developed in the late 16th cent., was encouraged by the introduction of new plants from the East. The tulip is first recorded in Europe in 1559 and in seventy-five years became the rage; 1634 was the year of tulipomania in Holland, when huge sums were paid for rare bulbs.

Tumbler cup: small, plain drinking-bowl with rounded base and straight sides. Extant from mid-17th cent. onwards.

Tumblers: units in a lock mechanism to retain the bolt. These are immovable to any but the right key which lifts them to predetermined heights and shoots the bolt.

Tunbridge ware: although the term acquired a wider meaning it was first applied to the simple, well finished marquetry and parquetry work (qq.v.), the 'ornamental woodwork' that made the Spa shops celebrated as gift emporiums. This work was introduced in the mid-1680s by the master wood-worker named Jordan and at first consisted of patterned veneers (q.v.) using various coloured native woods. The designs were mainly geometrical but included borders of heavy scroll-work and, in the 18th cent., repre-sentations of flowers and foliage, animals and so on. Large quantities of games boards were sold. When the

Games Act (1739) came into operation many indoor games were prohibited. The Tunbridge ware men set about evolving new games to evade the law and some of these are noted by Hoyle.

The furze, holly, yew and cherry, abundant in the Tunbridge Wells district, were used, as well as any wood of unusual colour or grain that gardeners at the numerous large resi-dences might find. Other woods came from London merchants of native and foreign hard woods. The marquetry work of Tunbridge Wells achieved such fame that the term Tunbridge ware was adopted by London special-ists, who took the opportunity of exploiting the fashion.

Rows of elongated triangles known as vandykes were a feature of Tun-bridge ware, arranged alternately in light and dark woods. These appear to have been derived from the pattern on backgammon and tric-trac boards which were among the first manu-factures. Vandykes might border par-quetry designs composed of various diamond and parallelogram shapes, so arranged as to produce effects of solid cubes viewed in perspective. Handles and spindles might be of lathe-turned stickwork (q.v.).

By the early 19th cent. Tunbridge ware had become a specialized branch of the small cabinet-making trade. This ware usually possessed a pine-wood base with kingwood, rosewood or walnut veneer as a setting for ornament in a wide variety of colourful woods

Robert Russell was a late worker in the Tunbridge style. He is known to have made dressing cases, work boxes and portable desks in the late 18th cent. and the catalogue of the Great Exhibition records him as having sent a 'Tunbridge ware marquetrie inlaid lady's work-box fitted with a till, etc. Made in the Gothic style from native woods.'

Turkey work: this was the name generally given in the 16th and 17th cent. to carpets, cushions and upholstery knotted in the manner of Near Eastern rugs. Apart from larger carpets and rugs, Turkey-work cushions appear to have been made in not inconsiderable numbers in England, though they are now rare. Examples can be dated throughout the 17th cent., and armorial cushions are noteworthy. In the 18th cent. cross-stitch embroidery took the place of knotted pile for upholstery.

Turkish rugs: the most numerous to be found in Europe are those from Anatolia and Asia Minor. Many were imported from the 18th cent. onwards, and due to their distinctive designs and fine quality, were not used on floors but as wall hangings and more often as table coverings, a custom which is still in general use in Holland. They came from Ghiordes, Bergama, Izmir, Kula, Melas, Oushak, Ladik, Konya and Mudjur; the main design is usually what is called the Mihrab, a representation of the mosque arch, often embellished by a hanging lamp between the pillars. Some were intended as prayer rugs. During the 14th and 15th cent. the Ottoman Turks invaded Persia on several occasions and enriched their own carpet and rug industries by importing skilled Persian craftsmen. The influence on these carpet weavers is most marked and a tradition of design and quality was established. The greatest period was during the reigns of Selim the Great and Sulliman the Magnificent, when the Persian carpet weaving was at its zenith. Contemporary specimens bear a marked resemblance to Persian rugs, but the national characteristics are clearly apparent. The flowing lines familiar in the finest products of Tabriz and Ispahan (qq.v.) have become bold and angular. The use of stronger colours and realistic flowers are other distinguishing features.

Turkoman rugs: throughout Turkestan, rugs are woven in traditional variations of the same motif, the octagonal gules, known as the 'elephant's foot', and generally dyed in deep, glowing red, with dark blue and black.

Turner: maker of turned wooden members. Furniture with turned supports was made in the Middle Ages. Turners were themselves chair-makers, and there are examples of early chairs consisting only of turned members, held together by a dowel joint, instead of the mortice-and-tenon joint of the joiner (qq.v.). In the 17th cent., turners were still the makers of cheap chairs with rush or wooden seats, of which the Windsor chair (q.v.) is an example and they continued to be so, producing a variety of simple forms, until well into the 19th cent.

Turner, John: (1738–67), an English potter who started his career as an apprentice to Thomas Whieldon (q.v.).

He was at Stoke from about 1756, then at Lane End from 1762–87. John Turner was, apart from Josiah Wedgwood (q.v.), the most famous Staffordshire potter of his time. Skilful, enterprising and successful in business, much of his work is equal in quality and similar in style to Wedgwood's.

Turner manufactured white stoneware in partnership with R. Bankes at the works of Josiah Spode (q.v.) in Stoke till 1762 when he moved to Lane End to manufacture on his own account, largely cream-coloured wares, stoneware and jasper (qq.v.).

In 1775 Turner was involved with Wedgwood in the opposition of the Staffordshire potters to the extension of Cookworthy's (q.v.) patent, which Champion (q.v.) tried to effect.

John Turner was a member of the New Hall porcelain (q.v.) company from 1781–2. He died in 1787.

William and John Turner succeeded their father, continuing successfully all the styles he had manufactured. But their prosperous business was ruined through its dependence on the Continental trade which was lost to them as a result of the French Revolution and the Napoleonic Wars. Their two factories closed in 1806, John Turner joining Thomas Minton (q.v.) as manager.
Marks:

TURNER   TURNER & CO.
Impressed   Impressed

Turner's Patent

In red

This mark was adopted for the firm's stoneware, usually painted in red, from 1800–05.

Turning: until about 1700 turning was one of the outstanding features of the legs of chairs, tables and stands, and of the uprights of chairs. It was carried out on the foot-operated pole lathe which rotated the wood while the turner's chisel cut the required shape. (See also Twist turning, Bobbin turning and Baluster turning.)

Turret clock: a clock for use in a church tower or other building.

Tutenag: see Paktong.

Twin-acorn thumbpiece: a thumbpiece (q.v.) in the form of two acorns rising from a wedge attached to the lid of pewter measures, etc.

Twin cusped thumbpiece: a thumbpiece (q.v.) in the form of two semispheres rising from a broad base found on pewter flagons (qq.v.), etc.

Twist turning: a variety of turning (q.v.) used by English furniture makers for the decoration of chair and table legs, etc., in the late 17th cent. It came to England from the Continent shortly after the Restoration and replaced the earlier bobbin turning (q.v.). At first the Flemish 'single rope' style was used, but this was followed by the English double rope or 'barley sugar' twist, finished by hand and sometimes pierced. The design was becoming less popular on chairs by 1685 but persisted on tables for some time longer.

Single rope   Barley sugar   Pierced

Two-handled cup: introduced in the late 17th cent., developing from porringer (q.v.) form and gradually replacing the earlier standing cup on a high stem. It is normally found with cover but is of great variety of size and decoration. Used for 'loving cup' (q.v.) ceremonies, race prizes and display generally.

Two-piece glasses: drinking glasses in which the stem is drawn in a piece from the bowl and a foot is added.

Two-seconds clock pendulum:
3.98 m (13 ft 0½ in). When making the
first two clocks for Greenwich Observatory, in 1676, T. Tompion (q.v.)
introduced 2-seconds pendulums and
year movements (q.v.), in an attempt
to secure the greatest accuracy. These
are thought to be the first clocks so
designed in England. When the clocks
were removed from Greenwich they
were converted to movements with
1-second pendulums; 2-second pendulums are now only found in some
turret clocks (q.v.).

Twyford toby jug: see 'Step' toby jug.

Tyg: a word of obscure origin used to
describe cylindrical drinking vessels
with from one to twelve handles: a
multiple-handled beaker.

Tz'ŭ Chou ware: The Tz'ŭ Chou
neighbourhood of China (Chihli Province) has made stonewares (q.v.) from
the Sung dynasty (q.v.) until the
present day. The characteristic body is
hard and greyish white, covered with
slips (q.v.) and glazes of creamy-white,
brown or black and occasionally green
colour, often ingeniously combined.
The Sung wares are remarkable for
bold, sensitive shapes – especially tall,
swelling vases and jars with loop-
handles at the shoulder. Plates and
dishes are rare. One type of decoration
has leafy floral designs strongly incised
or carved through the glaze to reveal
another colour beneath. Another is
bold painting in brown or black. Black
painting under a turquoise glaze was
popular about the 14th cent. Red,
green and yellow enamel painting is
sometimes of Sung date. Ming (q.v.)
wares employed similar techniques,
and elaborate landscape and figure
subjects became more common; but
there is a marked decline in their
vitality.

Uchiwa-ye: Japanese prints; fan-
shaped pictures.

Uki-ye: Japanese perspective prints.

Unaker: china clay (q.v.). It is mentioned in the patent specification of
Heylyn and Frye (q.v.) as 'the produce

of the Chirokee nation of America
called by the natives Unaker' (specification of patents No. 610, 6 December
1744). It was used with a frit (q.v.) to
make early Bow porcelain (q.v.).

American china clay was known to
Cookworthy (q.v.) by 1745. Richard
Champion (q.v.) received from his
brother-in-law, Caleb Lloyd of Charleston, S. Carolina, in 1765 a consignment of china clay, but the discovery
of the fine clays of Cornwall released
English potters from any necessity to
import the ingredients of their wares.

Under-glass painting: early examples of painting under glass belong
to Antiquity. In these examples, the
technique by which they were produced
consisted of engraving the picture on
the back of a piece of glass (usually a
goblet or similar container) through
a layer of gold leaf which had previously been attached to it. Sometimes
colour was added from behind.
Usually a second piece of glass was
used to seal this engraving from behind,
although this was more often omitted
in later work intended purely as
pictures and not as incidental decorations for glass vessels. Many such
pictures were made in Italy in the 14th
cent. and the method is known as
gold-glass engraving (q.v.). From this
method was developed that known as
verre églomisé (q.v.) in which the technique consisted of painting a picture
in reverse directly on to the underside
of a piece of glass and then backing
the whole of the glass with either metal
foil, wax or some other coloured pigment. From this to ordinary under-
glass painting was but another step,
and instead of the foil or pigment,
realistic or decorative backgrounds
could be painted in or, on the other
hand, especially in the case of silhouettes produced by this method, the
unpainted portion of the glass could be
left perfectly clear.

Another method of under-painting
was mirror painting (q.v.). This was
similar to the gold-glass engraving
process, excepting that an amalgam of
tin and mercury, to make it into a
mirror, was applied to the glass. The
parts to be painted were then scraped
away and painted in as required. Such

paintings were often made in China, where the technique is thought to have been introduced from Europe by Jesuit missionaries. Vauxhall bevelled plate glass was exported to China for this purpose in the 18th cent.

Underglaze decoration: decoration (painting or printing) applied to pottery or porcelain (qq.v.) in the biscuit (q.v.) condition before the application of glaze. The colours are absolutely permanent.

Union Glass Co.: an American glass manufacturing company established in 1854 in Somerville, Massachusetts, producing plain and pressed glass (q.v.), cut, engraved and silvered glass, and wares in the Art Nouveau (q.v.) style; also a variety of Venetian-style glass including encased gold-leaf (q.v.) decorated glasses.

Union Porcelain Works: In 1862 Thomas Carll Smith acquired the pottery of Boch Bros (q.v.) at Greenpoint, New York, and it became one of the few manufacturers of hard-paste porcelain (q.v.) in the United States. The factory produced artistic pieces, including imitations of Sèvres porcelain (q.v.), and tiles, hardware and industrial wares.

United States Pottery: an American pottery flourishing from 1852–8, producing porcelain and pottery (qq.v.) wares at Bennington, Vermont.

Universal table: a type of small dining table with draw leaves to extend the top, made in the late 18th cent. (See also Draw-leaf table.)

Uprights: the outer, vertical members of a chair-back.

Urbino maiolica: tin-glazed (q.v.) earthenware made in the city of Urbino in Italy. At Urbino and Castel Durante (q.v.) during the course of the 16th cent. the decorative designs previously employed gave way to pictorial designs in a warmer palette.

Urn: a decorative, two-handled vase with domed lid, of Classical derivation.

Urns as decorative adjuncts were used architecturally from the Renaissance (q.v.) onwards. They also appear as finials (q.v.) on furniture, metalwork, etc., during the 18th cent. and were particularly favoured as a decorative form by late 18th-cent. architects, designers and craftsmen, such as Robert Adam, Matthew Boulton, Josiah Wedgwood (qq.v.), etc.

Urn stand: see Kettle stand.

Urushi-ye: Japanese lacquer prints which involved the application of metal dusts.

Usk japanned ware: a break-away factory, manufacturing japanned ware (q.v.), established by two of the Allgood brothers (q.v.) in 1761, seven miles from Pontypool (q.v.) and operated by them until early in the 19th cent. Maintaining that they were the original makers of Pontypool japan they marketed their ware under that name. (See also Tôle.)

Valenciennes lace: pillow lace (q.v.). True Valenciennes is reputed to have been made in the town and false Valenciennes in the region around, the countrywomen continuing the older style of ground (q.v.) when the townswomen developed a new one early in the 18th cent. although both were 'true' in that they were worked pattern and ground in one operation. False Valenciennes included lace with mixed grounds while true Valenciennes had a clear open diamond mesh worked with four – later three – plaited threads. Patterns were mostly the old Flemish scrolls and conventional flowers without a cordonnet (q.v.) and worked with such exactitude that it became important, and rare, for one worker to complete a whole piece. Around the mid-18th cent. the four pieces for a lady's cap and lappets might cost £45 and represent two or three years' work. Since the early 19th cent. this lace has been made largely in Belgium.

Vamplate: see under Pole arms.

Van Briggle, Artus: (1869–1904), the foremost American Art Nouveau (q.v.) potter, and decorator at Rookwood Pottery (q.v.) 1896–9, having been sent by them to Paris on a scholarship. He moved to Colorado Springs because of ill health and established a pottery there under his own name in 1901. His early work was marked AA in monogram, often with Van Briggle and the date; later Colo.Spgs. was added instead of the date.

Vargueño: see Bargueño.

Variegated wares: earthenware made either by the use of different coloured clays extending throughout the body as in agate ware (q.v.) or by the mixture of colours in the glazes.

Vasa Murrhina: a technique, developed in 1882, whereby layers of different coloured glass are fused with mica, aventurine or coloured particles and covered with clear glass. The term is frequently misapplied to spangled, spattered or aventurine glass (qq.v.); it is in effect a mixture of all three.

Vase carpets: Oriental carpets bearing a design representing a stylized vase of flowers. The design is made up of graceful interlocking palmettes and floral designs, developing from a central motif.

Vaucanson, Jacques de: (1709–82), one of the earliest makers of automata (q.v.) of which records survive. Three of his figures were exhibited in Paris in 1738, and later in London, St Petersburg and in Germany. On the occasion of the London exhibition, a booklet was published, of which the title page reads: 'An account of the Mechanism of an Automaton or Image playing on the German Flute; As it was presented in a Memoire to the Gentlemen of the Royal Academy of Sciences at Paris. By M. Vaucanson, Inventor and Maker of the said Machine: Together with a Description of an artificial Duck, eating, drinking, macerating the Food, and voiding Excrements; pluming her wings, picking her feathers, and performing several operations in Imitation of a living Duck . . . .'. Vaucanson's figures caused sensations wherever they were shown and were the commencement of a long series of exhibition pieces.

Vauxhall Glasshouse: a manufactory of plate glass was commenced here about 1665 by George Villiers, second Duke of Buckingham. John Bellingham approached the Duke with a secret process for making mirrors, and as a result the Vauxhall factory was started and Bellingham was given the post of manager. Glasshouses continued to operate in Vauxhall until the end of the 18th cent., and old mirror plates are often referred to today as 'Vauxhall'.

Veneer: veneering was the chief decorative feature of walnut furniture introduced by cabinet-makers (q.v.) in the second half of the 17th cent. Since that period veneers of many other woods, such as yew, elm, mulberry, mahogany, rosewood, zebrawood, etc., have been used to achieve decorative effects by the cabinet-maker. Thin layers of wood, cut by hand-saw, perhaps one-eighth of an inch thick, are glued to the carefully prepared carcase (q.v.). Cut from the part of the tree which would show a delicate figuring, the veneer was applied to drawer fronts, door panels, table tops, etc., in such a way that the figure on the various parts would match. (See also Curl veneer and Burr veneer.)

Venetian flat point lace: needle-point (q.v.) with a solid *toilé* (q.v.), the fillings few and simple and the brides (q.v.) numerous and decked with picots (q.v.).

Venetian glass: thinly blown soda-glass, worked at a low temperature, cooling quickly, and requiring great speed of manipulation. The Venetian glassmakers, perhaps before the 15th cent., rediscovered the processes of decolorizing glass with manganese. The resulting 'cristallo' became the admiration of Europe and established a Venetian supremacy in the art of glassblowing which lasted until the late 17th cent.

Venetian grounded point lace: needlepoint meshed lace introduced to follow the 18th-cent. French fashion and much resembling Alençon (q.v.). The lace patterns were in the Rococo mood of their time and somewhat florid.

Venetian pillow lace: a minor product dating to the early days of pillow lace (q.v.) and much resembling early needlepoint (q.v.).

Venetian raised point lace: needle-point. This had a distinctively thick multi-thread cordonnet (q.v.) and no mesh ground (q.v.). It was used on the ends of men's cravats in the 17th and early 18th cent. and had a sumptuous effect of carved ivory.

Venetian rose point lace: needle-point (q.v.), lighter than raised point (q.v.). The cordonnet (q.v.) might have two or three rows of picots (q.v.) and more picots were introduced on the many brides (q.v.) which were dotted with tiny roses suggesting a powdering of snowflakes – hence its alternative name *point de neige*. Popular in England in the 17th and early 18th cent. for men's falling collars, ruffles, etc.

Venice porcelain: hard-paste porcelain (q.v.) was made at a factory in Venice started in 1720 by Francesco Vezzi with the help of an arcanist (q.v.) C. K. Hunger, who had previously been at the Du Paquier (q.v.) factory in Vienna. Both in form and in decoration Vezzi porcelain resembles that made by Du Paquier. The wares are marked 'va vena' or 'venezia' in underglaze (q.v.) blue or underglaze red. Another factory was started by Geminiano Cozzi in 1765, but in this case a variety of soft-paste (q.v.) was made, the wares largely imitating Meissen (q.v.). The factory existed until 1812, the mark used being an anchor in red.

Venisons: bowls 'made to fit into one another . . . in capacity ranging from a pint to a peck' (George Bourne), made at Frimley, Cove, and Farnborough, *c.* 1800–50.

'Verditure' or **verditer** (*verd de terre*) **wallpapers:** 18th-cent. name for plain blue-grey wallpapers.

Verdure: a tapestry with a design based principally on floral and plant forms. 16th-cent. verdures with wonderful scrolling foliage are especially noteworthy. In the second half of the 17th cent. formal verdure patterns changed into landscape-verdures. The many styles of verdure have always been favourite furnishing tapestries. Oudenarde, Enghien, Lille, Aubusson and Felletin (qq.v.) specialized in verdures.

Verge escapement: the original escapement (q.v.) for mechanical clocks. Date of invention unknown but perhaps the 13th cent. Although it is an escapement in its worst form, in that it never leaves the pendulum or balance free for an instant, nevertheless it was in its day as revolutionary an invention as was, later, the anchor escapement (q.v.). It held the field unchallenged for about four hundred years; even thereafter it remained in use for clocks and watches, along with better types, for another one hundred and fifty years. It was used in bracket clocks as long as there were only one or two in a house, and they were carried from room to room, since it does not need any very careful levelling.

Vermeil: (*Fr.*), silver-gilt (q.v.).

Vermicelli ground: a ground, usually of gold, used as a decoration on porcelain, formed by covering the surface with a continuous wriggling line.

Vermicular collar: a wavy trail of glass encircling the stem of a glass vessel or decanter neck.

Vernis Martin: a term applied generically to all varnishes and lacquers used for furniture and interior decoration in France during the 18th cent. It derives from the brothers Martin, who in 1730 were granted a monopoly to copy Chinese and Japanese lacquer. They also evolved a special kind of coloured varnish, which was applied in a large number of coats and then rubbed down to give it lustre. It was available in various colours, including grey, lilac, yellow and blue, but the most famous was the green, which was often applied to furniture. Vernis Martin was also used to decorate woodwork, carriages, fans and small boxes. The Martin family were much patronized by the Court and by Madame de Pompadour (see also Japan work).

Verre de fougère: (*Fr.*), Glass made in inland districts in France from potash obtained by burning bracken from the forests. Similar to the German *Waldglas* (q.v.).

Verre de Nevers :(*Fr.*), Nevers glass. This small French town became a centre of glass-making in the 16th cent., when Lodovico Gonzaga, by his marriage with Henriette of Cleves, became Duke of Nevers and brought Italian glassmakers from L'Altare to settle in the town. Glass in the Italian manner was made here until the 18th cent. In particular, small figures and 'toys' (q.v.), made of portions of glass rod, blown or manipulated, are ascribed to Nevers and appear to have been made throughout the period.

Verre églomisé: (*Fr.*), glass decorated at the back with designs in colour and gold and silver foils. It is a method that has been practised for many hundreds of years, but for some reason is named after an art-collector, J. B. Glomy, who died in France in 1786. Borders of *verre églomisé* in arabesque patterns and with coats-of-arms were used to frame mirrors *c.* 1695.

Verzelini, Giacomo: (1522–1606), a Venetian glass maker, believed to have come to England from Antwerp in 1571 and perhaps to have worked for Jean Carré (q.v.). In 1575 he obtained a privilege from Queen Elizabeth I for twenty-one years to make Venetian glass in London and to teach the art to Englishmen. He set up a glasshouse in Broad Street in London and the tradition which he founded was to dominate glass making in England until the last quarter of the 17th cent.

Vetro di trina: (*It.*), glass decorated with intricate patterns formed by threads of white glass embedded in the clear glass. Of Roman inspiration, this type of decoration was used in Venice in the 16th cent., the technique involving the arrangement of rods containing threads of white glass round a cylindrical pot which were taken up on a gathering of clear glass, the pattern being formed by twisting the gathering as required. Subsequently the shape was obtained by blowing and manipulating. This type of glass is also known as lace glass.

Vever, Henri: (1854–1942): one of the most influential French designers of Art Nouveau (q.v.) jewellery, and author of an authoritative work on French 19th-cent. jewellery. He and his brother Paul (1851–1915) inherited their father's jewellery firm in 1874 and developed a reputation second only to that of Lalique (q.v.). The characteristic style is somewhat formal and geometric.

Vezzi: see Venice porcelain.

Vicar and Moses: a popular subject with the Staffordshire figure makers during the second half of the 18th cent. first made by Ralph Wood (q.v.). It shows a parson in the pulpit asleep, with the parish clerk at the desk below conducting the service. Recorded with Ralph Wood glazes, as a 'white' figure group, and in enamel colours. Extensively pirated. The marks

R. WOOD   Ra Wood
                   Burslem

occur occasionally. The incised mark

R WOOD
1794

has been noted on a number of examples, some spurious.

Vienna porcelain: Claudius Innocentius Du Paquier, assisted by Christoph Conrad Hunger, an enameller and goldworker who had worked at St Cloud and at Meissen (qq.v.) and Samuel Stoelzel, an arcanist (q.v.) from Meissen, founded a factory at Vienna in 1717. He started by producing tableware derived from

silver shapes, decorated with Chinese motives and exotic flowers. About 1725 German flowers and European subjects were introduced in colours and in *schwarzlot* (q.v.), a black monochrome heightened with gold. Du Paquier figures formed at first parts of vessels only, supports, handles or finials (q.v.), but gained independence about 1730 and came into their own. The mingling of rustic pottery tradition with the urbanity of Meissen models gives these figures an air of wondering surprise. Financial difficulties forced Du Paquier to sell his factory to the State in 1744, when a complete reorganization took place. At that time the Vienna mark, a shield incised or, more often, in underglaze (q.v.) blue, was first introduced. New findings of kaolin (q.v.) in Hungary (1749) and sound management finally brought prosperity to the factory. L. Dannhauser and J. J. Niedermeyer modelled figures of great charm. During the latter part of the cent. the transition to Classicism took place under the direction of Konrad von Sorgenthal (1784–1805). Tablewares in the manner of Sèvres (q.v.) have coloured grounds and gold decoration of restrained design, including medallions with portraits or landscapes. Figures of the period are often biscuit (q.v.), to reproduce the effect of antique marble statues. These figures are clad in stylized Greek gowns, and their timid character seems due to a certain slackening of creative power. However, the factory carried on until 1864.

Vienna regulator: a weight-driven pendulum clock designed to hang on a wall, first made in Austria in about 1875. They were much copied in America and Germany.

Vignette: a small ornamental design or picture, not framed in a border, the edges being sometimes shaded off into the surrounding paper, used as a means of decoration in a book.

Villeroy and Boch: a German pottery firm established in 1836, producing earthenware, stoneware (qq.v.), etc., including art pottery (q.v.) with decorative coloured clay inlays.

Vinaigrette: small box fitted with a hinged inner lid or grille, sometimes simply perforated or, more often, pierced in elaborate and attractive designs. A perfumed sponge is secreted underneath this grille and the aroma escapes through it when the box is opened. Introduced in the late 18th cent., they were made to represent books, purses, eggs, etc. Usually in silver or gold, vinaigrettes are often beautifully engraved or chased.

Vincennes porcelain: see Sèvres porcelain.

Vinovo porcelain: a variety of soft-paste porcelain (q.v.) was made at Vinovo (Turin) between 1776 and 1820. The mark used consisted of several variations of the letter 'V' containing a cross.

Visor: that part of the helmet which protects the face and is pierced with slits to allow vision.

Vitruvian scroll: a border ornament consisting of a band of repeating scrolls resembling waves, much used as an architectural motif and on furniture during the 18th cent. During the Classical Revival of the latter part of the cent. this type of border ornament appears consistently upon carpets, ceramics, metalwork, etc.

Voider: large dish for collecting broken meats and table remnants. A Medieval term. The only known surviving example in silver is a 17th-cent. replacement of an earlier dish, belonging to the Drapers' Company.

Volkstedt porcelain: originally a soft-paste porcelain (q.v.) was made at Volkstedt in Thuringia about 1760, but later the factory secured a privilege from the Prince of Schwarzburg-Rudolstadt and acquired the secret of making hard-paste (q.v.). The body was greyish and of uncertain quality, frequently imitating the Meissen (q.v.) mark. From about 1799 onwards an 'R' for Rudolstadt was used.

Volute: a scroll form, as on an Ionic capital.

Voyez, John: (1735–1800), modeller and manufacturer of French extraction, brought to Staffordshire by Wedgwood (q.v.) in 1768 but quarrelled with him. Issued catalogue of seals and intaglios 1773 and did an extensive trade, undermining that of Wedgwood 1773–6; probably modelled for the Ralph Woods (q.v.), of Burslem; 'Fair Hebe' jug (q.v.) 1788 made for Richard Meir Astbury; in London 1791; disappears from record.

J VOYEZ
1788

Voysey, Charles Francis Annesley (1857–1941): An English architect and designer who devoted his artistic life to a search for simplicity in design, and whose work is a happy fusion between the ideals and the practices of Art Nouveau and the Arts and Crafts Movement (qq.v.). He designed furniture and other domestic wares, specializing in wallpaper and fabric.

Vulliamy family: a London family of clockmakers. The eldest, Justin, was active between 1730 and 1790, his son Benjamin from 1775 to 1820, and his grandson Benjamin Lewis, one of the last of the old school of London clock- and watchmakers, from 1809 to 1854.

Wager cup: a double cup formed as a skirted woman holding a swinging cup above her head, the skirt also forms a cup, both to be emptied without a spill. Made on the Continent from the 16th cent., a few rare examples survive in England from Charles II period and other copies made in late 18th and early 19th cent. Wager cups were also made in the form of a windmill, so that when they were inverted, the body of the mill acted as the bowl.

Wagon-spring clock: a clock using a similar spring to that used in a wagon, made in America c. 1825–55.

Wag-on-the-wall clock: an American term for a clock designed to hang on a wall. Frequently fitted with a pendulum, both weights and pendulum exposed.

Wainscot chair: modern jargon for a panel-back joined chair of the late 16th and early 17th cent.

Waiter: small tray for handing wineglass, letters, etc. Conforms generally to salver form (q.v.). In 18th cent. silver waiters were often found in pairs *en suite* (q.v.) with a larger salver. The small early, footed form often misnamed 'tazza' (q.v.).

Waldglas: (*Ger.*), glass made in inland districts from potash obtained by burning bracken from the forests.

Wall, John: (1708–76), Dr John Wall was the son of a one-time Mayor of Worcester and a successful local tradesman. Well-educated locally, he went to Oxford, became a Fellow of Merton, studied medicine at St Thomas's Hospital, London, and did some competent amateur painting. He was one of the original shareholders in the Worcester (q.v.) factory formed in 1751 for the manufacture of soapstone (q.v.) porcelain. He died in 1776. The first period of Worcester porcelain (q.v.) is known among collectors as the 'Dr Wall period' and is used to cover wares produced up to the year 1783, seven years after his death.

Wall bracket: the detachable wall bracket, as distinct from the fixed architectural feature, appeared towards the end of the 17th cent., and seems to have been used at first for displaying china. Its prominent position in the room singled it out for special decorative treatment in carving or gilding. In the early Georgian period the bracket was often used to support a bust or vase, and as a result it tended to become larger in size and more heavily ornamented; but with the return of the fashion for displaying china about 1750 and the growing use of the bracket for supporting lights, it became altogether more delicate in appearance, and was adapted to the various styles of the Chippendale and Adam (qq.v.) periods. The wall bracket supporting a clock was a popular form of decoration in the later 18th cent.

Wallendorf porcelain: see Limbach porcelain.

Wall-light: See Sconce.

Wallon sword: see *Pappenheimer*.

Wall pocket: flower or spill vase shaped as a mask, fish, or cornucopia, made in Staffordshire salt-glaze (q.v.), and in Liverpool and Lambeth delft (q.v.), 18th cent.

Walton, John, pottery figures: made from first decade of the 19th cent. until 1835, with tree backgrounds decorated with bright enamel colours, and Egyptian black (q.v.).
Often there is a large blue scroll on the base of the figures, which are sometimes marked within a scroll at the back. Occasionally the mark is underneath.

Wan Li period: (1573–1619), a period in which Chinese porcelain continued to be made in many of the Chia Ching styles (q.v.). Porcelain with enamels (q.v.) and underglaze (q.v.) blue painting (the *wu ts'ai*) are especially characteristic. The numerous blue-and-white (q.v.) export wares are very variable in quality, often with poor blue and careless drawing. Pieces expressly intended for Europe become common.

Warming pan: an enclosed metal pan, often with pierced or engraved cover and a long handle, used to contain hot embers for warming beds, made of brass or copper. Examples in silver are rare, but one or two late 17th-cent. versions survive.

Warner, Metford: the great entrepreneur of the British wallpaper industry in the late 19th cent., chairman of the firm of Jeffrey and Co. (q.v.). He placed great value on fine quality and was tireless in his search for new talent.

Warp: the series of threads placed lengthways in the loom over any desired width. Also called the chain or twist. An individual thread of warp is called an end.

Washing stand (or **basin stand**): specially adapted for bedroom use after 1750, and of two main kinds. There was a tripod stand with three uprights, a circular top fitted with a basin, and a central triangular shelf with a drawer (or drawers) and receptacle for soap. A four-legged version of this type was also made. A cupboard or chest of drawers on four legs with a basin sunk in the top, the latter covered by a lid or folding flaps was also made.

Wassail bowl: a two-handled loving cup, passed clockwise around the company on convivial occasions.

Watcombe Pottery: an English pottery established in Devon in 1869. Small terra cotta (q.v.) wares were produced, mainly in the Greek Revival style.

Water clock: a contrivance used in Egyptian, Greek and Roman times for measuring time by the regular flow of a stream of water changing the level in a container, on the surface of which floated a means of indication on a fixed scale. Water clocks in the 17th and 18th cent. were drums with internal pierced sloping divisions, causing the water to pass slowly from one to the other, making the drum revolve and its axis roll down a graduated framework. Very few genuine examples exist.

Waterford glass: the earliest record of flint-glass making at Waterford was discovered by Westropp in *The Dublin Journal*, 1729: 'a glasshouse near Waterford now producing all sorts of flint-glass, double and single . . . sold at reasonable rates by Joseph Harris at Waterford, merchant'. This glasshouse was at Gurteens, three miles from the city, and operated until 1739. The now celebrated Waterford glasshouse started production in 1784, financed with a capital of £10,000 by George and William Penrose, merchants. As works manager they employed John Hill, member of a family operating at the important Goalbournhill Glasshouse near Stourbridge. In evidence given before a committee examining commercial relations between Great Britain and Ireland in 1785, John Blades, a leading cut glass manufacturer in London, stated that 'Mr. Hill, a great manufacturer of Stourbridge has lately gone to Waterford, and has taken the best set of Workmen he could get in the County of Worcester'. The Penrose glasshouse was bought in 1799 by Ramsey, Gatchell and Borcroft, who built a new factory in Old Tan Yard, advertising the old premises to be let. Gatchell had become the sole proprietor by 1811 and with successive partners, the firm remained in the family. At the Great Exhibition of 1851, Gatchell exhibited a magnificent *Etagère* or ornamental centre for a banqueting table, consisting of forty pieces of cut glass, so fitted to each other as to require no connecting sockets of other material; quart and pint decanters cut in hollow prisms. Centre vase or bowl on detached tripod stand. Vases and covers. Designed and executed at the Waterford Glass Works'. This was Gatchell's swan song; his final effort to compete with England was a failure, and he closed the glasshouse later in the same year. It is difficult to distinguish Waterford glass from that made at other Irish glasshouses. Irish glass was said to display a slightly dusky tint although that from Waterford, by the first decades of the 19th cent., was claimed to be clear and colourless. No excise duty hampered the development of the Irish glasshouses in the 1780s and the glass produced was ideal for cutting in deep relief which became so popular. Much deep cut glassware was sent to England, where the Excise Duty, imposed under the Glass Excise Act of 1745 and increased later in the cent., discouraged heavy glass-making. The first Irish glass excise duty was imposed in 1825. The glasshouse ceased to function in 1851.

Waterloo Glasshouse Company, Cork: established in 1815 by Daniel Foley, a glass and china seller of Hanover Street, who set up as a specialist in extensive table services in cut glass (qq.v.) for military messes, particularly for regiments occupying France. By the end of 1816 he employed about a hundred men and women, many experienced workers deserting from the Cork Glasshouse Co. (q.v.) under the lure of higher wages. Glass trumpets were made for sale. A steam engine was installed to operate the cutting wheels and other machinery, thus drastically reducing costs.

Geoffrey O'Connell was taken into partnership during 1825, the firm operating as Foley and O'Connell, Waterloo Glass Works Co. They advertised that they had introduced a new annealing process which enabled them to guarantee their flint-glass to withstand hot water without breaking. The excise duty was too heavy a burden, and in mid-1830 the firm ceased operating. Fifteen months or so later it was reopened by O'Connell, who introduced up-to-date methods of blown-moulding and advertised that he had 'restored one hundred families to employment'.

The venture could not compete with English prices, however, and in 1835 he was made bankrupt owing to his failure to pay excise duties.

Watermark: a distinguishing mark, sometimes including the maker's initials, name or device, and occasionally the date, impressed in the pulp during the process of papermaking, and visible in the finished product when held against the light. They have been indexed, and approximately dated, in such works as Briquet's *Les Filigranes* (1282–1600), 1923, and Heawood's *Watermarks mainly of the Seventeenth and Eighteenth Centuries*, 1950.

Wauters family: tapestry weavers of Antwerp, Michael and Philip Wauters worked specially for the export trade in the latter part of the 17th cent. Apart from connections in Vienna, Paris, Lisbon and Rome, they studied the English market carefully and produced for it *pièces de petites dimensions à la mode d'Angleterre*. They imitated popular English tapestry sets, such as *Hero and Leander*, *Playing Boys*, *Metamorphoses*, and the Duke of Newcastle's *Horsemanship* series. Their mark is distinctive and their work can nearly always be distinguished from English weaving. Peter Wauters was also connected with them.

Wave pattern: see Vitruvian scroll.

Wax-flower modelling: groups of wax flowers and fruit in glass cases were a particular Victorian feature of decoration. At their best they are fascinating, although it is difficult to find specimens in perfect condition with the colours unfaded. Several Victorian books deal with the subject, notably *The Royal Guide to Wax Flower Modelling* (1851) (with four coloured groups of flowers to help the amateur modeller) by Mrs Peachey (artist to Her Majesty).

Waxjack: open-frame stand for coil of sealing wax taper threaded on central pin and led through nozzle above. Found from the mid-18th cent. onwards.

Web foot: see Duck foot.

Webb, Philip: (1831–1915), a leading British architect and designer. His set of uncut glasses made by James Powell and Sons (q.v.) for William Morris (q.v.) in 1859 embody the purest principles of simple form and good craftsmanship of the Arts and Crafts Movement (q.v.). He had a profound influence on glass design in the 20th cent.

Webb, Thomas and Sons: an English glass company founded in Staffordshire in 1837. The best period was while Thomas Wilkes Webb (1837–91) was the director. The firm's high reputation for craftsmanship is derived from the production of Woodall cameo glass, etched, rock crystal and engraved glassware by F. Kny (q.v.) and others, and also art glass.

Wedge thumbpiece: a thumbpiece (q.v.) formed by the extension of the lid attachment upwards to a point.

Wedgwood, Josiah: (1730–95), Josiah Wedgwood was born at Burslem. He left his brother's pottery, where he had been apprenticed in 1752 to go into partnership at Stoke with John Harrison and where he made agate, tortoiseshell and other staple wares until, desiring greater experimental opportunities, he joined Thomas Whieldon (q.v.) for a five-year partnership in 1754.

On leaving Whieldon in 1759 Wedgwood took over the Ivy House Works, which he retained until 1773 for the manufacture of useful pottery wares. In 1764 he rented the Brick House (or Bell Works). In 1766 he bought the Ridge House Estate where he proceeded to erect a factory which he named Etruria (q.v.). The same year he proposed a partnership to Thomas Bentley, a Liverpool merchant whose taste for Classical art accorded with his own. In 1769 Bentley joined him, the partnership lasting until Bentley's death in 1780. The Wedgwood & Bentley Etruria period was responsible for the finest products of the factory.

Wedgwood died in 1795, when the factory was inherited by his second son Josiah.

WHIELDON/WEDGWOOD partnership, 1754–9:
Wedgwood improved coloured glazes generally, and in the course of his experimental work devised 'a green glaze to be laid on common white (or cream-colour) biscuit ware'. He described this glaze as 'the result of many experiments that I made in order to introduce a new species of coloured ware to be fired along with the tortoiseshell or agate ware in our common glass ovens, to be of an even self-colour, and laid upon the ware in the form of a coloured glaze'.

IVY HOUSE, 1759–64:
Wedgwood continued the production of staple and Whieldon style wares but added green and, after 1760, yellow glaze, devising such shapes as the cauliflower and the pineapple to use the new colours to advantage.

Creamware (q.v.) was probably perfected by Wedgwood in 1762 when he presented Queen Charlotte with a caudle and breakfast set. After 1765, styled 'Potter to the Queen', the product was known as Queen's ware. The best examples are pale in shade, light in weight, often decorated in coloured enamels, with border patterns often of Neoclassical design. Most creamware and all Queen's ware items are impress marked, the earlier in upper and lower case, the later in upper case only. Manufacture has continued to the present day.

BRICK HOUSE or BELL WORKS, 1764–9:
Wedgwood concentrated on increasing output of useful wares in Queen's ware, though many items, both useful and decorative, were made in basaltes (q.v.). Items are impressed in upper and lower case, or in upper case; quality is high.

ETRURIA, opened 13 June 1769:
The first day's production consisted of six Etruscan ware vases thrown by Wedgwood while Bentley turned the wheel. They were painted with red classical figures and inscribed *Artes Etruriae Renascuntur* ('The Arts of Etruria are re-born'), a clear indication of the ambitions and tastes of the partnership and the style which was to dominate its period.

Before 1780 basaltes had been developed as a decorative body applied with endless variation to the manufacture of chimney ornaments, vases and decorative useful ware of the finest quality. The seal and wafer marks were used on vases and larger pieces, and the upper and lower case or upper case Wedgwood & Bentley mark impressed on smaller items. Encaustic (q.v.) and enamel decoration typify the basaltes of this period.

Creamware was developed decoratively, the 'surface agates' and other styles emulating polished stone, garnitures or suites of chimney ornaments being the most successful. These are often found with basaltes bases with the wafer or seal mark, or are otherwise impressed Wedgwood & Bentley.

It was also during the partnership that Wedgwood developed his most successful decorative ware. Called at first 'the white body', Wedgwood's intention was to devise a body with lapidary imitative possibilities, one capable of emulating Graeco-Roman objects in coloured glass or polished natural stone. Through 1773 to 1774 he experimented with 'white spars and earths', many of which had never been used before. By the end of 1774 he had developed a 'fine white terracotta of great beauty and delicacy' with a 'waxen' finish. By 1776 he had improved the body, which he then described as 'a fine white artificial jasper of exquisite beauty and delicacy, proper for cameos, portraits and bas-reliefs'.

Jasper (q.v.) was used with conspicuous success as a decorative body, a vast range of items being produced in it of great fineness and finish, including tea and chocolate ware, vases, plaques, bas-reliefs, and cameos in all sizes, in light and dark blues, green, black, lilac or lavender, and a peach-pink, usually with white reliefs. The jasper product of the partnership period is, however, largely blue-and-white or solid white, and is usually marked Wedgwood & Bentley, impressed, though many smaller items are found unmarked, being units of sets and sold as such.

While basaltes, jasper and Queen's ware are the most successful of Wedgwood wares, other 'dry' or unglazed bodies enjoyed a considerable market in both decorative and useful applications. These were all made from local marls to which various 'ochrous' earths were added to produce colour.

There are many variations of colour due to the quantity of admixture and the degree of firing. These wares were described by Wedgwood as
(a) Rosso antico: dark red to chocolate
(b) Cane ware: buff
(c) Terra cotta: light red
(d) Drab ware; olive grey
(e) White stone ware: pure white.

JOSIAH WEDGWOOD
Feb. 2nd 1805

Wedgwood & Bentley.

wedgwood   WEDGWOOD

Wedgwood & Bentley

Wedgwood & Bentley: Etruria

WEDGWOOD
WEDGWOOD

Wedgwood

W. & B.

Wedgwood & Bentley
356

WEDGWOOD & SONS   WEDGWOOD

L. Lysore

Wedgwood
& Bentley

Wedgwood
Wedgwood

WEDGWOOD

WEDGWOOD

Josiah Wedgwood II's conduct of the factory was unsuccessful due to his lack of interest coupled with the damage to trade caused by the Napoleonic Wars – so much so, that in 1811 he wrote 'the business is not worth carrying on, and if I could withdraw my capital from it, I would tomorrow'. Nevertheless, the period is distinguished by ten years of experiment in and production of bone china (q.v.) (1812–22). The ware found no great success.

By 1828 Wedgwood's trade had so declined that the London showrooms were closed, the stock of wares and old moulds and models being sold for £16,000, a considerable disaster to the firm and one from which it was unable to recover for many years.

In 1875 a London showroom was opened again and in 1878 the making of bone china revived. With the opening of the modern Wedgwood factory at Barlaston (started before and completed just after the 1939–45 War) the firm regained its eminent position.

Wednesbury: a South Staffordshire centre of the enamelling trade from 1776, when Samuel Yardley started there, and highly praised for its products in the early 19th cent. The last enameller, Yardley's grandson, gave up the trade in 1840.

Weesp porcelain: hard-paste porcelain (q.v.) was made at Weesp in Holland from about 1754, the factory moving first to Oude Loosdrecht in 1771 and then to Oude Amstel in 1784. The mark of crossed swords with a dot at the pommel of each hilt and three dots at the outside angles formed by the intersecting blades was in use while the factory was at Weesp. During the Oude Loosdrecht period an 'M.L' was used, either incised, in underglaze (q.v.) blue or in enamel colours, while at Oude Amstel the word 'Amstel' was employed, in either blue or black.

Weft or **woof:** in weaving, the threads which are woven across the width of the fabric.

Weisweiler, Adam: French cabinet-maker (q.v.). Born *c.* 1750 at Neuwied and trained in the workshops of Roentgen (q.v.). Established in Paris before 1777. Became a *maître-ébéniste* in 1778. He worked for the dealer Daguerre and, through him, supplied a large amount of furniture for the Royal palaces, and particularly for Queen Marie Antoinette at St Cloud. He was a good business man, and in consequence survived the Revolution safely, and was employed under the Empire, during which time he executed commissions for Queen Hortense. He was still in business in 1810. He used the stamp:

A·WEISWEILER

Weller, Samuel A.: (1851–1925), an American potter. He established a pottery at Zanesville (q.v.), Ohio, in 1882 and in 1895 bought the Lonhuda

Pottery (q.v.) which business he transferred to his own, producing art pottery (q.v.) similar to Rookwood (q.v.) wares.

Wellington chest: a tall narrow chest containing about a dozen drawers which can be locked by a single hinged flap securing all the drawers.

Welsh dresser: a cupboard intended for the display of plate, usually of oak, consisting of enclosed section with one or two doors below three drawers, and a superstructure holding shelves.

'Welshman' toby jug: a rare model of toby jug (q.v.), the figure being seated on a chair with the Welsh goat between his knees.

'Welsh' ware: shallow meat dishes with feathered slip decoration, in form like a gardener's trug, commonly made in Staffordshire, Sunderland (Scott's 'Superior Fireproof') and Isleworth, under this name.

West Country measure: a tavern measure (q.v.) with bulging body tapering to a narrow spouted neck. Of West Country origin. Examples of copper measures of this type are more frequently found than those of pewter.

What-not: a portable stand with four uprights enclosing shelves, in use after about 1800 for books, ornaments, etc.

Wheat-ear ornament: carved ornament in the form of a wheat ear, frequently used on late 18th-cent. chair backs of shield-shape design. Chair backs of this type were included in Hepplewhite's (q.v.) *Cabinet Maker and Upholsterer's Guide*.

Wheel barometer: a siphon-type in which the variation of the mercury level is magnified and registered on a circular dial.

Wheel engraving: glass, rock crystal and semi-precious stones can be decorated by means of the lapidary's wheel, which is in principle a grindstone, fed by water and abrasive and mounted with metal or stone discs of various sizes according to the pattern desired. Engraving on glass is the same process as cutting, the surface of the material being afterwards polished, although sometimes a matt surface is used to contrast with a polished surface. The technique of wheel engraving was used by the Romans and in modern times, was first employed as a means of decorating glass at the Court of Rudolf II in Prague in the late 16th cent. English wheel-engraved glass vessels date from the first quarter of the 18th cent., wine glasses bearing simple borders of scroll work and formal flowers being characteristic.

Wheeling Pottery Co.: Established in 1879 at Wheeling, West Virginia, this factory produced a general line of porcelain tablewares. Charles Craddock, head of the decorating department, came from Burslem, Staffordshire, where he had worked for Minton (q.v.).

Wheel lock: mechanism for igniting a gun, in which a piece of pyrites, fixed between the jaws of a cock, is pressed against the grooved edge of a wheel projecting through the bottom of the priming pan. The wheel is forced to rotate by a spring, released by the trigger, and rubs against the pyrites, causing a shower of sparks which ignite the powder. The lock is usually wound by means of a spanner, but on rare examples this is effected automatically when the cock is drawn back.

The earliest known illustration of a wheel-lock mechanism is that in the Codex Atlanticus of Leonardo da Vinci (d. 1519). There is, however, no evidence to show that this was ever made, the first practical wheel lock apparently having been produced in Germany in *c.* 1520. It is rarely found on military weapons, probably on account of the expense of manufacture, but it was much used for sporting and target guns until well into the 18th cent.

Whieldon, Thomas: (1719–1795), a potter who founded his factory in 1740. From 1754 until 1759 Josiah Wedgwood (q.v.) was his partner. He built up an extensive business and made a fortune estimated at £10,000 from his trade. He retired about 1780, and became High Sheriff of Staffordshire in 1786. No marks were used at his pottery.

Whieldon, one of the best known of English potters, had a strong and lasting influence on the tastes of his time and on the work of craftsmen to follow him.

He gave his name to a highly developed type of earthenware distinctive for its wide range of colours made possible by the use of coloured clays in the body and also by means of staining oxides in the glaze. Starting from the agate ware (q.v.) made at an earlier date, Whieldon revived and improved the methods formerly used, producing marbled wares of considerable merit. Simple shapes were customary in plates, dishes and other articles, the pieces relying mainly on colour for their appeal. 'Tortoiseshell' ware (q.v.) was among Whieldon's most successful productions. For decoration, applied reliefs often in paler clay are characteristic. Spouts and handles were often made in a lighter-coloured clay, and lead glazes were used.

Josiah Wedgwood was certainly in a great measure responsible for many of the improvements and developments which gave Whieldon his leading place amongst potters of his time. It was Wedgwood who revived the use of a brilliant green glaze, almost unused since the 16th cent., and put it to service in the making of 'pineapple' and 'cauliflower' pieces which were later to achieve great popularity.

Pieces made of black ware with gilt decoration were also made by Whieldon from about 1750. A similar body was used by potters at Jackfield (q.v.) in Shropshire at about this time and the two are often indistinguishable. Salt-glazed stoneware (q.v.) and earthenware were often made in the same shapes and from the same moulds. The formula for cream-coloured earthenware (q.v.) which formed the basis for many of Whieldon's productions was taken up by Wedgwood when he established his own factory and developed to become the Queen's

ware (q.v.) on which his early reputation rested.

About the middle of the 18th cent. Whieldon engaged in making figures, in both salt-glaze and earthenware. The subjects were those familiar to a rural community: musicians, equestrian figures of extremely lively conception, soldiers, gamekeepers, etc., all rendered in a simple manner and again relying on colour for their immediate effect.

The makers of such various kinds of Staffordshire wares of the time cannot usually be named with certainty. Many pieces are ascribed to Whieldon or Astbury. Whieldon made almost every type of ware in common use at this period, and added his knowledge and craftsmanship to the development of many of them. His pupils extended his influence, many becoming potters of repute.

Whistle tankard: see Blowhole.

Whitefriars Glass Works: a London glass manufacturing company established about 1680, producing good quality flint glass (q.v.). In the 19th cent. the factory made fine cut and engraved glass and various experimental coloured, mosaic and *millefiori* (q.v.) glass. The company is still in operation at Wealdstone, Middlesex.

White granite: a type of hard, white, opaque pottery bearing a close resemblance to porcelain (q.v.) and much used for tableware.

Whorl: circular ornament on Medieval (and later) furniture. The varying geometrical patterns employed were chip carved with the aid of a compass and set square. The terms whorl and roundel are both used to describe this type of ornament.

Wilkes, John: (*fl.* late 17th cent.), a well-known locksmith of Birmingham responsible for a series of signed locks, most of them in latten (q.v.), some in blue steel serving as a background to applied brasswork, or in engraved steel. Wilkes became celebrated for his Detector lock of which many examples exist *in situ* in England and on the Continent. This lock is ornamented with the figure of a late-Caroline soldier in relief. The left leg is extended by pushing a secret catch and this reveals the keyhole. The toe-cap of the boot then points to a number on the dial, by which the number of times the door has been opened is registered, as each turn of the key causes the number to change. The lock bolt is released by pushing back the hat.

Willard family: a famous family of American clockmakers. Aaron (1757–1844) was the most successful member, specializing in magnificent wall, tall, shelf and banjo clocks (qq.v.). His brother, Simon (1753–1848) and their two sons were also skilled in the craft.

Willets Manufacturing Co.: Established in 1879 at Trenton, New Jersey, by J., D., and E. Willets, this factory became a major manufacturer of American Belleek (q.v.) ware.

Williamite glasses: wine glasses dating from after the Rising of 1745, engraved with portraits of William III, the Orange Tree or suitable inscriptions.

Willow pattern: a popular pseudo-Chinese design used as a decoration on porcelain and first engraved by Thomas Minton, and known in numerous variants. Mintons, Spode, Turner, Davenport, Adams (qq.v.) and others in Staffordshire used a version of the pattern, as did the factories of Leeds, Swansea, Liverpool and Sunderland. Dated examples are rare: a plate with this design in Hanley Museum, Stoke-on-Trent, is lettered 'THOMASINE WILLEY, 1818'.

Wilton carpets: although a charter for clothiers was granted in 1701, it is doubtful whether carpets were then made there. Lord Pembroke introduced Brussels carpet or moquette (q.v.) looms in 1740. From that date Wilton was in keen rivalry with Kidderminster. The cutting of the looped velvet pile was probably an early speciality of Wilton, a type of carpeting subsequently called by its name. Wilton carpets, made on velvet or moquette looms in narrow strips with simple geometrical patterns, were certainly much used in 18th cent. houses, as well as the costlier knotted pile carpets. The Brighton Pavilion accounts, for example, record orders for both. It is unlikely that knotted pile carpets were made at Wilton until the acquisition of the Axminster looms (q.v.) in 1835, since when they have continued to work.

Wincanton pottery: a pottery at Wincanton worked by Thomas Lindslee (who came from the Limekiln Lane Works, Bristol) and Nathaniel Ireson, made tin-glazed (q.v.) earthenware in the second quarter of the 18th cent. Pieces dated 1737 to 1748 are known. A typical decoration includes motifs within panels reserved against a speckled manganese ground.

Windmills, Joseph: a London clockmaker of repute, active between 1671 and 1725.

Windsor chair: a simple chair of traditional design, the back consisting of turned spindles, the legs turned and splayed. Both the back spindles and the legs are fixed to the solid wooden seat by dowel joints. Also known as 'stick' chairs, existing examples date from the 18th and 19th cent., the basic form yielding little to the pressure of fashion. Early 18th-cent. types include the fan- or comb-back, with a horizontal cresting rail (q.v.) and sometimes a central vase-shaped splat (q.v.), flanked by turned spindles. Later examples have bow- or hoop-backs. The materials are beech, elm, ash or yew, the seat usually being of elm or ash and saddle-shaped in form. American Windsor chairs have no central splat, the back being formed entirely of spindles. They appear to have been first made about 1725 in Philadelphia, later in Massachusetts and Rhode Island. A type fitted with rockers, known as the Windsor rocker, is also found.

Wine bottles: tin-enamelled globular bottles were made at Lambeth (specimens dated 1629 to 1672) with initials, date, and name of wine in blue such as Sack, 'Whit', Claret, or 'Rhenish'.

Rackham and Read adopted the suggestion put forward by Frank Falkner that these were made for wine samples, being too small for use in such hard-drinking days (*English Pottery*, 1924), but they may have been intended for what appears, from contemporary diaries, to have been the customary gift, on 1 January, of a bottle of wine (F. H. Garner, *English Delftware*, 1948).

Wine-bottle stand: a silver oval bowl on moulded base for holding the early form of glass wine-bottle with rounded base dating from the early 18th cent. The very rare examples that survive are sometimes mistaken for sugar bowls.

Wine cistern: large oval vessel on base or separate feet for keeping bottles in cold water or ice. Wooden wine cisterns were lined with lead and came into wide use after *c.* 1730. Silver

survivals date from Charles II to the mid-18th cent. These can be regarded as important decorative pieces of a high standard of design and ornament.

Wine coaster: see Coaster.

Wine cooler: (also known as ice pail) a silver or plated vessel for keeping a single bottle in cold water or ice. A few survivals from early 18th cent. but not common till about 1780. Vase or tub shape, and occasionally of double oval form. Occur in pairs or sets of four or more. Usually fitted with liner and flat rim.

Wine cup: small, individual silver goblet on high stem, common in the late 16th and 17th cent. but revived in the Regency period. Also known as grace cup. Very small examples of mid-17th cent. have a small, trumpet-shaped foot in place of a stem.

Wine fountain: large vase-shaped silver urn with tap in body. Made in second half of 17th and early 18th cent., often *en suite* (q.v.) with wine cisterns (q.v.). They were used to keep wine, but were also used for the more humble purpose of holding water for washing up silver vessels. Numerous English examples survive, but very few from other European countries.

Wine funnel: tapering silver funnel with detachable strainer for decanting. Circular stands of saucer form with domed centres were used with the funnels.

Wine-glass cooler: a glass vessel resembling a finger-bowl but with one or two lips in the rim.

Wine label: pierced or chased label with the name of the wine hung by chain round decanter neck. A rarer form has neck ring in place of chain.

Made in silver and enamelled copper in many varieties of form and name, including plain initials (see also Bottle tickets), occurring from mid-18th cent. onwards.

Wine taster: small, shallow, silver circular bowl with one, two or no handles and slightly domed centre. The handleless form with plain spreading sides when reversed is occasionally mistaken for a trencher salt (q.v.). Examples occur from the mid-17th cent. onwards.

Wing bookcase: see Break-front bookcase.

Wing chair: upholstered armchair with a high back, stuffed arms, and wings. This type of armchair was introduced towards the end of Charles II's reign, and the form soon became standardized, remaining popular until after the middle years of the 18th cent. It was also known as a Grandfather chair.

Wing lantern clock: a type, popular for about a quarter of a cent. at the end of the 17th cent., where the pendulum was placed between the going and striking trains (q.v.), and took the form of an anchor, the flukes of which appeared each side of the main framework, and were protected by wings.

Wirework: among the rarest pieces of Sheffield plate are those constructed from plated wires, dating chiefly between 1785 and 1815. They were a direct result of George Whateley's patented invention of 1768, by which copper rods, round, flat, square, and triangular, could be silver-plated. Not until after the expiry of the patent in 1782 was this work carried out on a considerable scale, the demand being chiefly for a wide range of inexpensive table baskets, toast racks, and *épergnes* (q.v.). The wires at first were cut into short lengths, fitted into holes drilled into rim and base, and soldered into position. Early in the 19th cent. less expensive wire ware was made by bending lengths of wire into continuous curves forming patterns. These were

soldered to rim and base, thus saving the cost of drilling. Ball handles might consist of flat wire curved and spaced with balls or other ornament, or of twisted wire of various sections.

Witch balls: glass globes of 19th-cent. date made probably at Nailsea, Bristol (qq.v.) and elsewhere. They exist in many sizes, from a few centimetres (inches) to 46 cm (1 ft 6 in) in diameter and in several types, some with colours roughly painted on the interior of clear glass, others silvered or of coloured glass and with coloured pictures stuck to the inside of a clear globe.

Witch bottles: bellarmines (q.v.) have been so named, because they have been found frequently under the thresholds or hearths of old houses, or in ditches or river beds, usually filled with such things as pieces of cloth pierced with pins, twists of human hair, hand-made nails, finger-nail parings, and bones.

These charms were either intended to ward off the evil effects of witchcraft, or to inflict some injury upon another person by magical processes.

Wolfers, Philippe: (1858–1929), a Belgian sculptor, goldsmith and jeweller, specializing in ivory, gold and precious stones in Art Nouveau (q.v.) designs.

Wolverhampton lock: the finest English locks have been made here from early in the 17th cent. In 1660 Wolverhampton paid a hearth tax on 84 locksmiths' hearths and there were 97 in nearby Willenhall. The Georgian locksmiths of Wolverhampton maintained their high reputation and, when George III equipped the Queen's House, now Buckingham Palace, he specified that certain locks should be made in Wolverhampton.

Wood, Enoch: (1759–1840), Enoch Wood was the son of Aaron Wood, a celebrated block-cutter and modeller. He started to manufacture pottery in partnership with Ralph Wood (q.v.) about 1784, making useful earthenware, cane ware (q.v.), Egyptian black (q.v.), coloured bodies, and seals and cyphers. In 1790 he took into partnership James Caldwell of Linley Wood, and traded as Wood & Caldwell until 1818. Subsequently he took his sons into the business, who continued it under the style Enoch Wood & Sons until 1846 (six years after his death). Marks:

E. WOOD

ENOCH WOOD
SCULPSIT
(impressed or incised)

WOOD & CALDWELL

There are several variations.

W(✳ ✳ ✳)

Impressed

Enoch Wood was an accomplished modeller who did portraits of John Wesley from life, which became famous. Other busts were executed by him, notably Whitefield, Handel, King William IV, and Emperor Alexander of Russia. Large figure groups such as the 'Ariadne & Bacchus' after a sculpture by Houdon are characteristic. Toby jugs (q.v.) and groups representing 'The Night Watchman' or 'Parson and Clerk' (q.v.) are more attractive. Many pieces with a background of a tree or trees were made by him. These are usually enamelled over glaze, sometimes with the addition of touches of silver lustre.

Excellent blue-printed earthenware was made for the American market. Over sixty American views were produced, usually with an elaborate 'shell' border. English and French views were also made, and religious subjects.

Jasper (q.v.) wares and black basaltes in the style popularized by Wedgwood (q.v.) were made, and some experimental porcelain.

Wood, Ephraim: (b. 1773, d. after 1830), cousin of Enoch Wood (q.v.) and the younger Ralph Wood (q.v.); enameller, gilder and lusterer of earthenware, and manufacturer of pottery figures.

WOOD

EW
1788

π ◎

Wood, Ralph: there were three generations of potters of this name; Ralph Wood the elder (1715–72), was the son of a miller. He began manufacturing salt-glazed stoneware (q.v.), Whieldon (q.v.) ware, figures and toby jugs (q.v.) in Burslem in 1754 and built up a successful business which was continued by his son, Ralph Wood II (1748–95) and grandson Ralph Wood III (1781–1801) until 1801. Marks:

R. WOOD
(impressed)

Ra Wood
(impressed)

Ra Wood
Burslem

1770 Ralph Wood

Incised

A rebus mark in the form of a miniature representation of trees occurs on some Wood figures. Many Wood figures were impressed with mould numbers which have been tabulated and identified.

Ralph Wood figures and toby jugs of the early period are characterized by skilful modelling in relation to the glaze effects which the elder Ralph Wood introduced. These stained glazes, applied with a brush, were generally rather grey and washy in appearance but richer and deeper where the modelling or tooling was sharp.

Black basaltes (q.v.) figures were made and a number of excellent toby jugs. John Voyez (q.v.) is believed to have modelled for Ralph Wood. The younger Ralph Woods decorated their figures with bright overglaze (q.v.) enamel colours. (See also Vicar and Moses.)

Woodall, George (1850–1925) and **Thomas** (1849–1926): brothers, famous for the design and execution of cameo glass (q.v.). They worked at Thomas Webb and Sons (q.v.) from the 1880s.

Woodcut: a relief process, or black line process, obtained by cutting the plank of the wood with a knife.

Wood engraving: a very large number of engravings and, in particular, of book illustrations of the Victorian era were from wood blocks, the artists and engravers (often one and the same person) following after the great tradition started by Thomas Bewick (1753–1828). The illustrations of the 1860s were largely reproduced by wood-engravings.

Woolams, William and Co.: a London wallpaper firm which was in production for almost the whole of the 19th cent. It was famous for hand-made papers and goat-hair flock, and later for stamped gold and embossed leather.

Worcester porcelain: the Worcester manufactory was established in 1751 by a company of subscribers including Dr John Wall (q.v.), physician, William Davis, apothecary, Richard and Josiah Holdship (qq.v.), and Edward Cave whose association with the *Gentleman's Magazine* gave the factory products considerable free publicity.

Porcelain manufacture was commenced at Warmstry House, from a formula used at Bristol.

In 1772 the original company was reconstituted and Robert Hancock (q.v.) held shares in the business for two years. After the death of Wall in 1776 and Davis in 1783 (end of 'Dr Wall' period) the concern was bought by the London agent Thomas Flight for his two sons, Joseph and John, and Robert Chamberlain (q.v.) left the factory to form a rival company.

John Flight died in 1791, and in the following year Martin Barr joined the company, the successive partnerships being Flight & Barr, 1792–1807; Barr, Flight & Barr, 1807–13; Flight, Barr & Barr, 1813–40.

In 1840 Chamberlain's concern was amalgamated with the original business and from 1847 his premises used, in place of Warmstry House, as the porcelain manufactory.

Walter Chamberlain and John Lilly became owners of the business in 1848, and in 1850 were joined by W. H. Kerr. From 1852 the style was Kerr & Binns and from 1862 the Royal Worcester Porcelain Company.

A third Worcester factory for porcelain, started by Thomas Grainger in 1801, was absorbed by Royal Worcester in 1889, while a fourth, founded by James Hadley in 1896, experienced a like fate in 1905. The Royal Worcester Company continues.

Early Worcester porcelain was a soapstone (q.v.) paste, almost indistinguishable from that of Bristol of preceding years, thin and hard-looking, at first a creamy white, but soon somewhat greyish in tint, and finished with glaze which tended to shrink or recede from the foot-rings. Useful wares were made, teapots, cream jugs, cups and saucers, as well as other items; shapes were often derived from silver. Underglaze (q.v.) blue Chinoiseries (q.v.) in imitation of imported ,Nankin' china were among the earliest decorations. Sometimes the underglaze blue of early Worcester is blurred. Other pseudo-Chinese decorations were done in a brilliant palette of enamels, with delicate drawing.

In the Dr Wall period (1752–83) the settled conditions of productions resulted in a much wider range of wares and decorations, marked by excellent potting. Shapes of useful wares are generally dominated by silver forms. A thin glaze tending to shrink from the footring is still characteristic; it is never crazed. Landscape and figure subjects in the European style; fantastic crimson landscapes in reserved panels against yellow grounds; red landscapes painted upon relief scrolls superimposed on leaf dishes; flower painting in the style of Meissen (q.v.); transfer-printing (q.v.) in black, brown, purple or red, occasionally washed over in colour; all these may be found in the early Wall period. After Chelsea (q.v.) artists had been taken on at the factory about 1768, decoration became more elaborate and Meissen influence gave place to Sèvres (q.v.). Workmanship was always of the highest quality although decorations tended to hide the quality of the paste. The looser Kakiemon (q.v.) patterns were replaced with brocaded Imari (q.v.) all-over designs, panelled with fan-shaped and circular patches. Coloured grounds were extensively used in combination with reserved panels enclosing exotic birds, or foliage and figure subjects framed in gold. Sometimes grounds were diapered with patterns, such as the imbricated dark-blue ground generally known as 'scale blue'. A powder-blue ground was also used. Gilding was generally lace-like in quality and of excellent workmanship. Much Worcester porcelain in this period was decorated outside at James Giles's (q.v.) workshop in London. Vases with large reserved panels were supplied to John Donaldson (q.v.) to be filled with figure subjects, such as *Leda and the Swan* after Boucher, or to J. H. O'Neale (q.v.) to be painted with animals or long-limbed graceful mythological figures. Fluted jugs with Rococo handles, 'cabbage-leaf' jugs,

elegant candlesticks, Rococo flower holders, jugs with mask or foliated lips, flanged bottles and leaf dishes of many kinds were made from the 1760s

Black-pencilled Chinese subjects of a rather attenuated kind contrast with precise imitations of the Oriental in colour. Transfer-printing at Worcester was extensively used. From 1760, blue-and-white decoration, transfer-printed or painted, was characterized by a deep strong tone almost like indigo blue. Figures in Worcester porcelain have a certain rarity value but are lacking in accomplishment. The poses are awkward and stiff. Interest in paste diminishes towards the end of the 18th cent., and decoration becomes of supreme importance. Landscapes of a topographical kind were adapted from contemporary engravings usually of local or near-local subjects in the finished style popularized at Derby (q.v.). Classical subjects, shells, feathers, portraits, are typical of the Neoclassic phase of Worcester production. Armorial (q.v.) services, in this as in earlier periods were extensively produced. In the 19th cent. 'Japans' in the style of Derby or Spode (q.v.) became common; new ground colours were brought into use, covered with sea-weed and vermicelli (q.v.) patterns in bright mercury gilding (q.v.). Later Worcester porcelain of the 19th cent. has often distinctive, if not aesthetically satisfying qualities. The almost miraculous pierced wares of George Owen, emulating Japanese ivory carving, or the styles derived from Japanese export Satsuma (q.v.) are typical. Marks:

About 1755–65

1760

1760–95

1755–83

1780

Flight

In blue
1783–9

Flight

In red
1789–92

Flight & Barr

In red
1792–1807

1800

1820

B.F.B.

Incised

Barr,
Flight & Barr
1807–13

F.B.B.

Flight,
Barr & Barr
1813–40

Printed
Kerr & Binns

Impressed
1852–62

Printed
JamesHadley
& Sons
1896–1903

James Hadley
& Sons
1896–1903

Since 1862
Impressed

Work table: the name usually applied to the special table made in the second half of the 18th cent. for ladies' needlework, etc.

In Sheraton's (q.v.) time these tables were of several kinds; some, mounted on four tapered and reeded legs or on trestle feet, might include, in addition to a drawer, such fittings as a pouch for the work materials, an adjustable fire-screen and a writing-board or slide. Another type, the 'French Work-table', was a tray on trestle feet with a shelf or shelves below.

Wormed stem: see Air-twist stem.

Wreathing: spiral marks appearing as a defect in thrown porcelain wares. Some examples of Bristol hard-paste porcelain (q.v.) show wreathing.

Wrigglework: a form of engraved decoration on pewter (q.v.) and silver, employing a zigzag line cut by rocking a gouge from side to side in its progress. Used in conjunction with line engraving (q.v.) at certain periods, principally late in the 17th cent., for filling in spaces between engraved lines.

Writing-box stands: the post-Restoration writing box might be placed on a stand instead of a table. This had gate legs (q.v.) and the fall-down flap of the box opened on to them for writing. Even towards the end of the 17th cent. box and stand might be separate, although the box was acquiring the characteristic shape of the more elaborate desk, with the writing portion based on a chest of drawers. The simplest stands were without drawers, and resembled some of the first toilet looking-glass boxes. Early legs were turned and tapering, linked by flat, waved stretchers (q.v.). By about 1705 simple cabriole legs (q.v.) were coming into use.

Writing table: many varieties of small writing tables can be found dating from the end of the 17th cent., when they were first introduced. Early examples were made with turned baluster legs and folding tops, and were frequently used also as side- and card-tables. Gate legs (q.v.) were usual, and some were fitted with a drawer. Decoration with marquetry (q.v.) is often found. In the early 18th cent. small knee-hole writing tables (q.v.) were popular, with tiers of narrow drawers on each side of the central recess. Similar tables, it may be noted, were also used as dressing tables, and it is not always possible to determine their exact purpose. After the introduction of mahogany, when the fashion arose for larger pedestal tables in libraries, many versions of the convenient lighter table continued to be made. It was at the end of the cent. that perhaps the most elegant kinds of these smaller tables were seen, frequently of satinwood. Some closely resembled contemporary secretaires (q.v.) and cheverets; others were fitted with an adjustable board for writing and with a screen.

Wrotham pottery: slipware (q.v.) was made at Wrotham, Kent, and in the neighbourhood in the 17th and 18th cent., when the pottery there was extensive. A Wrotham pottery was in existence in 1612; no dated pieces are known after 1739. Owners are unknown, but it is suggested that Thomas Jull, whose initials appear on some Wrotham pieces, may have been one of them. Similar wares were being made in Staffordshire at this period making identification difficult in some

cases, but many pieces are marked 'WROTHAM', often in conjunction with the initials of the potter or eventual owner.

Wares for domestic use formed a large part of the production of Wrotham. Cups, jugs, tygs and posset-pots (qq.v.) were all made there, though dishes seem to have been comparatively rare. The body of the ware was usually of lead-glazed red clay, decorated with white or yellow slip in simple patterns; these were inscriptions in either applied or trailed slip, pads of white clay bearing initials or designs in relief. Some applied decoration is edged with an imitation of stitching, and other types of ornament derived from embroidery are used. Handles often bear a groove through their length which is filled with a twisted cord of white and red clay. Stars, masks and rosettes occur frequently as motifs. Many of the jugs are reminiscent of Rhenish stoneware (q.v.).

Wrought iron: literally iron which has been worked or formed by a blacksmith. The term has also come to mean a type of iron which contains practically no carbon but a considerable amount of slag which often gives it a grainy appearance. Wrought iron is readily worked and welded in the forge and is characterized by great toughness and ductility.

Wrythening: diagonally twisted or swirled ribbing or fluting on the bowl or stem of a glass vessel.

Wrythen-top spoon: a rare Medieval form of spoon in which the stem is surmounted by a spirally-fluted ovoid finial (q.v.).

Wu ts'ai (five-colour) wares: this generally implies the characteristic Wan Li period Chinese porcelain wares, painted in underglaze blue and enamel colours (red, green, yellow and purple). Some, however, date from Chia Ching (q.v.), and they continue into K'ang Hsi's (q.v.) reign, when the *famille verte* (q.v.) was introduced.

X-frame: chairs and stools covered all over with fabric, supported on an X-frame date from the Middle Ages. The frames and legs were usually of softwood. Early 17th-cent. examples survive. The X-frame was also used in the second quarter of the 18th cent. and returned to popularity during the Regency.

Yard-arm barometer: see Diagonal barometer.

Yard-of-ale: a drinking glass measuring a metre (3 ft) or so in length. There is a record of one dating from as early as the year 1685.

Considering their fragile nature it is not surprising that surviving yards-of-ale are seldom above a cent. old. The greater number of such survivors are not straightforward drinking vessels, but trick glasses. In them, the flared mouth tapers at length to a bulb at the foot, which ensures that the drinker cannot rest the vessel, and once started the glass must be drained completely or the contents will be spilled. The trick about these glasses is that when the liquid has been nearly all consumed and the glass is raised above the

horizontal to finish the remainder, the air trapped in the bulb by the action of lifting the glass forces the residuum violently into the face of the unlucky victim.

Yasuriko: (*Japanese* = file powder), a Japanese lacquer-work technique in which metal filings are sprinkled on the surface of the lacquer, often graduated in size but not deeply laid like *nashiji* (q.v.).

Year clock: a clock designed to go for one year with one winding.

Ye-goyomi: Japanese pictorial calendars.

Yellow ware: utilitarian earthenware of a yellow or cane colour, made especially from about 1868 by J. E. Jeffords' pottery in Philadelphia.

Yi-hsing stoneware: unglazed red and brown Chinese stoneware, used mainly for teapots which accompanied the new drink to late 17th-cent. Europe. They are often beautifully shaped, rounded or faceted, with incised or moulded relief decoration. Less pleasing are over-naturalistic forms of tree-trunks or fruit. Signatures of Ming (q.v.) potters are too common for credence; dating is difficult, but later pieces are generally of poorer quality. Crudely enamelled pieces are probably 19th cent. Imitations were made in Delft (q.v.) and elsewhere.

Ying ch'ing ('shadowy blue') ware: Chinese porcelain with a brilliant transparent glaze of a pale bluish or greenish tinge, made in Kiangsi and other provinces chiefly during the Sung dynasty (q.v.). The best examples are of a sugary fracture, thinly and delicately potted: lobed bowls, cups or vases. Freely incised or moulded designs often resemble those of Ting ware (q.v.).

Yoko-ye: Japanese prints; horizontal pictures.

Yomud rugs: Turkestan rugs which usually have diamond-shaped motifs, often composed of latch hooks and cloud-band borders.

York House: the factory engaged in making painted enamels, Battersea, London, owned by Stephen Theodore Janssen (q.v.), 1753–6. (See also Battersea enamel.)

Yorkshire chair: see under Derbyshire chair.

Youghal lace: needlepoint (q.v.), reproducing the Venetian rose point (q.v.) and flat point lace. This lovely lace was developed in Co. Cork in the late 1840s, but later was largely replaced by crochet.

Young, William, and Sons: Established in 1853 at Trenton, New Jersey, the company first made Rockingham (q.v.) and white wares. In 1857 the factory became known as the Excelsior Pottery Works. It won a bronze medal for porcelain hardware trimmings at the Centennial Exhibition in 1876. In 1879 it was acquired by the Willets Manufacturing Co. (q.v.).

Yüan dynasty: dynasty of the Mongol Emperors in China, covering the period 1279 to 1368. During this period, porcelain decorated in low relief known as *shu fu* (q.v.) or 'Privy Council' ware became important. With the adoption of painting in underglaze blue and the rise of the porcelain factories of Ching-tê-chên (q.v.), a change in taste took place.

Yüeh ware: celadon ware (q.v.) with grey porcellaneous body and thin, pale, greyish green or buff glaze, made in Chekiang Province in China from about the 3rd to 11th cent. Early examples often borrowed forms and moulded decoration from bronze work. Later pieces may be delicately potted, with lobed sides, and delicately incised designs.

Yung Chêng porcelain: porcelain made in the reign of the Chinese Emperor Yung Chêng (1725–35). This short reign brought a taste for softer colouring and somewhat feminine refinement, the *famille verte* enamels giving way to those of the *famille rose* (qq.v.) with their prominent rose-pink (introduced from Europe) and other semi-opaque colours. Thin 'eggshell' (q.v.) plates and bowls were adorned with delicately drawn flowers or ladies. Elegance of shape also distinguishes the monochromes, again expanded in range of colour. The classic Sung and Ming (qq.v.) styles, e.g. the Kuan and Ko ware (qq.v.), and the delicate *tou ts'ai* (q.v.) enamels were revived and imitated and, indeed, most underglaze blue or red wares of the Yung Chêng and Ch'ien Lung (q.v.) periods reflect the 15th-cent. (Hsüan Tê or Ch'êng Hua) style. From this time, too, wares with designs copied from European prints or with coats of arms supplied to order were much exported.

Zanesville: an American art pottery centre in Ohio, producing wares in imitation of Rookwood (q.v.).

Zuber, Jean: a French wallpaper firm which in the 19th cent. exported a large quantity of scenic papers to the United States.

Zürich: a Swiss porcelain and faience (qq.v.) factory founded in 1763 and directed by Adam Spängler. Soft-paste porcelain (q.v.) was produced, and hard-paste (q.v.) from 1765. After about 1790 faience formed the main output. The pieces were richly decorated and of fine craftsmanship, but there were financial difficulties and the factory closed soon after 1800. The mark was a Z in blue, or an incised Greek *zeta*.

Zwischengoldgläser: (*Ger.*), German glasses of the 18th cent. decorated with gold leaf (q.v.) applied and engraved. The tumbler thus decorated had been ground down for the greater part of its height so that a second, outer glass without a bottom could be fitted over it in order to protect the gilding.

Further Reading

General Works

BRIDGEMAN, HARRIET, and DRURY, ELIZABETH. *The Encyclopedia of Victoriana*, London, 1975.

BUTLER, JOSEPH. *American Antiques 1800–1900*, New York, 1965.

Collins Encyclopedia of Antiques, London and Glasgow, 1973.

COMSTOCK, HELEN. *The Concise Encyclopedia of American Antiques*, 2 vols, London, New York and Toronto, 1958.

The Collector's Encyclopedia, Victoriana to Art Deco, London and Glasgow, 1974.

The Connoisseur Complete Encyclopedia of Antiques, second ed., London, 1975.

DAVIDSON, MARSHALL B. (ed.) *The American Heritage History of American Antiques from the Revolution to the Civil War*, New York, 1968.

DAVIDSON, MARSHALL B. (ed.) *The American Heritage History of American Antiques from the Civil War to World War I*, New York, 1969.

DREPPERD, CARL W. *Primer of American Antiques*, New York, 1944.

METROPOLITAN MUSEUM OF ART. *19th-Century America*, catalogue of the exhibition, 2 vols, New York, 1970.

Arms and Armour

AKEHURST, RICHARD. *Antique Weapons for Pleasure and Investment*, London 1969.

BLAIR, CLAUDE. *European and American Arms*, London, 1962.

BLAIR, CLAUDE. *European Armour*, repr., London, 1972.

FRYER, DOUGLAS. *Antique Weapons A–Z*, London, 1969.

NICKEL, HELMUT. *Arms and Armour through the Ages*, London, 1971.

NORMAN, A. V. B. *Small Swords and Military Swords*, London, 1967.

PETERSON, HAROLD L. *Arms and Armour in Colonial America, 1526–1783*, Harrisburg, Penn., 1956.

Clocks, Watches and Barometers

ALLIX, CHARLES. *Carriage Clocks*, London, 1974.

BAILLIE, G. H. *Watchmakers and Clockmakers of the World*, London, 1947.

BRITTEN, F. J. *Old Clocks and Watches and their Makers*, London, 1956.

BRUTON, ERIC. *Clocks and Watches 1400–1900*, London, 1967.

CAMERER CUSS, T. P. *The Country Life Book of Watches*, London, 1967.

CLUTTON, CECIL, and DANIELS, GEORGE. *Watches*, London, 1965.

DE CARLE, DONALD. *Clocks and Their Value*, London, 1968.

DREPPERD, CARL W. *American Clocks and Clockmakers*, New York, 1955.

GOODISON, NICHOLAS. *English Barometers 1680–1860*, London, 1969.

JAGGER, CEDRIC. *Clocks*, London, 1973.

JOY, EDWARD T. *The Country Life Book of Clocks*, London, 1967.

LLOYD, H. ALAN. *Some Outstanding Clocks Over Seven Hundred Years 1250–1950*, London, 1958.

MIDDLETON, W. E. K. *The History of the Barometer*, Baltimore, Md., 1964.

SYMONDS, R. W. *A History of English Clocks*, London, 1947.

ULLYETT, KENNETH. *Watch collecting*, London, 1970.

ULLYETT, KENNETH. *Clocks and Watches*, London, 1971.

Furniture and Woodwork

ASLIN, ELIZABETH. *Nineteenth Century English Furniture*, London, 1962.

BORDES, MARILYNN JOHNSON. 'Furniture 1790–1910', *Britannica Encyclopædia of American Art*, Chicago, 1973.

COMSTOCK, HELEN. *American Furniture*, New York, 1962.

EDWARDS, RALPH. *The Shorter Dictionary of English Furniture*, third imp., London, 1969.

FASTNEDGE, RALPH. *English Furniture Styles from 1500 to 1830*, repr., London, 1969.

GLOAG, JOHN (ed.). *A Short Dictionary of Furniture*, rev. ed., London, 1969.

HAYWARD, HELENA (ed.). *World Furniture*, London, 1969.

JERVIS, SIMON. *Victorian Furniture*, London, 1968.

ODON, WILLIAM M. *A History of Italian Furniture from the Fourteenth to the Early Nineteenth Century*, New York, 1966–67.

ORMSBEE, THOMAS H. *Field Guide to American Victorian Furniture*, Boston, Mass., 1951.

OTTO, CELIA JACKSON. *American Furniture of the Nineteenth Century*, New York, 1965.

PINTO, EDWARD H. *Treen*, rev. ed., London, 1969.

VERLET, PIERRE. *French Royal Furniture*, London, 1963.

Glass

BARRETT, RICHARD CARTER. *A Collector's Handbook of American Art Glass*, Manchester, Vt., 1971.

BUCKLEY, W. *European Glass*, London, 1926.

BUCKLEY, W. *The Art of Glass*, London, 1939.

DAVIS, DEREK C., and MIDDLEMAS, KEITH. *Coloured Glass*, London, 1968.

ELVILLE, E. M. *Paperweights and other Glass Curiosities*, London, 1954.

GROVER, RAY and LEE. *Art Glass Nouveau*, Rutland, Vt., 1967.

GROVER, RAY and LEE. *Carved and Decorated European Glass*, Rutland, Vt., 1970.

HAYNES, E. B. *Glass through the Ages*, London, 1959.

HUGHES, G. BERNARD. *Old English, Irish and Scottish Table Glass*, London, 1956.

LEE, RUTH WEBB. *Victorian Glass*, Northboro., Mass., 1944.

LEE, RUTH WEBB. *Nineteenth Century Art Glass*, New York, 1952.

McKEARIN, HELEN and GEORGE. *American Glass*, New York, 1950.

McKEARIN, HELEN and GEORGE. *Two Hundred Years of American Blown Glass*, rev. ed., New York, 1966.

REVI, ALBERT C. *Nineteenth-Century Glass, Its Genesis and Development*, rev. ed., New York, 1967.

THORPE, W. A. *English and Irish Glass*, London and Boston, Mass., 1927.

THORPE, W. A. *A History of English and Irish Glass*, 2 vols., London, 1929.

THORPE, W. A. *English Glass*, London, 1935.

WAKEFIELD, HUGH. *Nineteenth Century British Glass*, London, 1961.

WHITLOW, HARRY. *Art, Colored and Cameo Glass*, Riverview, Mich., 1966.

WILSON, KENNETH M. *New England Glass and Glassmaking*, New York, 1972.

Jewellery

CLIFFORD SMITH, H. *Jewellery*, second ed., London, 1973.

EMANUEL, H. *Diamonds and Precious Stones*, London, 1865.

EVANS, J. *A History of Jewellery, 1100–1870*, second ed., London, 1973.

FLOWER, M. *Victorian Jewellery*, second ed., London, 1967.

FONTENAY, E. *Les Bijoux*, Paris, 1887.

JANSON, DORA JANE. *From Slave to Siren: the Victorian Woman and her Jewelry*, Durham, N.C., 1971.

LEWIS, M. D. S. *Antique Paste Jewellery*, London, 1970.

McCLINTON, KATHARINE M. *Collecting American Nineteenth-Century Silver*, New York, 1968.

STEINGRABER, E. *Antique Jewellery. Its History in Europe from 800 to 1900*, London, 1957.

VEVER, H. *La Bijouterie Française au XIX siècle*, 3 vols, Paris, 1906–8.

Metalwork

EBERT, KATHERINE. *Collecting American Pewter*, New York, 1973.

HUGHES, G. BERNARD. *Horse Brasses and Other Small Items for the Collector*, London, 1956.

KAUFFMAN, HENRY J. *Early American Ironware*, Rutland, Vt., 1966.

KAUFFMAN, HENRY J. *American Copper and Brass*, Camden, N.J., 1968.

MONTGOMERY, CHARLES F. *A History of American Pewter*, New York, 1973.

PEAL, CHRISTOPHER A. *British Pewter and Britannia Metal for Pleasure and Investment*, London, 1971.

WILLS, GEOFFREY. *The Book of Copper and Brass*, Middlesex, 1969.

Pottery and Porcelain

BARRET, F. A. *Worcester Porcelain*, London, 1953.

BEMROSE, GEOFFREY. *Nineteenth-Century English Pottery and Porcelain*, London, 1952.

BLACKER, J. F. *The A.B.C. of XIX Century English Ceramic Art*, London, ND (*c.* 1911).

BUSHNELL and DIGBY. *Ancient American Pottery*, London, 1955.

CHAFFERS, WILLIAM. *Marks and Monograms on European and Oriental Pottery and Porcelain*, fourteenth ed., London, 1946.

CLEMENT, ARTHUR W. *Notes on American Ceramics 1607–1943*, New York, 1944.

CLEMENT, ARTHUR W. *Our Pioneer Potters*, New York, 1947.

COOPER, RONALD. *Pottery of Thomas Toft*, Leeds, Yorks, 1952.

CHARLESTON, R. J. *Roman Pottery*, London, 1955.

CUSHION, J. P., and HONEY, W. B. *Handbook of Pottery and Porcelain Marks*, London, 1956.

DIXON, J. L. *English Porcelain of the Eighteenth Century*, London, 1952.

EYLES, D. *Royal Doulton 1815–1965*, London, 1966.

GARNER, F. H. *English Delftware*, London, 1948.

GAUNT, W., and CLAYTON-STAMM, M. D. E. *William de Morgan*, London, 1971.

GODDEN, G. A. *Victorian Porcelain*, London and New York, 1961.

GODDEN, G. A. *Encyclopedia of British Pottery & Porcelain Marks*, London and New York, 1964.

GODDEN, G. A. *Illustrated Encyclopedia of British Pottery and Porcelain*, London and New York, 1966.

GODDEN, G. A. *Minton Pottery & Porcelain of the First Period*, London and New York, 1968.

GODDEN, G. A. *British Porcelain, An Illustrated Guide*, London and New York, 1974.

GRAY, BASIL. *Early Chinese Pottery and Porcelain*, London, 1953.

HACKENBROCH, YVONNE. *Chelsea and other English Porcelain, Pottery and Enamel in the Irwin Untermeyer Collection*, London, 1957.

HAGGAR, REGINALD G. *English Country Pottery*, London, 1950.

HAGGAR, REGINALD G. *The Concise Encyclopedia of Continental Pottery and Porcelain*, London and New York, 1960.

HAYWARD, J. F. *Vienna Porcelain of the du Paquier period*, London, 1952.

HONEY, W. B., *The Ceramic Art of China and other countries of the Far East*, London, 1945.

HONEY, W. B. *Corean Pottery*, London, 1947.

HONEY, W. B. *Dresden China*, London, 1947.

HONEY, W. B. *German Porcelain*, London, 1947.

HONEY, W. B. *French Porcelain of the Eighteenth Century*, London, 1950.

HONEY, W. B. *A Dictionary of European Ceramic Art*, London, 1952.

HUGHES, G. B. *Victorian Pottery & Porcelain*, London, 1959.

HYDE, J. A. LLOYD. *Oriental Lowestoft. (Chinese Export Porcelain)*, Newport, Mon., 1954.

JENYNS, SOAME. *Later Chinese Porcelain*, London, 1952.

JENYNS, SOAME. *Ming Pottery and Porcelain*, London, 1953.

JEWITT, L. *The Ceramic Art of Great Britain*, rev. ed., London and New York, 1972.

JOHN, W. D., and BAKER, WARREN. *Old English, Lustre Pottery*, Newport, Mon., 1951.

KETCHUM, WILLIAM C., Jr. *Early Potters and Potteries of New York State*, New York, 1970.

LANE, ARTHUR. *Early Islamic Pottery*, London, 1947.

LANE, ARTHUR. *French Faience*, London, 1948.

LANE, ARTHUR. *Greek Pottery*, London, 1948.

LANE, ARTHUR. *Italian Porcelain*, London, 1956.

LANE, ARTHUR. *Later Islamic Pottery*, London, 1957.

MACKINTOSH, SIR HAROLD. *Early English Figure Pottery*, London, 1938.

MANKOWITZ, WOLF. *Wedgwood*, London, 1953.

MANKOWITZ, WOLF and HAGGAR, REGINALD G. *The Concise Encyclopedia of English Pottery and Porcelain*, London and New York, 1957.

MORLEY-FLETCHER, H. *Meissen*, London, 1971.

RACKHAM, BERNARD. *Medieval English Pottery*, London, 1948.

RACKHAM, BERNARD. *Early Staffordshire Pottery*, London, 1951.

RACKHAM, BERNARD. *Italian Maiolica*, London, 1952.

RHEAD, G. W. and F. A. *Staffordshire Pots & Potters*, London, 1906.

RICE, D. G. *Illustrated Guide to Rockingham Pottery and Porcelain*, London, 1971.

SANDON, H. *Royal Worcester Porcelain, from 1862 to the present day*, London, 1973.

SAVAGE, GEORGE. *Eighteenth-Century English Porcelain*, London, 1952.

SAVAGE, GEORGE. *Porcelain through the Ages*, London and New York, 1961.

SAVAGE, GEORGE. *Pottery through the Ages*, London and New York, 1963.

SAVAGE, GEORGE. *Eighteenth-Century German Porcelain*, London, 1967; New York, 1968.

SAVAGE, GEORGE. *Seventeenth- and Eighteenth-Century French Porcelain*, London, 1969.

TOWNER, DONALD. *English Cream-coloured Earthenware*, London, 1957.

TURNER, H. A. B. *Collector's guide to Staffordshire Pottery figures and Toby Jugs*, London and New York, 1971.

WAKEFIELD, H. *Victorian Pottery*, London, 1962.

WATNEY, BERNARD. *Longton Hall Porcelain*, London, 1957.

WEISS, GUSTAV. *Book of Porcelain*, London and New York, 1971.

WYNTER, HARRIET. *Introduction to European Porcelain*, London, 1971.

Prints and Silhouettes

HILLIER, J. *Japanese Masters of the Colour Print*, London, 1954.

HIND, A. M. *The Processes and Schools of Engraving*, fourth ed., London, 1952.

JACKSON, E. N. *Silhouette Notes and Dictionary*, New York, 1938.

LISTER, RAYMOND. *Silhouettes*, London, 1953.

MIDDENDORF, J. W., and SHADWELL, WENDY J. *American Printmaking: The First 150 Years*, Washington, 1969.

WEITENKAMPF, FRANK. *American Graphic Art*, repr., New York, 1970.
WILDER, F. L. *How to Identify Old Prints*, London, 1969.

Silver

BRADBURY, FREDERICK. *British and Irish Silver Assay Office Marks 1544–1968*, second ed., Yorkshire, 1969.
BUHLER, K. C. *American Silver 1655–1825*, New York, 1972.
BURY, SHIRLEY. *Victorian Electroplate*, London, 1971.
CLAYTON, MICHAEL. *The Collector's Dictionary of the Silver and Gold of Great Britain and North America*, London, 1971.
CULME, JOHN. *Nineteenth-century Silver*, London, 1977.
CULME, JOHN, and STRANG, JOHN G. *Antique Silver and Silver Collecting*, London, 1973.
DAVIS, FRANK. *French Silver 1450–1825*, London, 1970.
McCLINTON, KATHARINE M. *Collecting American Nineteenth-Century Silver*, New York, 1968.
OMAN, C. C. *English Domestic Silver*, rev. ed., London, 1968.
RAINWATER, DOROTHY T. *American Silver Manufacturers*, New York, 1967.
TAYLOR, GERALD. *Silver*, rev. ed., London, 1963.
WARDLE, PATRICIA. *Victorian Silver and Silver Plate*, London, 1963.

Textiles

BIGELOW-HARTFORD CARPET CO. *A Century of Carpet and Rug-making in America*, New York, 1925.
BOLTON, ETHEL STANWOOD, and JOHNSTON COE, EVA. *American Samplers*, Boston, Mass., 1921.
HARBESON, GEORGIANA BROWN. *American Needlework*, New York, 1938.
HENDERSON, PHILIP. *William Morris, His Life, Work and Friends*, rep., Harmondsworth, 1972.
KENDRICK, A. F. *English Embroidery*, London, 1905.
KENDRICK, A. F. *English Needlework*, London, 1933.
KENDRICK, A. F., and TATTERSALL, C. E. C. *Handwoven Carpets, Oriental and European*, 2 vols, London, 1922.
LOCKWOOD and GLAISTER. *Art Embroidery*, London, 1878.
MORRIS, BARBARA J. *Victorian Embroidery*, London, 1962.
MORRIS, BARBARA J. 'Victorian Textiles', *Connoisseur Period Guides*, Early Victorian, 1830–1860, London, 1958.
PETO, FLORENCE. *American Quilts and Coverlets*, London, 1949; New York, 1949; Toronto, 1949.
SWYGERT, MRS. LUTHER M. (ed.). *Heirlooms from Old Looms (Coverlets)*, Chicago, 1955.
THOMSON, W. G. *A History of Tapestry*, London, 1930.
VICTORIA and ALBERT MUSEUM. *Notes on Quilting*, rept., 1949. *Notes on Applied Work and Patchwork*, rept., 1949. *Catalogie of English Domestic Embroidery*, 1950. *Indian Embroidery*, 1951.
WATKINSON, RAYMOND. *William Morris as Designer*, London, 1967.